CARRYING THE BANNER OF FREEDOM

CARRYING THE BANNER OF FREEDOM

Poland's Government-in-Exile, 1939–1991

DAVID E. GRUS

Hippocrene Books, Inc.
New York

DEDICATION

This book is dedicated to all who served in
or supported the Polish Government-in-Exile.

Copyright © 2025 David E. Grus

All rights reserved.

Book design by Acme Klong Design and Mind the Margins, LLC.
Cover design by **Acme Klong Design**.

For more information, address:
HIPPOCRENE BOOKS, INC.
171 Madison Avenue
New York, NY 10016
www.hippocrenebooks.com

Cataloging-in-publication data available from the Library of Congress.

ISBN 13: 978-0-7818-1461-4

Printed in the United States of America.

CONTENTS

Timeline of Major Events	vii
A Few Words about Words	xi
London, Capital of Poland	1
Independent Poland	5
Invasion	23
An Abbreviated Presidency	33
Into Exile	47
The Troublesome Ally	89
Abandonment	113
"I Remain at My Post…"	141
Discord Among Exiles	165
From Discord to Division	191
Exiles Divided	219
Stanisław the Peacemaker	249
The Pretender	279
The Elder Statesman	293
The Scoutmaster	317
Exile's Last President	347
Exiles and the Third Republic	383
Changing the Course of an Avalanche	401
Abbreviations and Terms	405
Bibliography	413
Acknowledgements	429
Index	431

Timeline of Major Events

1918
November 11: Poland regains independence after 123 years of German, Austrian, and Russian subjugation.

1935
April 23: The Sejm approves the April Constitution, which provides for presidents to appoint their successors in times of national emergency.

1939
September 1: Germany invades Poland.

September 17: The Soviet Union invades Poland.

September 26: Bolesław Wieniawa-Długoszowski is named president but declines the nomination one day later.

September 30: Poland's government is reconstituted in Paris; Władysław Raczkiewicz is named president, and General Władysław Sikorski is prime minister.

1940
June 21: France capitulates to Germany; Władysław Raczkiewicz and the Polish government arrive in London.

1941
June 22: Germany invades the Soviet Union.

July 30: Poland and the Soviet Union sign the Sikorski–Maisky Pact, restoring Soviet recognition of Poland.

1943
April 25: The Soviet Union ends diplomatic recognition of Poland.

July 4: Władysław Sikorski is killed in an aircraft crash at Gibraltar.

1944
July 22: The Soviet-backed Polish Committee of National Liberation proclaims itself Poland's government.

1945

February 4–11: Stalin, Churchill, and Roosevelt meet at Yalta; they agree to recognize the Polish Committee of National Liberation and the new Polish-Soviet border demanded by Stalin.

June 29: The United States, the United Kingdom, and France cease to recognize Poland's exile government; Raczkiewicz declares the Soviet-backed government to be illegal and refuses to vacate the presidency.

July 17–August 2: Stalin, Churchill, Attlee, and Truman meet at Potsdam; they declare that Poland's exile government no longer exists.

1947

June 5: Władysław Raczkiewicz dies in Wales.

June 9: August Zaleski succeeds Raczkiewicz as president.

1954

June 9: Zaleski refuses to leave office after seven years in power, and Poland's émigré government formally splits into two factions: those recognizing Zaleski's presidency, and the Provisional Council of National Unity, which seeks to replace him.

1972

April 7: August Zaleski dies in London.

April 9: Stanisław Ostrowski succeeds Zaleski; his presidency is recognized by both émigré factions.

November 17: Juliusz Sokolnicki declares himself president of the Republic of Poland.

1979

April 8: Stanisław Ostrowski leaves office after seven years and is succeeded by Edward Raczyński.

1980

August 31: *Solidarność*, the first independent trade union in the Soviet bloc, is formally recognized; it is led by Lech Wałęsa.

1986

April 8: Edward Raczyński completes his seven-year term and is succeeded by Kazimierz Sabbat.

1989

July 19: Kazimierz Sabbat dies in London; Ryszard Kaczorowski takes the oath of office.

1990

December 9: Lech Wałęsa is elected president of Poland.

December 22: Ryszard Kaczorowski formally transfers presidential powers to Wałęsa.

1991

December 31: Liquidation of Poland's exile government is completed.

2010

April 10: Ryszard Kaczorowski is killed in an aircraft crash.

2022

November 3: The remains of Władysław Raczkiewicz, August Zaleski, and Stanisław Ostrowski are repatriated to Poland.

A Few Words about Words

WHEREVER PRACTICAL, APPROPRIATE, or useful, place names, names of organizations, and commonly used words are given in their original language. Thus, Kraków is used rather than Krakow or Cracow, Solidarność is used instead of Solidarity, PZPR is used rather than an acronym derived from an English translation, and *kresy*, not eastern borderlands, is used. Exceptions are made for Warsaw and Moscow; these names are used rather than Warszawa and Moskva due to the familiarity of their English forms. Likewise, Poland's postwar western border is depicted as the Oder–Neisse Line, the terminology commonly used in international relations, rather than the Odra and Nysa Łużycka, and Silesia is normally used in place of Śląsk.

Place names are rendered in their official forms at the time referenced. For example, the city of Lwów became Lemberg after the partitions, reverted to Lwów in independent Poland, and was renamed Lviv after the 1939 Soviet invasion. However, names of postwar organizations referring to an older name of a location, such as *Koło Lwowian*, are presented as they were named. Such use of place names is not a rejection of postwar borders, nor does it imply support for any revisions.

Proper names are given as rendered in their native language. Every effort has been made to present correct spellings, and any errors are the author's responsibility.

London, Capital of Poland

AT FIRST LOOK, nothing about the handsome townhouse at 43 Eaton Place seemed unusual. A flag flying above its entrance suggested that it was an embassy or consulate, a common sight in London's Belgravia district. On closer inspection, however, questions arose. The white-and-red flag signaled that the building was in the service of the Polish government, but its eagle was adorned with a gold crown, something not seen on the flag displayed at the Embassy of the People's Republic of Poland two miles away. A brass plaque at the door declared that this was the seat of the Republic of Poland, commonly known as the Polish Government-in-Exile.

Poland's government began functioning abroad after the joint German-Soviet invasion of September 1939. Rather than surrendering or risking capture, government officials reconvened abroad and provided leadership, direction, and funding for underground organizations, commanded the reconstituted Polish Army in the West and underground military groupings at home, maintained diplomatic relations with friendly nations, and planned for the restoration of a democratic government after the invaders had been defeated. Poland was not alone; London also hosted exiled governments from Czechoslovakia, Belgium, Greece, the Netherlands, Luxembourg, Norway, Yugoslavia, and France. Those exiles, however, returned to their homelands after liberation and participated in the creation of new governments. Poland's government was not given that opportunity. As the Red Army advanced into Polish territory, it installed a communist government. Within months, most nations recognized this new regime and terminated relations with the exiles, but the Polish government refused to capitulate and would continue to function for forty-five more years.

This government was surprisingly complex. It was comprised of a president, government ministries, a council, a judiciary, a treasury, an auditing body, and representatives in other countries. It cultivated an extensive network of contacts in the People's Republic of Poland and developed channels to provide financial and material aid to opposition groups and victims of repression. It published official journals and funded itself through donations. War veterans and refugees who could not or would not return to Poland comprised its primary support base; it also found support among the diaspora and a few British and American politicians.

Yet it toiled in relative obscurity. It rarely received attention from the Western media. When it did, it was usually portrayed as an oddity, a curiosity, or a futile endeavor by a group of old men in worn suits and tattered uniforms gathered under faded banners in a musty club, lamenting a lost world. This image persisted well after the government-in-exile ended its work; a 2001 article in Britain's venerable weekly *The Economist* characterized it as dusty and pointless and its leaders as uninspiring.

Such opinions cannot withstand even a cursory review. Far from being uninspiring, most exile leaders had survived unimaginable hardships and built new lives abroad but never forgot their homeland, their people, or their culture and took pains to ensure that their children knew their language and history. They tirelessly reminded the West about the fate of Poland and other Soviet Bloc nations, incessantly advocated for free elections and withdrawal of Soviet troops, and disseminated information about conditions in their now-totalitarian homeland.

Poland re-emerged in Western consciousness in the late 1970s and the 1980s with the election of Pope John Paul II and the emergence of *Solidarność* (Solidarity), the Polish trade union that grew into a broad social resistance movement and helped end Communist rule in Poland. Journalists seeking new sources of information, functionaries from Western governments searching for insights, and the merely curious rediscovered 43 Eaton Place. The British and American governments came to depend on it as a valuable, albeit informal, resource. Ryszard Kaczorowski, the exile government's last president, noted that visitors would arrive daily, even if only to see if the exiled government still existed.

Financial constraints hampered its scope of activities. Internal discord and conflict were inevitable, as were attacks from Warsaw and Moscow and meddling by Western governments. But despite these challenges, the government and its supporters soldiered on. Volunteers were found, money was raised, elections were conducted, protests were organized, schools were founded, and events were held. That people struggling to adapt themselves to life in foreign lands would gladly offer their time and money to the exile government seems remarkable. Examining their commitment in the context of Polish history provides insight into their motives. From late in the eighteenth century until 1918, Poland was absent from the map, having been partitioned by the German, Russian, and Austrian empires, but its people fought assimilation and struggled to regain independence throughout that period. Independence arrived because its partitioners collapsed during the Great War, but after a mere twenty years of freedom, it was again destroyed by those same nations.[1] Following the Second World War, Poland was nominally independent but remained under foreign military occupation and was governed by a party that espoused deeply unpopular ideology and maintained its hold on power through terror and repression. This was not the Poland that the exiles had fought for during independence and throughout the Second World War.

Polish exiles did not have the means to force out the communist government, and no help could be expected from Western nations, which were more concerned with peaceful coexistence than the plight of those millions consigned to life under Soviet domination. But they persisted, working within the realm of what was possible and continually defying attempts to relegate them to the dustbin of history.

---

[1] Austria had been incorporated into Germany in 1938.

Independent Poland

Józef Piłsudski, Marshal of Poland 1918-1935

JÓZEF PIŁSUDSKI AND HIS SECOND-IN-COMMAND, KAZIMIERZ Sosnkowski, stood on the cold platform of Warsaw's main rail station[1] talking with Adam Koc, commander of *Polska Organizacja Wojskowa* (POW, Polish Military Organization), and a handful of other comrades-in-arms and supporters. It was the morning of November 10, 1918. Few in Warsaw were aware that they had arrived, but word quickly spread. Piłsudski, former prisoner of Tsarist Russia, founder and commander of the Polish Legions, a man who preferred prison to subordinating the Legions to German command, and a living symbol of the struggle for independence, was in Warsaw.

In ancient legend, the brothers Čech, Rus', and Lech embarked on a hunting journey together, but their paths diverged. Čech traveled west, Rus' ventured east, and Lech headed north; each remained in the lands he found. Čech settled at Říp Mountain in the Bohemian flatlands, and Rus' near the Dnieper River. Lech observed a white eagle fiercely defending its nest and considered it to be a good omen; he settled nearby and named the place Gniezno (from *gniazdo*, or nest), adopting the white eagle as his symbol.

---

[1] This was *Dworzec Wiedeński* (Vienna Station), located at the corner of Aleja Jerozolimskie and Ulica Marszałkowska. It was destroyed in the Second World War.

Further to the south, a dragon was wreaking havoc on a settlement along the Wisła River. Daily, it emerged from its cave and claimed a victim—a cow, a sheep, a child. Attempts to slay it ended in failure, as axes and spears could not penetrate its scaly skin. The dragon's reign of terror continued until a cobbler named Krak obtained a dead sheep, filled it with sulfur, and placed it outside the dragon's lair while it slept. When the dragon awoke, it left its cave in search of food; seeing the sheep, the dragon hurriedly ate it. Soon, it had a terrible thirst; it dashed to the river and began to gulp down water, but its thirst still raged. The dragon's sides swelled as it continued to drink, until finally it burst. Freed from the dragon, the grateful townspeople made Krak their leader, and he built a castle on Wawel Hill, above the cave.

Such legends give shape to Poland's earliest centuries, a period about which few facts are known. That changed with the baptism of King Mieszko in 966, regarded as the year of Poland's founding. Mieszko was the first king of the Piast dynasty, rulers of the nation for three centuries. The Piasts united the Polish people under their government and fought incursions from the west and the east; the last Piast king, Kazimierz Wielki (Casimir the Great), died in 1370. Kazimierz died without a son and was succeeded by his nephew, Louis. His grandniece, Queen Jadwiga, married Jogaila, Grand Duke of Lithuania, who was baptized and took the name Władysław II Jagiełło, thus beginning the Jagiellonian dynasty and the union of Poland and Lithuania. Władysław II is well remembered for leading combined Lithuanian and Polish forces to victory over the Teutonic Knights at Grunwald in 1410. His dynasty endured until the last Jagiellonian king, Zygmunt II August, died in 1572 without leaving an heir. For the next two centuries, the Polish-Lithuanian Commonwealth's kings were elected by members of the nobility. This arrangement weakened the monarchy, increased the nobility's power, and provided an opening for other nations to subvert the Commonwealth. Several nations, most notably the Commonwealth's German, Austrian, Russian, and Swedish neighbors, had designs on its territory, but its military prevented them from realizing their aims. Indeed, in 1683, the Habsburg Empire was compelled to seek King Jan III Sobieski's assistance to stop the Turkish siege of Vienna, but in the following years the Commonwealth's military was irreparably weakened by nobles in the pay of foreign nations. Less than one hundred years later, the Habsburg Empire joined with the Prussian and Russian Empires in partitioning the Commonwealth.

In 1772, the Commonwealth's three powerful neighbors carved off about thirty percent of its area. Russia took territories in the north and east, the Habsburgs seized the southern lands around Lwów, Przemyśl, and

Związek Walki Czynnej (ZWC, Association for Active Struggle); it was headed by Władysław Sikorski, Marian Kukiel, and Kazimierz Sosnkowski. He also founded a ZWC training school in Kraków and organized a train robbery that seized over 200,000 rubles in tax revenues en route to St. Petersburg from Warsaw. At the outbreak of war in 1914, Piłsudski placed his units under Austrian authority and liberated the town of Kielce from Russian occupation. His now-renamed *Legiony Polskie* (Polish Legions) fought against the Russians, and he demanded that Germany and Austria grant independence to Poland. In 1916, they agreed and announced the creation of the Kingdom of Poland, hoping that more Poles would join the fight. The kingdom was governed by the *Rada Regencyjna* (Regency Council), but it was soon apparent that this was a puppet government with no real authority.[9] Piłsudski provoked Germany and Austria by refusing to allow Polish units to fight against the British and French. Their response was to compel Polish soldiers to swear an oath of loyalty to them. Piłsudski forbade the soldiers to do so and was arrested and imprisoned at Magdeburg, along with Sosnkowski. News of his arrest amplified his popularity in Poland.

ND was likewise active during the war. Its leader, Roman Dmowski, formed *Komitet Narodowy Polski* (Polish National Committee) in the Russian partition in 1914; in 1917, he refounded it in Switzerland. Along with Dmowski, its main activists were August Zaleski and the famed pianist Ignacy Jan Paderewski. *Komitet Narodowy Polski* initially allied itself with Russia and later with England and France. Its activities in Paris resulted in its formal recognition as the legitimate Polish government by the French, and its members cultivated extensive contacts in the West.

By November 1918, all three partitioning powers had ceased to exist. The Russian Empire had been overthrown the previous year, and Russia was engulfed in revolution; Austria-Hungary was dissolved in October; and in Germany the kaiser had abdicated, a republic had been proclaimed, and the new government had called for an armistice. On November 8, the German government released Piłsudski and Sosnkowski and placed them on a train to Warsaw in the hope that the two men would influence the emerging Polish state to be friendly towards Germany.

---

[9] *Rada Regencyjna* established two official publications: *Dziennik Ustaw Rzeczypospolitej Polskiej* (*Journal of Laws of the Republic of Poland*) and *Monitor Polski* (*Polish Monitor*). *Dziennik Ustaw* was founded as the official source of laws; any law published there was considered to be promulgated. *Monitor Polski* was founded as an official journal of the prime minister, but items published there are not considered to be officially binding. These publications have been produced regularly since their founding.

At the time of Piłsudski's arrival, Poland was governed by *Rada Regencyjna* and several other regional bodies that emerged to fill the vacuum created when its occupiers retreated. While *Rada Regencyjna* was unpopular, Piłsudski enjoyed widespread support. Just one day after he disembarked from the train, *Rada Regencyjna* appointed him commander in chief of the Polish Army and asked him to form a government, and in turn, he proclaimed an independent Polish state. Thus, November 11, 1918, is regarded as the day *Rzeczpospolita Polska* (Republic of Poland, also referred to as the Second Republic[10]) came into existence, bringing 123 years of foreign occupation and rule to an end.[11] Two days later, *Rada Regencyjna* dissolved itself and appointed Piłsudski *Tymczasowy Naczelnik Państwa* (Provisional Chief of State). Owing to his previous alliance with Germany and Austria, he was viewed with distrust by England and France. Their favor fell on Dmowski, but his *Komitet Narodowy Polski* had little support at home.

Paderewski crafted a compromise. Paderewski's international popularity, lack of party affiliation, and tireless work on behalf of Poland during the war[12] enabled him to obtain Western agreement for Piłsudski to remain in charge in Warsaw and for Dmowski to represent Polish interests at the Paris Peace Conference. Paderewski expended great effort to get Piłsudski and Dmowski to work together, but fundamental differences on crucial issues made that all but impossible. Piłsudski harbored an intense distrust of Russia, whereas Dmowski, twice elected to the Duma[13] as a Polish representative, favored aligning with Russia. Further, they held incompatible views on Poland's territory and demographics. Piłsudski envisioned the Second Republic as a rebirth of the Commonwealth, with its multiethnic citizenry, while Dmowski visualized a state populated by Poles. Further, Piłsudski's past affiliation with PPS was of great concern to the staunchly anti-socialist ND.

At Versailles, the fact of an independent Poland was a given. US President Woodrow Wilson had included Poland's restoration as one of his Fourteen Points: "An independent Polish state should be erected which

---

[10] In Polish historiography, the Polish-Lithuanian Commonwealth is regarded to have been the First Republic.

[11] *Rada Regencyjna* had declared independence on October 7. Polish society's acceptance of November 11 as its independence day reflects its low regard for *Rada Regencyjna*.

[12] Paderewski founded the Polish Relief Fund and the White Cross Society, hosted many fundraising events and concerts, and gave many speeches to promote the Polish cause. He urged Polish Americans to volunteer for the Polish armed forces in France. His influence led US President Woodrow Wilson to include creation of an independent Poland in his Fourteen Points.

[13] The *Duma* was the Russian legislature formed after Russia's 1905 Revolution.

should include the territories inhabited by indisputably Polish populations, which should be assured a free and secure access to the sea, and whose political and economic independence and territorial integrity should be guaranteed by international covenant."[14]

This aligned neatly with Dmowski's principles. He presented his proposal for Poland's borders in a five-hour session, declaring no interest in former parts of the Commonwealth that did not have a Polish majority, pushing for inclusion of Upper Silesia in Poland on economic grounds, and contending that prewar German census data had deliberately undercounted Poles. Poland was granted Poznań and its environs, parts of Upper Silesia, a section of the Baltic coast, and part of eastern Pomerania. Danzig was declared a free city under League of Nations supervision.[15] Dmowski was disappointed in the final Polish-German border, as he felt it should have been fixed further west. He also objected to Poland's being compelled to sign a treaty guaranteeing rights to minorities on the grounds that Germany was not required to sign a similar agreement, leaving Poles in Germany without legal protection.[16]

By early 1919, Piłsudski brought all of Poland's regions under Warsaw's authority, established a coalition government, negotiated the withdrawal of German troops, and formed the Polish Army.

Several new nations emerged in the Great War's aftermath, each asserting sovereignty over what it claimed to be its historic territory. Such claims were complicated by Europe's lack of ethnic uniformity. Centuries of migration, occupation, colonization, expulsion, and resettlement had left many cities and towns a mixture of nationalities, while the countryside, particularly in the east, was a patchwork of ethnically distinct villages. Defining borders was a highly contentious endeavor that led to a series of wars. Poland repulsed German campaigns to regain control over Wielkopolska and Upper Silesia, prevailed over the fledgling West Ukrainian People's Republic in its attempt to establish a Ukrainian state stretching from the Zbrucz (Zbruch) River to Nowy Sącz with its capital in Lwów (under the name Lviv), and took control of the Wilno (Vilnius) region from Lithuania. Poland fared less well in a dispute with Czechoslovakia over

---

[14] Woodrow Wilson, Address to Congress, January 8, 1918. https://www.archives.gov/milestone-documents/president-woodrow-wilsons-14-points
[15] Danzig was the name Germany gave to Gdańsk.
[16] Czechoslovakia, Greece, Romania, and Yugoslavia were required to sign similar agreements.

Cieszyn Silesia; it was awarded one third of the territory in question at the Spa Conference in 1920.

Amidst these territorial disputes, Poland's very existence was threatened by the Soviet Union. Revolution in Germany presented Moscow with an opportunity to export Bolshevism to an industrialized nation. In 1919, a portion of the Red Army advanced westward on an operation called Target Vistula;[17] its goal was to overrun Poland on its way to Germany and foment communist revolution in both countries. By August 1920, Soviet forces had reached the outskirts of Warsaw and appeared to be on the verge of taking the city, but Piłsudski and his commanders Władysław Sikorski, Kazimierz Sosnkowski, Józef Haller, Franciszek Latinik, Bolesław Roja, and Edward Rydz-Śmigły stiffened the city's defenses. Piłsudski planned and executed a counterattack that routed the Red Army and forced it back into Byelorussia.

There were attempts to define the Polish-Soviet border peacefully. In 1919, British Foreign Secretary George Curzon proposed a demarcation that became known as the Curzon Line. It was not implemented, but the idea was revived in July 1920 during the Polish-Soviet War. However, at that time the Red Army was pushing its way into Poland, and Lenin, confident of victory, rejected it. After the Polish victory, Warsaw and Moscow negotiated the Treaty of Riga. The new border was about 250 kilometers east of the Curzon Line, giving Poland 135,000 square kilometers more territory than it would have had were the Curzon Line adopted. This region, known as *kresy wschodnie* (eastern borderlands), was usually referred to as *kresy*.

When the territorial conflicts had been settled, the Second Republic had borders with Germany, Czechoslovakia, Romania, the Soviet Union, Lithuania, and Latvia. Its success in fixing its borders caused considerable resentment in most of those nations and made targets of Piłsudski and other prominent Poles. In September 1921, Piłsudski attended the opening of a trade fair in Lwów and was targeted in an unsuccessful assassination attempt by a Ukrainian independence activist.[18]

The Second Republic had challenges beyond creating a system of government and forming a military. It created a uniform economic structure and taxation system, instituted a common currency, and developed an

---

[17] Vistula is the English name for the Wisła River.
[18] Piłsudski's would-be assassin was Stepan Fedak. During the Second World War, he collaborated with the Germans; his last known whereabouts were in Berlin in 1945.

education system. The new government introduced reforms that included an eight-hour workday, free education, and women's suffrage. It embarked on major industrialization and infrastructure projects, including construction of a rail line connecting Warsaw and Kraków.[19] Port facilities were a crucial problem. The Free City of Danzig levied exorbitant tariffs on Polish imports and exports, and during the Polish-Soviet War, German stevedores refused to unload armaments shipped to Poland. Unable to rely on Danzig, Poland began to develop a new port at the small fishing village of Gdynia.[20]

Political stability was elusive. In 1919, Piłsudski's title had been changed to *Naczelnik Państwa*, removing the "provisional" qualifier, and a temporary constitution was implemented. The Second Republic's first prime minister was the socialist Jędrzej Moraczewski; in January 1919, Piłsudski appointed Paderewski to succeed Moraczewski. Hopes that Paderewski would be a unifying figure were dashed when his government failed to last a year. This instability was an unfortunate characteristic of the government. From 1918 to September 1921, the nation had five prime ministers: one from PPS, two agrarians from *Polskie Stronnictwo Ludowe "Piast"* (PSL "Piast," Polish Peasant Party "Piast"), one nationalist from ND's new political party *Związek Ludowo-Narodowy* (Popular National Union),[21] and one independent (Paderewski).

A new constitution was adopted in March 1921. It introduced a presidency, albeit a weak one; the legislative chambers held the greatest powers. In light of the very limited presidential powers, Piłsudski chose not to seek the office, and Poland's first president, Gabriel Narutowicz, was elected in November 1922.[22] He was not affiliated with a political party but was supported by PPS and two PSL factions and was a Piłsudski follower. He defeated ND's preferred candidate, Count Maurycy Zamoyski. Narutowicz took office on December 11, and on December 14, Piłsudski handed over his powers, ending his service as *Naczelnik Państwa*. Narutowicz served a mere five days. He was assassinated on December 16 by Eligiusz Niewiadomski, a painter, art critic, and ND supporter, at an exhibition at the National Gallery of Art. Niewiadomski later claimed he originally wanted

---

[19] Warsaw and Kraków had been under the rule of two different partitioning powers; neither had interest in building a rail line between the two cities.
[20] Danzig's German population scoffed at Gdynia, thinking it impossible for Poland to successfully execute a project of this massive scale. By the mid-1930s, Gdynia was handling most Polish freight, Danzig's economy was nearing collapse, and its government demanded that Poland use its port facilities.
[21] *Związek Ludowo-Narodowy* was formed in 1919 to succeed *Stronnictwo Narodowo-Demokratyczne*.
[22] Under the March Constitution, the president was elected by *Sejm* and *Senat* deputies.

to kill Piłsudski, but since Piłsudski had not run for the presidency, he killed Narutowicz instead. In December, Stanisław Wojciechowski from PSL *Piast* was elected president.[23]

Sejm and *Senat* sessions regularly descended into partisan bickering, and neither the president nor the prime minister had the power to stop it. In Piłsudski's view, the *Sejm* and *Senat* were consumed with petty squabbles, and their inability to set aside partisan differences to address more urgent matters was leaving the nation economically and militarily vulnerable. Germany started a trade war with Poland in 1925, and that same year, Germany signed a series of agreements, known as the Locarno Treaties, that normalized relations with France, Belgium, Italy, and the United Kingdom and fixed its western borders. Conspicuously, Locarno left Germany's eastern borders open for revision. Both Poland and Czechoslovakia had sent representatives to the conference, but they had no say in the deliberations. Locarno diminished Poland's trust in France, led to the downfall of the government,[24] and convinced Piłsudski that his nation would need a strong military to defend itself.

Poland's efforts to define its borders and defend itself from Russian and German revanchism led to difficult relations with Czechoslovakia, Lithuania, Germany, and the Soviet Union and resentment from a portion of the Ukrainian people. In 1920, a group of Ukrainians formed the Ukrainian Military Organization (UVO); this group was responsible for the 1921 attempt on Piłsudski's life.[25] Lithuania resented the loss of Wilno, Czechoslovakia remained displeased with the division of the Cieszyn region, Germany seethed at the "free city" status of Danzig and Polish rule over Wielkopolska and Upper Silesia, and Moscow was upset that its plans to export revolution had been checked. Germany began covertly supporting UVO with money and arms. Poland's economy was racked by inflation, the military needed to be modernized, and there was no shortage of road, rail, bridge, and other infrastructure projects that needed to be funded, such as a much-needed rail line connecting Upper Silesia with Gdynia. Yet Poland's politicians still could not find a way to work together to improve matters; since 1921, there had been another seven prime ministers and nine governments.[26]

---

[23] *Sejm* Marshal Maciej Rataj temporarily succeeded him.
[24] Prime Minister Władysław Grabski's government failed in the wake of Locarno.
[25] Stepan Fedak was a UVO member.
[26] Such instability was not uncommon in interwar Europe. During this period, Hungary had sixteen governments, Romania had twenty-five, France had forty-three (five in 1933 alone), and Yugoslavia had seventeen. Between 1918 and the end of their existence in 1938, Austria had seventeen governments and Czechoslovakia had ten.

Piłsudski felt strongly that these issues should take precedence, and his frustrations peaked in May. In a newspaper interview, Piłsudski condemned the excessive power wielded by *Sejm* and *Senat* deputies and declared that he was ready to restore the nation to political health.[27] On the night of May 11, the Warsaw military garrison was placed on alert; some units marched to the town of Rembertów, east of Warsaw, and declared their support for Piłsudski. The following day, they advanced on Warsaw and took control of bridges crossing the Wisła. The government declared a state of emergency. At five in the afternoon, Piłsudski met President Wojciechowski on the Poniatowski Bridge. Piłsudski demanded the resignation of Prime Minister Witos and his Council of Ministers; in return, Wojciechowski demanded that Piłsudski call off his supporters and submit to the government's authority. Neither budged from his position, and open fighting broke out that evening.

The following morning, the Roman Catholic Church began negotiations, but no resolution was reached. PPS called for a general strike in support of Piłsudski. Crucially, the Railwaymen's Union joined and prevented government reinforcements from reaching the capital. Wanting to prevent a civil war, Wojciechowski and Witos resigned. Piłsudski saw to the creation of a new government under Kazimierz Bartel and took the position of minister of military affairs for himself. Ignacy Mościcki was elected president, but it was clear that Piłsudski held the power.

Piłsudski's promise to restore the nation to political health was realized in a movement called *Sanacja*,[28] which later formed a non-party organization called *Bezpartyjny Blok Współpracy z Rządem* (BBWR, Nonpartisan Bloc for Cooperation with the Government). BBWR's stated purpose was to provide a political structure that placed the good of the state ahead of party interests; in practice, however, it was a grouping of Piłsudski's supporters.

BBWR made its electoral debut in the March 1928 legislative elections. It took the most seats but did not achieve a clear majority in either the *Sejm* or *Senat*, and those seats it did not win were divided among an even larger number of parties.[29] Kazimierz Bartel, a BBWR member, was appointed prime minister. This fragmentation caused great concern among Piłsudski's opponents, and in 1929, a group of centrist and leftist parties

---

[27] The interview was with the newspaper *Kurier Poranny*. The edition containing his interview was confiscated by the government.

[28] *Sanacja* took its name from *sanatio*, Latin for healing, and reflected Piłsudski's intent to morally heal political life.

[29] In 1922, twelve parties held *Sejm* seats, and eight parties held *Senat* seats. In 1928, almost twice as many parties (twenty-three) won *Sejm* seats, and twelve parties were represented in *Senat*.

formed the *Centrolew* coalition as a consolidated opposition.[30] *Centrolew* succeeded in securing a vote of no confidence in Bartel's government, and the legislature was dissolved, necessitating new elections. Wanting a clear majority, the *Sanacja* government arrested twenty opposition party leaders in the run-up to the 1930 elections on charges of plotting a coup and imprisoned them in a fortress in Brześć. BBWR won majorities in both the *Sejm* and *Senat*. *Centrolew* again attempted a vote of no confidence, but this time it failed, and the coalition itself crumbled in 1931. Its failure was hastened by the nation's generally positive view of Piłsudski and its lack of faith in *Centrolew's* ability to forestall an economic crisis stemming from the global economic depression. ND also reorganized; it dissolved *Związek Ludowo-Narodowy* in 1928 and replaced it with *Stronnictwo Narodowe* (SN, National Party).

In the late 1920s, Josef Stalin took power in the Soviet Union and began aggressive industrialization and militarization programs. Adolf Hitler's National Socialist Party emerged as a strong force in German politics, playing on resentments from postwar loss of territory and crippling reparation payments to grow his power. Piłsudski saw both as existential threats. Poland's industrial capabilities lagged behind both Germany's and the Soviet Union's, and Piłsudski grasped that their military capabilities would soon be superior to Poland's. He needed to buy time to strengthen the economy and military, and he strategically began to pursue treaties with both countries. After several years of negotiations, Poland and the Soviet Union signed a non-aggression pact in 1932, pledging peaceful relations. It was effective for three years; in 1934, both sides agreed to extend it to December 31, 1945. In January 1934, Poland and Germany agreed to a non-aggression pact with a term of ten years.

Piłsudski and the government then faced the problem of funding expansion of the military. About one third of the national budget was allocated to the military, a percentage significantly higher than in other European nations, but Poland's much smaller economy and budget meant that its total military expenditures were comparatively modest. Since sufficient funds were not available from the budget, the government sought other sources. In 1933, *Fundusz Obrony Morskiej* (FOM, Maritime Defense Fund) was created to solicit private contributions for the navy. It was very successful: the nation contributed about 10.7 million *złoty*, most of which

---

[30] The term *Centrolew* reflected its composition of centrist (*centrowiec*) and leftist (*lewicowiec*) parties.

was used to fund construction of the submarine ORP *Orzeł*[31] and several fast gunboats.[32]

In June 1934, a Ukrainian activist assassinated Minister of Internal Affairs Bronisław Pieracki. The assassin was a member of the Organization of Ukrainian Nationalists (OUN), a group created in Vienna in 1929 out of UVO. Over the course of its existence, OUN claimed responsibility for over sixty murders, five bombings, numerous robberies, and many acts of sabotage. A wave of police raids followed, resulting in dozens of arrests and confiscation of hundreds of documents, some of which confirmed German, Czechoslovak, and Lithuanian support for OUN activities. Two days after Pieracki's assassination, *Sanacja* opened a prison at Bereza Kartuska to detain persons viewed as a "threat to security, peace, and social order." In addition to terrorists, Bereza Kartuska would be used to detain communists, criminals, and prominent opponents of the government.

Creation of a strong presidency remained one of Piłsudski's goals. After the 1926 coup, the March Constitution was amended to reduce powers held by the *Sejm* and *Senat*, but he wanted a more permanent solution. This was achieved in the new constitution adopted in April 1935.[33] Legislative acts now required presidential approval to become law, the president gained the right to dissolve the *Sejm* and *Senat*, one third of *Senat* seats were presidential appointees, and the president had the power to issue decrees. Opponents of Piłsudski and *Sanacja* considered these changes to be contrary to democratic principles and categorized the April Constitution as authoritarian. Mostly overlooked in the controversy was Article 13 (2)(b), a clause that empowered the president to name his successor in wartime.

At the time the April Constitution was implemented, few knew that Piłsudski's health had been in decline. For several years he had suffered from liver cancer, and he died on May 12, 1935. The announcement of his death came as a shock to the nation. Most of his opponents expressed their condolences civilly; even SN kept its criticism to a minimum. Poland's communists, however, denounced him as a capitalist and fascist;

---

[31] ORP *Orzeł* was commissioned on February 2, 1938.
[32] Creation of FOM was rooted in 1923's *Liga Obrony Powietrznej i Przeciwgazowe* (LOPP, League of Air and Anti-Gas Defense), instituted to collect funds for military aviation.
[33] The April 1935 Constitution is generally known as the April Constitution; the March 1921 Constitution is typically called the March Constitution.

their condemnation was seconded by German, Ukrainian, and Lithuanian extremists. In contrast, many of the Second Republic's ethnic minorities mourned his passing, as did the Orthodox, Protestant, Jewish, and Islamic communities. His body was carried to Kraków on a funeral train; thousands lined the tracks to see it pass. He was laid to rest in the crypt of the cathedral on Wawel, and his heart was entombed in the grave of his mother in Wilno.

Piłsudski left a void that could not be filled. Neither President Mościcki nor General Edward Rydz-Śmigły, who took charge of the military, commanded the same respect afforded to Piłsudski. For the next few years, the Second Republic was governed by what were derisively called "Piłsudski's colonels" or simply "the colonels." These were his close associates from the Legions and included Minister of Foreign Affairs Józef Beck and Adam Koc. His opponents, however, now saw an opportunity to break *Sanacja* rule. Prominent among them was General Władysław Sikorski.

Sikorski had opposed the 1926 coup. Piłsudski had punished him in 1928 by relieving him of his command and not giving him a new assignment. With no responsibilities, he devoted his time to studying and writing books about military history and theory. He spent a great deal of time in France writing on military matters, working with the École Supérieure de Guerre (French war college), and cultivating contacts with the French government and military. He remained in contact with Paderewski, who was living near Morges, Switzerland. In 1936, they formed an alliance of centrist political parties that became known as *Front Morges*. Their goals were to form a new government—with Paderewski as president and Wincenty Witos as prime minister—to undo what they considered to be authoritarian policies and to cultivate closer ties with France. *Front Morges* received little publicity or support in Poland, but its followers formed a new party, *Stronnictwo Pracy* (SP, Labor Party).

BBWR ceased to exist a few months after Piłsudski's death. Adam Koc organized most of its remnants into *Obóz Zjednoczenia Narodowego* (OZN, Camp of National Unity), a group dedicated to a strong military and defense of the new constitution. SN continued to function, although Dmowski's health was worsening and he restricted himself to writing books and articles. When he died in January 1939, over one hundred thousand attended his funeral, but the government declined to send an official representative.

During this time, Warsaw viewed growing German and Soviet military strength with alarm. The military's budget remained insufficient to deter or repulse an attack by either neighbor; additional funding was crucial. Inspired by FOM's success, Mościcki issued a decree in April 1936 creating *Fundusz Obrony Narodowej* (FON, National Defense Fund). FON collected funds from the sale of state property, loans from abroad, and donations from the population. Citizens gave cash, jewelry, paintings, silver, and real estate; even schoolchildren contributed. By May 1939, FON had raised about one billion *złoty*; about 37.7 million was from public donations. This represented over one *złoty* per capita, a highly impressive response considering the economic environment.

Contributions came from around the world, and ethnic minorities joined in the effort, with significant contributions made by the Jewish, Ukrainian, and Byelorussian populations. Cash donations were used immediately to purchase arms and munitions. Gifts of gold and silver objects were prepared for conversion into bullion.

Mościcki and Rydz-Śmigły were right to be concerned. Germany's aggressive foreign policy had troubling implications for Poland. In 1936, the German military had occupied the Rhineland, a direct violation of the Versailles treaty. Two years later, under the pretext of unifying German-speaking people, Germany annexed Austria. Neither move brought more than faint protests. Later in 1938, Hitler demanded annexation of Czechoslovakian territories populated by ethnic Germans, and in late September he met with Italian dictator Benito Mussolini, British Prime Minister Neville Chamberlain, and French Prime Minister Édouard Daladier to press his case. Chamberlain and Daladier acquiesced. Germany incorporated areas it referred to as Sudetenland; the remainder formed the short-lived Second Czechoslovak Republic, which Germany later divided into the Slovak Republic and the Protectorate of Bohemia and Moravia, both under German supervision. German aggression extended to Lithuania; in March 1939, it demanded and received the Klaipėda region.

Stalin was similarly aggressive. He had forcibly imposed Soviet authority in Ukraine in 1932–1933 by inflicting the Holodomor, an engineered famine that took several million lives. Afterwards, he consolidated his authority by ruthlessly eliminating political enemies and even some of his allies in a period known as the Great Terror. He viewed Soviet citizens who were ethnic Poles with suspicion, and the head of the NKVD, the Soviet Union's security service,[34] issued Order No. 00485, "On the liqui-

---

[34] NKVD's official name was People's Commissariat for Internal Affairs.

dation of Polish sabotage and espionage groups and units of the POW." Stalin ordered the NKVD to eliminate the Poles. NKVD officers made lists of Poles, sometimes by looking for Polish names in telephone directories. About 110,000 Poles were killed, and another 28,000 were deported into the depths of the Soviet Union. Most of those killed were men; women were deported, and children were placed in orphanages and brought up with no knowledge of their origins.

By all appearances, Germany and the Soviet Union were headed to war. Nazi Germany railed against communism, while the Soviet Union unequivocally condemned fascism. Both began to look for allies, and each pressured Warsaw to grant their military free passage. From Poland's perspective, both requests were essentially seeking consent to occupy Poland. Sikorski, understanding that his nation was in peril, returned from France, put aside his dislike of *Sanacja*, and offered his services. He petitioned Rydz-Śmigły for an assignment but was refused.

Beck, Edward Raczyński, Poland's ambassador in London, and Juliusz Łukasiewicz, Poland's ambassador in Paris, worked feverishly to obtain British and French support. Both the United Kingdom and France pledged to guarantee the independence of Poland, Belgium, Romania, Greece, and Turkey; Britain went further by agreeing to form a military alliance with Poland. England, France, and the Soviet Union started talks to contain German aggression. Britain and France pressured Poland to permit the Red Army to pass through its territory if Germany attacked, but Beck refused, stating his government's concerns that if the Red Army entered Poland, it would never leave. Poland's situation was complicated by Hitler's April declaration that the Polish-German non-aggression agreement of 1934 was void.

While the British–French–Soviet talks were ongoing, People's Commissar for Foreign Affairs Vyacheslav Molotov welcomed German Foreign Minister Joachim von Ribbentrop to Moscow. On August 23, stunning news reached the West: they had concluded the Treaty of Non-Aggression between Germany and the Union of Soviet Socialist Republics, better known as the Molotov–Ribbentrop Pact. Officially, it was a guarantee that neither would attack the other or ally itself with the other's enemies. What was not known at the time was that it included a secret protocol defining a division of central Europe between them.

Molotov–Ribbentrop provided Raczyński with the leverage he needed to conclude the Agreement of Mutual Assistance between the United Kingdom and Poland, a pact committing the United Kingdom to declare war on

Germany were it to attack Poland. Warsaw also relied on its long-standing alliance with France, which had been renegotiated in May, obliging both armies to support one another in the event of a German attack.[35] Maurice Gamelin, Commander of the French Army, promised a strong offensive within three weeks of a German attack on Poland. As Rydz-Śmigły began to mobilize the military, Sikorski again made it known that he was ready to accept an assignment but was again rejected.

On August 30, Łukasiewicz received word that Hitler had met with the British ambassador and had demanded that Poland abandon its claims to Danzig and cede Pomerania and parts of the Poznań and Śląsk regions to Germany.[36] Hitler had added an ultimatum: Beck had twenty-four hours to come to Berlin and sign an agreement to this effect.

Throughout Germany, the military was moving. Tanks, armored vehicles, artillery, and infantry massed along the Polish border. Ships and submarines took positions on the Baltic coast. More than two thousand aircraft prepared to go into action. These moves were apparent to Poland as well as Britain and France, but both London and Paris pressured Warsaw to not mobilize its military for fear of provoking Germany. On August 31, German troops dressed in Polish uniforms conducted attacks on a radio station in Gleiwitz, a customs station at Hochlinden, a railway at Jablunka Pass, a forest station in Pitschen, a communications station in Neubersteich, and a railroad station in Alt-Eiche. Berlin declared these acts to be proof of Polish aggression against a German nation that only wanted peace. To bolster their claims, they placed bodies of executed concentration camp prisoners dressed in Polish uniforms at the sites of their provocations. In the early morning hours of September 1, Germany unleashed its military against Poland.

---

[35] Although the renewed Franco–Polish agreement, known as the Kasprzycki–Gamelin Convention, had been signed in May 1939, the French government did not ratify it until September 4.
[36] Hitler's demand would have deprived Poland of its access to the Baltic Sea, including surrendering Gdynia to Germany.

Invasion

Władysław Sikorski,
Prime Minister of the Republic of Poland 1939-1943

FRIDAY WAS MARKET DAY IN Wieluń, a town of fifteen thousand about twenty miles east of the German border. At half past four in the morning, some farmers were already taking their places in the main square. As they prepared for a busy day selling their produce, the calm was shattered by the wail of air-raid sirens, but nobody panicked; they knew that a practice alert was scheduled. Within a few minutes, however, they heard the drone of aircraft followed by the shriek of dive bombers, the screech of falling bombs, and the roar of explosions. Wieluń, a town with no military presence and of no strategic value, was under attack. Within minutes the town center was aflame, the hospital had been reduced to rubble, and people fleeing the carnage were strafed. Waves of bombers relentlessly pounded Wieluń for the next nine hours. About three-quarters of the town was obliterated, and an unknown number of residents lost their lives.[1]

Eighteen minutes after the first bombs fell on Wieluń, the German battleship *Schleswig-Holstein*, in Danzig on what was reputed to be a friendly

---

[1] The exact number of people killed in the attack on Wieluń is not known. According to IPN, 127 deaths have been confirmed beyond doubt; this is the minimum number. Norman Davies claims over 1,000 were killed, and Sylwia Słomińska contends that 1,200 were killed, although in 2013 historian Mateusz Jan Piątkowski stated that the figure of 1,200 was the total number of victims in all of the Wieluń area during the early days of the war. In communist Poland, propaganda claimed anywhere from 1,200 to 2,169 victims. Many were buried in mass graves by the invader, making an accurate count impossible.

visit, trained its guns on the Polish garrison on the Westerplatte peninsula and opened fire. Simultaneously, German police and paramilitary troops took to the city's streets. Their actions to seize the Polish post office complex were particularly savage. After several unsuccessful attacks, they pumped gasoline into the basement and tossed in a hand grenade.

At the break of dawn, the German Army breached Poland's northern, western, and southern borders. Infantry poured across the frontier in the wake of mechanized units, while artillery shells and bombs rained down indiscriminately on military, government, and civilian targets. That morning, Hitler delivered a fiery speech in the Reichstag contending that the invasion was in response to Polish aggression. He was referring to the German provocations from the previous day.[2]

As reports of the attacks streamed in, the Ministry of Foreign Affairs struggled to contact its embassies. Finally reaching Łukasiewicz at nine, the Ministry briefed him, ordered him to inform the French government, and directed him to apprise Raczyński to do the same in London. Łukasiewicz instructed his deputy Feliks Frankowski to contact Raczyński and rushed off to meet with Foreign Minister Georges Bonnet. Poland received assurances of France's support; Bonnet promised Łukasiewicz that France would live up to its obligations.

Immediately after speaking with Frankowski, Raczyński hurried to Number 10 Downing Street and met with Foreign Secretary Lord Halifax. Raczyński invoked the agreement they had signed barely a week earlier; Halifax concurred. They concluded their brief meeting as Britain's Cabinet assembled; Chancellor of the Exchequer Sir John Simon grasped Raczyński's hand and assured him that the United Kingdom didn't abandon its friends.

Poland's strategy was to halt the invader's advance while France and Britain mobilized and attacked Germany's lightly defended western border, but help was slow in coming. Łukasiewicz stormed into the Ministry of Foreign Affairs on September 2 demanding to know why France had not declared war and accusing Bonnet of abandoning Poland. One day later, both France and Britain declared war against Germany, and British troops began to land in France. France was obliged to launch aerial attacks immediately but did not do so; further, it refused to permit Britain's Royal Air Force (RAF) to attack Germany from French airfields for fear of reprisals. Gamelin refused to meet with any Polish military envoys and went so far

---

[2] Germany's provocation was known variously as "Operation Himmler," "Operation Konserve," or "Operation Canned Goods."

as to issue orders barring them from contacting him. Already in Poland there was talk that France was betraying its commitment, but Poland continued to await a western offensive. On September 7, the French Army made a tenuous advance into German territory. Despite meeting negligible resistance, it ventured no further; in little more than a week it withdrew. Other than this operation, French assistance was limited to sending shiploads of military equipment to Poland via Romania, and Bonnet himself was responsible. Prior to the German attack, he urged Daladier to pressure Poland into renouncing any claims to Danzig and wanted to end the Franco-Polish military alliance; after the invasion, he argued in a cabinet session against declaring war. Britain did little more. Royal Navy ships blockaded Germany, and the RAF launched an ineffective air raid on a German naval base. Thus, Poland fought alone.

Although Poland's military fought tenaciously, Warsaw was in danger of being overrun. Mościcki knew that the government and treasury had to be evacuated a safe distance from the invaders. On September 6, he and the government arrived in Lublin, but continued pressure forced them to abandon Lublin for Krzemieniec on the ninth. Again under attack, they moved to Zaleszczyki on the thirteenth.[3] On September 14, Mościcki appointed Marshal Edward Rydz-Śmigły as his successor; he and his government then proceeded to the town of Kuty,[4] across the Czeremosz River[5] from Romania.

Bank Polski evacuated its gold reserves, valued at 363 million *złoty* ($68 million),[6] first to Lublin and then to Łuck.[7] Government and Bank Polski officials, concerned that Łuck was also vulnerable, decided on September 10 to evacuate the gold to the West and asked Bucharest, London, and Paris for assistance. The Romanian government gave permission to transit the country, Britain offered assistance to transport the gold from Romania to Lebanon, and France agreed to take it from Beirut to a Banque de France vault. On the evening of September 13, Poland's gold arrived at the rail station in Śniatyn, near the Romanian border. That night, a detail of Polish soldiers took it across the border and headed for the Black Sea port of Constanța. Late in the evening of September 15, 66 tonnes of gold bullion were loaded onto the British tanker SS *Eocene*.[8] Chagrined that

---

[3] Zaleszczyki is now the Ukrainian city of Zalishchyky.
[4] Kuty also is now in Ukraine; it is still known as Kuty.
[5] The Czeremosz River is now known as the Cheremosh and lies in Ukraine.
[6] This equated to 62 tonnes of gold. Poland held another 17.5 tonnes on deposit in other nations.
[7] Łuck is now in Ukraine and is named Lutsk.
[8] Poland left four tonnes of gold in Bucharest, sold one tonne, and left the remaining three tonnes in Bucharest for the duration of the war.

the gold was about to escape their grasp, German agents pressured the Romanian government to seize the ship and its cargo. Before they could act, Captain Robert E. Brett and his crew doused the ship's lights, cast off quietly, and eased out of port under cover of darkness. They stealthily made their way along the coast and arrived in Istanbul on the nineteenth with their cargo intact. The gold was offloaded into waiting freight cars and hauled overland through Syria to Beirut. The French Navy took it to France; by the middle of October, Poland's gold was safely in the vaults of Banque de France in Nevers.

Evacuating FON holdings was a greater challenge. Its assets, a mix of cash, coins, securities, checks, jewelry, and a hoard of gold and silver objects, were worth one billion *złoty* ($187 million). Its custodians packed everything into containers, loaded them into several automobiles, and departed on September 9. This convoy navigated clogged roads to the Romanian border, traveling mostly after dark, and made it unscathed. This arduous evacuation was completed on September 26, when the assets arrived intact at the Polish embassy in Bucharest.

Władysław Sikorski and his wife, Helena, departed Warsaw on the night of September 6 and headed southeast to Osmolice, a village on the Wieprz River near the town of Ryki. Their temporary refuge was the manor house of the Leśniowski family, parents of Władysław and Helena's son-in-law, Stanisław.

Anticipating the need for covert activity, Sikorski called a group of trusted associates to the manor house, and they created a framework for an underground civil and military structure. At two in the morning on September 10, Sikorski left for Lwów. One week later, he authorized creation of *Centralny Komitet Organizacji Niepodległościowych* (CKON, Central Committee of Independence Organizations), consisting solely of apolitical groups and groups opposed to *Sanacja*.[9] He then crossed into Romania.

After fifteen days, German progress had slowed. Resistance was more tenacious than anticipated, Poland's army was launching counterattacks, and heavy rains impeded operations. *Armia Małopolska*, under the command of General Sosnkowski, defeated two German divisions on the sixteenth, taking several thousand prisoners in the process. Poland's

---

[9] CKON was headed by *Biuro Polityczne* (Political Bureau). More than a dozen resistance organizations recognized its authority, including *Organizacja Wojskowa* (OW, Military Organization). Sikorski viewed OW as the core of a future Polish army. CKON and its affiliated groups would later receive funds from the government-in-exile.

government remained in control of the eastern half of the country, including Wilno and Lwów. Combat aircraft continued to roll off a production line in Pińsk. Border crossings with Lithuania, Latvia, the Soviet Union, Hungary, and Romania remained open; the Romanian border, referred to as the "Romanian bridgehead," was of paramount importance as it allowed French shipments of tanks, aircraft, artillery, and ammunition to flow into Poland.[10] Worse for Berlin, Poland's oil fields remained beyond its grasp, and this became a worry. With practically no oil reserves, Germany was on the verge of running out of fuel. For Mościcki, his government, and the military, there remained hope that Germany could be repelled.

That hope evaporated in Moscow at three in the morning on September 17. Wacław Grzybowski, Poland's ambassador to the Soviet Union, was summoned to the People's Commissariat for Foreign Affairs;[11] when he arrived, he was taken to the office of Vladimir Petrovich Potemkin, First Deputy of the People's Commissariat for Foreign Affairs. Grzybowski later recounted that he expected bad news but was utterly unprepared for what awaited him. Potemkin proceeded to read a diplomatic note from Molotov claiming that Poland had lost all of its industrial and cultural centers, contending that the Polish government had ceased to exist, and declaring that all Polish–Soviet agreements were now irrelevant. He went on to inform Grzybowski that the Red Army had been ordered to cross the prewar border to protect the Ukrainian and Byelorussian people. The note ended with the charge that the Polish government bore responsibility for the war.

Grzybowski emphatically protested. He pointed out that Poland's government was still functioning, that eastern Poland remained under government control, that normal services continued to function outside war zones, and that Poland's military continued to fight and was launching successful counterattacks. Grzybowski refused to accept the note, advised Potemkin that he would inform his government of this exchange, and returned to the embassy. According to diplomatic protocols, the note had to be delivered to Poland's ambassador. Since Grzybowski refused to accept it, Potemkin had the note delivered to the Polish embassy in the morning mail.

This note was a diplomatic cover and an attempt to create a veneer of legitimacy; the Red Army's invasion of Poland was a foregone conclusion. After signing the Molotov–Ribbentrop Pact, Germany and the Soviet

---

[10] Although this equipment was most welcome, it could not compensate for the lack of French military action.

[11] The People's Commissariat for Foreign Affairs was the name used at that time for the USSR's Ministry of Foreign Affairs.

Union had agreed on their plans to invade Poland.[12] One hour after Grzybowski's meeting with Potemkin, the Red Army violated Poland's eastern border with an invasion force of over 500,000 soldiers. The Polish government issued a communique declaring, "The Polish Ambassador in Moscow has refused to accept the Note presented to him today by the Soviet Government." It went on to state, "The Polish Government solemnly protest [sic] against the unilateral violation of the Non-Aggression Pact by Russia and against the invasion of Polish territory at a moment when the whole Polish Nation is making a supreme effort to repel the German aggressor. The Polish Government protests against the motives alleged in the Note of the Soviet Government because the Polish Government are carrying on their normal activities and the Polish Army is successfully resisting the enemy."[13]

The London embassy followed with a statement citing the specific agreements that had been abrogated and concluded with a sharp rebuke of Moscow: "Therefore, by the act of wanton aggression committed this morning, the Soviet Government stands self-condemned as a violator of its international obligations, thus contradicting all the moral principles upon which Soviet Russia pretended to base her foreign policy since her admittance into the League of Nations."[14]

The Soviet invasion dashed Poland's hopes of survival. Mościcki realized that any realistic chance of holding out was gone, but neither he nor his generals considered surrender; the fight would continue from abroad. Prior to the Soviet invasion, France had agreed to host the Polish government and military.[15] Commanders ordered their soldiers to leave for Romania, Hungary, Lithuania, or Latvia and make their way to France to regroup.

Romania was the preferred route, but that country was under intense German and Soviet pressure to prohibit passage. The Romanian government had officially declared neutrality on September 6, and on September 15, the country's Crown Council issued a decree sealing its border. Despite this, on the sixteenth, Beck petitioned the Romanian government to allow the Poles to transit Romania on their way to France, and on the seventeenth, King Carol II decided to disregard foreign pressure and agreed.

---

[12] In 1948, the US Department of State published a book of documents captured from German archives titled *Nazi–Soviet Relations, 1939–1941: Documents from the Archives of The German Foreign Office*. Among other information, it contained secret protocol. The Soviet Union responded quickly; that year, the Soviet Information Bureau published a book titled *Falsifiers of History*, an attempt to rebut the American book. Stalin personally edited and revised it.

[13] *Polish–Soviet Relations, 1918–1943*, pp. 97–98.

[14] *Polish–Soviet Relations, 1918–1943*, pp. 96–97.

[15] During the Great War, France had granted the Belgian government *droit de résidence* (right of residence), allowing it to function on French territory until its territory had been liberated. France granted Poland this same right, following the Belgian precedent.

Both nations signed an agreement that afternoon in Kuty. Mościcki issued a statement that he was moving the government abroad. That evening,[16] Mościcki and his government crossed the border into Romania and were promptly interned.

The Red Army was accompanied by thousands of NKVD officers. Communist sympathizers fashioned triumphal arches from tree branches and flowers and welcomed the invaders into their towns and cities with bread and salt. Disinformation claiming that the Red Army had mobilized to assist the Polish Army blared from loudspeakers, leaflets rained from the skies exhorting Polish soldiers to desert and to attack their officers, and peasants were showered with propaganda urging them to use their tools to beat "Polish lords."

About 660,000 Polish officers and soldiers were captured in September. In some cases, enlisted men were disarmed and released, but this was not universal practice. It was common for the Red Army's prisoners of war to be deported to gulags, although some were executed immediately, at times with horrendous barbarity.[17] Officers who were not murdered were separated from enlisted men and transported to special prisons; the largest were at Starobelsk, Kozelsk, and Ostashkov. Soviet propaganda alleged that Polish officers were oppressors and were hated by their men, a charge that was belied by the number of soldiers who concealed the identities of officers and chaplains to protect them from worse treatment.

Civilians were not spared. The NKVD entered Poland with lists of people to arrest; these ranged from government officials to professors, teachers, priests, policemen, journalists, and businessmen. They seized jails, filled them to overflowing, and tortured their prisoners. Nor did children escape Soviet wrath. Tank crews were known to lash Polish children to their armor, reasoning that Polish soldiers would not fire on them.[18]

The invaders were nearing realization of their shared objective. Elements of their armies began to meet. On September 22, they held a joint

---

[16] Historian Ludwik Łubieński puts the time of the border crossing at 11:15 p.m.

[17] In some cities and towns, captured Polish soldiers and civilians were bound together, laid on a road, and crushed alive by Red Army tanks. In Grodno, Red Army soldiers tied up Polish prisoners of war and dragged them behind tanks. In a military hospital in Grabowiec, the Red Army executed all doctors, staff, and patients.

[18] Thirteen-year-old Tadeusz Jasiński failed in his attempt to throw a gasoline bomb at a Red Army tank in Grodno. He was shot five times but didn't die; Red Army soldiers then tied him to the front of a tank. Two Polish women risked their lives to rescue him and hurried him to a hospital. His wounds were too severe, and he died in his mother's arms. In 2009, President Lech Kaczyński awarded him the Commander's Cross of the Order of Polonia Restituta.

victory parade in Brześć.[19] Final pockets of resistance were subdued in the next two weeks. An exhausted Warsaw, under attack since the first hours of the war, held out until September 28; off the coast of Gdynia, the garrison on Hel Peninsula fell on October 2. On October 6, the final battle ended at Kock, north of Lublin, when Polish forces ran out of ammunition and food. All the territory of the Second Republic was now occupied by Germany and the Soviet Union. In the Supreme Soviet, Molotov declared that the German Army and the Red Army had made quick work of the "bastard of the Treaty of Versailles."

Both invaders declared that Poland would never again exist and set about dismembering the country. Germany annexed northern and western Poland, Germanized place names, and expelled Poles. Danzig was incorporated into Germany, ending its "free city" status. Soviet authorities began referring to the areas they occupied as Western Byelorussia and Western Ukraine, claimed that the population had spontaneously requested incorporation into the Soviet Union, and conducted fraudulent plebiscites. Place names were changed, governments were established following the Soviet model, and education in Polish was forbidden. In a series of operations led by NKVD General Ivan Serov, ethnic Poles were forcibly expelled to the far reaches of the Soviet Union.

Lithuania benefited from Poland's partition. Soviet forces had occupied Wilno early in their invasion; in October, the Soviet Union and Lithuania concluded a mutual assistance treaty that granted Wilno and the surrounding area to Lithuania in exchange for establishment of Soviet military bases on Lithuanian territory.[20] Wilno then became Vilnius, and Lithuanian authorities began a campaign to eradicate Polish identity, culture, and language. Ethnic Poles were treated as Lithuanians who had been Polonized over several centuries and needed to embrace their true identity; they were forced to use the Lithuanian spelling of their names, their schools were closed, and they were forbidden to use the Polish language.

Britain and France refused to involve themselves in the Polish–Soviet conflict. A secret protocol in Poland's alliance with the United Kingdom specified that Britain would assist if Poland were attacked by Germany; a Soviet attack was not included in their treaty, and Prime Minister Neville

---

[19] Shortly thereafter, Brześć was renamed Brest-Litovsk; today it is known simply as Brest.
[20] To be fair, Lithuania's government signed the agreement under duress. Stalin told their government that regardless of a treaty, the Red Army would garrison troops in Lithuania. In short, the Red Army would either be invited or would invade. The Lithuanian president expressed doubts that the price to gain Wilno/Vilnius was too steep, but the Red Army was already moving to the border and was prepared to enter regardless.

Chamberlain issued only a vague condemnation. Britain's government wanted to maintain good relations with the Soviet Union for trade and as a potential ally against Germany. France declined to take any action or offer any assistance.

Two days before Warsaw fell, General Michał Tokarzewski-Karaszewicz approached General Juliusz Rómmel, commander of the city's defense, with a proposal to create an armed resistance organization and underground government. Later that day, Major Edmund Galinat arrived in Warsaw from Romania and reported to Rómmel. Galinat had been sent by Rydz-Śmigły with a proposal to create an underground military organization with Galinat in command. After considering both, Rómmel placed Tokarszewski in command of the military in occupied Poland.

Having received his orders, Tokarszewski organized *Służba Zwycięstwu Polski* (SZP, Service for Poland's Victory).[21] SZP's goals were to continue the fight against the German occupiers until Poland was liberated and prewar borders were restored, to reconstruct and reorganize armed forces in Poland, and to establish a temporary government structure in occupied Poland. Tokarszewski named Colonel Stefan Rowecki[22] as his deputy. SZP built a communications network, collected weapons, and started producing false identification papers. In November, SZP published the first issue of *Biuletyn Informacyjny (Information Bulletin)*, a newspaper that would grow into a national publication.[23] Tokarszewski also organized a political body, *Główna Rada Polityczna* (GRP, Main Political Council). GRP acted as a surrogate *Sejm*; its members came from PPS, SN, *Stronnictwo Ludowe* (SL), and *Stronnictwo Demokratyczne* (SD). A more unusual organization grew out of *Związek Harcerstwa Polskiego* (ZHP, Polish Scouting Association). German occupation authorities banned ZHP and executed some of its members, but many of those who avoided that fate reorganized as *Szare Szeregi* (Gray Ranks). They engaged in a broad range of activities such as sabotage, armed resistance, transporting munitions, acting as liaisons and couriers, conducting surveillance, smuggling Poles out of the Soviet zone, and assassinations.

---

[21] SZP was created on September 27, 1939, one day before Warsaw fell.
[22] Rowecki's pseudonym was "Grot." He is sometimes referred to as Stefan Grot-Rowecki.
[23] *Biuletyn Informacyjny* grew into a national publication with print runs nearing 50,000.

After Germany and the Soviet Union dismembered Poland, what remained was a section of the central and southern regions that included Warsaw, Kraków, Lublin, and Radom. This area was occupied by the German Army, administered by Germany, and designated as the *Generalne Gubernatorstwo* (General Government). German policy was to reduce the Polish population to the status of slaves; when the Poles had died off, the area was to be resettled by Germans. A program of cultural destruction ensued. Works of art were seized and shipped to Germany. The National Library in Warsaw was burned; over 3.6 million volumes were lost. All universities, secondary schools, and seminaries were closed. Jews were segregated and forced to live in overcrowded ghettos.

Poland was occupied, and tens of thousands of its soldiers and citizens were dead, wounded, or imprisoned. Wholesale expulsions were underway to clear Poles from areas where their presence was inconvenient. Cities, towns, and villages were pocked with smoldering ruins of government buildings, factories, schools, businesses, apartment buildings, houses, and churches. Roads, railways, and bridges had been obliterated. Irreplaceable artifacts, books, works of art, and cultural treasures were looted or destroyed. But Poland had not surrendered. The nation was one generation removed from German, Russian, and Austrian occupation, and a collective consciousness of survival and resistance under foreign subjugation remained strong. Thousands of soldiers evaded capture and headed to France, the government was in neutral Romania, and the treasury and some of the most important national treasures had been evacuated. Soldiers, government officials, and ordinary citizens remaining in Poland formed resistance organizations.

Unfortunately, the government was unable to leave Romania. Mościcki would have to find a solution to ensure the Second Republic's continued existence.

An Abbreviated Presidency

Bolesław Wienawa-Długoszowski,
President of the Republic of Poland 1939

IGNACY MOŚCICKI WAS in King Carol II's hunting lodge in the village of Bicaz, deep in the Carpathian Mountains. Prime Minister Składkowski and his Council of Ministers were about three hundred kilometers away in Slănic, and Rydz-Śmigły was more than four hundred kilometers away in Craiova. All were under guard, and their communications were monitored, making it impossible for them to act in their official roles. Raczyński and Łukasiewicz vigorously solicited the assistance of the British and French to persuade Romania to allow them, or at least Mościcki, to depart for France, but to no avail; neither Britain nor France made much effort on their behalf.

As Łukasiewicz was lobbying the French government and announcing the formation of the Polish Army in France,[1] he began to receive disconcerting information from Frankowski: Poland's ambassador to Romania, Roger Raczyński, and Romanian Minister of Foreign Affairs Grigore Gafencu had been discussing the need for Mościcki to appoint a successor.[2]

---

[1] On September 19, Łukasiewicz issued an appeal to Poles in France announcing the formation of the Polish Army in France and calling on them to register for military service.

[2] Roger Raczyński was Edward Raczyński's brother.

Two days after Mościcki and the government were interned, Gafencu informed Raczyński of their whereabouts and divulged that Germany had threatened to declare war on Romania if the Polish leaders were permitted to leave. Raczyński recounted their conversation: "Without seeking any legal justification, he told me honestly that he was in an extremely difficult situation. It is extremely difficult for him, and he is sorry that he has to stop the President of the Republic of Poland and the Polish Government in Romania for the time being, not being able to expose his country to an unequal war with Germany, which would have to end with disastrous results as in Poland."[3]

On September 20, Raczyński met with Mościcki in Bicaz, and the president considered his options. Clearly, Rydz-Śmigły could not succeed him, nor could Sosnkowski, whose precise whereabouts were unknown.[4] His pool of candidates was limited to people already in the West and to those in Romania who were free to depart. Raczyński proposed Ignacy Paderewski, Cardinal August Hlond, former Foreign Minister August Zaleski, and former *Senat* Marshal Władysław Raczkiewicz.[5] After discussing their merits, Mościcki handed Raczyński a large, sealed envelope and ordered him to get it to Łukasiewicz; he also instructed Raczyński to call as soon as he received a message from Łukasiewicz about the "Konecki family." Raczyński immediately returned to Bucharest and sent a coded telegram to Łukasiewicz advising him that an important envelope was being brought to him.

The next day, Raczyński called on Léon Noël, France's ambassador to Poland. Noël and his secretary were about to depart for Paris, and Raczyński entrusted them with Mościcki's envelope. At the same time, Minister Flondor, marshal of King Carol II's court, visited Mościcki and confirmed that he and the government would not be permitted to leave.[6] Mościcki decided to send Stanisław Łepkowski, head of his civil chancellery, to Paris to personally see to it that his orders were carried out, specifically instructing that his successor was to be in place before Warsaw

---

[3] Waldemar Kowalski, "Kryzys prezydencki 1939 roku" ("The Presidential Crisis of 1939," https://muzhp.pl/wiedza-on-line/kryzys-prezydencki-1939-roku).
[4] At the time Mościcki and Raczyński were meeting in Bicaz, Sosnkowski was still in Poland and in command of *Front Południowy* (Southern Front).
[5] Paderewski was in the United States. Cardinal Hlond had left Poland along with the government and traveled to Rome. Zaleski had left Poland to evacuate the assets of Bank Handlowy. Raczkiewicz left Poland on September 17 but was not interned.
[6] Romania's government was also under internal pressure from *Garda de Fier* (Iron Guard), a domestic fascist movement that supported the German invasion of Poland. *Garda de Fier* assassinated Prime Minister Armand Călinescu on September 21.

fell.⁷ Since Łepkowski was not a member of the government, he was permitted to leave Romania, doing so under the premise that he needed to go to Budapest to attend to his wife and their sick child. Łepkowski left Bicaz on September 22 and arrived in Bucharest the next morning. Before he departed for Paris, he telephoned Bolesław Wieniawa-Długoszowski, Poland's ambassador in Rome, advised him that Mościcki had ordered him to Paris, and arranged for them to meet in Milan.

Noël and his secretary arrived on September 24, accompanied by Władysław Sikorski. Noël's secretary went directly to the Polish embassy and delivered the envelope to Łukasiewicz. He found it contained two smaller envelopes, one addressed to him; in it were instructions to personally deliver the other envelope to Długoszowski.

At noon on the twenty-fifth, Długoszowski and Łepkowski reached Paris. Długoszowski immediately telephoned the embassy and was instructed to report without delay. When he arrived, Łukasiewicz gave him the envelope; it contained a decree appointing him president, a personal letter suggesting that he designate Cardinal August Hlond as his prime minister,⁸ and instructions to send a message to Raczyński in Bucharest stating that the Konecki family is fine (this was to let Mościcki know that Długoszowski had received his instructions). That evening, Raczyński received Długoszowski's message and telephoned Bicaz. Shortly thereafter, Łukasiewicz received this message from Bucharest: "Please ask Wieniawa to take care of the Konecki family."⁹ At about six that evening, Edward Raczyński arrived in Paris. Łukasiewicz advised him of the succession decree, and Raczyński was pleased. However, they were troubled when Łepkowski reported that Roger Raczyński met frequently in Bucharest with Sikorski, August Zaleski, and Stanisław Stroński, all opponents of Mościcki and *Sanacja*.

Early in the morning of September 26, Łukasiewicz handed a note to French Undersecretary of Foreign Affairs Auguste Champetier de Ribes announcing Długoszowski's presidency. Champetier de Ribes stated that this was precisely what should have been done and asked no questions. Łukasiewicz sent a coded message to Mościcki confirming that he could now notify King Carol II of his resignation; an edition of *Monitor Polski* was printed announcing the new president. With the matter of succession

---

⁷ The president's civil chancellery is his staff. The head of the civil chancellery is the equivalent of the chief of staff for a US president.
⁸ Długoszowski did ask Cardinal Hlond to take on the role of prime minister; Hlond declined.
⁹ Kowalski, "Kryzys prezydencki 1939 roku."

apparently resolved, Edward Raczyński returned to London to present a note to Lord Halifax announcing the appointment.

Bolesław Ignacy Florian Wieniawa-Długoszowski was a medical doctor, poet, polyglot, translator of literature, painter, soldier, former prisoner of the Soviet Union, aide to Józef Piłsudski, diplomat, politician, journalist, and one of the Second Republic's most colorful figures. He was born on July 22, 1881, in Maksymówka, near Stanisławów; his father, Bolesław, was a veteran of the January Uprising, an ardent patriot, and a member of a noble family under the Wieniawa heraldry. When he was quite young, his family moved to Bobowa, a town near Gorlice. In his youth, Długoszowski was a difficult student and changed schools several times; he later claimed this was due to his temperament and his dislike of Greek grammar. At his own request, he attended a Jesuit-run school in Chyrów, but its strict discipline was too much for him; he completed his secondary education in Nowy Sącz.[10]

Although his interests were artistic, Długoszowski acceded to his father's wishes and attended medical school at the University of Lemberg.[11] He had transformed himself into an excellent student, led an abstemious life, and graduated with honors in 1906. Despite his rigorous studies, he made time to immerse himself in the artistic community and frequented cafés favored by artists.

While in medical school, he was briefly engaged to the daughter of the university rector;[12] after graduation, he married opera singer Stefania Calvas.[13] They lived in Berlin for a year while he studied at the Academy of Fine Arts and then moved to Paris, where he practiced medicine and pursued his interest in art.[14] He also left his teetotaling ways behind, frequenting cafes and parties and engaging in a series of extramarital affairs, although not all women succumbed to his charms. Bronisława Berenson, a medical student and wife of attorney Leon Berenson, not only resisted his advances but warned other young ladies of his ways. Despite her initial

---

[10] He attended I Liceum Ogólnokształcące im. Jana Długosza (Jan Długosz Secondary School), named for Jan Długosz, a Roman Catholic priest considered to be Poland's first historian. Długosz was also a member of a noble family entitled to use the Wieniawa heraldry.

[11] Lemberg was the name the Austrians assigned to Lwów during the partitions.

[12] His first fiancé was Maria Balastis.

[13] Długoszowski and Calvas were married in the village of Słotwina, near Brzesko. Słotwina was incorporated into Brzesko in 1951.

[14] Along with sculptor Stanisław Kazimierz Ostrowski, Długoszowski founded Towarzystwo Artystów Polskich (Association of Polish Artists).

aversion to him, she would later prove to be an important figure in his life. Through his friends, he became involved in *Związek Strzelecki* (Riflemen's Association), a paramilitary cultural and educational organization that served as a legal front for ZWC. Długoszowski first met Piłsudski when he visited France in 1914 to inspect *Związek Strzelecki* branches.

This meeting changed his life. In a letter to his brother, he proclaimed that he had found his commander and now felt like a soldier. He left for Kraków in 1914 and began his military career in the infantry. He soon transferred to the cavalry, where he displayed ability, courage, and a willingness to take on difficult assignments; he also began to display his characteristic wit and sense of humor. In one incident, a captured Russian officer asked him what exactly the Polish legionaries were fighting for. Długoszowski replied, "We fight for freedom, and you for what?" The Russian responded, "And we for honor." "Apparently everyone is fighting for what they lack," answered Długoszowski.

In 1915, Długoszowski was assigned to be Piłsudski's adjutant and accompanied him on his travels until Piłsudski was arrested and imprisoned. Długoszowski was then conscripted into the Austrian Army, but he deserted and joined POW. He was sent on a mission to the Soviet Union to make contact with the French military mission in Moscow and with General Józef Haller, commander of a formation of Polish soldiers formerly in the Imperial Russian Army. After completing his tasks, he boarded a train in Moscow bound for Murmansk; from there he planned to travel to Paris with several French diplomats. His trip was interrupted when the *Cheka*[15] arrested him on the charge of being a POW member and imprisoned him in Moscow's Lubyanka and Taganka prisons.[16]

His release came about in an unlikely way. While in Petrograd he had unexpectedly met Bronisława Berenson. Her husband, Leon, had been *Cheka* founder Felix Dzerzhinsky's lawyer prior to the revolution, and she visited Długoszowski regularly in prison. Using her name and contacts, she prevailed on the authorities to release him to house arrest. In October, Długoszowski, accompanied by Bronisława, escaped from the Soviet

---

[15] *Cheka* was the original name of the Soviet Union's secret police. It was later known by several other names, most notably NKVD and KGB.
[16] Built in 1898 as the main office of the All-Russia Insurance Company, Lubyanka was seized after the Bolshevik Revolution and used for purposes far removed from insurance. It became the headquarters of the *Cheka* and was used as a prison. In Stalinist times, prisoners of special interest to the NKVD were imprisoned here. Prisoners referred to the Lubyanka as the building with the best view in Moscow because you could see Siberia from the basement. Taganka was a purpose-built prison dating back to 1804; it was razed in the 1950s.

Union.[17] After reaching Poland, Bronisława divorced Leon and married Długoszowski, who had himself divorced in 1918.[18]

Długoszowski resumed service as Piłsudski's adjutant during the Polish–Soviet War. After hostilities ceased, Długoszowski wanted nothing more than to command a cavalry regiment and remain in Warsaw, where he could immerse himself in its flourishing artistic community and enjoy its vibrant social life. This disappointed Piłsudski, who thought Długoszowski's intelligence, fluency in several languages, and charm made him an ideal candidate for diplomatic service. Piłsudski did appoint him military attaché to Romania, where he played a crucial role in negotiating an alliance, but much to Piłsudski's frustration, Długoszowski refused any further such assignments. He was often seen at restaurants, cafes, parties, and cabarets and was popular in artistic and literary circles. He had a regular table at Warsaw's *Mała Ziemiańska* cafe, a noted meeting place for artists. He wrote poetry, translated literature, and painted; his reputation among the artistic and literary community was enhanced by his actions to assist them when they were in need. For example, the writer Aleksander Wat mentioned in his memoirs that when he was imprisoned for publishing the magazine *Miesięcznik Literacki*, the unofficial organ of the Communist Party of Poland, he had received a hamper of vodka and caviar from Długoszowski to ease his circumstances.[19]

His exploits and sense of humor were widely known in Poland, as was his enjoyment of alcohol.[20] Długoszowski's attachment to the cavalry encompassed its historically chivalrous aspects. Although duels were illegal,[21] Długoszowski considered them to be matters of honor and was known to

---

[17] Both used forged French passports. Berenson used one bearing the name Jeanne-Liliane Lalande.

[18] They were married on October 2, 1919, in the Lutheran church in Gawłów, a village between Kraków and Tarnów (Bronisława was Lutheran; her family had converted from Judaism when she was a child). Her name is recorded in the church marriage register as Lalande. In 1934, after the death of Stefania Calvas, they remarried in the Catholic Church.

[19] Wat fled to the Soviet Union in September 1939; in 1940, he was arrested and imprisoned in the Lubyanka. His experiences in the Soviet Union dashed his sympathies for communism.

[20] In one story, Długoszowski and Colonel Józef Szostak had agreed that when they went out, one of them must remain sober. After a number of outings, Szostak asked Długoszowski when it would be his turn. In another, when he was appointed to command a cavalry regiment, Piłsudski admonished him:
  —"Listen, Wieniawa, you have to watch the cavalrymen so that they do not drink too much!"
  —"Commander! I dutifully promise they won't drink any more than me!"
  —"It does not comfort me that much," sighed the marshal with resignation.
Długoszowski often told such stories about himself; some were true, and others were his own fabrications.

[21] At this time, duels were fought using sabers.

engage in them;[22] he also was known to intervene when he saw women being mistreated.[23]

When Piłsudski withdrew from public life in 1923, Długoszowski and several close associates followed him.[24] Długoszowski left active duty and remained inactive for a year, until Sikorski ordered him to undergo additional training. He returned to service and was appointed to the general staff and given command of a cavalry regiment, but he remained loyal to Piłsudski and was at his side during the 1926 coup. In 1932, he was promoted to brigadier general; this meant that he would no longer command his beloved cavalry. He accepted his appointment with a heavy heart and ordered business cards bearing the inscription, "General Wieniawa-Długoszowski, former colonel."

The brooding, ascetic Piłsudski and the fun-loving Długoszowski seemed an unlikely pair, but Długoszowski had valuable traits and skills. He was clever and able to quickly evaluate complex matters; Piłsudski frequently entrusted him with sensitive diplomatic missions. He also could make Piłsudski laugh when nobody else could. The day before the marshal's death, Długoszowski visited him and was said to be the only person who could bring a smile to his face.

Długoszowski's reputation did not sit well with the opposition, who viewed him as unserious, a frivolous womanizer and an alcoholic. But after Piłsudski's death, Długoszowski publicly critiqued *Sanacja* figures. In 1938, he was named Poland's ambassador to Italy. Although his opponents believed this would be disastrous, Długoszowski was highly effective in the role; his deputy Aleksander Zawisza later noted that he was regarded as one of the most respected diplomats in Rome. He abstained from alcohol; at receptions he drank nothing stronger than tea.

It was no coincidence that General Władysław Sikorski was on the same Bucharest–Paris train as French Ambassador Léon Noël. Since his arrival

---

[22] He engaged in at least three duels. One was with a major who publicly called him a "Jewish henchman," referring to his wife and friends. Długoszowski won; his opponent claimed his bandaged head resulted from an automobile accident. Another duel took place during his time at the higher military school. A colonel treated him brutally; Długoszowski called for a duel and defeated the colonel, sending him to the hospital for an extended recovery. A third was in April 1926 with Wacław Drozdowski, secretary of the editorial office of *Gazeta Warszawska*; for this Długoszowski was tried by a military court.

[23] One evening in Warsaw's elegant *Adria* restaurant, he observed a customer forcibly pulling a young lady to his table. Długoszowski approached him and, without saying a word, struck him. He fell to the floor, and Długoszowski turned to the young lady, stood at attention, and proclaimed, "Beautiful lady, free passage." He was applauded by other guests.

[24] Józef Beck also left the military at that time. He was later minister of foreign affairs.

in Bucharest, Sikorski had been meeting with French and British diplomats, and along with Zaleski and Stroński, he had been in regular contact with Roger Raczyński. Sikorski and his *Front Morges* associates placed full responsibility for Poland's inability to repel the German and Soviet armies on *Sanacja* and charged Mościcki and his government with failure to adequately prepare for war. Their internment presented a long-sought opportunity to remove *Sanacja* from power. For more than ten years, Sikorski had cultivated relationships with French government and military officials, and now he was using his contacts to influence events.

In the days leading up to Długoszowski's arrival, members of the political opposition began to call on Łukasiewicz; first Stroński, then Zaleski and Adam Pragier, a former *Sejm* member who had been jailed by *Sanacja* in 1930. On September 24, Sikorski's secretary called the embassy requesting a meeting with Łukasiewicz; they met at noon on the twenty-sixth. Although they differed politically, Łukasiewicz approached this meeting with the intention of overcoming their differences. He was unable to inform Sikorski about the succession since he did not have confirmation that Mościcki had received his message, but he promised to provide further information in a few hours. They were interrupted by a telephone call from Champetier de Ribes asking Łukasiewicz to come to *Quai d'Orsay* immediately.[25] Łukasiewicz apologized to Sikorski and asked to resume their meeting later.

Łukasiewicz was startled to learn that the French government disagreed with the appointment of Długoszowski and replied that this appeared to be interference in Poland's internal affairs. Champetier de Ribes asserted that, as the host of the Polish government and armed forces, France had the right to make their position known; in response, Łukasiewicz said that he would be willing to discuss a revision to their agreement. Champetier de Ribes replied that France did not wish to revisit the agreement but thought that Długoszowski would not be accepted by Poles in exile; Łukasiewicz disagreed. Champetier de Ribes ended their meeting by asking that their conversation be kept confidential until the matter was resolved, and Łukasiewicz took their discussion as nothing more than an attempt at influence.

After returning to the embassy, he learned he was wrong. He was informed that Edward Raczyński had presented a note to Halifax announcing Długoszowski's appointment; Halifax had no objections but said he understood France had reservations. He learned that Adrien Thierry,

---

[25] *Quai d'Orsay* is the location of France's Ministry of Foreign Affairs.

France's ambassador to Romania, had informed Roger Raczyński that France would not recognize a government headed by Długoszowski. He also discovered that the opposition had proposed four candidates: Hlond, Paderewski, Zaleski, and Raczkiewicz. And he recalled rumors that, while in Bucharest, Sikorski and other opposition leaders had lobbied the French ambassadors to Poland and Romania to influence French policy towards Poland. Realizing the seriousness of these developments, Łukasiewicz asked Długoszowski to send Mościcki a telegram asking to be released from his nomination; Długoszowski agreed.

Łukasiewicz and Sikorski resumed their meeting at four. Łukasiewicz advised him that Mościcki had designated Długoszowski as his successor. Sikorski responded with a mixture of surprise and indignation. Not knowing that Łukasiewicz had met with Długoszowski immediately after his arrival, Sikorski declared that he was an alcoholic and was drunk when he had arrived in Paris. Łukasiewicz refuted his assertion and suggested that Sikorski meet with Długoszowski, but Sikorski refused, stating that he had nothing to say to him. Further, Sikorski claimed he had asked Roger Raczyński to tell Łepkowski to discuss nomination options with Mościcki; however, Łepkowski contradicted him, stating that he had never received instructions of this sort.

After their meeting, Łukasiewicz became concerned that Sikorski and his associates would attempt to form a rival government that would have French backing. Łukasiewicz contacted Roger Raczyński, who agreed to immediately drive to Bicaz to inform Mościcki of Thierry's message. Łukasiewicz also received word from Edward Raczyński that the British Foreign Office was startled by France's position and shocked by their interference.

At this point, it was clear to Łukasiewicz that he would need to work with Sikorski and the opposition to identify an acceptable president. He found assistance in the person of Colonel Adam Koc, who had played a significant role in evacuating Poland's gold reserves. Sikorski and the opposition based themselves in Hotel du Danube, and Łukasiewicz began to use Koc as an intermediary. Through Koc, Łukasiewicz learned that the opposition wanted an orderly succession that followed the constitution; however, Sikorski refused to meet with Łukasiewicz.

On September 27, Władysław Raczkiewicz arrived from Bucharest and reported to the embassy, where Łepkowski revealed that he was in possession of two blank sheets, signed by Mościcki, that were to be used if it were necessary to select a different president.

Early in the morning of September 28, Roger Raczyński sent a telegram to Łukasiewicz stating that Mościcki had requested a list of candidates that would be acceptable to France. Later that day, Sikorski was named commander of Polish forces in France. When accepting this responsibility, Sikorski declared to Łukasiewicz and to General Stanisław Burhardt-Bukacki, head of the Polish military mission to France, that he would place himself under Sosnkowski's command were he to arrive in France. Later, Łukasiewicz, Edward Raczyński, Długoszowski, Łepkowski, and Stanisław Janikowski, counselor at the Polish embassy to the Vatican, met to discuss the candidates. Due to his advanced age, Paderewski was not seen as a good choice; Cardinal Hlond and August Zaleski were also rejected. They agreed on Raczkiewicz with the provision that, if Sosnkowski arrived, Raczkiewicz would transfer the office to him. When news of this discussion reached Sikorski, he declared his firm support for Paderewski.

The next day, Łukasiewicz sent a telegram to Mościcki listing the acceptable candidates and stating their recommendation; he also received a note from Daladier formally stating that France would not recognize a government with Długoszowski as president. Łukasiewicz then met with Anatole de Monzie, a member of the French Parliament with whom he had a good working relationship. Łukasiewicz stated that he had never expected France to meddle in Polish affairs at such a time. De Monzie shared that, at a Council of Ministers meeting on the twenty-sixth, it had been reported that the new president would be a general (no name was given) who was an alcoholic and had arrived in Paris in an inebriated state; on that basis, Daladier had decided to oppose the nomination. When he learned that the general in question was Długoszowski, he was unpleasantly surprised. After Łukasiewicz assured him that Długoszowski had not been drunk on arrival, they discussed other nominees. De Monzie had no objections to Raczkiewicz and contacted Daladier, confirming that France would accept him. Łukasiewicz advised Mościcki, who then resigned in a letter to King Carol II.

By September 30, succession appeared to be settled. Łukasiewicz presented a note to Champetier de Ribes announcing Mościcki's resignation and Raczkiewicz's appointment, advising that he was only awaiting confirmation of receipt of the note. Łukasiewicz also sent a note to the *Quai d'Orsay* addressing Daladier's rejection of Długoszowski; Daladier stated that he could not acknowledge the note since doing so would be interfering in Poland's internal affairs.

At the embassy, Raczkiewicz set up his office and began to name his government. The Hotel du Danube group was not necessarily pleased, but

Raczkiewicz began talks directly with Sikorski, Zaleski, and Stroński on the composition of the new government; Stroński was assigned the task of forming it.

Raczkiewicz's swearing in was planned for noon on the thirtieth; however, the deed of the oath was not ready due to the painstaking calligraphy required. At 1 p.m., Sikorski proposed reconvening two hours later; all agreed, and he returned to the Hotel du Danube. But when 3 p.m. arrived, Sikorski had not come back, so Łepkowski called him at the hotel. Now Sikorski had a hostile attitude, declaring that the opposition was being cheated and that, based on information from Champetier de Ribes, French acceptance of Raczkiewicz was not assured. When Łepkowski mentioned the constitution, Sikorski retorted that he cared nothing about it.

Koc immediately went to the Hotel du Danube and found that Sikorski and his fellow opposition members believed they were being deceived and that Raczkiewicz would form a government quite different from what they had discussed the previous day. Koc was able to defuse the situation by reporting on de Monzie's assurances that France would not oppose Raczkiewicz. Finally, at about 4 p.m., Sikorski, Zaleski, and Stroński arrived at the embassy. They had been in contact with Paderewski, who requested that Sikorski, not Stroński, be named prime minister. Raczkiewicz agreed; after this, he was sworn in and signed the decrees forming the new government and dissolving the previous one.

The new government consisted of General Władysław Sikorski as prime minister and minister of military affairs, Stanisław Stroński as vice prime minister, August Zaleski as minister of foreign affairs, Adam Koc as minister of the treasury, and General Józef Haller and Aleksander Ładoś as ministers without portfolio. Długoszowski returned to Italy and resumed his duties as ambassador.

With a successor in place, continuity of government was assured. Mościcki had held Swiss citizenship prior to Polish independence, and he now sought to return to Switzerland. Romania agreed, but Germany continued to oppose his departure. After US President Franklin Roosevelt intervened, Romania permitted him to leave; in an unexpected display of compassion, Sikorski ordered the Polish embassy in Bucharest to assist him. At the end of 1939, he left for Switzerland; en route he passed through Italy, meeting with Długoszowski in Milan.

Mościcki initially lived in Fribourg, resuming his work as a chemist and teaching at the University of Fribourg; he also began to write his memoirs and donated money to the Polish Army in France and for aid to Polish war prisoners. Needing more income, he moved to Geneva in 1940 and worked in a chemical laboratory. He died in October 1946 in Versoix, Switzerland.

Scuttling Długoszowski's presidency proved easier than removing him from the diplomatic corps. Sikorski dismissed Łukasiewicz in November and refused to permit other diplomats closely associated with Beck to serve, but dispensing with Długoszowski was impossible. While Italy had not declared war on Poland and continued diplomatic relations,[26] the Italian government had signaled that, were Długoszowski to be recalled, it would refuse to accept his replacement, thus ending relations. Sikorski was forced to keep him in Rome.

Długoszowski's continued presence proved beneficial. Polish soldiers who entered Italy were safe from imprisonment as prisoners of war; further, Italy showed no interest in interning them. This made passage through Italy en route to France a viable option. Through Długoszowski's influence, Italy considered Polish soldiers to be seasonal workers and permitted them passage to France. Długoszowski and his staff issued travel documents and provided material aid, making it possible for thousands to join the Polish military in France.

Germany's 1940 attack on the Low Countries and France marked the end of Długoszowski's time in Rome. Mussolini's government declared war on the United Kingdom and France on June 10; three days later, Italy severed relations with Poland and ceased to recognize the Polish ambassador. Długoszowski and his family left Rome on June 20 and moved to New York. He contacted representatives of the Polish Army but was unable to get an assignment, so he worked in bookbinding and wrote for the *Dziennik Polski (Detroit)* newspaper. In April 1941, he secured a meeting with Sikorski in Washington, DC. Although the subject of their discussion remains unknown, on April 18, 1942, Długoszowski was appointed to a diplomatic posting in Havana as envoy to Cuba, the Dominican Republic, and Haiti. It was not an ideal assignment, but it allowed him to support his wife and daughter better than he could have as a journalist.

---

[26] Although Italy later severed diplomatic relations, it never declared war on Poland.

In New York, Długoszowski met with Wacław Jędrzejewicz, Ignacy Matuszewski, and Henryk Floyar-Rajchman, associates of his from pre-war Poland. All four had been supporters of Piłsudski, had held positions in the military or the *Sanacja* government, and had been dismissed from the exile government due to their *Sanacja* past. On June 20–21, they founded *Komitet Narodowy Amerykanów Polskiego Pochodzenia* (KNAPP, National Committee of Americans of Polish Extraction). KNAPP's purpose was to lobby for Poland's independence, press for restoration of Poland's prewar borders, bring attention to the Soviet Union's intentions, and oppose any compromise with Moscow. In practice, KNAPP was opposed to Sikorski and critical of his government. Długoszowski was simultaneously a member of Sikorski's government and a member of KNAPP, an organization opposed to Sikorski's government. His KNAPP associates could not understand how he could bring himself to work with Sikorski and accused him of betraying Piłsudski's memory. He endured their barbs and placed Poland and the welfare of his family ahead of partisan squabbles.

But eventually the pressures on Długoszowski pushed him in a tragic direction. At about 9 a.m. on July 1, a taxi driver was parked across the street from the apartment building at 3 Riverside Drive in New York City. He looked up at the building and saw a man jump from the third-floor terrace. Police identified the victim as Bolesław Wieniawa-Długoszowski. In his pocket was a note:

> My thoughts get confused and break like matches or straw. I cannot remember the simplest names of places, names of people and simple events in my life. Under these circumstances, I do not feel able to represent the Government, because instead of helping it, I could harm the case. I am aware that I am committing a crime against my wife and daughter, leaving them to their fate and indifferent people. I am asking God to take care of them. God save Poland. B.

His renewed status as a government employee provided his wife and daughter with a small pension. Floyar-Rajchman later fulminated that Długoszowski's acceptance of a government position was a disgrace.[27]

His former deputy Aleksander Zawisza memorialized him for his talents, patriotism, honor, character, loyalty, and love of Poland. Długoszowski's

---

[27] Conspiracy theories later emerged that his erstwhile allies in KNAPP had convened, judged him to be guilty of betrayal, and forced him to commit suicide. Many years later, Wacław Jędrzejewicz debunked these claims in the London *Wiadomości*, although the claims were revived by the newspaper *Wprost* in 2017.

funeral was attended by many American dignitaries, including General George Patton. Although he had the briefest possible term of office, the Third Republic recognized him as one of Poland's presidents.

Into Exile

Władysław Raczkiewicz,
President of the Republic of Poland 1939-1947

IN THE FAR SOUTHEASTERN REACHES of Europe, the Greater Caucasus Mountains span the territory between the Caspian and Black Seas. On their southern slope, the Rioni River begins its path towards the Black Sea; in the Georgian plains, it flows through the ancient city of Kutaisi. Near the Rioni, a bust of Władysław Raczkiewicz stands in a prominent position in a small park dedicated to Georgian–Polish friendship; an inscription on the statue's base reads in part: "Władysław Raczkiewicz, 1885–1947, Born in Kutaisi, President of the Republic of Poland." At 1,500 miles from Warsaw, Kutaisi seems an unlikely birthplace for a Polish president, but his family was part of a sizeable Polish diaspora in the Russian Empire that traced its origins to expulsions after failed uprisings.

As punishment for fighting against Russia in the January Uprising (1863–1864), Benedykt Raczkiewicz's property was confiscated, and he and his family were exiled to Siberia along with about 80,000 of their countrymen.[1] After a few years, the Russian government granted him permission

---

[1] Historian Norman Davies estimated the total deportation at 80,000, making this the largest deportation in the history of Tsarist Russia. Later deportations by the Soviet Union would greatly surpass this figure.

to resettle his family in the rather more pleasant climate of Georgia. Benedykt's son Józef became a judge in Kutaisi, and on January 28, 1885, Józef's wife, Ludwika, gave birth to Władysław.

After his early years in Kutaisi, Władysław completed secondary school in Tver, began studies in mathematics at St. Petersburg Imperial University, and joined a clandestine organization of Polish students. *Związek Młodzieży Polskiej* (Association of Polish Youth, typically referred to as *Zet*) was founded to organize Polish students, train future leaders, and conduct military training. *Zet* ran an underground publishing house and educated its members in Polish language and history. *Okhrana*, the Tsarist secret police, closely watched them and periodically arrested *Zet* activists. The young Raczkiewicz was taken into custody but was released due to his age and permitted to resume his studies at the University of Dorpat;[2] he earned a law degree in 1911. After graduation, he practiced law in Mińsk and married Jadwiga Niesłuchowska in 1912.

Raczkiewicz was conscripted into the Imperial Russian Army during the Great War. When Russia's February Revolution erupted in March 1917, the more than 700,000 Poles in the Russian military began to organize themselves; in June, the First General Congress of Military Poles met in Petrograd and created *Naczelny Polski Komitet Wojskowy* (Supreme Polish Military Committee, widely known as *Naczpol*) with Raczkiewicz at its head. *Naczpol* organized *I Korpus Polski w Rosji* (First Polish Corps in Russia) to defend ethnic Poles and to work towards creation of an independent Poland. *Naczpol* was dissolved in February 1918 and replaced by the Supreme Council of the Polish Armed Forces, also led by Raczkiewicz.

In independent Poland, he headed the Military Department of the Committee for the Defense of the Eastern Borderlands, followed by an appointment as Deputy General Commissioner of the Eastern Lands. He continued in military service, commanding a volunteer unit defending Wilno in the Polish–Soviet War. After that war, Raczkiewicz turned his focus to government service. In November 1920, he became head of the short-lived Temporary Board of Frontier Areas, established as the civil administration of territories that were part of the former Russian partition. After its dissolution, Raczkiewicz was delegate to the government of Central Lithuania in Wilno.

Raczkiewicz's next move was to Warsaw. In June 1921, he was appointed minister of the interior, but this assignment ended in September

---

[2] The University of Dorpat is now the University of Tartu; Dorpat is now known as Tartu, Estonia. Dorpat was the name given to this city by the Germans.

with the dissolution of the Witos government. He then took a position as *wojewoda*[3] of Nowogródek *województwo*,[4] serving until August 1924, after which he became delegate to Wilno. In June 1925, he was again called upon to be minister of the interior under Prime Minister Władysław Grabski, and he continued in this office under Aleksander Skrzyński. When this government ended, he was appointed *wojewoda* of Wilno. He left this role in November 1930, when he was elected to the *Senat* and served as *Marszałek Senatu* (Marshal of the Senate).[5] After Raczkiewicz's time in the *Senat*, Prime Minister Marian Zyndram-Kościałkowski appointed him minister of the interior; Raczkiewicz held this position until June 1936. He also served briefly as *wojewoda* of the Kraków *województwo* from August to October 1935. After Zyndram-Kościałkowski's government was dissolved, he was appointed *wojewoda* of the Pomorskie *województwo*[6] in July 1936, a position he held until September 1939. In 1934, he was also placed in charge of *Światowy Związek Polaków z Zagranicy* (World Association of Poles Abroad, commonly known as *Światpol*); in this role, he became well known in Polish communities around the world. On September 12, 1939, President Mościcki tasked him with organizing the Polish community in the United States to provide aid to the people of Poland. Along with other members of the government, Raczkiewicz crossed into Romania on September 17, but he was not interned and was permitted to leave for France.

Władysław Raczkiewicz was not the president Sikorski or Paderewski would have preferred, but his conciliatory nature suited him to their purposes. Indeed, Raczkiewicz's style was to minimize conflicts and seek compromise, a tendency Piłsudski had noted some years prior. There was also the possibility that Raczkiewicz would not be president for long; in early October, he was diagnosed with leukemia. His prognosis was good, but to ensure continuity of government, he designated Sikorski as his successor. Neither his illness nor Sikorski's appointment were made public, but less than two weeks after becoming president, Raczkiewicz offered to resign—not due to health concerns but to the arrival of Kazimierz Sosnkowski in France.

---

[3] In the Second Republic, Poland was divided into sixteen administrative regions known as *województwo* (voivodeship); a *wojewoda* was the governor of the *województwo*.

[4] Nowogródek was a region in the northeast of Second Republic; after the September 17 invasion, the Soviet Union forcibly annexed it. Most of its territory is now in present-day Belarus, the remainder is in Lithuania.

[5] *Marszałek Senatu Rzeczypospolitej Polskiej* is the presiding officer of the *Senat*.

[6] *Województwo pomorskie* included territories in the northwest reaching from Gdynia and the Baltic coast to Toruń.

At the time Mościcki was deciding on his successor, Sosnkowski was ordering his soldiers to disband and head for Hungary. He made the journey himself, reaching France on October 11. Raczkiewicz offered to appoint him as his successor and then resign. Sosnkowski declined, expressing his concern that another change in the presidency in such a short period would reflect poorly on Poland. Despite his September 28 declaration, Sikorski did not place himself under Sosnkowski's command; he was the de facto commander in chief, but Rydz-Śmigły had not yet resigned. In late October, a courier brought Rydz-Śmigły a handwritten letter from Raczkiewicz politely requesting his resignation. He obliged, clearing the way for Sikorski. Sosnkowski asked Sikorski to place him in charge of the underground army.

Sikorski strengthened his position by pressuring Raczkiewicz into a power-sharing agreement that came to be known as *Umowa Paryska* (Paris Agreement). Under its terms, the prime minister became the most powerful government figure, securing veto power over presidential decisions, including changes in ministerial appointments. In practice, this meant that the prime minister could block his own removal.[7] Raczkiewicz also agreed to consult with the prime minister and political parties before appointing his successor. He publicly announced the agreement in his November 30 speech to Poland, which was broadcast by the Polish radio service in France: "Under the April Constitution, I decided on those provisions that entitle me to act independently, to do so in close consultation with the Prime Minister."[8] Details were published in the December 9, 1939, issue of *Monitor Polski*. Raczkiewicz also stated that his successor would be bound by this agreement. Although *Umowa Paryska* was an official presidential declaration, legally it was no more than an agreement between the president and the prime minister; the constitution was unaltered. Regardless, Sikorski and his political allies had extracted significant concessions. However, Sikorski was not pleased that, in his speech, Raczkiewicz announced that his successor was Sosnkowski. Sikorski responded with a letter admonishing Raczkiewicz for violating *Umowa Paryska*.

There remained only one constitutional check on Sikorski's newfound powers, and it could not be used. The *Sejm* had the power to demand resignation of the Council of Ministers or of an individual minister,[9] but it hadn't met since September 2 and could not convene under occupation.

---

[7] Article 28 of the April Constitution states: "The Prime Minister and the Ministers are politically responsible to the President of the Republic and may be dismissed by him at any time." Thus, ceding this power to Sikorski in *Umowa Paryska* violated the Constitution.

[8] *Monitor Polski*, Nr. 271–276, 9 grudnia 1939, Angers, France (published December 9, 1939).

[9] This power was specified in Article 31, section 2(a).

It was impossible to conduct elections for an exile *Sejm*, so Raczkiewicz created *Rada Narodowa Rzeczypospolitej Polskiej* (National Council of the Republic of Poland) as a temporary substitute and dissolved the *Sejm* on November 2. *Rada Narodowa* consisted of representatives of prewar opposition political parties and the Jewish community; notable by their absence were representatives from *Sanacja* and non-Jewish minorities. Raczkiewicz issued his decree creating *Rada Narodowa* on December 9 and appointed members in December and January. Paderewski was named chairman; vice chairs were Tadeusz Bielecki (SN), Stanisław Mikołajczyk (PSL), and Herman Lieberman (PPS). In total, he appointed twenty members. *Rada Narodowa* was an advisory body and held no constitutional powers.

Although the government and military were firmly in the hands of the prewar opposition, they were gripped with anxiety that *Sanacja* would re-establish itself. Having amassed powers rivaling those enjoyed by Piłsudski, Sikorski first used them to weaken presidential powers to approximate those defined in the March Constitution and then employed them to expunge *Sanacja* from public life. Initially, he did not bar *Sanacja* from government service; indeed, two of his four government ministers, Adam Koc and August Zaleski, were *Sanacja* associates.[10] This balance did not last long. In October he added five new ministers; four were from opposition parties and the fifth was the politically unaffiliated Sosnkowski.[11] In December, another minister from the opposition was added, and Kot departed and was replaced by another *Sanacja* associate.[12]

The prewar opposition began to circulate accusations that *Sanacja* had failed the nation by leaving the military unprepared,[13] charges that aligned with Western perceptions. Regardless of their accuracy, such perceptions were useful in discrediting and marginalizing *Sanacja*.[14] The government used its influence to block *Sanacja* members from entering France. Colonel Zakrzewski, Poland's military attaché in Bucharest, screened requests for French visas

---

[10] The other minister was Stanisław Stroński from SN.

[11] The other four ministers were Jan Stańczyk (PPS), General Józef Haller (SP), Aleksander Ładoś (SL), and Marian Seyda (SN). Sosnkowski was affiliated with *Sanacja*, although he had supporters in the opposition. He favored allowing *Sanacja* members to serve in government, a stance that caused members of the opposition parties to isolate him.

[12] Stanisław Kot (SL) joined the Council of Ministers along with Henryk Strasburger, who took the place of Adam Koc. Like Koc, Strasburger was affiliated with *Sanacja*.

[13] Charges that *Sanacja* left Poland unprepared should be evaluated in the context of the Second Republic's financial position. Journalist Melchior Wańkowicz managed to meet with the interned Rydz-Śmigły in Romania and asked him about military preparations. Rydz-Śmigły responded that Poland simply could not afford fortification and armaments.

[14] Considering Poland's economic difficulties in the 1930s, it is highly unlikely that the events of September would have been forestalled by a non-*Sanacja* government. Poland had insufficient funds to adequately prepare its military for the attacks it suffered.

and recommended for approval only those acceptable to Sikorski's government.[15] Many former officials were thus sidelined, unable to rejoin the fight even in diminished roles. Some appealed directly to Sikorski and were met with accusations of dereliction of duty. The case of General Tadeusz Kasprzycki, minister of military affairs in the last prewar government, is illustrative. Kasprzycki wrote to Sikorski from Romania requesting permission to join the Polish Army in France. Sikorski responded by charging him with leaving Poland unprepared for modern warfare, thus making him responsible for the defeat; he closed with a blunt statement that his service was not needed.

Sikorski also took the unusual action of issuing an instruction regarding prewar officials directly to heads of Polish diplomatic missions, bypassing Minister of Foreign Affairs Zaleski: "There is no excuse for the foreign, internal, military and economic policy that led to the defeat. The attempt to defend or excuse this policy is to be treated as a line-of-duty offense and will be followed by respective consequences."[16]

There was little to stop Sikorski from placing culpability for the defeat on *Sanacja*. This effort became institutionalized on October 10 with the creation of the Fact-Finding Commission to Enquire into Recent Events in Poland. Its members were Stanisław Stroński, General Józef Haller, Aleksander Ładoś, and General Izydor Modelski. According to the announcement of its creation, the commission's responsibility was to "collect comprehensive information, materials and documents relating to the course of recent events in Poland and to determine their causes." But its true mission was rather more limited: its members were to assemble evidence against Mościcki's ministers, regardless of whether their ministries had any bearing on military preparedness. Their common bond was their affiliation with Piłsudski and *Sanacja*.[17]

---

[15] According to historians Andrzej Grzywacz and Marcin Kwiecień, government officials facilitated the movement of opposition loyalists to France and hindered the evacuation of those suspected of Sanacja leanings.

[16] Archiwum Akt Nowych w Warszawie. Akta Władysława Sikorskiego, sygn. 21[mkf 27604], k. 21. *Instrukcja dla kierowników placówek w sprawie propagandy* (Polish Central Archives of Modern Records in Warsaw. Władysław Sikorski's Files, sign. 21 [mcf 27604] Col. 21. Instruction to heads of diplomatic agencies on matters of propaganda).

[17] Commission targets were: Prime Minister and Minister of Internal Affairs General Felicjan Sławoj-Składkowski; Deputy Ministers of Internal Affairs Bronisław Nakoniecznikow-Klukowski and Władysław Korsak; Minister of Military Affairs General Tadeusz Kasprzycki and his deputy ministers General Janusz Głuchowski and General Aleksander Litwinowicz; Minister of Foreign Affairs Józef Beck and his deputy ministers Jan Szembek and Mirosław Arciszewski; Minister of the Treasury Eugeniusz Kwiatkowski and his deputies Tadeusz Grodyński and Kajetan Morawski; Minister of Trade and Industry Antoni Roman and his deputy Adam Rose; Minister of Communications Juliusz Ulrych and his deputies Aleksander Bobkowski and Julian Piasecki; Minister for Post and Telegraphs Emil Kaliński and his deputy Tadeusz Argasiński; Minister of Religious Denominations and Public Enlightenment Wojciech Świętosławski; Minister of Justice Witold Grabowski; Minister of Social Welfare Marian Zyndram-Kościałkowski and his deputy Tadeusz Garbusiński; and Minister of Agriculture and Agrarian Reform Juliusz Poniatowski along with his deputy Tadeusz Wierusz-Kowalski.

In the Council of Ministers, anti-*Sanacja* fervor at times reached extremes. On January 2, 1940, Jan Stańczyk submitted a motion demanding that Rydz-Śmigły, General Tadeusz Kasprzycki, General Felicjan Sławoj-Składkowski, and former Minister of Foreign Affairs Józef Beck be brought before a military tribunal. To their credit, Sikorski and most other ministers recommended postponement since it would have been impossible to do and would have been poorly received by the French and British. Stańczyk persisted, but the motion was eventually defeated. However, those investigated by the commission had no chance to serve in government or military positions, as exclusion of anyone linked to *Sanacja* became policy. As Stanisław Kot later recounted, "When organizing offices, the presidium of the Council of Ministers accepted only people known for their political activity in the opposition camp, without any difference between the parties."[18]

France provided facilities for the Polish government in Angers; Raczkiewicz's residence was at Château de Pignerolle in the adjacent town of Saint-Barthélemy-d'Anjou. Sikorski and his officers established military bases in Coëtquidan and Parthenay; they also opened a military academy. Poland's military in France was formed by expatriates and by soldiers who had eluded capture; they came to France by way of Sweden, Yugoslavia, Italy, Syria, and Lebanon. German propaganda derisively labeled them "Sikorski's tourists," but they came to embrace this epithet; by June 1940, about 85,000 of them had arrived. Some were *Sanacja* supporters. Sikorski dealt with them by ordering a new military camp to be opened in Cerizay. Officially, it was for officers awaiting assignment; in practice, its residents were officers whom Sikorski held responsible for the September defeat. To an outsider, this camp looked innocuous. There were no fences, guard posts, or barracks; internees lived in boarding houses or hotels and paid for their accommodations out of their own pockets. To Cerizay's involuntary residents, it was quite clearly a prison. They were under observation, subjected to searches, and required to report to camp headquarters daily. All correspondence was censored, and none of the internees could leave the camp without authorization.[19] None was given a reason for his detention.

France had no reason to suspect that Cerizay was anything but a reserve center until the French president received a letter from General

---

[18] S. Kot, "Wspomnienia z początkowego okresu II wojny światowej" ("Memories from the first period of World War II"), *Przegląd Polonijny*, 1981, p. 126.
[19] About 100 officers were held in Cerizay.

Stefan Dąb-Biernacki, one of its inmates.[20] Dąb-Biernacki had escaped to Hungary in September but was planning to return to Poland when he received a telegram from Lieutenant Colonel Bagiński, a member of Sosnkowski's staff, ordering him to report to General Marian Kukiel in France.[21] Several Polish officers escorted him to Paris and deposited him at La Santé prison. After a month, he was taken to Cerizay, where a military prosecutor charged him with culpability for the defeat, squandering his army, and anti-government agitation while in Hungary. With Sikorski controlling the military, Dąb-Biernacki understood that his conviction was a foregone conclusion. Seeing no other course of action, he decided to have a letter smuggled to the French president, informing him of Cerizay's purpose. In the letter, Dąb-Biernacki described Cerizay as "a punitive and disciplinary place, a kind of isolation camp for officers removed from the cadres of the Polish Army in France," and he renounced his French Legion of Honor decoration, contending that as a prisoner it would be disrespectful for him to wear it.[22] Both France and Britain disapproved of such persecutions, and it later emerged that some members of Sikorski's government did as well. Kukiel, who served as deputy minister of national defense, later called Cerizay a mistake that damaged Poland's image.

Sikorski was displeased with the unwanted scrutiny but continued to isolate his perceived opponents. Cerizay's existence and purpose became known among internees in Romania as did other of Sikorski's actions. General Wacław Stachiewicz had slipped out of internment, gotten to Belgrade, and made contact with Polish authorities. With the connivance of the French government, Stachiewicz was sent to Algeria and was incarcerated in Oran. By early 1940, the situation in Europe was deteriorating. Sikorski's government decided to evacuate those still in Romania and started by ordering twenty officers to leave for French North Africa and await further orders. Word of Stachiewicz's fate had reached them, and many refused.

Anti-*Sanacja* attitudes divided the Polish underground as well. Although SZP's political body GRP was composed of representatives from both sides

---

[20] Dąb-Biernacki had sided with Piłsudski in the 1926 coup and had a reputation for harshly treating generals who had been on the other side of the coup. In September 1939, he commanded *Armia Prusy* and had to rush it to the front before it was fully operational. Several officers accused him of poor leadership and deficient command. By most accounts, he did not distinguish himself during the German–Soviet invasion.
[21] Neither Sosnkowski nor Kukiel was aware of the telegram.
[22] Dymarski, "Polskie obozy odosobnienia" ("Polish Isolation Camps"), *Dzieje Najnowsze*, Rocznik XXIX - 1997, 3.

of the divide, some groups aligned with the prewar opposition considered it to be a *Sanacja* front. CKON refused to include any groups linked to *Sanacja*. Such was the discord that Colonel Klemens Rudnicki delayed his escape to France to intervene. He and Colonel Tadeusz Komorowski[23] worked to bring the various groups under common leadership and sent Sikorski a detailed report that reinforced his distrust of Tokarszewski. Unwittingly, Tokarszewski then made a fateful mistake. He prepared his first report to Sikorski, addressing it to the commander in chief without specifying his name, and gave it to a Hungarian military attaché who was to get it to the Polish government. The attaché traveled to Romania and gave it to Rydz-Śmigły, who forwarded it to Sikorski. In Sikorski's eyes, this meant that Tokarszewski considered Rydz-Śmigły to be the commander in chief. Tokarszewski sent three more reports, each addressed to Sikorski by name and sent directly to him, but the damage was done.

Sikorski decided to replace SZP. He sent Lieutenant Jerzy Szymański to Warsaw to coordinate activities between the underground and the government, ordering him to contact Rowecki but forbidding him to meet with Tokarszewski. On November 13, Sikorski and Sosnkowski formed *Związek Walki Zbrojnej* (ZWZ, Union of Armed Struggle) and subordinated SZP to it. Rowecki was given command of territory under German occupation and was based in Warsaw, while Tokarszewski was in charge of areas under Soviet occupation and headquartered in Lwów. On the surface this seemed logical; Tokarszewski had served in that city prior to the war and was familiar with the area. However, this assignment was highly perilous, as he was well known in Lwów district and would be easily recognized.[24] This danger was realized in March 1940 when Tokarszewski was arrested by the NKVD while crossing into Soviet-controlled territory. Rowecki then took command of both districts.

CKON remained independent of ZWZ. The two functioned in parallel until CKON's leaders were arrested by the Germans in April 1940. Rather than join ZWZ, CKON's remnant formed *Komitet Porozumiewawczy Organizacji Niepodległościowych* (KPON, Committee of Underground Independence Organizations). KPON had a brief existence; it evolved into *Konfederacja Narodu* (KN, Confederation of the Nation) and eventually merged into ZWZ. Some CKON member groups did not join KPON or KN; the largest was *Bataliony Chłopskie* (BCh, Peasants' Battalions).

---

[23] Colonel Tadeusz Komorowski would later be promoted to general and was known as Bór-Komorowski; Bór was a code name.

[24] Historian Arkadiusz Adamczyk contends that sending Tokarszewski to Lwów was an attempt to eliminate him.

In the months following the invasion, underground groups continued to form. Some, such as Żydowski Związek Wojskowy (ŻZW, Jewish Military Union), cooperated with ZWZ,[25] while others, including SN's *Armia Narodowa* (National Army), chose to remain independent.[26] PPS went further by creating its own political structure, PPS-WRN (*Polska Partia Socjalistyczna – Wolność, Równość, Niepodległość*, Polish Socialist Party – Freedom, Equality, Independence), as well as a military organization, *Gwardia Ludowa WRN* (People's Guard of the WRN).

1940 brought increased repression. Poles living in territories annexed by Germany were expelled to the General Government or sent to Germany as slave labor, while some children were forcibly taken from their parents for Germanization. Cultural artifacts were looted, and higher education was forbidden; only basic education was permitted. Germany's plan was to use the Poles as slave labor; eventually they would die off, and Germans would resettle Polish lands.[27] In the town of Oświęcim, German authorities began using a former Polish Army facility as a prison camp; its first inmates were prisoners of war. In June, a transport of 728 men arrived, consisting of Polish soldiers caught attempting to make their way to France, resistance organizers, Catholic priests, political figures, and other intellectuals, including a number of Jews. This was the beginning of the Auschwitz concentration camp.

Those areas taken by the Soviet Union had been annexed, with the Red Army claiming that they had liberated the population from Polish exploitation. Ethnic Poles were removed from their positions in government and schools, education in the Polish language was eliminated, and Polish-language textbooks were burned. Like their German allies, the Soviet Union looted art and cultural artifacts. Polish citizens were forced to take Soviet citizenship. In February, a series of deportations began under the command of General Ivan Serov. About 1.2 million ethnic Poles were deported into the depths of the Soviet Union; over sixty percent of

---

[25] ŻZW was formed by a group of Polish Army officers and non-commissioned officers of Jewish origin. ZWZ provided ŻZW with weapons and training.

[26] *Armia Narodowa* changed its name somewhat frequently. It was next known as *Organizacja Wojskowa Stronnictwa Narodowego* (Military Organization of the National Party), then as *Narodowe Oddziały Wojskowe* (National Armed Units); finally, in July 1941, it took the name *Narodowa Organizacja Wojskowa* (National Military Organization). Although it recognized the authority of the government in France, SN's military arm did not subordinate itself to SZP.

[27] This was Germany's policy of *Lebensraum* ("living space"), a concept first proposed in the 1890s and embraced by Hitler and the Nazi party. *Lebensraum* entailed conquering neighboring nations and gradually eradicating their population, thus opening territory for German colonization, providing additional farmlands to feed the expanding population, and claiming natural resources to fuel the economy.

them would die within eighteen months. Their homes were turned over to Ukrainians or Byelorussians.

In 1940, an underground network of political and military leaders created *Delegatura Rządu Rzeczypospolitej Polskiej na Kraj* (Government Delegation for Poland, typically referred to as *Delegatura*) to maintain continuity of government institutions, document war crimes and actions of the occupiers, protect cultural assets, and prepare for governing postwar Poland. It was headed by the *Delegat*, an executive overseeing a remarkably complex organization. Its departments were Internal Affairs, Information and Press, Labor and Social Affairs, Education and Culture, Industry and Trade, Agriculture, Justice, Liquidation of the Effects of the War, Public Works and Reconstruction, Treasury, Post Offices and Telegraphs, and Communications. The Department of Justice ran underground courts, conducting trials of criminals, traitors, and collaborators; in some cases, defendants were captured German Army soldiers, Gestapo officers, and SS officials. Internal Affairs employed an underground police force, *Państwowy Korpus Bezpieczeństwa* (PKB, National Security Corps), to conduct criminal and intelligence investigations, gather reports on activities of the occupiers, and enforce verdicts handed down from underground courts. Internal Affairs provided security for *Delegatura* and was responsible for Żegota, an organization that assisted Jews by providing food, medical care, money, and false identification documents. Information and Press published bulletins, leaflets, posters, and books, published news from abroad, and prepared reports for the government. Labor and Social Welfare provided material assistance to families of victims of the occupiers. *Delegatura* also built an organization to assist escaped Allied prisoners of war. Education and Culture operated on an astonishing scale. Its largest section, *Tajna Organizacja Nauczycielska* (TON, Secret Teaching Organization), provided primary and secondary education.[28] Talmudic schools were organized in Jewish ghettoes. Secret universities were created, offering degrees in a large range of disciplines, including medicine and law; nearly ten thousand master's degrees and several hundred doctorates were awarded during the war. Military academies were organized in the larger cities, and underground seminaries operated throughout the country.[29] Combined, these organizations formed *Polskie Państwo Podziemne* (Polish Secret State); it would grow into the largest and most extensive underground of the war.

---

[28] It is probable that over two million students received their primary education and hundreds of thousands more received secondary education through the efforts of TON.

[29] The best-known graduate of Cardinal Adam Sapieha's underground seminary in Kraków was Karol Wojtyła, later known as Pope John Paul II.

As underground structures grew in number, size, and sophistication, GRP (Main Political Council) sought greater influence over them. In late February, GRP members from PPS, SL, SN, and SP reorganized themselves into *Polityczny Komitet Porozumiewawczy* (PKP, Political Coordinating Committee).

Neither Germany nor the Soviet Union were done with their aggression. The Soviet Union had been pressuring Finland to cede territory since 1938, and in October 1939, it made a final demand, which Finland refused. In November, the Red Army attacked. This conflict lasted into March 1940, when both sides agreed to a peace treaty. Soviet territory was further expanded in June with the invasion and forcible annexation of Estonia, Latvia, Lithuania, and the Romanian regions of Bessarabia and Northern Bukovina. In April, Germany invaded Norway and Denmark.

Poland's government and military anticipated that their time in France would be relatively brief. Their stay was indeed short, but not for the expected reasons. On May 10, 1940, Germany launched a westward attack. The German Army swept through Belgium, Luxembourg, and the Netherlands and stormed into France. Morale in the French military and government fell quickly, so much so that by May 15, Prime Minister Paul Reynaud declared to Winston Churchill that the fight was hopeless. Indeed, in mid-May, the French government was burning its archives and preparing to flee Paris.

Sikorski had a particularly high opinion of the French military. His faith was so great that, even as Paris was about to fall, he embarked on an inspection tour of Polish units and was out of contact with the Polish government. On June 13, Poland's government received word that France was discussing terms of surrender. With the situation deteriorating and Sikorski unreachable, Raczkiewicz called a Council of Ministers meeting at 3:55 a.m. on June 14 to plan evacuation to the United Kingdom. Later that day, the German Army marched into Paris unopposed. On June 17, the Polish government received official word that France would surrender; this ended Poland's obligation to fight for France. Raczkiewicz and a number of Polish soldiers boarded HMS *Arethusa* at Bordeaux on June 17. For several days their ship was under German air attack, and Raczkiewicz designated Edward Raczyński as his successor in the event of his death. Raczkiewicz arrived in London on June 21. That same day, France surrendered to Germany.

Finally understanding that the fight for France was over, on June 19, Sikorski broadcast a radio bulletin ordering Polish soldiers to make their way to the coast for evacuation to the United Kingdom. About 85,000 Polish soldiers had fought in France; of them, 1,400 were killed in action, 4,000 were wounded, 16,000 were captured, and 13,000 were interned in Switzerland. Between 20,000 to 35,000 Polish military personnel were evacuated to the United Kingdom; there were reports that local French authorities attempted to prevent them from boarding ships, intending to intern them. Officers interned in Cerizay headed for the coast when they found that their guards had abandoned their posts. Poland's gold reserves were evacuated by the French government to its African territories. Sikorski's delay in ordering evacuation prevented some of his soldiers from reaching the United Kingdom, and he was now in the unexpected position of being criticized for his actions. His opponents charged that he had misused the army and contended that his lack of action resulted in the failure to secure Poland's gold reserves, placing them outside of Poland's control.

Before his inspection tour, Sikorski had contacted the British and American governments about their potential intervention on behalf of Poles in the Soviet Union. He also met with his ministers to discuss having Sir Stafford Cripps, British ambassador to the Soviet Union, intervene to prevent further repressions and deportations and to consider forming Polish military units on Soviet territory. Moscow had used Stefan Litauer, the London correspondent of *Polska Agencja Telegraficzna* (PAT, Polish Telegraphic Agency) and the Soviet press agency TASS, to inform Sikorski that such actions might be possible. Sikorski did not think Soviet overtures would amount to much, but he had Litauer explore the idea. Sikorski had embarked on this initiative without the knowledge or consent of Raczkiewicz and Zaleski. When they learned about it, they terminated further discussions. Further, Raczkiewicz demanded dismissal of Minister of Internal Affairs Stanisław Kot for exceeding the limits of his office and for obstructing evacuation from France; he also demanded that Minister of Finance, Industry, and Commerce Henryk Strasburger be dismissed for his failure to secure the Polish gold reserves. Sikorski refused to remove them, so Raczkiewicz dismissed him from the office of prime minister for independently conducting his own foreign policy initiatives.

Replacing Sikorski turned out to be impossible. Raczkiewicz first approached Sosnkowski, but he declined. Raczkiewicz then appointed Zaleski, but he was unable to form a government. Further, *Rada Narodowa* declared its support for Sikorski, and several Polish generals pressed

Zaleski to refuse the nomination. Foreign influence in Poland's affairs again became an issue; this time, British Foreign Secretary Lord Halifax told Raczyński that the United Kingdom would find a change in prime ministers to be undesirable.

It was clear to Raczkiewicz that he would not be able to replace Sikorski as prime minister. He considered resigning, but Sosnkowski pressed him to stay in office and brokered an agreement keeping Sikorski as prime minister and appointing Stanisław Mikołajczyk to the position of deputy prime minister. Raczkiewicz's position was further weakened by the incident, and Sikorski and his ministers treated him with distrust and, at times, outright hostility.

London was now Poland's temporary capital, and Poland was now the United Kingdom's most significant ally, a point underscored by King George VI when he personally greeted Raczkiewicz on his arrival at Victoria Station. Britain was a solicitous host, providing facilities, military equipment, and financial support to Poland and to exile governments and militaries from Czechoslovakia, France, and Belgium. Their presence was crucial; the United Kingdom was under attack. German bombs fell on British cities daily, and the German Army was massing across the English Channel. The Polish Army was pressed into service to defend Scotland's east coast. Three Polish destroyers and two submarines evaded capture and destruction and were attached to the Royal Navy.[30] Poland had more sailors than it could deploy, while the Royal Navy did not have enough trained crews to man its ships. This problem was solved easily enough; several ships were transferred to the Polish Navy. The RAF created several Polish squadrons that included a number of Czechoslovak pilots. They made a disproportionately large contribution and were lauded as heroes in the British press. Commander in Chief of Fighter Command Hugh Dowding was effusive: "I must confess that I had been a little doubtful of the effect which their experience in their own countries and in France might have had upon the Polish and Czech pilots, but my doubts were soon laid to rest, because all three Squadrons swung into the fight with a dash and enthusiasm which is beyond praise. They were inspired by a burning hatred for the Germans, which made them very deadly opponents. The first Polish squadron (No. 303) in No. 11 Group, during the course of a month,

---

[30] *Błyskawica* served the Allied cause for the duration of the war, including the D-Day landings at Normandy; after retirement from active service, it was docked in Gdynia as a museum ship.

shot down more Germans than any British unit in the same period."[31]

On another occasion, Dowding continued his praise for the Polish airmen, stating, "Had it not been for the magnificent material contributed by the Polish squadrons and their unsurpassed gallantry I hesitate to say that the outcome of battle would have been the same."[32]

Former residents of Cerizay found that a new home had been prepared for them: *Stacja Zborna Oficerów Rothesay* (Officer Concentration Station Rothesay) in the town of Rothesay on the Isle of Bute. Like Cerizay, its official purpose was to be a staging point for officers awaiting assignment; in practice, it was a larger version of Cerizay. Eventually, over fifteen hundred were held here. Among Poles, Bute had the unofficial name of *Wyspa Wężów* (Isle of Snakes). Like Cerizay, Rothesay had no fences, barbed wire, or cells. Its prisoners were billeted in hotels that they paid for themselves (they were paid sixty percent of their normal salaries), and they had to report to the camp commander daily. Travel off base was practically impossible, and all correspondence was censored. Rothesay prisoners found that they were treated with suspicion by locals; they later learned camp authorities spread the word that they were there for criminal activity, cowardice, treason, drunkenness, and sexual offenses. Rothesay's purpose was made plain by Sikorski in the July 18 *Rada Narodowa* meeting when he declared, "There is no Polish court, and those who make intrigues will be in a concentration camp."[33]

Sympathy for Poland ran high in the United Kingdom, but few in government or among the public knew much about their newfound ally. Poland's Ministry of Information and Documentation remedied this by providing information in English. In early 1940, the Ministry published *Official Documents Concerning Polish–German and Polish–Soviet Relations 1933–1939 – Polish White Book* describing and documenting Polish–German relations and negotiations prior to the war. A second volume, *German Invasion of Poland*, followed. In July, the Ministry began to publish *Polish Fortnightly Review*, a press bulletin providing information on conditions under occupation.[34]

---

[31] Air Chief Marshal Sir Hugh C. T. Dowding, "The Battle of Britain," Supplement to *The London Gazette* of Tuesday, September 20, 1946 (His Majesty's Stationery Office, London, 1946), pp. 4553–4554, paragraph 164.

[32] Ministry of Defence and Prime Minister's Office, 10 Downing Street, "The World's War in Europe," April 27, 2015 *(https://www.gov.uk/government/news/the-worlds-war-in-europe)*.

[33] Dymarski, "Polskie obozy odosobnienia," *Dzieje Najnowsze*, Rocznik XXIX - 1997, 3.

[34] A total of 119 issues of *Polish Fortnightly Review* were published, beginning on July 15, 1940. The final issue was dated July 1, 1945.

Itscontents made for unpleasant reading. It detailed atrocities such as arrests, deportations, executions, looting, and cultural eradication, none worse than the extermination of Europe's Jews in purpose-built camps. *Polish Fortnightly Review* regularly included articles about these camps. An early example was "Oświęcim[35] Concentration Camp" in the November 15, 1941, issue. In July 1942, the *Review* carried a number of reports about the mass killing of Jews, conditions in Auschwitz, Zyklon-B gas, and medical experiments on prisoners. *Dziennik Polski*,[36] the largest émigré newspaper in the United Kingdom, published similar articles, and the BBC broadcast information about the camps.

In 1941, the Ministry of Information released a 240-page report, *German Occupation of Poland – Extract of Note Addressed to The Allied and Neutral Powers*, that described atrocities committed by the Germans. This campaign continued in 1942 when the Ministry of Information published a 750-page report, *The Black Book of Poland*, that detailed German crimes from September 1939 through June 1941, including over 400,000 murders. This book was a collection of documents, photographs, eyewitness accounts, and depositions detailing massacres, torture, expulsion of the indigenous population, persecution of the Jews, plunder, religious persecution, and cultural destruction. Each report was published in Polish, English, French, and German.

In the early days of the war, Western public opinion regarded Stalin and Hitler as equally malevolent. *Time* magazine went so far as to declare Stalin "Man of the Year" for 1939, printing his picture on the cover of its January 1, 1940, issue and characterizing him as Hitler's rival for the dubious title of the world's most-hated man. Stalin was Hitler's loyal ally, providing fuel and raw materials in exchange for weapons and manufactured goods and permitting Germany to establish a naval base near Murmansk. Gestapo and NKVD agents coordinated actions against the Polish resistance. Poland's objective was defeat of both invaders and restoration of the nation, but despite its contribution to the war effort and its role in the defense of the United Kingdom, the exile government could not get support for action against the Soviet Union. Prime Minister Winston Churchill's sole

---

[35] Oświęcim is the Polish name for the town widely known by the German name Auschwitz.
[36] *Dziennik Polski* (*Polish Daily*) was first published on July 12, 1940, and was the most popular Polish émigré newspaper in the United Kingdom. On January 1, 1944, it merged with *Dziennik Żołnierza* (*Soldier's Daily*, also founded in 1940) and was published under the title *Dziennik Polski i Dziennik Żołnierza*.

goal was defeating Germany, and for some time he had been working to draw Moscow into an alliance.

On June 22, 1941, Hitler facilitated British policy by turning on his ally. A force of nearly four million invaded the Soviet Union and quickly made deep incursions. Stalin was shocked; his initial reaction was disbelief that Hitler would turn on him. For Churchill, it was an opportunity not to be squandered. He immediately embraced the Soviet Union as an ally and offered all possible aid and cooperation. Churchill did realize that he had a public relations problem. Although there were sizable pro-Soviet currents in the United Kingdom, most public opinion was negative. Understanding the magnitude of the problem, Churchill remarked, "I have only one purpose, the destruction of Hitler, and my life is much simplified thereby. If Hitler invaded Hell I would make at least a favourable reference to the Devil in the House of Commons." In Parliament on June 24, he received considerable praise for his stance.

In his haste, Churchill placed no conditions on British support, although he had the leverage to do so. Stalin was in a vulnerable position. His military was unable to halt the German advance, Moscow and Leningrad were under threat, his government had to move its functions to Kuybyshev,[37] his factories were relocated to the east, and cultural assets were evacuated.[38] Foreign Secretary Anthony Eden and Sikorski opposed Churchill's lack of conditions but were powerless to stop his plan, and Churchill pressed Sikorski to open negotiations with Moscow. Sikorski had been placed in a difficult position. He could scarcely overlook the September 17 invasion and its aftermath, and he had to consider the precarious situation of Poles in the Soviet Union.

Sikorski and Zaleski prepared for negotiations. Their desired conditions were for the Soviet Union to declare its treaties with Germany to be null and void, recognize all Polish–Soviet treaties in force before September 1939, return or pay for plundered goods, and release all Polish prisoners of war and deportees. Sikorski provided this list to Eden on July 2. Eden advised moderation and compromise, suggesting that talks should start if the Soviets revoked their agreements with Hitler, renewed diplomatic relations with the Polish government, enabled relief committees for Polish citizens to be formed in the Soviet Union, and released prisoners of war and deportees to form a Polish army in the Soviet Union.

---

[37] Kuybyshev was originally named Samara. In 1935, the city was renamed in honor of Bolshevik leader Valerian Kuybyshev. After the USSR collapsed, the city's name was changed back to Samara.
[38] Cultural artifacts evacuated included the Hermitage collections and Lenin's body.

Sikorski received authorization from his Council of Ministers to negotiate; he and Zaleski began talks with Soviet Ambassador to the United Kingdom Ivan Maisky on July 5. Sikorski opened by proposing a return to the Treaty of Riga border, annulment of the Molotov–Ribbentrop agreement, normalization of relations, and appointment of a Polish ambassador to Moscow. Six days later, Maisky responded by offering to recognize an independent Poland within ethnic borders, annul German–Soviet agreements disadvantageous to Poland, renew diplomatic relations, create a Polish army in the Soviet Union under Soviet command, and not form an alternative Polish government.

While Sikorski and Zaleski were reviewing Maisky's response, the Soviet Union and the United Kingdom signed an agreement, and British pressure increased. Sikorski and Maisky sharply disagreed on the border question. Sikorski insisted on the border defined in the Treaty of Riga, while Maisky held to his vague formulation based on ethnic boundaries. Considering the mixed ethnicity of eastern Poland, Maisky's proposal could be interpreted in any number of ways, and this vagueness was of great concern to Sikorski and the government. Sikorski held firm on this issue and received an official note stating that the United Kingdom would not recognize any territorial changes in Poland without Polish agreement. The Soviet Union objected, demanding that this British guarantee not influence the final resolution of borders.

Absent from these negotiations was Raczkiewicz. Sikorski had proceeded without obtaining his approval, and Raczkiewicz held that, under the April Constitution, Sikorski was overstepping his role;[39] he also contended that the agreement did not contain sufficient protections for Polish citizens in the Soviet Union. Raczkiewicz considered resigning but was advised by the British that it would be catastrophic to Poland if the Sikorski–Maisky agreement were not signed; Sosnkowski also had a hand in persuading him to remain in office.

Sikorski's choice was either to agree to the terms presented and possibly save thousands of his countrymen or to reject the agreement and abandon them. The Council of Ministers debated the agreement, and on July 25, a majority voted to accept it. Zaleski, Sosnkowski, and Marian Seyda voted against and resigned. Churchill sent a note to Sikorski assuring him that no territorial changes to Poland's borders as of August 1939

---

[39] Raczkiewicz was correct. Article 12(g) of the April Constitution states that the President of the Republic "concludes and ratifies treaties with other States." Sikorski was acting without Raczkiewicz's authorization; therefore, he did not have legal authority to conduct negotiations with Maisky.

would be recognized. With this note in hand, Sikorski signed the agreement and sent his friend Dr. Józef Retinger to Moscow to establish an embassy.

The agreement's final text had significant differences from Poland's starting positions. Notably absent was a definition of borders, acknowledgment of prewar Polish–Soviet treaties, release of all Polish prisoners and deportees, or restoration of (or restitution for) plundered assets. Raczkiewicz refused to sign it and notified Sikorski that, under the constitution, the agreement could not be considered binding. Sikorski replied with a letter stating that Raczkiewicz's objections would not prevent the agreement's implementation. General Józef Haller attempted to defuse the situation. Raczkiewicz once again considered resigning but instead proposed a major restructuring of the government. Sikorski refused to consider this proposal and in turn demanded the dismissal of Zaleski as head of Raczkiewicz's civil chancellery, a position he had taken after resigning from the government. Support was also lacking in *Rada Narodowa*; it dissolved itself in protest.

Per the agreement, Poles in Soviet captivity were to receive amnesty, a term that many in the government objected to. Ambassador Cripps questioned Stalin on this topic, but Stalin asserted that Soviet criminal law had provided sufficient grounds for all arrests and deportations. Sikorski and the government may have opposed the term, but it had to be accepted if there were to be an agreement.

Regardless of terminology, Sikorski–Maisky meant that the Polish government could secure the release of its citizens and was permitted to create an army on Soviet soil. Sikorski designated General Stanisław Haller to lead the army. Unfortunately, Haller had been taken prisoner during the Soviet invasion, and his captors would not disclose his whereabouts. Sikorski had to find another commander.

General Władysław Anders had become accustomed to what he called the sinister silence of Moscow's Lubyanka prison. Guards spoke with prisoners only in whispers; in the thickly carpeted corridors, speaking was forbidden. On June 22, 1941, this silence was shattered by the sounds of falling bombs and intense anti-aircraft fire. Anders immediately understood that Germany had turned against its ally.

Anders began his military career in the Imperial Russian Army and joined the First Polish Corps after the Russian Revolution. He commanded a regiment in the Polish–Soviet War; after hostilities ceased, he studied at the French military academy. Although he opposed Piłsudski during the 1926 coup, he avoided repercussions. In September 1939, he and his soldiers fought well, but after the Red Army invasion, he led his brigade towards Romania. In late September, he was wounded twice and taken prisoner by the Red Army. After being told that Poland would never exist again and being admonished for fighting against the Red Army, he was taken to a hospital in Lwów. As he recuperated, Soviet officers offered him a position in a Soviet-backed Polish government and a command in the Red Army. After an unsuccessful escape attempt, he rejected another offer to join the Red Army and was charged with being a spy and with betraying the proletariat by fighting against the Red Army in 1919–1920 and in 1939. He was imprisoned in Lwów's Brigidki prison and remained there until he was transported to Moscow in February 1940. His first stop was the Lubyanka. After a few weeks of interrogation, he was transferred to solitary confinement in Butyrka prison. In September, he was sent back to the Lubyanka. Colonel Kondratik conducted his interrogations using a variety of methods ranging from cordial conversation to beatings and torture. This was his routine until bombs began to fall.

After a few days, Anders was taken to Kondratik's office. His now-smiling interrogator was the picture of courtesy and asked about his health; Anders responded by confronting him about the new war. Initially reticent, Kondratik finally admitted that Germany and the Soviet Union were at war, that the Soviet Union was now an ally of the United Kingdom, and that the Soviet Union and Poland were in talks. Anders immediately saw great improvement in his treatment. On August 4, the prison commander escorted him to an office where two men introduced themselves as Lavrentiy Beria, head of the NKVD, and Vsevolod Merkulov, one of Beria's top subordinates. Anders asked if he was free; he was told that he was. Beria and Merkulov then explained that the Germans had unexpectedly attacked and now the Soviet Union and Poland were allies. They also advised Anders that a Polish army would be formed and that General Sikorski had appointed him to command it.

Throughout the conversation, Beria and Merkulov were extremely courteous, solicitous about Anders's health,[40] and apologetic that some of his belongings had been lost. Kondratik was assigned to assist Anders, resulting in his awkward attempt to explain his behavior during interrogations. When their meeting ended, Anders was driven to an apartment building in a limousine. His new home had four rooms and a kitchen; he

---

[40] Anders noted the irony, since it was their organizations that had caused his health issues.

was also assigned a maid and a cook. When he entered the dining room, he was shocked to see a table laden with food and bottles of vodka, cognac, and French wine; it was quite the contrast to his prison rations. Although Anders was no longer a prisoner and was being treated as an honored guest, he understood that he was still under surveillance. He found concealed microphones and received telephone calls in the evenings from unknown women asking to visit, a standard tactic used to compromise foreign officials.

Anders's first Polish guests were Colonel Zygmunt Berling and Lieutenant Colonel Kazimierz Dudziński. Both were vague about their experiences after capture, insisted on close cooperation with the Soviet Union, and were highly critical of pre-war Poland. From newspaper reports, Anders learned that a Polish military mission headed by Major General Zygmunt Bohusz-Szyszko had arrived in Moscow. When they finally met, Anders learned of all that had happened since he was taken prisoner and of Polish military efforts in France, Norway, and the Battle of Britain. He also met with General MacFarlane, head of the British military mission, who gave him a letter from Sikorski placing him in command of the Second Polish Corps pending the return of General Stanisław Haller, who had also been taken prisoner by the Soviet Union in 1939 and could not be located.

On August 14, Poland and the Soviet Union signed a military agreement clearing the way for officers to be released from prison. Anders set about assembling his staff and making arrangements for recruitment, training bases, rations, uniforms, supplies, and equipment. Anders got permission to form two divisions and a reserve regiment; the Soviet Union authorized an army of 30,000. Before he could start recruiting, Anders was told that his army should be ready for action by October 1. This left barely six weeks to recruit, assemble, and train soldiers, and the army had no equipment or uniforms. Anders later said that he didn't bother to object as it would have been a waste of time. A week later, Anders was told that his headquarters would be in Buzuluk and that Polish military camps would be in Tatistchev and Totskoie.

Stanisław Kot was appointed as Poland's ambassador to the Soviet Union. During his first conversation with Anders, Kot demanded exclusion of all former officers of Piłsudski's Legions from the army. Anders rejected Kot's request, informing him that he would accept anyone willing to fight for Poland, that differences of opinion were to be set aside, and that Kot should refrain from interfering in military matters.

Even before Poland and the Soviet Union resumed diplomatic relations, the Polish government began planning an organization to assist Poles in the Soviet Union. On July 30, the government formed a welfare committee; when relations resumed, the Polish embassy took over. The embassy sought to obtain names of deportees and prisoners, ascertain the number of people released from prisons and gulags, determine what help was needed for them, get them to better climates, and establish contact with their families in Poland through the International Red Cross. Anders and the embassy sought to recruit as many people as possible, establish an auxiliary corps, and direct skilled workers and specialists to the Soviet war industry. Recruiting started when a team of newly released officers traveled to a prisoner-of-war camp for enlisted men; among them were twenty-three officers and one chaplain.

Word of the amnesty spread erratically. Some camp commanders claimed they needed the labor and refused to release anyone, while others suppressed the news altogether. Amnestied Poles on their way to the army were frequently delayed and forced to work in factories or on farms. Poland's embassy was frustrated in its efforts to obtain lists of Poles and was given false information about where they could be found; the NKVD declared there were no Poles in some places where many were known to be.

Reports of noncompliance filtered back to Kot, and he addressed these problems to Deputy Commissar for Foreign Affairs Andrey Vyshinsky. Those fortunate enough to obtain their release learned that they could expect no help from Soviet authorities. Many had no idea where to go and simply made their way to major rail junctions, hoping to find someone with information. Fortunately, consular staff had fanned out across the Soviet Union to assist them, providing food, money, documents, and instructions. Soviet officials disliked these people, seeing them as political operatives.[41] Soviet authorities also refused to permit the Polish Red Cross to operate on Soviet territory.

Anders arrived in Buzuluk, a small provincial city with few paved roads, on September 10 and was moved by the sight of the Polish flag flying over his headquarters at the corner of Lenin and May 1 Streets. He now had to build an effective army out of thousands of former prisoners and deportees. They were exhausted and malnourished; many were ill. They wore the tattered remnants of uniforms or the clothing they were wearing when

---

[41] Of the 352 delegates proposed by Poland to assist the amnestied, the Soviet Union accepted only 131.

arrested; quite a few had no boots or shoes. Anders had to house them, but he was not allocated barracks and had to billet them in tents. They needed uniforms, but the Soviet Union struggled to provide them; Raczkiewicz and Sikorski had to persuade the British military to issue 100,000 uniforms. Medical supplies were scarce. A military hospital was established; at one point, 300 to 400 men were dying every month. Some were so weakened and had suffered so many injuries from their ordeals that no amount of medicine would have saved them, but others could have lived had medicine been available. Food supplies were insufficient, and Anders worried that his soldiers would starve. An unknown number died on their way to the army, with more dying after arrival. A Polish military cemetery was established in Buzuluk, beginning a long trail of cemeteries on foreign soil.

Recruits reflected Poland's ethnic composition. Most were ethnic Poles, and a substantial number of Ukrainians, Byelorussians, and Jews[42] reported for duty; there were even twenty-two Tatars among the recruits. Anders expected all citizens of prewar Poland to be eligible to enlist, but the Soviet Union wanted to limit enlistment to ethnic Poles. For a time, Poland's position prevailed. Soviet officials were surprised by the large number who reported, far exceeding their plan for 30,000. Another shock was the number of chaplains: twenty Roman Catholic priests, two Uniate priests, two Orthodox priests, five rabbis, and one Protestant minister were among the recruits. A large number of Polish civilians also made their way to Buzuluk. The Soviet Union gave them no support, and Polish soldiers shared their meager rations with them. Despite these challenges, the soldiers were determined to succeed. Anders was thrilled to see that all were shaven and conducted themselves with military discipline; their bearing amazed General Zhukov when they marched in review.

Although they had been freed, the Poles understood that the NKVD had no intention of leaving them unmonitored. Colonel Okulicki, Anders's chief of staff, would repeatedly tap metal objects with his pencil during confidential conversations to disrupt listening devices. Examination of the headquarters proved him correct; microphones were found throughout the building.

Sikorski visited the Soviet Union in December 1941 and was overwhelmed by his reception at Buzuluk. Soldiers viewed him as their rescuer and showered him with gratitude. He was concerned about conditions for the Corps. He had earlier proposed basing the Corps in Baku to defend the Soviet oil fields, and in his upcoming meeting with Stalin he planned

---

[42] About 5,000 Jewish soldiers joined the Second Polish Corps in the Soviet Union.

to demand this. He and Anders were under constant Soviet pressure to accelerate deployment; they responded by challenging their hosts to provide food and equipment as promised and regularly reminded them of the physical condition of their soldiers and the need for them to regain their strength. Training was also hampered by a lack of officers. Although several thousand officers had been held in Starobelsk, Kozelsk, and Ostashkov, a fact confirmed by Berling and Dudziński, none of them arrived in Buzuluk. Every recruit was asked if they had encountered anyone who had been in those camps; none had.

The missing officers were discussed in nearly every meeting with Soviet officials, but responses were inconsistent. Molotov assured Kot that they had all been released and were delayed by administrative issues and a lack of transportation; Molotov also gave him a note stating that all prisoners had been released. Edward Raczyński received a note from the Soviet ambassador in London assuring him that all Polish officers on Soviet territory had been freed. Deputy Commissar for Foreign Affairs Vyshinsky assured the Poles that he had records of all prisoners and promised to provide them; several months later, he denied any such lists existed. In a discussion with Sikorski, Stalin suggested that they had escaped to Manchuria. Anders was told they had been released in 1940 and sent to the German occupation zone.

This last claim was refuted by the underground: the prisoners had not returned home and were not in German camps, and all correspondence from them had ended in April–May 1940. More troubling were answers received from Merkulov and from NKVD General G. S. Zhukov. When Berling asked Merkulov about the missing officers, he blurted out that a mistake had been made with them. Zhukov, who had been very helpful in obtaining the release of many Poles, made clear to Bohusz-Szyszko that he could not help in this matter. Further, *Polska*, the Polish government's newspaper in the Soviet Union, was prohibited from publishing inquiries about the missing officers. Despite these difficulties, it appeared that the Soviet Union and the Republic of Poland were functioning reasonably well as allies. These appearances were deceiving. Early indications of Soviet plans for Poland were revealed soon after the invasion. Soviet officials made overtures to Anders, General Mieczysław Boruta-Spiechowicz, General Marian Januszajtis, and General Wacław Przeździecki to collaborate, but their efforts failed. Another source of potential collaborators was the group of officers being held in Kozelsk, Starobelsk, and Ostashkov. A small number displayed favor towards the Soviet Union and formed the "Red Corner" in the camp barracks, holding political discussions and openly voicing support for their captors. Although the other prisoners shunned them, the NKVD studied them carefully and eventually selected several for further instruction, including Berling, Dudziński, Captain Narcyz Łopianowski, Lieutenant Colonel Marian Morawski, and Major Józef Lis.[43] They were taken by train to an NKVD villa in the town of Malakhovka; the Poles nicknamed it the "Villa of Bliss." Here, they received political indoctrination, learned the organization of the Red Army, and studied Red Army manuals. Morawski prepared a proposal to create a communist Polish state and organize a Polish division in the Red Army; however, he also discussed Poland's eastern border and the treatment of Polish soldiers in Soviet captivity. His comments were not well received; he was sent to Butyrka.

Over the course of his nearly eighty years, Ignacy Paderewski had interspersed government service with his career in music. He had advocated for a free Poland during the Great War, served as Poland's prime minister, organized *Front Morges*, a group opposing Sanacja, and chaired the exile government's national council. In late 1940, he traveled to the United States to gain support for the fight against Germany and for the Polish cause. He gave speeches, made radio broadcasts, wrote letters, and lobbied Franklin Roosevelt to pressure Vichy France to permit Poles to leave. He spent the winter in Florida and was invited to several parties given by Eleanor Roosevelt and other socialites, but he was troubled by their indifference to Europe's plight. In 1941, Sikorski visited the United States and Canada and spent Easter with Paderewski.

With the return of warm weather, Paderewski returned to New York and resumed his work despite his weakened condition. In late June, he was diagnosed with pneumonia. He rested in his hotel, but his condition declined. On June 29, he received extreme unction. At five in the afternoon, he suddenly awoke and asked for champagne. His astonished caretakers quickly found a bottle. He drank a glass and fell asleep for the last time. At 10:59 that evening, he died.

Thousands queued to pay their respects. His funeral was on July 3 in St. Patrick's Cathedral; afterwards, a military escort accompanied his casket

---

[43] The others were Colonel Eustachy Górczyński, Lieutenant Colonel Leon Bukojemski, Lieutenant Colonel Leon Tyszyński, Captain Kazimierz Rosen-Zawadzki, Lieutenant Włodzimierz Szumigalski, Lieutenant Michał Tomala, Lieutenant Janusz Siewierski, Lieutenant Tadeusz Wicherkiewicz, Lieutenant Roman Imach, Second Lieutenant Stanisław Szczypiorski, and Second Lieutenant Franciszek Kukuliński.

to the Polish embassy in Washington, where he lay in state. On July 5, he was buried with full military honors in the crypt of the USS *Maine* Memorial in Arlington National Cemetery. Roosevelt had arranged for that to be Paderewski's temporary resting place until he could be returned to a free Poland.

While Anders was forming an army, the anti-German alliance continued to grow. Earlier in 1941, the United States began supplying military equipment, food, and oil to the United Kingdom, the Free French Army, and the Republic of China; the Soviet Union began to receive American aid after the German invasion. On August 14, Churchill and Roosevelt issued the Atlantic Charter, a statement declaring their postwar policies, including their "…desire to see no territorial changes that do not accord with the freely expressed wishes of the peoples concerned" and their respect for "the right of all peoples to choose the form of government under which they will live."[44]

Britain sponsored creation of the Inter-Allied Council, comprised of Belgium, Czechoslovakia, Greece, Luxembourg, the Netherlands, Norway, Poland, the Soviet Union, and Yugoslavia; the Council also included representatives of the French exile government. At a meeting in September, the Council endorsed the Atlantic Charter. Of great importance to Raczkiewicz and Sikorski were the points regarding territorial changes, particularly in light of Soviet attitudes towards Poland's eastern border and their forcible incorporation of Polish territory into the Soviet Union. Included in the Inter-Allied Council statement was a quote from Soviet Ambassador Maisky: "The Soviet Union defends the right of every nation to the independence and territorial integrity of its country and its right to establish such a social order and to choose such a form of government as it deems opportune and necessary for the better promotion of its economic and cultural prosperity." He added that the Soviet Union advocated the necessity of collective action against aggressors and that "the Soviet Government proclaims its agreement with the fundamental principles of the declaration of Mr. Roosevelt and Mr. Churchill."[45]

Not all Polish citizens were upset by the destruction of their state. Indeed, most Polish communists viewed it as another step towards the inevitable

---

[44] Atlantic Charter, August 14, 1941.
[45] Inter-Allied Council Statement on the Principles of the Atlantic Charter: September 24, 1941.

global revolution. They supported the Red Army in the 1919–1920 war; in 1925, they formed *Komunistyczna Partia Polski* (KPP, Communist Party of Poland). KPP backed Piłsudski's coup based on his socialist past, a position Comintern considered to be incorrect.[46] KPP was viewed with distrust by Comintern; suspicion rose when it was learned that government agents had infiltrated it. Government investigations resulted in the arrest of a number of activists, including Bolesław Bierut, Władysław Gomułka, Edward Ochab, Stefan Jędrychowski, Aleksander Zawadzki, and Mieczysław Moczar. Ironically, *Sanacja* had saved their lives. During Stalin's great purge, forty-six members and twenty-four deputy members of KPP's Central Committee were summoned to Moscow; upon arrival, they were arrested, tried, found guilty, and executed. Their imprisoned comrades were beyond Moscow's grasp and thus avoided sharing their fate. Most surviving KPP members ceased their activities but remained loyal to the communist cause, so much so that they chose to flee into the Soviet Union in September 1939 rather than attempt to survive under German occupation.

Opportunity awaited them. Writers such as Wanda Wasilewska found work at communist newspapers, including Lwów's *Czerwony Sztandar (Red Banner)*, a Polish-language daily featuring pro-Soviet propaganda, slanders against the Second Republic, and attacks on the clergy; she also wrote for its companion journal *Nowe Widnokręgi (New Horizons)*.[47] Wasilewska gained prominence in the Soviet Union. She joined the Communist Party of the Soviet Union in September 1939, became a member of the Supreme Soviet, and was the only Pole with a special telephone giving her direct access to Stalin.[48] Paweł Finder and Marceli Nowotko worked as government officials in Soviet-occupied Białystok. In 1940, Finder, Nowotko, and Bolesław Mołojec began working with Soviet authorities to create a new Polish communist party. Beria took interest in their cause and requested permission to create a Polish division in the Red Army and a Polish section in Comintern's political school.[49] Mołojec was one of its first students.

---

[46] Comintern is short for Communist International. Comintern was founded in 1919 to foster world communism and was led by the Soviet Union. Comintern's goal was to "struggle by all available means, including armed force, for the overthrow of the international bourgeoisie and the creation of an international Soviet republic as a transition stage to the complete abolition of the state." Stalin dissolved it in 1943 to allay Churchill's and Roosevelt's fears that the Soviet Union was pursuing a policy of fomenting revolution in other countries.

[47] Wasilewska was editor of *Nowe Widnokręgi*.

[48] Her telephone was known as a "*vertushka*" or "*vyertushka*." These had no dialing mechanism and were linked directly to the Kremlin.

[49] Comintern's political school was in Pushkino, a few kilometers from Moscow.

Bolesław Bierut warrants particular attention. He was a mysterious figure; even his birth name and his parents' names are unclear.[50] Details of his early years are straightforward enough; he joined PPS prior to the Great War and gravitated to KPP in independent Poland. In the second half of the 1920s, he attended the International Lenin School in Moscow and the NKVD academy, became an NKVD officer, and worked in Austria, Czechoslovakia, and Bulgaria under the name Jan Iwaniuk. From this point, accounts diverge. In one, he returned to Poland in 1932, was secretary of KPP's Central Committee in Łódź, and worked as a Soviet military intelligence agent. He was arrested for espionage in 1933 and sentenced to seven years' imprisonment; he was languishing in a prison in Rawicz when KPP was dissolved and its leadership liquidated. Released under a 1938 amnesty, he worked as an accountant in Warsaw until the German invasion. However, former NKVD agent Alexander Orlov claimed that in 1935 Bierut was an NKVD interrogator in Lubyanka prison, using the name Bolesław Rutkowski. Bierut was also alleged to have been the NKVD's director of Polish espionage in 1936. These activities would have been impossible were Bierut in Rawicz.

Bierut's whereabouts in the first years of the war are also contested. One version of events holds that he first went to Kowel[51] and worked on a commission to aid political prisoners and then moved to Kiev and worked in construction. In another, he was in Lwów in 1939 and 1940 preparing lists of people to be deported. In yet another, he was involved in organizing and carrying out plebiscites in Polish territories seized by the Soviet Union. He next surfaced in German-occupied Minsk in November 1941 as an employee of the municipal board; considering his NKVD affiliation, it can reasonably be assumed that he would have been an undercover operative.

Other Polish communists served Moscow in various capacities, invariably becoming Soviet citizens.[52] Preparations for a Soviet Poland were underway in the first half of 1941, and Polish communists in the Soviet Union formed its core. Nowotko and Mołojec headed the Polish section of Comintern's political school. In the Villa of Bliss, Dudziński and several other officers wrote a declaration condemning the Second Republic and

---

[50] In some accounts, his parents were Wojciech Bierut and Marianna Salomea. Others claim that they were Henryk (or Wojciech) Rutkowski and Barbara (or Maria) Biernacka and that he created "Bierut" by combining the first syllables of his mother's maiden name and his father's surname. Yet another version holds that he was born Bolesław Biernacki.

[51] Kowel was absorbed into the Soviet Union in 1939 and renamed Kovel.

[52] Many Polish communists joined Wasilewska, Finder, Nowotko, Mołojec, and Bierut in the Soviet Union. Among them were Alfred Lampe, Włodzimierz Sokorski, Jan Krasicki, Stanisław Skrzeszewski, Stefan Jędrychowski, Jakub Prawin, Jakub Berman, Hilary Minc, Piotr Jaroszewicz, Edward Ochab, Stanisław Radkiewicz, Roman Zambrowski, Aleksander Zawadzki, Julia Brystiger, and Józef Różański, people who would play prominent roles in postwar Poland.

expressing their hope that Poland would join the Soviet Union. *Nowe Widnokręgi* published it. Two officers, Lis and Łopianowski, refused to sign. By the end of the month, both were removed from their comfortable quarters in Malakhovka, taken to the Lubyanka, and later transferred to Butyrka.[53]

In early June 1941, the Soviet Union formally authorized creation of a Polish division in the Red Army; it would be commanded by Berling since no generals had agreed to cooperate. The German invasion of the Soviet Union ended this plan. After the Sikorski–Maisky agreement was signed, these officers were inducted into the Second Polish Corps. Most officers of the Corps, knowing their background, were reluctant to trust them.

About two weeks after the German Army invaded the Soviet Union, Comintern authorized formation of *Polska Partia Robotnicza* (PPR, Polish Workers' Party)[54] and formed a Polish group at its school in Kushnarenkovo to serve as PPR's core.[55] Comintern began Polish-language broadcasts from *Radiostacja im. Tadeusza Kościuszki* (Tadeusz Kościuszko Radio Station, typically referred to as Radio Kościuszko). It claimed to be based within occupied Poland; in reality, it broadcast from Moscow. Programming was the responsibility of a group of Polish communists led by Zofia Dzierżyńska[56] and Jakub Berman, and their programs included attacks on the Polish government and the Second Polish Corps.[57] A few weeks after the German attack, a Pan-Slav Committee was formed in Moscow with the stated purpose of creating racial solidarity among the Slavic nations. In its first meeting, the Committee called on all Slavic nations to establish armed forces to fight the Germans and sabotage the German war effort. In attendance was Wanda Wasilewska; she delivered a speech exhorting the Polish nation to join the fight against the Nazis.[58]

---

[53] Captain Łopianowski's presence in the "Villa of Bliss" was not due to pro-Soviet sympathies; he was there on the orders of Brigadier General Wacław Przeździecki. His assignment was to determine Soviet plans for the Polish officers in the villa. He was released under the Sikorski–Maisky agreement and joined the Second Polish Corps; he was parachuted into Poland, fought in the Warsaw Uprising, was captured by the Germans, and was liberated from a prisoner-of-war camp by the US Army. He remained in the West until his death.

[54] On Stalin's orders, the term "communist" was not to be used in the party's name.

[55] Comintern had run the International Lenin School until its dissolution in 1938. In 1940, it was re-established, but its true purpose was concealed; officially, it was an agricultural school.

[56] Zofia Dzierżyńska was the widow of Feliks Dzierżyński; he is better known as Felix Dzerzhinsky, founder of the Cheka.

[57] In addition to his duties at Radio Kościuszko, Berman was an instructor at the Comintern school in Kushnarenkovo.

[58] The first Pan-Slavic Committee meeting began on August 10. Wasilewska's comments can be construed as a deliberate slight against the London-based government, since Poland had fought Germany since September 1, 1939; she ignored the considerable efforts of the Polish military in the West and the Polish underground.

When Soviet government functions were relocated east, Radio Kościuszko began broadcasting from Ufa, *Nowe Widnokręgi* resumed publishing in Kuybyshev, and another group of Polish communists began to function in Saratov. On December 12, while Sikorski was in Moscow meeting with Stalin, the Soviet newspaper *Izvesta* reported on a demonstration organized by Polish communists in Saratov who called themselves the representatives of the Polish people. In a direct challenge to the Polish government's welfare and relief efforts, the Saratov group announced that an organization created in Lwów in 1939 would be responsible for the care of Poles released from prisons, labor camps, and collective farms. Radio Kościuszko broadcast claims that communists had played a leading role in the defense of Warsaw and in the September campaign and announced the formation of a Soviet-sponsored Polish Army in Siberia.

Alumni of the Kushnarenkovo school formed *Grupa Inicjatywna PPR* (PPR Initiative Group) and were charged with establishing PPR in German-occupied Poland. They planned to parachute into Poland on September 26, 1941, but their aircraft crashed shortly after takeoff; one died and three others were injured.

That Moscow would sponsor creation of a Polish communist party and an army, engage in propaganda attacks against the government and military, and send agents into Poland after having restored diplomatic relations with the Republic of Poland and authorizing it to form a Polish army on Soviet territory betrayed its plans for Poland and illustrated its true attitude towards the Sikorski–Maisky agreement.

As Polish communists were retreating towards the Ural Mountains, Edward Rydz-Śmigły was heading towards the Germans. He had disregarded the May 1940 order commanding internees to leave Romania for the West; instead, he escaped in December and crossed into Hungary. He was returning to Poland. Sikorski received news of his presence in Hungary with alarm. He sent a message to ZWZ Commander Stefan Rowecki declaring that the government would regard Rydz-Śmigły's return to Poland as an act of sabotage and instructing Rowecki that, were he to encounter Rydz-Śmigły, he was to order him to travel to South Africa via Istanbul.

In October 1941, Rydz-Śmigły left Hungary for Slovakia; by the end of the month, he was again in Warsaw. His intent was to engage in partisan actions against the Germans, and he wanted to meet with Rowecki to discuss including *Obóz Polski Walczącej* (OPW, Camp of Fighting Poland) in the fight,[59] although it is not known if they met.

Late in November, Rydz-Śmigły suffered a heart attack. After several days in the care of a friend, he died on December 2. He was buried in Powązki Cemetery under the name Adam Zawisza;[60] a simple wooden cross marked his grave. A note tucked into his pocket revealed his true identity.

On December 7, 1941, Japan's military attacked American and British bases in the Pacific Ocean and southeast Asia. Both the United Kingdom and the United States declared war on Japan, and Germany responded by declaring war on the United States. The United Kingdom and Poland now had two large and powerful allies, and Poland's significance declined sharply. Its military was dwarfed by the vast armies of the Soviet Union and the United States. Further, both new allies possessed immense manufacturing capabilities and seemingly limitless reserves of oil and raw materials. Polish–Soviet relations were shaky at best; Poland's hope was that America's large Polish population would help influence American policy in its favor.

British and American propaganda was needed to present the Soviet Union as a palatable ally. What followed was a thorough campaign to rehabilitate the image of Stalin and the Soviet Union. Stalin was now frequently referred to as "Uncle Joe" and was again *Time* magazine's Man of the Year, but this time he was portrayed as a wise and heroic leader and ally. *Life* magazine published an issue dedicated to the Soviet Union with Stalin's photo gracing its cover; inside, Lenin's photo was featured, and the NKVD was described as a law enforcement body analogous to the FBI. Similar articles appeared in other national publications. Several feature films emerged from Hollywood presenting the Soviet Union in the most positive light possible.[61] This strategy achieved its intended effect.

---

[59] *Obóz Polski Walczącej* was formed by members of the prewar *Obóz Zjednoczenia Narodowego* (OZN, Camp of National Unity), a group that strongly supported Rydz-Śmigły. One of its founders was Adam Koc.

[60] In 1991, Adam Zawisza's true identity was revealed. In 1994, a new marker was placed on his grave. It bore the inscription "*Marszałek Polski Edward Śmigły Rydz, 1886–1941, Naczelny Wódz WP 1939*" ("Marshal of Poland Edward Śmigły Rydz, 1886–1941, Supreme Commander of the Polish Army 1939").

[61] Frank Capra's *The Battle of Russia*, part of his "Why We Fight" series, was a notorious example. It contained no references to Soviet aggression and atrocities in 1939–1940. Other pro-Soviet films included *The Boy from Stalingrad, Days of Glory, Mission to Moscow, The North Star, Song of Russia,* and *Three Russian Girls*. During the Cold War, these films were considered embarrassing and withdrawn from circulation.

Public opinion of the Soviet Union became positive, with the corollary perception that opposition to Soviet policies was in essence a betrayal of the allied cause.

In late December, a second attempt was made to parachute *Grupa Inicjatywna PPR* into Poland. This was more successful, although one agent was injured and their radio was lost. Another group joined them in early January; they made their way to Warsaw, began PPR activities, and sought recruits. They created a partisan military organization, choosing the name *Gwardia Ludowa* (GL, People's Guard), an obvious copy of *Gwardia Ludowa WRN*. PPS-WRN leadership did not fail to notice this appropriation and denounced PPR's perfidy.

Communism remained unpopular in Poland, and PPR and GL struggled to attract members. Their Comintern affiliation was to have been secret, although it was not difficult to work out their connection to Moscow and they were treated with suspicion and distrust. Few underground organizations cooperated with them, and the great majority of potential GL recruits instead joined ZWZ or BCh. By the end of 1942, GL and PPR had perhaps five thousand members each, whereas ZWZ had about two hundred thousand. In February 1942, ZWZ renamed itself *Armia Krajowa* (AK, Home Army) to more clearly define its function and reflect its size. BCh remained nominally independent but partially integrated itself into AK, while SN's military organization, now known as *Narodowe Siły Zbrojne* (NSZ, National Armed Forces), opted to remain independent, although its commanders often coordinated operations with AK. New underground groups continued to emerge, such as *Żydowska Organizacja Bojowa* (ŻOB, Jewish Combat Organization), comprised of Jews in the Warsaw Ghetto.

AK based its strategy on its assessment that Germany's military was overextended. Germany was forced to rely on soldiers from its allies and volunteers from occupied territories,[62] and AK's leaders reasoned that as new fronts opened and casualties mounted, a weakened German Army would be more vulnerable. Until that time came, AK took into account the German policy of collective responsibility and disproportionate retaliation and planned its actions to minimize reprisals against civilians.[63] AK defended the population against attacks, conducted sabotage operations,

---

[62] Germany's allies were Italy, Romania, and Hungary; volunteer units came from France, Norway, Denmark, the Netherlands, Belgium, Russia, Ukraine, Estonia, and Latvia.

[63] If a German was killed, a much larger number of Poles would be publicly executed without regard for their culpability.

and gathered intelligence while building strength in preparation for an uprising.[64]

In contrast, GL agitated for frequent and indiscriminate attacks, but its actions did not match its exhortations. Throughout its existence, GL operations against the Germans were typically acts of sabotage and assaults on soft targets such as administration buildings, theaters, and cafes. GL's relations with the Jewish population are best described as uneven. Some GL units had a large number of Jewish soldiers, and some Jews called GL their best defenders among the underground organizations. However, other GL units refused to accept Jews into their ranks and had no qualms about robbing, attacking, or killing them.

Publicly, PPR maintained that its objectives were defeating Germany and establishing democracy. Behind the scenes, it was engaged in activities to weaken and destroy *Delegatura* and AK. In 1942, GL units began attacking AK and NSZ units and killing their soldiers. PPR, GL, and Soviet agents established an information department that was functionally a part of Soviet intelligence and planted agents to collect information and disrupt activities; some went so far as to use the Germans to achieve their goals. Marceli Nowotko, a *Grupa Inicjatywna* member, was suspected of passing names, code names, and addresses of *Delegatura* and AK members to the Gestapo. On November 28, his bullet-ridden corpse was found near the Warszawa Zachodnia railroad station. He had last been seen in the company of another PPR activist, Bolesław Mołojec, who was nowhere to be found. For three days, other PPR activists searched for Mołojec. When he was finally located, he claimed that he and Nowotko had talked briefly and then went their separate ways. A few days later, he changed his story; now he claimed that they had been attacked and that he had managed to escape, adding that the perpetrators may have been from AK. With Nowotko dead, Mołojec took over as PPR first secretary, but his story and subsequent actions seemed suspicious. After some investigation, his fellow PPR leaders concluded that he had killed Nowotko. Mołojec was executed in late December.

Stalin and Sikorski agreed to relocate the Second Polish Corps to a warmer climate. Stalin did not authorize this move out of concern for the Corps;

---

[64] AK intelligence observed a massive buildup of German soldiers and equipment near the German–Soviet demarcation line and informed the government in London, suggesting that it could be in preparation for a German action against the Soviet Union. The Polish government informed its hosts; the British government passed this intelligence on to the Soviet Union. It was ignored.

he was thinking about railroads. The Soviet Union was unable to produce enough arms and equipment. Allied aid was indispensable, and the Trans-Iranian Railway was a crucial route. Iran was no less important to Britain; it relied on Middle Eastern oil and had already intervened in Iraq to defeat a pro-German government. A friendly Iran was vital to both nations, but its pro-German ruler presented a problem. They solved it by jointly invading Iran, removing the shah, and replacing him with his son;[65] since the new shah was dependent on their support, he was subservient to his sponsors.

Maintaining control was an issue, as Germany desperately needed oil and neither the British nor the Soviets could spare sufficient troops to protect the region, so Stalin and Churchill agreed to move the Corps to Soviet Central Asia; from there it could be deployed into Iran. Britain also took on increased responsibility for supplying the Poles. In late December, the Second Polish Corps began moving to Soviet Central Asia, with headquarters at a disused military camp at Yangi-Yul[66] and bases throughout the region.[67] Recruits continued to pour in, and permission was received to further increase the army's size; from December 1941 to March 1942, the army grew from 30,000 to 66,000. Old problems such as inadequate food supplies and NKVD surveillance continued, and new problems arose. Some Poles who ventured off base disappeared, and a few were abducted from their camps. All were exposed to mosquito-borne diseases such as typhus, typhoid fever, and malaria, and the medical corps did not have sufficient drugs or facilities to handle the ensuing epidemic. Illness ravaged the Corps; about three thousand were buried in twelve military cemeteries established in Soviet Central Asia.

Ethnic composition of the Corps again became an issue. Red Army policy was to permit most people from west of the Molotov–Ribbentrop demarcation line to join the Polish Army; those from areas east of the line would be allowed to join only if they were ethnic Poles. Jews were forbidden to enlist. This was enforced by requiring all recruits to register with the Red Army, but anyone determined to join the Corps could easily do so. A common tactic was to declare that one's identification papers had been lost or stolen; another was to claim a birthplace in western Poland. Ukrainians and Byelorussians would write their names following Polish

---

[65] The new shah was Mohammad Reza Pahlavi; he was deposed in the Iranian Revolution of 1979.
[66] Now known as Yangiyo'l in independent Uzbekistan.
[67] When the Soviet Union collapsed, Soviet Central Asia splintered into several independent nations. Former locations of Polish bases can be found in what is now Uzbekistan, Kyrgyzstan, and Turkmenistan.

spelling conventions, and Jews would declare themselves Catholic or state that they had no religion. Other restrictions existed that were harder to circumvent. Poles forced into the Red Army and those working in factories were not permitted to enlist.

Soviet officials were increasingly impatient that the Corps was not ready for the front. Zhukov demanded that Anders immediately deploy one division to the front, insisting that it would be a political victory. Anders refused, contending that deployment required healthy, well-fed, trained, and properly equipped soldiers; the Poles were none of these. He pointed to Soviet failures to deliver promised equipment and food and proposed June 1942 as the date when the Corps would be ready, provided that sufficient supplies were delivered. Anders insisted that the Second Polish Corps should be deployed as a unified force; he also wanted the Corps to fight on the Soviet front. Sikorski agreed with Anders, as it would place the Corps in a better position to help liberate Poland.

Underlying these issues was mutual distrust. Poles did not forget the Soviet invasion, arrests, interrogations, torture, deportations, gulags, and repeated failures to deliver promised aid. From the Soviet perspective, the Poles were a demanding group of foreigners who, rather than being grateful for their release, did not respect Soviet laws and wasted few opportunities to display their patriotism by flying flags, singing patriotic songs, and conducting public religious services. To compound the matter, Soviet citizens were surreptitiously attending religious services offered by Polish chaplains. Reflecting the situation's severity, Zhukov let Anders know that he was dissatisfied with anti-Soviet views expressed by members of the Polish army, warning of forthcoming arrests and gulag sentences.

By March 1942, it became quite clear that the Soviet Union was determined to impose its will. Stalin decided to reduce the Polish Army's size by seventy-five percent and send surplus soldiers to work on collective farms. Soviet officials began confiscating citizenship documents from Poles, forbidding them to travel, and closing Polish assistance and recruiting centers. Anders was notified that rations would be reduced to a level that would support only 26,000 people; with over 70,000 in the army, this meant certain starvation. Sikorski negotiated a solution that maintained the army's size, provided rations for 44,000, evacuated the rest of the army to Iran, removed restrictions on recruitment, obtained weapons for a second division, and permitted Poles in the Red Army to join the Second Polish Corps. The last three of these promises were not kept. Evacuation to Iran was allowed to proceed, and in March the first group boarded trains headed to the Caspian Sea; from there, they sailed to Iran. By April 5, 44,000 had been evacuated. Despite these developments, Sikorski wanted to adhere to the Polish–Soviet military agreement and maintain an army in the Soviet Union; he also wanted to increase its strength to 96,000.

June came, and the army still was not ready for combat, Soviet pressure increased, and the situation was becoming untenable. Further obstacles emerged in July, when the Soviet Union advised the Polish embassy that its delegations would no longer be allowed to function, claiming that they were engaged in anti-Soviet activities. Delegates and their staff members were arrested and imprisoned; food, clothing, and medical supplies were seized, and their bank accounts were frozen. Polish military commanders planned to resist if force was used against them. They needn't have worried; Stalin was ready to send them to the British. On July 26, Anders received a telegram from Zhukov stating that the Soviet government would not hinder evacuation of the Polish Army to the Middle East and claimed that the Polish government was unwilling for the Corps to deploy alongside the Red Army. Both sides agreed that all soldiers and their families would leave in August, but those from eastern Poland who had been forced to take Soviet citizenship were excluded. Soviet officials forbade evacuation of Jewish civilians. After considerable negotiations, wives and children of Jewish soldiers would be allowed to leave, but no other relatives could join them. Soviet authorities conducted detailed inspections of evacuation transports and threatened to cease them if the Poles violated this agreement. When Jews rejected from evacuation approached the NKVD, they were told that the Soviet Union had no objection to their departure and that it was the Poles who were preventing it. Those denied permission to leave tended to blame the Poles.

Anders proposed leaving members of his staff behind to continue recruiting, but this was rejected. Evacuation proceeded with surprising ease. The same Soviet government that had such difficulties providing equipment, food, and transportation was now able to quickly marshal trains and ships. In all, about 115,000 were evacuated; this was less than ten percent of the total number of Poles in the Soviet Union.[68]

With the Second Polish Corps out of Soviet territory, Stalin was free to implement his own plans for Poland. A few officers did not leave. Anders had chosen Berling to take charge of the evacuation center in Krasnovodsk,

---

[68] A far larger number of Poles were left in the Soviet Union. Some returned to Poland when the Soviet Union established a Polish Army under their complete control. Others returned after the war, and the rest disappeared into the depths of the USSR. Small Polish communities populated with descendants of deportees remain, scattered throughout the former Soviet Union.

but when the time came to leave, an NKVD officer advised Anders that Berling did not have permission to do so. Anders ordered Berling to report to Yangi-Yul, but Berling requested reinstatement in the Red Army instead and went to Moscow with three other officers. They declared their independence from the London government, renounced claims to territories seized by the Soviet Union, demanded a western border on the Odra (Oder) and Nysa Łużycka (Neisse) rivers, and stated that the Polish army formed in the Soviet Union would fight alongside the Red Army. Berling and two other officers were tried *in absentia* by a military court of the Second Polish Corps. They were charged with desertion and found guilty; the court recommended expulsion from the army and sentences of death for treason.[69]

1942 began with a display of allied unity. On January 1, twenty-six nations, including Poland and the Soviet Union, reaffirmed their commitment to the Atlantic Charter. At the time that Poland's ambassador to the United States, Jan Ciechanowski, signed this declaration, some semblance of normalcy had returned to Polish political life. Sikorski, having successfully deflected several challenges to his position, continued to exercise extensive powers and maintained considerable influence with Churchill and other British politicians. He was also forging closer ties with other captive nations. On January 19, 1942, Hubert Ripka, secretary of state in the Czechoslovak government-in-exile, and Edward Raczyński, now minister of foreign affairs, signed a joint declaration pledging to create a postwar confederation with a common foreign policy, economic policy, and military.

Five months after *Rada Narodowa* resigned, Raczkiewicz appointed a new council. *II Rada Narodowa Rzeczypospolitej Polskiej* convened on February 3, 1942, with Stanisław Grabski chairing the thirty-one-member body. Members included representatives from political parties, several people with no party affiliation, and two representatives from the Jewish population; six members had formerly served on the first *Rada Narodowa*.

Raczkiewicz was still president, but he had no illusions regarding his level of support or his influence. His health remained a concern and continued to affect his ability to be more active in political life, and presidential succession again became an issue. In May 1942, Minister of Information Stanisław Stroński proposed that Raczkiewicz change his successor to Sikorski. His concerns were twofold: Raczkiewicz was in poor health,

---

[69] When he became commander in chief, Sosnkowski vacated these penalties.

and his named successor Sosnkowski was in conflict with Sikorski and his Council of Ministers over the Sikorski–Maisky agreement. Sikorski disagreed with the proposal, reminding his ministers that Raczkiewicz was the legitimate president and that such a move would have to be initiated by him. Sikorski did, however, leave the door open to discuss the proposal with Raczkiewicz. During a meeting in June, Sikorski presented the proposal, although he took pains to make it clear that this was not his idea. For perhaps the first time since *Umowa Paryska*, Raczkiewicz had the upper hand. He rejected the proposal, stating that such a change could only be made for reasons of utmost importance and not merely due to a political conflict; he also noted that the proposal was unconstitutional and could easily be viewed as a step towards dictatorship. This was the last attempt to place Sikorski in line for the presidency.

Throughout these developments, nothing changed in Rothesay and Tighnabruaich. Officers and some political figures sat and waited; Polish military intelligence monitored their activities. Some managed to leave by finding jobs, pursuing further education, or obtaining an assignment with the British Army. Morale was low, drunkenness was rampant, and pro-*Sanacja* political activities flourished. A few, driven to despair, committed suicide. Dąb-Biernacki was court-martialed, dismissed from the army, and served time in a British prison.[70] No thought was given to assign any of them to the Second Polish Corps to alleviate its shortage of officers.

Herbert Morrison, a Labour MP, was in Rothesay visiting his sister when he encountered several Polish officers whose only activity seemed to be playing cards. He learned that they had no assignments and had little hope of returning to active duty; he also discovered that there were several hundred others similarly situated. He raised the issue in the House of Commons, and Sikorski's practice of isolating his political opponents was exposed and condemned. Under British pressure, the camps were dissolved and officers were permitted to return to duty. Only the sick and elderly remained.

In December 1942, Edward Raczyński took an extraordinary step. He sent a diplomatic note to the member governments of the United Nations describing German actions to exterminate the Jewish population and making them aware that one million Jews had already been murdered. The Ministry

---

[70] Dąb-Biernacki was released from prison due to poor health. After Sikorski's death, Sosnkowski permitted Dąb-Biernacki to emigrate to Ireland.

of Foreign Affairs published his note under the title "*The Mass Extermination of Jews in German Occupied Poland*" and made it available to the public. His actions ensured that no Western government could deny knowledge of the Holocaust. Unfortunately, many prominent figures chose to not believe him or eyewitness accounts. Jan Karski, an AK officer who had gone undercover to observe conditions in the Warsaw Ghetto and at a transit station for the Belzec death camp, slipped out of Poland and traveled to the United States. He met with Roosevelt, members of the government, the media, and prominent members of the Jewish community, but his report was received with varying degrees of incredulity.

Late in 1942, Germany began to transport Jews from the Warsaw Ghetto. In January 1943, ŻZW and ŻOB fought back. AK and GL units outside the Ghetto supported them by attacking German positions. After several days, the Germans resorted to systematically burning the Ghetto block by block. Most Ghetto inhabitants died in the fighting or were transported to death camps; a handful escaped.

German plans to resettle Poland began in earnest in the Zamość area. In November 1941, two thousand peasants were expelled from six villages and replaced with Germans. A second phase ran from November 1942 through March 1943, and a third began later in 1943. German troops would surround a village, herd the population to one location, and separate them into groups: forced labor in Germany, slave labor for colonists, children selected for Germanization, or transport to death camps. To avoid capture, people fled into the forests and were helped by AK, BCh, and GL; underground soldiers attacked the German military, fought pitched battles, freed Poles from jails, and attacked, harassed, and killed German colonists. Faced with such firm resistance, the occupier halted colonization efforts.

Zamość and the Warsaw Ghetto Uprising were noteworthy for two reasons. First, both were rare examples of GL directly engaging the Germans in open battle. Second, in both operations, GL cooperated with AK and BCh. Normally, GL did not coordinate actions or conduct joint operations with any group loyal to London; quite the contrary, it was more likely to attack AK and NSZ units, murder individual AK, NSZ, and *Delegatura* members, or betray them to the Gestapo. Many GL units confiscated food from villagers and engaged in banditry, singling out churches and larger houses for particular attention. Such acts, coupled with communist ideology, were repugnant to many potential recruits. GL's precise size is not known, but the most generous estimate is eleven thousand, many of whom were Russian, Byelorussian, and Ukrainian.

PPR regularly transmitted optimistic reports to Moscow, but the reality was quite different. Neither PPR nor GL had much success recruiting members, and efforts to form alliances with PPS and SL failed. Early in 1943, PPR issued an open letter to *Delegatura* and AK urging active armed resistance, calling on the government to condemn prewar Poland's anti-Soviet policies, and requesting talks. AK viewed PPR's overture as a ploy: temporary compromises to improve its position. Suspicions ran high, and Sikorski was consulted. He was hesitant but authorized talks.

Delegatura and AK opened discussion by requesting that PPR and GL recognize the London government, *Delegatura*, and AK's command, comply with AK directives, end independent military actions, end agitation against *Delegatura* and AK, and declare the inviolability of Poland's eastern borders. Władysław Gomułka, PPR's primary negotiator, countered by proposing creation of a new government that would include all political forces except for *Sanacja* and groups on the political right, permitting GL commanders to join AK's general staff while maintaining organizational independence, abandoning AK's policy of preparing for an uprising, and launching an active insurgency. PPR negotiators claimed they wanted a democratic government but evaded requests to expand on their definition of the term; they also falsely declared that PPR was not affiliated with Comintern. Talks failed; Gomułka claimed that *Delegatura* and AK had set conditions that were impossible to accept. *Delegatura* and AK viewed PPR's demands as unacceptable and believed that its objective was to legitimize itself, discredit AK, and isolate the London government. Soon, another motive became apparent: AK and *Delegatura* figures who had met with PPR were denounced to the Gestapo and arrested; among them was *Delegat* Jan Piekałkiewicz who, after enduring months of interrogation and torture, was murdered at Gestapo headquarters in Warsaw.[71] AK and *Delegatura* had no choice but to break off contact with PPR and GL; those who had met with them were quarantined to prevent additional people from being exposed.

Moscow continued to reinforce PPR with Poles trained in the Soviet Union. In July, Bolesław Bierut arrived in Warsaw and joined PPR's Central Committee.[72] Despite his relatively undistinguished career, he grew in stature; his rapid ascent clearly indicated that he was trusted by Stalin. But

---

[71] Piekałkiewicz's brother, Major Stanisław Piekałkiewicz, was a victim of the Katyń massacre; he was murdered at Kharkov.
[72] On his return to Poland, Bierut used the name Bolesław Birkowski.

something about him appeared to be different. People who had known him before the war, such as Piotr Jaroszewicz, later remarked that the Bierut of 1943 was not the same person as before the war.[73]

Moscow also began to support *Polska Armia Ludowa* (PAL, Polish People's Army), an outgrowth of the prewar PPS. PAL established itself in April 1943 and operated in the environs of Warsaw, Lublin, Kielce, and Łódź. Like GL, most of its activities involved sabotage and attacks on softer targets.[74]

Several months had passed since the Second Polish Corps departed the Soviet Union, but hundreds of thousands of Polish citizens remained, and the Polish government continued to provide them with aid and citizenship documents. This abruptly ended in January 1943. First, the Soviet Union revoked its permission for the Polish embassy to grant passports, claiming that "the demands of the Polish government collide with the sovereign rights of the Soviet Union." A few days later, the embassy was informed that, since there were now few Polish citizens in the USSR, the Polish government's relief organization was no longer necessary and was not permitted to function. Those who approached the Polish embassy were arrested and, in some cases, publicly beaten; those who had received passports were summoned to NKVD offices and ordered to surrender them and accept a Soviet passport. They were blackmailed, interrogated, tortured, and threatened; those who continued to refuse were taken to court and sentenced to a gulag. Embassy staff themselves were under pressure to accept Soviet passports. Those who refused were imprisoned.

Poland's government viewed these actions as unmistakable signs that the Soviet Union did not intend to adhere to the terms of the Sikorski–Maisky agreement, and Raczkiewicz's supporters considered them to be proof that his criticism was correct. Discontent ran high in the Second Polish Corps, so much so that Anders sent a letter to Raczkiewicz. He bluntly criticized the government's inability to protect Polish citizens and called for Sikorski and his government to step down. Sikorski refused to consider resignation, but he felt compelled to heal this rift. He planned an inspection of the Second Polish Corps so he could meet with his officers and soldiers. Before he left, German radio made a shocking announcement that would permanently alter the relationship between the Republic of Poland and the Soviet Union.

---

[73] During the war, Jaroszewicz was an officer in Berling's army; later, he was prime minister.
[74] PAL was dissolved in January 1945; most of its members joined Polish communist military units.

The Troublesome Ally

ON APRIL 11, the German news service reported that a mass grave of ten thousand Polish officers had been found in a forest near the village of Katyń, a few kilometers from Smolensk. The next day, Moscow countered with a broadcast on Radio Kościuszko denouncing the report as propaganda. German radio followed up on the thirteenth with a bulletin describing the graves-and the manner of execution. News of the discovery swept through occupied Poland, the Polish Army, and the exile community. Anders immediately sent a message to Minister of Defense Kukiel detailing the search for thousands of missing officers while the army was still in the Soviet Union, advising him of the mood of his soldiers, and demanding that the government obtain an official Soviet explanation. Two days later, the Soviet Information Office issued a reply placing blame on Germany, claiming the officers were engaged in construction work and had been captured by the Germans in the summer of 1941.

Sikorski's Council of Ministers resolved to demand an explanation from the Soviet embassy, request an investigation by the International Red Cross, and issue a statement on the matter from Kukiel. Sikorski and Raczyński met with Churchill and Under Secretary of State for Foreign Affairs Alexander Cadogan. Churchill warned them to not raise the issue publicly, but Sikorski responded that he had to do so since he was responsible to the Polish people and had irrefutable proof of Soviet guilt. Churchill could not dissuade Sikorski, who insisted that his government needed to take a clear stand. On April 17, Poland formally requested an investigation by the International Red Cross. Reaction from Moscow was swift. *Pravda*, the official newspaper of the Communist Party of the Soviet Union, ran an article on April 19 titled "Hitler's Polish Collaborators," accusing the Polish government of siding with the Germans.

Raczyński wrote to the Soviet ambassador recounting the many unsuccessful efforts to receive information on the officers and asking again for detailed information on their fate. He received no reply.

Soviet response was harsh; it threatened to break relations with Poland. Eden met with Sikorski on April 24 to present Stalin's demands. Stalin insisted that Poland withdraw the request to Red Cross and officially acknowledge that the Germans were to blame. Eden followed by asserting that the United Kingdom did not believe the German report and could not estrange the Soviet Union. Sikorski replied that he would not press for a Red Cross investigation, but he could not place responsibility on the Germans in the face of significant evidence of Soviet guilt. As Eden and Sikorski met, Churchill assured Moscow that his government would oppose an International Red Cross investigation. However, he had doubts. He asked Owen O'Malley, the British ambassador to Poland, to investigate further. O'Malley analyzed all available evidence and determined that it pointed clearly to Soviet guilt. His report concluded by examining the moral dilemma facing the United Kingdom, contending that good relations with Moscow took precedence and stating that "We have in fact perforce used the good name of England [...] to cover up a massacre...."[1]

O'Malley's report was sent to Churchill, members of the War Cabinet, and King George VI. After reading it, Churchill remarked to Eden, "All this is merely to ascertain the facts, because we should none of us ever speak a word about it." Churchill passed the diplomat's comments to Roosevelt in a letter, taking care to ask for the letter to be returned. Roosevelt's reaction was callous. He called the Polish government fools, stated that he had no more patience for it, and declared that the matter was not worth the uproar. He did ask John F. Carter, a journalist working for the government, to investigate and prepare a report. When Carter returned with his conclusion that the Soviet Union was responsible, Roosevelt suppressed his report.

It appeared that Churchill was convinced of Soviet guilt. He discussed the matter with Sikorski in a private meeting, but his refusal to alienate Stalin took precedence. In an official meeting, Eden asked Sikorski to issue a statement calling the massacre a Nazi fabrication. Sikorski refused. It was clear that keeping the Soviet Union as an ally was paramount to British and American policy. Seeing that there would be no repercussions, the Soviet Union broke relations with Poland. At 11:30 p.m. on April 25, Polish Ambassador to the Soviet Union Tadeusz Romer received a telephone call from Molotov's office informing him that Molotov wanted to meet. On arrival he was ushered into Molotov's office. Molotov proceeded to read a note declaring that Poland had made no attempt to discuss the Katyń discovery with the Soviet Union, accusing Poland of treachery and collusion with Germany, and declaring that the Soviet Union was terminating diplomatic relations with Poland.

---

[1] Memo from Mr. O'Malley to Mr. Eden, May 24, 1943, paragraph 20.
https://webarchive.nationalarchives.gov.uk/ukgwa/20121212135632/http://www.fco.gov.uk/Files/kfile/Omalley_Whole.pdf

When Molotov finished, he attempted to hand the note to Romer, but Romer refused to accept it and left. Later that day, the Soviet authorities delivered the note to Romer's residence, but he returned it. He immediately advised London and closed the embassy. Polish citizens in the Soviet Union were placed under the care of the Australian embassy, and Romer and his staff left the country.

There is considerable irony that this note was composed and delivered by Vyacheslav Molotov, the same person who had signed the Molotov–Ribbentrop Pact allying the Soviet Union with Germany and dividing Poland between them. And who, it would later be revealed, was one of the signatories of the order to execute the Polish officers.

In the aftermath of the Soviet invasion, thousands of Poles were taken prisoner. Most enlisted men were deported to gulags; unbeknownst to the NKVD, a number of officers removed their rank insignia and passed themselves off as privates among their own soldiers.[2] Officers were sent to separate camps, the largest of which were Kozelsk, Ostashkov, and Starobelsk; all were former Orthodox monasteries now serving as NKVD prisons. Interrogations, incessant propaganda broadcasts over loudspeakers, and indoctrination sessions were the norm, a program designed to identify those positively disposed towards the Soviet Union who could potentially serve in the Red Army, in a Soviet-sponsored Polish army, or in a Soviet-backed government. The results were dismal. Those who would not cooperate presented a problem; Beria proposed resolving that problem by eliminating them.

On March 5, 1940, Beria issued a memo to the Politburo enumerating the number of officers in captivity and the potential threat they presented to Soviet power if released; he concluded by recommending a final examination of their cases followed by execution. Stalin approved the proposal and signed it along with Molotov, Kliment Voroshilov, and Anastas Mikoyan. Later that day, the Politburo issued a decree to carry out the decision.

Throughout March 1940, Kozelsk prisoner Lieutenant Stanisław Swianiewicz had been hearing rumors that the camp would be disbanded; some were told by their guards that they would be sent to German-occupied Poland. The

---

[2] Timoshenko's exhortation for soldiers to turn on their officers fell on deaf ears; no cases were found where soldiers exposed officers hidden in their ranks.

first rumor proved true; on April 3, groups of officers began to be taken from Kozelsk. Swianiewicz was in the April 24 group. He and his fellow prisoners were given bread and herring and searched for sharp objects; they were then loaded into trucks, taken to a rail siding, and crammed into Stolypin cars.[3] Six days later, he caught sight of Smolensk through a crack in the railcar wall; about ten miles later, the train stopped. He heard the sounds of truck motors, a large number of people moving about, and officers barking out orders. After about thirty minutes, an NKVD officer entered the railcar and ordered Swianiewicz to take his belongings and follow him. He was taken to an empty Stolypin and locked inside. A guard was in the corridor, but he wasn't paying attention to his prisoner, so Swianiewicz climbed onto the top bunk and looked out through a hole. He saw a road alongside the rail track, a small bus with whitewashed windows, and a group of NKVD guards with bayonets fixed to their rifles cordoning off the area; the officer who had taken him from the transport appeared to be in command. The bus backed up to a Stolypin, and prisoners stepped directly into the bus. When full, the bus was driven off; thirty to forty-five minutes later, it returned and the process was repeated. When the train was completely unloaded, Swianiewicz was taken from the railcar, locked in a prison van, and driven to the NKVD prison in Smolensk. Six days later, he was transferred to the Lubyanka.

When the bus arrived at its destination, each prisoner was disembarked individually and led into a small room with red walls. An officer verified his identity; the guards then bound his hands and took him through a door into an adjacent room. One wall was made of logs and the other three were thickly padded; there was a sloping concrete floor with a drain at the bottom, a spigot, and a hose. The guards led the prisoner to face the log wall and restrained his arms; an executioner approached from behind, positioned a pistol on the base of the prisoner's skull, and fired. Two guards then dragged the lifeless body out a back door and stacked it on a truck while another hosed off the floor.[4] Loaded trucks were driven to a trench, and the bodies were stacked in layers. When the trench was full, it was

---

[3] A Stolypin car was a railroad carriage with passenger compartments and livestock pens. Its name came from Pyotr Stolypin, a Russian prime minister in the first decade of the twentieth century. Stolypin promoted a plan to voluntarily resettle Russian peasants in Siberia, and the railcar bearing his name was designed to facilitate their transport. After the revolution, the Cheka found them useful for prisoner transport; guards occupied the passenger compartments, and prisoners were locked into the livestock pens. Typically, Stolypin cars would be coupled immediately behind the engine or to the end of a train.

[4] In some cases, prisoners were shot at the trench, but this method was an exception.

covered with soil and planted with pine saplings. This continued until all of the camps were emptied.

Execution and burial of Kozelsk prisoners was at Katyń. Starobelsk prisoners were executed and buried at Kharkov; Ostashkov prisoners met their end at Mednoye. A total of 21,857 were killed; about 448 were spared. Non-military victims included landowners, government officials, university professors, physicians, lawyers, engineers, teachers, writers, journalists, pilots, and one prince. Military victims included ten generals, one admiral, about 300 colonels and lieutenant colonels, 500 majors, 2,500 captains, and 5,000 lieutenants and second lieutenants; in all, about half of Poland's military officers were murdered. Among the victims was General Stanisław Haller.

Germany reasoned that Katyń could be leveraged to drive a wedge between the Soviet Union and its newfound allies and dispatched investigators in April 1943 to collect and document evidence. They determined that the rope used to bind prisoners was of Soviet manufacture, that bayonet wounds matched a type used only by the Soviet Union, that none of the letters, personal journals, or newspapers found on the deceased bore dates later than April 1940, and that saplings over the graves were two to three years old. Although the ammunition used was German, it was a type that had been exported to the Soviet Union in large quantities prior to the German invasion. Forensic studies of decomposition pointed to burial in 1940, and local residents testified that they saw trainloads of Polish officers arriving almost daily in April 1940. Germany created a commission consisting of forensic experts from twelve countries.[5] Two American prisoners of war, Colonel John H. van Vliet and Captain Donald B. Stewart, were taken to Katyń; both sent coded messages to their superiors indicating that they saw proof of Soviet guilt.[6] German authorities attempted to include Polish experts on their commission, but they refused to participate,[7] although

---

[5] Germany's team of forensic experts were from Belgium, Bulgaria, Croatia, Denmark, Finland, France, Hungary, Italy, the Netherlands, Romania, Switzerland, and Slovakia. All of these nations were either neutral, allied with Germany, or occupied by Germany.

[6] After his release in 1945, Colonel John H. van Vliet submitted a report on Katyń to Major General Clayton Bissell concluding that the Soviet Union was responsible for the massacre; Bissell classified the report as top secret and ordered van Vliet to remain silent on the matter. In 1950, van Vliet re-created his report. In 2014, a copy of the original report was discovered in France.

[7] Writer Ferdynand Goetel was one of the witnesses; after the war, an arrest warrant was issued for him, and he escaped Poland using a fake passport. Also after the war, Bulgarian representative Marko Markov and Czech representative František Hájek were forced by their new communist governments to recant and blame the Germans. Croatian pathologist Eduard Miloslavić escaped to the United States to avoid prosecution.

representatives from the Polish Red Cross were permitted to conduct their own review. They steadfastly refused to make statements or to appear in photographs; their concern was identifying the deceased.[8] Germany also called for an International Red Cross examination.

The Soviet Union retorted that the officers had been killed in summer 1941, but this did not square with physical evidence. All of the exhumed bodies were wearing winter greatcoats, appropriate for April in Smolensk but not for summer. Boots and uniforms showed much less wear than would be expected if the Poles had been engaged in road construction work as Moscow claimed. Soviet insistence that the slain officers had fallen into German hands was inconsistent with the multiple explanations proffered by Soviet authorities.

Both the United Kingdom and the United States ignored the evidence and accepted the Soviet position for fear of losing their powerful ally. Both nations had already invested considerable effort into remaking the Soviet Union's image, and it would have been embarrassing to admit that they were allied with a nation capable of such atrocities. Pro-Soviet activities were already commonplace in Britain; in February 1943, the British government sponsored official celebrations of Red Army Day. Much of the British press had taken a pro-Soviet and anti-Polish orientation; charges of anti-Russian prejudice and a lack of common sense among Poles became the norm and had been offered as explanations for Poland's unwillingness to cede territory to the Soviet Union. British and American publications attacked the Polish government as feckless troublemakers striving to destroy the alliance with the Soviet Union; widely read magazines and newspapers including *Life, Newsweek, The Spectator,* and *Stars and Stripes* published insulting criticisms of the Poles.

Regardless, Poland remained an ally, and Churchill needed the Second Polish Corps to reinforce British units that had suffered large losses in Africa. But the damage was done, and Poland's reputation was tarnished; even the heroic Polish efforts in the Battle of Britain were forgotten. Yet Raczkiewicz and Sikorski had no choice but to pursue the matter. Katyń was a question of justice and truth, and failure to seek the truth would

---

[8] When the Germans announced the discovery of the graves, they put up posters inviting people to volunteer for a committee to inspect them. *Akcja N* reproduced the poster, beginning with the German declaration but then continuing: "In this connection, the General Government has ordered that a parallel excursion be organized to the concentration camp in Auschwitz for a committee of all ethnic groups living in Poland. The excursion is to prove how humanitarian, in comparison to the methods employed by the Bolsheviks, are the devices used to carry out the mass extermination of the Polish people..." This poster was so convincingly done that some German officials pasted them up.

have been viewed by the nation as a betrayal. Poland's government may have committed a diplomatic error by requesting an International Red Cross investigation before seeking clarification from the Soviet Union, but it didn't matter. Preparations had been underway for some time to create a Soviet-sponsored Polish government and to create a pro-Soviet Polish army. Had it not been Katyń, another pretext would have been found to break relations.

At the time that Molotov attempted to deliver his note to Romer, the Soviet Union had already taken its first steps towards creating a Polish government more to its liking. In January 1943, Alfred Lampe and Wasilewska sent a letter to Molotov proposing creation of a Polish organization in the Soviet Union that would function as a counterweight to the London government. Their proposal was well received; the following month Stalin summoned Wasilewska, Hilary Minc, and Wiktor Grosz to a meeting. Declaring that it was only a matter of time before the Soviet Union severed relations with the Polish government, Stalin gave his approval for creation of *Związek Patriotów Polskich* (ZPP, Union of Polish Patriots);[9] its establishment was announced in its newly founded newspaper *Wolna Polska* (Free Poland)[10] on March 1, 1943. ZPP's first congress was held in Moscow on June 9 and 10. Wasilewska chaired the meeting; Berling was among those present. ZPP emphasized the need for alliance with the Soviet Union to ensure security of Poland's borders and renounced the border defined in the Treaty of Riga. Their declaration stopped short of calling for a new government, but the London government was criticized for operating under the "anti-democratic" April Constitution. Sikorski was singled out for condemnation, claiming that he was acting to the detriment of the Anglo–Soviet–American bloc.

News of ZPP's creation was cause for consternation in London and Washington. Stalin insisted it was an internal Soviet organization founded solely to represent Poles who were Soviet citizens and assured Churchill and Roosevelt that it was not the basis of a future government. There was a kernel of truth in this; ZPP's first mission was to support Poles in the Soviet Union by providing material assistance and education.[11] But Stalin

---

[9] According to Wasilewska, Stalin himself gave the organization its name; she claimed that Stalin wanted a name vague enough to appeal to all Poles regardless of their political leanings.
[10] Wasilewska was editor of *Wolna Polska*.
[11] ZPP had taken over these responsibilities from the London government.

and ZPP had greater ambitions; they were anxious to field a regular army. Now that the Second Polish Corps had departed Soviet territory, Berling resumed his work that had been interrupted by Sikorski–Maisky. Berling and ZPP formally proposed creation of an army in April 1943. One day after the Polish ambassador departed Moscow, Stalin granted permission for the formation of *1 Polska Dywizja Piechoty im. Tadeusza Kościuszki* (Polish 1st Tadeusz Kościuszko Infantry Division) under operational command of the Red Army and under ZPP's political control. Its creation was announced in *Wolna Polska* on May 8. Berling, recently promoted to general, was placed in charge.[12] Recruits were Poles unable to join the Second Polish Corps, such as gulag prisoners who did not learn of the amnesty in a timely manner, deportees, prewar Polish citizens, and ethnic Poles who were Soviet citizens.[13] As they reported for duty, Berling claimed to be shocked by their physical condition; they arrived clad in rags and were almost uniformly in poor health.[14]

When assembling his officer corps, Berling felt reverberations from Katyń. There was a dearth of officers, as most had departed with the Second Polish Corps. To compensate, vacancies were filled with Red Army officers who did not speak Polish and had no intention of learning. This created communications difficulties and caused resentment among the Poles. Soldiers were required to swear loyalty to the Soviet Union and brotherhood with the Red Army, but the political character of the division typically had little influence on recruits; most simply took advantage of an opportunity to leave the Soviet Union. ZPP's attempts at political indoctrination had little impact. Many soldiers skipped lectures to rest or repair their gear, and their political reliability was suspect. At one point, the NKVD warned Wasilewska that she might not be safe among rank-and-file soldiers. On the positive side, Berling's army was well supplied. Unlike the Second Polish Corps, Berling's army was provided sufficient rations and equipment. However, they were not allowed enough time to regain their health and strength or to properly train.

In August, the division was declared ready for combat and saw its first action on October 12, a mere four months after it was created. The Battle of Lenino was disastrous. Berling's soldiers, poorly trained and in ill health, ran out of ammunition and for a time were inadvertently shelled

---

[12] Appropriation of Kosciuszko's name for the army division, as well as for the radio station, was particularly galling to the Polish government and military. Kościuszko was famous for his role in the fight for a free Poland against Russian imperialism; now his name was being invoked by an imperialistic Soviet government.

[13] One of Berling's soldiers was Wojciech Jaruzelski, who would later rise to the rank of general.

[14] This should not have been a shock to Berling; he would have seen this same appalling and inhumane sight when he served under Anders.

by Soviet artillery. Casualties were staggering. Nearly three thousand soldiers, about thirty percent of the division, were killed, wounded, captured, or missing.[15] Regardless, the Soviet Union and ZPP considered Lenino to be a victory since they could claim that their military had seen combat before the Second Polish Corps and could paint Anders as being more interested in leaving the Soviet Union than in fighting the Germans. The division was taken out of action for further training and to rebuild its depleted ranks; it did not see combat again until the following summer.

Sikorski remained the personification of Poland in Western eyes. He met regularly with British and American officials and with leaders of other exiled governments. However, his political position within the Polish émigré community had weakened. Discovery of the Katyń graves greatly impacted the soldiers of the Second Polish Corps, particularly since most of the soldiers had known the victims. This made his planned inspection of the Second Polish Corps imperative. Before he departed, he visited General Kukiel and his wife. Kukiel described a Sikorski intent on repairing relationships with Raczkiewicz and within the exile community.

In late May, Sikorski departed and spent the next few weeks with the Second Polish Corps. He stopped in Gibraltar on his return to London. Shortly after 11 p.m. on July 4, 1943, his B-24 took off. Less than a minute later, it crashed into the sea. Sikorski and ten other passengers, including his daughter, were killed; only the pilot survived.

Sikorski's coffin lay in state in the Cathedral of St. Mary the Crowned in Gibraltar until ORP *Orkan* arrived to take it to the United Kingdom; upon arrival in Plymouth, it was taken by train to London. Sikorski lay in state at the Polish government's headquarters in Kensington Palace Gardens; Raczkiewicz decorated his coffin with the medal and ribbon of *Order Orła Białego* (Order of the White Eagle). His funeral was held at Westminster Cathedral. In attendance were Raczkiewicz, the Council of Ministers, Czechoslovak Prime Minister Jan Šrámek, and members of the British government including Churchill and Eden; Churchill himself delivered a eulogy. The next day, his coffin was taken to the Polish Military Cemetery in Newark-upon-Trent, where a special brick-lined grave had been prepared; his body was to be returned to Poland after the war. After the coffin was lowered into the grave, Raczkiewicz knelt and scattered a handful of

---

[15] After the battle, the ZPP arrogated to itself the right to award the *Virtuti Militari* and *Krzyż Walecznich* decorations to division soldiers.

Polish soil on it. Sikorski's posthumous image was that of a Polish patriot who had led the struggle for freedom, independence, and democracy for his country in difficult times. Many soldiers of the Second Polish Corps were particularly devoted to him.

The circumstances surrounding Sikorski's death were controversial. A British Court of Inquiry was convened and determined that the crash had occurred due to jammed controls but could not find a cause and ruled it an accident. Despite the ruling, doubts emerged. At the Gibraltar airport, Sikorski's plane had been left unguarded and was parked next to Soviet Ambassador Ivan Maisky's airplane; if someone wanted to, they could have easily accessed it without detection.[16] Although no proof exists of Soviet involvement, there is no doubt that Sikorski's death was quite convenient. After his death, it would be impossible for another Pole to obtain such prominence and visibility in the West, no matter how charismatic a leader they may have been. Thus, Sikorski's death made the Soviet Union's plan to install its own government much easier.

Sikorski's untimely demise left vacant the offices of prime minister and commander in chief. Raczkiewicz was determined that there would be no repeat of Sikorski's consolidation of power. He appointed Sosnkowski commander in chief; however, outside influences asserted themselves in the selection of a prime minister. Churchill lobbied for a prime minister who would follow Sikorski's political line; he also made the ominous remark that the British Army did not have any divisions available to defend Poland's border. Raczkiewicz, understanding the message, offered the position to Mikołajczyk; he accepted under the condition that *Umowa Paryska* remain in force.

Mikołajczyk objected to Sosnkowski's appointment and made attempts to weaken or abolish the position of commander in chief. He would not permit Sosnkowski to serve in his Council of Ministers, and he attempted to reduce Sosnkowski's authority over AK by transferring some responsibilities to Minister of National Defense Kukiel.[17] Relations between Mikołajczyk and Sosnkowski were hostile. Aside from Mikołajczyk's desire to have control over the military, they held incompatible views on Poland's policy towards the Soviet Union. For his part, Sosnkowski requested

---

[16] In 1963, another suspicious circumstance came to light. Kim Philby had been in charge of British intelligence operations in Spain and Portugal for much of the war and was in Gibraltar at the time of Sikorski's death. Philby had been a Soviet agent since the 1930s, and in 1963 he defected to Moscow when he was about to be unmasked. After his defection, his presence in Gibraltar in 1943 raised the question of his potential involvement in the crash.

[17] Mikołajczyk had long wanted control of AK. When he was in Sikorski's government, he demanded subordination of AK to him in his capacity as minister of the interior. Sikorski refused.

appointment of a deputy prime minister who would be his contact, allowing him to avoid Mikołajczyk as much as possible. Mikołajczyk's appointment also caused concern in the military. Telegrams from AK commander General Bór-Komorowski and *Delegat* Jan Jankowski expressed concern among the Polish population, while Anders starkly declared that the Second Polish Corps did not trust Mikołajczyk's government. Raczkiewicz was once again saddled with a prime minister not of his choosing, who showed him little respect. Mikołajczyk's regard for Raczkiewicz is illustrated by an incident in June 1944. On his return from a meeting with Roosevelt in Washington, Mikołajczyk landed in Scotland. As it happened, Raczkiewicz was nearby, inspecting Polish troops. Mikołajczyk proceeded on to London without meeting with the president.

The increasing flow of Soviet agents and Soviet-trained Polish communists into Polish territory was causing alarm, particularly as they seemed more interested in undermining *Delegatura* and AK than in fighting the Germans. Moscow's termination of diplomatic relations with the Republic of Poland left no official channels of communication between the two nations, and the Poles had to consider the prospect that the Red Army could again occupy Poland.

After a series of messages between London and Warsaw, Sosnkowski and Bór-Komorowski created a new organization, NIE, an abbreviation of *niepodległość* (independence). Its commander was General Leopold Okulicki; he was assisted by General Emil Fieldorf. Its mission was to engage in anti-communist activities in the event of a protracted Soviet occupation; its initial activities were intelligence gathering, disseminating anti-communist propaganda, and engaging in defensive actions. NIE did not engage in sabotage or guerrilla attacks against communist forces. It was a highly secretive organization; Sosnkowski kept it so confidential that even Raczkiewicz did not know that it existed.[18] Its first members were high-ranking AK members, and they were required to sever contacts with AK.

PKP had transformed itself into *Krajowa Reprezentacja Polityczna* (KRP, National Political Representation) in August; its intent was to strengthen cooperation among underground organizations and between political parties. Concerned by the failure of *Delegatura* and PPR to reach an agreement, KRP formed *Społeczny Komitet Antykomunistyczny* (Public Anticommunist Committee) in October; its purpose was to neutralize

---

[18] Raczkiewicz and the government learned of NIE's existence only after Sosnkowski resigned.

PPR's presence. Around the same time, *Delegatura* and AK created *Akcja Antyk* (an abbreviation of the phrase *Akcja Antykomunistyczna,* or Anti-Communist Action) to counter communist propaganda and reveal PPR's intentions. *Antyk* printed newspapers, pamphlets, and leaflets critical of the Soviet Union and PPR, illustrating parallels between Nazi and Soviet actions.[19]

Early in 1943, the tide had turned in the Soviet Union, and the German Army was on the defensive. The Red Army began to push westward. The British and American armies had finally defeated Germany in North Africa and landed in southern Italy in early September. By October, the Red Army had taken Smolensk, and the Soviet Union seized the opportunity to present the Katyń massacre as a German crime. NKVD officers flooded the area, destroyed cemetery markers, removed evidence, and exhumed bodies to plant forged documents supporting the Soviet timeline. Witnesses were threatened with arrest for collaboration with the Germans if their testimony did not match the official version of events. On January 11, 1944, the NKVD issued a preliminary report placing blame on the Germans. It was signed by Vsevolod Merkulov, who had supervised the murders.[20] Shortly after, the Extraordinary State Commission for Ascertaining and Investigating Crimes Perpetrated by the German-Fascist Invaders and their Accomplices was formed; headed by Nikolai Burdenko, president of the USSR Academy of Medical Sciences, it was commonly known as the Burdenko Commission. Its final report blamed the Germans for committing the murders, manipulating evidence, intimidating witnesses, and murdering Russians who had been forced to dig graves. Western journalists were brought to Katyń to view the graves, examine evidence, and listen to witness testimony, but they left unpersuaded by the Soviet version of events.[21]

America's official position was that Germany was responsible, despite two official intelligence reports that pointed to Soviet guilt. But Roosevelt appeared to have doubts. In 1944, he assigned Captain George Earle, his special emissary to the Balkans and a family friend, to gather information

---

[19] *Antyk* activities included graffiti campaigns. Messages such as "*PPR – zdrajcy*" (traitors) and "*PPR – płatne pachołki Rosji*" (paid servants of Russia) appeared on walls and fences.

[20] In the March 5, 1940, memo to Stalin from Beria in which execution of the Polish officers was proposed, Merkulov was named as one of the three people assigned to examine cases and carry out decisions.

[21] Burdenko himself may have shared their doubts. Shortly before his death in 1946, he allegedly told a family friend that, based on his medical knowledge, he knew that the murders had occurred in 1940.

on the massacre. Based on information from contacts in Romania and Bulgaria, Earle concluded that it was the work of the Soviet Union. Roosevelt rejected and suppressed Earle's report, stating that he was convinced the massacre was the work of the Germans; he also issued a written order rejecting Earle's request to publish the report. Earle was then assigned to Western Samoa and remained there until the war ended.

Britain and America continued to publicly accept the Soviet version of events. Neither wanted their ally's unsavory acts to become public knowledge.

As the German threat to the Middle East faded, there was no longer a need for the Second Polish Corps to protect its oil fields. While in Iran, the Polish Army finally received the rations, supplies, and armaments it needed and was now ready for deployment.[22] Britain's command in the Mediterranean desperately needed reinforcements, so the Poles were moved across Syria into Palestine. On reaching Tel Aviv, several thousand Jewish officers and soldiers chose to remain there. Technically, this was desertion, but Minister of Defense Kukiel declared that any such deserters should not be pursued and would be permitted to retain Polish citizenship. Nearly 3,000 of the 4,500 Jewish soldiers in the Second Polish Corps remained in Palestine.[23]

In November 1943, the Second Polish Corps moved to Egypt and was issued new weapons and equipment. Its soldiers assembled at the port of Alexandria and boarded transport ships. On December 16, the first units of the Corps set sail, accompanied by the destroyer ORP *Ślązak*. On the twenty-first, they disembarked at Taranto, Italy. Over the next three months, more than fifty thousand members of the Second Polish Corps made the same journey.

As the Second Polish Corps was preparing to land in Italy, Moscow and PPR stepped up their campaign to tarnish the government-in-exile and to justify the Soviet seizure of eastern Poland. A communist publication in Warsaw likened the London government to Germany's, and Maxim Litvinov, the Soviet ambassador in Washington, asserted that Poles would need to live within their ethnic borders. This was consistent with Maisky's stance during his 1941 negotiations with Sikorski and signaled that the

---

[22] Soviet propaganda later cited the Polish Army's departure from the USSR as proof of cowardice since they would not go to the front.
[23] A notable member of the Second Polish Corps who remained in Palestine was Menachem Begin (original name Mieczysław Biegun), the sixth prime minister of Israel; General Tokarszewski granted him a leave of absence.

Soviet Union had no intention of revisiting its annexation of Poland's eastern territories.[24]

In late 1943, ZPP created *Polski Komitet Narodowy* (PKN, Polish National Committee), directly contradicting Stalin's assurances that ZPP was not the nucleus of a future government. Its architect was Alfred Lampe, a former KPP member who was in prison in 1939. Lampe's fundamental belief was that for communists to attain power in Poland, they had to simultaneously destroy competing political structures and gain the acceptance of Polish society; he felt that a coalition government of communists and non-communists would not work. PKN was to be composed of ten Poles from the Soviet Union, two from the United States, two from London, one from what was vaguely referred to as the near east, and five from within Poland itself. Jakub Berman served as secretary of its organizational commission.[25] But ZPP knew little about events in Poland. In November, the Gestapo disrupted communications between PPR and Moscow by arresting Małgorzata Fornalska, the PPR Central Committee member who had been responsible for maintaining radio contact with the Soviet Union. The following month, the Gestapo arrested PPR First Secretary Paweł Finder. Władysław Gomułka was elected to replace Finder, and under his leadership PPR declared its political program in a document titled, "*O co walczymy?*" ("What Are We Fighting For?"). PPR demanded territorial concessions from Germany in the north and west, claimed that the Polish government had no right to take power in postwar Poland, and called for a planned economy, nationalization of industry and banks, and land redistribution without compensation to previous owners. Gomułka's election and PPR's declaration occurred without ZPP's knowledge or authorization.

It was also evident that PPR had equally little knowledge about ZPP's activities. Gomułka and the PPR leadership, unaware that PKN had been created, established *Krajowa Rada Narodowa* (KRN, State National Council) on December 31, 1943. KRN declared itself to be the actual political representation of the Polish nation and empowered itself to act on behalf of the nation until the German occupation was over. It viewed the Polish

---

[24] Some months later in Parliament, Captain Alan Graham posited that Stalin's border demands were rooted in a fear that a large Byelorussian and Ukrainian population outside Soviet borders would provide what he called "centripetal nuclei for an independent White Ruthenian or Ukrainian state independent of Russia." See Hansard HC Deb. "War and International Situation," vol. 397 col. 733–734, February 22, 1944.

[25] Berman was chosen for this position by Stalin.

government as illegitimate and claimed that the April Constitution was invalid and had never been accepted by the Polish people. On January 1, 1944, KRN renamed and restructured GL, now calling it *Armia Ludowa* (AL, People's Army). GL Commander Michał Rola-Żymierski took the same role in AL but extended his duties by claiming command of all Polish forces, whether in Poland or in the West.

Gomułka's moves were received poorly in London, Moscow, and Poland itself. He had attempted to convince leftist parties such as PPS and SL to join KRN, but none agreed; only a handful of PPS members joined independently of their party. In London, the Polish government condemned KRN as an illegal body. But the most severe reaction came from the Soviet Union. Comintern General Secretary Georgi Dimitrov learned of the arrest of Finder on January 17; shortly thereafter, news reached him of Gomułka's election and of KRN's creation. Dimitrov and the ZPP leaders became concerned that Gomułka was acting independently and were suspicious of his motives; they also viewed KRN's program to be inconsistent with Comintern's plans. To regain control of the situation, the Communist Party of the Soviet Union created *Centralne Biuro Komunistów Polski* (CBKP, Central Bureau of Polish Communists) in January. CBKP declared that it had oversight and control over PPR, although they didn't trouble themselves to inform PPR that it had a new overseer. Among CBKP's leadership were Aleksander Zawadzki, Jakub Berman, Wanda Wasilewska, and Hilary Minc, all ZPP leaders. For the first few months of its existence, CBKP functioned as a secret organization and asserted its preeminence over PPR and AL by starving them of funds and weapons and undermining their authority. In January, Gomułka sent a message to Moscow pleading for funds; in March, he sent a message begging for weapons for AL. His requests went unanswered.

Gomułka realized that he had to justify his actions. In January he wrote a letter explaining his rationale, stating that PPR took the initiative to create KRN since domestic matters should be resolved by people in the country, while ZPP's role should be to handle Polish issues in the international sphere; he proposed that the two organizations would complement one another. He took pains to write this letter in a manner that would convince both ZPP, to whom the letter was addressed, and the Soviet authorities, whom he knew would also read it. He felt compelled to send a delegation to Moscow to meet with ZPP and Soviet authorities. On March 15, Marian Spychalski, Edward Osóbka-Morawski, Kazimierz Sidor, and Jan Haneman left for Moscow, but they were intercepted by Soviet partisans and detained for several weeks.

At first, these actions mattered little. Gomułka was viewed with suspicion by ZPP and the Soviet Union, and PPR, KRN, and AL continued to receive scant material support. Soviet attitudes towards KRN are illustrated by a comment made on April 24 by Molotov to Oskar Lange, a native of Poland who had been teaching economics at the University of Chicago since 1938 and was a naturalized American citizen. Lange was visiting the Soviet Union at the request of Stalin, who considered him a potential member of a new Polish government. When their conversation turned to KRN, Molotov commented that it had been formed without consulting the Soviet Union or ZPP.

While the KRN delegation was languishing at the partisan base, CBKP created a new military formation, *Polski Sztab Partyzancki* (PSzP, Polish Partisan Staff). PSzP was organized in the town of Szpanów, near Równe in the Wołyń district, in April and became operational in May. Nominally, its commander was CBKP head Aleksander Zawadzki, but in actuality it was Siarhei Prytytski, a Red Army colonel from Byelorussia. When PSzP units were sent into Poland, they were under CBKP's command and maintained radio contact with Moscow. PSzP units were ordered to act independently of KRN, PPR, and AL and not recognize their command; they also made efforts to subordinate non-PSzP partisan units to their command.

On May 17, the KRN delegation was finally brought to Moscow and was quite probably stunned to receive a warm reception from Stalin himself after two months of detention. They learned that Stalin had come to favor Gomułka's creation and decided to make use of it. One week later, ZPP recognized KRN as the highest political body of the Polish nation, but the very existence of CBKP remained unknown by KRN; it wasn't until July that Gomułka learned of it.

Although KRN had been legitimized, PPR leaders held differing views on how to implement communism in Poland. Bierut advocated imposition of communism using the force of the Red Army and NKVD, installation of a new government, and brutal elimination of opposition. Gomułka favored cultivation of popular support; he feared that imposition of a new government by force would be politically harmful and would make it difficult to gain acceptance. Gomułka also preferred a more measured approach towards the opposition, gradually isolating and eliminating them. In June, Bierut sent a letter to Dimitrov accusing Gomułka and two of his supporters of a series of transgressions and requesting dispatch of an emissary to bring order to PPR.

Over the course of the war, Poland's image in the West underwent an astounding transformation. In September 1939, Poland elicited widespread sympathy as victim of German and Soviet aggression and terror. The following summer it was celebrated by the United Kingdom as its most important ally. By December 1941, it had been relegated to the position of a minor partner, and after the Katyń graves were discovered, Poland was considered a troublesome ally. Poland's hopes rested in the Atlantic Charter, but its signatories so valued their alliance with the Soviet Union that they gave Stalin a free hand.

In late 1943, Churchill, Roosevelt, and Stalin met in Teheran to coordinate military strategy and discuss the landscape of postwar Europe.[26] They made initial plans to divide Germany in order to weaken it; they also agreed on a general outline for Poland's borders. Stalin demanded revising Poland's eastern border to follow the Curzon Line, which happened to coincide almost exactly with the Soviet Union's western border as defined in the Molotov–Ribbentrop Pact. Churchill and Roosevelt agreed and compensated for the territorial loss by relocating Poland's western border to a line defined by the Oder and Neisse rivers (known as the Oder–Neisse Line) and ceding most of Germany's Prussian territory to Poland. Roosevelt requested that the border agreement remain confidential as he was running for re-election in less than a year and needed Polish-American votes.

On his return to London, Churchill met with Mikołajczyk to belatedly seek his agreement. Mikołajczyk's satisfaction in hearing that Britain desired a strong, independent, and free Poland quickly turned to alarm when Churchill added that Britain supported a Poland situated between the Odra and the Curzon Line. Mikołajczyk objected, and Churchill retorted that Britain had gone to war to defend Poland's independence from Germany, but borders were not part of the guarantee. He pressed Mikołajczyk to agree in principle to these borders, intimated that doing so would open the path for resumption of Polish–Soviet relations and Red Army–AK coordination, and pressed for a decision before the Red Army advance rendered their discussion moot. Mikołajczyk countered that Stalin was using Poland as a test case for how Soviet power would be imposed elsewhere, but Churchill refused to discuss the matter further. Mikołajczyk advised the government and *Delegatura* of these demands, and they refused to accept them. He gave Churchill Poland's official response on February 15, rejecting the "dictatorial demand" of the Soviet Union.

Churchill began to campaign for the Curzon Line in Parliament. He stated that the United Kingdom had never guaranteed Poland's borders

---

[26] Teheran was the English-language spelling of Tehran at the time of the conference.

and that he did not agree with the prewar border, calling Stalin's demand reasonable and just. In the ensuing debate, a few MPs defended Poland's government. John McGovern, a member of the Independent Labour Party from Glasgow, reminded Parliament of the full extent of the Soviet role in the war: "As Hitler is receding, the partner with whom Hitler entered into his aggressive crimes in 1939, is taking the place of Adolf, and as Germany is disgorging territory, it is being swallowed up by Russia. [...] When does aggression cease to be aggression? Is it aggression only when perpetrated by Hitler and the Nazi party, or does it cease to be aggression when it is perpetrated by Stalin and the Bolshevik party?"[27]

Moscow had invested considerable time, money, and effort into creating a government for Poland, but installing it was a delicate matter. Despite its diminished importance to the Allied cause and its vilification in the Western media after the Katyń revelation, Poland continued to elicit sympathy. It was not forgotten that the war began with Germany's invasion of Poland, and the suffering of its citizens was well known. Moscow could not simply impose a new government as it would elicit comparisons of Hitler's tactics in German-occupied nations and damage the Soviet Union's carefully constructed self-portrayal as a victim of German aggression; worse, it could revive memories of the Molotov–Ribbentrop Pact, the Soviet role in Poland's dismemberment, and Soviet actions in Estonia, Latvia, Lithuania, Finland, and Romania.

However, Stalin had a plan. Nobody would object to replacing the governments of Germany's allies; therefore, Soviet propaganda would recast Poland as a German ally. Constant repetition of this message would cause Westerners to accept this new portrayal of Poland.[28] At the same time, AK, BCh, NSZ, and *Delegatura* had to be disrupted or destroyed, and PPR, GL, and the NKVD had no qualms about using the Germans to achieve this goal. Communist agents constantly attempted to infiltrate underground structures loyal to the government; those who succeeded collected intelligence and information. They sent anonymous letters to the Gestapo with lists of names and at times would claim they were communist collaborators. One of those named had been taken to the Katyń graves by

---

[27] Hansard HC Deb. "War and International Situation," vol. 397, col. 736, February 22, 1944.
[28] This is called the "big lie." Adolf Hitler described it as a lie so enormous that nobody would believe that someone "could have the impudence to distort the truth so infamously." Its propagators repeat it incessantly until incredulity is worn down. The Soviet Union frequently used this tactic to discredit its enemies and to justify its actions.

the Germans to serve as a witness. On occasion, AL conducted joint operations with the Germans; one such incident involved a raid on a Warsaw apartment jointly conducted by AL and the Gestapo to seize a cache of *Delegatura* files. Their raid provided the Gestapo with information it needed to identify and arrest AK soldiers and gave AL information on agents who had penetrated communist structures. The communists then proceeded to pursue those agents, who responded by defending themselves. To the British, Stalin depicted this as Poles murdering Soviet personnel, and he went on to declare that the Poles were collaborating with the Germans.

It was inevitable that the Red Army, with Berling's renamed *Ludowe Wojsko Polskie* (LWP, Polish People's Army) in tow, would be first into Poland.[29] Sosnkowski and his AK commanders had developed a plan for this scenario: *Akcja Burza* (Operation Tempest). As the Germans prepared their defenses against the advancing Red Army, AK would attack and seize control of occupied areas, *Delegatura* representatives would restore Polish authority, and AK and government members would greet the Red Army to the newly liberated area. If conditions rendered this approach infeasible, AK commanders were to reveal themselves to the Red Army and conduct joint operations to liberate the area.

There were a few cases where *Burza* went according to plan, but in most engagements the Red Army accepted AK's help and then arrested its officers and soldiers after the operation was complete. If they were fortunate, officers would be imprisoned and enlisted men would be forcibly conscripted into LWP; in many cases, they were executed. As word spread, many units abandoned the *Burza* strategy and defended themselves against Soviet forces. Soviet protests ensued. Britain received complaints from Moscow and was informed that AK and *Delegatura* members were being arrested to ensure security in the rear of the Red Army. The British government passed this information on to the Polish government; it replied that AK wouldn't be compelled to defend itself if the Soviets would stop arresting its people.

Like its predecessors, KRP had been a political advisory group similar to *Rada Narodowa*. In January 1944, *Delegatura* took action to create *Rada Jedności Narodowej* (RJN, Council of National Unity), an underground *Sejm*. It was initially composed of parties in KRP; throughout the year RJN added representatives from other parties.

---

[29] Ludowe Wojsko Polskie (LWP, Polish People's Army) was the common name for the Polish Armed Forces in the East.

In March, RJN issued a declaration titled, "*O co walczy Naród Polski?*" ("What is the Polish Nation Fighting For?"). It detailed RJN's postwar vision, calling for disarming Germany, bringing war criminals to justice, forcing Germany to pay reparations, restoring the prewar Polish–Soviet border, and redrawing the Polish–German border; Poland would also have a role in the postwar occupation of Germany. Poland would be a parliamentary democracy with minority rights guaranteed, and the April Constitution would be amended to "formulate the principles of universal civil freedom, freedom of religion, conscience, political opinion, speech, print, assembly and association, and the principles of equality of civil rights with equal responsibilities and the independence of the judiciary." Foreign policy would be based on alliances with the United Kingdom, France, the United States, and Turkey; normal relations with the Soviet Union would be conditioned on Moscow's recognizing the prewar border and refraining from interfering in Poland's internal affairs. A planned economy and land reform were proposed, as was an international organization for keeping peace among nations.

"*O co walczy Naród Polski?*" presented a very different vision than did PPR in its statement "*O co walczymy?*" Although both agreed on the need for land reform, a planned economy, and revised borders with Germany, PPR proposed nationalization of banks, transportation, and large industry. PPR's foreign policy was based on alliance with the Soviet Union, and it refused to allow the London government any role in postwar Poland.

Anders and the Second Polish Corps moved north with the British Army; their task was to break the German line obstructing the way to Rome. German defenses were centered on the ancient Benedictine abbey of Monte Cassino, situated on a hill towering over the town of Cassino. From there, the Germans had a commanding view of the town and surrounding area. In January, February, and March, the allies launched three assaults on the hill; each failed, and the abbey itself was reduced to ruins in the February attack.

The fourth attack began on May 12. A combined force of American, British, Polish, French, South African, and New Zealander soldiers began after midnight. For five days, the battle raged as positions were taken, lost, and retaken. On the seventeenth, Anders led the Second Polish Corps on a fresh assault. After a day of brutal fighting, the Corps forced the Germans from the hill. In the morning, a bugler played the *Hejnał mariacki* beneath the Polish flag that had been raised above the ruins.³⁰ From Cassino, the Corps moved north alongside the British and American armies and liberated Ancona.

In the West, a massive Allied force landed at Normandy on June 6; Polish RAF squadrons and Poland's navy provided support for the landings. In July, the First Polish Armored Division, commanded by General Stanisław Maczek, landed in France and joined an operation to encircle the Germans at Falaise; Maczek was given the job of blocking the escape route. For two days, the Germans directed furious attacks at the division, but the Poles held firm. About fifty thousand Germans were captured as a result of Polish efforts; thousands more were killed, and hundreds of their tanks and armored vehicles were destroyed or abandoned.

Poland presented a difficult problem for Roosevelt. He hadn't troubled himself to become familiar with its history and cared little for its fate, but he was acutely aware of America's substantial Polish minority. His popularity was falling, and he needed the Polish-American vote to win re-election, but admitting that he had made an agreement on Poland without its government's consent or knowledge could send him to electoral defeat. He chose to handle the problem through prevarication.

In June 1944, Mikołajczyk met with Roosevelt in the White House. When asked what had been decided about Poland's borders at Teheran, Roosevelt replied that he was opposed to the Curzon Line and expected to mediate the issue, but Stalin didn't want to discuss it. Later, Roosevelt said he was sure he could broker an agreement that included Silesia, East Prussia, Königsberg, Lwów, Tarnopol, and Drohobycz within Poland's borders, but he doubted Poland would retain Wilno. Roosevelt ended by asking Mikołajczyk to visit Stalin to discuss Polish issues; Mikołajczyk agreed immediately. Roosevelt then alerted Stalin, and Stalin refused the meeting.

Before his trip to Washington, Mikołajczyk met twice with Viktor Lebedev, the Soviet Union's ambassador to governments-in-exile of Allied countries.³¹ When Mikołajczyk returned to London, they met again, and Lebedev advised him that he had been ordered to discuss Poland's future with him. Mikołajczyk offered the full cooperation of the underground government and military with the Red Army and stated that his government's

---

³⁰ *Hejnał mariacki* is a trumpet call played every hour from the north tower of Kraków's *Bazylika Mariacki* (St. Mary's Basilica), the large church in the northeast corner of the city's main square.
³¹ From January 1945 to March 1951, Lebedev was the Soviet Union's ambassador to Poland.

position was to put off discussions of the border until the postwar peace conference. Lebedev stated that he was certain that any difficulties could now be resolved. Three days later, Lebedev returned with his government's proposals. The Soviet Union requested the dismissal of Raczkiewicz, Sosnkowski, Minister of Defense Kukiel, and Minister of Information Kot and their replacement by Poles from Britain and the United States; Lebedev then demanded that the newly formed government denounce the government that had brought Katyń to the attention of the International Red Cross. Mikołajczyk could not believe what he was hearing and asked if Lebedev expected him to denounce the government that he had served in. Lebedev nodded; an astonished Mikołajczyk ended the meeting.

In a coordinated action, AK and the Red Army liberated Chełm on July 21. The next day, *Polski Komitet Wyzwolenia Narodowego* (PKWN, Polish Committee of National Liberation) proclaimed itself the governing body in Poland. Four days later, PKWN established itself in its temporary seat of Lublin. It became commonly known as the Lublin Committee. PKWN claimed to be a broad coalition of leftist parties, and a cursory examination would confirm this, as some members indicated that they were members of PPS, SL, and SD. However, neither the SL nor the SD in PKWN were connected to the prewar SL or SD that had been part of the Polish government since its reconstitution in France and had been operating underground in Poland; both were created by PPR in 1944. PPS representatives could actually trace themselves to the legitimate PPS, although they were part of a splinter group that had separated itself from PPS in 1943 and did not recognize Raczkiewicz and his government.

Edward Osóbka-Morawski chaired PKWN. His deputies were Andrzej Witos from the PPR-sponsored SL and Wanda Wasilewska. Its manifesto declared that the only legal power in Poland was KRN and denounced the London government and *Delegatura* as illegal, labeling them "self-proclaimed." It deemed the April Constitution to be unlawful and fascist and declared that it would operate under the March Constitution until a new one could be written. PKWN also ceded Poland's eastern territories to the Soviet Union. Names of PKWN members were listed on the manifesto, with one exception: Soviet Ambassador General Nikolai Bugnanin, whose powers extended far beyond those of an ambassador and included control over the Soviet-subordinated Polish Army. Stalin approved PKWN's manifesto, and it was announced on Radio Kościuszko. Soon, posters of the manifesto were plastered on walls throughout areas under Red Army control.

By the middle of 1944, Sosnkowski had fallen into deep disfavor. Although he had been Raczkiewicz's successor since October 1939 and had survived the 1942 attempt to have his nomination revoked, by 1944 he had amassed several powerful foes. Mikołajczyk's antipathy towards him was well known. Kot was another adversary. Displeased with Sosnkowski's appointment as commander in chief, Kot suppressed the announcement and began a campaign against him in émigré and British papers. PAT and TASS correspondent Stefan Litauer also maligned him. Soviet criticisms first appeared in 1943; by January 1944, Stalin was demanding his removal.[32] In July, Churchill finally gave in to Stalin's incessant pressure and promised he would persuade Raczkiewicz to do so.

First came his removal from presidential succession. RJN took the position that the next president should be someone who had spent the war in occupied Poland, and *Rada Narodowa* agreed, passing a resolution calling on Raczkiewicz to change his succession to avoid an excessive concentration of power in one person. Mikołajczyk agreed, and Raczkiewicz gave in. RJN submitted a list of three candidates from which Raczkiewicz chose Tomasz Arciszewski. A PPS member since 1896, Arciszewski was a veteran of the Polish Legions in the Great War, served in the *Sejm* in the 1920s and 1930s, fought in the defense of Warsaw, and was an RJN member. Now he was next in line for the presidency and had to get to London.

Late in the evening of July 25, Arciszewski stood at the edge of a dark field a few kilometers from Tarnów.[33] Surrounding the field were AK soldiers, some of whom scanned the sky and strained to hear aircraft; the others nervously watched the perimeter for any indication that their operation had been compromised. After several tense minutes, the AK commander gave a signal, and a detachment of soldiers lit torches and formed two lines to mark a landing strip. A British C-47 transport plane emerged from the night sky and landed in knee-deep grass. As it rolled to a stop, the field buzzed with activity. Soldiers doused their torches, four

---

[32] In January 1944, Stalin had demanded dismissal of Sosnkowski as well as Kot and Kukiel; he went on to demand that Oskar Lange and two other Polish-American communist sympathizers take their places.

[33] This field, known as *Motyl*, was along the Kisielina River near the village of Wał-Ruda, about 18 km. from Tarnów. *Motyl* had been used previously by the AK for a similar operation.

soldiers exited,[34] about one thousand pounds of cargo was unloaded, and Arciszewski and four others boarded.[35] The plane should have been on the ground for only about ten minutes, but its landing gear was bogged down in the damp field; it finally took off on the fourth attempt. As the plane flew out of sight, the soldiers melted into the fields, woods, and villages. A few hours later, the C-47 landed at an airfield near Brindisi, Italy; from there, Arciszewski proceeded to London by way of Cairo. His wife, Melania, remained in Warsaw.

Raczkiewicz agreed not to announce Arciszewski's nomination until he was safely in London. Now that he had arrived, Raczkiewicz needed to clear the path. He expected Sosnkowski to voluntarily resign but he refused, although he indicated that he would abide by Raczkiewicz's decision in the matter, forcing his dismissal. On August 7, Raczkiewicz issued a letter to Sosnkowski withdrawing his nomination and officially named Arciszewski as his successor. Although no longer in line for the presidency, Sosnkowski remained commander in chief.

---

[34] *Cichociemni* (Silent and Unseen) were special operations soldiers trained for covert actions. Their name indicated their ability to "appear silently where they are least expected, play havoc with the enemy and disappear whence they came, unnoticed, unseen."

[35] Also on the plane were German V-2 rocket components captured by the Polish underground.

Abandonment

Stanisław Mikołajczyk,
Prime Minister of the Republic of Poland 1943-1944

AS THE RED ARMY approached Warsaw in July 1944, Poland's underground leaders contemplated their options. Launching an uprising was risky, although AK considered that the German Army would be weakened and demoralized by its recent string of defeats. A successful uprising would mean that the Red Army would be greeted into free Warsaw by the Polish government and AK; defeat would demonstrate that AK had fought to the end in the Allied cause. In either case, Soviet efforts to install a new government would be seen as the act of a conqueror, not an ally. Standing idly by while the Soviet military expelled the Germans would clear the path for the Soviet Union to install its own government, risk civilian acceptance of such a government, and fuel Moscow propaganda claiming that *Delegatura* and AK were either neutral or allied with Germany. RJN unanimously approved an uprising.

On July 29, posters appeared in Warsaw claiming that Bór-Komorowski and *Delegat* Jan Jankowski had fled the city. They were signed by Colonel Julian Skokowski, commander of a small PPR-aligned military group. He called on the population to follow his leadership.[1] Also that day, Radio Kościuszko broadcast an exhortation to the people of Warsaw to rise up against the Germans. A day later, it broadcast another message calling for

---

[1] Skokowski was a member of *Polska Armia Ludowa*.

an uprising and for the people of Warsaw to assist the Red Army in crossing the Wisła.

On August 1, 1944, Bór-Komorowski issued a message to engage the Germans in open combat. At five in the afternoon, Poland's underground military emerged. Units of AK, NSZ, and AL[2] joined forces to attack German positions. Within a few days, they took control of the Old Town, the city center, and parts of other districts. After these initial gains, German reinforcements poured in with orders to crush the uprising and destroy the city. The poorly armed and outnumbered Poles were no match. The Germans systematically retook the city, killing soldiers and civilians alike, but fierce resistance slowed their progress.[3] Eventually, the Poles were unable to continue the fight, and the uprising ended on October 2. Both the United Kingdom and the United States declared Polish soldiers to be combatants and therefore subject to treatment according to the Geneva Convention, forcing the German military commander to treat them as prisoners of war.

Warsaw was evacuated. Some soldiers were sent to prisoner-of-war camps; many soldiers and civilians were sent to Germany as forced labor, some were released in other parts of occupied Poland, and about sixty thousand were sent to Auschwitz and other concentration camps. Bór-Komorowski was held in a German prisoner-of-war camp until the end of the war.[4] German units were sent into now-deserted Warsaw with flamethrowers and explosives to destroy everything they could, particularly monuments, libraries, and archives. They completed their pillage in December, leaving eighty-five percent of the city in ruins.

Throughout the uprising, the Red Army sat across the river in the Praga district and did nothing. Its official explanation was that it had faced setbacks on the way to Warsaw and could not engage the Germans. However, the Red Army's lethargic advance into Praga stood in stark contrast to its rapid moves to capture other objectives. It was later revealed that Stalin had given orders to cut off Warsaw from outside assistance; the Red

---

[2] This was one of the few times AL cooperated with AK and perhaps the only time it cooperated with NSZ.

[3] As the Germans advanced in the Wola and Ochota districts, they shot all inhabitants and burned their bodies. The most brutal perpetrators were members of SS Sturmbrigade RONA (Russian National Liberation Army), consisting of Soviet citizens who had joined the Germans. On the other end of the spectrum, units of the Royal Hungarian Army stationed around Warsaw as part of the German occupation force refused to participate in attacks; some passed information, food, equipment, and supplies to the Poles, assisted civilians fleeing from the fighting, protected wounded soldiers from the Germans, blocked German units pursuing Poles, and jammed German radio frequencies.

[4] After his release, Bór-Komorowski went to London. Raczkiewicz appointed him commander in chief, replacing Anders.

Army received a direct order from the Kremlin to halt its advance on Warsaw on August 1, and tank units stopped receiving fuel shortly after. An order issued on August 23 directed the Red Army to prevent Polish units in Soviet-controlled areas from reaching Warsaw.

Only one attempt at assistance was made from Praga. After watching helplessly for weeks, in mid-September Berling ordered several units of the First Polish Army to cross the Wisła and link up with Warsaw's defenders; unfortunately, they were beaten back by the Germans. A few days later, Berling was abruptly relieved of his command and replaced with a Soviet-born general.

In the early days of the uprising, the Soviet Union and ZPP claimed it wasn't happening. Wasilewska flatly denied that there was an uprising, and Bierut falsely declared that he was in Warsaw on August 4 and that there was no fighting. In Moscow, Mikołajczyk met with Molotov and Stalin and handed them a message from Colonel Kalugin of the Red Army. Kalugin was in contact with AK, and his message was sent by AK to London for re-transmission to Moscow. Stalin responded by stating that he didn't know Kalugin. As Mikołajczyk was leaving, Osóbka-Morawski met him and claimed that Bór-Komorowski was not in Warsaw or anywhere near the fight. In the United Kingdom, *Daily Worker*, a Soviet-friendly newspaper that had previously published denials that there was any fighting in Warsaw, printed a bulletin from TASS calling the London government's claims that the Soviet Union was not assisting libelous. Other left-leaning British papers joined *Daily Worker* in parroting the Soviet line.

Yet PKWN was anxious to present a positive image of its sponsors. At a Moscow press conference, Osóbka-Morawski claimed that the Red Army was providing equipment to the Warsaw fighters. He claimed AK commanders were deliberately avoiding contact with the Red Army, called Bór-Komorowski a war criminal, and promised to prosecute him. Churchill wanted to send airlifts of supplies to Warsaw and repeatedly petitioned Stalin to allow British aircraft to land in Soviet-controlled territory to refuel, but he was bluntly told that any flight crews landing in Soviet-controlled territory would be taken prisoner. British, Polish, and South African flight crews later made several round-trip flights from Italy to provide supplies, but these were insufficient to change the course of the battle. After the Warsaw Uprising ended, Soviet radio labeled the people of Warsaw traitors for surrendering. The Red Army entered the ruins of Warsaw unopposed on January 17. Thousands of potential opponents of the Soviet-sponsored government were dead or in German captivity.

One month into the uprising, Sosnkowski's frustrations were mounting. His soldiers were fighting an uneven struggle against a larger, better-armed opponent. The Red Army not only failed to join the fight as it had intimated that it would; it actively hindered British and American assistance. His pleas for help were refused, at times with explanations that the risk to Allied air crews was too great. Sosnkowski contrasted Allied excuses with Poland's efforts on their behalf. He thought about the invaluable military intelligence delivered by Polish couriers. And he concluded that Poland's allies were showing a lack of gratitude and support when it was Poland that needed help. As commander in chief, he was obligated to inform his soldiers. On September 1, he issued a message to AK soldiers in Warsaw declaring that Poland's allies had abandoned them, countering Allied claims that assistance would cost too many lives and too much equipment with a reminder of the losses taken by Poles in the Battle of Britain, demanding that the allies live up to their treaty obligations, and assuring them that he would not stop trying to get help. He closed by praising their efforts and sacrifices.

Mikołajczyk saw an opportunity to further his campaign against his rival. In the September 7 Council of Ministers meeting, he claimed Sosnkowski was inciting military disobedience against the government, called his words offensive to the Polish nation and tantamount to German propaganda, and demanded his dismissal. The Council of Ministers issued a statement announcing that it did not endorse Sosnkowski's message and intensified the pressure by sending Raczkiewicz a formal request on September 22 to dismiss Sosnkowski. Likewise, Churchill stepped up his efforts to influence the matter. Sosnkowski received support from Generals Anders, Głuchowski, Bór-Komorowski, and Tokarzewski-Karaszewicz, all of whom defended his integrity and trustworthiness; General Kopański added that the resolution from the Council of Ministers violated military discipline. But Raczkiewicz was unable to withstand the internal and external pressure and twice asked Sosnkowski to resign. Sosnkowski refused both times, contending that his resignation would appear to be submission to Soviet demands; in return, he urged Raczkiewicz to dismiss Mikołajczyk, citing his collaborationist position towards the Soviet Union and PKWN. Raczkiewicz refused to consider his request.

Finally, Raczkiewicz gave in to Mikołajczyk and summoned Sosnkowski on September 30. With tears welling in his eyes, he handed Sosnkowski a dismissal letter. He then appointed Bór-Komorowski as his replacement and named Anders as acting commander in chief.

On the day the Warsaw Uprising ended, Charles Rozmarek received a long-awaited invitation to meet with U.S. President Franklin Roosevelt. Rozmarek was president of the recently formed Polish American Congress (PAC) and had been requesting a meeting for four months. PAC's origins were rooted in the Polish-American community's disproportionate contribution to the war effort. About four percent of the population was ethnically Polish, but Poles made up more than eight percent of the military, and Polish organizations and Polish-American citizens purchased inordinately large quantities of war bonds. However, practically all Polish organizations were fraternal, religious, educational, or charitable; a unified political voice was lacking. Leaders of most Polish organizations and 2,600 delegates met in Buffalo, New York, at the end of May to form a national body to lobby the government to support restoration of a free and independent Poland within its prewar borders and to support Raczkiewicz and his government.[5] Rozmarek, president of the Polish National Alliance, was elected PAC's president. Rozmarek and PAC's board sought a meeting with Roosevelt to make their views known.

Rozmarek's problem was that Roosevelt didn't want to meet. Every request was rebuffed under the pretext of Roosevelt's busy schedule and health issues; even Congressman John Dingell and Senator James Mead were unable to sway him with assurances that PAC was friendly to him. Rozmarek finally secured a meeting through the efforts of Chicago mayor Edward Kelly. He lobbied one of Roosevelt's advisors at what turned out to be an opportune time: election day was less than two months away, and Roosevelt's popularity was ebbing. His opponent, Thomas Dewey, had announced his plans to attend New York City's Pulaski Day Parade,[6] and Roosevelt fretted that Dewey's appearance and his campaign in the Polish-American community might win him their votes. To counter Dewey, Roosevelt resolved to secure PAC's endorsement. Now that he had a reason, Roosevelt's aides scheduled a meeting for the symbolically significant date of October 11, Pulaski Day.

---

[5] Two left-wing, pro-Soviet groups did not join PAC: the American Polish Labor Council and the American Slav Congress. Both groups were later classified as communist front groups by the American government.
[6] Pulaski Day honors General Kazimierz Pulaski, a Pole who served under George Washington in the American Revolution.

A delegation headed by Rozmarek[7] was escorted into the Oval Office, where they were greeted by Roosevelt seated at his desk; behind him was a large map of prewar Poland. Rozmarek requested an unambiguous declaration that American foreign policy would follow the Atlantic Charter and Roosevelt's own "Four Freedoms"[8] and asked for assurances that the president would support Poland's territorial integrity and independence. Roosevelt made no commitments; instead, he responded with generalities. This did not satisfy the delegation, and they did not endorse him. But news stories featured a photo of Roosevelt flanked by the delegates with the map as their backdrop. Polish-American publications viewed the meeting positively, and the map was widely interpreted as Roosevelt's policy. Roosevelt's popularity among Polish voters remained high, but endorsement eluded him. One week before the election, Roosevelt was in Chicago and invited Rozmarek to a private meeting. Roosevelt assured him that he would uphold the principles of the Atlantic Charter. Rozmarek gave him his personal endorsement, which Roosevelt's campaign rendered as the official position of PAC and the PNA. Roosevelt won re-election, taking ninety percent of the Polish-American vote.

More than fifteen thousand AK, BCh, and NSZ soldiers died during the Warsaw Uprising and a like number were taken prisoner. For PKWN, this was a positive development, as it considered all soldiers, *Delegatura* members, and indeed anyone recognizing the authority of the London government to be its enemies. On August 31, PKWN issued a decree "on punishment for fascist-Nazi criminals guilty of murder and abuse of civilians and prisoners of war, and for traitors of the Polish Nation." PKWN labeled those not aligned with it and the Soviet Union as "reactionaries," "fascists," and "Hitlerite collaborators"[9] and routinely referred to AK, BCh, and NSZ soldiers as criminals and adventurers, thus making them subject to the August 31 decree.

---

[7] In addition to PAC and PNA President Rozmarek, attendees included PRCUA President Jan Olejniczak, Polish Women's Alliance President Honorata Wołowska, Polish Falcons Alliance President Teofil Starzyński, Congressman John Dingell, Judge Thaddeus Adesko, and Frank Dziob.
[8] Roosevelt set forth the "Four Freedoms" in a January 1941 speech. He declared that all people should have freedom of speech, freedom of worship, freedom from want, and freedom from fear.
[9] "Dekret Polskiego Komitetu Wyzwolenia Narodowego z dnia 31 sierpnia 1944 r. o wymiarze kary dla faszystowsko-hitlerowskich zbrodniarzy winnych zabójstw i znęcania się nad ludnością cywilną i jeńcami oraz dla zdrajców Narodu Polskiego," ("Decree of the Polish Committee of National Liberation of August 31, 1944, on the punishment of fascist-Nazi criminals guilty of murder and abuse of civilians and prisoners of war, and of traitors to the Polish Nation"), *DzU RP* Nr 4 (Lublin), dnia 13 września 1944 r., poz. 16, s. 17.

In October, PKWN created *Milicja Obywatelska* (MO, Citizens' Militia, commonly referred to as *Milicja*),[10] a national police force with a scope ranging from everyday police functions to identification and detention of political opponents. *Milicja* was part of the security structure defined at PKWN's founding, charged with fighting the "reactionary underground," combatting "political banditry," and observing PKWN's opponents; it operated outside the jurisdiction of local governments. *Milicja* coordinated its activities with Soviet military and security, although the Red Army and NKVD were free to pursue and eliminate the opposition without Polish oversight or approval.

In July, elements of the 1st Byelorussian Front under the command of Marshal Konstantin Rokossovsky entered the farming village of Kąkolewnica in the vicinity of Lublin and seized buildings, houses, livestock, and crops. Public buildings became temporary headquarters for the military and NKVD. Interrogation rooms and jail cells were constructed in their basements and were soon filled with captured AK, BCh, and NSZ officers and soldiers. Kąkolewnica had been transformed into a processing center for those considered to be enemies of the Soviet Union and PKWN. About three kilometers west of the village lay *las Baran* (Ram's Forest). In the autumn, military guards were stationed around its perimeter. Local residents reported hearing gunshots at night and seeing military trucks driving back and forth between the village and the forest. In the forest, pits were dug that became mass graves. Some prisoners were killed in the village, and their bodies were hauled to the forest; others were shot in the back of the head at the edge of their graves. Victims had their arms and legs tied with cable before execution; some were savagely beaten before being killed. Executions continued well into 1945; of the estimated 2,500 to 3,000 prisoners who passed through Kąkolewnica, an estimated 1,200 to 1,800 are buried in the forest. When the camp was closed, pine saplings were planted over the graves. This forest became known as *Uroczysko Baran*;[11] it is also known as *Mały Katyń* (Little Katyń).

Those recognizing the London government's authority were not the only people PKWN wished to remove. On September 9, it signed an agreement with the Ukrainian SSR to relocate Ukrainians from Poland; it signed a similar agreement with the Lithuanian SSR on September 22.[12]

---

[10] Before the war, Poland's police force was called *Policja*.
[11] "*Uroczysko*" means a solitary and mysterious place.
[12] SSR is an abbreviation for Soviet Socialist Republic.

Unaware of the decisions made in Teheran, Mikołajczyk persisted in his efforts to come to an agreement that would preserve Poland's borders and forestall imposition of a new government. Churchill succeeded in securing an invitation for him to meet with Stalin, and he arrived in Moscow during the first week of August. Stalin demanded that Mikołajczyk accept the Curzon Line and come to an agreement with the Lublin Committee. Mikołajczyk found the Committee to be uninterested in compromise, but Bierut offered to appoint him prime minister if he went to Warsaw with them and recognized Bierut's presidency. An astonished Mikołajczyk unequivocally rejected his proposal but offered to go to Warsaw to negotiate an agreement with RJN. Bierut declared that if he were to go to Warsaw as prime minister of the London government, the Lublin Committee would have him arrested.

After his return to London, Mikołajczyk prepared a proposal for a postwar government composed of SL, SN, PPS, SP, and PPR; under his plan, each party would have equal representation, and *Sanacja* would be excluded. The government and the *Delegatura* approved it, and on August 30, he submitted it to the British, American, and Soviet governments. Both the British and American governments reacted favorably; no Soviet reply was received.

Churchill invited Mikołajczyk to accompany him and Eden to Moscow for further discussions.[13] Mikołajczyk presented his plan to Stalin, Molotov, Churchill, Eden, and the American envoy Averell Harriman. Churchill requested a larger role for the Lublin Committee. Stalin seconded Churchill's request and demanded that Mikołajczyk accept his border. Molotov then exclaimed that these questions had already been resolved at Teheran. As the British and Americans fell silent, Molotov reviewed their accord on the border and their agreement to keep the matter confidential.

Mikołajczyk was stunned; this completely contradicted what Roosevelt had said in June. First, he turned to Harriman, who looked at the floor. Then Churchill looked at Mikołajczyk and quietly admitted that Molotov was correct. Churchill's somber demeanor quickly turned to anger; he demanded compliance from Poland, reminded Mikołajczyk of Britain's aid to Poland, and claimed it was his duty to accept Britain's agreement. Mikołajczyk retorted that he didn't come to Moscow to participate in a new partition of Poland. Churchill offered that the deal could be kept secret for now, but Mikołajczyk again refused. Churchill countered that Mikołajczyk should accept the border as temporary, with final adjustments

---

[13] Mikołajczyk was accompanied by Romer and Grabski.

to be made at the peace conference. An indignant Stalin interjected that there would be no future border adjustments. The meeting ended. Mikołajczyk, Churchill, Eden, and Harriman left silently.

Mikołajczyk later met with Churchill and Eden. Churchill blamed him for not appeasing Stalin earlier in the year, claiming that his unwillingness to acquiesce led to creation of the Lublin Committee and threatening to abandon Poland. Mikołajczyk reminded Churchill of his speeches that condemned taking of territory by force and pointed out how much better the Allies were treating Italy and Romania, who fought on the side of Germany. Churchill responded by belittling Mikołajczyk, contending that he and his government were consumed with their own interests and had no regard for people in Poland. It was clear to Mikołajczyk that there was no possibility that Poland could retain its prewar border. He relented and advised Churchill that he would endorse an agreement that left Wilno and Lwów in Poland. Churchill proposed this to Stalin, along with a request that Mikołajczyk serve as prime minister in the new government. Stalin rejected both proposals.

Mikołajczyk returned to London on October 20. It was now his duty to present the grim details to the Council of Ministers and *Rada Narodowa*. He warned that the Polish government would lose any opportunity for positive relations with the Soviet Union and influence in postwar Poland if it did not accept the Curzon Line and PKWN. He advised that Poland would get other territories to compensate for losses in the east, but this would be settled at the peace conference. He made it clear that no assistance could be expected from the United Kingdom or the United States. Lastly, he affirmed that he had made no commitments.

Churchill was anxious to settle the matter. He summoned Mikołajczyk, Romer, and Raczyński on November 2 and demanded an immediate answer, but the Poles were able to defer the decision until after their next Council of Ministers meeting. One day later, the ministers unanimously resolved that they could not agree with these demands and asked to meet with the British, American, and Soviet leaders. Mikołajczyk, Eden, Romer, and Raczyński met to discuss next steps, and they agreed to wait until they could verify Roosevelt's position. When Harriman stopped in London in November on his way to Moscow, he handed Mikołajczyk a letter from Roosevelt confirming that the United States would not guarantee Poland's borders.

Poland's government maintained its uncompromising stance, but it meant nothing without backing from its allies. A rift developed in the Council of Ministers. Most members contended that Mikołajczyk was compromising too much; he countered that Poland would be left without any democratic representation if a solution could not be found.

Mikołajczyk contemplated Poland's plight. Its fate was being decided by others, and a Soviet-controlled government would be installed. He reasoned that the London government had to cooperate with PKWN if postwar Poland were to have any semblance of democracy. He decided that if his government would not yield, he and SL would cooperate with PKWN.[14] He advised Harriman that all parties except SL firmly opposed border changes and stated that he may need to resign. The next day, Mikołajczyk resigned from the government. A new government was formed a few days later with Tomasz Arciszewski as prime minister. Arciszewski's government was supported by PPS, SP, and SN; Mikołajczyk and SL refused to participate.

Churchill distanced himself from Arciszewski's government and placed himself squarely on the side of Mikołajczyk and SL. He indirectly referred to the new government in a December speech in the Commons: "The Polish Government has, in fact, been almost entirely reconstituted in a form which in some respects I am not able to applaud. Mr. Mikołajczyk and his friends remain in the view of His Majesty's Government the only light which burns for Poland in the immediate future."[15] He continued by blaming the Polish government for its predicament, asserting that there would have been no Lublin Committee had Poland agreed to the border, and echoing the Soviet line on Katyń.

Churchill could now legitimately claim that there were Poles in exile who were willing to work with PKWN and accept the imposed borders. He was preparing to abandon the Polish government and recognize Mikołajczyk as the legitimate representative of the Polish nation in the West, a highly irregular move since the British government had not ceased recognizing Raczkiewicz and his government and since Mikołajczyk had no position in the government and could not officially represent Poles in the West.

Even though SL was not part of the new government, Mikołajczyk declared his support for Arciszewski, but this did not last long. He began publishing *Jutro Polski* (*Poland Tomorrow*), a magazine advocating for a settlement with the Soviet Union. Arciszewski was caught in the aftermath. Churchill labeled him as uncompromising and unyielding and would not

---

[14] From Mikołajczyk's perspective, the Soviet Union was in complete control of Poland, and neither the United Kingdom nor the United States had the ability to alter that fact; therefore, the only possible option was to work with Poland's Soviet-imposed government.

[15] Hansard HC Orders of the Day, vol. 406, col. 1481–1482, December 15, 1944.

meet with him. Further rifts followed. General Stanisław Tatar, transferred from Warsaw to London shortly before the Uprising, declared that he did not recognize General Leopold Okulicki as AK's commander.

Piłsudski's followers had never been trusted by Sikorski or Mikołajczyk, and their resentment at being marginalized deepened over time. Many had been imprisoned at Cerizay and Rothesay, and only a very few had meaningful roles in the government or seats in *Rada Narodowa*. They comprised a large proportion of Polish society but were not welcome in the mainstream political parties. In Poland and in the West, they banded together in organizations and informal associations.

Sanacja supporters interpreted Mikołajczyk's trip to Moscow as acquiescence to the Soviet Union and contradictory to Poland's war objectives. Their response was to create a new political party, *Liga Niepodległości Polski* (LNP, Polish Independence League), espousing their commitment to the April Constitution and the prewar Polish–Soviet border, accepting the Oder–Neisse Line, and rejecting cooperation with the Soviet Union. Formed on October 3, 1944, LNP had as its founders former prime minister Janusz Jędrzejewicz, former Rothesay prisoner Michał Grażyński, former ambassador to France Juliusz Łukasiewicz, and former deputy *Sejm* speaker and co-author of the April Constitution Bohdan Podoski. By uniting Piłsudski followers into a single party, LNP filled a political void that had existed since the Polish government had reconstituted itself in France.

On the first day of 1945, PKWN changed its name to *Rząd Tymczasowy Rzeczypospolitej Polskiej* (RTRP, Provisional Government of the Republic of Poland), declared itself to be the legitimate government of Poland, and asserted that the April Constitution was fascist and invalid.[16] The Soviet Union officially recognized RTRP as Poland's government. If it was not already clear that RTRP would implement a government modeled after the Soviet Union, its creation of *Ministerstwo Bezpieczeństwa Publicznego* (MBP, Ministry of Public Security) removed any doubts. MBP's origins were in *Resort Bezpieczeństwa Publicznego* (RBP, Resort of Public Security),[17] founded in Moscow on July 21, 1944, one day before the creation of PKWN was announced, but its origins reached further back. In April 1944, a group

---

[16] This gave RTRP the basis to declare that the president in exile was an illegitimate president.
[17] In the Polish language, *resort* is a synonym for department.

of about twenty Poles began a course at the NKVD school in Kuybyshev; by mid-year, over two hundred future RBP officers had been trained in Kuybyshev, Gorky,[18] and Smolensk, along with officers of communist security services in other countries occupied by the Red Army. When MBP succeeded RBP on January 1, its scope of duties included secret police, intelligence, and counterespionage. MBP was organized into field offices known as *Urzędy Bezpieczeństwa Publicznego* (UBP, Public Security Offices), better known as *Urząd Bezpieczeństwa* (UB, Department of Security).[19]

After the Germans completed their destruction of Warsaw, those Red Army divisions that had ensconced themselves in Praga for four months finally returned to action. As they resumed their push towards Germany, NKVD and UB canvassed every captured city, town, and village and arrested anyone suspected of loyalty to the London government. This included the 500,000 to 750,000 AK, BCh, and NSZ soldiers and officers, every *Delegatura* member, and every person who worked in any capacity for the underground government.[20] PKWN considered every one of them to be a threat to be eliminated. In the face of intensified persecution, Okulicki requested permission to dissolve AK, and Raczkiewicz agreed. From the railroad station in Częstochowa, Okulicki issued his final order on January 19. He urged his soldiers to continue to recognize Raczkiewicz, work in the spirit of regaining full independence, protect the population, and act as guides to the nation; he then released all AK members from their oath. Poland's underground army, the largest such organization in the war, was no more.

Dissolution made no difference. On January 20, the Polish government received a report that Bierut had ordered the arrest and trial of all AK members and anyone recognizing the authority of the London government. Seeing no alternative, some AK soldiers disregarded Okulicki's orders and remained in action to defend the population and themselves.

Churchill, Roosevelt, and Stalin met in Yalta in early February 1945 to refine their plans for postwar Europe. At the conclusion of their conference,

---

[18] Gorky was originally named Nizhny Novgorod. In 1932, its name was changed to honor Soviet writer Maxim Gorky. In 1990, the city's name reverted to Nizhny Novgorod.

[19] The common appellation for a UB officer was *ubek*.

[20] AK was the largest underground army in Europe. At its founding in 1942, it consisted of about 100,000 officers and soldiers; within a year it grew to approximately 200,000. By the middle of 1944, its strength was an estimated 300,000 to 500,000. BCh, the second largest group, numbered about 160,000, and NSZ was third largest, with about 70,000 members. Altogether, the Polish government's underground military strength was between 500,000 and 750,000 at its peak. In contrast, AL's strength never exceeded 30,000.

they issued a joint statement outlining their decisions regarding Germany, the liberated nations, and an upcoming international conference that would create the United Nations. In their Declaration on Liberated Europe, they invoked the Atlantic Charter by affirming "the right of all peoples to choose the form of government under which they will live."[21] Their statement paid particular attention to Poland and Yugoslavia. In Poland, RTRP would be the basis of a new government that was to include "democratic leaders from Poland itself and from Poles abroad" and would be called the Provisional Government of National Unity. American, British, and Soviet representatives would appoint members to the government; "free and unfettered elections" were to be conducted "as soon as possible on the basis of universal suffrage and secret ballot," and "all democratic and anti-Nazi parties" had the right to participate and nominate candidates.[22]

The United States and the United Kingdom pledged to extend diplomatic recognition to this new government. Poland's eastern border was to closely follow the Curzon Line; in the north and west, it would receive territory from Germany. Absent was any role for the Polish government in London. When the matter of Poland's government was taken up, Roosevelt stated that he did not attach importance to the continuity or legality of any Polish government since he felt that, in reality, for some years there had been no Polish government. Late one evening, a clearly tired Roosevelt wanted to end discussion for the day, but Churchill pressed on. Churchill stated that British sources believed that the Lublin Committee would be supported by perhaps one third of the people and therefore had no right to claim it represented the nation. Roosevelt interjected, "Poland has been a source of trouble for over five hundred years."[23]

Poland's legitimate government was not consulted. One day after the conference ended, Raczyński received a copy of the decisions; the following day, the Council of Ministers reviewed and rejected them. The government issued a statement declaring that it did not accept the agreements, emphasized that they violated the Atlantic Charter, and reiterated its willingness to cooperate in the formation of a truly representative government. But the decision had been made. Molotov, Harriman, and Sir Archibald Clark Kerr, the United Kingdom's ambassador to the Soviet

---

[21] "Protocol of the Proceedings of the Crimea Conference," February 11, 1945.
[22] "Protocol of the Proceedings of the Crimea Conference," February 11, 1945. Stating that all anti-Nazi parties could participate was unusual, as no Polish pro-Nazi parties existed.
[23] Zygmunt C. Szkopiak, ed., The Yalta Agreements - Documents prior to, during and after the Crimea Conference 1945 (Polish Government-in-Exile, London, 1986), p. 89.

Union, proceeded to choose delegates in preparation for a conference in Moscow.[24]

Churchill now had to present the Yalta agreements to Parliament. His policies towards Poland had come under criticism in the Commons before, but he muted those debates in deference to the war effort. This debate would be different. Germany's defeat was imminent, and questioning policy could no longer reasonably be construed as detrimental to strategy. He decided to request a formal vote of confidence on the agreement.

At noon on February 27, Churchill opened the debate by introducing a resolution to accept the Yalta agreements. He followed with a two-hour speech, much of it dwelling on Poland.

He declared the revised Polish–Soviet border to be "just and right," further claiming that, "If I champion this frontier for Russia, it is not because I bow to force."[25] In an echo of his December speech, he blamed the Polish government for its predicament, contending that, "… there would have been no Lublin Committee or Lublin Provisional Government in Poland if the Polish Government in London had accepted our faithful counsel given to them a year ago. They would have entered into Poland as its active Government, with the liberating Armies of Russia." He declared the Soviet Union to be a paragon of trustworthiness: "I feel also that their word is their bond. I know of no Government which stands to its obligations, even in its own despite, more solidly than the Russian Soviet Government. I decline absolutely to embark here on a discussion about Russian good faith."[26] But he then obliquely contradicted his defense of Soviet honor by indirectly acknowledging that exile soldiers may not be safe in postwar Poland, stating that, "It may be possible to offer the citizenship and freedom of the British Empire, if they so desire."[27] Churchill concluded his speech with a call to walk forward together and yielded the floor.

What followed was a mixture of dissent, support, and acquiescence. Labour MP Arthur Greenwood decried the lack of Polish participation at Yalta, declaring that, "… it is foreign to the principles of British justice that

---

[24] Yugoslavia received a far different treatment. It was permitted to form a parliament that included members of the last prewar parliament; the only exceptions were anyone who had collaborated with the Germans during the war.
[25] Hansard HC Deb. "Crimea Conference," vol. 408, col. 1275, February 27, 1945.
[26] Hansard HC Deb. "Crimea Conference," vol. 408, col. 1284, February 27, 1945.
[27] Hansard HC Deb. "Crimea Conference," vol. 408, col. 1284, February 27, 1945.

the fate of a nation should be decided in its absence and behind its back."[28] Conservative MP Lord Dunglass rejected Churchill's claim that Poland's revised eastern border was just: "When the Prime Minister says that he accepts this as an act of justice, I must take a fundamentally opposite view. [...] I accept it as a fact of power, but I cannot be asked to underwrite it as an act of justice."[29]

After Dunglass came a speaker supporting the Curzon Line,[30] one defending the Soviet Union's honor and contending that it had no desire to have puppet states,[31] and one asserting that Polish claims to the prewar border were imperialist.[32] These speakers were rebutted by Captain John McEwen, a Conservative from Berwick and Haddington, who charged that Yalta "...amounts to little more or less than a complete acceptance of the Russian point of view."[33]

Captain Alan Graham questioned the exclusion of the Polish government from the conference and Churchill's refusal to meet with Arciszewski; he also gave Churchill an uncomfortable reminder of whom he was asking them to trust: "Commissar Molotov is the one who, in 1939, signed with Ribbentrop the agreement to wipe off the Polish State, who can be held responsible for the deportation of one million and a half of Poles, who took away Polish citizenship from all Poles in the Soviet Union. In spite of this, in the Big Three's opinion the Polish people should trust Molotov more than President Raczkiewicz [...]."[34] Graham concluded by enlightening the Commons with facts about repressions, arrests, and executions at the hands of NKVD and UB.

After the debate was adjourned for the day, twenty-five members drafted an amendment to the motion acknowledging Britain's failure to adhere to the Atlantic Charter. The following day, Maurice Petherick introduced it. He went on to question the agreement's statement that only anti-Nazi parties would be permitted to function, pointed out that none existed in Poland, and predicted that the Soviet Union and the Lublin Committee would use this clause to exclude any party opposing them. Victor Raikes, a

---

[28] Hansard HC Deb. "Crimea Conference," vol. 408, col. 1298, February 27, 1945.
[29] Hansard HC Deb. "Crimea Conference," vol. 408, col. 1304–1306, February 27, 1945.
[30] Speech was made by Sir William Beveridge, member of the Liberal Party from Berwick-on-Tweed.
[31] Speech was made by Denis Pritt, Independent Labour member from Hammersmith North. Pritt was an ardent supporter of the Soviet Union and had been expelled from the Labour Party in 1940 for supporting the Soviet invasion of Finland.
[32] Speech was made by M. Philips Price, member of the Labour Party from Forest of Dean.
[33] Hansard HC Deb. "Crimea Conference," vol. 408, col. 1326, February 27, 1945. Speech was made by Captain John McEwen.
[34] Hansard HC Deb. "Crimea Conference," vol. 408, col. 1333–1334, February 27, 1945.

Conservative from Essex, reproached Churchill and Eden for ignoring the Polish government, cautioned that Britain's reputation as "the friend and hope of the weak"[35] was at stake, and called Churchill's tone as "...rather that of a man who regards Poland as a defeated country which has to get the best it can after defeat."[36] Raikes warned that Churchill was setting a dangerous precedent: "He [Churchill] said that after thirty years during which British, Russians, Americans and French had struggled against Germany, all the three great Allies had agreed what Poland should receive. If that is to mean throughout the world that any treaty made in Europe between 1914 and 1944 can come to an end because there has been war in between, I tremble for the future of Europe and of the world."[37] Arguments continued through the afternoon. In the early evening, Petherick's amendment was defeated 396–25.

Debate resumed on March 1 with a call to discuss other aspects of the agreements, such as Yugoslavia, Greece, and the postwar administration of Germany, but the Polish question remained central. John McGovern aimed a particularly biting remark at Churchill: "The Prime Minister and the President of the United States would not admit that they were compelled to accept the decision because their pride would not let them do otherwise."[38]

And so went Parliament's debate. Most members acquiesced, accepting the agreements as the best that could be had. In the late afternoon of March 1, Churchill's resolution was put to a vote and received near unanimous approval: 413 members voted in favor and none voted against; however, there were thirty abstentions. Henry Strauss, a Conservative from Norwich and holder of a minor office in Churchill's government, resigned from the government in protest.

Around the time that Parliament was concluding its debate, Roosevelt was addressing Congress. He struck an optimistic tone: "I come from the Crimean Conference with a firm belief that we have made a good start on the road to a world of peace." Most of his speech addressed the administration of postwar Germany and progress towards defeat of the Axis powers. Turning to Poland, Roosevelt claimed he did not agree with all of the border settlement, but he also justified the eastern border by claiming that ethnic Poles were very much in the minority east of Stalin's line.[39] Unlike

---

[35] Hansard HC Deb. "Crimea Conference," vol. 408, col. 1491, March 1, 1945.
[36] Hansard HC Deb. "Crimea Conference," vol. 408, col. 1491, March 1, 1945.
[37] Hansard HC Deb. "Crimea Conference," vol. 408, col. 1493, March 1, 1945.
[38] Hansard HC Deb. "Crimea Conference," vol. 408, col. 1608, March 1, 1945.
[39] Report to Congress on the Crimea Conference, March 1, 1945. https://www.presidency.ucsb.edu/documents/address-congress-the-yalta-conference

Churchill's debate, this was a speech, so there were no rebuttals.

Charles Rozmarek and his fellow PAC officers were furious. Only four months earlier, Roosevelt had given his word to uphold the principles of the Atlantic Charter; now, his perfidy was on public display. Rozmarek requested a meeting; Roosevelt refused. Rozmarek and PAC's officers, along with Congressmen John Lesinski, Martin Gorski, and William Link, then sent an impassioned letter to Roosevelt. They condemned the injustices committed against Poland at Yalta, declared that the Four Freedoms and the Atlantic Charter had been ignored, decried the imposition of the new eastern border, and closed by calling it tragic that Roosevelt had assisted in a partition of Poland and the installation of a Soviet-sponsored puppet government. Their tone was not diplomatic, nor did they hope to induce Roosevelt to reconsider his position. Rather, they understood that Roosevelt had deceived them and, having obtained what he wanted, discarded them, and they were expressing their frustration. Roosevelt was indignant. He chose to reply not to Rozmarek but to Congressman Lesinski. His draft response was so heated that his advisors counseled him to tone down his rhetoric. In his final letter, he complained of his irritation with PAC and labeled them unrealistic, nationalistic, and anti-Russian.

Bierut's order to arrest all AK soldiers and anyone supporting the Polish government caused considerable alarm in London. Churchill and Eden proposed providing a list of names of underground leaders to Stalin with a request to protect them from arrest. Despite its misgivings, the Polish government provided names of four leaders—Jan Stanisław Jankowski, Antoni Pajdak, Stanisław Jasiukowicz, and Adam Bień—accompanied by a request for assurances that they would indeed be safe. Not long after, Jankowski received a letter from a Colonel Pimenov inviting him to a meeting with a Colonel-General Ivanov to settle "very important problems" and giving his word as an officer that his safety was guaranteed. Okulicki received a similar letter. Having been imprisoned in the Lubyanka, he was familiar with Soviet methods and believed it was a cleverly conceived trap. Declining would be viewed negatively by the British and Americans and would bring further charges from Moscow that the Polish government was an enemy of the Soviet Union and therefore an opponent of the Allied cause. Accepting meant delivering themselves into NKVD custody. They advised their superiors in London, who in turn briefed the British and American governments; both urged the Poles to attend.

The invitees cautiously began talks with Pimenov. He claimed that the Soviet Union wanted to ensure law and order at the rear of the Red Army and that the underground authorities were critical to achieve this goal. Pimenov further agreed to place an airplane at their disposal to allow them to fly to London after their conference for consultation with the Polish government. As part of the discussions, they were invited to a lunch meeting with Marshal Zhukov. The underground leaders still suspected a trap but knew they had no choice. Knowing that the Polish, British, and American governments were aware of the situation, they agreed to attend.

On March 27 and 28, sixteen leaders of the Polish underground presented themselves to Soviet authorities. They were AK Commander Okulicki, *Delegat* Jankowski, his deputy Antoni Pajdak, Minister of Internal Affairs Adam Bień and his deputy Stanisław Jasiukowicz, RJN chair Kazimierz Pużak and his deputy Aleksander Zwierzyński, RJN members Kazimierz Bagiński, Eugeniusz Czarnowski, Józef Chaciński, Stanisław Mierzwa, Zbigniew Stypułkowski, Franciszek Urbański, Stanisław Michałowski, and Kazimierz Kobylański, and the delegation's translator, Józef Stemler. They were taken to a manor house and greeted by Pimenov. Their host advised them that their lunch with Zhukov would be held a few miles away, and they were driven to the Warsaw suburb of Włochy.

From that point, there was no communication from any member of the delegation. Their colleagues waited in vain for their return and notified London. On April 6, *Polska Agencja Telegraficzna* issued a statement outlining the Soviet invitation, the purpose of the proposed meeting, and Pimenov's guarantee of safety, ending with the news that there had been no word from the Poles since they had presented themselves for the meeting. British and American diplomats broached the issue with their Soviet counterparts but received only denials and claims that the charge was a fabrication by "fascist Poland."

The disappearance of the sixteen, coupled with reports of Soviet repressions in Poland, led to intensified scrutiny of Churchill's policy towards Poland in Parliament. In April, Eden was peppered with questions regarding Soviet detention and deportation practices, the arrests of Melania Arciszewska and a contingent of Polish Red Cross members, and consequences stemming from the disclosure of names of underground leaders. One MP, Vice Admiral Ernest Taylor, presciently asked if the provisional government was even to be composed of Polish citizens.

In early 1945, preparations were underway for the founding conference of the United Nations, sponsored by the United States, the United Kingdom, the Soviet Union, and the Republic of China. On March 5, the sponsors issued invitations to forty-four countries and two constituent republics of the Soviet Union. Excluded from the conference were the Axis nations, their allies, and Poland. Although Poland was one of the signatories of the United Nations Declaration in 1942, no invitation was issued, purportedly because there was no consensus on the postwar government. Since Raczkiewicz's government was recognized by all participating nations with the exception of the Soviet Union, Czechoslovakia, and Yugoslavia, Poland's exclusion was another example of Stalin imposing his will. PAC President Charles Rozmarek attended the conference as an unofficial representative.

On April 25, the conference began in San Francisco. Artur Rubinstein had been invited to perform a concert for the delegates. A native of Łódź and a strong supporter of Poland, Rubinstein was incensed when he learned that Poland was not represented. As he took the stage, Rubinstein angrily pointed out the absence of a Polish flag and commanded the audience, including delegates from the Soviet Union, to stand. He then played the Polish national anthem loudly and slowly; the audience responded with thunderous applause. Such dramatic gestures were of no help. At a Politburo meeting in Warsaw in May 1945, Jakub Berman remarked that the Soviet Union was binding the West with agreements that it had no intention to keep, just as it had at Yalta.

At the time the United Nations conference began, the fate of the missing underground leaders remained unknown in the West. Clark Kerr repeatedly pressed the Soviet government without result, and at a press conference an RTRP representative denied any knowledge of the delegation.

The truth came out on May 3. Anthony Eden hosted a cocktail party at San Francisco's Mark Hopkins Hotel. Eden and Secretary of State Edward Stettinius were talking when Molotov and his entourage entered. Molotov approached Eden and complimented him on the party. Turning to Stettinius, Molotov casually revealed that the sixteen Polish leaders had been arrested. Before either could say a word, Molotov walked away. Stunned, Eden and Stettinius adjourned to another room to decide how to reply. The next day they issued a note to the Soviet ambassador feebly condemning the arrests. It was ignored.

It was later learned that after the underground leaders had arrived at Włochy, they were kept waiting with excuses that Zhukov was attending to matters at the front. Late in the evening they were ushered to rooms in groups of four under the pretext that they needed rest. In each, there were two NKVD officers. In the morning, they again received apologies and were told that Zhukov wanted to meet them at his field headquarters and that they needed to fly there immediately, but once they took off, they realized they were not headed west, towards the front, but to the east. Their plane landed in the Soviet Union, and they were driven to a rail station and placed on a train to Moscow. They were then driven to the Lubyanka, and interrogations commenced.

Two days after Molotov's remarks to Eden and Stettinius, the Soviet Union officially admitted that the sixteen had in fact been arrested and were charged with a series of crimes against the Soviet Union, including collaborating with Nazi Germany, planning a Polish–German military alliance, carrying out intelligence-gathering and sabotage at the rear of the Red Army, engaging in terrorism, owning a radio transmitter, printing machines, and weapons, disseminating propaganda against the Soviet Union, and being members of underground organizations. The Polish government immediately protested the arrests, demanded the prisoners' release, and appealed to the United States and the United Kingdom to intervene. On May 6, *Polska Agencja Telegraficzna* issued its first bulletin outlining the incident and naming the arrested. A number of bulletins followed, along with appeals to attendees at the United Nations conference and an appeal to parliaments of other nations. Even some Polish communists raised objections. PPR General Secretary Gomułka intervened on their behalf with Stalin, arguing that the arrest and trial violated Poland's sovereignty and would have unfavorable consequences for PPR, the new government, and the Soviet Union. Stalin dismissed his complaints.

Now that the arrests were public knowledge, a correspondent for *The Times* of London submitted a list of questions regarding the sixteen arrestees to Stalin. On May 19, he received Stalin's reply. He stated that the arrests were agreed to by RTRP and denied that they were invited for negotiations. This was not all Stalin had to say on the matter. When American envoy Harry Hopkins asked Stalin to release the prisoners, Stalin replied, "There is no point in linking the case of the Trial of the Sixteen with the support for the Soviet-backed government of Poland because the sentences will not be high."

The trial of the sixteen men began on June 18 and concluded on the twenty-first. In attendance were a number of foreign press correspondents and observers from the United Kingdom and the United States. Prosecutors presented fabricated and falsified documents; no witnesses for the defense were permitted. Contrary to Stalin's remarks to Hopkins, not all sentences were light. Okulicki received a ten-year sentence; Jankowski's was eight years; Bień, Jasiukowicz, and Pajdak each received five years.[40] Pużak was sentenced to eighteen months, Bagiński to one year, Zwierzyński to eight months, and Czarnowski to six months. At four months each, Chaciński, Stypułkowski, and Urbański received the lightest sentences. Michałowski, Kobylański, and Stemler were acquitted and released.[41]

Poland's underground state had been deprived of its top leaders, who would have been obstacles to the imposition of a Soviet-sponsored government. Apart from protesting, the United Kingdom and United States did nothing. It later emerged that General Ivanov, the person with whom the sixteen were summoned to meet, was actually General Ivan Serov.

In April 1945, as the United Nations conference was beginning, Britain, the United States, and the Soviet Union had yet to agree on delegates to the conference that would create Poland's provisional government. Among Clark Kerr's nominees were Kazimierz Bagiński, Józef Chaciński, and Franciszek Urbański, still unaccounted for after their meeting with

---

[40] Pajdak was not tried with the others; he was sentenced to five years in a separate trial. After his release in 1950, he was sent to Siberia in forced labor and was finally released in 1955.

[41] After trial and sentencing, the Sixteen met with varied fates. Okulicki died in captivity; circumstances of his death are unclear. He may have been murdered on December 24, 1946. Jan Jankowski died on March 13, 1953; his death is suspected to have been murder. Adam Bień was released in 1949 and returned to Poland. He died on March 4, 1998. Stanisław Jasiukowicz died in Butyrka Prison on October 22, 1946. Kazimierz Pużak was released in November 1945; he refused to emigrate, was arrested in 1947 and sentenced to ten years. He died as a result of injuries sustained when he was pushed down a flight of stairs in prison. Aleksander Zwierzyński was released in November 1945 and returned to Poland. Kazimierz Bagiński was released in November 1945 and returned to Poland, where he was an activist in the PSL and was again arrested in 1946; he was amnestied in 1947 and was compelled to emigrate. Eugeniusz Czarnowski returned to Poland. He died on January 30, 1947. Józef Chaciński returned to Poland. He died on May 6, 1954. Stanisław Mierzwa returned to Poland after his release in August 1945 and was arrested again in 1947. He was sentenced to ten years in prison and was released in 1953; he died on October 10, 1985. Zbigniew Stypułkowski returned to Poland, where he was threatened with arrest, forcing him to emigrate; he died in London on March 30, 1979. Franciszek Urbański returned to Poland after his release and died on December 7, 1949. Stanisław Michałowski returned to Poland, where he was arrested by the security service on charges of sabotage and sentenced to nine years in prison. Released in 1952, he remained under surveillance; in 1980 he became involved in NSZZ Solidarność. He died on September 30, 1984. Kazimierz Kobylański returned to Poland and was arrested in September 1945 but was released on November 11. He was arrested again in July 1947 and sentenced to eight years in prison; he was released in December 1954 and died on May 11, 1948. Józef Stemler returned to Poland; in 1955, he was sentenced to six years in prison for alleged participation in an American intelligence operation. He died in 1966. Antoni Pajdak returned to Poland in 1955; he was one of the founders of KOR and a member of ROPCiO. He died in 1988.

Pimenov. In late May, the new US president, Harry Truman, sent Harry Hopkins to Moscow to break the impasse.[42] He and Stalin agreed that five delegates would come from Poland, three from the émigré community, and four from the Lublin Committee; however, Stalin stipulated that three or four of the delegates from Poland and one of the émigré delegates must be sympathetic to the Lublin Committee.

For the émigrés, Hopkins proposed Mikołajczyk, Stanisław Grabski, and Jan Stańczyk. Stalin did not agree and insisted that the group include Antoni Kołodziej, head of the Polish Seamen's Union in the United Kingdom. Hopkins countered with Karol Popiel; Stalin replied that it was all right with him if Popiel replaced Stańczyk and would only accept Józef Żakowski, an engineering professor at the University of Liverpool, in place of Kołodziej.

From Poland, Hopkins proposed Wincenty Witos, Zygmunt Żuławski, Stanisław Kutrzeba, Archbishop Adam Sapieha, and Wojciech Trąmpczyński. Stalin demanded inclusion of Adam Krzyżanowski and Henryk Kołodziejski in this group. They agreed on Witos, but he declined and was replaced by longtime PSL activist Władysław Kiernik.[43] Sapieha also declined, and Trąmpczyński was not included in the final group. They were replaced by Krzyżanowski and Kołodziejski.

The final group consisted of Władysław Gomułka, Bolesław Bierut, Edward Osóbka-Morawski, and Władysław Kowalski from the Lublin Committee, Mikołajczyk, Stańczyk, and Kołodziej for the émigrés, and Żuławski, Kutrzeba, Kiernik, Krzyżanowski, and Kołodziejski from Poland.

While the Trial of the Sixteen was underway, in another part of Moscow the Soviet government had convened a conference to define the composition of Poland's new government. In attendance were representatives from PPR, RTRP, and Mikołajczyk's newly created *Polskie Stronnictwo Ludowe* (PSL, Polish People's Party).[44]

Mikołajczyk had considered not attending. He interpreted the Trial of the Sixteen as an unmistakable signal that Stalin didn't want Poles not under his control to participate in the new government, but he relented after Churchill pleaded with him to participate. By now, Churchill's optimism, his trust of Stalin, and his faith in the Polish communists had evaporated. He prodded Mikołajczyk to go, acknowledged that the Lublin Committee

---

[42] Roosevelt died in April 1945 and was succeeded by Vice President Harry S. Truman.

[43] Mikołajczyk had suggested Kiernik, but he later observed that Kiernik was not the same after imprisonment by the NKVD.

[44] When Mikołajczyk returned to Poland, PSL continued to function in London and other émigré communities under the name *Stronnictwo Ludowe Wolność* (SL Wolność, People's Party Freedom).

was widely unpopular, and threatened to end his involvement in Polish affairs if he refused. Mikołajczyk considered his options and concluded that he had to attend. He also knew he was exposing himself to danger. A Polish communist in London had even offhandedly remarked to Mikołajczyk that he might be killed in an accident on his way.

PPR and RTRP had little interest in considering differing viewpoints. PPR members expounded on the love that the Polish people had for them and were contradicted by Kutrzeba and Żuławski, both of whom had been in Poland throughout the war; the meeting was immediately adjourned. When Mikołajczyk delivered his proposal for the new government's structure and demanded release of AK prisoners, repatriation of Poles from the Soviet Union, withdrawal of the Red Army, and dismissal of Soviet officers from the Polish Army, an angry Bierut declared that there could never be an agreement with PSL and ended the meeting. Edward Osóbka-Morawski was proposed as prime minister because Stalin favored him. Despite these incidents, after several days an agreement was reached that allowed all political parties the freedom to operate and to publish, provided amnesty for political prisoners, and called for evacuation of the Red Army and NKVD.

At the conference's conclusion, Poland had a new government: *Tymczasowy Rząd Jedności Narodowej* (TRJN, Provisional Government of National Unity). Its initials mimicked the acronym for the Polish government's underground parliament. TRJN included ministers from PPR, PPS, SD, SL, and PSL and had the outward appearance of a coalition government, but PSL was the only party outside PPR's control. Osóbka-Morawski was prime minister, Gomułka was deputy prime minister and minister of regained territories, and Mikołajczyk was deputy prime minister and minister of agriculture and agricultural reform. PPR and its subsidiary parties dominated the new government: seven ministers were from PPR, six from PPS, three from SD, and two from SL, and they controlled the most critical ministries, including National Defense, Public Security, Foreign Affairs, Justice, Information and Propaganda, and the Treasury. Four of the twenty-one ministries were held by PSL, none of which was of high importance.[45]

Poland's new government arrived in Warsaw on June 27. Except for Mikołajczyk, most of its members were relative unknowns. Karol Popiel returned from London with plans to re-establish SP. On June 28, KRN issued a decree announcing creation of TRJN.

---

[45] PSL members were in change of the Ministries of Agriculture and Agricultural Reform (Mikołajczyk), Public Administration (Władysław Kiernik), Posts and Telegraphs (Mieczysław Thugutt), and Education (Czesław Wycech).

Despite Soviet recognition of RTRP and the arrest of the underground leaders, Poland's government continued to make known its readiness to work with the Soviet Union. On April 21, the government issued a statement to that effect. This gesture was ignored. The same day, Stalin and Osóbka-Morawski signed an agreement for a twenty-year treaty of alliance and friendship between the Soviet Union and Poland.

Realizing that their time abroad would be considerably longer than anyone had anticipated, a group of younger government employees contemplated the Republic's predicament. Political divisions were still strong among the older generation, and the younger group viewed these attitudes as detrimental to their cause. Prolonged exile would bring the risk that Polish culture and traditions would be lost, particularly among the young. In their view, a movement was needed that would cultivate Polishness, patriotism, and traditions among the émigrés, a movement that could bridge political divisions. They formed a new political group independent of the legacy parties called *Polski Ruch Wolnościowy Niepodległość i Demokracja* (Polish Freedom Movement Independence and Democracy, abbreviated as PRW NiD or simply as NiD). Romuald Piłsudski, a distant relative of the late marshal, was the first chairman. Members included AK officers and wartime couriers such as Jan Nowak-Jeziorański.

NiD also took on the task of winning support for the Polish cause among the British and countering communist propaganda. Piłsudski edited *Whitehall News*, a weekly sent to members of Parliament and other government officials. NiD conducted letter-writing campaigns to British newspapers and encouraged émigré Poles to make their British friends, neighbors, and co-workers aware of Poland's plight. For the émigré community, NiD began publishing the monthly *Trybuna*.

As Captain Alan Graham remarked in the Commons during the Yalta debate, Soviet and Polish security services were actively persecuting anyone who had served in *Delegatura*, AK, BCh, or NSZ, or who recognized London's authority. Persecution took two forms: physical destruction and moral destruction.

Physical destruction encompassed arrest, imprisonment, deportation, and in many cases, execution. By May 1945, over 60,000 AK and NSZ soldiers had been arrested; 50,000 of them had been deported to Soviet gulags.

NKVD prisons sprang up in the wake of the Red Army's advance. Any suitable facility that came to hand was used and was soon filled to overflowing. In Lublin, the castle and a monastery were now prisons, and the Majdanek concentration camp was reopened under Soviet management. Zgoda, a former Auschwitz-Birkenau subcamp, became an NKVD prison in February 1945 and was turned over to UB in March. Approximately 6,000 prisoners were held there; about 1,800 died. When Zgoda was liquidated, those released were forced to sign statements swearing they would never discuss what happened in the camp.[46]

Moral destruction entailed ruining reputations of people and organizations by leveling false accusations of collaboration with the Germans. Images had to be ruined, questions had to be obscured, and an official version of history in which communists were the war's heroes had to be promulgated. TRJN and the Soviet Union disseminated propaganda portraying AK and NSZ as fascists. Posters became ubiquitous; one portrayed an AL soldier in a heroic pose, rifle at the ready, facing left (i.e., towards Germany); at his feet stood a much smaller, unarmed man in civilian clothing, a banner draped over his neck bearing the inscription "AK," shouting insults at the AL soldier. Beneath, the caption read "*Olbrzym i zapluty karzeł reakcji*" ("Giant and the putrid reactionary midget"). Communist newspapers denounced AK and NSZ under blaring headlines such as: "We will abolish AK from the face of the earth;" "AK murders peasant wives and children;" "Let the traitors of the nation under the signs AK and NSZ go to their Nazi friends;" and "Put on trial the AK and NSZ murderers, Hitler's helpers!"

Głos Ludu, PPR's newspaper, printed a claim that NSZ was an auxiliary formation of the SS and Gestapo. LWP political officers received a propaganda guideline, "On the mobilization of hatred of reactionary thugs," that provided approved terminology to be used by all soldiers when referring to AK and NSZ; they were to be called "bastards of the NSZ and AK." Political officers were exhorted to "brand with all your strength the criminal activities of the bastards of the NSZ and AK, Hitler's emulators. Develop hatred among the soldiers and push them against the reactionaries." Non-communist Polish insurgents were to be referred to as "bandits," "traitors," "anti-Semites," and "Jew-killers." Political officers contended that AK fought against the Jewish insurgents in the Warsaw

---

[46] After the camp closed, Morel continued to serve in the UB and was commander of the Jaworzno concentration camp. After the fall of communism, he emigrated to Israel. The Polish government failed in its attempts to extradite him to face charges; he died in Tel Aviv in 2007.

Ghetto Uprising. Propaganda proclaimed AK and NSZ complicity in the Holocaust.

Veterans of non-communist formations were forced to engage in self-defense. Some AK veterans formed *Zrzeszenie Wolność i Niezawisłość* (WiN, Freedom and Independence) in September. WiN's commanders knew they had no hope of defeating the communists and had no intention of trying. Rather, they focused on assisting AK veterans by providing false documents and money to help them discreetly return to society.[47] WiN also acted to free prisoners from the NKVD; in 1944, AK, NSZ, and BCh units began conducting operations to release their comrades.[48] On rare occasions, WiN and NSZ would fight open battles with occupiers; WiN agents would also carry out executions of communist agents and informers, much as AK had done during the war. Other former AK soldiers joined with NSZ members to form *Narodowe Zjednoczenie Wojskowe* (NZW, National Military Union) specifically to oppose the communists. Having learned from *Burza*, NZW units never revealed themselves to the Red Army and never attempted to cooperate with communist forces.

Raczkiewicz, the exile government, and political parties in the West took on the imposing job of refuting propaganda emanating from Moscow and Warsaw. Appeals to United Nations delegates and Western governments to intervene for those accused in the Trial of the Sixteen contained background information on Poland's war record. PAT published reports detailing repressions, arrests, deportations, and executions and reiterated the facts of Katyń. Raczkiewicz and Arciszewski issued statements reminding the West of how TRJN ascended to power. *Rada Polskich Partii Politycznych* (Council of Polish Political Parties) petitioned the British government to reconsider encouraging repatriation.

At the beginning of 1945, it was plain that Germany had no hope of staving off defeat. From the east, the Red Army was moving towards Berlin; from the west, the American, British, Canadian, and other Allied armies were

---

[47] Despite the omnipresent NKVD and UB, many thousands of people recognizing the London government evaded detection and arrest. WiN would certainly have played a role in their safety and liberty.

[48] A noteworthy example was the NKVD prison in Rembertów, a transit point for deportation to the Soviet Union. Prisoners were permitted to receive food parcels from their families, which the NKVD typically stole. AK used this to its advantage. On the evening of Saturday, May 20, family members brought food parcels that included large amounts of alcohol; as expected, guards confiscated them. Soon, the guards were sufficiently drunk and offered little resistance when AK attacked; about 800 prisoners were freed.

pouring into the country; from the south, American and British armies were working their way northward through Italy. Polish armies played significant roles in all three advances, although they faced unique challenges from the Germans and from their own allies.

After liberating Ancona, the Second Polish Corps continued northward. Its members closely followed news from the Warsaw Uprising and were distressed by its failure, but reports from Yalta nearly broke their will. On learning of the betrayals of Roosevelt and Churchill, Anders submitted his resignation and requested that the Second Polish Corps be withdrawn from service. This caused alarm in London. Raczkiewicz summoned Anders to defuse the situation. In a lengthy meeting, Raczkiewicz assured him that the government was equally surprised by the news from Yalta and tried to prevent him from resigning; he later appointed Anders commander in chief. Anders met with Mikołajczyk to dissuade him from joining TRJN. Mikołajczyk insisted that he and his party would ensure fair elections; Anders countered that there was no question that elections would be fraudulent, warning that he would likely end up in prison.

Anders also had a terse meeting with an unsympathetic Churchill, who again attempted to place the blame for Yalta on the Poles and claimed that the United Kingdom no longer needed the Corps. Britain's generals did not agree. Before he left for London, General Richard McCreery, commander of the British Eighth Army, told Anders that it would be impossible to withdraw his soldiers as there were no other units that could replace them. Chief of the Imperial General Staff General Alan Brooke later commented that the Allied advance through Italy would not have been possible without the Corps.[49]

Like McCreery and Brooke, the Germans understood the value of the Second Polish Corps, and Yalta gave them an opportunity to drive a wedge between the Allies. Radio broadcasts urged the Poles to abandon their positions and offered them help to return home. Leaflets bearing messages such as "You are marching round Italy, while the Bolsheviks invade Poland" were dropped on Polish positions. German propaganda was ineffective. The Second Polish Corps fought on, adding more soldiers along the way as Poles forcibly conscripted into the German Army abandoned their posts and joined their countrymen.[50] In April, the Corps liberated Bologna.

---

[49] General Alan Brooke later received a lordship and was known as Lord Alanbrooke.

[50] As casualties mounted, the German military forcibly conscripted some Poles into its ranks. These were perhaps their least effective soldiers and had to be forced into action at gunpoint; they sought any opportunity to cross lines and surrender. The Soviet Union pointed to Poles forced into German service as proof of a Polish–German alliance.

In Western Europe, Major General Stanisław Sosabowski and *1 Samodzielna Brygada Spadochronowa* (1st Independent Parachute Brigade) had been deployed quite against their wishes to the Netherlands. The brigade had been formed and trained for operations in Warsaw, but the British command ordered it to participate in Operation Market Garden, an ambitious but poorly planned effort to seize a key crossing on the Rhine River, sixty miles behind enemy lines. Sosabowski warned Field Marshal Montgomery about flaws in his plan, but his concerns were ignored. Market Garden failed, and the allies were forced to retreat. Montgomery wrote a letter to Sosabowski praising the bravery of his soldiers, but a few days later he sent a letter to his commanders blaming the Poles for the defeat. Poland's General Staff was forced to relieve Sosabowski of his command, and Churchill used the incident to prod Mikołajczyk into cooperation with TRJN.

General Maczek's First Polish Armored Division fared better. After Falaise, it drove east, forcing the Germans out of a number of towns and cities. In France it liberated Saint-Omer, and in Belgium it freed Ypres and Ghent. Then it crossed into the Netherlands. As they approached Breda, Maczek led his division in a maneuver that pushed the German Army away from the city without any civilian casualties. Cheering crowds lined the streets to welcome their liberators; Maczek's soldiers were greeted with signs bearing the message "*Dziękujemy wam Polacy*" ("Thank you Poles"). In early 1945, the Division entered Germany, and on May 6 it seized the naval base at Wilhelmshaven; Maczek accepted the surrender of the fortress, naval base, fleet and several infantry divisions.

As the First Polish Armored Division was approaching Wilhelmshaven, a Polish flag fluttered in the breeze atop the Berlin Victory Column. Two kilometers away, a Soviet banner flew above the Reichstag. For blocks in all directions, streets were choked with rubble, the twisted remains of military equipment, and bodies. Hitler had committed suicide a few days earlier rather than face capture, and Germany was about to unconditionally surrender. LWP had moved into Germany along with the Red Army. Volunteers, including AK, BCh, and NSZ soldiers seeking to avoid arrest and deportation, and forcibly conscripted underground soldiers had swollen its ranks to about eighty thousand. LWP joined the Red Army's encirclement and subsequent capture of Berlin. Some German units fled Berlin and headed west, preferring to be prisoners of the Americans or British rather than the Soviets. The Red Army unleashed a wave of destruction that left about eighty percent of Berlin in ruins.

"I Remain at My Post…"

AFTER THE EVENTS at Yalta, loss of international recognition for Poland was simply a matter of time. Czechoslovakia ended relations with the Republic of Poland and recognized TRJN in January 1945;[1] two months later, Yugoslavia's new communist government followed suit.[2] On June 29, France severed diplomatic ties. In response, Raczkiewicz issued a statement recounting Poland's sacrifices and suffering. After emphasizing that Poland had not yet regained its freedom, he declared that neither he nor the Republic of Poland would capitulate:

> The Constitution of the Polish Republic imposes on me the duty of transferring the office of President of the Polish Republic after the conclusion of the war into the hands of my successor, chosen by the nation in democratic elections, free from violence and threats of any kind. I shall do it immediately when our nation is in a position to hold such an election. For the time being I remain at my post in accordance with both the provisions of the Constitution now in force and also, I think, with the will of the immense majority of the Polish people.[3]

On July 5, the United Kingdom and the United States ended recognition. Poland's diplomats responded with protests; Edward Raczyński's note to the British government was particularly blunt, declaring that Poland's new government had been installed by force and comparing it with puppet governments established by Germany during the war.

Polskie Państwo Podziemne could not continue to function and scuttled itself to protect its members. Stefan Korboński had been appointed *Delegat* after Jankowski's arrest. On June 28, he was arrested by the NKVD. His successor was Jerzy Braun, a writer, poet, and playwright. During the war, Braun headed *Unia*, a Catholic political and military organization that later merged with AK and SP, edited an underground cultural journal, and fought in the Warsaw Uprising. After the fall of Warsaw, he relocated to

---

[1] President Edvard Beneš was basing his foreign policy on good relations with Moscow. His government ended relations with Poland at the end of January.
[2] Yugoslavia's communist-dominated government under Marshal Tito ended relations on March 30.
[3] "The President of the Polish Republic…," PAT (London, June 29, 1945), AJPIA 701/9/7, No. 17.

Kraków. On July 1, RJN met for the last time.[4] Its concluding act was to issue *Rada Jedności Narodowej do Narodu Polskiego i do Narodów Zjednoczonych* (Manifesto of the Council of National Unity to the Polish and Allied Nations) and *Testament Polski Walczącej* (Testament of Fighting Poland). These recounted the struggle against German occupation, outlined Poland's war objectives and postwar vision, documented Soviet actions in Poland, explained RJN's dissolution, and called for termination of Soviet occupation, cessation of political persecution, and implementation of self-government. Both documents were published in the final issue of *Rzeczpospolita Polska*.[5] With that, RJN dissolved itself.[6] Poland's underground state was no more, and the last *Delegat* had completed his very brief tenure.

Nearly two million Red Army soldiers were on Polish soil. They, along with the omnipresent NKVD and UB, mercilessly eliminated their opponents. Germans were expelled; some moved west of the Oder–Neisse Line while others were deported to the Soviet Union. Arrested Poles were deported to the Soviet Union and imprisoned along with captured German SS officers and soldiers. One German prisoner later remarked that the Soviets treated Poles worse than Germans. Association with the London government was not a prerequisite for arrest; Poles freed from forced labor in Germany who had the misfortune to come to the attention of the NKVD or UB were also deported. In October, RTRP announced amnesty for underground members loyal to London. About thirty thousand revealed their identities, identified their commanders, and surrendered their weapons. NKVD and UB officers used this information to launch a new round of arrests, deportations, and murders.

In Potsdam, a small city near Berlin's ruins, Red Army soldiers had taken up shovels and hammers. They were readying Cecilienhof Palace and its surroundings for what would be the final conference of the American, British, and Soviet leaders. They repaired roads, renovated palace rooms, appropriated furniture from area residences, and planted trees, bushes,

---

[4] In attendance were Braun, Zygmunt Zaremba of PPS, Jan Matłachowski of SN, Zygmunt Kapitaniak of SD, and Józef Krasowski of *Racławice*.

[5] *Rzeczpospolita Polska (Republic of Poland)* was *Delegatura's* official publication. It contained government declarations, official statements, and news.

[6] Braun was active in the SP after the war; he was arrested on December 11, 1948, and imprisoned until 1956. He lost one eye and all of his teeth from torture in custody. Zaremba, threatened with arrest, left for France in 1946 using a forged passport. Matłachowski left for London in 1945 to avoid arrest; he returned to Poland in 1961. Kapitaniak was a lawyer and judge in postwar Poland. Krasowski was arrested in 1945 and died in prison on October 28, 1946.

and flowers; a floral rendering of the Soviet red star highlighted their landscaping.

Churchill hadn't wanted to meet in the Soviet occupation zone, but Stalin and Truman agreed to meet near Berlin.[7] Churchill was accompanied by Labour Party leader Clement Attlee, expected to be the next prime minister when results of the United Kingdom's general election were announced. In a conference from July 17 to August 2, Stalin, Churchill, Attlee, and Truman defined their plans for postwar Europe. Their primary topic was disarming and administering conquered Germany, but the matter of Poland consumed no small amount of time. They declared that the Polish government in London no longer existed[8] and that Polish soldiers serving in the West would be allowed to return to Poland, but they made no guarantees regarding their safety.[9] Poland's western border was agreed to on a provisional basis, pending final settlement in the expected peace conference,[10] and the Soviet Union took responsibility for settling Poland's claims out of its share of reparation payments.

Poland's delegation included Bolesław Bierut, Edward Osóbka-Morawski, Stanisław Grabski, Stanisław Mikołajczyk, Wincenty Rzymowski, Zygmunt Modzelewski, and Michał Rola-Żymierski. During discussions on the western border, Mikołajczyk began to suspect that a Soviet game was being played. When Bierut and Rzymowski demanded territories from Germany, Mikołajczyk perceived that they worded their demand in a manner intended to provoke British and American dissent. In his opinion, if they successfully dissuaded the British and American governments from granting the territories in question to Poland, the Soviet Union and TRJN could regard the Yalta agreements as void. Privately, Mikołajczyk urged the British and Americans to accept the new western border; he was later asked to express his views to Molotov, Eden, and Byrnes. Mikołajczyk's justification of the new western border included hampering Germany's ability to manufacture armaments by weakening its industrial capacity, removing German control of the Oder River by giving

---

[7] Truman distrusted Stalin, viewing his actions to be at variance with his commitments at Yalta.
[8] From the Potsdam Agreement: "We have taken note with pleasure of the agreement reached among representative Poles from Poland and abroad which has made possible the formation, in accordance with the decisions reached at the Crimea Conference, of a Polish Provisional Government of National Unity recognised by the Three Powers. The establishment by the British and United States Governments of diplomatic relations with the Polish Provisional Government has resulted in the withdrawal of their recognition from the former Polish Government in London, which no longer exists."
[9] This declaration refuted Churchill's claims in Parliament during the Yalta debate, in which he pledged that Polish troops who returned to Poland would be afforded "every safeguard."
[10] No peace conference was held, making Poland's western border unsettled for decades.

Stettin[11] to Poland, and providing land needed to resettle Poles from the Soviet Union. Eden and Byrnes agreed, and the new border was delineated in the final agreement.

Derecognition was no simple matter for the United Kingdom. As the Polish government's host and sponsor for five years, the British government had loaned it a considerable amount of money, provided facilities, and taken in thousands of refugees. Now there were debts to be settled, properties to be vacated, people to repatriate, and a military to demobilize. Britain's government started the process by forming the Interim Treasury Committee for Polish Affairs (ITC) to conduct an orderly shutdown of the Polish government. ITC's founders were facing considerable obstacles: the Polish government had no intention of being shut down, it did not entertain any thoughts of recognizing, cooperating with, or acknowledging TRJN, and it was determined to safeguard as much information and as many assets as possible. On June 27, prior to ITC's creation, Arciszewski and the Council of Ministers formed a commission to handle problems resulting from the impending loss of recognition and designated Edward Raczyński as its head.

Raczyński handled the transfer of Poland's embassy to TRJN in a novel manner. On July 4 he signed a deed of assignment transferring the embassy building and other state-owned property to the British treasury; one day later he formally consigned the embassy and its contents to the British government. It thus became Britain's responsibility to pass title.

During the preceding months, the Republic of Poland had discreetly transferred a considerable amount of financial and material assets to trusts, rendering them private property and therefore inaccessible to the Warsaw government. It also anticipated that TRJN would be keenly interested in government and military archives as a means to identify those who had served in the armed forces and the underground. To protect them, the government had to secure their archives in a manner that would make them inaccessible to Warsaw. Fortunately, an ideal solution was at hand. On May 2, the General Sikorski Historical Institute had been founded in London with the mission of facilitating research into Sikorski's career and his times; Helena Sikorska, the general's widow, had donated her husband's papers and memorabilia. The Institute had been organized as a trust and had no connection with the government; indeed, it was deliberately

---

[11] Stettin was incorporated into Poland and renamed Szczecin.

established without any input or direction from the Polish government to avoid any pressure from the British government or Warsaw. This made it an ideal home for the archives, and the government donated them in their entirety. This meant that Warsaw had no legal means to obtain the materials. As a result, countless people were protected from unwanted attention by communist security agencies.

ITC claimed to have assumed the official powers of the Polish government, but its members, none of whom were Poles, quickly understood that they could not function without Polish support. Raczyński was appointed to help, and he brought with him a delegation of government members. As they assisted ITC's British civil servants, they took control over internal affairs and maintained influence over other departments. Thus, Raczkiewicz's unrecognized government retained a somewhat official function. However, it was powerless to stop Britain from cutting off funding. By early August, over half of the Republic of Poland's employees in the United Kingdom had been dismissed from their jobs. Raczyński's commission coordinated plans to vacate British-owned properties. Stratton House at 5 Stratton Street had been the seat of government after the embassy at 47 Portland Place had been damaged in a bombing raid. Military headquarters had been in the Rubens Hotel at 39 Buckingham Palace Road.[12] Raczkiewicz's office was at 56 Great Cumberland Place. Other government and military offices were housed in various locations throughout London; in total, Poland had to leave forty-nine properties in London alone.[13] One property remained: Raczkiewicz's private residence at 43 Eaton Place. Warsaw had no claim to it, and the government relocated its considerably diminished functions there.

Henryk Strasburger[14] and his fellow TRJN diplomats arrived in London in late July. Strasburger ran the treasury in Sikorski's government and held a ministerial position under Mikołajczyk, giving him extensive knowledge of the Republic of Poland's financial affairs, assets, and records. He had returned to Poland around the time Mikołajczyk did, began to work in the diplomatic corps, and was posted to London, where his familiarity with the British government and knowledge of the exile government were expected to be useful. And now, back in London, he was not pleased. Although he and his staff took possession of the embassy from the

---

[12] After the war, the Rubens Hotel resumed commercial operations. A plaque at the main entrance commemorates the hotel's role during the war; photos of Sikorski, Churchill, and other leaders are displayed in the lobby.

[13] A list of these properties accompanies Raczyński's note to the British government handing over title of 47 Portland Place.

[14] Henryk Strasburger served as Warsaw's ambassador to the United Kingdom until 1949. He cut his ties with Warsaw and remained in London until his death in 1951.

British, government archives and many assets were missing. He found that Raczkiewicz's government refused to disband and had an active, if unofficial, role in ITC. To compound his problems, TRJN was widely ignored by the émigrés. He and his staff peppered the British government with a mixture of accusations and demands. They leveled charges that the British were complicit in the continued existence of the exile government and demanded relinquishment of all assets. They contended that the Potsdam Agreement had specifically safeguarded all assets, and they had a valid point,[15] but the transfers had been executed in conformance with British law and could not be reversed.

Strasburger and his staff viewed ITC as an impediment to their work and a refuge for their opponents, and they sought to neutralize it. They found an opportunity in financial matters. Britain, having transferred its recognition to TRJN, had also transferred responsibility for Poland's considerable wartime debts to it; as of mid-1945, Poland had borrowed over £40 million from the British treasury. Part of Poland's gold reserves were held in the Bank of England's vaults[16] but the value amounted to less than half of its outstanding debt.[17] It is not clear if the United Kingdom had contemplated claiming Poland's gold as partial payment; even if it had, it would have been deterred by the considerable remaining debt and the risk of a diplomatic rift. Strasburger made the question of settling Poland's debts contingent upon TRJN gaining control of ITC.

Thus, relations between TRJN and Britain started on a sour note, and they continued to deteriorate. Mindful that elections had been promised, Britain wanted to maintain cordial relations and did not press the matter, but Strasburger did not relent and continued to press for control of ITC. In March 1946, the Foreign Office chose to close ITC and dole out its functions to other government agencies; these included seeing to the welfare of Polish refugees within the empire, funding education, and assisting with passport complications.

---

[15] From the Potsdam Agreement: "The British and US Governments have taken measures to protect the interests of the Polish Provisional Government, as the recognised Government of the Polish State, in the property belonging to the Polish State located in their territories and under their control whatever the form of this property may be. They have further taken measures to prevent alienation to third parties of such property. All proper facilities will be given to the Polish Provisional Government for the exercise of the ordinary legal remedies for the recovery of any property belonging to the Polish State which may have been wrongfully alienated."

[16] Ownership of Poland's gold was transferred to the Warsaw government, although the gold itself remained in London. Exile Minister of the Treasury Jan Kwapiński was criticized for not blocking this transfer, but as the gold reserves were deposited in British vaults, he could not have prevented it.

[17] In mid-1945, the value of Poland's gold reserves in Bank of England vaults was between £18 million and £19 million.

Poland's postwar border with the Soviet Union was defined in an agreement signed on August 16. TRJN formally ceded territories that had been seized by the Soviet Union in September 1939. Poland received part of former German East Prussia, including Danzig, now officially named Gdańsk. The border with Germany was set along the Oder and Neisse rivers as agreed at Potsdam, but no treaty was signed; this area was designated as temporarily administered by Poland. These areas were referred to as the "Recovered Territories." In practice, the presence of the Red Army in eastern Germany and all of Poland ensured that this border was respected.

With new borders drawn, populations had to be adjusted to conform to the new reality. It was politically inconvenient and contradictory to Soviet policy for Poles to live in areas that had been declared to be eternal and inviolable parts of Ukraine or Byelorussia, so they needed to be removed. Likewise, with Poland now contained within its so-called historic ethnographic borders, there could be no question of Ukrainians or Byelorussians living there, to say nothing of Germans in the Recovered Territories. Thus began the spectacle of entire cities relocating. Many of Wrocław's new citizens were former residents of Lwów, and Opole was the new home for many from Stanisławów. Officially, these massive population transfers were called repatriation, an unusual term to describe uprooting people from their homes in cities, towns, and villages where their families had lived for centuries and resettling them in places they had never been. Cities, towns, and villages east of the Polish border had already been renamed; now, their Polish residents were expelled and any traces of association with Poland were obliterated.

Along with the people came institutions. Academics from Lwów's *Uniwersytet Jana Kazimierza* and Wilno's *Uniwersytet Stefana Batorego* set up in the vacant buildings of the former Breslau University and formed the faculty of *Uniwersytet Wrocławski* (University of Wrocław). Their task was enormous: nearly seventy-five percent of the university buildings had been destroyed, and a substantial part of the library's collection was burned by the Red Army four days after the Germans surrendered the city. Lwów's famed Ossolineum was likewise uprooted. Founded in 1817 by Count Józef Ossoliński as a library of historical and archival materials and a publishing house, by 1939 it had grown into one of the largest libraries in Poland. At war's end, Ossolineum was an unacceptable symbol of Polish Lwów. Ukrainian authorities divided the collection into two parts: materials originating from or referring to areas east of the Curzon Line were to stay; anything solely referring to Poland west of the line could be released. Two trainloads of materials were sent to Wrocław, where the Ossolineum was reconstituted; it was called a gift from the Soviet people to the Polish people. Over eighty percent of the collection remained in the Soviet Union.[18]

Resettled Poles faced other challenges created by their occupier. Legnica was one of the cities where displaced Germans were being replaced by displaced Poles. Although it had been a Polish city for centuries, Legnica was annexed into the Kingdom of Prussia in the eighteenth century, and its Polish population had gradually been replaced by Germans. Now, it fell inside Poland's new borders, and in May 1945, Poles expelled from the Soviet Union began to settle there. When the German Army retreated, it abandoned a large, mostly intact military base. This came to the attention of Rokossovsky, who had been looking for a suitable permanent Red Army base. Liking what he saw, he decided to use this base for what came to be known as the Northern Group of Forces. Housing would be needed, and Rokossovsky solved this problem by claiming about one third of the city. Residents were given twenty-four hours to vacate; often, they had been there for only a few days. Frequently, furniture and other belongings were requisitioned. Poles were not permitted in the Soviet district, and the Polish government and military had no authority there or over the military base. The Russian language was so common on the streets and in shops that Legnica acquired the nickname *Mała Moskwa* (Little Moscow).

Poland's ethnic composition was profoundly altered. The Second Republic was a multiethnic society with about thirty percent of the population comprised of minorities. Postwar Poland was almost entirely ethnically uniform, but a sizable number of Poles who had survived the war were missing. Over two million citizens who had lived within the Second Republic's borders were now scattered across the world. About half were in the Soviet Union; some were in prisons or gulags, others were deportees who had not been repatriated, and still others hadn't gone anywhere but now found themselves on the Soviet side of the newly drawn border. The rest were outside of Soviet control. Displaced Poles languished in camps in Germany, Austria, and Italy, refugees were scattered across the globe, the Second Polish Corps was in Italy, the First Polish Armored Division was in Germany, and many functionaries from the exile government and military were in London.

---

[18] Ossolineum's vast archive of Polish periodicals was not permitted to leave the city; it was stored in the Church of Saints Peter and Paul, which was being used as a warehouse. This invaluable collection was destroyed a few decades later as part of an ongoing Soviet effort to obliterate any traces of Polish culture in the city.

For the United Kingdom, the exile government and military presented a thorny problem. Politically, the presence of a large Polish army under British command and the existence of an alternative Polish government on British soil hindered good relations with the Soviet Union and TRJN. Financially, the Polish military was a burden. Socially, the prevailing opinion in Britain was that Poland had been liberated from German occupation, so Poles in the West could now return home. Further, a sizable segment of British society had supported Labour and other leftist parties in the recent elections and considered the Poles to be anti-socialist.[19] The ideal solution was for the Poles to simply go back to Poland, and it appeared that their nation wanted them. Warsaw was issuing appeals to soldiers and refugees encouraging them to return home and participate in rebuilding their nation, and government agents in refugee camps were exhorting people to take their place in the new Poland.

Anders made matters more difficult for both Britain and Warsaw. In March 1945, he had submitted a memo to his government on the matter of the military's future. In it, he declared that Allied recognition of the Soviet-backed government would not be followed by the Polish military's subordination to it, and he proposed maintaining the military under British command. Britain disagreed and was anxious to demobilize, while Warsaw regularly criticized Britain for keeping the military active as long as it had. Anders knew his proposal was unlikely to be accepted, and in 1946 he created *Polski Instytut Historyczny* (PIH, Polish Historical Institute) with the official purpose of documenting Poland's military history during the war. Unofficially, PIH was his military office and the core of a future general staff. Also that year, *Stowarzyszenie Polskich Kombatantów* (SPK, Association of Polish Ex-Combatants) was formed to maintain connections between veterans and to coordinate political and social activities.[20]

On November 20, a team of American, British, French, and Soviet prosecutors and judges began proceedings against German leaders in Nuremburg. Crimes against humanity were to be prosecuted by France and the Soviet Union, with France bringing indictments for crimes committed in Western Europe and the Soviet Union handling those committed in Eastern

---

[19] Socialist sympathies in parts of British society were so strong that they launched a campaign called "Hands Off Russia" opposing government support for the so-called "White armies" fighting the Bolsheviks in the Russian Civil War. This carried over into the Polish–Soviet War of 1919–1920, when many union members refused to load ships with arms bound for Poland.

[20] Many veterans considered themselves to be on extended leave, not demobilized.

Europe. Chief prosecutor for the Soviet Union was Roman Rudenko,[21] a member of the prosecution team in the Trial of the Sixteen a few months earlier. Seeking international acceptance of the Soviet version of events, Rudenko chose to include the Katyń massacre in the indictment.

Deputy Chief Prosecutor Pokrovsky presented his evidence for the Katyń massacre. It consisted solely of the Burdenko Commission report. Defense counsel requested admission of other materials into evidence, but the Soviet prosecutors objected, claiming that the Burdenko report was definitive proof of German guilt. They also objected to allowing testimony from a witness who had served in the German unit that the Soviet Union accused of committing the massacre. Despite Soviet arguments, the court allowed six witnesses to testify. It became clear to Rudenko that this court would not follow the rules of Soviet jurisprudence and his bid to pin Katyń on the Germans would not succeed. He quietly dropped the matter. No mention of Katyń could be found in the final verdicts.

American, British, and French recognition of TRJN was swiftly emulated. By late summer, most of Europe ceased recognizing the London government, as did China, Canada, Mexico, and Turkey. Most, but not all, then recognized TRJN. With this increased legitimacy, Poland could now join the United Nations, and a TRJN delegate signed the United Nations Charter on October 16. Most other nations ended recognition of the London government during the remainder of 1945 and into 1946. Raczkiewicz's government was recognized only by Cuba, Lebanon, the Republic of Ireland, Spain, and the Vatican.

Under TRJN, Poland's official calendar took on a new look. Three new holidays appeared: National Victory Day on May 9, celebrating Germany's surrender,[22] National Day of the Rebirth of Poland on July 22, marking the anniversary of PKWN's establishment, and Great October Socialist Revolution Day on November 7, commemorating the Bolshevik Revolution of 1917. Missing from the calendar was Independence Day on November 11. In 1946, May 3rd Constitution Day vanished, although May 3 and November 11 continued to be observed by the government in

---

[21] After the trial, Rudenko became commander of the Sachsenhausen concentration camp, which the NKVD used to imprison Nazi functionaries, German military officers, anti-communists, and Russians who had served in units allied to Germany. At least 12,000 prisoners died in the camp during his command.

[22] Germany actually surrendered late in the evening of May 8, but as it was after midnight in Moscow, the Soviet Union considered the surrender to have occurred on May 9.

London and in Polish communities in the West and were surreptitiously celebrated in Poland.

Changing the calendar was just one part of fundamental changes to Polish society, politics, and economics. Throughout 1945 and 1946, the Soviet-installed government issued a series of decrees seizing assets owned by Germans, nationalizing abandoned property and all businesses that employed fifty or more people, and nationalizing all property in Warsaw. In practical terms, this meant that building owners could not rebuild to suit their own desires or budgets; they had to have government approval to ensure restoration or new construction met official aesthetic guidelines.[23] Nationalization resulted in government ownership of ninety percent of Poland's economy.

While TRJN was seizing assets, the Soviet Union was appropriating vast areas for its own uses. Soviet army bases and airfields sprang up in every part of the country, and Soviet naval bases dotted the Baltic coast. Poland was being garrisoned; ultimately, nearly eighty Soviet bases were on Polish soil hosting tens of thousands of troops, thousands of tanks, and hundreds of aircraft and ships. These did not appear on official maps, and even the highest levels of Poland's government and military were not permitted entry.[24] Not only did TRJN accommodate this and virtually every other whim of its sponsors, it lavished honors on its patrons. In April 1946, Bierut awarded NKVD General Ivan Serov Poland's highest military honor, *Virtuti Militari*.[25]

One year after the war in Europe ended, London was busily preparing for a victory celebration featuring a tremendous parade. At ten in the morning of June 8, King George VI and his family left Buckingham Palace and were driven along the parade route to their reviewing stand, where they were joined by Clement Attlee and Winston Churchill. An estimated twelve million people, one fourth of the combined population of England, Scotland, and Wales, lined the streets to view the spectacle of a nine-mile-long column of commanders, soldiers, sailors, and pilots from the United

---

[23] Issued on October 26, 1945, it was officially titled *Dekret o własności i użytkowaniu gruntów na obszarze m. st. Warszawy* (Decree on the ownership and use of land in the area of the capital city of Warsaw) but was commonly known as *Dekret Bieruta* (Bierut Decree). Its defenders asserted that the decree was necessary to prevent Warsaw from becoming a hodgepodge of architectural styles and that it enabled reconstruction of historically significant districts such as *Stare Miasto* and *Nowe Miasto*.

[24] During the nuclear era, several Soviet bases in Poland housed nuclear missile launch sites, a fact that the Soviet Army neglected to mention to the Polish government or military.

[25] In 1995, President Lech Wałęsa revoked Serov's decoration.

Kingdom, Australia, New Zealand, Canada, Rhodesia, and Britain's colonies and from the United States, France, China, Belgium, Greece, and other Allied nations, followed by a fly-by featuring 300 aircraft. Three Allied nations did not attend: the Soviet Union, Yugoslavia, and Poland.

Both the Soviet Union and Yugoslavia were invited but declined; Yugoslavia used a diplomatic tiff with the United Kingdom as its excuse. Poland's situation was, as always, complicated. Britain invited the Warsaw government to send a contingent but did not invite anyone from the Polish military who had fought under British command. This immediately became a controversy. Churchill, several MPs, and a number of RAF officers protested, calling it an offense; members of the Polish forces in the West and their supporters also declared that the Warsaw government had no right to represent them. After these protests and other public criticism, the British government invited a small number of Polish pilots who served in the RAF plus General Kopański and several others. They all refused to attend and protested the omission of their fellow soldiers and sailors. Warsaw then refused to send any representatives; its reason was that the Polish RAF pilots had been invited.

A few days before the parade, ten MPs issued a letter protesting Poland's exclusion. In it, they reviewed the list of participants and concluded by asking if the United Kingdom had lost its perspective and its sense of gratitude. This protest did not matter. Poland, the nation that had fielded the fourth-largest military on the Allied side, was not represented.

Neither communism nor the Soviet Union were popular in Poland. No amount of propaganda could make the population forget the Soviet Union's role in starting the war, nor could it paper over the brutality of the current occupation. Regardless of how it was presented, the official image of the Soviet Union as liberator and protector was widely rejected. Pressure was also mounting to hold the "free and unfettered elections" committed to at Yalta. PPR leaders understood these facts quite well and knew they would lose truly free elections.

To stand any chance of gaining popular support, Gomułka understood that perceptions of PPR had to be drastically altered, and he wanted to ensure the Recovered Territories were repopulated. This would take time, and *Sejm* elections had to be delayed as long as possible. Improving PPR's image started with creating *Blok Demokratyczny* (Democratic Bloc), consisting of PPR, PPS, SL, and SD, presented as a united front of parties with a shared commitment to democracy. This was a façade; behind the public image of a multiparty coalition, PPR was in control. Neither PSL nor SP joined, and PPR portrayed them as anti-democratic. It didn't matter. Most of the population saw *Blok Demokratyczny* as a ruse and held to their anti-Soviet sentiments.

To hone its methods for conducting elections, *Blok Demokratyczny* decided to hold a referendum. It crafted three questions expected to garner widespread support, anticipating that its image would be burnished by a highly visible campaign in favor of the proposals. The questions were:

1. Are you in favor of abolishing the *Senat*?
2. Do you want the new constitution to safeguard the economic system introduced by the land reform and by the nationalization of the basic branches of the national economy while preserving the rights of private initiative?
3. Do you want to fix the western borders of the Polish State on the Baltic, Odra, and Nysa Łużycka?

There was logic in the choice of these questions. Abolition of the *Senat* had been proposed prior to the war, and PSL was known to be in favor. Land reform had been a constant issue in the Second Republic; even the government in London and *Delegatura* had been advocates. Public acceptance of the new borders in the north and west was also viewed as a certainty, particularly among those who had been resettled from the east. Mikołajczyk and the other PSL leaders agreed to the questions, and the campaign began.

PPR wanted a "yes" vote on all three questions, and its campaign slogan was "*Trzy Razy Tak*" ("Three Times Yes", abbreviated as *3xTAK*). A deluge of propaganda followed: over 84 million posters, leaflets, and brochures were distributed, and over 15 million pieces of propaganda were dropped by airplane—this in a country with a population of about 24 million.[26] Posters were plastered on walls, fences, bus stops, and seemingly any available surface; *3xTAK* was daubed on buildings, walls, and fences.[27] PPR propaganda ranged from emotional appeals such as imploring mothers to vote *3xTAK* for their children, to socialist realist imagery of strong workers boldly choosing *3xTAK*, to cartoonish depictions of those who presumably opposed PPR's program. Senators were portrayed as aristocrats decked out in top

---

[26] In the census of February 14, 1946, Poland's population was 23,930,000.
[27] Some 40 years after the referendum, faded *3xTAK* messages could still be seen on some walls.

hats and tails; capitalists and landowners as well-dressed, fat, and clutching bags of money; anyone opposed to the border question was invariably rendered as a Nazi. Although Germany was occupied, disarmed, and had been rendered incapable of attacking, caricatures of German soldiers appeared with the message, "You don't want his return." Trucks drove through cities and towns carrying propaganda billboards and oversized portrayals of perceived opponents. One could hardly step onto a street without encountering PPR exhortations, but home was no refuge either: *3xTAK* propaganda was pervasive on the radio, whether overtly in campaign speeches or by subtle inclusion in news stories and interviews.

Opponents of PPR considered the referendum an opportunity to show their strength and popularity while simultaneously exposing society's rejection of PPR and its program. All of the opposition—PSL, WiN, NSZ, and Catholic lay organizations—urged supporters to vote "no" on the first question; they differed somewhat on questions two and three. Theoretically, PPR's opponents had the right to present their viewpoints and to campaign; in practice, their efforts were routinely thwarted. PSL activists reported that their posters were torn down or covered with PPR posters and their newspapers were frequently seized. Paper was made available to PPR's opponents only in limited quantities, whereas PPR had seemingly unlimited resources.

In this atmosphere, the population went to vote on June 30. Despite its relentless propaganda, PPR did not expect the vote to go its way, but it was prepared. Ballot boxes were stuffed, ballots with "no" votes were discarded, blanks were counted as "yes" votes, and legitimate ballots were replaced with false ones. In some cases, ballots were not counted and predetermined results were reported. Understanding that unanimous or near-unanimous results would be questioned by Western governments, it permitted some dissenting votes to show in the final tally. PSL officials reported that "no" ballots were found in the trash. These actions were in stark contrast to the pre-election PPR poster depicting a vote being cast into a sealed ballot box.

Officially, question one was approved by 68 percent of the voters, question two was approved by 77 percent, and question three was approved by 91 percent; 68 percent were reported to have voted *3xTAK*.[28] Although fraud was pervasive throughout Poland, PSL was able to keep the votes in Kraków safe from tampering, and actual results were published. PPR officials then labeled that city as a bastion of reaction.

---

[28] Actual results were uncovered after the fall of communism in UB files: question 1, 27% yes and 73% no; question 2, 42% yes and 58% no; and question 3, 67% yes and 33% no.

Opposition groups viewed the referendum as proof of PPR's weakness. They failed to grasp that it was a dress rehearsal for the upcoming *Sejm* elections. As for those in the West inclined to question the referendum's legitimacy, their attentions would be diverted by news from Kielce.

Allied liberation of German death camps confirmed what the Polish government had been reporting about the Holocaust since 1940, and the Nuremburg trials brought the appalling details to the world's attention. As the trials entered their eighth month, correspondents in Poland reported a deadly attack on Jews in Kielce on July 4. According to TRJN, allegations that a boy had been abducted by Jews and held captive in the basement of a building housing Holocaust survivors sparked a riot that ended with the deaths of thirty-seven Jews and three Poles. Twelve civilians were arrested and tried a week later; nine were sentenced to death and immediately executed. TRJN alleged that uniformed WiN soldiers incited the crowd, and the head of the Ministry of Public Security declared that the incident was committed by the London government, Anders, and AK.

One day after the alleged perpetrators were executed, results of the *3xTAK* referendum were announced. They were little noticed by Western reporters; their focus remained on Kielce. Had they examined the massacre in greater depth, they would have found a rash of inconsistencies, suspicious actions, and unusual coincidences. With NKVD, UB, *Milicja*, and ORMO (*Ochotnicza Rezerwa Milicji Obywatelskiej*, Volunteer Reserve of the Citizens' Militia)[29] flooding every city, town, and village, it would have been impossible for a mob to form without their permission. Although security officers had cordoned off the area around the building and refused to allow government officials and priests to intervene, workers from a nearby factory reached the building unimpeded. *Milicja* officers spread rumors that Christian children were being held in the basement of that building and were being ritually murdered by Jews.[30] Soviet military intelligence officers had been brought to Kielce a few weeks prior to the massacre and left soon afterward. Lastly, the building in question had no basement.

---

[29] ORMO was created in February 1946 as a volunteer paramilitary organization comprised of volunteers. ORMO members could expect bonuses and special privileges, such as new apartments, cars, vacations, access to better health care, and better jobs. Most of its members were also PPR members.

[30] This was the "blood libel," which alleged that Jews used the blood of Christian children when making matzoh bread for Passover. Once widely disseminated, it had long been rejected in Western Europe but clung to life in tsarist Russia.

July 4 was a slow news day in the United States, and reports from Kielce appeared in many newspapers. With Germany defeated and the Holocaust's surviving architects on trial, these reports lent credence to Soviet claims that Poles loyal to the London government were allied with the Germans. News reports from Kielce created an image of a deeply antisemitic nation morally comparable to the German perpetrators of the Holocaust.[31]

Attlee inherited Churchill's pledge to assist military personnel unwilling to return to Poland, but he preferred to eliminate the problem altogether and started a campaign encouraging soldiers to return.[32] Attlee reasoned that the average soldier wanted to return but was under intense pressure from his commanding officers to refuse; he thought that taking the decision directly to the soldiers would yield positive results. He questioned Warsaw's diplomats about the reception they would receive and was assured that they would be warmly welcomed.

Britain's government prepared a pamphlet for the soldiers containing a message from Foreign Secretary Bevin and an appeal from Warsaw to accept the new government and return home to participate in rebuilding Poland. Britain supervised distribution of the pamphlet to ensure that the Polish command did not interfere. British officers were instructed to prevent Polish military newspapers from publishing any articles counseling soldiers not to return or any items questioning TRJN's legitimacy. They were also told to make it clear that the British government could not fund the Polish military indefinitely and to discourage any thoughts that Polish soldiers could remain on British territory. Anders, his commanders, and

---

[31] After the massacre, the boy, Henryk Błaszczyk, changed his story, claiming he went to stay with friends and lied to his father to prevent punishment. It was later learned that Walenty Błaszczyk was employed as an informer for UB. The Kielce incident occurred on the same day that Katyń was raised at Nuremberg. Kielce had the hallmarks of a Soviet provocation, but it did not matter; Poland's reputation was permanently damaged. In 1998, Henryk Błaszczyk was interviewed by Anna Stempniak of Polskie Radio. He now claimed he had stayed two nights with an unnamed family in a nearby village and was treated well; he also stated that his father instructed him to stick with the Jewish abduction story. For years afterward, he claimed to have received threats of dire consequences should he break his silence. Soviet actions at Kielce were spectacularly successful. For decades, the Kielce pogrom tainted Western opinions of Polish society. The United States Holocaust Museum conflated the pogrom with the Holocaust and continues to offer it as a proof of Polish antisemitism. Arthur Bliss Lane advanced the theory that Kielce was staged to coincide with 3xTAK; its purpose was to simultaneously discredit WiN and NSZ while drawing the attention of British and American correspondents away from the referendum to a more sensational story.

[32] It is to the United Kingdom's credit that they did not attempt to force Poles to return as they and the Americans did in Operation Keelhaul, a forced repatriation of anti-communist Russians, Ukrainians, Croatians, and Hungarians. Those unfortunate subjects of Keelhaul who didn't commit suicide were imprisoned, exiled to labor camps, or executed upon return.

their press obliged. Pamphlets were distributed in March 1946 without incident, but the results were not what Attlee had hoped. Some stated that they would ignore the message from Warsaw, while others refused to accept the pamphlet altogether; compounding the matter was the poor translation of Bevin's message.[33] Attlee had also failed to consider geography. Most Second Polish Corps officers and soldiers were from areas forcibly incorporated into the Soviet Union, and their home cities, towns, and villages now lay east of the border. They had no homes to return to.

Despite these obstacles, about half of the soldiers expressed an interest in returning, but TRJN abruptly complicated the matter by declaring that it no longer recognized Polish forces under British command as part of the Polish military and now required anyone desiring repatriation to apply individually. Adding to the problem, thousands of underground soldiers fleeing persecution joined the Second Polish Corps, bringing with them news that returnees from the West were being deported to gulags. Still, some were undeterred and chose to return; many were immediately arrested on arrival, interrogated, beaten, charged with being British spies, and deported into the depths of the Soviet Union.

Attlee was obliged to come up with a new plan. His solution was the Polish Resettlement Corps (PRC, *Polski Korpus Przysposobienia i Rozmieszczenia*), announced by Bevin on May 22, 1946. PRC was designed to keep Polish refugees under British military command while they transitioned to civilian life. Brigadier General Stanisław Kopański shared command with General William Bain Thomas. Participation in PRC was voluntary; enlistees would receive pay and housing and were offered language instruction, vocational training, further education, and assistance finding employment. It was expected to be dissolved when all enlistees either found employment in Britain, emigrated onwards, or returned to Poland. Most Poles recognized PRC to be a generous offering; about 115,000 joined.

Some segments of British society thought it too generous. Anti-Polish, pro-Soviet sentiment continued to shape public opinion, and Bevin's office was flooded with letters from unions, councils, and individuals demanding a change in policy and calling for the Poles to be ejected from Britain. Such letters were frequently rife with misinformation, including claims that the Polish soldiers had been allied with Hitler and that they were fascists. Others included allegations that the Poles wanted to avoid hard work at home

---

[33] Compounding the problem, many Poles remembered Bevin's personal involvement in blocking military assistance to Poland during the Polish–Soviet War of 1920 and thus considered him to be acting in Moscow's interests.

and intended to live off British taxpayers. Members of the Trades Union Congress and other large unions viewed their introduction into the labor market as unwanted competition for jobs. Anti-Polish sentiments grew into open hostility. Near Polish bases, messages such as "Poles go home" and "England for the English" were scrawled on walls and fences. Even venturing into nearby towns and villages became unsafe. Knowing they would likely encounter a cold reception, Poles shied away from pubs; reports of verbal and physical assaults in the streets became frequent. Anti-Catholic prejudices surfaced as well; protests arose over allowing the mostly Catholic Poles to settle in an overwhelmingly Protestant nation. The Protestant Action Society organized its first anti-Polish rally in Edinburgh in June 1946; others would follow. A Gallup poll from July 1, 1946, showed that 56 percent of Britons opposed PRC; in Scotland, opposition reached 75 percent. In the face of opposition and protests, Attlee and Bevin pressed on, and PRC began recruiting in September.

In Warsaw, TRJN held firm to its statement in the repatriation brochure: "There will not be, and must not be, any Polish Army that does not recognise the Government of National Unity." As PRC was a British military formation, TRJN's position was that enlistment was an act of treason against the Polish state and grounds for loss of citizenship. Having obtained a list of seventy-five officers who had enlisted, TRJN made an example of them by passing a resolution depriving them of Polish citizenship. Not on the list was General Władysław Anders, an omission not missed by Mikołajczyk. Minutes from the September 26 Council of Ministers meeting attribute the following to him: "Citizen Deputy Prime Minister points out that General Anders, who is the main perpetrator, is not on the list of officers who are to be deprived of Polish citizenship. It so happens that the main culprit will not be covered by the resolution and other good soldiers will suffer the consequences."

Mikołajczyk was advised that Anders was not named in the resolution because his name did not appear on the list of officers who had joined PRC and that his case was being considered separately.[34] The need to quickly pass the resolution took precedence. The resolution was adopted unanimously. A separate resolution stripping citizenship from Anders was passed later.

Truman's policies towards Poland differed little from Roosevelt's. Truman accepted TRJN, withdrew recognition from the London government,

---

[34] Anders never joined PRC.

and acknowledged Poland's new borders. Rozmarek criticized these decisions, calling them a tragic blunder. PAC continued to advocate for the elections pledged at Yalta. In the summer of 1946, with no *Sejm* elections forthcoming, PAC declared that the Yalta agreements did not contain the necessary provisions to ensure that free elections would be conducted in a timely manner and called on the US government to renounce the Yalta agreements, cease recognition of TRJN, and re-establish relations with the London government until free elections could be held. The Americans brushed off PAC's demands, opting for diplomatic pressure.

Even those commitments made by the Americans at Yalta and confirmed at Potsdam came into question. Secretary of State James Byrnes gave a speech in Stuttgart outlining America's revised policy on German reconstruction. He touched on the question of the Polish–German border, stating, "At Potsdam specific areas which were part of Germany were provisionally assigned to the Soviet Union and to Poland, subject to the final decisions of the Peace Conference," and "The United States will support revision of these frontiers in Poland's favor. However, the extent of the area to be ceded to Poland must be determined when the final settlement is agreed upon."[35] PAC's leaders were alarmed and interpreted this as a signal that the United States now considered the Oder–Neisse line to be provisional, a significant shift in policy since Potsdam, where Byrnes himself had strongly supported the border. Byrnes's speech caused much consternation in the West, but Moscow and Warsaw were pleased. Poland's alliance with the Soviet Union could now be portrayed as the only means to guarantee the western border, and the United States could plausibly be accused of abandoning the Poles.

By the middle of 1946, TRJN had been in power for a year and was recognized by most nations. It could legitimately claim to be a coalition of multiple parties. But it had yet to conduct *Sejm* elections, and British and American pressure was mounting as were calls from Mikołajczyk to conduct elections and to withdraw the Red Army as Stalin promised at Potsdam. Neither Stalin nor Bierut were willing to conduct elections unless the outcome was certain. Stalin and his agents had badly miscalculated in Hungary, where even the presence of the Red Army and the NKVD could

---

[35] Restatement of United States Policy on Germany: Address by the Secretary of State (Byrnes) at Stuttgart, Germany. September 6, 1946. Department of State *Bulletin*, September 15, 1946, pp. 496–501.

only bring the communists 16 percent of the vote. Clearly, the election had to be carefully planned and managed.

First came an effort to convince Mikołajczyk to bring PSL into *Blok Demokratyczny*. This would reduce the elections to a show, as voters would be deprived of alternatives and PPR would allocate *Sejm* seats after the election. Mikołajczyk refused; he was confident that in a fair election PSL would emerge victorious. Likewise, Popiel expected a good showing for SP, and he prepared for his party's congress with optimism. A few days before the congress, SP's headquarters was raided, its newspaper was confiscated, its employees were arrested, the congress was canceled, and the government appointed a new party chairman.

Unable to co-opt Mikołajczyk, PPR launched a relentless campaign against him and PSL. *Milicja* and ORMO forcibly dispersed PSL rallies, beating and arresting those present. The editor and several staff members of *Gazeta Ludowa*, PSL's newspaper, were arrested. *Milicja* turned a blind eye to vandalization of PSL offices, campaign signs, and posters. PSL members were dismissed from their jobs, evicted from their farms, arrested, beaten, and murdered. New laws enabled a purge of more than 409,000 voters, mostly AK and NSZ veterans, from the electoral rolls; another 80,000 were arrested prior to the election. Some PSL candidates were arbitrarily rejected, about 150 were arrested, and a few were murdered. *Gazeta Ludowa* was heavily censored; not even obituaries of PSL members were permitted. PSL was saddled with oppressive restrictions on its campaign activities, whereas *Blok Demokratyczny* was unencumbered by any limits. *Blok Demokratyczny* also took steps intended to confuse voters. A new party, PSL "Nowe Wyzwolenie" (PSL "NW"),[36] had been formed shortly before the referendum by PSL members opposed to Mikołajczyk and was permitted to run independently from the *Blok*; there were now two parties calling themselves PSL in the election.

Electoral procedures used a pattern unfamiliar to those accustomed to secret ballots. Parties and groupings submitted lists of candidates for every electoral district, and the electoral commission assigned a number to each list. *Blok Demokratyczny* had an advantage: their list was numbered "3" throughout Poland, whereas list numbers for PSL and SP varied by district. This simplified *Blok Demokratyczny's* campaign propaganda while complicating efforts of the other parties. At the polling station, voters would select a paper with their desired list number away from the view of others, place it in an envelope, and drop the envelope into the ballot box

---

[36] *Polskie Stronnictwo Ludowe Nowe Wyzwolenie* (PSL NW, PSL New Liberation) was founded on June 6, 1946. Its use of "PSL" was certainly meant to confuse.

in full view of all. But even this modicum of freedom was attacked. In the weeks leading up to election day, voters were barraged with exhortations to vote openly (i.e., to openly show their ballot) to demonstrate support for so-called "democratic forces;" those who did not would be labeled "reactionary" and "anti-democratic," and veiled threats were made that the authorities would remember those who obstructed progress and democracy. Workers were pressured to proceed to the polls *en masse* and vote as a group. One final disinformation effort was made the day before the election: thousands of PSL officials and members received a telegram falsely claiming that Mikołajczyk had been killed in an aircraft accident.

Voters went to the polls on Sunday, January 19, 1947. American Ambassador Arthur Bliss Lane observed that many voters openly showed their ballot before casting it, and he saw officials noting the names of anyone who did not do so. Voting was conducted under the watchful eyes of armed ORMO troops. United Nations observers were barred from the polling stations, and only a small number of PSL observers were permitted. British and American proposals to supervise and observe the elections were rejected by the Soviet Union.

Even with this level of intimidation and pressure, PPR left nothing to chance. Official results were readied in advance, and ballot boxes filled with votes for list 3 were prepared before election day. Official results showed an overwhelming victory for *Blok Demokratyczny*; the grouping garnered 80 percent of the vote and took 394 Sejm seats. Mikołajczyk's PSL came in a distant second, tallying 10 percent of the vote and twenty-eight seats, followed by SP with about 4.75 percent of the vote and twelve seats, and PSL NW with about 3.5 percent of the vote and seven seats.[37] The remaining three seats were won by unaffiliated candidates. PSL claimed fraud; their appeals to examine the election results were dismissed.[38] Protests were issued by the British and American ambassadors. Lane, convinced he had failed the Polish people, resigned.

Mikołajczyk, Stefan Korboński, and twenty-six of their fellow PSL candidates won seats, but their situation was precarious. They were openly attacked and threatened in the *Sejm* but persisted, considering it the last place they could speak freely and counting on foreign correspondents to

---

[37] Stalin, interested in gauging PPR's true level of support, had MGB officer Aron Palkin prepare a report on the actual outcome. Palkin concluded that Blok Demokratyczny received 50% of the votes. Palkin had also taken an active role in rigging the 1946 referendum; for that effort he was awarded the Order of the Red Banner.

[38] Based on reports from PSL observers in the few polling places where they were admitted, between 65% and 85% of the vote went to PSL lists.

report what they saw and heard in *Sejm* sessions. Poland's newly elected *Sejm* convened for the first time on February 4. One of its first acts was to elect Bierut, a citizen of the Soviet Union, to the office of president.[39] About two weeks later, it issued a temporary constitution, *Mała Konstytucja z 1947* (Small Constitution of 1947), a conglomeration of the PKWN manifesto and the March Constitution.

Later in the year, Bierut was targeted in an assassination attempt at Kraków's Hotel Francuski. According to Piotr Jaroszewicz, Bierut was shot repeatedly by a member of the anti-communist underground disguised in an NKVD uniform. Witnesses reported seeing a dead body removed from the hotel. Half an hour later, Bierut appeared and calmed the crowd. This odd event, coupled with observations that the wartime Bierut differed from the prewar Bierut and with reports of his activities in Moscow while he was in prison in Poland, led to speculation that the Soviet Union had introduced a double in the 1930s. This was not unknown; the NKVD had been known to replace people with similar-looking doubles known as *matryoshkas*,[40] although no firm evidence has been found to indicate that Bierut had one.

For two years, NKVD and UB units had doggedly pursued underground soldiers loyal to London. Tens of thousands had been arrested, more than fifty thousand were deported to gulags, and thousands more had been executed, and yet tens of thousands remained at large. Many were with their units in the countryside, some had joined LWP, UB, or *Milicja* in an attempt to hide in plain sight, and others used false papers issued by WiN to blend into postwar society.

Their continued ability to elude arrest was an ongoing frustration to Warsaw. Those thousands of security personnel allocated to the hunt were not resolving the problem quickly enough, so Bierut decided to revisit an earlier strategy. In February, the *Sejm* approved an amnesty and appealed to underground soldiers to register; by doing so, they would avoid prosecution. Applicants were required to report to the amnesty committee at a UB station, surrender any weapons, and provide their name, pseudonym, rank, organization, and address; they were also required to furnish the name, address, and pseudonym of their commander. Propaganda was

---

[39] UB officer Józef Światło was closely connected to Bierut; he received orders directly from him. In the 1950s, Światło reported that Bierut had been an NKVD agent.
[40] This theory was documented by journalist Bohdan Roliński in his book *Przerywam milczenie* (*I Am Breaking Silence*) and was based on his conversations with Piotr Jaroszewicz.

sufficiently convincing to compel around 55,000 soldiers to present themselves; another 23,000 already imprisoned applied in hopes of obtaining their release.

Amnesty closed in late April. Almost immediately, UB began to summon applicants to return for additional questioning. Many were arrested, as were those they had identified. Those who had not applied for amnesty numbered fewer than two thousand, and information gleaned from applicants facilitated the capture of many of them.

Leukemia had been a constant factor in Raczkiewicz's life since 1939; at times it sapped his strength to the point that he was forced to limit his activities. Throughout the war he managed to function, but in December 1946 his health worsened, and he sought treatment at the Duff House Sanatorium at Ruthin Castle in North Wales. As his health faded, Raczkiewicz reconsidered his successor. In August 1944, he had designated Arciszewski, but he was a nonentity with the British. He decided that August Zaleski would be a better option and summoned him to Ruthin on April 15. Raczkiewicz informed Zaleski that he planned to designate him as his successor and would then resign. Zaleski disagreed with his resignation but agreed to accept the presidency. On April 26, Raczkiewicz appointed Zaleski; it was announced on June 6 in *Dziennik Ustaw,* one day after Raczkiewicz's death. He was buried in the Polish Military Cemetery in Newark-upon-Trent, next to Sikorski.

Even in death, Raczkiewicz could not escape Warsaw's scorn. Britain's government received a note from the Polish embassy protesting its decision to send representatives to his funeral and to allow full military honors by units of the Polish Resettlement Corps. In response, the British government stated that this was done in recognition of Raczkiewicz's wartime role and had no political significance.

When Władysław Raczkiewicz became president, he was the leader of a country under attack by two hostile nations. France and the United Kingdom regarded Poland as an important ally in the war against Germany, and Poland's fate engendered worldwide sympathy. At the time of his death, however, over six million Polish citizens had been killed, two million more had been forcibly relocated, and Poland lost one third of its territory to the Soviet Union. Poland was occupied by a military that treated it as a defeated foe. A new and alien form of government was imposed, thousands of buildings had been destroyed, and Warsaw had been obliterated.

Countless factories were stripped of their equipment. Art and cultural artifacts were looted. Poland's legitimate government lost recognition from nearly every nation. Britain and America had abandoned Poland to Soviet occupation and control. And there was nothing Raczkiewicz could have done to prevent it.

Discord Among Exiles

August Zaleski,
President of the Republic of Poland 1947-1972

POLAND'S NEW PRESIDENT, August Zaleski, had considerable experience in diplomacy, many contacts within the British government, great familiarity with the United Kingdom, and fluency in English, all qualities needed in the new reality. Born in Warsaw on September 30, 1883, he graduated from *gimnazjum* in the city's Praga district and continued his education abroad at the London School of Economics. He intended to pursue a career in academia and accepted a position in Warsaw's Krasiński Library, but his plans changed when the Great War began. He threw himself into political activity and was dispatched to London in 1915 to represent *Komitet Narodowy Polski* (KNP, Polish National Committee), a group advocating for Poland's independence. To support himself, he taught the Polish language at King's College.[1]

After the Great War, Zaleski joined the Ministry of Foreign Affairs and proved himself to be a skilled diplomat. His initial posting was to Switzerland where he was *chargé d'affaires*; he then served in Poland's delegation at the Paris Peace Conference. After the conference he returned to Warsaw and briefly took charge of the Great Powers department at the Ministry, and in 1920 he was dispatched to Athens as an envoy. The following year he returned to Warsaw as director of the ministry's political department. This proved to be another short assignment; in 1922, he was named

---

[1] This marked the first time that the Polish language had been taught at King's College.

ambassador to Italy. He stayed in Rome for nearly four years, returning in early 1926. After Piłsudski's coup, Zaleski was appointed minister of foreign affairs and held that position until 1932. During his tenure, he signed several major agreements, including a trade treaty with Germany, the non-aggression treaty with the Soviet Union, and the Kellogg–Briand Pact.[2] He secured Poland a seat on the League of Nations Council and for a time served as the Council's president; he also represented Poland at the Hague Conference on Reparations and at the World Disarmament Conference. His policy was to strengthen Poland's ties with Western nations, particularly France and the United Kingdom. In addition to his responsibilities at the Ministry, Zaleski held a *Senat* seat from 1928 through 1935.

In 1932, he left the Ministry and entered the private sector as chairman of the supervisory board of Poland's largest privately owned bank, Bank Handlowy w Warszawie.[3] When Germany invaded, Zaleski hurried to Paris to protect the bank's assets from seizure. For Sikorski, the presence of such an experienced diplomat in Paris was fortuitous; he appointed him minister of foreign affairs. Apart from Raczkiewicz's ill-fated attempt to install him as prime minister, Zaleski headed the Ministry until he resigned in protest of the Sikorski–Maisky agreement. Raczkiewicz then appointed him head of the Presidential Civil Chancellery. Zaleski remained in this position until Raczkiewicz's death.

Despite his qualifications, Zaleski's appointment met with fierce opposition. Members of the prewar opposition disliked his *Sanacja* connections, and PPS saw it as an affront to Arciszewski.

In his final weeks, Raczkiewicz contemplated the challenges the government would face in exile and concluded that Zaleski was better suited to lead the government. Arciszewski would have little if any influence with the British, whereas Zaleski had extensive contacts. On April 26, Raczkiewicz wrote a decree announcing Zaleski's appointment, a letter to Anders and Tadeusz Tomaszewski charging them with informing Arciszewski, and a letter to Arciszewski informing him of his decision and the reasons behind it. Raczkiewicz declared that he wanted continuity and did not want the government to have a new president and prime minister simultaneously; further, he noted that Zaleski would be impartial, as he was not a member of any political party.

---

[2] The Kellogg–Briand Pact was an agreement rejecting war as a means to resolve issues and committing its signatories to resolve conflicts using peaceful means.
[3] Chairman of the supervisory board is equivalent to chairman of the board of directors.

Rumors had been circulating that Raczkiewicz was being influenced by *Sanacja* to appoint a new successor; however, Arciszewski heard nothing from him, so in late May he visited Raczkiewicz and asked if he was being replaced. Raczkiewicz said there were no plans to do so. On June 3, while Arciszewski was still in Ruthin, Anders and Tomaszewski handed him the letter. He refused to recognize the change. The following day, Arciszewski, Anders, Tomaszewski, and Zaleski met with Raczkiewicz to resolve the issue. In Arciszewski's account, Raczkiewicz claimed it was a misunderstanding and recommended talks to resolve the issue; in these talks, Zaleski is said to have offered to take the presidency provisionally for two weeks until succession could be resolved, but Raczkiewicz died before that could happen.

On June 6, *Dziennik Ustaw* published the decree, the letter to Arciszewski, the letter to Anders and Tomaszewski, and an announcement by them that they had informed Arciszewski and therefore had discharged their responsibility. In these circumstances, August Zaleski took office on June 9, launching a period of division, distrust, and intrigue that endured until the end of the Second Republic itself.

PPS responded four days later. It issued a bulletin to party members explaining the situation and the party's position, citing three reasons that it considered Zaleski's appointment to be invalid. First, Raczkiewicz did not consult with Arciszewski to obtain his approval, thus violating *Umowa Paryska*. Second, PPS claimed that, although the constitution permitted Raczkiewicz to name his replacement, it did not allow him the right to change his nomination.[4] Third, PPS called the move counter to the

---

[4] This claim cited Article 13 of the April Constitution:
  (1) The President of the Republic enjoys personal rights constituting his prerogatives.
  (2) These prerogatives include: (a) the designation of one of the candidates for the Presidency of the Republic and the calling of a referendum; (b) the appointment of his successor in time of war; (c) the nomination and dismissal of the Prime Minister, the First President of the Supreme Court, and the President of the Supreme Board of Control; (d) the appointment and dismissal of the Commander in Chief and of the Inspector-General of the Armed Forces; (e) the nomination of the judges of the Tribunal of State; (f) the nomination of the Senators receiving their mandate by the President's selection; (g) the appointment and dismissal of the Director and officials of the President's Household; (h) the dissolution of the *Sejm* and *Senat* before the expiration of their term; (i) impeachment of members of the Government before the Tribunal of State; (j) application of the right of pardon.

Items (h), (i), and (j) were not considered relevant. PPS claimed that Article 13 gave the president power to dismiss only the prime minister, commander in chief, and director and officials of the president's civil chancery—items (c), (d), and (g)—since these were the only offices for which the power of dismissal was enumerated. As dismissal was not specified for item (b), PPS contended that, once the president named a successor, he had no authority to change it (except, presumably, in the event of death, incapacitation, or resignation of his designee). The flaw in this argument is that appointment of a successor was fundamentally different from appointment of judges and senators. The president had the power to appoint, but not dismiss, judges of the Tribunal of State and one third of the *Senat*. Since they served while the president who appointed them was in office, allowing the president power to remove them would have afforded him excessive powers to interfere in judicial and legislative matters. Constitutional remedies, not presidential prerogatives, were specified for removal of judges and senators. The president's successor took office after the presidency became vacant; it would have made no sense to define a presidential right to dismiss his successor and therefore such a power was not granted; likewise, it made no sense to deprive the president of the flexibility to change succession before he left office.

expressed will of RJN that the next president come from Poland and not the exile community.⁵ Its declaration concluded with the statement that PPS did not recognize Zaleski's presidency and demanded that Arciszewski take office.⁶ Arciszewski refused to resign from the office of prime minister, claiming that there was no legitimate president to whom he could tender his resignation. Zaleski dismissed Arciszewski and his government and appointed Tadeusz Bór-Komorowski.⁷

PPS, SP, SD, and NiD formed *Koncentracja Demokratyczna* (Democratic Concentration) and announced this new creation on June 30. Its political program was incoherent: it advocated agricultural reform and nationalization of major industries while leaving member parties to set their policy on all other issues; it was more of an opposition grouping than a political coalition with a common program. Cracks soon appeared. NiD favored making an agreement with Zaleski and joining Bór-Komorowski's government; in contrast, PPS refused to recognize Zaleski, although its foreign committee accepted Bór-Komorowski as prime minister. SP suspected that PPS was trying to form a bloc with SN and *Sanacja* and agreed to join the government only under the condition that the PSL also join. Bringing PSL into the discussion was no ruse. Mikołajczyk had returned to London.

After the election in Poland, Mikołajczyk resigned from the government but remained in the *Sejm* along with twenty-seven other PSL deputies. *Gazeta Ludowa* was heavily censored and was not permitted to print *Sejm* speeches made by PSL deputies, and PSL was not permitted radio airtime. The only avenue left to express their opinions was on the *Sejm* floor, and PSL deputies agreed to continue promoting their program there with the hope that foreign news correspondents would make their positions and protests known in the West.

This state of affairs did not last long. In October, Mikołajczyk learned that he, Stefan Korboński, and Wincenty Bryja were to be stripped of their

---

[5] Note that RJN had dissolved itself on July 1, 1945, nearly two years before Raczkiewicz changed his successor.

[6] The PPS claim that the constitution did not permit the president to change his successor presented an awkward problem, since Sosnkowski, who was very much alive and in good health in 1944, had not resigned the nomination; Raczkiewicz advised him that he was no longer the successor—that is, Raczkiewicz changed the nomination. PPS skirted this issue by claiming that Sosnkowski had resigned.

[7] After Bór-Komorowski's release from German captivity, Raczkiewicz appointed him commander in chief, but the British refused to recognize him. Compelled to find employment, he worked as an upholsterer.

parliamentary immunity, arrested, tried, and sentenced to death at the beginning of the next *Sejm* session. He understood Stalinist justice and knew there would be no semblance of a fair trial. Further, he feared that their executions would spark protests followed by violent repressions, and he wanted no further bloodshed. He decided to leave Poland.

On Friday, October 17, Mikołajczyk sent an urgent message to an official at the American embassy asking for a meeting; that evening, Embassy First Secretary George D. Andrews went to his residence. Mikołajczyk detailed the information he had received, explained his conclusion that he needed to leave, and appealed for assistance. Andrews reported to Ambassador Stanton Griffs, who without hesitation agreed to help. Over the weekend, British and American officials identified three feasible escape routes and reviewed them with Mikołajczyk. Their first option was to make use of an American truck convoy in Warsaw to retrieve the bodies of American war dead buried in Poland; Mikołajczyk would be concealed in a casket. However, the convoy's departure date would cause Mikołajczyk to miss a PSL meeting, and his absence would undoubtedly raise suspicion and prompt UB to issue an alert; further, it would be embarrassing for him and PSL if he were to be caught hidden in such a manner. Another option was to slip across the Polish–Czechoslovak border, head west, and cross into the American zone of Germany. The risks in this plan were the need to cross two borders and transit Czechoslovakia itself, which was increasingly under communist control.[8] Their third option was to spirit him out on a foreign ship through Gdynia; this was the plan chosen.

On Monday, while Mikołajczyk attended his PSL meeting, workers at the American embassy loaded a truck with crates belonging to the British chargé d'affaires destined for London. Early that evening, Mikołajczyk crawled into a void in the crates, and the truck left for Gdynia. Along the route it was stopped at nine checkpoints but was subjected to only one cursory inspection. At 3:30 a.m., it arrived at the house of Walpole Davis, head of the Moore–McCormack Steamship Lines office; the truck proceeded to the port. Mikołajczyk rested briefly, and at 6:45 a.m., Davis drove him to a pier where the British cargo ship *Baltavia* was preparing to depart. While Mikołajczyk waited in the car, Davis walked to the ship. Seeing the crates from the British embassy, Davis put on a show for the guard stationed at the gangplank, expressing his exasperation at having to

---

[8] Concerns about the safety of escape through Czechoslovakia were valid. Wincenty Bryja and two other PSL activists (Maria Hulewiczowa and Mieczysław Dąbrowski) left Poland using this route and were captured. They were returned to Warsaw and imprisoned without charges until 1951, when they were tried and found guilty of being saboteurs and spies.

accommodate them at the last minute. His ploy was effective; he persuaded the guard to bring this to the attention of the customs office. While the guard was away, Mikołajczyk hurried aboard, and the captain concealed him in the ship's sick bay. *Baltavia* sailed at 9:30 and crossed into international waters at noon. Mikołajczyk had escaped.[9]

His return to London could hardly be called triumphant. He received a frosty reception from much of the émigré political community and was considered a traitor to the Polish cause. He called on Churchill, who expressed his surprise that he was alive. Churchill gave him warm words, but no assistance. His usefulness had been spent.

However, Mikołajczyk still held considerable sway. Many Western politicians respected him, and his escape from Warsaw made him a symbol of resistance to communism. He had supporters in the émigré community, particularly in the United States and France. *Koncentracja Demokratyczna* sought to bring PSL into the fold, but Mikołajczyk had greater ambitions. Unlike Zaleski and the exile parties, he could claim that, under adverse conditions, PSL had won a national election in Poland; that it was unable to form a government due to wholesale fraud and persecution only bolstered his image. In effect, he could lay claim to a mandate from the people in Poland and fashion that into an assertion that he was free Poland's leader. The most promising field for him to press his claim was the United States.

As the postwar world took shape, the United States emerged as the Soviet Union's principal rival, and Mikołajczyk saw it as the only effective counterweight to Soviet power. He also recognized that, while the Polish politicians were in the United Kingdom, the bulk of Polonia was across the Atlantic. More than five million Americans were of Polish descent, and a good number held political offices. Their political potential had been demonstrated by Roosevelt's efforts to conceal the Yalta agreements until after the 1944 election and by the backlash in the 1946 congressional elections.[10] Moreover, the Polish-American community was well organized. In contrast, Poles were a small minority in Britain, numbering perhaps 160,000.[11] Other than a handful of friends in Parliament, they enjoyed little political influence, and there were no Polish MPs.

---

[9] In his book, Mikołajczyk presented a different scenario for how he left Poland and makes no mention of American or British assistance. Since his book was published in 1948, this presumably was a subterfuge to protect those who had helped him.

[10] In the 1946 American elections, Democrats lost a number of what they considered to be "safe" congressional seats due to the Polish vote. When analyzing losses in Chicago, Gael Sullivan, a Democratic Party operative, faulted the Poles for abandoning the party, calling them selfish for thinking Roosevelt abandoned Poland at Yalta.

[11] In 1949, an émigré organization counted 162,200 Poles in the UK.

Arthur Bliss Lane had become well acquainted with Mikołajczyk during his time in Warsaw.[12] Pleased by his extrication from Poland, Lane invited him to the United States. In December, Mikołajczyk traveled to Washington accompanied by fellow PSL escapees Kazimierz Bagiński, Stefan Korboński, and Paweł Zaleski.[13] They met with members of Congress, made public appearances, and gave lectures. They conferred with Department of State officials, who focused their attentions on Mikołajczyk. Their crucial event was a meeting with PAC President Rozmarek on December 15–16, 1947, where Mikołajczyk and Rozmarek reached an agreement for PSL to cooperate with PAC. Through this stroke of luck, Mikołajczyk and PSL had gained access to PAC's organizational apparatus and the Polish-American press. His influence and power base now appeared to be considerable. But American adulation for Mikołajczyk was not universal. Of the sixteen members of PAC's executive committee, four opposed the agreement. Critics pointed out its weak condemnation of Yalta, failure to mention the matter of Poland's eastern border, and lack of any reference to the London government; they also rebuked Rozmarek for not consulting the executive committee prior to coming to agreement.

Regardless, Mikołajczyk embarked on a speaking tour in January 1948, starting in Chicago and culminating in May at the PAC convention in Philadelphia. Rozmarek formally announced the agreement but did not get the reception he had expected. As Mikołajczyk stepped up to the podium, shouts of "Traitor!" rang through the hall, and the KNAPP representatives left before he could speak. In the aftermath, KNAPP formally withdrew from PAC, followed by the Polish Roman Catholic Union of America.

Almost from its inception, *Koncentracja Demokratyczna* was ineffective. Proposals were floated to expand, restructure, or replace it, and PSL figured prominently in each. SD suggested forming a coalition of what it called "truly democratic" parties that had counterparts in Poland—that is, SD, SP, PPS, and PSL. Another concept was a caucus of leftist parties. PPS and NiD held talks with PSL to draw it in, but Mikołajczyk vetoed this idea, claiming that *Koncentracja Demokratyczna* had abandoned its democratic principles by holding talks with Zaleski's government and had reduced itself to chasing money and position. Mikołajczyk also differed

---

[12] Arthur Bliss Lane was ambassador to Poland from August 4, 1945, until February 24, 1947. In 1948, he published *I Saw Poland Betrayed*, a memoir of his time in Poland.
[13] Korboński and his wife escaped to Sweden shortly after Mikołajczyk left Poland.

from *Koncentracja Demokratyczna* parties on the very need for an exile government.

The appellation "legalists" gained currency to describe people holding firm to the principle of government continuity in the form used since September 1939. While *Koncentracja Demokratyczna* parties may have opposed Zaleski's presidency, in the main they respected legalist principles and based their programs on them. However, some exiles rejected legalism, considering it to be irrelevant, anachronistic, and a hindrance to cooperation with Western governments. Their preferred alternative was a national committee composed of representatives from a cross-section of political and social groups, a structure in favor among other émigré communities from Soviet Bloc nations. Its greatest advantage was that Western nations could cooperate with a national committee without causing major diplomatic rifts, whereas recognition of a government would be construed by Warsaw and Moscow as a break in relations. Unfortunately for proponents of a national committee structure, most émigré politicians saw no need to form one since they had a government that had not ceded power and therefore had a legitimate claim to continuity.

Mikołajczyk and PSL championed the concept of a national committee. In contrast, PPS held a firmly legalist position, and SP claimed these issues to be of secondary importance that could be tackled later. In June 1948, leaders of PSL, PPS, and SP met in Paris to negotiate an agreement. Some weeks later, they agreed to a formula that would not base itself on the constitution, and in mid-November they announced the creation of *Porozumienie Stronnictw Demokratycznych* (PSD, Accord of Democratic Parties). Its socialist-leaning program included drafting a new constitution, nationalizing major industries and banks, and land reform. Opponents of the Yalta border were cheered by the declaration that Poland was not bound by Soviet annexation of Polish lands. PPS leadership was pleased that the agreement prevented Mikołajczyk from forming a national committee, whereas Mikołajczyk and his associates, delighted that they were not compelled to renounce their anti-legalist and anti-constitution positions, claimed victory.

Agreement by party leaders did not mean party members were united behind them. Dissent was particularly strong in PPS. Jan Kwapiński, a PPS leader, refused to sign the agreement and sent letters criticizing it to PPS members. Arciszewski, who signed the agreement, received irate letters from party members demanding an explanation. Émigré newspapers in the legalist camp were harshly critical. None of this deterred Mikołajczyk.

A few days after PSD was announced, he gave a speech at a PSL congress in France. He launched into a spirited defense of his actions in postwar Poland, rejected the concept of legalism, and repudiated the April Constitution. There was no doubt where he stood politically, and he underscored this by relocating to the United States.

Despite these differences, PSD member parties had common ground in their opposition to Zaleski, and he provided a fresh justification by appointing *III Rada Narodowa*, reactivating an institution that hadn't existed since 1945. Zaleski acted in response to a campaign calling for reorganization of the exile government to make it more representative of the émigré community. Participation by legacy political parties was out of the question, so Zaleski populated *III Rada Narodowa* with over forty men and women from LNP, SL *"Wolność,"* the Foreign Committee of SP, military veterans, and the clergy. Its first session was held in June 1949. PSD dismissed *III Rada Narodowa* as non-democratic and non-representative.

As *III Rada Narodowa* convened, PSD was drifting from its founding principles. Growing tension between the West and the Soviet Union fueled expectations that war was imminent, and émigré politicians from Soviet-controlled nations saw the possibility of liberation. Now, cooperation with Western governments became perceived as an urgent necessity. PSD sought to meet that need, but to do so it had to expand to include political opponents. In Western Europe, preparations were underway to form the Council of Europe, and PSD took on the task of creating a delegation. Its proposal would have brought SN, SD, and NiD representatives into the delegation, but they could not reach agreement. Arciszewski, who had a strong desire to bring in SN, was critical of PSD's inability to achieve tangible results. PSL blamed PPS and Arciszewski for PSD's ineffectiveness.

American interest in exile politics was intensifying; specifically, Washington was considering the role political exiles could play in the Cold War. In 1949, a group called the National Committee for a Free Europe (NCFE) was founded in New York. NCFE was presented as a private organization advocating for freedom for nations under Soviet control; its most visible component was Radio Free Europe. NCFE and Radio Free Europe conducted public fund drives in the United States, but their functions were overseen by the Department of State and the Department of Defense, and most of their funding came from the CIA. Exile politicians and parties, perennially strapped for cash, were enticed to join by NCFE's offer of money, offices, and support. Governments-in-exile could not participate;

only national committees would be admitted and could receive funding.[14] Committees representing Bulgaria, Czechoslovakia, Hungary, Poland, Romania, and Yugoslavia were invited to join. Zaleski and members of his government could not engage with NCFE. Mikołajczyk was another matter, and he seized this opportunity to advance his vision. A committee would require broader political representation than PSD provided. SN and NiD would have to be included, but neither was about to abandon legalism; further, strong support of legalism had also become clear within PPS. A further motivation to resist Mikołajczyk was the underlying concern that he would use such a body to advance his personal authority. This was no irrational fear. Mikołajczyk had many contacts in the United States and was held in high esteem by the American government, and he had received assurance from one of NCFE's founders that no Polish committee would be recognized unless it included PSL.

Mikołajczyk's expectation that American financial support would prove to be irresistible was incorrect. PPS, SN, and NiD formed *Rada Polityczna* (Political Council) in October 1949 with legalism as a founding principle. It planned to expand by bringing in SP and SD and aimed to include PSL, but knowing that Mikołajczyk would never agree, its approach was to persuade two of his associates, Korboński and Bagiński, to join. Both were expelled from PSL for their actions, and they created an offshoot party, PSL *"Odłam Jedności Narodowej"* ("Group of National Unity"). Despite its best efforts, *Rada Polityczna* was unable to persuade SP and SD to join; they remained allied with PSL. But formation of *Rada Polityczna* spelled the end of PSD. In May 1950, PSL, SP, and SD established *Polski Narodowy Komitet Demokratyczny* (PNKD, Polish National Democratic Committee).

Three political groups were now competing for the loyalty of the émigré community and for the attention of Western governments: Zaleski's government, *Rada Polityczna*, and PNKD. *Rada Polityczna*, however, was about to debase itself by becoming entangled in a tragic scandal.

Illicitly crossing into Poland was risky, but during the first postwar years, experienced couriers could make the journey with a high probability of success. Their services were in great demand; couriers delivered money and equipment to WiN and other opposition groups and smuggled news

---

[14] This stipulation was necessary since the United States had recognized the Soviet-sponsored governments in each country.

into the country, most notably *Przegląd Polski (Polish Review)* in quantities often reaching two thousand copies.[15] American intelligence services had their own needs. They sought reliable information from within an increasingly opaque Poland and wanted to establish a covert network. They had the financial wherewithal to support this, but it would take time to build their own operations. Poland's exiles presented an opportunity to accelerate these plans.

As early as 1948, representatives from SN were meeting with the CIA. In a 1949 meeting with the Department of State, SN President Tadeusz Bielecki declared that his party had many unofficial channels into Poland. Convinced it had found the right partner, the CIA reached agreement with SN in the second half of 1950. SN agreed to expand its network of agents and informants, prepare a radio network, and interrogate refugees; in return, the United States would provide financial and material assistance. In 1951, SN concluded a similar agreement with British intelligence. SN established two communications bases in West Germany: *Północ* (North) was initially located in Oerlinghausen and later relocated to Mülheim; *Południe* (South) first was in Rotach, then was moved to Munich and later to Berg.

A source of potential couriers was readily available in the nearly one hundred refugee camps still functioning in western Germany. Their residents had been waiting years for an opportunity to resettle in the West, and several hundred were enticed to volunteer with offers of money, new clothing, a trip to the United States, and the opportunity to take action against the communist government. After training, they would travel to Poland, deliver money, equipment, and publications to their contacts, collect information, and return to base.

Neither SN nor its recruits fully understood the risks. UB agents had been operating in refugee camps practically from their first days,[16] and it did not take long for them to infiltrate this operation. Their work was unwittingly facilitated by SN personnel who were almost without exception inexperienced in covert operations and at times acted amateurishly. Couriers were being arrested on arrival, relieved of their shipments, and interrogated. Some agreed to work for UB, while others divulged their contacts. Hundreds of thousands of dollars intended for underground groups fell into UB's hands, and over four hundred people, couriers as well as underground contacts, were arrested. Most were imprisoned, and some were executed.

---

[15] *Przegląd Polski* was published in London starting in 1946; it ceased publication in 1949 due to lack of funds.

[16] UB was not alone. Both the United States and the United Kingdom had agents active in refugee camps.

By the end of 1952, UB decided to expose the operation by staging a defection. In December, two of its operatives from *Południe* traveled to Berlin and made their way to the Polish consulate. There, they identified themselves as agents employed by the London government and claimed they no longer wanted to serve the Americans and British. Their story was broadcast on Radio Warsaw on December 31; on January 1, *Trybuna Ludu* ran an article titled "*Nie chcą więcej służyć wywiadowi USA*" ("They no longer want to serve American intelligence"). The London government was depicted as in the pay of the United States and the United Kingdom, and those loyal to it were portrayed as pawns.

The news reverberated through Polish London and was dubbed "*Sprawa Bergu*" (Berg matter) and "*afera Bergu*" (Berg affair). Zaleski charged *Rada Polityczna* with spying; journalist Stanisław Mackiewicz accused them of "trading in death." It was soon learned that SN had received more than one million dollars from American and British intelligence agencies. SN's inept foray into covert operations intelligence was more than an embarrassment; it tainted the reputations of *Rada Polityczna* and SN for years to come.[17]

WiN, one of the intended recipients of American aid, had also been penetrated. WiN was so thoroughly compromised that, for the last five years of its existence, its commander was an undercover UB officer. By December 1952, WiN, the last underground military organization loyal to the London government, had been completely destroyed.[18]

UB's success in penetrating the Berg organization and WiN came on the heels of its profitable venture to seize FON's assets. At war's end, FON's holdings were considerable: 350 kilograms of gold, 2,408 kilograms of silver, and $2.5 million in gold and silver coins and banknotes. As a military asset, FON was the responsibility of General Marian Kukiel, head of the Ministry of National Defense. Kukiel decided to use FON to help AK veterans and their families. Delivering this assistance presented a challenge since he needed to find an organization independent of the Warsaw government. Caritas,[19] a Catholic relief organization, provided food and medical care throughout Poland, and Kukiel chose it for this task. He appointed

---

[17] *Egzekutywa Zjednoczenia Narodowego*, successor to *Rada Polityczna*, conducted an investigation of *Sprawa Bergu*. EZN's report can be found in *Zeszyty Historyczne* #79.

[18] A few individual WiN soldiers carried on after the organization was disbanded; no longer able to effectively mount resistance, their motive for staying in hiding was to avoid prosecution. The last WiN soldier, Józef Franczak, was killed by a ZOMO unit in a village near Lublin in October 1963.

[19] Caritas had been active in Poland prior to the war and resumed activities in 1945.

General Stanisław Tatar to transfer FON to Caritas. Tatar was assisted by Lieutenant Colonel Marian Utnik and Colonel Stanisław Nowicki; they were known as "*Komitet Trzech*" (Committee of the Three).

After the war, Warsaw attempted to gain control of Second Republic assets in the West but achieved limited success. FON, however, remained a tantalizing objective, and Tatar was known to have an accommodationist attitude towards the Soviet Union. Intelligence agents learned that Tatar was planning a trip to Paris in 1945, and Poland's ambassador to Switzerland, Jerzy Putrament,[20] was dispatched to make contact with him. Putrament succeeded in tracking him down and proposed transferring FON to the government, arguing that it could best ensure secure control and distribution. Tatar agreed to hand over a small amount as a test. Late in 1945, Tatar gave $100,000 in cash and one hundred gold coins to a consul named Sobolewski from the Polish embassy. Sobolewski and the funds promptly vanished. Although Sobolewski later resurfaced, the funds were never accounted for.

Despite this, Tatar remained in contact with Warsaw's representatives. Colonel Józef Kuropieska had been posted to London as part of the Polish military mission, and in 1946 he began meeting with Tatar. Initially, Kuropieska used him as an unofficial advisor on émigré policy matters; as their collaboration progressed, he directed their discussions to financial affairs. In early 1947, Tatar handed him a note stating that FON's assets were valued at about $3 million. Kuropieska convinced him that these funds would have a greater public impact if they were used to fund Warsaw's three-year plan. In March, Tatar met with Colonel Stanisław Flato[21] in London and confirmed that *Komitet Trzech* intended to hand over FON. Knowing they were acting contrary to orders, Tatar, Utnik, and Nowicki surreptitiously prepared the transfer. Ten metal chests were filled with 350 kilograms of gold, $2.5 million in cash, and more than five hundred files from the archives of the Polish Army General Staff. The date and location of the transfer are unclear. In one account, the transfer occurred on June 19. Another claims that two shipments were made in July. The first left London on July 3, and the second accompanied the coffin of General Lucjan Żeligowski,[22] who had planned to return to Poland but died on

---

[20] Jerzy Putrament would later be portrayed as Gamma, the Slave of History, in *The Captive Mind* by Czesław Miłosz.

[21] Col. Stanisław Flato served in Division II of the General Staff of the Polish Army, a military intelligence unit.

[22] General Lucjan Żeligowski had been an officer in the Imperial Russian Army officer and was one of the organizers of the 1st Polish Corps in Russia. He escaped to France after the fall of Poland in 1939 and moved to London, serving on *Rada Narodowa*. After the war, Żeligowski planned to return to Poland but died before he could do so.

July 9. Tatar arranged shipment of his remains to Warsaw. Boxes filled with FON assets accompanied Żeligowski's remains.

Tatar, Utnik, and Nowicki brought the wrath of the exile community on themselves. In contrast, Warsaw rewarded them. In 1947, Tatar was issued a consular passport.[23] In July 1948, Tatar and Nowicki were awarded the Order of Polonia Restituta *(Order Odrodzenia Polski)*, and Utnik was promoted to colonel while Tatar was promised a leadership position in LWP. On November 4, 1949, the three returned to Poland and, to their surprise, were arrested upon arrival and charged with stealing gold from FON and attempting to use it to fund espionage activities. For the next two years, they were incarcerated, interrogated, and tortured; in 1951, they were put on trial. On August 13, 1951, Tatar was sentenced to life imprisonment; Utnik and Nowicki each received a 15-year sentence.[24]

With the exception of the silver in Tolouse, FON's assets were held by military intelligence. In 1948, they were transferred to *Narodowy Bank Polski* (NBP, National Bank of Poland). Records indicate that 208 kilograms of gold and less than $100,000 were received by NBP. A total of 142 kilograms of gold and more than $2 million was unaccounted for. NBP records indicate that 122 kilograms of gold was melted into bars in 1951. The most valuable jewelry was given to the civil chancellery of the president of Poland and was then given as gifts to dignitaries. Other jewelry was sold in Desa and Jubiler shops;[25] the rest was transferred to *Muzeum Narodowe* (National Museum).[26] None of FON's assets were used to assist AK veterans as Kukiel had intended or as Putrament had promised.

Tatar, Utnik, and Nowicki had returned to a country rapidly undergoing Sovietization. Bierut ousted PPR General Secretary Gomułka and took control of the party, now known as *Polska Zjednoczona Partia Robotnicza* (PZPR, Polish United Workers' Party). PZPR was formed by forcibly incorporating PPS into PPR in 1948. Two other parties, SD and ZSL, held *Sejm* seats, but both were controlled by PZPR. Stalin ordered Bierut to appoint Rokossovsky as minister of defense and marshal of Poland. Rokossovsky assigned several thousand Soviet officers to Poland's military. A Soviet

---

[23] Consular passports were issued by the Warsaw government to Poles living abroad.

[24] Tatar, Utnik, and Nowicki were released from prison and rehabilitated in 1956, but none returned to military service. Nowicki died in 1963, Tatar in 1980, and Utnik in 2003.

[25] Desa was a chain of shops created by the Communist government to deal in antiques and art; Jubiler was a state-owned chain of jewelry shops.

[26] Some of the remaining FON artifacts are displayed at the Royal Castle in Warsaw.

admiral commanded the navy, a Soviet general commanded the air force, and by the end of 1952, forty-three of the fifty-six generals in the Polish Army were Soviet.

PZPR's objective was to build a new Poland based on the Soviet model. Emphasis was placed on heavy industry, such as steelmaking, vehicle manufacturing, and shipbuilding at the expense of consumer goods and housing. All but the smallest businesses were nationalized after the war,[27] and agriculture was to be collectivized. The economy was centrally planned to the extent that prices for food and consumer goods were set in Warsaw. New schools were built throughout the country, and illiteracy was sharply reduced; however, only Soviet-approved versions of history were taught, and economics education adhered to Marxist-Leninist principles. The sole approved form of artistic expression was Socialist Realism, a genre in which smiling, tanned, muscular workers were portrayed as heroic figures. Historic figures who were uncomfortable for PZPR or Moscow were erased from public life. Their names were replaced by those of acceptable, if occasionally obscure, socialist heroes or politicians currently in power.[28]

PZPR controlled most aspects of society except for religious life. UB had infiltrated every religion,[29] but over ninety percent of the nation belonged to the Roman Catholic Church, making it the most formidable obstacle in PZPR's path to attaining absolute power. PZPR would not tolerate the existence of an alternative authority, but neutralizing the Church would be problematic. Severing it from the Vatican was unacceptable, as this would cause international repercussions and infuriate the very people it was governing. PZPR developed a strategy of publicly supporting freedom of religion while attacking the Church from within. Warsaw funded repair and reconstruction of war-damaged churches and made no effort to restrict religious practice, and it courted the Church's hierarchy for support. Simultaneously, UB took steps to gain control of the Church. It set up *Stowarzyszenie PAX* (PAX Association) and recruited priests who would cooperate with PAX in exchange for material rewards; PZPR referred to them as "patriotic priests." By the late 1940s, bishops, priests, and nuns

---

[27] Nationalization is the seizure of private business by the state; in the Soviet model it is done without compensation.
[28] In 1952, *Uniwersytet Wrocławski* (University of Wrocław) was renamed *Uniwersytet Wrocławski im. Bolesława Bieruta* (Bolesław Bierut University of Wrocław). It retained this name until 1989.
[29] For example, UB took control of the Polish Autocephalous Orthodox Church in the postwar period, and its successors maintained that control until the fall of communism. Collaborators were recruited from all ranks of the clergy to ensure control over church activities. In 1989, every member of its Holy Council of Bishops was a collaborator.

were being arrested.³⁰ Trials were held, and priests were sentenced to death; PAX publicly supported these actions. Terrorizing the Church did not work as intended. Parishioners avoided "patriotic priests" and would not budge from their support for arrested and imprisoned religious leaders.

Infiltration and persecution weren't achieving the desired results, so UB began a project to replace the Church altogether. It turned its attention to *Polski Narodowy Kościół Katolicki* (PNKK, Polish National Catholic Church), a small independent church with its roots in the United States³¹ that took over some abandoned German Evangelical churches in the Recovered Territories. UB viewed PNKK with suspicion owing to its fealty to an American bishop but was intrigued by its similarities to the Roman Catholic Church. Clergy used the same titles and wore the same clerical garments and vestments, and their church buildings were practically indistinguishable from one another. Their two most visible differences were language (Mass in Roman Catholic churches was in Latin, while in PNKK churches it was in Polish) and clerical celibacy (PNKK permitted married clergy). For UB, it was an appealing substitute.³² In 1951, PNKK succumbed to UB pressure, declared itself autonomous from PNCC, and refashioned its name to *Kościół Polskokatolicki* (Polish Catholic Church). Priests opposed to communism were expelled, PZPR's national holidays were celebrated in church services, congratulatory messages were sent to Party figures, and bishops appeared with communist authorities on state occasions.³³ UB was confident that, with the right leadership, *Kościół Polskokatolicki* would supplant the Roman Catholic Church in twenty to thirty years.

---

[30] Bishop Czesław Kaczmarek of Kielce was among the arrested. He was the ordinary of Kielce during the 1946 pogrom. His report placed responsibility on the NKVD, and he gave a copy to American Ambassador Arthur Bliss Lane. When arrested, he was charged with espionage on behalf of the United States and the Vatican and for illegal currency trading. He was tortured, tried, and sentenced to twelve years imprisonment.

[31] PNCC emerged from a conflict between some Polish priests and the predominantly Irish and German hierarchy in the United States. Several bishops assigned Polish priests to parishes with few if any Poles and assigned Irish or German priests to Polish parishes. Laypeople in Polish parishes complained that they could not communicate well with their priests, could not understand their sermons, and could not make good confessions due to their struggles with English. When appeals to the Vatican were rejected, several priests and their congregations rejected the authority of their bishops and created the Polish National Catholic Church, aligning itself with the Old Catholic Church in Utrecht. Although this was not part of the reason for the schism, PNCC eschewed Latin in favor of Polish for services. PNCC also adopted new doctrines, including rejection of the First Vatican Council and permitting married clergy.

[32] As usual, Moscow provided a template. In the early 1920s, a reform movement had emerged in the Russian Orthodox Church that was exploited by the Cheka to weaken the church and its influence on society. The Soviet authorities used this movement to provoke a schism.

[33] The appearance of bishops at official events was meant to give the impression that the Roman Catholic Church supported the communists. Since *Kościół Polskokatolicki* bishops and priests dressed in the same manner as their Roman Catholic counterparts, it was impossible to tell that they belonged to a different church simply by looking at them.

It found its leader in Maksymilian Rode, a suspended Roman Catholic priest. He supported the new government, was frustrated that his career was not advancing as rapidly as he would have liked, and was alleged to have violated his vow of celibacy. In 1956, he left the priesthood and got married, but his time in the secular state was short. *Urząd do Spraw Wyznań* (UdSW, Office for Religious Affairs) summoned Rode to Warsaw and informed him that he would become vicar general of *Kościół Polskokatolicki*. Rode obliged, was ordained bishop, and took charge of his new church. He received generous assistance from the government; he and his bishops and priests received salaries from the state. Rode considered Cardinal Wyszyński to be his rival and frequently attacked him in the press. Initially, his government handlers were pleased with his efforts to grow his church, but by the middle of the 1960s he was criticized for his growing independence from UdSW, his failure to attract converts, and what was viewed as his excessive pride, this last charge stemming from having himself declared primate of *Kościół Polskokatolicki*. He was removed from his position; his replacement fared little better in winning converts but worked well with UdSW, and he and his hierarchy continued to support PZPR.[34]

Kultura, a Paris-based periodical, was a threat to Poland. That was the logical conclusion to draw from Warsaw's ban of it in 1950. Its publisher, *Instytut Literacki*, was founded in Italy in 1946 by Jerzy Giedroyc to meet military and civilian demand for books in the Polish language. Within a year, he introduced *Kultura*. It published works from a profusion of notable writers, many of whom were not in favor with the communist authorities; subject matter ranged from literature and poetry to history and current events. Polish writers such as Gustaw Herling-Grudziński, Witold Gombrowicz, and Czesław Straszewicz shared pages with the likes of George Orwell, T. S. Eliot, Albert Camus, Arthur Koestler, and Antoine Saint-Exupéry; in time they were joined by writers from inside the Soviet bloc. *Kultura* quickly became a highly influential émigré publication and was widely read in Poland and in the West. Its independence from both Warsaw and London earned it the admiration and trust of its readers.

Warsaw's proscription of *Kultura* did not eliminate demand or interest. Copies were regularly smuggled in and were widely circulated amongst the intelligentsia, and writers in Poland had their works printed in the periodical, usually under pseudonyms.

---

[34] Rode's successor was Bishop Julian Pękala.

As Zaleski made plans to convene *III Rada Narodowa*, Bór-Komorowski requested to be released from the duties of prime minister. Zaleski agreed and replaced him with Tadeusz Tomaszewski. In 1939, Tomaszewski was appointed to head *Najwyższa Izba Kontroli* (NIK, Supreme Audit Office)[35] and stayed in this position throughout the war and the immediate postwar years. Although he had been a PPS member since 1901, Tomaszewski was expelled when he agreed to serve in Zaleski's government. He was appointed prime minister on April 7, 1949, and was named as Zaleski's successor on June 9.

Stanisław Dołęga-Modrzewski,[36] head of the Treasury and Budget Commission for *III Rada Narodowa*, called a meeting for the evening of August 10 to review funding for the proposed budget. After Tomaszewski spoke for the second time, he slumped into his chair. Commission members immediately provided first aid. An ambulance arrived within ten minutes and rushed him to St. Mary Abbot's hospital,[37] but nothing could be done. He was pronounced dead that evening.

Tomaszewski's funeral was held on August 16 in the Polish church on Devonia Road, Islington.[38] In attendance were Zaleski, Anders, members of Tomaszewski's government, *Rada Narodowa* members, and hundreds of others. He was buried at St. Mary's Catholic Cemetery, Kensal Green; his grave is next to that of his wife, who had died in 1941.

To fill the unexpected vacancy, Zaleski selected General Roman Władysław Odzierzyński. The new prime minister was a native of Lwów and a veteran of the Austro-Hungarian Army in the Great War. He later joined the Polish Army, fought in the Polish–Soviet War of 1919–1920, and continued in the military throughout the interwar period. He avoided captivity in 1939 and arrived in France by way of Romania. In 1942, he was dispatched to Iraq and took command of the artillery in the Second Polish Corps. After the war, he settled in the United Kingdom and served as minister of defense and minister of the interior in Tomaszewski's government.

Zaleski also needed a new successor. He chose Władysław Anders.

---

[35] *Najwyższa Izba Kontroli* was (and remains) an independent body responsible for auditing government spending. In the April Constitution, the president named NIK's head.

[36] His real name was Stanisław Kauzik; he used the pseudonym Dołęga-Modrzewski in exile.

[37] St. Mary Abbot's Hospital was located on Marloes Road in Kensington; it closed in 1992.

[38] In 1930, the Polish Catholic Mission in England and Wales purchased a church building at 2 Devonia Road, Islington; this became the permanent location of the first Polish parish in the United Kingdom. Its official name is *Polska Parafia pw. Matki Boskiej Częstochowskiej i św. Kazimierza* (Polish Parish of Our Lady of Częstochowa and St. Casimir).

Around the time of Tomaszewski's death, the pro-Warsaw, London-based newspaper *Tygodnik Polski* ceased publication in what would become embarrassing circumstances for the Polish embassy. For Warsaw, the abundance of Polish-language newspapers and magazines published in the West was a problem. Almost without exception, these publications were unfriendly towards, if not openly hostile to, the communist government and hampered efforts to convince émigrés to return to Poland. They also constituted an opposition press that was only too happy to bring to light what Warsaw would have preferred to keep under wraps. *Tygodnik Polski* was launched as a component of Warsaw's plan to advance a positive image of the new Poland while simultaneously providing a platform to influence public opinion about exile political and military leaders. Its editor, Bernard Singer, had served in the Polish Army during the war but was now collaborating with Poland's intelligence service.[39] Ostensibly published by a citizens' council, *Tygodnik Polski* was funded by the embassy.

The appearance of this new paper was accompanied by speculation about the source of Singer's funding. Rumors intensified as the paper's praise for the Warsaw government became more effusive while its tone towards exile figures and organizations was increasingly harsh. In 1948, Singer went too far. *Tygodnik Polski* ran an article by an anonymous author claiming to have attended a recent SPK congress. The author accused SPK's board of corruption and fraud and called for their arrests; he further accused SPK's newspaper *Polska Walcząca* of complicity by covering up the scandal. *Tygodnik Polski* claimed that these transgressions led to resignations by several SPK leaders and demanded publication of detailed meeting minutes and financial statements.

On June 30, the former president of SPK's British section and ten board members filed a libel suit against Singer and the printer demanding compensation; they also filed an injunction prohibiting *Tygodnik Polski* from publishing further defamatory allegations. Singer had no documentary evidence to support his accusations, nor could he produce any witnesses to corroborate his story. The English lawyer retained by the embassy concluded that the plaintiffs were almost certain to win the case and would likely be awarded substantial damages, so the embassy decided to pursue a settlement.

Warsaw was anxious to end the case quietly; it would have been highly embarrassing if the connection between *Tygodnik Polski* and the embassy

---

[39] Singer's code name was "Rex."

were exposed. It also did not want to risk an outcome that would have resulted in closure of *Tygodnik Polski*. Its efforts were focused on reaching a financial settlement that would not come from the embassy or from Singer; it also wanted to avoid an apology by Singer. In March 1949, the plaintiffs dropped their demand for a printed apology and accepted a £6,000 settlement and an agreement prohibiting the defendants from publishing similar articles. News of the settlement was published on the first page of *Polska Walcząca* along with a report that Singer had apologized to the offended parties. *Dziennik Polski i Dziennik Żołnierza* made it clear that it understood who was behind *Tygodnik Polski* and noted that the slur significantly improved SPK's financial position.

Singer, however, had not learned his lesson. In 1950, *Dziennik Polski i Dziennik Żołnierza* filed another libel suit against *Tygodnik Polski*. Again the embassy paid a settlement, but this time *Tygodnik Polski* would not survive. Publication ended that summer.

Civil disputes such as these, as well as criminal cases, fell under the jurisdiction of British courts, but there was no system to adjudicate matters of honor. Shortly after the war, AK veterans established a court of honor that heard cases involving dishonorable actions or breaches of etiquette, and ZPWB organized an adjudicating committee to resolve disputes within the émigré community.[40] In 1947, Bór-Komorowski's government took the first steps towards creating a judicial system. In 1947, it developed a detailed outline of a civil court system and drafted a presidential decree to announce its establishment. It was never implemented,[41] but the matter was not dead. In July 1950, Tomaszewski presented his proposal for a judicial system at a Council of Ministers meeting and justified it by noting the existence of adjudicating committees and citizens' courts in many exile communities. He included a mechanism for handling civil cases to provide émigrés with an affordable venue to resolve issues in their own language. *Rada Narodowa* unanimously approved his proposal in August, and Zaleski announced its creation in September.

Sądy Obywatelskie na Obczyźnie (Citizen's Courts Abroad) claimed no authority over criminal matters. Submission to its authority was voluntary, and parties to a case had to reside within the territory over which the court had jurisdiction. Its first (and, as it transpired, only) embodiment, *Sąd Obywatelski w Londynie* (Citizens' Court in London), claimed jurisdiction over

---

[40] *Zjednoczenie Polskie w Wielkiej Brytanii* (ZPWB, Federation of Poles in Great Britain) was founded in 1946 as an umbrella group to promote Polish culture, preserve Polish history, and promote the interests of Poles residing in the United Kingdom.

[41] No documentation has been found explaining why the decree was not published.

matters in the United Kingdom and consisted of two divisions: *Wydział Ogólny* (General Division) and *Wydział Cywilny* (Civil Division).

Wydział Ogólny was a court of honor empowered to hear three categories of cases: rehabilitation, violation of honor, and violation of ethics. It had the authority to restore honor to those whose character had been wrongly impugned, issue reprimands, bar individuals from holding positions in the government, exclude individuals from public life, and levy financial penalties.

Rehabilitation petitions were brought by individuals seeking to clear their names of what they contended were false accusations. These typically dated from the war and involved charges of collaboration or fraternization with German or Soviet occupiers. Rehabilitation accounted for half of the cases considered by *Wydział Ogólny*, and its rulings were respected by the émigré community. Violation-of-honor cases were brought by individuals contending that they had been victims of slanderous or libelous statements. Allegations of contact with the Warsaw government and accepting funds from its embassy fell into this category, as did accusations of financial irregularities within émigré organizations. In these cases, plaintiffs sought retraction of the statements in question. Violations of ethics were actions contrary to civic ethics or detrimental to Poland's image. Actions contrary to civic ethics meant cooperation with officials of the Warsaw government; actions detrimental to Poland's image are best illustrated by *Sprawa Bergu*, and this case showed the inherent weakness of *Wydział Ogólny*. Minister of Justice Okulicz petitioned the court to begin proceedings against those responsible, but the court declined to initiate action against two of the accused since they lived in West Germany, outside of the London court's jurisdiction, and those living in the United Kingdom refused to submit to the Court's authority.

Wydział Cywilny was an arbitration court, and its judgments were accepted as valid under British law. It provided émigrés with a venue to resolve financial and property disputes, but it was little used.

Sąd Obywatelski was an ambitious effort to create a judicial structure, but it also was little used. From 1951 through 1954, *Wydział Ogólny* considered twenty-six cases; in the same period, a total of nine cases were brought to *Wydział Cywilny*. No cases were heard after 1954 in either venue. The effectiveness of *Sąd Obywatelski* was hampered by its voluntary nature and its limited jurisdiction;[42] as émigrés became accustomed to their host countries, the need for a Polish civil court dwindled. Judicial appointments continued after 1954, but the court existed only on paper.

---

[42] Discussion of establishing a similar court in France came to nothing.

After the Second World War, Germany was administered by France, the United Kingdom, the United States, and the Soviet Union.[43] At first, they governed jointly, but within a few months the Soviet Union set up a communist government in its zone and, in 1949, officially named it the German Democratic Republic, commonly known as East Germany. That same year, the other powers ended administration of their zones and the Federal Republic of Germany, often referred to as West Germany, came into existence. East and West Germany had different political and economic systems but shared resentment over Germany's loss of territory. Those relocated from former East Prussia and the Recovered Territories numbered in the millions and had to be absorbed within Germany's new borders, but many clung to the hope that they would one day return to their home regions. This hope was nurtured by one fact: there had been no final peace conference and no border treaty.

This ambiguity caused uneasiness among the residents of the Recovered Territories. People evicted from east of the new Soviet border feared they were at risk of losing their new homes and their livelihoods if the German border was revised. Moscow-pressured East Germany signed the Agreement Concerning the Demarcation of the Established and the Existing Polish–German State Frontier, also known as the Treaty of Zgorzelec, in July 1950. Despite American and British assent at Yalta and Potsdam, neither recognized the Treaty of Zgorzelec's border, nor did France. West Germany considered the Recovered Territories to be "under Polish and Soviet administration." This suited the Soviet Union. For years, Moscow and Warsaw propagandized the border question by portraying the Soviet Union as Poland's friend and defender and depicting West Germany as an existential threat.

Moscow applied a different standard to Poland's eastern border. In 1950, it forced an exchange of 480 square kilometers near Zamość for a similar amount near Sanok. The Soviet Union took developed land that included towns, industry, farmland, and extensive coal deposits and gave Poland a depopulated area with no appreciable natural resources. The

---

[43] Initially, the United Kingdom had proposed a Polish zone of occupation in addition to the American, British, French, and Soviet zones. General Maczek and the First Polish Armored Division were the de facto occupation force in a 6,500-square-kilometer area of northwestern Germany bordering the Netherlands and had administrative headquarters in the city of Haren (Bór-Komorowski dubbed it *Maczków*, after General Maczek). This British proposal was abandoned due to Soviet opposition.

population was evicted and could take only what they could carry; most were resettled in the Recovered Territories. All houses, barns, buildings, and industrial equipment was now the property of the Soviet Union, and no compensation was paid. Within a few years, the Soviet Union had opened four large coal mines in the area. In return, Poland received rugged, mountainous land that was poorly suited for development.[44] But Moscow wanted more and was planning another exchange for an additional 1,300 square kilometers in the same area. It was only Stalin's death in 1953 that put an end to this scheme.

Mikołajczyk's venture into engaging the Polish-American community was soon emulated by Zaleski and by *Rada Polityczna*. In March 1950, *Rada Polityczna* opened an office in the United States headed by Stefan Korboński; it also opened an office in France. *III Rada Narodowa* completed its term on June 5, 1951; soon after, Zaleski began naming members to *IV Rada Narodowa*. Of its seventy-six members, eleven were from the United States.

As the government and *Rada Polityczna* expanded their presence, Mikołajczyk lost influence when his relationship with PAC soured. Rozmarek had already paid a high price for their agreement, and in the ensuing years he came to understand that Mikołajczyk styled himself as the leader of free Poland and expected PAC to subordinate itself to him. At the Polish National Alliance convention in 1951, Rozmarek declared that PAC was no longer cooperating with PNKD. He aligned PAC with Korboński's PSL faction and appealed to Zaleski, *Rada Polityczna*, and PNKD to put aside their differences and unify.

Zaleski's government was impoverished and needed revenue to fund its activities and maintain its properties. Assets that had been secured before recognition ceased were insufficient, so the government turned to the émigré community.

Skarb Narodowy (National Treasury) was created by a presidential decree and was incorporated as Danina Polska Ltd.[45] It was headed by Anders, and its source of revenue was donations. Every October, *Skarb Narodowy* conducted its annual appeal.

---

[44] No significant economic development occurred in this region until 1960, when construction began on a dam and hydroelectric plant on the San River. In 1969, the Solina Dam was completed and began generating electricity.

[45] Danina Polska Ltd. was incorporated March 1, 1950.

Émigrés responded with enthusiasm. In 1950, its first full year of operations, *Skarb Narodowy* collected £18,199; this increased to £22,000 in 1951, £30,000 in 1952, and £37,000 in 1953. Frequently, contributions were true sacrifices by donors of modest means.[46] *Skarb Narodowy* conducted well-attended annual public meetings. The 1952 meeting was held in Caxton Hall. A Polish eagle adorned the wall, along with charts and tables showing revenues, expenditures, and locations of its offices. Zaleski presided, and Anders was the main speaker; people from both sides of the political divide were in attendance. This occasion is notable since it was the last major event at which both Zaleski and Anders were present.

In 1952, Warsaw was still emerging from ashes and rubble. Its historical core was being painstakingly reconstructed, drab apartment blocks were built, and construction began on a massive, excessively ornate building along Ulica Marszałkowska, *Pałac Kultury i Nauki im. Józefa Stalina* (Josef Stalin Palace of Culture and Science). Officially a gift from the Soviet Union, it was nevertheless funded by Poland. With forty-two floors, it would dominate the city's skyline[47] and serve as a symbol of Soviet dominance.[48]

A few months later, and exactly eight years after PKWN declared itself to be the government, Poland had a new constitution and a new name. *Konstytucja Polskiej Rzeczypospolitej Ludowej* codified a socialist system based on the Soviet model and renamed the country *Rzeczpospolita Polska Ludowa* (PRL, Polish People's Republic). It made the *Sejm* the highest state authority and abolished the presidency, replacing it with the seventeen-member *Rada Państwa* (Council of State). PZPR was not mentioned, but it remained the true power; *Rada Państwa* and the *Sejm* simply approved and carried out its decisions. Stalin personally edited its draft.

Stalin's oversight came to an end within a year. On March 6, 1953, TASS announced that he had died the previous day from a cerebral

---

[46] In the early 1950s, even a £1 contribution was a significant sum. To put this amount into perspective, Krzysztof Głuchowski's first job as a draftsman in postwar London paid just over £7 per week.

[47] In 1956, the building was renamed *Pałac Kultury i Nauki*, shedding its dedication. Its architecture was in what is commonly known as the "Stalinist wedding cake" style and closely resembles several buildings in Moscow. Its aesthetics made it the object of scorn and the butt of jokes; one perennially popular joke claims that the best view of Warsaw can be had from its observation deck, since you can't see the building from there. In post-communist Poland, several campaigns have been launched to have it demolished, but it has survived, and some consider it to be one of the symbols of the city.

[48] Like *Cytadela Warszawska* and the Russian Orthodox Cathedral of St. Alexander Nevsky, *Pałac Kultury i Nauki* was viewed by Warsaw's citizens as an imposing symbol of Russian domination.

hemorrhage, and the Soviet Bloc went into an official period of mourning. Behind the somber atmosphere and solemn testimonies, speculation about what would happen next ran rampant through PZPR and all of society, and some cautious steps towards liberalization were made in the Soviet Union and several Bloc nations. UB was dissolved in 1954, but its demise was not a result of post-Stalin reforms. Rather, it can be traced to a shop in the French sector of Berlin on an early December day in 1953.

For years, prisoners of the Bierut regime feared Józef Światło. He had served as a political officer in Berling's army and later transferred to UB. His work included arrest, interrogation, and torture of former AK members; he also played a role in the arrest of the sixteen underground leaders in 1945. Światło himself arrested Władysław Gomułka, Marian Spychalski, General Michał Rola-Żymierski, and Cardinal Stefan Wyszyński, and he often received orders directly from Bierut. He had risen to the position of deputy director of the 10th Department, was charged with protecting the Party from provocateurs and dissenters, and had extensive files on UB personnel and leading Party members. His interrogation methods were so brutal that prisoners referred to him as "the butcher," but now it was he who was afraid. Światło was well aware that after Stalin's death, Beria was arrested along with several subordinates and associates; they were all executed and blamed for "criminal activities against the Party and the State." It took little imagination to visualize a similar event in Poland. Światło sought an opportunity to flee the Soviet Bloc to save his own life.

His wait was brief. In November, he and his superior Anatol Fejgin went to East Germany to confer with the *Stasi* on liquidation of a Polish journalist who had defected and was now broadcasting on Radio Free Europe.[49] After a meeting on December 5, Fejgin and Światło were riding the underground back to their hotel and missed their stop. They exited the train in the French sector and needed to purchase tickets to get back to their hotel, but as they were no longer in the Soviet sector, they needed West German currency. Stopping at a shop, Światło asked Fejgin to wait outside while he exchanged money. After a few minutes, Fejgin grew impatient; as time passed, his attitude turned to concern, then to alarm. Fejgin entered the shop, but Światło was not there. He stepped back outside and watched the street for an hour, but there was still no sign of him.

---

[49] Wanda Brońska, a prewar communist, was the target. During the Great Purge, her parents were executed, and she was sentenced to forced labor in the Magadan gold mines. After the war, she worked as a journalist and defected while on assignment in Berlin; on Radio Free Europe she broadcast information about the gulag system. Brońska was not killed by the security apparatus; she lived until 1972.

Fejgin then returned to the hotel, expecting Światło to turn up. When he failed to appear, Fejgin returned to Warsaw, convinced that he had been abducted.

Fejgin was incorrect. Światło had not been abducted; he had defected. When he entered the shop he made for the back door, slipped out into an alley, and hurried through the streets until he arrived at the American military mission. He introduced himself to the guards and requested asylum. That night he was flown to Frankfurt; by Christmas, he was in Washington. For several weeks, he underwent extensive debriefings in which he provided extensive details of the structure, methods, and operations of PZPR and UB. He made his first public appearance in the West at a press conference in September 1954 and then made a series of appearances on Radio Free Europe broadcasts detailing political arrests, torture, murder, and power struggles.[50] The next month Warsaw admitted that Światło had defected and labeled him a traitor and a provocateur.[51] Late in 1954, UB was dissolved and replaced by a smaller organization, *Służba Bezpieczeństwa* (SB, Security Service). Several UB leaders were arrested, others reassigned to duties outside the security apparatus. UB's chokehold on the nation had been broken, but in time its replacement proved to be only slightly less repressive.

---

[50] Transcripts of Światło broadcasts were dropped into Poland using balloons.
[51] Józef Światło lived out the remainder of his life under great secrecy in the United States; even the year of his death is uncertain. He was under government protection and had plastic surgery to conceal his true identity.

From Discord to Division

KAZIMIERZ SOSNKOWSKI OBSERVED the political maneuverings of Zaleski, *Rada Polityczna*, and PNKD from across the Atlantic. After his dismissal, he traveled to Canada, but when he prepared to depart, he learned that neither the United Kingdom nor the United States would grant him a visa. Confined to Canada for the foreseeable future, he bought a 25-acre farm in Arundel, Quebec, and took up carpentry. His visa status prevented him from accepting a nomination to serve as minister of defense, and in 1947 he was released from military service.

He remained popular. He was far removed from exile political intrigues, burnishing his image of being above the fray. By 1949, he was again permitted to enter the United Kingdom and the United States, and he made speeches and granted interviews in both countries. American politicians sought to capitalize on his burgeoning popularity. Late in the 1952 presidential campaign, both Dwight Eisenhower and Adlai Stevenson met with him; he presented them with his proposals for American recognition of the Polish exile government, unambiguous acceptance of Poland's western border, and support for restoration of Poland's prewar eastern border. Although both declared their willingness to work for Polish independence, they stopped short of endorsing his plan.

Sosnkowski continually advocated for unification in Polish politics. He officially returned to public life in 1951 when Zaleski appointed him to the Main Commission of the National Treasury. Viewed positively by Zaleski and *Rada Polityczna*, Sosnkowski was well positioned to lead the drive to unify. Michał Grażyński of LNP took the first step by imploring him to direct the unification effort. Sosnkowski's reply called for unity in the context of legalism and proposed a plan for compromise. His letter, publicly read at the Polish Independence Day celebration in Manchester in November 1952, favored neither Zaleski nor *Rada Polityczna*. Both saw elements in his plan that that they agreed with and invited him to London. Work began in earnest when he arrived in London in December. *Dziennik Polski i Dziennik Żołnierza* published his statement declaring the trip to be his civic duty and proposing compromise, but he made no promises. He met with Zaleski on December 21 and presented twelve principles of unification. These included establishment of *Rada Jedności Narodowej* (Council of National Unity) to replace *Rada Narodowa*; an increase in powers for the prime minister at the expense of the president; a reduction in the number of political parties; and the possibility of relocating the seat of government to the United States. Under the agreement, Sosnkowski would succeed Zaleski. Many of the twelve principles were a codification of *Umowa Paryska*. Zaleski gave a positive response but made the start of unification contingent on acceptance of Sosnkowski by all parties. He underscored the importance of legalism in a speech to military veterans at St. Pancras Town Hall.[1] Émigrés, weary of political divisions, responded with enthusiasm.

It took little time for Zaleski's condition to be met; within two weeks all political parties, including PPS, agreed to Sosnkowski's succession. Acceptance by PPS was significant; it indicated tacit recognition of Zaleski's presidency and marked the end of its demand for Arciszewski to take office. Zaleski abided by his promise. On January 7, he offered to immediately name Sosnkowski as his successor, but the general demurred, proposing to accept the appointment only after the political parties agreed to the unification plan. Sosnkowski assigned Zaleski's government and *Rada Polityczna* the task of jointly drafting an act of reconciliation and returned to his farm. Optimism ran high; the pages of *Dziennik Polski i Dziennik Żołnierza* were filled with messages of support for Sosnkowski and his mission from throughout the émigré community. *Kultura* conducted a survey of its readers and published statistics that indicated strong support for legalist principles. Yet beneath the veneer of agreement, undercurrents on both sides threatened to derail the process.

Sosnkowski had barely left London when *Dziennik Polski i Dziennik Żołnierza* began reporting on rumors of dissent within the government over weakening the presidency. A planned conference of government and *Rada Polityczna* representatives failed to achieve its goal of jointly developing a basis for the republic's foreign policy. Sosnkowski's plan for both groups to work together to draft an act of reconciliation also failed; when he returned to London, he received two different documents. His patience was faltering. Upon his return to the United Kingdom in April 1953, he deplored their inflexibility. On May 3, Sosnkowski again made a speech in Manchester; this time, he appealed to both sides to remember that the cause of unity must take precedence. Again, his speech was very well received.

Zaleski took the next step. On May 16, he released a statement in which he noted that the authors of the April Constitution had not foreseen that the Republic of Poland might be in an extended period of war

---

[1] Since 1965, St. Pancras Town Hall has been known as Camden Town Hall.

and had not fixed a term for presidents appointed under Article 13. He decided to apply the seven-year term specified in Article 20, announced that his term would end on June 9, 1954, and declared that Sosnkowski would succeed him.[2] He expressed his hope that Sosnkowski would follow his precedent by limiting himself to a seven-year term. But he would not leave it at that. He labeled attacks on the presidency as anti-constitutional and declared that he supported unity but not at the price of the constitution. *Rada Polityczna* took offense, dismissing his claims of attacks as a feature of the democratic process and charging that he had damaged the dignity of his office. But Zaleski's comments illustrated his growing concern that *Akt Zjednoczenia Narodowego* (National Unity Act) amounted to an attempt to revise the constitution.

Sosnkowski was unwilling to accept Zaleski's terms. He drafted a compromise version of the act, brought both groups together, and threatened to renounce the presidency and abandon unification if they could not agree, but both sides drifted further apart. PPS returned to its previous stance towards Zaleski, while Zaleski himself was increasingly leery of the wisdom of the agreement. His doubts were fueled by two considerations: first, in his view the agreement would destroy the constitution and the continuity of state; second, *Sprawa Bergu* caused him to question the trustworthiness of *Rada Polityczna* in general and SN in particular. As his reluctance grew, he embarked on a project to transform *Rada Narodowa* into a more democratic body.

Since its inception, *Rada Narodowa* members were appointed by the president. This was a sensible approach during the war as it would have been nearly impossible to conduct elections, but by 1953 this was no longer the case. In response to criticism that *Rada Narodowa* was undemocratic, in December Zaleski announced his plan to replace it with *Rada Rzeczypospolitej Polskiej*. In this new body, just over fifty percent of its ninety seats would be filled through open elections with seats apportioned by country based on size of the émigré population. Political parties and groups would appoint about one third of the seats. The remainder would be appointed by the president; some of his appointments would be made in consultation with religious leaders or non-political organizations.[3] Even this was contentious within the government. Prime Minister Odzierzyński proposed

---

[2] Notably, Władysław Raczkiewicz was president for nearly eight years.
[3] Global dispersion of postwar emigration is illustrated by the allocation of seats up for election. The United Kingdom was allocated twenty-six seats, France and the United States were granted fifteen seats each, Canada and Australia each had nine seats, and the Benelux countries as a group were allotted six seats, as was West Germany. Argentina and Brazil had four seats between them.

delaying the election in deference to the ongoing unification talks, since unification would render the election pointless. In response, three of his ministers (Hanke, Rusinek, and Hryniewski) resigned. Odzierzyński then met with Zaleski; after this, he also resigned. His replacement, Jerzy Hryniewski, was appointed on December 29, 1953, and formed a government on January 18.

Like his predecessor, Poland's new prime minister came from the Austro-Hungarian partition. Born Mikołaj Dolanowski in the village of Olszanka in the Wołyń district, he adopted the pseudonym Jerzy Hryniewski during his time in POW, and he fought in the Polish–Soviet War. In independent Poland, he served in the *Sejm* as a BBWR representative. He was an AK soldier and fought in the Warsaw Uprising; after the war he was under threat of arrest and left Poland. He settled in the United Kingdom in 1947 under the name Jerzy Hryniewski and immersed himself in exile politics; he was vice president of the Main Commission of the National Treasury from 1950 to 1954, held a seat in *III Rada Narodowa*, and was minister of internal affairs under Odzierzyński. He was a founding member of LNP, but his fellow party members disapproved of his acceptance of the position of prime minister.

A week after Hryniewski formed his government, Sosnkowski returned to London. He managed to shepherd the opposing groups into a compromise, even reaching an agreement on how PNKD could participate. But now, Zaleski appeared to have changed his mind and invoked *Sprawa Bergu* as justification. He convened a meeting with Anders, Sosnkowski, Hryniewski, and Minister of Justice Okulicz. In this meeting, Okulicz presented documents illustrating *Rada Polityczna's* financial dependence on foreign intelligence. Although Anders and Sosnkowski both condemned the actions of those involved in the scandal, they opposed bringing the matter to *Sąd Obywatelski* as it would harm prospects for unification. Sosnkowski pressed on, and by March 14 he had collected approvals from all political parties on both sides of the divide. One day later, he went to 43 Eaton Place and presented the agreement. Zaleski asked him to leave the documents for him to review and sign. Sosnkowski informed him that PPS would not permit him to sign *Akt zjednoczenia* since it did not recognize him as president; it would only agree to him signing Sosnkowski's nomination. Zaleski asked Sosnkowski how he could have agreed to such absurdity and rejected the agreement.

Zaleski made his rationale clear two weeks later at a Council of Ministers meeting. He declared the agreement to be unconstitutional and contended that it would deliver the government into the hands of those behind *Sprawa Bergu*. In late March, PPS responded by rejecting cooperation with Zaleski and confirming that it would not take part in any unity council convened by him. Two months of charges and countercharges followed, along with calls to put aside differences for the good of the nation. On May 5, the Council of Ministers met and adopted a resolution calling on both sides to agree and to resolve differences over time. Again, Zaleski refused to sign; in response, an exasperated Hryniewski resigned. Zaleski finished the matter by claiming he did not believe Sosnkowski would observe the constitution; therefore, he could not appoint him. Sosnkowski and *Rada Polityczna* blamed Zaleski for the failure of *Akt Zjednoczenia Narodowego*. Zaleski, however, saw it differently and attributed its demise to respect for the constitution.

The charge of foreign meddling was quite serious. Objections to Soviet interference in Poland were common to all exile political parties; likewise, memories of British and American pressures over Katyń, the Tehran and Yalta agreements, and the removal of Sosnkowski, to name a few, remained vivid. Adam Pragier, the former *Sejm* member and *Sanacja* prisoner who founded the émigré socialist party after the war, connected acceptance of foreign funds to acceptance of foreign control and depicted Zaleski as the one party in the negotiations who would not allow this.

Fault for the failure of *Akt Zjednoczenia Narodowego* can fairly be apportioned to both sides. After initial optimism gave way to the reality of compromise, the primary antagonists gravitated towards their original positions. Zaleski appears to have been influenced by people within his inner circle. Likewise, both PPS and SN had long been distrustful of Zaleski due to his Piłsudskiite past and neither had accepted his presidency. Further recriminations followed. Throughout the unification efforts, Anders had backed the president, but now he renounced his support. Anders handed Zaleski a letter stating that he no longer considered him to be president. His letter was published in *Dziennik Polski i Dziennik Żołnierza*. Zaleski immediately dismissed Anders from his post of inspector general of the armed forces, declaring, "I am sorry that such a distinguished soldier has tarnished his reputation among future generations by rebelling against his rightful authorities, and by usurping the rights which, both by law and by good political practice, do not belong to him."[4] Anders countered that

---

[4] "Komunikaty Kancelarii Cywilnej Prezydenta Rzeczypospolitej" ("Announcements of the Civil Chancellery of the President of the Republic of Poland"), *DzU RP* Nr. 8 (Londyn), dnia 14 sierpnia 1954 r., s. 51.

he respected the constitution but that Zaleski did not respect the will of the exiles, dealing a harsh blow to Zaleski's reputation and prestige.[5] In a speech in Montreal, Sosnkowski blamed Zaleski for the failure of *Akt Zjednoczenia Narodowego*, asserted that he was in conflict with the majority of émigrés, and proposed applying constant pressure on 43 Eaton Place.

The failure of unification talks did not end efforts to replace Zaleski. *Rada Polityczna* asserted that his May 16 statement was legally binding and therefore his term would end on June 9, 1954. Zaleski rebuffed their claim, stating that it was nothing more than an expression of his will and that he could change it if he wanted. *Rada Polityczna* refused to accept this. On June 10, one day after what would have been his final day in office, it issued a statement proclaiming Zaleski was no longer president and announcing the creation of *Tymczasowa Rada Jedności Narodowej* (TRJN, Provisional Council of National Unity);[6] its mission was to implement *Akt Zjednoczenia Narodowego* and install Sosnkowski as president. To accomplish the latter, TRJN planned to invoke the April Constitution. Under Article 23, the *Senat* marshal would assume the presidency if the office was vacant.[7] Bogusław Miedziński had been marshal when *Senat* was dissolved in 1939; under TRJN's plan, Miedziński, now living in the United Kingdom, would claim presidential powers and then appoint Sosnkowski. However, he refused to take office under these circumstances and would only accept the presidency if Zaleski were to resign. Otherwise, there would be two presidents, which would unquestionably be contrary to the constitution.

Unable to install Sosnkowski, TRJN created *Rada Trzech* (Council of Three) as a substitute for the president until Zaleski vacated the office and formed *Egzekutywa Zjednoczenia Narodowego* (EZN, Executive of National Unity). The opposition had developed a structure where TRJN substituted for the *Sejm*, *Rada Trzech* acted as head of state, and EZN was the Council of Ministers; its chair was the equivalent of a prime minister. Leadership positions were held by familiar names. TRJN was chaired by Tadeusz Bielecki of SN. *Rada Trzech* members were Anders, Arciszewski, and Raczyński. Odzierzyński chaired EZN; he also was responsible for national defense.

---

[5] According to Zaleski, Anders demanded that Zaleski transfer the presidency to him immediately and without conditions.

[6] Although they used the same acronym, *Tymczasowa Rada Jedności Narodowej* should not be confused with *Tymczasowy Rząd Jedności Narodowej*, the body formed in Moscow in 1945 to succeed PKWN.

[7] Article 23 reads: "While the office of the President of the Republic is vacant, the Speaker of the Senate exercises the functions of the President in his place, and should the Senate be dissolved, the Speaker of the dissolved Senat; he then enjoys all the rights vested in the office of the President of the Republic."

Adam Ciołkosz served as deputy chairman, Jan Starszewski managed foreign affairs, Zbigniew Stypułkowski handled internal affairs, Bolesław Wierzbiański was in charge of information, and Kazimierz Sabbat oversaw fiscal matters. To fund its operations, including its plans to establish diplomatic missions abroad, the opposition established *Skarb Narodowy Zjednoczenia* and began competing with *Skarb Narodowy* for contributions; it also began a venture to make the situation in the Soviet Bloc more comprehensible to British readers. It launched a quarterly English-language journal, *Polish Affairs*, that covered political, economic, sociological, cultural, religious, and foreign policy issues in Poland and the Soviet Bloc. Its title was later expanded to *Polish Affairs and Problems of Central & Eastern Europe* to better reflect the breadth of its coverage.[8]

Rada Trzech considered Sosnkowski to be the legitimate president and declared its intent to entrust him with presidential powers,[9] but he held out hope that a resolution could be reached. In February 1956, TRJN debated granting presidential powers to *Rada Trzech*, but the matter was tabled when Sosnkowski objected and pushed for talks to resume. This would be the end of his influence over the TRJN group, though: in August, he renounced his nomination to the presidency, and TRJN granted executive powers to EZN.

Zaleski was officially president, had his office in 43 Eaton Place, and held the symbols of authority. He and his government became known as *Zamek* (Castle, a reference to 43 Eaton Place). Anders and the opposition were referred to as *Zjednoczenie Narodowe* (National Unity), and Mikołajczyk continued to lead PNKD. All were vying for the allegiance and financial support of the émigré community, and both were dwindling. Seemingly incessant bickering and infighting soured many émigrés on exile politics, and contributions declined. *Skarb Narodowy* revenues had already dropped sharply from £37,000 in 1953 to about £10,000 per year prior to the split; the year after *Akt Zjednoczenia Narodowego* failed, it took in only £2,000.[10] *Rada Trzech* fared better; it took in over £20,000 in its 1954–1955 campaign.[11]

With hopes for unification dashed, Zaleski needed to appoint a new prime minister. After Hryniewski's resignation, he ventured outside the

---

[8] *Polish Affairs and Problems of Central & Eastern Europe* ended publication in 1990 after a total run of 127 issues.
[9] In its August 16, 1954 issue, *Dziennik Polski i Dziennik Żołnierza* published a statement from *Rada Trzech* declaring this.
[10] It would take a decade of painstaking work for revenues to recover.
[11] *Rada Trzech* needed the revenue to support its government and to establish diplomatic missions in France, Spain, Portugal, the Netherlands, the Vatican, and the United States.

realm of generals and conventional political figures and chose Stanisław Mackiewicz, best known as a political journalist. During the Second Republic, he founded, published, and edited the Wilno-based *Słowo*. His political views fell outside the positions held by mainstream political parties: he argued for restoration of the lands that had comprised the Polish-Lithuanian Commonwealth, thought the Treaty of Riga to be shameful, and at one point advocated for Piłsudski to be crowned King of Poland and Grand Duke of Lithuania. His ideal Poland was multiethnic and based on allegiance to the state rather than to any ethnic group. From 1928 to 1935 he was a *Sejm* deputy from BBWR, but this affiliation did not translate into support for the government after Piłsudski's death. His criticism of *Sanacja* government earned him seventeen days in Bereza Kartuska.[12] The government justified his incarceration with the claim that he "… influences public opinion in a way leading to undermining trust in the state's defense capabilities, degrading state authorities and spreading defeatist sentiments regarding the internal and external situation of the state, and acting against national unity during the general consolidation of Polish society."[13]

In September 1939, Mackiewicz crossed into Lithuania on his way to France. Despite some opposition, he was appointed to *Rada Narodowa*. He resumed publication of *Słowo* and published attacks on Mościcki and prewar *Sanacja* politicians; these enraged Raczkiewicz. *Słowo* also published criticisms of Sikorski's government. Sikorski's response was to ban publication of all political newspapers except for *Dziennik Polski i Dziennik Żołnierza*, citing the need for national unity. Mackiewicz denounced the decision as a violation of freedom of the press and called Sikorski a totalitarian. In return, several government and *Rada Narodowa* members accused him of political subversion. France fell before this confrontation could escalate further, and Mackiewicz publicly urged Raczkiewicz to join France in surrendering. When *Rada Narodowa* reassembled in London, it convened a court of honor that accused Mackiewicz of being in league with the Germans. Mackiewicz was on his way to removal from *Rada Narodowa* when the *Rada* itself was dissolved.

After the war, Mackiewicz eked out an existence by publishing the weekly newspaper *Lwów i Wilno*, contributing to the London-based *Wiadomości*, and

---

[12] Ironically, Mackiewicz had been a strong proponent of the establishment of Bereza Kartuska.

[13] Jacek Gzella, "Cenzura wobec relacji 'Słowa' o zesłaniu Stanisława Cata-Mackiewicza do Berezy Kartuskiej w 1939 roku" ("Censorship of the 'Słowa' report on Stanisław Cat-Mackiewicz's exile to Bereza Kartuska in 1939"), *Klio. Czasopismo poświęcone dziejom Polski i powszechnym*, 17/2011, s. 115, https://repozytorium.umk.pl/bitstream/handle/item/805/KLIO.2011.029%2CGzella.pdf?sequence=1

selling pieces to *Kultura*, *Dziennik Polski (Detroit)*, and wherever else he could. Despite his appearance before *Sąd Honorowy* in 1941, he was appointed to *III Rada Narodowa*, *IV Rada Narodowa*, and *I Rada*.

On June 8, 1954, Mackiewicz was appointed prime minister and formed his government; he also served as minister of foreign affairs. His combative personality served neither him nor Zaleski well, as he clashed with most of his Council of Ministers. His accomplishments in office were few; he opposed *Sprawa Bergu* but did little to address it, and he advocated for the émigré community to protect cultural artifacts that were spirited out of the country when the war began but failed to develop concrete plans to do so. Just about a year later, Mackiewicz himself concluded that he could do nothing for Poland in his position and resigned on June 21, 1955. Paradoxically, he remained in government, serving as a minister without portfolio in the next government. He returned to writing for *Wiadomości* and other émigré publications; late in 1955, the readers of *Wiadomości* voted him their favorite writer.

Zaleski underscored his rejection of *Akt Zjednoczenia Narodowego* and his break with Sosnkowski by nominating a new successor. He offered the position to Professor Tadeusz Brzeski, a noted economist formerly on the faculty of *Uniwersytet Warszawski*, but he declined. Zaleski then turned to Eustachy Sapieha, a member of an illustrious noble family. Sapieha had been a Piłsudski supporter, was briefly minister of foreign affairs, and held a *Sejm* seat between the wars. In September 1939, he was arrested by the NKVD, interrogated in the Lubyanka, tried, and sentenced to death; by a stroke of luck, his sentence was reduced to ten years in a gulag.[14] Freed under the Sikorski–Maisky agreement, he left the Soviet Union with the Polish Army. From Tehran, he moved to Nairobi, Kenya, where he was living when Zaleski appointed him. Sapieha was a wise choice; he was widely respected in the émigré community and belonged to no political party. And Zaleski was quite pleased that Sapieha was willing to support him at a time when so many notable figures were in opposition.

There was no longer a reason to postpone elections to *Rada Rzeczypospolitej Polskiej*, and an election calendar was published in August; voting would be in person where possible or by mail. In November, for the first time since before the war, a Polish government conducted free elections, although far fewer votes were cast than anticipated and plans for a

---

[14] The only prominent Sapieha family member to remain in Poland throughout the war was Cardinal Adam Sapieha, Archbishop of Kraków, noted for his courage in his dealings with the German (and later, Soviet) occupiers. Cardinal Sapieha also holds the distinction of having ordained Karol Wojtyła to the priesthood.

ninety-member *Rada* were scaled back. On December 18, the fifty members comprising *Rada Rzeczypospolitej Polskiej* convened for their first session.

For the remainder of Zaleski's life, the exiles would be split. He would retain his title and remain at 43 Eaton Place. *Rada Trzech*, EZN, and TRJN would continue to meet but would refrain from naming an alternative president. And Warsaw would portray the London politicians as a petty, argumentative group bickering over nothing while PZPR was doing the hard work of rebuilding their devastated country.

After Mackiewicz's contentious year as prime minister, Zaleski counted on Hugon Hanke to bring harmony. Hanke was neither divisive nor polarizing; quite the opposite, he was well liked and had no known enemies in exile. He was a native of Siemianowice Śląskie in Upper Silesia and was an SP activist prior to the war. In September 1939, he fled to southeastern Poland ahead of the German advance; when the Red Army invaded, he crossed into Romania. He joined the Polish Army in France but was captured in 1940 and interned in a prisoner-of-war camp in Strasbourg. Not willing to give up the fight, he escaped in 1941 and, via Spain and Ireland, rejoined the army in the United Kingdom. He served in the First Polish Armored Division until 1943, when the government assigned him to work in the Ministry of the Interior. After the war, he remained in the United Kingdom and remained active in SP. This changed when a rift developed in SP between those supporting *Rada Polityczna* and a minority that supported Zaleski. As one of the pro-Zaleski group's leaders, Hanke became chairman of the SP faction loyal to the president, and he continued to support Zaleski throughout the attempt at unification. He served as a minister without portfolio in the Odzierzyński and Hryniewski governments and was a member of *IV Rada Narodowa*. Hanke appeared to be a safe and prudent choice, but appearances were deceiving: he was an informant in the pay of SB.

On July 23, 1952, six months after he had been appointed to Odzierzyński's government, Hanke approached the Polish Military Mission office in London and identified himself as Woliński, an employee of the exile government. He claimed to have access to secret documents, including plans to create an intelligence and sabotage network in Poland. Stating that his motives were to prevent unnecessary bloodshed, he showed an agent three documents as proof of his capabilities. He dangled the prospect of providing information that would show routes used to infiltrate

Poland, identify Western agents in the Warsaw government, and provide names of underground figures. In his second meeting, he disclosed his true name, revealing that his wife and three children were still in Poland and that he regularly sent them packages.[15] SB considered Hanke to have great potential and assigned him the codename *Ważny* (Important). For the next two years, Hanke met regularly with his contact and provided documents, although SB determined that they were of minor importance. His handlers considered steps to force him to provide more useful information, including blackmailing him or threatening his family. Nevertheless, he continued to be paid.

With the collapse of unification talks, Hanke took on a larger role in *Zamek*. He was a member of *Rada RP* and was given a seat on *Tymczasowa Komisja Skarbu Narodowego* (Temporary National Treasury Commission). Hanke capitalized on his ascent by providing information that was of greater use to SB, particularly government activities, details of unification talks, treasury reports, and materials on *Sprawa Bergu*. His handlers now weighed their options. There was considerable inclination to leave him in London, as he was SB's highest-placed source, but proponents of his return to Poland prevailed, bolstered by Hanke's expressed desires. When Hanke was named to replace Mackiewicz, his propaganda value grew immensely, and in the middle of August, the decision was made.

Hanke's departure from London raised no suspicions; he was headed to Rome under the guise of seeking an audience with Pope Pius XII. He arrived in Rome on September 5, 1955, and disappeared; three days later, he resurfaced in Warsaw. On September 10, his return was reported on Polish Radio; later that day, he held a press conference and called on émigrés to return. At first, the government and *Rada Narodowa* assumed that he had been abducted and forced to make pro-Warsaw and anti-emigration statements. A search of his apartment yielded incontrovertible evidence of his collaboration with SB.

Warsaw began a media campaign aimed at the London government with Hanke as its centerpiece. News of such a highly placed exile politician transferring his allegiance was sensational news and was reported around the world. He gave interviews, made public appearances, and held press conferences in which he elaborated on *Sprawa Bergu*, criticized political figures, and urged Poles to return. But his usefulness was quickly spent. Before the war, Hanke was little known outside of Silesia, and the

---

[15] Hanke's claim that he was supporting his family contrasts with his wife's claims that he rarely sent any packages and her frequent letters to him in which she begged for assistance.

Warsaw authorities found that his return did not cause much of a stir. By the following summer, SB had given up on him as a useful asset. A now-embittered Hanke held a series of unimportant positions and spent his spare time writing to exiles urging their return. He died a forgotten man in Warsaw on December 19, 1964.

For the seventh time since he took office and the fourth time in less than two years, Zaleski needed to appoint a prime minister. His next choice was Antoni Pająk. Pająk had evaded arrest during the Soviet invasion only to be banished to a labor camp in the depths of Siberia in the mass expulsion of June 1940. He regained his freedom thanks to the Sikorski–Maisky agreement and went to work as a delegate of the Polish embassy in the Yakutia region. In July 1942, he was arrested and expelled; from there he went to London and held several government positions. He was a prolific journalist: he founded *Wolność*, a monthly publication of PPS, edited the newspaper *Gazeta Polska* from 1946 to 1948, and assisted in founding the magazines *Tygodnik, Gazeta Powszechna, Głos Powszechny*, and *Rzeczpospolita Polska*. During the first years of Zaleski's presidency, Pająk firmly aligned himself with the government by founding a breakaway socialist party. In Mackiewicz's government, he was minister of the treasury and minister of citizen's affairs; under Hanke, he was again minister of the treasury, a responsibility he continued in his own government. In his first address as prime minister, he confirmed his commitment to legalism and declared that recognition of the April Constitution was a mandatory component in the struggle for a free Poland. For the next ten years, Pająk would be prime minister. His presence brought much needed stability to *Zamek*.

Tomasz Arciszewski's *Rada Trzech* tenure was brief. He died in London on November 20, 1955, and was buried in Brompton Cemetery. Tadeusz Bór-Komorowski was chosen to fill the vacant seat.

TRJN and EZN met at The Polish Institute and Sikorski Museum at 20 Prince's Gate. Anders also maintained his office there, but an important person was beginning to object to his presence. Helena Sikorska, the Institute's honorary patron, was increasingly convinced that Anders had actively opposed her late husband, and she was influenced by conspiracy theories contending that Anders himself had played a part in his death. She demanded that Anders and his associates vacate the premises. He refused.

Soviet power continued to grow in the years following Germany's defeat. Communist governments ruled Poland, East Germany, Czechoslovakia,

Hungary, Romania, Bulgaria, Yugoslavia, Albania, North Korea, and China; most enjoyed Moscow's support and assistance. Concurrently, British and American attitudes towards the Soviet Union deteriorated as fears of a war with the Soviet Union grew. Only three years after the war ended, an opinion poll indicated that nearly three-quarters of Americans expected a war with the Soviet Union within a decade. In 1949, the United States and Canada joined the United Kingdom and a group of West European nations to form the North Atlantic Treaty Organization (NATO), a military group that was a counterweight to the Soviet Bloc. War in Korea revived the prospect of a third world war that some émigrés hoped would result in the final defeat of the Soviet Union and restoration of independence to Bloc nations. Anders went so far as to seek a military role for émigré Poles. In 1950, he met with the US Department of Defense and offered to reconstitute the Polish Armed Forces in the West.

American inquiries began into previously ignored Soviet war crimes. In September 1951, Congress convened the Select Committee to Conduct an Investigation and Study of the Facts, Evidence, and Circumstances of the Katyn Forest Massacre.[16] Chaired by Congressman Ray Madden, it became known as the Madden Committee. After hearing testimony from more than eighty witnesses and reviewing thousands of pages of documentary evidence, the committee unanimously concluded that the NKVD was responsible and recommended that the case be heard by the International World Court of Justice. Radio Free Europe regularly transmitted reports on the work of the committee.

NCFE grew in importance to the American government. Its sponsors, the Free Europe Committee, provided headquarters in New York City across the street from the United Nations; NCFE took advantage of this by hanging a succession of banners on their building calculated to embarrass or irritate Soviet Bloc delegates. In 1954, it took a new name, Assembly of Captive European Nations (ACEN), added exile representations from Albania, Estonia, Latvia, and Lithuania, and broadened its scope to include two international political groupings: the International Peasant Union and the Christian Democratic Union of Central and Eastern Europe. Poland's representation continued to be problematic. No national committee had been formed, and none was in the offing, yet Poland was too large to exclude. NCFE's solution was to allot a portion of Poland's seats to *Rada Polityczna* and the remainder to PNKD, and this arrangement

---

[16] PAC had lobbied strongly for a congressional investigation of the Katyń massacre; the Madden Committee's very existence was testimony to PAC's influence and persistence.

continued in ACEN. Pressure to unify came from within ACEN and from Polish American organizations, but the division between Mikołajczyk and Korboński was too deep.[17]

Nikita Khrushchev took control of the Communist Party of the Soviet Union in 1953 and launched a series of reforms to mitigate the worst excesses of the Stalinist era. Hopes for reform were fanned by a speech he delivered at a closed session of the 20th Congress of the Communist Party of the Soviet Union. Titled "On the Cult of Personality and its Consequences," it was highly critical of Stalin and his methods. Although intended to be heard only by those in attendance, copies of the speech were clandestinely circulated far beyond Soviet borders, raising hope that Soviet control over its satellite nations would be loosened.

Khrushchev sought to improve relations with the West. He proclaimed a policy of peaceful coexistence and signaled his intention to visit Western nations. Britain's government agreed to host him and Prime Minister Nikolai Bulganin in April 1956. Most émigré Poles did not consider Khrushchev to be a reformer and viewed his upcoming visit with skepticism. Zaleski and Pająk sent an official diplomatic note to the British Foreign Office requesting that the British–Soviet talks include restoration of the 1939 Polish–Soviet border, release of Poles in Soviet camps and prisons, accountability for Katyń, an explanation of the Trial of the Sixteen, and sovereignty for nations under Soviet control. Although the Foreign Office did not act on these requests, the fact that the note was accepted was a positive sign.

Dziennik Polski i Dziennik Żołnierza urged its readers to seize this opportunity to remind Britain of the fate of all nations under Soviet control. The paper invited its readers to offer suggestions on how to best greet Khrushchev and Bulganin; most respondents suggested public demonstrations. *Dziennik Polski i Dziennik Żołnierza* also launched a petition calling on the British government to raise the subjects of free elections, release of political prisoners, and the Katyń massacre. Its editors exhorted readers to sign the petition and to gather signatures from family, friends, neighbors, and coworkers; about 60,000 signed. A pre-visit rally was planned for the Royal Albert Hall, but the venue canceled; eventually, it was held in Manchester.

---

[17] It should be noted that the Poles were not the only exile group to have internal disputes. Differences existed within every national delegation, understandable when considering the range of political, social, and economic viewpoints represented.

On Sunday, April 22, Archbishop Józef Gawlina offered Mass at the Brompton Oratory for victims of Soviet repression. Afterwards, twenty thousand people began a silent protest march outside the Oratory, led by scouts bearing a wreath and standard bearers holding national flags aloft. Following them were Anders, Raczyński, Adam Ciołkosz, Zbigniew Stypułkowski, and Malcolm Muggeridge. Then came contingents of Czechs, Bulgarians, Hungarians, Yugoslavs, Estonians, Latvians, and Lithuanians. Next was Bór-Komorowski leading a group of AK veterans, followed by uniformed veterans from the Polish Armed Forces in the West. Completing the march were other émigré Poles. Marchers hoisted banners calling for Soviet withdrawal and freedom for political prisoners. They walked three miles through the streets of central London to the Cenotaph,[18] where Anders laid a wreath opposite one placed by Khrushchev three days earlier. The assembled marchers sang the national anthems of Poland, Great Britain, Czechoslovakia, Bulgaria, Hungary, Yugoslavia, Estonia, Latvia, and Lithuania; then, the editor of *Dziennik Polski i Dziennik Żołnierza*, the president of the Federation of Poles in Great Britain, and Muggeridge delivered ten volumes of petitions to 10 Downing Street.

British reaction was quite supportive. Along the route, Londoners stopped and applauded; the march received positive coverage on television and in newspapers. On Monday, Anders and Raczyński met with Foreign Secretary Selwyn Lloyd to discuss the march and the petition. This was the exile government's first official meeting with the British government since July 1945.

These protests did not change Poland's situation, nor did they compel the British government to intercede. But they demonstrated that the émigré community was deeply concerned about the fate of its homeland and was willing to act, regardless of exile disunity. Britain's acceptance of the note from *Zamek*, its acceptance of the petition, and its meeting with Anders and Raczyński showed that, although Poland's exile government was not recognized, it was not ignored.

Bierut had been in Moscow for the 20th Congress but did not attend Khrushchev's "secret speech." After the congress, the Polish delegation returned to Warsaw without him. His health had been fading for some months; since at least the middle of the previous year, he had suffered from bouts of influenza and pneumonia as well as kidney disease and

---

[18] London's Cenotaph is the United Kingdom's official national war memorial.

atherosclerosis. He was now in a Moscow hospital. In Warsaw, rumors began to circulate about Khrushchev's speech. Central Committee members demanded an immediate report, regardless of Bierut's availability, and a meeting of PZPR activists was held. The first order of business was to review the speech; this soon evolved into frank discussions on Stalinism in Poland and turned into criticisms and attacks on Bierut, Berman, and other party leaders. On March 12, Bierut suffered heart failure and died in a Moscow hospital.[19] Circumstances of his death became the subject of considerable speculation; he was not the first Soviet Bloc leader to die during or after a trip to Moscow.[20]

Bierut's regime had been particularly brutal. He led the effort to forcibly impose a Soviet system on Poland, including rigging the 1947 *Sejm* elections. He and his cohorts had established a police state with an omnipresent security apparatus: as of January 1953, UB had files on more than five million individuals. Prisons and labor camps, including detention centers for adolescents, had been established throughout the country. Former AK, NSZ, and WiN members had been pursued relentlessly and subjected to show trials and executions. Prominent victims were General Emil Fieldorf, Captain Witold Pilecki, and Lieutenant Colonel Łukasz Ciepliński; Bierut himself had approved their executions. Hundreds of priests and nuns, along with dozens of bishops, were arrested, jailed, and in some cases executed. Bierut himself ordered the arrest and imprisonment of Cardinal Stefan Wyszyński.[21] In all, during Bierut's reign, nearly 400,000 Poles had been arrested for political reasons.

Mackiewicz absented himself from the Khrushchev protests. He saw little point in the demonstrations and dismissed them as futile and useless. Not two months later he returned to Poland, arriving in Warsaw amidst great fanfare. But this was no impulsive decision; he had been discussing his return with PRL agents for nearly ten years.

Several factors were behind his decision. He was convinced that there would not be a war between the United States and the Soviet Union and

---

[19] At Bierut's funeral, Khrushchev told PZPR activist Stefan Staszewski that he was to blame for Bierut's death. According to Khrushchev, Bierut read transcripts of the conference every day and became agitated; Khrushchev claimed that Staszewski's speech upset Bierut to the point that he suffered a heart attack.

[20] In 1946, Bulgarian Communist Party chairman Georgi Dimitrov suddenly became ill after the 19th Congress and died near Moscow; in 1953, Czechoslovakia's party chairman Klement Gottwald died in Prague shortly after returning from Moscow.

[21] For this act, Bierut brought upon himself the penalty of excommunication.

therefore Poland would not be liberated from Soviet rule; in his view, this meant that there was no point in the continued existence of the London government and that the émigré community needed to come to terms with reality and return to Poland. Mackiewicz did not like London or the British people, and his family was still in Poland. He was also facing financial difficulty. However, he was neither a communist nor a sympathizer and was concerned that he would be viewed unfavorably by Warsaw; he feared arrest and imprisonment. Even if he were to remain free, he was concerned that he would not be able to find work and would lead as meager an existence in Poland as he had in London.

In 1947, Mackiewicz initiated contacts with Warsaw by writing to a prewar friend who was now a *Sejm* deputy; he also contacted Bernard Singer. These moves resulted in Mackiewicz presenting himself at the embassy to negotiate terms. His actions soon became known in the émigré community. He denied accusations that he was an agent or informer and continued discussions with Singer and other agents, but he became frustrated when it became clear that Warsaw wanted him to remain in London as an informant. He ended negotiations, though his impulse to return remained.

Zaleski's appointment of Mackiewicz to head the government rekindled Warsaw's interest and his case was reopened, but he had no discussions with agents while in office. Shortly after his resignation, he offered to resume talks. This aligned with Warsaw's renewed efforts to encourage repatriation, divide the émigré political community, and neutralize the London government. Return seemed quite probable. Mackiewicz offered to write books and articles critical of the London government and to encourage Poles to come home; in return he wanted to publish his works and lecture in Russian literature at the University of Warsaw. In the ensuing months, the tone of his *Tygodnik Polski* columns became increasingly strident, culminating on June 2 when he announced his return. This was treated with derision in the émigré press, but it also spawned another reaction. In 1950, Tadeusz Żenczykowski had won a libel judgment for £4,000 against Mackiewicz that had not been paid. Now that Mackiewicz was leaving the country, Żenczykowski's lawyers launched insolvency proceedings against him; had Mackiewicz declared bankruptcy, leaving the United Kingdom would have been almost impossible. He left the United Kingdom on June 14, 1956, ahead of legal proceedings against him.

A propaganda campaign immediately began. Mackiewicz was well known in Poland prior to the war, giving his return higher propaganda value than Hanke's. Mackiewicz did his part by writing books and articles highly critical of the London government and émigré community, calling them unnecessary and harmful. He wrote for several periodicals and lectured on Russian literature.[22]

Émigrés had been building lives for themselves in other countries since the war ended, either finding employment or starting businesses. Although millions of Poles were dispersed around the globe, the United Kingdom was the epicenter of postwar emigration, London was the hub of émigré life, and a stretch of Cromwell Road was at its heart. Passengers on the number 74 bus would occasionally hear the conductor call out "Polish Corridor" when announcing stops between Exhibition Road and Earls Court. In this area, Polish restaurants, groceries, bakeries, pharmacies, law offices, and medical practices sought to meet the needs of their fellow émigrés; the Polish language could be heard everywhere.

Physicians, dentists, lawyers, architects, engineers, and accountants were usually able to resume their careers in the United Kingdom. Those unable to demonstrate professional qualifications typically found work as unskilled laborers. This group included many high-ranking military officers who were now living in exile with no pensions;[23] they usually found menial work.[24] Some younger, energetic, and enterprising exiles launched their own businesses. In 1942, there were only two Polish-owned businesses in the United Kingdom; by the mid-1950s, there were about one thousand; more than four hundred were in London. Many light manufacturing companies were established, such as Limba Trading Company Ltd., founded by Polish Army veteran Kazimierz Sabbat to produce blankets and quilts. A number of import and export firms such as Tazab and Haskoba were formed, specializing in shipping food, clothing, pharmaceuticals, and supplies to Poland; many exiles used them to provide material assistance to family at home. Business

---

[22] Mackiewicz eventually became disillusioned with Poland's communist government as well. When he objected to censorship, he was removed from his positions on several editorial boards and was not permitted to publish. He then began to write for *Kultura* under a pseudonym, resulting in charges of publishing false information about the government. He died before he could be put on trial. Mackiewicz earned for himself the distinction of being prosecuted by *Sanacja*, Sikorski's exile government, and the PRL.

[23] Their situation contrasts with former German officers living comfortably on government pensions.

[24] General Stanisław Maczek worked as a bartender at the Grosvenor Hotel in Edinburgh. General Tadeusz Bór-Komorowski was an upholsterer. General Zygmunt Bohusz-Szyszko opened his own business repairing and restoring porcelain. General Józef Zamorski worked as an elevator operator. General Ludwik Kmicic-Skrzyński was a factory laborer in Manchester. General Władysław Bortnowski took a job as a hospital nurse. General Marian Przewłocki was a warehouse worker at Continental Food Supply. General Stanisław Sosabowski performed physical labor in a diesel engine parts warehouse.

owners tended to hire their fellow exiles. Tazab and Haskoba employed many older Poles who had few other prospects. Other émigrés scraped together enough money to buy a house and rented rooms.

As émigrés settled into their new homes and jobs, their daily lives increasingly resembled those of their neighbors and coworkers, but they typically held firm to their Polish identity and patronized Polish businesses. Groceries provided familiar foods, and Polish-language newspapers were in abundance. *Dziennik Polski i Dziennik Żołnierza* provided news from the diaspora as well as from within Poland. Weekly newspapers included the Catholic publication *Gazeta Niedzielna*, *Orzeł Biały*, targeted towards military veterans, the weekly *Wiadomości*, focusing on social and cultural topics, *Życie*, a weekly religious and social publication, *Jutro Polski*, PSL's paper, and *Trybuna*, a monthly published by PRW NiD. Polish-language books were available from the *Orbis* bookstore or could be borrowed from a Polish library; the London-based *Gryf Publications Ltd.* published books in Polish and in English.

Most children attended the same schools as their neighbors. To ensure they remained connected to their cultural heritage, children spent their Saturday mornings learning the Polish language at *Polska Macierz Szkolna* (Polish Educational Society), established on the initiative of Anders. Two Polish boarding schools were available for families who could afford them. Primary and secondary education for girls was offered at Holy Family of Nazareth Convent School in Pitsford, Northamptonshire; this school was operated by Polish nuns. For boys, Divine Mercy College at Fawley Court, Buckinghamshire, provided secondary education. Many children were involved in scouting. ZHP units were established in refugee camps during the war and continued afterward. *Związek Harcerstwa Polskiego poza granicami Kraju* (ZHP pgK, Polish Scouting Organization Operating Outside the Country) was based in London and was active in Polish communities throughout free Europe, North America, South America, and Australia. Thousands of young Poles were members of ZHP pgK troops. Émigré leaders strongly emphasized the importance of university education, and since 1949, students had the option of attending *Polski Uniwersytet na Obczyźnie* (PUNO, Polish University in Exile).[25]

Regardless of the availability of familiar foods and publications in their own language, émigrés were living in a foreign culture with quite different customs and social mores. Restaurants provided an atmosphere of

---

[25] PUNO continued the mission of *Uniwersytet Polski za Granicą* (Polish University Abroad), founded by the exile government in late 1939 in France.

home and community. Daquise, a mile from 43 Eaton Place, was a regular destination for émigré politicians, including most of the presidents. Many sought solace in the abundance of organizations and clubs where they could socialize with their fellow Poles, observe national holidays, celebrate weddings, baptisms, and other important events, and hear familiar music. Organizations for military veterans abounded, such as *Stowarzyszenie Polskich Kombatantów* (SPK, Polish Combatants' Association) in Queen's Gate Terrace, *Klub Lotników Polskich* (Polish Airmen's Club) in Collingham Gardens, and *Samopomoc Marynarki Wojennej* (Navy Mutual Aid Association) on Chelsea Embankment.

At the apex of émigré clubs stood *Ognisko Polskie* (Polish Hearth). Its very name reflected its purpose: to provide the warmth and familiarity of home. *Ognisko Polskie* opened under the patronage of the Duke of Kent[26] and became the favored meeting place for members of the military and government. After the war, *Ognisko Polskie* was the center of Polish social and cultural life in London. Its building at 55 Exhibition Road housed several other organizations, including the Polish Red Cross, the Anglo–Polish Society, *Związek Artystów Scen Polskich* (ZASP, Association of Polish Stage Artists), the Polish Research Centre, and the Polish University College. The building's large hall hosted meetings, balls, weddings, and commemorations. A restaurant and a club room provided venues to meet and socialize. Generals Anders, Kopański, Kukiel, Rudnicki, Bohusz-Szyszko, Bór-Komorowski, Sosabowski, Odzierzyński, Dembiński, Ząbkowski, Smoleński, Grudziński, and Pragłowski convened at what came to be known as the "Generals' Table." Political figures including Raczyński, Bielecki, Rowmund Piłsudski, and Lidia and Adam Ciołkosz were also frequent guests. Noted personalities from art, literature, and theater regularly visited, including Artur Rubinstein, Stanisław Mackiewicz, painter Feliks Topolski, and poet/lyricist Marian Hemar. A theater on the premises hosted dramatic productions, musicals, and cabarets.

The arts held an important place in émigré culture. Mateusz Grabowski, a pharmacist with several shops in the Polish Corridor and nearby Chelsea, owned an avant-garde art gallery next to one of his stores on Sloane Avenue.[27] At the *Orzeł Biały* club, the *Piekiełko* cafe was home to regular

---

[26] The Duke of Kent's family have continually supported *Ognisko Polskie* since its founding.

[27] Grabowski built a highly successful business that included one of the first mail-order pharmacies in the United Kingdom; he exported much-needed pharmaceuticals to Poland. The M. B. Grabowski Foundation funded Polish programs at Cambridge, Oxford, Stirling, and University College London. After the fall of communism, his private art collection was donated to museums in Poland.

cabaret performances. One of its performers, Marian Hemar, later established the satirical and political Hemar Theater. Cabaret performer Feliks Konarski, better known as "Ref-Ren," operated *Teatr Ref-Ren* in *Ognisko Polskie*.[28] Singer Zofia Terné opened her own club, Chez Sophie. Many others, such as Polonia Theater, could be found nearby.

Religion was central in émigré life. *Polska Misja Katolicka* (Polish Catholic Mission) ministered to Poles in Western Europe. Its first parish in the United Kingdom was in Islington, but its size was not adequate to accommodate the throngs of Poles who desired to attend Mass, hear sermons in their own language, and sing familiar hymns, and its distance from the Polish Corridor made it inconvenient. For several years, *Polska Misja Katolicka* offered Sunday Mass in the Brompton Oratory. In time, church buildings were acquired, and parishes were established across London and throughout the United Kingdom. First was St. Andrew Bobola Church (*Kościół św. Andrzeja Boboli*) in Hammersmith; this became the unofficial garrison church for the Polish military in the West and was the home parish for many veterans. Where a permanent church could not be obtained, Mass would be offered in local parishes or at *Dom Polski* (Polish Home), a social, cultural, and self-help institution that could be found in almost every Polish community. Further illustrating the community's resolve to look after its own, London was home to two Polish retirement homes and Mabledon Hospital, a psychiatric facility for veterans and refugees traumatized by the war.

Newsagents in London began to sell *Głos Powszechny* in June 1955, a new weekly with an editorial line staunchly supportive of Zaleski and Zamek. Its appearance was fortuitous, as the government did not publish an official newspaper. Its publisher Zygmunt Kotowicz printed official announcements and decrees issued by the government; in turn, he received financial assistance. But the interminable quarrels between political groups wore on him, and his pro-Zaleski attitude began to fade. He continued to print official statements from Zaleski and Pająk, though his paper's divergence from government positions culminated in its publication on January 26, 1957, of a message from *Polska Agencja Telegraficzna* distancing the government from the newspaper. Yet government subsidies continued, as 43 Eaton Place needed a media outlet. Kotowicz, however, had already decided to move in a different direction. In mid-January, he began working with PRL intelligence, agreeing to provide information on émigré politics in exchange for funding; he also agreed to adopt a pro-Warsaw tone. By

---

[28] Konarski wrote the lyrics to *Czerwone maki na Monte Cassino* (Red Poppies on Monte Cassino).

March, *Zamek* terminated funding, and Kotowicz was losing contributors who no longer wanted to be associated with him. In 1958, Scotland Yard opened an investigation into the newspaper's funding; meanwhile, PRL intelligence determined that the paper had limited influence and ended funding. The next year, Kotowicz and his family returned to Poland. Fortunately for him, in 1957 Wacław Grubiński and Xawery Glinka founded the biweekly *Rzeczpospolita Polska – Republic of Poland* as the official press organ of the government. It published accounts of government activities, political news from Poland and in exile, and reports on activities of émigré political groups.

In Sweden, Waldemar Sobczyk published *Nasz Znak*, that country's official PSL organ. Like Kotowicz, Sobczyk tired of contentious politics in the wake of the failed unification efforts, and *Nasz Znak* took a strongly critical stance towards *Zamek* and *Rada Trzech*; increasingly, it echoed Warsaw's line. PRL intelligence contacted Sobczyk and reached an agreement to provide funds in return for information on émigrés and for adopting an overtly pro-Warsaw editorial stance. Suspicions grew in PSL, culminating in a declaration that *Nasz Znak* was not affiliated with PSL and did not reflect its views. When Sobczak was expelled from PSL a few months later, he focused editorial attacks on Mikołajczyk, accusing him of betraying PSL's ideals and of embezzlement. Sobczak continued his activities for years, although PSL declared his paper to be a communist front.

PRL efforts to influence émigré opinion extended beyond *Nasz Znak*. It also funded publication of the weeklies *Odgłosy*, *Kronika*, and *Oblicze Tygodnia*, all advocating cooperation between émigrés and the Warsaw government.

Work to remake Polish society and industry in the Soviet model proceeded without pause. Streets, factories, buildings, schools, and even entire cities were renamed in honor of Lenin, Stalin, Dzierżyński, Luksemburg, Nowotko, and other communist luminaries; many streets and public squares took names commemorating communist holidays. This obsession reached its peak when Katowice was renamed Stalinogród shortly after Stalin's death. Names of national heroes who opposed communism or whose legacy could not be adapted to serve communism were excised from public spaces and history books. Place names that commemorated national holidays such as May 3 were changed. Poland's economy was now centrally controlled, and all but the smallest companies were nationalized.

Food prices were set by a government ministry, as were production quotas for state-owned factories. Trade unions were of no help to workers, as they were run by the government and were nothing more than propaganda mouthpieces.[29] Many government and military officials were Soviet citizens and spoke little or no Polish; resentment grew among Poles who didn't appreciate having to speak Russian to their own leaders or commanders. The Soviet Army was omnipresent. These conditions might have been tolerable if the promised improvements in economic conditions had been realized, but food prices were high, apartments and houses were scarce, and living standards were falling.

In Poznań in June 1956, these factors converged into a volatile mixture. Workers at the ZISPO railcar factory were frustrated that they were unable to maintain an adequate standard of living for their families due to rising food prices, increased production norms, and higher taxes. After attempts to negotiate failed, they walked out on the morning of June 28 and were joined by other workers. When they reached the city center, their numbers swelled to about 100,000. They tore down red flags, smashed radio-jamming equipment, and broke into the SB building and destroyed files. Polish Army tanks roared into the streets. Rokossovsky dispatched Deputy Minister of National Defense General Stanislav Poplavsky[30] to Poznań, and he sent in more tanks, along with infantry units. Sporadic fighting continued into the night. By morning, Poznań was under military occupation, and protestors were being rounded up and arrested. Between fifty and one hundred protestors were killed; their funerals were held at night under guard with only immediate family present. Those prosecuted were charged with being American or West German agents. Pacification was complete the following day.

After Poznań, mass meetings and public protests erupted throughout the country. As in Poznań, demands went much further than basic economic issues. Protestors called for the release of Cardinal Wyszyński, return of the Eastern territories, a truthful accounting for the Katyń massacres, elimination of the Russian language requirement in schools, and dismissal of Rokossovsky and other Soviet citizens from political and military positions. Concurrent with the protests, several thousand visitors and journalists from the West had been attending an industrial trade show in Poznań, and their reports, eyewitness accounts, and photographs

---

[29] This was by design. Lenin's purpose for labor unions was to be "transmission belts" for instructions from the Party to the workers.

[30] Like Rokossovsky, Poplavsky was a Soviet general of ethnic Polish descent assigned to a command in the Polish Army.

appeared in the Western press. Anders organized *Komitet Pomocy Rodakom w Kraju* (Committee to Aid Compatriots in the Country); its mission was to provide financial and material aid to those arrested or wounded and to the families of those killed. Joining Anders as patrons were Archbishop Gawlina,[31] Sosnkowski, Raczyński, and Rozmarek. Zaleski and the government issued a condemnation of Warsaw's actions and appealed to the people of Poland to remain calm and refrain from unnecessary actions. The government's representative in Washington presented a note to his American contact protesting the violent repression of the demonstrators. Radio Free Europe broadcast a detailed critique of the repressions and an analysis of the issues facing Poles under the communist government. And *Nasz Znak* demonstrated Sobczyk's new sympathies, claiming that the protests had been planned outside of Poland long in advance.

Tensions ran high after Poznań, but PZPR felt secure that it had society under control. Its bloody repression of protestors signaled its willingness to use force against its opponents, and it was confident that it had completely intimidated the Roman Catholic Church. In August, PZPR learned that it had badly miscalculated.

At the highest point in the city of Częstochowa stands the monastery of Jasna Góra. Its greatest treasure is the famed Black Madonna, an ancient icon of Mary and the infant Jesus. For centuries it has been a popular pilgrimage destination, with the largest crowds coming for the feast day of Our Lady of Jasna Góra on August 26. Normally, this occasion attracted hundreds of thousands, but in 1956, PZPR was certain that after its crackdowns far fewer would venture to Częstochowa. PZPR failed to accurately gauge society's mood. 1956 was a notable year, as it marked the 300th anniversary of the Miracle of Częstochowa, when a handful of defenders held off Swedish and German invaders for six weeks, ultimately forcing them to abandon their siege of the monastery. As August 26 neared, thousands upon thousands poured into Częstochowa from all of Poland, many making the journey by foot; to PZPR's astonishment, over one and a half million flooded the fields below the monastery's walls by the morning of the 26th. Cardinal Wyszyński's empty chair was carried in procession along the walls, an enormous bouquet of white and red roses filling his seat. When the pilgrimage concluded, the crowd dispersed peacefully and went home without incident. It was plain to PZPR that its tactics were not working. Terror and fear, until then its reliable tools, had lost much of

---

[31] *Sprawa Bergu* continued to cast its shadow. Archbishop Gawlina made his participation conditional on the exclusion of anyone connected with Berg.

their effectiveness. Workers walking off their jobs and attacking PZPR and SB buildings demonstrated that the people were losing their fear. Jasna Góra revealed rejection of the anti-religion program.

Poznań and Jasna Góra had a lesson for émigré politicians as well: Poland's people were taking initiative.

PZPR's leaders realized that changes were needed to restore order and maintain their hold on power. A new leader was needed, but prominent figures from the Stalinist era would be unacceptable. They turned to one well-known person who, since he had been imprisoned by Bierut's government, was decidedly not expected to maintain the status quo: Władysław Gomułka. In October, he was elected to the position of first secretary. Although he was viewed positively in Poland, his election, coupled with Hungary's liberalization program, alarmed Khrushchev. Accompanied by most of the Soviet Union's leadership, Khrushchev flew to Warsaw,[32] demanding an explanation. Gomułka skillfully calmed him down, defended PZPR's moves, and convinced the Soviet visitors that Poland would remain a faithful ally. Power would remain in PZPR's hands, and the Soviet Army would remain at its Polish bases.[33]

Now that he had Soviet support, Gomułka made a series of moves to ingratiate himself with society. UB leaders and functionaries arrested in the aftermath of Światło's defection, including Fejgin, Roman Romkowski, and Józef Różański, were tried. Cardinal Wyszyński was released, as were about 35,000 unjustly convicted people, including many AK veterans. Another 29,000 Poles were repatriated from the Soviet Union. Artists and musicians were freed from the restrictions of Socialist Realism, and the obligatory inclusion of communist propaganda in films was ended. Publications and monuments related to the Warsaw Uprising and AK were permitted. Jamming of Western radio broadcasts was suspended. Religion classes were allowed to resume in schools. Professors removed from their positions in Stalinist Poland were allowed to return to work. Special shops for PZPR and SB members were closed. Finally, Stalin himself was erased from Poland: Stalinogród reverted to its previous name of Katowice, Warsaw's Palace of Culture and Science was no longer dedicated to him, and

---

[32] Among Khrushchev's entourage were Vyacheslav Molotov, Anastas Mikoyan, and Lazar Kaganovich; all three had approved the Katyń massacre.
[33] Hungary was not so fortunate. Khrushchev ended its liberalization program by deploying the Soviet Army to occupy Hungary, remove its government, and install new leadership.

across the country his name was removed from institutions and factories.³⁴

Gomułka went on to remove Soviet officers from the military. Rokossovsky himself was ethnically Polish and never attempted to conceal that fact, but his inaction during the Warsaw Rising and his postwar repressions earned him the enmity of much of the population; he was widely regarded to be a Russian.³⁵ Gomułka dismissed him and other Soviet officers.

Not all of these changes would last, but Gomułka had signaled that the era of Stalin and Bierut was over. He did not, however, abandon their methods. Late in December, *Milicja* and ORMO were bolstered by the creation of *Zmotoryzowane Odwody Milicji Obywatelskiej* (ZOMO, Motorized Reserves of the Citizens' Militia). Officially, ZOMO's role was to respond to natural disasters, provide security for large public events, pursue criminals, search for missing persons, and build hospitals; its real role was to provide a readily available force that could rapidly respond to civil disturbances such as those in Poznań. ZOMO officers were highly trained, heavily armed, and brutal; their first actions, in 1957, were to secure *Sejm* elections and to disrupt strikes and student protests.

Throughout these events, *Zamek's* financial position continued to deteriorate. In 1949, the government closed its Cuban consulate due to lack of funds, and in late 1956, it ended consular functions in Lebanon.³⁶ In 1957 *Zamek* closed its Dublin consulate,³⁷ leaving a diplomatic presence only in Spain and the Holy See. Zofia Zaleska, sister-in-law of August Zaleski, had worked at the Dublin consulate since the war ended and headed it from late 1952 until its closure. With no further role in the exile government, Zaleska moved back to Poland and was soon under the scrutiny of intelligence.

SB now set its sights on Zaleski himself, to whom it assigned the codename *Arbuz* (Watermelon). Its objectives were to have him resign, recognize

---

³⁴ ZISPO, short for *Zakłady Metalowe im. Józefa Stalina w Poznaniu* (Josef Stalin Metal Works in Poznań), reverted to its previous name of *Zakłady Przemysłu Metalowego H. Cegielski w Poznaniu, Przedsiębiorstwo Państwowe* (H. Cegielski Metal Industry Complex in Poznań, National Enterprise).
³⁵ When Rokossovsky left Poland in 1956, he bitterly remarked to General Franciszek Cymbarewicz: "Oh, Cymbarewicz, irony of fate, in Russia I was a Pole and in Poland I was a Russian."
³⁶ Although the Polish consulate in Beirut had closed, Zygmunt Zawadowski retained his diplomatic privileges and remained in Lebanon as an unofficial representative of the Republic of Poland until 1971.
³⁷ Closure of a Polish consulate or embassy did not necessarily mean recognition of the Warsaw government. After the Dublin consulate closed, Paweł Czerwiński remained in Ireland and headed the Polish diplomatic office there from 1957 to 1958. Likewise, Portugal withdrew recognition in 1945 but refused to recognize the Warsaw government. Continued Portuguese acceptance of the London government is illustrated by the announcement in 1964 of the appointment of an honorary consul in Lisbon. Portugal only formally recognized the Warsaw government in 1974.

the Warsaw government, and hand over the presidential seals, the banner of the Republic, the April Constitution,[38] and government archives. Warsaw expected Zaleski to be susceptible to its overtures and looked at Zaleska as a channel to approach him. An intelligence agent met with her in 1958. She confirmed *Zamek's* poor financial situation, provided a few details about the divisions in London, and offered to establish contact with Zaleski. Her willingness to assist raised suspicion that she was not trustworthy. Though the matter was set aside, it was not dismissed.[39]

---

[38] For all their dismissive rhetoric about the April Constitution, Poland's communists displayed an obsession with that document. In 1943, KRN declared that constitution to be illegal and invalid, as did the PKWN Manifesto of 1944, yet the PRL still wanted the original document to be turned over to them, just as it wanted Zaleski to formally acknowledge its primacy.

[39] Zaleska eventually returned to London, where she died in 1974.

Exiles Divided

WITH ÉMIGRÉ POLITICS in a protracted stalemate, Zaleski labored to grow support outside of the opposition political parties. He dissolved *Rada RP* in December 1957 and replaced it with *II Rada RP* the following March. It was comprised of fifty-six members, fifteen elected from émigré communities, eighteen appointed by political parties, seventeen appointed by Zaleski, and six from the prewar *Sejm* or *Senat*. Over half of its members claimed no party or social group affiliation. Those who did represented *Konwent Walki o Niepodległość* (Convention for the Fight for Independence, a faction that emerged from a split in LNP), *Stronnictwo Chrześcijańskiej Demokracji* (Christian Democracy Party, an SP spinoff), *Związek Socjalistów Polskich na Obczyźnie* (Association of Polish Socialists Abroad, a group of former PPS members), *Związek Ziem Wschodnich* (Union of the Eastern Territories, representing *kresy* expellees), and *Ruch Odrodzenia Narodowego* (National Rebirth Movement). A new pro-*Zamek* political entity, *Niezależny Ruch Społeczny* (Independent Social Movement), appeared in 1957. Its purpose was to foster the creation of community groups supportive of the government outside political parties.

Eustachy Sapieha withdrew from presidential succession in 1959.[1] Zaleski now chose his trusted associate Aleksander Zawisza. He was an experienced diplomat, beginning with service as Paderewski's adjutant at the Paris Peace Conference. From 1922 to 1935 he worked in the Ministry of Foreign Affairs. In 1935, he was posted to the Polish embassy in Rome, serving until 1940. He was then *chargé d'affaires ad interim* to the Czechoslovak government-in-exile and held a succession of diplomatic postings in Africa, first as consul general in Lusaka, Northern Rhodesia;[2] he later held the same position in Salisbury, Southern Rhodesia,[3] and Nairobi, Kenya. After the war, he moved to the United Kingdom. He was appointed to *III Rada Narodowa* in 1949 and was minister of foreign affairs under Hanke and Pająk.

---

[1] Eustachy Sapieha remained a resident of Kenya for the remainder of his life; he died in Nairobi on February 20, 1963.
[2] Northern Rhodesia is now the Republic of Zambia; Lusaka remains its capital.
[3] Southern Rhodesia is now the Republic of Zimbabwe; Salisbury was renamed Harare.

After Pope Pius XII, an ardent opponent of communism, died in October 1958, Kazimierz Papée, ambassador to the Vatican since 1939, expected trouble. Papée was concerned that the new pope would require him to present his credentials, and the split in London had the potential to complicate the matter. His fears were realized when he met with Secretary of State Tardini in November. Tardini confirmed that the Vatican intended to cease recognition of the Republic. His justification was Papée's inability to submit his credentials, the Vatican's desire to alleviate pressure on the Church in Poland, and opposition to maintaining the embassy from the Catholic hierarchy within Poland. Papée offered letters from Zaleski and Anders accrediting him as ambassador; Tardini rejected them. Papée argued that loss of recognition would not help the Church in Poland and asked Tardini if the Church in Czechoslovakia was in any less peril since it did not have representation at the Vatican; Tardini refused to answer. Papée did not believe Cardinal Wyszyński wanted the embassy closed and suspected SB disinformation.[4] Wyszyński subsequently assured him that he had not called for the embassy's closure. Papée informed Tardini of this in later meetings, but he refused to accept that Wyszyński had sent Papée such a message.

Tardini's position was a component of John XXIII's policy of opening dialogue with the communist world, and closure of the Polish embassy was expected to be received as a goodwill gesture. However, Tardini backed down. The embassy was permitted to remain open, but Papée was now recognized as manager of embassy affairs. As he was no longer accepted as an ambassador, he and his staff were not recognized as diplomats. Poland was not alone. Lithuania's legation to the Vatican was downgraded at the same time; it also was permitted to continue to function in a diminished capacity.

Poland had suffered staggering cultural devastation in the war, but not everything had been lost. Since 1940, many of the nation's most precious artifacts, including *Szczerbiec*, the coronation sword of Polish kings, had been secured in Canada and were cared for by Józef Polkowski, a former curator at Wawel Castle. He and another curator, Stanisław Świerz-Zaleski,

---

[4] Considering the infiltration of the Roman Catholic Church in Poland by agents of the security service and the cooperation of some priests with the authorities (the "PAX" priests), and in light of the multiple messages Papée claimed to have received from Poland, it is plausible that a message from Wyszyński to the Vatican expressing his opposition to the continued operation of the embassy was a fabrication.

brought them from Kraków to Canada by way of Romania and France and deposited them in the National Archives. Towards the end of the war, the curators and Poland's envoy to Canada Wacław Babiński resolved to protect them from Moscow's grasp.[5] They deposited some in a Bank of Montreal branch in Ottawa and the rest in a monastery and a convent.

In 1945, Alfred Fiderkiewicz, head of the new government's diplomatic delegation, met with Polkowski and Świerz-Zaleski and thanked them for their efforts. He then asked where the artifacts were stored, but they refused to answer. Polkowski thought that the Soviet Union could not be trusted, but Świerz-Zaleski began to think otherwise.[6] By June 1946, Świerz-Zaleski decided to cooperate and attempted to retrieve the artifacts, but he was unable to remove anything from the bank without Polkowski's concurrence, and Polkowski had already moved the other items out of the monastery and convent. Quebec Premier Maurice Duplessis, a staunch Catholic and strong opponent of communism, agreed to help and moved everything to the Quebec Provincial Museum, announcing the items would stay there until a competent authority could decide on ownership and resolution.

They remained there through the 1950s. Polkowski made regular visits to perform conservation work, but as he neared seventy years of age, he realized that he could not continue much longer, nor could he afford to. The London government was perennially short of cash and provided no funds for upkeep of the Wawel treasures. He lived modestly, working in a grocery store and living in a rented room, leaving him very little money to spend on the collection. Meanwhile, Duplessis had died, and his successor was willing to enter into discussions with Warsaw. A consul from the embassy contacted Polkowski to discuss preservation, and he received an invitation to meet with Witold Małcużyński, an émigré concert pianist with extensive contacts in Poland. They discussed the Wawel treasures and Polkowski, believing there was no longer a threat of Soviet confiscation, agreed that they could best be cared for in Poland. Małcużyński promised to discuss this with Warsaw. Clearly, he knew the right people; in a few weeks, an agreement was reached. Polkowski agreed to release the items under the

---

[5] This was a valid concern. The 1944–1945 Red Army advance across Poland into Germany was followed by wholesale looting.

[6] Polkowski's perspective was that most of the items under their care had been looted from Poland by the Russian Empire during the partitions. A large number of tapestries had not survived their Russian sojourn; many were destroyed when Russians cut openings for doors and windows in them. To him, allowing Warsaw to reclaim them opened the possibility of further damage or complete loss. Świerz-Zaleski took the opposite approach. He felt that the Soviet Union could be trusted in this matter, as some of the items they were looking after had been returned to Poland by the Soviets.

condition that they were to be handed over to the people of Poland and not to the government. He asked *Rada Trzech* and *Zamek* for approval. Anders sent *Rada Trzech's* approval, but no word came from 43 Eaton Place, so Polkowski contacted *Zamek's* Montreal representative and received his approval. By December 1958, all items were released from the bank and the museum. After examination and inventory, they were shipped to Boston, loaded on the Polish ship *Krynica*, and sailed for Gdynia.

In 1960, the treasures were again in Wawel, but *Zamek* disagreed with its representative in Montreal. In January 1961, *Polska Agencja Telegraficzna* released the text of a protest note sent on January 4 to Ottawa. It claimed that the items were under Canadian protection and that Canada had no right to release them, charged Ottawa with caving to communist pressure, and claimed that the Soviet Union's denouncement of the 1921 Treaty of Riga opened the door to confiscate the collection. That did not occur, and the Wawel treasures remained securely in Kraków.

If division and conflict were, as Zaleski contended, the inevitable fate of all émigré communities in the world, such unpleasantries usually remained internal to the community, although some became visible to outsiders. Such an event happened in February 1960 when Sir John Athworth, a judge in London's Royal Courts of Justice,[7] opened proceedings in a libel case. Anders was the plaintiff; the defendants were Michał Kwiatkowski and Adam Gaś. Kwiatkowski was editor and publisher of *Narodowiec*, a Polish-language daily newspaper published in France. At issue was an item written by Gaś and published in the January 28, 1956, edition of *Narodowiec* that claimed Anders refused to fight in the 1920 Battle of Warsaw and that during the Second World War he was an enemy of Sikorski's government and expected Germany to win.

Anders would not allow these allegations to go unchallenged. He filed suit against Kwiatkowski and Gaś for libel.[8] Although his claims complemented Warsaw propaganda, Gaś was acting independently and was a Mikołajczyk supporter. SB took note, however, and initiated contacts with Gaś; by 1959, he was a paid agent. And Warsaw was only too happy to provide support for the defense. At the request of Kwiatkowski and

---

[7] The Royal Courts of Justice are often referred to simply as the "Law Courts." They are located in a monumental, grey-stone Victorian Gothic building on The Strand.
[8] This was not the first time Anders was involved in a libel suit in the United Kingdom. In 1951, he won a judgment of £5,000 against the *Daily Worker*, a British communist newspaper, for implying that he was a traitor and a renegade.

Gaś, documents from the Nowogródek Cavalry Brigade, commanded by Anders in September 1939, were made available, and Captain Jerzy Klimkowski, Anders's former adjutant, was permitted to travel to London to serve as a witness. General Juliusz Rómmel, whom Anders had requested as a witness, was denied a passport. They were also in regular contact with the embassy and with Mikołajczyk.

Public interest in the case ran high. For every session of the three-week trial, the gallery was filled to capacity; daily reports appeared in *Dziennik Polski i Dziennik Żołnierza* and in British newspapers. Anders was on the stand for fifteen hours. Three senior British officers testified in his support. During cross-examination, Gaś distanced himself from the *Narodowiec* article. He claimed that he had merely written opinions that were circulating in London and that he had not bothered to check their veracity. He contended that he bore no ill will towards Anders; he even agreed that Anders was a courageous man who had served the Polish cause. Mikołajczyk made a rare appearance in London for the trial, and his testimony had a very different tone. He insisted that Anders bore moral responsibility for Sikorski's death.

Klimkowski was not called to testify. His history with Anders may have been a factor: while in the Second Polish Corps, Klimkowski had approached the NKVD and offered to cooperate to keep the Corps on Soviet soil. His plans and the materials he had gathered were discovered, and he was tried by a Polish military court, expelled from the army, and imprisoned. In July 1945, he was released and returned to Poland. During Anders's testimony, the judge asked him if he knew Klimkowski. Anders responded in the past tense: "*Znałem*" ("I knew him").

The jury ruled in favor of Anders on all points except for the characterization that he was an enemy of the Sikorski government; they found this to not be libelous. *Narodowiec* was ordered to pay £7,000 in damages to Anders and to reimburse him for two thirds of his legal costs. Anders was responsible for paying the remainder of his legal fees, which amounted to more than the damages he was awarded. For Anders, this was a mostly positive outcome, since he had been cleared of the three most serious allegations. But Sikorski's widow Helena Sikorska, already poorly disposed towards Anders, again demanded that he vacate his office in the Sikorski Institute. Once more, he refused.[9]

Klimkowski's trip had not been unproductive. By chance, he spoke with Major Marceli Kycia, brother-in-law of Helena Sikorska, and learned that

---

[9] Sikorska's dislike of Anders and his supporters was widely known; she was incensed that his associates had taken control of the Institute's board without her agreement.

she was in poor health, dissatisfied with her living conditions, and willing to return to Poland. Klimkowski reported this conversation to SB. A few months later, Kycia was approached by an intelligence officer. He confirmed that Sikorska missed Poland, had resolved to return, and had decided that her husband's remains belonged there. In 1961, Sikorska made plans to remove some of Sikorski's papers and memorabilia from the Institute and deliver them to the embassy. These plans came to nothing, and the matter was closed, but it was not forgotten by either Sikorska or Warsaw.

Throughout the 1950s, *Kultura's* influence continued to grow on both sides of the Iron Curtain. In 1962, *Instytut Literacki* commenced publication of *Zeszyty Historyczne* (Notebooks of History), a forum for research into Polish history, focusing on topics that had been distorted or ignored in Warsaw's version of history.

SB targeted *Instytut Literacki* and made an ill-fated attempt to recruit a *Kultura* contributor as a collaborator. Warsaw also tried to confuse *Kultura* readers by merging two periodicals, *Nowa Kultura* and *Przegląd Kulturalny*, into a new publication it chose to name *Kultura*. This fooled nobody, and its version was commonly referred to as *Kultura warszawska*.[10] Regardless, most of the prominent writers in Poland had little choice but to write for it if they wanted to be published.

In light of Warsaw's inability to provide for its own citizens, parcels from abroad kept many families fed, clothed, and supplied with medicines. At its peak, the import/export firm Haskoba shipped an average of over one thousand packages every week. But in the early 1960s, Warsaw sharply increased customs duties, and many impoverished recipients could not afford to pay. Their benefactors stopped sending material aid; Tazab saw parcel volume decline by 80 percent. Yet émigrés still wanted to help, and their alternative was to send money. Their only reliable option was *Bank Powszechna Kasa Oszczędności* (Bank PKO). Émigrés also wanted to visit, and Warsaw had liberalized travel policies. They were now able to more easily visit family and friends and bring them money, clothing, and other goods.

These developments launched a competition among émigré businesses to obtain the right to be official representatives of Bank PKO, LOT Polish

---

[10] When asked about the Warsaw *Kultura*, writer Janusz Głowacki stated that the title was stolen from Giedroyc. Głowacki had written for both Giedroyc's *Kultura* and the Warsaw *Kultura*.

Airlines,[11] or the state-owned Orbis travel bureau. As usual, SB saw opportunities to recruit informants. Owners of the export firms Tazab, Haskoba, and Fregata were targeted, and each was offered the desired business opportunities in exchange for cooperation. None agreed, although some events during their failed recruitment bordered on comical. SB questioned Tazab's owner on his connections with Anders and challenged his trustworthiness; in response, he pointed out that Tazab was an official representative of the Soviet travel bureau Intourist and asked why Warsaw would not trust him if Moscow did. Fregata's owner caused his own difficulties. He managed to obtain rights to represent Orbis without having to collaborate with PRL intelligence, but his passion for gambling caused him to run up debts that he covered by delaying payments to Orbis. He further embarrassed SB by leaking news to the émigré press that Prime Minister Józef Cyrankiewicz had purchased a new Jaguar automobile. SB came up empty; no one cooperated.

It was ironic that *Zamek*, accused by *Zjednoczenie Narodowe* of acting contrary to democratic principles, had twice conducted *Rada* elections, while TRJN had been an appointed body since its inception. This was not by design. Elections had been discussed since 1956, but it was not until 1962 that *Zjednoczenie Narodowe* parties finally agreed on electoral procedures. In June and July, TRJN conducted elections to *Zjazd Polaków w Wielkiej Brytanii* (Congress of Poles in Great Britain). Of the 60,000 to 80,000 eligible voters, about 13,000 cast ballots to elect 536 representatives. In October, they convened at Cathedral Hall in Westminster[12] to articulate their positions on foreign, domestic, and exile affairs. They called for Poland's freedom, restoration of the prewar Soviet border, acceptance of the Oder–Neisse border, compensation from Germany, free elections, an end to religious persecution, and closer economic and cultural ties to the West, and they rejected armed actions. Representatives finished their work by issuing an appeal for unity among exiles and by electing members to TRJN's replacement, *Rada Jedności Narodowej* (RJN, Council of National Unity). RJN would hold its initial meeting in December.

In just over two months since RJN first met, a split emerged in *Zjednoczenie Narodowe*. Political parties and groups that refused to accept RJN

---

[11] In the Polish language, LOT Polish Airlines is known as *Polskie Linie Lotnicze LOT*.

[12] All 536 *Zjazd Polaków w Wielkiej Brytanii* representatives paid for travel to London, lodging, and other expenses out of their own pockets.

seats formed *Federacja Ruchów Demokratycznych* (Federation of Democratic Movements) in March 1963. Their disaffection dated to 1956 and was rooted in disagreements about the role of émigrés in the wake of the Poznań events. This new group was composed of NiD, SD, a faction of SP, and PSL "*Odłam Jedności Narodowej.*" NiD was by far the largest constituent group. *Federacja Ruchów Demokratycznych* appears to have been under considerable outside influence. Two PSL activists contended that it was created and controlled by ACEN; it was also heavily infiltrated by SB.

As *Zjednoczenie Narodowe* labored to solidify its standing among émigrés, *Zamek* asserted its constitutional authority. In February 1964, RJN conducted a debate regarding citizenship. Many exiles wrestled with the question of accepting citizenship in their new home countries; some did so out of necessity but hoped to retain their standing within the community.[13] RJN declared that acquiring foreign citizenship did not mean loss of Polish citizenship or rights within the émigré community but cautioned that anyone who did should not occupy leadership positions in émigré society. *Zamek* took exception to RJN's declaration, calling it illegal and contending that RJN had violated the April Constitution by assuming legislative prerogatives. *Zamek* issued a statement reminding émigrés that dual citizenship was prohibited under Polish law,[14] pointing out the perils of dual loyalties, and dismissing RJN's declaration as nothing more than a private statement. Later that year, the Council of Ministers appealed to military veterans to avoid ceremonies conducted by Anders and his associates by reminding them of their oath to guard the constitution and to submit to the law and the president; it concluded that Anders had violated his oath when he declared that he no longer considered Zaleski to be president.

Zamek also involved itself in international matters. In 1959, the West German government declined to prosecute those who committed atrocities during the 1939 invasion on the grounds that Germany's twenty-year statute of limitations on murder had expired. As the twentieth anniversary of Germany's defeat drew near, there was a very real possibility that war criminals who had avoided prosecution thus far would escape punishment. *Zamek* protested to the West German government and called on it to abolish the twenty-year limit for war crimes; it sent a copy of its protest to all United Nations delegations.[15]

---

[13] This was a valid concern. In 1966, a *Rada RP* member was dismissed for accepting British citizenship.

[14] The law referenced was promulgated on January 20, 1920.

[15] Initially, Poland's protest made no difference; in November 1965, Bonn declined to consider the matter. West Germany later reversed its position.

II Rada RP reached the end of its five-year term on March 28, 1963, and was followed by the eighty-five member *III Rada RP*. Its composition was somewhat different; fourteen seats were Zaleski appointees, eight had been members of the previous *Rada*, six were former *Sejm* or *Senat* members, eight had been government ministers, twenty-two were filled by popular vote in London, Manchester, and Edinburgh, and the remaining twenty-seven were appointed by political parties. Again represented were *Konwent Walki o Niepodległość, Związek Ziem Wschodnich*, and *Ruch Odrodzenia Narodowego*. *Stronnictwo Chrześcijańskiej Demokracji*, now simply known as Chrześcijańska Demokracja, was also represented, along with *Związek Socjalistów Polskich na Obczyźnie* (Association of Polish Socialists Abroad). For the first time, *Niezależny Ruch Społeczny* was represented. *III Rada* convened on September 14, 1963, chaired by Adam Pragier.

For nearly ten years, *Zamek* benefited from the steadying presence of Antoni Pająk. Since 1955, he had served as prime minister, managed the treasury, and briefly oversaw the Ministry of Polish Political Emigration. He had been a *Rada RP* member since its inception. In Pająk, Zaleski had a functionary, not a politician; he faithfully carried out presidential directives while maintaining tight control over the government. Dissenting views and alternative perspectives had little chance to come to light. Tadeusz Machalski, a minister in two of Pająk's governments, described their meetings as monologues. Not that he was complaining. He noted that Pająk concentrated on financial issues and matters of everyday life while rarely venturing into what he considered to be futile discussions of strategic topics. But Pająk could not avoid political conflicts. Zaleski dismissed his first government in 1957, entrusted him to form a new one, and then dismissed that one in 1963. Disputes with opposition politicians carried into Pająk's third government. His patience exhausted, Pająk resigned in June 1965. On the night of November 25, he died unexpectedly of heart failure and was buried in South Ealing Cemetery.[16] Zaleski called on his trusted associate and designated successor Aleksander Zawisza to form a new government. Zawisza's style of governance proved to be quite similar to Pająk's.

The matter of Zaleski returning to Poland came up again, but this time the initiative came from Bolesław Świderski, a London-based book publisher and editor of the weekly newspaper *Kronika*. He had no loyalties to any exile political faction; in his view, exile politics was not only

---

[16] Pająk's first wife Maria had died in 1959; they had been married for forty years. In 1963, he remarried; his second wife Jadwiga was to later hold a position in the treasury in Kazimierz Sabbat's government. He was buried next to Maria.

meaningless but harmful to the Polish cause. He also believed that émigré journalism's generally anti-communist and anti-Soviet stance prevented those abroad from appreciating developments in Poland and supporting their homeland. Świderski had no qualms about cooperating with Warsaw; he obtained funding for *Kronika* from the embassy. *Kronika* presented PRL in a positive light while exposing disarray and dysfunction in émigré politics, with RJN and Anders singled out for specific criticism.

Świderski's involvement in the *Arbuz* case began in May 1965. He had recently returned from his second visit to Poland and claimed that former Minister of the Treasury General Tadeusz Machalski had approached him prior to his trip asking him to meet with communist officials to discuss the possibility of Zaleski's return. Świderski contended that Zaleski thought the exile government was a fiction and was prepared to recognize the Warsaw government and hand over *Zamek's* assets. He further claimed to have informed Zaleski that Warsaw saw no obstacles to his return and to have offered to arrange a meeting between Zaleski and the Polish consul. Nothing came of the matter.

A final incident occurred in October 1966 at the Polish embassy in Paris. General Antoni Zdrojewski, president of *Związek Uczestników Polskiego Ruchu Oporu we Francji* (ZUPRO, Union of Participants of the Polish Resistance Movement in France), was there for the Polish Army Day celebration and entered into conversation with two employees who were actually intelligence agents. Zdrojewski claimed that Zaleski wanted to transfer his authority to the Warsaw government and that he would be the intermediary. It soon became clear that Zaleski had made no such statement, and the agents concluded that Zdrojewski was out for personal gain.

Zdrojewski's overture was the last time PRL intelligence considered the matter of Zaleski's return. His case was closed after intelligence concluded that the importance of the exile presidency was so diminished that bringing him back to Poland would be of little significance.[17]

SB's assessment of Zaleski's minimal propaganda value and the low turnout for émigré elections demonstrated how far the relevance of exile politics had fallen. Reversing the trend would require repairing the rift, and Zaleski and Anders stood in the way of unification. Offers to reconcile emanating from either camp were typically demands to concede. Pająk made one such effort in 1961, proposing creation of a unified political

---

[17] Historian Krzysztof Tarka suggested that Zaleski may have been playing a game with his London opponents, using the threat of handing over the symbols of power to get them to recognize him as president.

center; his terms were for *Rada Trzech* to recognize the government-in-exile and concede that Zaleski was the legitimate president. *Rada Trzech* refused, although in the following months Raczyński had intermittent conversations with *Zamek* representatives. Émigré organizations issued resolutions imploring the factions to resolve their differences,[18] individuals petitioned them to find a solution,[19] and prominent Poles attempted to intervene. Cardinal Wyszyński called for politicians to "abandon disagreement, close ranks and cease disputes."[20] Prince Stanisław Radziwiłł[21] met with Anders and insisted on "settling the *Zamek* crisis."[22] Anders insisted that unification had to be based on *Umowa Paryska* and *Akt Zjednoczenia Narodowego* and dismissed Zaleski's position, stating: "I stood and I stand [...] on the basis of the 1935 constitution" and, in reference to *Akt Zjednoczenia Narodowego*, "I do not see anything that would be contrary either to the spirit or the letter of the constitution." Anders went on to declare that the prerequisite to resolving the split was a "statement by A. Zaleski that he has ceased to hold the office which, as we know, he held legally from 1947 to 1954."[23] Zaleski refused to yield. He insisted that unification would be accomplished when *Rada Trzech* unconditionally recognized him as the legitimate president, accepted the April Constitution, and dissolved itself.

In time, Zaleski did offer some concessions. In August 1965, *Zamek* presented a unification plan that proposed merging RJN with *Rada RP* and dissolving *Rada Trzech* and EZN; Zaleski would then appoint a new government composed of people from both sides. Anders and his supporters rejected it.

Advocates for unification persisted. In June 1965, *Stowarzyszenie Lotników Polskich w Londynie* (Association of Polish Airmen in London) called for unification. Its president, Colonel Aleksander Gabszewicz, met with General Bronisław Duch and General Stefan Dembiński at a memorial service in the Polish Aviators' Cemetery in Newark-upon-Trent in

---

[18] For example, in January 1961, *Komitet Główny Milenium Polski Chrześcijańskiej w Kanadzie* (Main Committee of the Millennium of Christian Poland in Canada) petitioned *Rada Trzech* to end the dispute.

[19] In late 1961, some of Zaleski's American supporters wrote to him suggesting that he resign the presidency.

[20] Anna Siwik, "Polska emigracja polityczna" ("Polish Political Emigration"), *Dzieje Najnowsze*, Rocznik XXVI 1994, 1.

[21] Stanisław Radziwiłł, as a member of the Radziwiłł family, was entitled to claim the title of prince. He had served as a cavalry officer in September 1939 and had made his way to Paris via Hungary and Yugoslavia. During the war he lived in Geneva, where he represented the Polish Red Cross and served as representative to the League of Nations. After the war, he rarely involved himself in affairs of the exile government.

[22] Anna Siwik, "Polska emigracja polityczna," *Dzieje Najnowsze*, Rocznik XXVI 1994, 1.

[23] Anna Siwik, "Polska emigracja polityczna," *Dzieje Najnowsze*, Rocznik XXVI 1994, 1.

November, and the three agreed to start what they called a "noble conspiracy" to end the division. Their efforts were bolstered by an appeal for unity jointly made by the American and Canadian councils of *Stowarzyszenie Lotników Polskich*. Gabszewicz understood that, despite popular support for unification, he had to proceed carefully to avoid alienating either side. His plan was to have Anders draft a letter to Zaleski requesting a meeting that would require his response. When both accepted each other's letter, the meeting would be scheduled. Anders placed no preconditions on the proposed meeting and agreed to Zaleski's request that he retract the 1954 letter in which he broke with Zaleski.

Anders's letter struck a conciliatory tone. Zaleski convened a meeting with Zawisza and the Council of Ministers and asked them to prepare a reply. Their response was so antagonistic that Gabszewicz, Duch, and Dembiński agreed it could not be given to Anders; Dembiński worked with the government to tone it down. *Zamek's* final draft included a proposal for a meeting between delegates from *Zamek* and *Zjednoczenie Narodowe* prior to the Zaleski–Anders meeting. Anders agreed, and a timeline was fixed for the preliminary meeting.

And nothing happened. The preliminary meeting was never held, nor did Zaleski and Anders meet. *Zjednoczenie Narodowe* remained skeptical that Zaleski would yield the presidency, while *Zamek* viewed Anders's willingness to reconcile as an opportunity to extract further concessions. This was made plain in an article by Minister of Justice Stanisław Lubodziecki in *Rzeczpospolita Polska*. Lubodziecki referred to *Zjednoczenie Narodowe* as "*grupa rozłamowców*" (group of dividers) and laid out conditions to achieve reconciliation; these can be summarized as admitting that culpability for the split lay solely upon the opposition, dissolving its institutions, and subjecting all of its actions to review. But dissent was surfacing in *Zamek*. At a meeting of *III Rada RP*, Janusz Witołd Alexandrowicz charged Zawisza, Lubodziecki, and Zygmunt Muchniewski[24] with doing "everything in order to prevent reconciliation," including concealing the very existence of the Anders letter from the *Rada*.[25]

Zaleski's opponents frequently portrayed him as an autocrat who had no intention of leaving office; in essence, a president for life. He disputed these accusations in a 1966 talk with Włodzimierz Srokowski.[26] Zaleski

---

[24] Zygmunt Muchniewski was minister of émigré political affairs.
[25] Anna Siwik, "Polska emigracja polityczna," *Dzieje Najnowsze*, Rocznik XXVI 1994, 1.
[26] Włodzimierz Scholze-Srokowski was a career military officer who remained in the United Kingdom after the war. Zaleski promoted him to the rank of Brigadier General in 1964.

maintained that he had every intention of stepping down in 1954 but was unable to accept *Akt Zjednoczenia Narodowego*, which he claimed would have effectively replaced the constitution with the rule of party politics. He proposed forming an arbitration committee from both sides to negotiate a new agreement, after which he would form a council of state with representation from all political parties. Zaleski reiterated that he would step down if the opposition truly intended to reconcile.

Gabszewicz, Duch, and Dembiński persevered. They believed staunch opponents of Anders and his circle within *Zamek* had inordinate influence on Zaleski, and they sought to counter it by expanding his exposure to pro-unification voices within *Zamek* and to public opinion within the émigré community. In 1967, they sent a letter to Zaleski reviewing their efforts and imploring him "to believe in the sincere intentions of the General." They proposed a private meeting between Zaleski and Anders in a neutral location without any delegates. But Zaleski would not take a position contrary to that of his advisors.[27] Again, an effort to reconcile opposing groups that had broad support among émigrés came to nothing.

In 1948, Mikołajczyk had become president of another American-sponsored organization, the International Peasant Union (IPU), a coalition of exile agrarian political parties. IPU claimed to be the legitimate representatives of farmers in their homelands and advocated free multiparty elections. Mikołajczyk's colleagues at NCFE and IPU learned what exile politicians already knew: he was difficult to work with. Those same traits he had exhibited in London were on display in America, and his tenure at IPU was marred with conflict. In 1953, a long-running dispute between Mikołajczyk and IPU Secretary-General G. M. Dimitrov ignited and was resolved only when NCFE interceded. NCFE's American operatives also found him to be a challenge. Its political advisor Lewis Galantiere summarized their meeting in February 1955 by noting that Mikołajczyk spoke for nearly two hours without interruption and didn't trouble himself to respond to comments.

If anything, his forceful personality was more pronounced within his own party. PSL Vice President Franciszek Wilk noted his aversion to consulting with his staff and his tendency to act unilaterally. Mikołajczyk came under attack for his domineering traits, muddy financials, and the party's dwindling international influence. His response was to dismiss three leading

---

[27] Anna Siwik, "Polska emigracja polityczna," *Dzieje Najnowsze*, Rocznik XXVI 1994, 1.

party members,[28] who then formed a breakaway party they named PSL-NKW. Meanwhile, PNKD was crumbling; SD had left PNKD in 1954. All that remained was Mikołajczyk's faction of PSL and Karol Popiel's branch of SP.

By the late 1950s, PNKD's activities had all but ceased, but it was not formally dissolved; at an ACEN meeting in 1962, Mikołajczyk was introduced as president of PNKD. Mikołajczyk had little interest in London politics and few followers in the United Kingdom, yet American politicians and American-funded organizations continued to hold him in high regard. He continued to hold the IPU presidency and made frequent appearances on Radio Free Europe. In 1962, he was called upon to testify before the Subcommittee on Europe of the House Committee on Foreign Affairs, and he used this forum to reject the American policy towards Poland and called for an economic blockade against the Soviet bloc. He resigned the IPU presidency in 1964, but animosities lingered. Ferenc Nagy, his colleague from IPU and ACEN, was interviewed in 1965 by a journalist from the Warsaw newspaper *Express Wieczorny* and called Mikołajczyk a reactionary and difficult to work with. Mikołajczyk responded by dispatching a furious letter to Nagy; he sent copies to the chairs of every national delegation of ACEN and to the American leaders of FEC. At about the same time, Mikołajczyk published a harsh criticism of Korboński in the Chicago publication *Orka*,[29] accusing him of neglecting Polish issues in ACEN, supporting Gomułka, and other offenses. These conflicts ended when Mikołajczyk died in his home in Chevy Chase, Maryland, on December 13, 1966. He was buried at Mount Olivet Cemetery in Washington, D.C. With him died the last vestiges of PNKD.

Mikołajczyk had left PSL in disarray. For nearly two years after his death, it remained splintered into several factions. This state of affairs was finally resolved in October 1968. Representatives from all émigré PSL groups convened for a congress in Brussels where they were able to resolve their differences and develop a common program. Franciszek Wilk took the presidency of the reunited party. Stanisław Bańczyk, whom Mikołajczyk had expelled some years earlier, became head of PSL's supreme council.

With respect to the divide between *Zamek* and *Zjednoczenie Narodowe*, nothing had changed. PSL remained on the sidelines.

---

[28] The expellees were Stanisław Bańczyk, Stanisław Wójcik, and Władysław Zaremba.

[29] *Orka*'s complete title was "*Orka*" Biuletyn Informacyjny Polskiego Stronnictwa Ludowego Związku Przyjaciół Wsi Polskiej w Ameryce ("'Orka' Information Bulletin of the Polish People's Party of the Association of Friends of Polish Villages in America"). As its name indicates, *Orka* was a publication of the PSL and of the ZPWP (*Związek Przyjaciół Wsi Polskiej w Ameryce*, or Association of Friends of the Polish Village in America).

As the millennium of King Mieszko I's baptism[30] approached, the Polish nation and diaspora prepared to commemorate this singular event. Warsaw portrayed it as a purely secular event commemorating Polish statehood and began celebrations in 1960 with observances of the 550th anniversary of the Battle of Grunwald and the launch of a program to build one thousand new schools. Activities reached their peak on July 22, 1966, with a massive military parade in Warsaw. Cardinal Wyszyński and the hierarchy maintained that Mieszko's baptism inextricably linked Christianity with Poland's statehood, and Wyszyński's program emphasized this bond. It began in 1957 when he declared a nine-year period of prayer leading to the millennium. As the date neared, banners appeared on churches bearing messages such as *"Sacrum Poloniae Millenium"* ("Poland's Sacred Millennium"), *"Poloniae semper fidelis"* ("Poland always faithful"), and *"Naród z Kościołem"* ("Nation with the Church").

Warsaw made a concerted effort to overshadow the millennium's religious aspects and to disrupt religious celebrations. On April 15, 1966, Archbishop Karol Wojtyła's Mass in Gniezno was disrupted by the roar of cannon salvos fired as part of a government ceremony. In Poznań one day later, Gomułka derided Wyszyński and the Church for portraying Mieszko's baptism as the baptism of the nation. Gomułka would not permit Wyszyński to leave the country to visit Polish communities abroad, nor would he allow Pope Paul VI to visit Poland.[31] At the millennium Mass at Jasna Góra, Paul VI was represented by his portrait and an empty throne on which lay a bouquet of white and yellow roses.

Poles in the United Kingdom held commemorations, most notably a May 22 Mass at White City Stadium,[32] filled to its capacity of 45,000. Prior to Mass, military veterans paraded across the field with regimental banners; they were followed by scouts and émigré organizations.

In the days prior, 220 delegates from seventeen countries met in Westminster Cathedral Hall for *Światowy Zjazd Polski Walczącej* (World Congress of Fighting Poland). As with the 1962 *Zjazd Polaków w Wielkiej Brytanii*, attendees were *Zjednoczenie Narodowe* supporters. They passed a

---

[30] Mieszko I was baptized on Holy Saturday, April 14, 966. The specific location is unknown but is believed to be either Gniezno, Poznań, or Ostrów Lednicki (an island on Lake Lednica, between Gniezno and Poznań).

[31] Even if Gomułka had relented on allowing a papal visit, it would have been vetoed by Leonid Brezhnev, who explicitly forbade it.

[32] White City Stadium was demolished in 1985.

resolution confirming that Sosnkowski's unification act of 1954 was the basis for émigré politics and affirmed their recognition of *Rada Trzech* and EZN. *Zamek* took exception to the resolution. *Rada RP* issued a statement declaring that, by adopting this resolution, *Światowy Zjazd Polski Walczącej* was attempting to negate the April Constitution and abolish legal continuity. *Rada RP* drew a parallel between the resolution and ongoing actions from Warsaw, contending that the resolution made *Rada Trzech* a de facto ally of the Warsaw regime.

Kazimierz Sabbat was one of the congress's organizers. *Rada Trzech* had high confidence in his organizational skills; in 1970, he was appointed co-organizer of *Kongres Kultury i Nauki Polskiej na Obczyźnie* (Congress of Polish Culture and Science Abroad).

Maria Danilewiczowa and her staff at *Biblioteka Polska* (Polish Library) had adapted themselves to their cramped quarters. Tightly packed bookshelves reached the ceilings of their small rooms, with even more books stored in the damp basement. *Biblioteka Polska* had been established in 1942 and funded by the British government, but that support ended after the war. Rather than letting the library close, the Polish University College Association Ltd. (PUCAL) made space for it in their building. PUCAL had itself been formed during the war as Polish Polytechnic and continued its mission to educate engineers after the war. PUCAL had obtained a building at 9 Princes Gardens and shared it with PUNO, *Biblioteka Polska, Stowarzyszenie Techników Polskich w Wielkiej Brytanii* (Association of Polish Engineers in Great Britain), and *Rada Akademickich Szkół Technicznych* (Council of Academic Technical Schools). That these organizations were able to function in such a limited space was admirable, but the narrow building was hardly an ideal location. New accommodations were needed.

With more than one hundred Polish organizations in London, the idea of a common facility had been discussed for years but had not proceeded beyond talk until Roman Wajda took it upon himself to turn the concept into reality. Wajda, a former gulag prisoner and Second Polish Corps veteran, was a professor at Polish University College and at Battersea College of Technology. He was intimately familiar with 9 Princes Gardens and had a thorough understanding of the problems faced by its occupants. He envisioned a large building with space for all member organizations, classrooms, a theater, and function rooms; revenues would come from tenants and from venue rental. It took little effort for him to bring all occupants of 9 Princes Gardens on board, and they created *Polski Ośrodek Społeczno-Kulturalny* (POSK, Polish Social and Cultural Association) in 1963.

Challenges were numerous. POSK needed to recruit members, raise funds, purchase property, design its building, obtain permits, and oversee construction. Wajda and his team took a model of the proposed building to meetings with organizations and individuals throughout Britain to gain their support and financial assistance. Hammersmith was chosen as POSK's new home after Mieczysław Sas-Skowroński pored over the London telephone directory for days to determine the highest concentration of Poles in the city. After one year, fifty-two organizations and 112 individuals joined. POSK also had a number of influential supporters, including Anders, Bór-Komorowski, Raczyński, and Kopański. Giedroyc and the staff of *Instytut Literacki* joined as individual members and promoted POSK in the pages of *Kultura*. But POSK had opponents, the most vocal of whom was Karol Poznański, former consul general in Paris and London. Poznański conducted a vigorous campaign against POSK and used his clout to prevent many organizations from joining. Wajda and his team pressed on. In 1968, they found suitable property at 240–244 King Street, and the arduous task of obtaining planning permission began. They commenced publication of *Wiadomości POSK* (POSK News) to promote the organization and publicize its activities.[33]

Although 43 Eaton Place belonged to the government-in-exile, August Zaleski's name was on the lease. That changed in August 1968. The government registered a new company, Cytadela (Eaton Place) Limited, to hold the property in trust; its trustees were Bohdan Wendorff and Paweł Jankowski. The president held most of the shares in this new structure, and his successor was the only person authorized to receive them.

Rada RP approved this change, and in January 1969, Zaleski announced this company's creation. Its trustees would regularly communicate with their law firm to confirm or update presidential succession.

Gomułka enjoyed a period of popularity after he faced down Khrushchev in 1956, but this waned within a few years. Workers began to view him as a poor communicator and out of touch with the masses, and his position within PZPR was weakening. An opposition faction calling itself

---

[33] By the late 1960s, property values in the Earls Court ("Polish Corridor") area had increased to the point that it was financially untenable for Polish residences and businesses to remain. Hammersmith and Ealing became new areas of Polish concentration, as well as Lewisham and Balham, across the Thames.

"*partyzanci*" (partisans) emerged, a group of GL/AL veterans holding a strong nationalist ethos and opposing inclusion of non-ethnic Poles in PZPR, the government, and higher education. Its leader was Minister of the Interior Mieczysław Moczar,[34] and he leveraged his position to launch a campaign to purify PZPR.

International developments favored him. In June 1967, Israel defeated Egypt, Jordan, and Syria in the Six-Day War. Israel was backed by the United States, while the Soviet Union supported its opponents. For many Poles, it was a welcome slap in Moscow's face, made all the sweeter by the presence of a number of Polish Army veterans in the Israeli military.[35] For Moscow, it was an embarrassing defeat, and it responded by terminating diplomatic relations with Israel, as did Poland and other Bloc nations. Moscow backed its anti-Israel campaign with a broader anti-Semitic offensive. Anti-Jewish articles appeared in the press, anti-Jewish books were published, and thousands of Soviet Jews sought permission to emigrate. Moczar viewed these developments as a clear signal that he could proceed with his purge.

Zjednoczenie Narodowe made its opposition clear. Sabbat issued a statement on behalf of EZN declaring émigré support for Israel, and Anders sent his congratulations to Israeli General Moshe Dayan. Jan Starzewski, head of EZN's Foreign Affairs Department, responded to Warsaw's termination of diplomatic relations with Israel by sending a letter to the Israeli government assuring them that the Polish people did not agree with Warsaw's actions.

Difficulties continued to mount for Gomułka. His wife was Jewish, making them both targets of Moczar's campaign. Poor economic conditions led PZPR to raise food prices, increase work norms, and lower wages, fueling discontent among workers. In 1968, PZPR sparked a series of protests by canceling a production of Adam Mickiewicz's epic *Dziady (Forefathers' Eve)* staged by *Teatr Narodowy* (National Theater) in Warsaw. PZPR considered *Dziady* to be anti-Russian, anti-Soviet, and overtly religious. Protests erupted after the last performance, and students, intellectuals, and writers petitioned the *Sejm* to end censorship. *Uniwersytet Warszawski* (University of Warsaw) worsened the situation by declaring two Jewish students to be dissidents and expelling them. In response, protests broke out across the

---

[34] Moczar's father was Belorussian; his mother was Polish. This mixed ethnicity made his drive to purge non-Poles from the PZPR rather perplexing.

[35] Many Israeli officers and soldiers had served in the Polish Army prior to or during the war; this included a number of veterans of the Second Polish Corps who remained in Palestine. Many Poles took pride in this, tormenting Soviets with the taunt, "Our Jews beat your Arabs."

country, and participants were attacked by ZOMO, ORMO, and plainclothes police officially called "worker activists." Thousands of students were expelled and forcibly conscripted into the military, and dozens of professors lost their jobs. Several thousand Jews emigrated to avoid expected persecution by Moczar and his apparatus, further tarnishing Poland's image. But Moczar and his allies were not strong enough to take down Gomułka. In November, Gomułka was re-elected to the position of PZPR First Secretary, and in the ensuing months, he removed Moczar's supporters from their positions. Moczar retained his position as minister of the interior, but his support base had been dissipated.

Dramatic though these events were, they were overshadowed by developments in Czechoslovakia. In response to a series of reforms that Moscow considered threatening to communist power, the Soviet Army, backed by Hungarian, Polish, and Bulgarian units, flooded into Czechoslovakia and installed new leadership.

Zamek and *Zjednoczenie Narodowe* condemned both repressions. In an April speech to *III Rada RP*, Zaleski declared that the student protests were a manifestation of Polish society's dissatisfaction with the Warsaw government and placed ultimate responsibility on Moscow. Zawisza gave a lengthy speech condemning repressions in Poland and Czechoslovakia and holding the Soviet Union accountable. EZN Chairman Sabbat declared Polish participation in the invasion of Czechoslovakia to be one of the saddest events in Poland's history. On Radio Free Europe, Sabbat asserted that Polish participation in the invasion had caused irreparable damage in relations with the Czech and Slovak peoples.

Later in 1968, Poland closed its diplomatic outpost in Spain, leaving only the embassy to the Vatican. Kazimierz Papée continued to represent the Republic as administrator of the embassy despite the reduced recognition afforded him by the Vatican.

Janusz Zawodny was next to attempt reconciling Zaleski and Anders. He was an AK veteran and commanded a company in the Warsaw Uprising. He was liberated from a German prisoner-of-war camp by the Americans, joined the Second Polish Corps, and moved to the United States after demobilization. He studied at the University of Iowa and supported himself by working as a farm laborer; he earned his Ph.D. from Stanford University and published *Death in the Forest: The Story of the Katyn Forest Massacre* in 1962. His academic credentials, reputation, and lack of political affiliation made him a respected neutral party among émigré Poles, and he was dismayed by the ongoing division in London. In 1969, he embarked on an initiative to organize a meeting between Zaleski and Anders. At first, his effort looked promising. Both sides initially agreed, but the matter soured when *Zamek* demanded that Anders apologize for his 1954 letter as a precondition. Anders would not, and Zawodny's effort ended unsuccessfully.

Sosnkowski had played no role in any reconciliation efforts since 1954. He lived on his farm in Canada and limited his role in émigré life and politics mainly to North America. His activities were limited by faltering health. He suffered two heart attacks in 1958, and in the ensuing years he became increasingly ill; by the late 1960s, he was almost completely blind. On October 11, 1969, Sosnkowski died in Arundel. He had wanted to be buried in Poland, but only when independence was restored. Until then, he wanted to be as close as possible to Poland, and his remains were taken to France. After a brief period at a Polish church in Paris, his remains were moved several miles away to the cemetery in the town of Montmorency,[36] where dozens of his countrymen were also buried.

At the age of seventy-seven, Anders still bore himself with soldierly discipline and had an air of authority about him. But he was not aloof; he was known for his sense of humor and his patience. He had an almost fatherly concern for his soldiers and their families and was in a position to help. Almost uniquely among Poles who had served under British command, the United Kingdom granted him a military pension, and his financial security enabled him to devote much of his time to the exile community. He received thousands of requests for assistance and helped as many people as he could. Anders was a strong proponent of education and encouraged young Poles to attend university. He never wavered in his belief that Poland would again be free.

Among his many friends were Kamil Czarnecki and his wife, actress and singer Irena Delmar-Czarnecka. Anders took on the responsibility for educating Kamil and his brother Marian after their parents died; both later served as officers in the Polish Army. Kamil and Irena had built successful lives in exile, and their house was a hub of activity; artists, military officers, and politicians could often be found there. Since his wife's birthday was

---

[36] A number of notable Poles moved to Montmorency after the failure of the November 1830 Uprising; the Les Champeaux cemetery is the final resting place for many notables of 19th- and 20th-century Polish society.

only a few days away from that of Irena Anders, Kamil had the idea to celebrate with a party for both of them. The chosen date, May 11, 1970, turned out to be a beautiful spring day, and about eighty guests joined the celebration. Anders was, as always, popular with the guests; he talked, joked, and laughed throughout the evening. Around midnight, he planned a game of bridge with Czarnecki and two other friends for the next evening. With that, Władysław and Irena Anders retired for the evening. Anders did not sleep well. He woke at about 3 a.m., feeling ill; he did not realize it, but he was suffering a stroke. He died later that day, the twenty-sixth anniversary of the final assault on Monte Cassino.

His flag-draped coffin lay in state in St. Andrew Bobola Church; thousands filed in to pay their respects. Westminster Cathedral was filled with veterans, émigrés, and representatives of the British and American governments and military for his funeral Mass,[37] and uniformed veterans held aloft regimental banners. At his request, Anders was laid to rest with his soldiers in the Polish Military Cemetery at Monte Cassino; the RAF provided a transport aircraft. On May 23, 1970, scores of Poles, accompanied by an Italian honor guard and British and French military officials, ascended the hill to the cemetery for his burial. Western newspapers provided extensive coverage, but his passing received scant attention in the official Polish press. Most newspapers printed the same brief notice, deliberately buried amidst minor news items. *Życie Warszawy* and *Żołnierz Wolności* were the exceptions, both running articles that impugned his character and were dismissive of his accomplishments. And yet, this news was on the lips of most Poles. Despite Warsaw's efforts, he remained a heroic figure.

A few days after Anders was buried, Helena Sikorska met with the Polish ambassador. She reaffirmed her desire to return to Poland and declared her intent to finalize arrangements for the return of her husband's remains. For Warsaw, the timing of this meeting could hardly have been better, as such an announcement would divert public attention from the death of Anders.

But Sikorska's timeline did not align with Warsaw's. It was not until September that she officially declared her intent in a letter to the ambassador. Although the opportunity to overshadow Anders was gone, there was still significant propaganda value to be reaped. Sikorska proposed returning her husband's remains in 1971 to coincide with his ninetieth birthday, and she notified the British War Graves Commission of her intentions.

---

[37] British representatives included the sons of Prime Ministers Winston Churchill, Clement Attlee, Anthony Eden, and Harold MacMillan. General Mark Clark, former commander of American forces in Italy, also attended.

Warsaw soon encountered an unexpected obstacle: Sikorska insisted that her husband's tomb was to be in the crypt of Wawel Cathedral. For Warsaw, burial in Wawel would have cast undesirable religious overtones on the event and was unacceptable. Its intent was to bury Sikorski in Warsaw; specifically, he was to be reinterred in Powązki Cemetery along *Aleja Zasłużonych* (Avenue of the Meritorious), near such communist luminaries as Bolesław Bierut. Confident that its plan would be accepted, Warsaw continued quietly preparing for the event.

In 1970, less than three weeks before Zawisza would have marked his fifth year as prime minister, he presented Zaleski with a request to dismiss his government. Zaleski accepted, and on July 20, he entrusted Zygmunt Muchniewski with the task of forming a new government. At first glance, this did not signal changes in *Zamek's* attitude towards unification, but Muchniewski emerged as a champion of unity. On his first day in office, he issued an appeal for unity to the émigré community. It was more than empty words; he outlined a specific plan and assigned Minister of Foreign Affairs Jerzy Gawenda, General Ludwik Ząbkowski, and Lieutenant Janina Płońska to establish cooperation with those who desired unification.

His move achieved quick results. EZN chairman Sabbat contacted him, and they met on September 17. Three weeks later, Sabbat and Jerzy Starzewski, chair of EZN's Foreign Department, met with Gawenda's committee. Sabbat was sufficiently convinced in their sincerity that he created a commission, *Komisja Scaleniowa* (Unification Commission), to work with them. Another important *Zjednoczenie Narodowe* figure then made a substantial concession. In a November interview with the *Daily Telegraph*, Raczyński stated that he assumed Zaleski would name his successor and that both sides would consider that person to be their leader.

Negotiations and correspondence continued for several months, initially focusing on cooperation between *Zamek* and *Zjednoczenie Narodowe* and on merging their treasuries. Most *Zamek* and *Zjednoczenie Narodowe* supporters in the United Kingdom strongly supported unification, and messages urging reconciliation came from émigrés around the world.

Gomułka needed a political victory to bolster his image, and he got one courtesy of Moscow. In 1970, the Soviet Union and West Germany normalized relations, clearing the way for Gomułka to do the same. This culminated in the Treaty of Warsaw. Poland and West Germany accepted the border as defined at the Potsdam Conference and committed to nonviolence in their mutual relations. Prime Minister Cyrankiewicz and Chancellor Willy Brandt signed the treaty on December 7, 1970, in Warsaw's Palace of the Council of Ministers.[38] This would be Gomułka's final triumph.

After a quarter century in power, it was entirely reasonable to hold PZPR accountable for domestic economic conditions. There had been no significant disruptions in the global economy; quite the contrary, export markets were expanded when the Soviet Bloc liberalized trade with the West. There had been no wars and only one brief deployment of Polish troops in another country.[39] And yet PZPR struggled to meet basic material needs. In the 1960s, real wages and the standard of living steadily declined, and demand for housing far exceeded supply. Inefficient government enterprises could not build enough units to meet demand, and families languished on waiting lists for years to be allocated apartments of dubious quality. Major appliances were scarce, and automobiles were out of reach for many; those who could afford one typically had to wait years for delivery. But food was the largest problem: by 1970, it was common for a family to spend half of its budget to eat.

In this precarious situation, PZPR received the grim news that 1970's harvest would fail to meet projections. Unable to make up the difference through imports, the party chose to raise prices on forty-six items. An effort was made to temper the bad news by bundling it with price reductions for consumer goods and building materials such as clothing, televisions, refrigerators, vacuum cleaners, sewing machines, and paint. Forty items saw price reductions, but none were food.

At eight in the evening of Saturday, December 12, Gomułka announced the changes. Sunday's newspapers provided the painful details: on average, meat would cost 17.6 percent more, fish prices were raised by 11.7 percent, flour increased by 16 percent, milk was up 8 percent, lard came in at a staggering 33.4 percent higher, and coffee nearly doubled, jumping 92.1 percent. A further shock was that the prices went into effect immediately, meaning there was no chance to stock up before the increase. Stunned workers were faced with the realization that they would not be able to afford enough food for their families. Compounding the blow, these increases took effect two weeks before Christmas.

---

[38] Since 1994, the Palace of the Council of Ministers has been the official residence of the president and was renamed the Presidential Palace.

[39] Since the end of the Second World War, the only time Polish troops had been used abroad was in Czechoslovakia in 1968.

Gomułka had emphatically declared that society would follow PZPR's instructions, but the Politburo placed *Milicja* on alert. On Monday, workers at *Stocznia Gdańska* (Gdańsk Shipyard)[40] went on strike, marched into the city, and were attacked by helmeted *Milicja* officers brandishing rubber truncheons and heavy plastic shields. That night, the dull roar of tanks and armored vehicles echoed through Gdańsk. Poland's army was deployed and took up positions in the streets, at the shipyard, and at the port. By morning, the strike had spread to more shipyards and factories in Gdańsk, Gdynia, and Szczecin. Strikers were careful to frame their problems as economic; handmade banners bearing slogans such as "*strajk ma podłoże ekonomiczne a nie polityczne*" ("this strike is economic, not political") appeared. Protestors returned to the streets and were attacked by *Milicja*. Gomułka ordered the army to respond with force. Workers leaving the shipyard were fired on; three were killed. *Milicja* and the military prevented ambulances from reaching the victims.

On Wednesday, shipyard workers in Szczecin marched into the city and were attacked by *Milicja* and the army. On Wednesday evening, Deputy Prime Minister Stanisław Kociołek made a televised speech summoning workers to return to their jobs. Workers did not know that their shipyards, factories, and ports had been ringed by the army; Kociołek had set a trap. On Thursday morning, workers arrived at Gdynia's *Stocznia im. Komuny Paryskiej* (Paris Commune Shipyard) and were confronted by a wall of *Milicja* drumming their truncheons on their shields; behind them were a line of army tanks. Loudspeakers blared a message that the shipyard was closed and ordered the workers to return home, but as more workers arrived for their shifts, a tank cannon roared, followed by rifle fire. Injured and dead workers fell to the pavement.

When the shooting ended, the workers gathered their dead and marched to the city center, led by marchers bearing bloodstained Polish flags and followed by six men carrying a door on which lay the body of an unknown worker.[41] Chants of "Murderers!" echoed through the streets. Protests spread to other cities along the coast; as in Gdynia, they were forcibly suppressed. By Saturday, a state of emergency had been declared, and the shipyards and factories were closed. Forty lost their lives; the two

---

[40] In 1967, the shipyard had been renamed *Stocznia Gdańska im. Lenina* (Lenin Shipyard in Gdańsk).
[41] He was later identified as eighteen-year-old Zbigniew Godlewski, a worker from Elbląg. Krzysztof Dowgiałło, an author, saw the image of Godlewski's body being carried through the streets and wrote *Pieśń o Janku z Gdyni* ("Song about Janek from Gdynia," better known as *Janek Wiśniewski padł*, or "Janek Wiśniewski Fell"). Not knowing his name, Dowgiałło gave him the symbolic name Janek Wiśniewski.

youngest victims were fifteen, and the oldest was fifty-eight. Their burials were conducted in the middle of the night, and their immediate families were summoned on very short notice.[42] Another 1,165 were wounded. Over 3,000 were arrested, beaten, and tortured.

In London, a Polish student group organized a demonstration at Speakers' Corner in Hyde Park. On December 20, four thousand people gathered under the slogan "*Wolności, cheba dla Polski*" ("Freedom, bread for Poland"). After a series of speeches, *Rada Trzech* and EZN members led the group on a march to the embassy on Portland Place. Sabbat and Starzewski issued a protest to the United Nations about the conduct of the Warsaw government, and Sabbat called for creation of a fund to assist the victims.

Gomułka fell ill during the crisis; under that pretext, he was removed from power and replaced by Edward Gierek. After appealing for calm, Gierek proposed changes to the five-year plan, including increased wages to compensate for price increases. Stanisław Kociołek was shunted off to Belgium as an ambassador. Among the workers, a new generation of leaders was emerging, including a 27-year-old electrician from Gdańsk named Lech Wałęsa.

Over the years of his presidency, Zaleski had established the custom of delivering a speech to his government and supporters on the first Sunday of January. In 1971, his brief but pointed comments ranged from the December events in Poland to Soviet expansionism; he concluded with a warning to Western governments about Moscow's intentions. He gave no indication that he and his government were taking meaningful steps towards unity. Muchniewski followed with a somewhat longer address; he announced that committees comprised of *Zamek* and *Rada Trzech* supporters had been formed the previous year and were working on unification plans.

Considerable progress had been made. Muchniewski and Sabbat were corresponding regularly. *Komisja Scaleniowa* met three times in December and again in January;[43] by late January, it had composed principles of consolidation that recognized the April Constitution, *Umowa Paryska*, and select provisions of *Akt Zjednoczenia Narodowego*. Its members also agreed that the united government would follow the *Zamek* structure of president, government, and a representative body, although some crucial questions remained unresolved.

---

[42] Conducting funerals in this manner was designed to prevent crowds from gathering and demonstrations from erupting.
[43] Their meetings were held on December 1, 15, and 30, 1970, and on January 19, 1971.

Unification had opponents on both sides of the divide. In *Zjednoczenie Narodowe*, an increasingly assertive SN was its most strident foe. For six years, SN had been waging a campaign to claim the leading role in *Zjednoczenie Narodowe*; it disagreed with Sabbat's appointment to chair EZN, and at one point, its chairman Antoni Dargas flatly demanded that all opposition parties subordinate themselves to its authority. In February, Sabbat presented *Komisja Scaleniowa's* work to EZN, and SN adamantly opposed it. However, a majority of EZN members supported it, and *Rada Trzech* received appeals from émigré communities overseas imploring them to reach an agreement.

Their next step was to agree on a new president, and Gawenda declared that within two weeks he would present *Zamek's* nomination for *Zjednoczenie Narodowe's* approval. Gawenda had a candidate in mind: Witold Czerwiński, publisher of *Dziennik Polski i Dziennik Żołnierza*, RJN member, and former EZN chair. Zaleski met with Czerwiński, showing his willingness to consider a candidate from the opposition. Muchniewski also proposed a candidate, the politically unaffiliated Stanisław Ostrowski, a physician and former president of Lwów. On January 4, Zaleski suspended his 1968 decree that detailed the manner of appointing members to *Rada RP*. He was planning a new form of *Rada*.

At this late point, several obstacles threatened to derail their work. A Canadian paper published an interview with Sabbat that referred to him as prime minister; some in *Zamek* viewed this as disrespectful and offensive. Next, Sabbat refused to participate in a public meeting that was to focus on consolidating exile political structures. Lastly, Zaleski issued a decree announcing Stanisław Ostrowski as his successor and nullifying his 1959 appointment of Zawisza. Although appointing Ostrowski signaled his intention to mend the split, Zaleski acted without consulting *Zjednoczenie Narodowe* as Gawenda had promised. A letter from Ząbkowski to *Zjednoczenie Narodowe* informing them that the agreement reached by the committees was too vague to be acceptable made matters worse. In response, *Zjednoczenie Narodowe* reiterated its commitment to unification, implored Ząbkowski to not waste this opportunity, and expressed its willingness to clarify any questions and revise the agreement if necessary.

To *Zjednoczenie Narodowe*, it appeared that *Zamek* was once again attempting to define the direction and terms of unification. *Zamek* responded by reiterating that the constitution and the office of president were not negotiable. It proposed a transitional government composed of the current government and EZN representatives, which would then nominate members to a new body, *Rada Państwa* (Council of State); after *Rada Państwa* was appointed, EZN would dissolve. *Zamek* declared its intent to sign such an agreement immediately; *Zjednoczenie Narodowe* declined.

And yet, talks continued and steps towards unification proceeded. In November 1971, Zaleski announced the creation of *Rada Stanu Rzeczypospolitej Polskiej* (Council of State of the Republic of Poland), replacing *IV Rada RP*. Zaleski appointed twenty-six members to this new body on March 24, including former Prime Minister Jerzy Hryniewski, who was again using his birth name, Mikołaj Dolanowski. It would be Zaleski's last decree.

In her discussions with the ambassador, Helena Sikorska requested handling the matter of her husband's reinterment quietly, but negotiations could not be kept out of the public eye for long. In early January 1971, Radio Free Europe broadcast a report detailing PRL's plans to rebury Sikorski in Powązki. A wave of protests, appeals, and pleas followed. Jan Nowak-Jeziorański sent Sikorska a private letter urging her to reconsider. Articles opposing the move were printed in *Dziennik Polski i Dziennik Żołnierza* and other émigré publications, and the board of *Stowarzyszenia Lotników Polskich* passed a resolution appealing to Sikorska to change her mind. Several British newspapers and magazines joined the debate, but it was for naught. Sikorska dismissed their appeals and protests and refused to discuss the matter.

The only obstacle was agreement on the burial site. Warsaw was adamant that Sikorski would be laid to rest in Powązki or in Hyżne, a village where he had lived during his childhood. Sikorska was equally unwavering, insisting that her husband's remains would be returned to Poland only under the condition that they were buried in Wawel. She had received permission from Cardinal Wyszyński and Cardinal Wojtyła and refused to yield. She also amended her will to include the stipulation that her husband's remains could only be entombed in the Wawel crypt. This stalemate continued until the end of her life.

Helena Sikorska died on February 1, 1972. Her burial in a British cemetery was temporary; five months later, her remains were transported to Zakopane. About five thousand people attended her funeral Mass in *Kościół Najświętszej Rodziny* (Holy Family Church), most of whom spilled out of the church into the courtyard, down the steps, and onto the street below. Sikorska was buried in her family tomb in the parish cemetery. General Mieczysław Boruta-Spiechowicz delivered a brief speech, declaring that Sikorski would one day join Kościuszko, Poniatowski, and Piłsudski in Wawel.

Passersby on King Street had become accustomed to the fence stretching from 238 to 246. At first, the roof of a vacant Baptist church and the upper levels of disused commercial buildings could be seen; as the weeks passed, these gradually disappeared. For a few months, nothing was visible, although the din of construction could be heard along with the rumble of trucks that periodically entered or exited through the gate. By 1971, a new edifice had begun to emerge above the fence. Construction of the new POSK building was well underway.

Roman Wajda and his team had tirelessly labored to gather support for the concept of POSK, collect money, agree on a design for their building, and obtain the necessary permits. Fundraising ranged from soliciting donations from individuals and organizations to collecting spare change outside Polish churches. Polish organizations from throughout the United Kingdom frequently toured the construction site.

On a Wednesday in early March 1971, Bishop Władysław Rubin ascended the front steps of POSK accompanied by Wajda, the mayor of Hammersmith, and notable figures from the Polish émigré community. Several hundred people assembled below to observe Bishop Rubin bless the cornerstone. A significant amount of work remained, and the POSK building would not open for three more years. But Wajda's vision was steadily becoming a reality, despite the efforts of POSK's opponents.

In January 1972, Kamil Czarnecki received a letter from Mieczysław Hara, the consul general in London. Considering his standing with respect to the Warsaw government, this was rather unusual; Czarnecki was one of the seventy-five officers who had been stripped of citizenship by Warsaw for joining PRC, and he had little reason to hear from the embassy. Hara's letter was brief; he informed him that the People's Republic of Poland had canceled the 1946 resolution depriving him of Polish citizenship.

Citizenship had been restored to all those officers who had been sanctioned for joining PRC; in many cases, this act was posthumous. Czarnecki and his fellow officers were now at liberty to claim citizenship in the People's Republic. Clearly, Gierek's policies towards the émigré community differed from Gomułka's, but there were still limits to Warsaw's magnanimity. Even in death, the status of Anders and Mikołajczyk remained unchanged.

More normal relations with the Soviet Union had softened its image in the eyes of many Americans. Public interest in the plight of ACEN's member nations faded through the 1960s, and ACEN's ability to influence American opinion was declining. This made the Free Europe Committee's 1971 decision to cease funding ACEN easier.

The Free Europe Committee's 1972 budget had been cut by its parent organization, the CIA. Faced with decisions on allocating fewer funds, the Committee's leadership decided to terminate its subsidies to ACEN, which effectively meant ACEN would end operations. In January 1972, ACEN closed its offices and ended its publishing activities.

Stefan Korboński was not willing to let ACEN fade out of existence. He registered a successor organization, ACEN Inc., in New York later in the year, but it was even less influential than its predecessor.

Zaleski lived his final days in London's Hospital of St. John and St. Elizabeth.[44] He had been admitted on March 15, 1972, and underwent surgery on April 4. On the morning of April 7, PAT issued a statement that he had been hospitalized for several weeks and was in serious condition. At 3:25 that afternoon, August Zaleski died. The Council of Ministers declared a period of national mourning from April 8 through April 22; flags were to be flown at half-mast until after his funeral. His requiem Mass was in St. Andrew Bobola Church on April 13, and he was buried two days later at the Polish Military Cemetery in Newark-upon-Trent; his grave was adjacent to that of Raczkiewicz.

Ewelina Zaleska saw to it that her late husband was remembered through gifts to two American universities. She donated his papers to the Hoover Institution Library at Stanford University and gave a grant to Harvard University for a lecture series: *The August Zaleski Lectures in Modern Polish History*

---

[44] The Hospital of St. John and St. Elizabeth was run by the Knights of Malta and was also known as the Maltese Hospital.

Stanisław the Peacemaker

Stanisław Ostrowski,
President of the Republic of Poland 1972-1979

SEVEN MONTHS INTO the 1863 January Uprising, Michał Ostrowski was wounded, taken prisoner, and sentenced to six years of hard labor in Siberia. After completing his sentence, he returned to historically Polish territory and settled in Lemberg in the Austro-Hungarian partition. It was here that Michał and Maria Ostrowski's son Stanisław was born on October 29, 1892.

Stanisław Ostrowski spent his early years in Lemberg, graduating from V Gimnazjum in 1912 and studying medicine at the University of Lemberg. He joined Zet, ZWC, and Związek Strzelecki. In 1914, he joined the Polish Legions and served in the medical corps until he was captured by the Austrians in early 1918 and interned for the remainder of the war. He returned home; however, home was now Lwów in the Republic of Poland. He fought in the defense of Lwów against the West Ukrainian People's Republic; about three thousand of his fellow soldiers were buried in Cmentarz Obrońców Lwowa (Cemetery of the Defenders of Lwów), including young defenders of the city (the Lwów Eaglets) and French and American volunteers.

As that war ended, another began. Ostrowski served in the medical corps during the Polish–Soviet War, rising to the rank of captain. Throughout his military service, Ostrowski continued his studies and was awarded his medical degree in 1919. After he left active duty, Ostrowski began his career in civilian medicine, first taking a position as senior assistant in the dermatology department at the University of Warsaw. In 1925, he returned to Lwów and was appointed head of the dermatology ward in the state general hospital and was on the staff at *Uniwersytet Jana Kazimierza* (Jan Kazimierz University);[1] in 1928, he was promoted to head the hospital. He continued his studies and research, earning an advanced degree in 1930. In 1931, he began teaching at the university. During this period, Ostrowski published a significant number of research papers in domestic and foreign medical journals.

Ostrowski also became involved in politics. In 1930, he was elected to the *Sejm* as a BBWR deputy and was re-elected twice. He was elected Lwów's vice president in 1934 and president in 1936. Ostrowski developed close links with leaders of the city's Jewish and Ukrainian communities.[2] Under difficult economic conditions, his administration created a jobs program for the unemployed and embarked on ambitious modernization programs to expand municipal water service, extend tram lines, and bring electricity to nearby villages. His wife, Kamila, led several charitable organizations that provided food and medical care for children.

Lwów was under attack from the first days of Germany's invasion. Ostrowski remained at his post to direct relief and defense efforts as refugees flooded in from western Poland and as German bombs and shells rained down. He, General Władysław Langner,[3] and General Franciszek Sikorski[4] rejected German demands to surrender, but the Soviet invasion ended their hopes to defend the city. On September 22, Ostrowski and Langner prepared the conditions of surrender. Ostrowski requested that the Soviet Union commit to maintaining hospitals, orphanages, schools, geriatric homes, social welfare institutions, and utilities; the conditions also included official recognition for all languages in common use in the city, freedom of religion, and respect for priests, nuns, and other religious figures. The Soviet authorities accepted the surrender of Lwów and agreed to permit privates and non-commissioned officers to return home

---

[1] In 1919, Lwów's university was renamed *Uniwersytet Jana Kazimierza* (Jan Kazimierz University) in honor of its founder, King Jan Kazimierz.

[2] Between the wars, Lwów's ethnic composition was 65% Polish, 25% Jewish, and 10% Ukrainian.

[3] After the surrender of Lwów, General Władysław Langner evaded capture and crossed the border into Romania; he rejoined the Polish Army in France and moved to the United Kingdom when France fell. After the war, he retired to a farm near Newcastle-upon-Tyne, where he died in 1972.

[4] General Franciszek Sikorski was captured by the Red Army and imprisoned in Starobelsk; in 1940, he and 3,819 of his fellow Polish officers were executed by the NKVD near Kharkiv as part of the Katyń massacres.

after registering with Soviet authorities and to permit officers to leave the country, but they rejected all conditions proposed by the municipal administration. Red Army units entered the city, followed closely by the NKVD. By noon, the Soviet forces had already violated their agreement and arrested every Polish officer they found.[5] They seized government buildings, police stations, and jails and confiscated city archives. Guards were posted at all official buildings, and Ostrowski was constantly accompanied by guards. Once these initial objectives were achieved, Red Army soldiers looted the city and raped women unlucky enough to fall into their hands. Ostrowski protested these crimes but to no avail.

On the morning of September 23, Ostrowski said goodbye to his wife and went to his office. Three NKVD officers interrupted his work and requested that he accompany them him to a meeting with General Semyon Timoshenko, commander of the Red Army's Ukrainian Front; the officers told him that Timoshenko wanted to have a brief discussion regarding city government. Instead, their car took him to the police building on Ulica Łącki. He was interrogated and accused of repressing workers and mistreating the city's Ukrainian and Jewish population. After his third interrogation, an NKVD officer took him into the building's basement and ordered him to face the wall. The officer then took out his revolver and clicked off the safety. Ostrowski waited for a shot that did not come, and after a few minutes the officer handed him over to a guard to take him to a cell. His cell had a bunk but no blankets. There was a broken window about four meters above the floor, making nights very cold. Soon, he was joined by a Ukrainian colleague from the Lwów government, the eighty-year-old Dmytro Levytsky;[6] Ostrowski let him have the bunk and slept on the floor. In the evenings, he heard Polish soldiers being executed in the courtyard.

Ostrowski was interrogated for about three weeks at Ulica Łącki and was then moved across the city to the Brygidki prison. In late October, he was ordered out of his cell, taken to the prison courtyard, loaded into the back of a truck, and taken to a freight train station. There, he was placed in the compartment of a railcar. The train took seven days to reach its destination. On arrival, Ostrowski was taken directly from the train into the back of a van and driven to a prison. He was now in Moscow, his home for the next eighteen months, although he later related that he didn't know

---

[5] Most of the arrested officers met their end as victims of the Katyń massacres.
[6] After the Sikorski–Maisky agreement, Polish authorities intervened to get Levytsky released from the gulag. However, due to his poor health, he stayed in a nursing home run by the Polish consulate in Bukhara in the Uzbek SSR. He died there in 1942.

what the city looked like since all his time there was spent either in prison or in the back of a truck. He soon learned that he was in the Lubyanka.

Ostrowski was placed in a cell with six other prisoners. Five were Soviet citizens, one of whom was a general; the other was a Swede. None of them knew about the war. In a few hours, he was taken to his first interrogation and then transferred to a different cell. This time, he was in the company of a former Soviet official who had the misfortune of being a friend of Nikolai Yezhov;[7] his other companions were the president, prime minister, and nine government ministers of Mongolia. Ostrowski realized that his survival could depend on learning Russian, and he was permitted to request books. Prisoner management and isolation was so comprehensive that Dmytro Levytsky, Ostrowski's colleague from Lwów, was in the cell next door for fourteen months and neither of them even knew that the other was in the same prison, let alone the next cell.

Ostrowski was questioned about government functions in Lwów, the structure of each government department, and the city's economic structure, school curriculum, and ethnic relations. He was ordered to write reports on the Polish government and on Polish–Ukrainian relations. Interrogators questioned him about the whereabouts of Ukrainian *Sejm* deputies and pressed him to give names of his colleagues; he gave names of the deceased, people in the West, and people whom he assumed would be spared from arrest due to advanced age or poor health. He was pressured to criticize Polish government and military officials. Sometimes interrogations were conducted in whispers; other times his questioners would shout. Eventually, Ostrowski learned what the charges against him were. Since he had been born in Lwów and was now incorporated into the Soviet Union, he was retroactively considered to be a Soviet citizen; therefore, his service in the Polish Army prior to the Soviet invasion, particularly during the Polish–Soviet War of 1919–1920, made him a traitor. Further, he was accused of being a fascist, a German agent, and a traitor, since he had stayed at his post when the Red Army entered Lwów. As city president, he was charged with suppression of the proletariat and with firing and otherwise mistreating seasonal Ukrainian workers, failure to provide food for children, and Polonizing Lwów. To complete the picture, he was charged with espionage.

His next stop was Butyrka prison. Interrogations were frequent, and he was transferred to a different building and assigned a private cell. Later,

---

[7] Nikolai Yezhov headed the NKVD during the Great Purge; he fell out of favor and was executed in 1940.

he learned he was in a death cell and would either be executed or dispatched to a gulag. One night, he was ordered to gather his belongings and was brought to a hall where there were between 300 and 400 other prisoners. All were searched and then sent to large cells. Ostrowski met Poles, Finns, and German communists. The Germans claimed they knew nothing about Soviet prisons or gulags until they were imprisoned themselves.

After a few days, Ostrowski was led to a different building and directed to join a queue of prisoners leading to a desk where an NKVD officer was seated. When it was his turn, Ostrowski approached. The officer checked his name, age, and father's name and informed him that a panel of three Soviet officials had heard his case, found him to be a socially dangerous element, and sentenced him to eight years in a correctional labor camp. Ostrowski's response was laughter. Surprised, the officer asked the reason for this; Ostrowski replied that he was amused that he had not been allowed to testify or even attend this trial. The officer sternly retorted that he shouldn't joke, that those eight years were enough for him to rot in a labor camp, and if he survived, he would get more time.

The next day, he and his fellow convicts were loaded onto a train destined for Siberia; nearly eighty years after Michał Ostrowski had been deported, his son took the same journey. In May 1941, his transport arrived in Krasnoyarsk, and the prisoners were herded through showers and disinfection. During this process, an individual wearing a medical coat asked if any of the prisoners had medical experience. Ostrowski identified himself as a doctor and was ordered to report to the infirmary in the evening to assist the staff. This assignment did not exempt him from physical labor; during the day he worked in the forest felling trees before his evening shifts in the infirmary. This workload, combined with the inadequate gulag rations, was difficult for much younger men; for the forty-eight-year-old Ostrowski, it was nearly unbearable.

After three weeks, Ostrowski was transferred to a camp in the Chita region; he arrived in June and was put to work as a doctor. At about the time he arrived, Germany invaded the Soviet Union, and Ostrowski learned about the Sikorski–Maisky agreement, amnesty for Poles, and formation of the Polish Army. He sent a letter to camp authorities requesting release under the terms of the Sikorski–Maisky agreement; the camp commander's response was that he was a prisoner of Moscow and only Moscow could release him. Ostrowski sent another letter; this time he got no answer.

In the ensuing weeks his hopes for release waned, until late one November night, when a sharp knock on the barracks door roused the prisoners to their feet. A guard entered, called Ostrowski's name, ordered him to gather his belongings, and escorted him to the back of a truck. He was taken to the central camp at Chita and assigned to a special barracks where the most dangerous criminal prisoners were held. He was ordered to hard labor. He protested that he was in poor health and demanded to be taken to the infirmary. Once there, he informed the staff that he was a doctor and had worked in that capacity prior to his transfer; the staff immediately put him to work. After a few days, the deputy camp commander moved him to a barracks for technical personnel, where conditions were much better. He learned from a fellow prisoner that he was to be released, and camp officials began to treat him with unexpected kindness. He was permitted to shave, was issued new clothing, and was allowed to go to the camp office without a guard.

After a few days, the commander informed him that he had been released from his sentence and was now a full citizen of the Soviet Union; as such, he had the right to join the Red Army as a doctor, or he could choose to report to the Polish Army. Ostrowski politely acknowledged the offer to join the Red Army but declined due to his limited knowledge of the Russian language; he chose instead to join the Polish Army. He was given instructions to travel to Kuybyshev and report to the NKVD. He found a Polish military recruiting office in Ufa; from there, he made it to Kuybyshev.

Before the war, Kuybyshev did not have a significant role in Soviet government, but this changed in October 1941. As the German military advanced on Moscow, much of the government and most embassies were evacuated to Kuybyshev.[8] Ostrowski decided to report to the Polish embassy instead of the NKVD. A tired, ragged Ostrowski called on Ambassador Stanisław Kot, who sent him to a hotel for a long rest to regain strength before reporting to the army. An NKVD agent posted at the hotel ordered him to produce a passport; when he did, he was ordered to get permission to stay in Kuybyshev. At the NKVD office, he was ordered to leave the city. Instead, he slipped through the snow-covered streets back to the embassy. Indignant about the treatment Ostrowski had received, Kot sent him directly to the Polish Army headquarters in Buzuluk.

On December 19, 1941, Stanisław Ostrowski rejoined the Polish Army. He was now a member of the Second Polish Corps under the command of fellow Lubyanka alumnus General Władysław Anders. Ostrowski was

---

[8] A special bunker was also built in Kuybyshev that was designed to be Stalin's command post in the event of his evacuation; he never used it.

assigned to the medical corps and served throughout its journey from the Soviet Union through the Middle East, Africa, and Italy.

When the war ended, Ostrowski considered his options. He was in Italy, Poland was occupied by the Red Army, and Lwów was now in the Soviet Union and had been renamed Lviv. Returning home was out of the question;[9] the city's remaining Polish population was being expelled. Repatriating to another location within Poland's new borders was also not feasible. As an officer in the Polish Army and a former NKVD prisoner, there was a high probability he would have been arrested upon arrival. Ostrowski had no real choice; instead of attempting to rejoin his wife in Poland, he had to join thousands of his countrymen in exile. He moved to the United Kingdom.

Britain's government housed the thousands of Poles who refused to return in disused military bases converted into refugee camps. Several well-equipped field hospitals were also turned over to the Poles. In North Wales, Penley Hall no. 129 General Hospital, built to handle D-Day casualties, became Polish Hospital No. 3. The Second Polish Corps field hospital relocated to Penley, and Ostrowski took charge of the dermatology department.[10] As camp residents adapted to their new surroundings and found homes, resettlement camps were wound down. Military hospitals were consolidated and evolved into Polish-language hospitals. When Polish Hospital No. 3 closed its dermatology clinic, Ostrowski took a position in the Mossley Hill military hospital in Liverpool.

In 1956, Ostrowski and his wife were finally reunited. Kamila Ostrowska had remained in Poland throughout the war, but in the postwar Stalinist atmosphere she had little chance of leaving. After Stalin's death and the subsequent thaw, Kamila was granted permission to join her husband, and they remained together until her death in 1962. After her passing, Ostrowski retired, moved to London, and immersed himself in a broad range of émigré organizations. He joined *Związek Lekarzy Polskich w Londynie* (Polish Medical Association in London) and was president of that organization for a time; he also was active in *Polskie Towarzystwo Naukowe na Obczyźnie* (Polish Society of Arts and Sciences Abroad). As a veteran of Piłsudski's Legions, he joined *Związek Legionistów Polskich* (Union of Legionnaires). He was honorary president of *Koło Lwowian* (Lwów Circle), had honorary memberships in the Józef Piłsudski Institute in New York

---

[9] Ostrowski was the only Lwów government official to survive the war.
[10] In addition to Penley, the Second Polish Corps took over military hospitals at Llanerch Panna and Iscoyd Park, also in Wales.

and in London, was one of POSK's founders, and was a patron of *Biblioteka Polska*. He inaugurated celebrations for the 300th anniversary of the establishment of the university in Lwów.

Although unable to return to his home city, Ostrowski closely monitored events there. Soviet authorities renamed streets, public buildings, and landmarks and removed or obscured street signs to eradicate evidence of the city's Polish history.[11] Other inconvenient reminders of Polish culture were also targeted. Ostrowski was particularly upset by the vandalism and destruction visited on *Cmentarz Obrońców Lwowa*. Desecration of the cemetery began in the 1950s, when it was used as a garbage dump, and after a few years it was converted into a truck depot. Destruction began in earnest in the 1960s, when monuments to foreign soldiers, sculptures, and the colonnade were destroyed. Tanks were used to demolish the triumphal arch, and military bulldozers were employed to raze tombs. Ostrowski was powerless to stop the destruction, but he formed the Defense Committee of the Eaglets Cemetery. As chairman, he informed the émigré press and the English press; the committee also protested to several governments.[12] Ostrowski and General Tokarszewski-Karaszewicz established a memorial in St. Andrzej Bobola Church in London.

On February 27, 1971, August Zaleski chose Ostrowski to succeed him; the next day, Ostrowski's nomination was announced in *Dziennik Ustaw*. Zaleski had made a wise choice. Ostrowski was respected by most of the exile community and was known in Poland for his military, medical, and government service.

Stanisław Ostrowski took the oath of office on April 9, 1972. His priority was to reconcile *Zamek* and *Zjednoczenie Narodowe*. He made this clear in his first speech, declaring that there should be forgiveness and that there could be no victors and no defeated. Within a few weeks, negotiators had drafted an agreement. Presidential powers would be those defined in the April Constitution as interpreted in *Umowa Paryska*. Government structure would follow the *Zamek* model. Independence was reaffirmed as the government's primary goal, the western border was accepted, calls were

---

[11] Soviet efforts were not very thorough. In the 1970s, Radosław Sikorski saw faded Polish street signs on some buildings and Polish symbols on several facades.

[12] After the collapse of the Soviet Union and the Ukrainian declaration of independence, the Polish and Ukrainian governments agreed on plans to restore the cemetery. Initially, restoration was opposed by Ukrainian nationalists; opposition declined after Poland supported Ukraine's Orange Revolution in 2004. The restored cemetery reopened in 2005.

made to void treaties that revised the eastern border, cooperation with other nations in central and eastern Europe was proposed, and aspirations to join the European Economic Community were declared.[13] Ostrowski accepted the proposed agreement and released it to the émigré press; on May 22, he appealed for its acceptance.

SN and SP rejected the agreement, but PSL, PPS, NGS, and LNP signed on June 9. Alfred Urbański, a PPS member and *Rada Trzech* member since 1969, was named prime minister, and Stanisław Kopański, part of *Rada Trzech* since 1970, was appointed Inspector General of the Armed Forces. After some debate, Ostrowski succeeded in gaining approval for Edward Raczyński to succeed him.[14] Raczyński, Kopański, and Urbański gathered on July 8 for the final meeting of *Rada Trzech*. They dissolved RJN and EZN, officially recognized Ostrowski as president, transferred their powers to him, and brought *Rada Trzech's* existence to its end. *Rada Stanu Rzeczypospolitej Polskiej* was dissolved a few days later.[15] Urbański formed a government composed of *Zamek* and *Zjednoczenie Narodowe* supporters. PAT issued a press release announcing reconciliation, Urbański's appointment, and the government's aims; it also included an overview of the government's budget and reminded readers that the main source of funding was donations.

With *Rada Stanu* and RJN no longer in existence, Ostrowski established *Komisja Tymczasowa Okresu Przejściowego* (Temporary Committee for the Transitional Period) to serve as an advisory council until a more permanent body could be seated. Like the Council of Ministers, *Komisja Tymczasowa* included people from both sides; its membership was evenly divided between former RJN and *Rada RP* members. *Komisja Tymczasowa* reviewed and approved the unification agreement's final text, coming to agreement on interpretation of the constitution, consolidation of treasuries, citizenship requirements, and composition of the next *Rada Narodowa*. *Komisja Tymczasowa* submitted proposed guidelines granting eligibility to those who were Polish citizens as of September 1, 1939, and their children. Ostrowski accepted the recommendations and issued a decree declaring that accepting another citizenship would not result in loss of Polish citizenship; he went on to state that children of at least one Polish citizen would have citizenship rights.

Komisja Tymczasowa did not limit itself to internal matters. A member reported that Warsaw's security apparatus was attempting to blackmail émigrés into making statements calling for the closure of Radio Free Europe; in

---

[13] The European Economic Community later became known as the European Union.
[14] PSL had proposed Stefan Korboński to succeed Ostrowski.
[15] *Rada Stanu Rzeczypospolitej Polskiej* was dissolved on July 12, 1972.

response, *Komisja Tymczasowa* passed a resolution calling on the government to inform its representatives and Polish organizations of Warsaw's actions and requesting that the government take appropriate actions to neutralize them. Creating a unified treasury was another priority. Following the recommendations of *Komisja Tymczasowa*, Ostrowski issued a decree merging both treasuries into a single entity and placed it under the supervision of *Komisja Tymczasowa* until *Rada Narodowa* could be reconstituted.

Émigré communities around the world responded enthusiastically and expressed their appreciation financially. In Victoria, Australia, *Komisja Skarbu Narodowego* reported a sharp increase in contributions after unification was announced. Detroit's committee announced plans to expand its fundraising campaign. In Canada, *Skarb Narodowy Rzeczypospolitej Polskiej* and *Skarb Narodowy Zjednoczenia* anticipated the unified treasury by placing themselves under common leadership; they noted that many émigrés stopped contributing during the period of political division and that efforts were needed to bring them back into active support.

On November 17, Ostrowski declared his acceptance of the unification agreement and pledged to leave office after seven years. *Komisja Tymczasowa* completed its work in May 1973; its conclusions were published in *Dziennik Ustaw*.

Unification had been achieved, but resentments simmered. Ostrowski was mayor under *Sanacja* and had been affiliated with LNP in exile but had mostly remained outside of the fray. But now, he had appointed *Rada Trzech* in its entirety to important positions, and *Zjednoczenie Narodowe* supporters constituted half of the Council of Ministers.[16] This did not sit well with some *Zamek* loyalists, who for years had maintained that they were the defenders of the constitution and that *Zjednoczenie Narodowe* was the rebellious group. Resentments would simmer among some *Zamek* adherents for years to come, but in general they respected the authority of Ostrowski, Urbański, and Kopański. Such was not the case with SN.

Along with SP, SN spurned the unity agreement. For SN, the matter went beyond the legitimacy of Ostrowski; once squarely on the side of legalism, SN's position had completely shifted, and it now questioned the

---

[16] Members of Zygmunt Muchniewski's Council of Ministers who retained seats in Urbański's government were Jerzy Gawenda, Stanisław Nowak, Brigadier General Stanisław Kuniczak, Sylwester Karalus, and Wiesław Strzałkowski; they were joined by *Zamek* supporter Brigadier General Stefan Brzeszczyński. Council members from *Zjednoczenie Narodowe* were Urbański, Józef Poniatowski, Stanisław Wiszniewski, Stanisław Borczyk, Zbigniew Scholtz, and Jan Starzewski.

necessity of the presidency itself. In SN's view, détente had altered international relations to the point that the post-Yalta political landscape was ripe for collapse. SN, along with parts of PPS, SP, and *Federacja Ruchów Demokratycznych* (which itself had split in May), formed *Polskie Zjednoczenie Narodowe* (PZN, Polish National Union) on December 2, 1972. PZN declared the exile government structure to be useless.

Regardless, Ostrowski pressed on. In June 1973, he dissolved *Komisja Tymczasowa* in preparation for reestablishing *Rada Narodowa Rzeczypospolitej Polskiej*. On December 15, 1973, *V Rada Narodowa Rzeczypospolitej Polskiej* convened with Franciszek Wilk as its chairman. With 234 members, this would be the largest *Rada* yet.[17] Consistent with its refusal to support Ostrowski, SN was not represented.

It had been over a decade since Kazimierz Papée had his credentials revoked by the Vatican. He remained in Rome, continued to run the embassy, and provided what assistance he could to his countrymen. Funds from London were far from sufficient, and Papée pared expenses. Michał Bojczuk, a *Skarb Narodowy* representative in Chicago, had been alerted to the embassy's issues and contacted Papée with an offer to solicit help from American Polonia. He attempted to enlist the support of nearly two hundred leading figures, but most spurned his appeal. In a letter to Papée, PAC Vice President Władysław Zachariasiewicz lamented their indifference. He affirmed that American Polonia had the means to support the embassy, but no individual or organization would do so.

Financial issues were not the cause of the embassy's closure. That was Warsaw's doing, and it used the Vatican to accomplish the task. Dioceses in the Recovered Territories had been canonically irregular since new borders were imposed in 1945. In the absence of a formal treaty recognizing the Polish–German border, the Vatican could not subordinate them to the Primate of Poland. They were administered directly by the Vatican, and this temporary solution stood for twenty-five years until Poland and West Germany signed their border treaty in 1970.

The Vatican and the PRL began talks in 1971 to obtain agreement on a proposed diocesan structure. The result was the Papal bull *Episcoporum Poloniae coetus*, which established new dioceses and updated the Church's

---

[17] Of the 122 elected members, 56 were elected by émigrés in the United Kingdom and 66 by émigrés in other Western nations. Ostrowski appointed 23 members, of whom three were representatives of religious groups. Political parties appointed 61 members, and 28 were appointed by social, cultural, veteran, and youth groups.

administrative structure in Poland. One of PRL's conditions was that the Vatican had to end relations with the government-in-exile. Paul VI, like his predecessor, pursued a policy of rapprochement with communist states, and if the Republic of Poland's embassy was an impediment to that end, it would have to go. On October 19, 1972, Vatican Secretary of State Cardinal Villot informed Papée that permission to have an embassy had been revoked. The Republic's last bastion of international recognition was gone.[18]

Moscow's standing had suffered in the aftermath of its 1968 actions in Czechoslovakia, and it was anxious to improve its image in the West. To accomplish this, it launched a series of diplomatic initiatives and proposed an international security conference. This grew into the Conference on Security and Co-operation in Europe (CSCE).[19] Moscow's goals were to expand economic cooperation on terms favorable to the Soviet Bloc and to obtain acceptance of postwar borders. CSCE began with a 1973 meeting of foreign ministers in Helsinki, Finland, and a series of negotiations began later that year in Switzerland. Moscow signed a number of agreements and treaties with Western nations, creating the impression that it was abandoning expansionist policies and was evolving into a trustworthy partner.

Émigré organizations from Bloc nations were suspicious. Poland's exile government was certain that Soviet motives for these conferences and treaties were less than pure. Apprehension over anticipated Soviet designs for CSCE led émigrés to form the Polish Committee for Cooperation and Security in Europe in 1973.[20] It began a lobbying and media campaign starting with a telegram to the Foreign Office urging the British government to reject any proposals endorsing the single-party system in Poland and to call for general elections and a constitutional assembly.[21] The Committee followed with letters to representatives of Western governments at the conference reminding them of past Soviet actions, outlining anticipated Soviet aims, and calling on them to negotiate based on universal human rights, self-determination, free elections, and withdrawal of Soviet troops.

---

[18] Although the PRL insisted on the closure of the Republic of Poland's embassy to the Vatican, it did not enter into formal relations with the Vatican until 1989.

[19] Andorra and Albania were not represented. Owing to its status of a principality headed by the French president and Spain's Bishop of Urgell, Andorra's interests were represented by France and Spain. Albania's government refused to attend.

[20] The Committee's members were Adam Ciołkosz (chairman), Kazimierz Sabbat (vice chairman), Jerzy Zaleski (secretary), Witold Czerwiński, Bronisław Hełczyński, Adam Pragier, Franciszek Wilk, Stefan Soboniewski, and Józef Żmigrodzki.

[21] Contents of this telegram were reproduced in the pamphlet *Poland and the Conference on Security and Co-operation in Europe - Three documents - one telegram and two appeals*.

It took its campaign to the public, purchasing newspaper advertisements laying out the state of affairs in Poland and calling for free elections.[22]

An arms reduction conference was planned for Vienna in 1974, and the government-in-exile's representative in Austria delivered a memorandum to the conference secretariat and to Western delegations cautioning that the NATO reductions desired by the Soviet Union would give the Soviets a significant military advantage; the memorandum also petitioned its readers to press for withdrawal of Soviet military units from Warsaw Pact nations. Its counsel emanated from ongoing analysis of conditions in Poland and the Soviet Bloc and a comparison of Moscow's rhetoric with its actions. The exile government's views ran counter to optimistic attitudes prevalent in Western governments and were disregarded, but at the time of the Vienna conference American intelligence was surreptitiously receiving information from deep within Poland's military that confirmed the government-in-exile's assessment and added alarming particulars about Moscow's intentions. As an officer of the Polish General Staff, Colonel Ryszard Kukliński had detailed knowledge of Warsaw Pact military plans, and he discovered a stark disparity between rhetoric and plans. To the West, Soviet Bloc nations portrayed themselves as peaceful societies that desired harmonious coexistence. To their citizens they depicted the United States and the United Kingdom as aggressors and imperialists; their underlying theme was that the Soviet Union had no aggressive intentions. Kukliński found that Soviet military plans were almost exclusively offensive in nature; worse, they anticipated that Poland would be a major battleground. Further disillusioned by the invasion of Czechoslovakia and the use of army units to attack protestors in 1970, Kukliński became convinced that Poland's alliance with the Soviet Union was contrary to the nation's interests. In 1972, he made contact with American intelligence and became one of the most prolific agents in the Soviet Bloc;[23] the information he provided left no doubt as to Soviet intentions.[24] The government-in-exile did not know it, but Kukliński had validated its position.

---

[22] Their advertisements included the caption, *"This advertisement was paid for by the Polish National Fund, a voluntary organisation supported by donations and contributions of free Poles all over the world."*
[23] Between 1972 and 1981, Kukliński provided over 35,000 pages of secret documents including strategic plans for use of nuclear weapons, precise locations of Soviet Bloc military bases, technical specifications for many weapons systems, and plans for martial law in 1981.
[24] Fearing that his unmasking was imminent, Kukliński, his wife, and their two sons were spirited out of Poland late in 1981. Kukliński paid a high price for his actions. Both of his sons died in suspicious circumstances: Waldemar was run down by a truck with no license plates, and Bogdan, an expert sailor, died when his boat capsized in calm waters. Kukliński was sentenced to death in absentia; after the fall of communism his sentence was reduced and later vacated. He remains a controversial figure in Poland, viewed by some as a patriot and others as a traitor. He died in Tampa, Florida, in 2004.

Exile politicians were not alone in their distrust of Moscow. While CSCE negotiations were underway in Geneva, a group of Swiss academics and officials took the initiative to organize a conference on human rights and national self-determination. This conference, held in Lucerne in March 1974, was attended by the president and vice president of the European Parliament and other Western politicians, intellectuals, and journalists; also attending were exile politicians from Hungary, Czechoslovakia, Poland, Romania, Byelorussia, Ukraine, and Georgia. Poland's delegation was led by Jerzy Gawenda, included representatives from Polish communities in France, Switzerland, Italy, and Israel, and served as a bridge between Eastern and Western delegations. At the conclusion of the conference, the delegations passed a resolution calling for the political unification of Europe and respect for human rights and civil rights. They went on to reject the "Brezhnev Doctrine"[25] that a threat to socialist rule in any Soviet Bloc state in Europe was a threat to the entire Bloc, and they proceeded instead to create a permanent body for the defense of human rights and self-determination of European nations.

By 1974, passersby on King Street, Hammersmith could see the upper floors of the POSK building above the construction fencing, but POSK's ability to finish the job was uncertain. Inflation was rapidly driving up costs, and interest rates for loans were reaching unprecedented levels. If the building were to be opened on schedule, more money was needed.

Ostrowski and the Council of Ministers issued appeals. Ostrowski invoked the opening words of the April Constitution as a reminder to Poles of their duty to their nation.[26] He called on all Poles in the West to put aside political differences and contribute to a cause that would benefit all of Polonia through preservation of culture, provide facilities and organizations to prepare the next generation of émigré leaders, and serve as a monument to the determination of émigré Poles. The Council of Ministers implored organizations and individuals to contribute, linking the project to the Polish Library that émigrés founded in Paris in 1838. It noted its contribution to POSK and warned that the building's full opening would

---

[25] The Brezhnev Doctrine was used to justify Soviet military intervention in Afghanistan in 1979.
[26] Article 1 of the April Constitution begins with these statements:
(1) The Polish State is the common weal of all its citizens.
(2) Resurrected by the efforts and sacrifices of its worthiest sons it is to be bequeathed as a historic heritage from generation to generation.
(3) It is the duty of each generation to increase the power and authority of the State by its own efforts.
(4) For the fulfilment of this duty each generation is responsible to posterity with its honour and good name.

be delayed if sufficient funds were not raised. Their appeals brought the needed contributions. By Christmas, fencing that had obscured the construction site had finally come down, revealing a muscular concrete and glass facade. Pavements were swept and the building was cleaned of dust until it gleamed in the thin December sun. POSK was ready for its occupants.

On December 29, 1974, Stanisław Ostrowski, the Council of Ministers, *Rada Narodowa* members, clergy, representatives of the Borough of Hammersmith and Fulham, and a mass of Polish veterans, émigrés, and their children gathered at POSK for its opening. They viewed PUNO's classrooms, visited offices of SPK and other member organizations, and marveled at the theater. Roman Wajda's vision, eleven years in the making, had at last been realized. Britain's Polonia had a spacious, modern home.

Wajda was not there to see his work fulfilled. He had passed away on December 8.

In a Tolouse bank vault, 2,408 kilograms of silver, all that remained of FON, had sat undisturbed for more than twenty-five years. Warsaw had been unable to secure it, but Edward Gierek's rise to power presented a new opportunity.

Gierek had a particular advantage in his dealings with France: his family had emigrated there in 1923. He had lived in France and Belgium for twenty-two years, worked in coal mines, and developed an excellent command of the French language. This enabled him to converse with French president Valéry Giscard d'Estaing without a translator, allowing them to build a close relationship. He put this to use in the matter of FON, and in 1975 the two reached an agreement. It took a few months to work out the details, and in 1976 the silver departed Tolouse. For Gierek, FON was a matter of prestige and not an opportunity for plunder. Public exhibitions were held in several cities, a sharp contrast with the shroud of secrecy that concealed the 1947 FON shipment from London.

Ostrowski had no power or ability to prevent the transfer. He and the government-in-exile watched helplessly as more property of the Second Republic was handed over to the communist government.

Like Zaleski, Ostrowski faced an opposition that did not recognize him. Unlike Zaleski, however, he had broad support among the opposition. Of those who followed émigré politics, the vast majority backed Ostrowski, the Council of Ministers, and *Rada Narodowa*. PZN, his primary opposition, lacked widespread support and could not claim a patron who transcended party lines. PZN had a narrow base that was held together by rejection of legalism. By the mid-1970s, it had dwindled to little more than SN and several disaffected SP members, and SN activists dominated the organization. Even so, disputes within SN threatened PZN's existence; in late 1973 and early 1974, an SN publication questioned the value of cooperation between SN and SP.

Despite this internal issue within SN, PZN continued its efforts to extend its influence. In 1975, PSL "*Odłam Jedności Narodowej*" split into two; Franciszek Wilk led a London-based faction, and Stanisław Bańczyk headed a group based in Brussels. Bańczyk was backed by PZN.

In July 1975, Poland was preparing to welcome US President Gerald Ford.[27] Two days before his visit, the London government issued an official statement recognizing America's role in the re-establishment of an independent Poland in 1918, recalling Poland's postwar fate, and reiterating its position that PRL's government was not legitimate. The statement concluded with an assurance that Ford would be warmly received by the Polish people.

After Poland, Ford traveled to Helsinki for the final CSCE session. Long-held suspicions about Soviet motives and Western accommodationist policies were substantiated when the American press reported that Secretary of State Henry Kissinger had proposed recognition of the Soviet Union's forcible annexation of Estonia, Latvia, and Lithuania. The ensuing uproar was contained only when Ford met with representatives of exile groups and pledged that American policy towards the Balkan States would not change.

At the conclusion of the CSCE meetings, Moscow was convinced that it had scored a diplomatic triumph. Although the Final Act was not accorded the status of a treaty, there was agreement on the inviolability of borders, economic and scientific cooperation, and improved transportation links. But Moscow and its satellites had not considered the implications of their signatures on the Final Act's declarations guaranteeing respect for human rights, freedom of thought, freedom of conscience, freedom of religion, and the right to self-determination.

---

[27] Ford's visit was the second by an American president. Richard Nixon visited in 1972.

Edward Gierek was preparing to amend Poland's 1952 Constitution. This was not unusual in itself, but the proposed changes were highly controversial. He intended to codify the socialist character of the nation, PZPR's leading role, and Poland's permanent alliance with the Soviet Union. Further, rights of citizens would be dependent on their fulfillment of obligations to the country. Proclamations of the leading role of the communist party were common in Bloc constitutions as were declarations of friendship and alliance with the Soviet Union,[28] but none contained a clause making rights conditional. Gierek's planned constitutional amendments contradicted the Helsinki Final Act. Seeing this disparity, a group of writers, artists, professors, lawyers, priests, and other notable figures resolved to exercise their rights as enumerated in the Final Act. They prepared a protest letter highlighting deficiencies in the constitution, criticizing the proposed amendments, and illustrating their contradiction with the Final Act. Edward Lipiński, an economist and PZPR member,[29] submitted it to the *Sejm* Chancellery.[30] Initially this letter, known as *List 59* (Letter of 59, named for the number of signatures it bore), was ignored until Western journalists learned of it. Then, it was denounced by Gierek and PZPR. Such critiques failed to dissuade its authors; indeed, in January more people added their signatures, including a large number of émigrés and exiles such as Raczyński, Adam Ciołkosz, and Lidia Ciołkosz. *Rada Narodowa* declared its opposition, noting that the *Sejm* was not freely elected, that codifying PZPR's leading role would give constitutional sanction to dictatorship, and that binding Poland to the Soviet Union would forfeit the nation's latitude to conduct an independent foreign policy. Its declaration included an expression of support for those Poles protesting the amendments and calling for civil rights and free elections.

List 59 achieved results. In the final text, "steering role of the Party in the nation" became "steering role of the Party in the building of socialism," "alliance" with the Soviet Union was changed to "friendship," and citizens' rights were no longer dependent on fulfillment of obligations. For the signatories of *List 59*, this was a victory, although Poland was far from compliant with the Helsinki Final Act. Unbeknownst to them, they had

---

[28] For example, the constitutions in effect in Czechoslovakia, Hungary, and Romania in 1976 all contained declarations of the leading role of their respective communist parties; the Czechoslovak and Romanian constitutions also referred to their alliance with the Soviet Union.

[29] Lipiński was expelled from PZPR in 1977.

[30] *List 59* was submitted to the Chancellery on December 5, 1975. The act of submitting such a letter was not illegal; Polish law guaranteed safety for those who wrote to government authorities. Although none of the signers was officially sanctioned, afterwards many did have employment difficulties, and writers could not get published.

achieved something greater. They had laid the groundwork for the Soviet Bloc's first civic opposition group.

Ostrowski had become accustomed to Soviet gestures of goodwill that masked malevolent designs, and he viewed CSCE as another example of Moscow's duplicity. He made this plain in his 1975 "*Polski Nowy Rok w Londynie*" speech, calling this Soviet attempt to present itself as the leading architect of world peace a gross deception.[31] However, he was willing to work with CSCE and nominated Sabbat to serve on its émigré committee. Ostrowski saw other subjugated nations as potential allies and sought to strengthen ties with their exile governments, paying particular attention to Lithuania and Ukraine. Ostrowski and Urbański met with the Ukrainian exile prime minister and deputy prime minister; they agreed to strengthen ties and work cooperatively in the struggle for freedom. All expressed their hopes that good relations in exile would continue once independence had been won; Ostrowski and the exile Ukrainian President Mykola Livytskyi later signed a mutual declaration.

In the immediate wake of unification, *Skarb Narodowy* reported indications that émigrés would respond positively. Three years later, there was no doubt. In 1974, contributions were fifty percent higher than in 1972, and the year ended with a sizable surplus, enabling nearly £11,000 to be retained for future needs. *Główna Komisja Skarbu Narodowego* had consolidated two networks into a far-reaching organization with representatives in communities throughout the West. This structure worked to restore trust among émigrés, dispel lingering misconceptions that contributions to *Skarb Narodowy* favored specific political factions, and minimize costs. None of its staff received salaries; representatives largely paid their own expenses. But inflation was a problem, and *Skarb Narodowy* strove to keep ahead of rising costs with efforts to attract new contributors and solicit increases from current donors. In October, the month of *Skarb Narodowy*,[32] Ostrowski issued a declaration thanking its members and contributors for their support and appealing for increased contributions.

Polish émigrés and exiles, part of the community yet separate, distinctive, and demanding no special treatment, continued to pique British

---

[31] Zaleski started the tradition of New Year's speeches, referred to as "*Polski Nowy Rok w Londynie* ("Polish New Year in London"). His successors carried on this tradition as well as his yearly bestowal of awards, honors, and decorations at the end of December.

[32] *Skarb Narodowy* had been founded in October 1949. To commemorate the anniversary, special appeals for contributions were made every October.

curiosity. Evidence of this enduring interest was a 1976 BBC1 television program titled "Polish Government-in-Exile." After a brief history of the invasion of Poland and the government's arrival in London, viewers learned about the continued existence of the government in London. They saw Ostrowski, Urbański, fragments of a Council of Ministers meeting and a *Rada Narodowa* session, and brief interviews with Urbański, Adam Ciołkosz, and Wiesław Strzałkowski, a *Rada Narodowa* member and government minister. This was favorable publicity for the government and reminded the British people why the Poles were still there.

In the early 1970s, Gierek had launched an ambitious plan to modernize industry, expand production of consumer goods, and increase exports. Initial funding would come from Western loans; proceeds from exports would be used to repay these debts. For about two years, this plan was on track, and the standard of living improved significantly. His plans were shattered by events outside of his control. In October 1973, Egypt and Syria attacked Israel, and OPEC cut oil exports to nations that supported Israel. Sharp increases in oil prices sparked a recession in the United States that spread to Western Europe, causing a drop in demand for manufactured products. Poland's exports declined, but loan payments were still due. To avoid default, Gierek increased exports of coal and agricultural products, a strategy that might have worked had the weather cooperated. In 1974 and 1975, Poland's farmers were hampered by inclement weather, and harvests failed to meet domestic needs. PZPR attempted to rectify the situation by purchasing grain from the West using credit meant for industrial investment, but imports weren't enough to satisfy demand. Farmers reduced their herds, and meat shortages followed. Government officials conducted unsuccessful searches of farms for hidden grain. None was found, and the farmers were now irritated.

Gierek was now facing the same problem Gomułka had five years previously: the need to raise food prices. Heavy subsidies had kept prices low, but by late 1975 Poland's economic situation had deteriorated to the point that the state could no longer afford them and needed to revise its fiscal plan. Gierek and the Politburo decided to increase food prices, but they were determined to not repeat Gomułka's mistakes. At the December PZPR conference, Gierek assured the public that prices would remain unchanged for the Christmas season but alluded to changes ahead.

Gierek and the Politburo planned price increases for June without pay increases. Expecting trouble, *Milicja*, ORMO, and ZOMO units were placed on alert, detention space was prepared, and about seven thousand people thought to be potential protest and strike leaders were called up for military service. Newspapers and television news programs ran a series of stories about rising food prices worldwide and unemployment in the West.

On June 24, Prime Minister Piotr Jaroszewicz announced the increases. They were worse than the 1970 increases. Strikes erupted throughout the country. Workers at Warsaw's Ursus tractor factory tore up a section of track on the international rail line, protests raged throughout the day in Płock, and protests turned violent in Radom. Two workers were killed, about two thousand were injured, and hundreds were arrested and beaten. Many were dismissed from work; others were unofficially banned from employment. As reports of strikes and violence poured into Warsaw, the Politburo hastily announced cancellation of the price increases. In the following days, media reports placed blame for the unrest on criminals and anti-socialist elements, claiming that drunks and hooligans were responsible.

All of this was widely reported in the West. *Dziennik Polski i Dziennik Żołnierza* reported on Jaroszewicz's speech and published the new prices. Reports and analyses were featured in the émigré and British press. *Gazeta Niedzielna*, a UK-based Catholic weekly, opined, "Nowhere in the world is the working class so disregarded and deceived as in communist-ruled countries."[33] Radio Free Europe provided extensive coverage in its broadcasts. 43 Eaton Place issued a statement on July 2. In the government's analysis, the "...deteriorating economic situation in the country is caused not only by the insistent implementation of the insane communist doctrine, but also by Soviet colonial exploitation." It declared that, by striking and protesting, the "...Polish nation has once again demonstrated that it will never come to terms with communist tyranny." Its statement concluded with a call for a free, independent, and democratic Poland.[34] *Rada Narodowa* followed with a unanimous resolution declaring support for the workers who "reacted immediately and decisively to the party's attacks on the standard of living of working people."[35]

Fourteen *List 59* signatories protested these brutalities in a letter to the authorities, but they realized that the workers and their families needed

---

[33] Krzysztof Tarka, "Prasa polskiej emigracji politycznej w Wielkiej Brytanii wobec protestów robotników w kraju w czerwcu 1976 roku" ("The press of the Polish political emigration in Great Britain in the face of the workers' protests in the country in June 1976"), *Rocznik Historii Prasy Polskiej*, T. XIX (2016) Z. 4 (44), s.127–141.

[34] PAT, "Oświadczenie Rządu" ("Government Statement"), Nr. 9/76, Londyn, 2 lipca 1976, AJPIA 701/9/13, No. 83.

[35] Tarka, "Prasa polskiej emigracji" ("The Press of Polish Emigration"), *Rocznik Historii Prasy Polskiej*, T. XIX (2016) Z. 4 (44), s. 127–141.

more tangible help. In July, arrested Ursus workers were encouraged by an unexpected display of support. Those fourteen had collected money to help jailed and unemployed workers and their families, and they soon expanded their efforts to assist Radom workers. This was the beginning of *Komitet Obrony Robotników* (KOR, Workers' Defense Committee), a previously unknown type of organization in the Soviet Bloc.[36] KOR members, a group of intellectuals, writers, lawyers and clergy, sent open letters of protest to the government, helped the accused to secure better legal representation, obtained medical diagnoses to prove abuse and torture, and worked with Western journalists to have accurate information published.[37]

Émigré Poles and British sympathizers met at *Ognisko Polskie* on August 6 and passed a resolution stating, "The June workers' protest was a mass demonstration against the dictatorial methods of the communist authorities in Poland, wishing to transfer to the world of work the burden of the ineptitude of their own government." They demanded the right to strike, independent unions, amnesty for those arrested and sentenced, reinstatement to their jobs, and punishment of security personnel responsible for abuse; they also reprimanded the communist authorities for their propaganda.[38]

Ostrowski knew that Poland's workers and KOR needed more substantive help. He also knew that émigré Poles had a history of sending help to their countrymen and would contribute generously to a relief fund; indeed, some already had. Adam Ciołkosz and his PPS colleagues conducted a fundraising campaign and sent its proceeds to KOR. The government-in-exile possessed the means to expand this effort throughout the entire émigré community, and Ciołkosz, through his contacts with KOR member Edward Lipiński, was able to establish a channel to deliver funds. On October 8, Raczyński, Ciołkosz, and several others[39] founded *Obywatelski Komitet Zbiórki na Pomoc Ofiarom Wydarzeń Czerwcowych* (Civic Committee of the Collection to Aid the Victims of June Events).[40] It issued appeals to Polonia for donations that would be used to help workers and

---

[36] *List 59* and KOR inspired opposition movements in other Soviet Bloc nations. These included Czechoslovakia's *Charta 77* (Charter 77), the Moscow Helsinki Group, and its spinoff groups in Lithuania, Ukraine, Georgia, and Armenia. KSS "KOR" assisted *Charta 77* by using its Western media contacts to publicize repression of Czechoslovak dissidents.

[37] One of KOR's members was Antoni Pajdak, a defendant in the Trial of the Sixteen.

[38] Tarka, "Prasa polskiej emigracji," *Rocznik Historii Prasy Polskiej*, T. XIX (2016) Z. 4 (44), s.127–141.

[39] Joining Raczyński and Ciołkosz were *Dziennik Polski i Dziennik Żołnierza* publisher Witold Czerwiński, Maria Leśniakowa, Artur Rynkiewicz, Franciszek Wilk, Andrzej Zakrzewski, Father Karol Zieliński, Tadeusz Żenczykowski, and Mikołaj Dolanowski (Jerzy Hryniewski).

[40] PZN did not participate in *Obywatelski Komitet Zbiórki na Pomoc Ofiarom Wydarzeń Czerwcowych*.

their families and enlisted *Skarb Narodowy* representatives to collect contributions. By December 31, it had raised £6,000; by mid-1977, it raised an additional £26,000. *Kultura* and Polish organizations in Canada and the United States also collected funds.

Ostrowski and *Rada Narodowa* grasped the importance of KOR. Ostrowski recognized its emergence as an unprecedented development in postwar Poland, and Sabbat called the cooperation of workers, intellectuals, and the Church "a key phenomenon for the future," noting that society had lost its fear of the authorities and refused to be intimidated by them.[41] In its resolution, *Rada Narodowa* declared, "We acknowledge with satisfaction and joy the solidarity of intellectuals, intelligentsia, and clergy with the working class, workers and peasants that has recently been manifested. In this solidarity, we see a preview of a better future for the Polish nation and state."[42] *Rada Narodowa* also protested exploitative new accounting rules implemented by the Soviet Union for trade with Comecon states, called for free trade unions, and demanded an end to repression against protestors.

KOR members knowingly exposed themselves to harassment. Several lost their employment, students were subjected to academic sanctions, many received anonymous threats, and one member was fined for "illegal fundraising." KOR members were arrested, beaten, and held without charges. Several who remained outside of jail began a hunger strike. Polish London circulated news of these repressions, and protests began to pour in from Western politicians and intellectuals. Embarrassed by the unwanted attention, the government released all imprisoned workers and KOR members by July 1977.

Having achieved its goals, KOR transformed itself into *Komitet Samoobrony Społecznej "KOR"* (KSS "KOR," Committee for Social Self-Defense "KOR") and expanded its role into a nationwide civil rights organization that aimed to break PZPR's control over society. KSS "KOR" joined *Ruch Obrony Praw Człowieka i Obywatela* (ROPCiO, Movement for Defense of Human and Civic Rights), formed in March with the objective of holding the government to its commitments made at Helsinki.[43] KSS "KOR" and ROPCiO operated openly. A steady flow of contributions from the West

---

[41] Tarka, "Prasa polskiej emigracji," *Rocznik Historii Prasy Polskiej*, T. XIX (2016) Z. 4 (44), s.127–141.

[42] PAT, "Uchwała Rady Narodowej R.P. w sprawie wydarzeń w Kraju" ("Resolution of the National Council of the Republic of Poland regarding the events in the country"), Nr. 11/76, Londyn, 5 lipca 1976 r., AJPIA 701/9/13, No. 82.

[43] Although some of ROPCiO's founding members had been involved in KOR, their political orientations differed. KOR's leaders tended to have socialist leanings; many were former or current PZPR members, and some could accurately be described as disillusioned former Party members. Political orientation of ROPCiO's leaders were rooted in the Second Republic, AK, and WiN.

enabled both organizations to function,⁴⁴ and they printed newsletters and published banned books.⁴⁵

After KOR became *KSS "KOR,"* leaders of *Obywatelski Komitet Zbiórki na Pomoc Ofiarom Wydarzeń Czerwcowych* decided that a realignment would better enable Polonia to support the opposition. They dissolved their committee and planned to replace it with a new organization, the Committee of Solidarity with the Democratic Movement. Unfortunately, this was never realized. A dispute over legalism emerged during discussions and derailed the effort, leaving Polonia with no central fundraising structure through which it could aid its fellow countrymen.

While Poland was in turmoil, Urbański submitted his resignation. Ostrowski appointed Kazimierz Sabbat to succeed him. His council of ministers had a majority of former oppositionists, including Urbański, who was minister without portfolio. Again, *Zjednoczenie Narodowe* people predominated in the unified government, and simmering resentments among former *Zamek* adherents were stoked again; another "dissident" was in charge.

Sabbat and his council of ministers were sworn in on August 7. Ostrowski thanked Urbański and his government for their work, particularly for their efforts to unify émigrés; he then reiterated the need for the government-in-exile's work and gave a brief defense of the April Constitution. Sabbat emphasized the need to involve younger Poles in the government: "We will also pay special attention to the need for the young generation to take responsibility for the fate of the Polish Case. It's time for us to change generations. The continuity of our work can only be ensured by the adoption of our ideals and our work by the next generation."⁴⁶

Katyń had been mostly absent from Western consciousness since publication of Zawodny's *Death in the Forest* in 1962. That changed in 1971, when *The Times* of London reviewed a new edition of Zawodny's book, Louis

---

⁴⁴ *Kultura* frequently printed acknowledgements of contributions to KSS "KOR" and ROPCiO.
⁴⁵ KOR's publishing venture was *Niezależna Oficyna Wydawnicza NOWA* (Independent Publishing House NOWA). Its publications included works from Polish authors in the West, including Czesław Miłosz and Jan Nowak-Jeziorański; authors who remained in Poland but were refused permission to publish, such as Jerzy Andrzejewski; and Western authors, including Arthur Koestler and Kurt Vonnegut. NOWA survived communist Poland and successfully transitioned into a free-market publisher. *Wydawnictwo Biblioteka Historyczna i Literacka* was founded by ROPCiO members.
⁴⁶ PAT, Nr. 13/76, Londyn, dnia 10 sierpnia 1976, AJPIA 701/9/13, No. 76.

FitzGibbon published *Katyn: A Crime Without Parallel*, and the BBC announced a documentary on the subject. Moscow's ambassador lodged a protest claiming that the program would damage British–Soviet relations and demanding that the British government block its airing, but the government refused to intervene. BBC2 broadcast *The Issue to be Avoided* in April. In the House of Lords, several members called on the government to declare Soviet responsibility.

There was no suitable memorial for the victims. At Katyń itself, the marker erected by the Soviet Union placed responsibility on the Germans and bore the date 1941. In Poland, official commemorations followed the Soviet line, although unofficial memorials could be found throughout the country.[47] In the West, there was no public memorial. For a group of British notables and Polish émigrés, it was now an opportune time. They formed the Katyn Memorial Fund and busied themselves with designing the monument, finding a location, and soliciting contributions.[48]

Moscow took note. Britain's ambassador was summoned to the Ministry of Foreign Affairs, but he declined to get involved. However, the Foreign Office was concerned. British–Soviet relations had lately been improving, and it intended to maintain this trend. If the committee could not be dissuaded from constructing a memorial, the Foreign Office preferred that it be inconspicuous and unprovocative, characteristics quite the opposite of what was envisioned. Initial plans called for a twenty-foot obelisk mounted on a stand twenty feet square; it would be located across the street from the Victoria and Albert Museum at the junction of Thurloe Place and Cromwell Road, on a wedge of land known as the Cromwell Road Triangle. Foreign Office officials were in a quandary; this monument would draw the ire of Moscow and Warsaw, yet two hundred members of the Commons declared their support for it. Britain's secretary of state opined that such a memorial would be of no help to either the victims or the living. No inscription had been announced, but judging from the

---

[47] No official memorial for the victims of Katyń had been permitted in the PRL, but authorities could not prevent unofficial memorials from springing up. "Katyń" and "1940" typically were not displayed, but society had an unspoken understanding of what was commemorated. In Warsaw's Powązki cemetery, there was a cobbled square that had no monument and bore no inscription, but flowers, wreaths, and candles were always present. Upon learning that it was a Katyń memorial, the Soviet ambassador demanded its destruction. Gierek reportedly responded that it was no use; he could bulldoze all of Poland and the people would find a place to commemorate Katyń.

[48] The Katyn Memorial Fund was chaired by Lord Barnby; his deputies were Lord St. Oswald, MP Airey Neave, and Toby Jessel. Louis FitzGibbon was honorary secretary, and former Foreign Secretary George Brown was a member. Among the Fund's patrons were Lord Salisbury, Lord Arran, Sir Roy Bucher, Sir John Sinclair, and Winston Churchill, grandson of Sir Winston Churchill. Polish members included Major Eugeniusz Lubomirski and Colonel Stefan Zamoyski; his son Adam Zamoyski is a noted historian and prolific author.

content of appeals and letters sent by the Fund committee to solicit contributions,[49] it was probable that responsibility would be affixed to the Soviet Union. The Foreign Office recommended placement inside a church or cemetery, and the government refused to permit the memorial to be placed on Crown property, thus ruling out the Cromwell Road Triangle.

With its preferred location rejected,[50] the committee applied to the Royal Borough of Kensington and Chelsea's council to locate the memorial in St. Luke's Gardens, a park located next to St. Luke's Church and a short distance from Cromwell Road. The council gave its provisional approval, but the Church of England needed to give its assent. St. Luke's rector was opposed, citing expected damage to nearby church grounds by visitors. Diocesan approval was doubtful; a diocesan official stated that such a memorial in a churchyard would be inconsistent with the church's ministry of reconciliation. While this site was under consideration, the committee announced further design elements, including a crowned Polish eagle surrounded by a ring of barbed wire and the year 1940. A lawyer for the Church of England proposed replacing 1940 with 1941, calling it a compromise; the memorial committee rejected his suggestion. Ultimately, permission was denied.

As the Foreign Office had feared, the memorial was becoming an issue with Moscow and Warsaw. In 1972, Foreign Secretary Sir Alec Douglas-Home met with Polish Minister of Foreign Affairs Stefan Olszowski to discuss trade; during the meeting, Olszowski brought up the memorial, declared that it had the potential to cause trouble in Polish–British relations, and stated that the victims of the Katyń massacre could not, after all, be brought back to life. Douglas-Home countered that the memorial would most likely go unnoticed if Warsaw did not bring attention to it. A few months later, Douglas-Home met with Soviet Ambassador Mikhail Smirnovsky, who made a formal statement declaring that the

[49] Katyn Memorial Fund's appeal for contributions included the following: "...the 14,500 Polish officer prisoners of war who disappeared from 'special' camps at Kozielsk, Starobielsk and Ostashkov in the USSR during the spring of 1940, of whom the bodies of nearly 4,500 were found in mass graves in the Katyn forest near Smolensk in the spring of 1943...". Colonel Stefan Zamoyski, a member of the Fund, wrote to the British prime minister, secretary of state, and other officials asking for their support. His letter explicitly placed responsibility on the Soviet Union: "The death of 4,500 Polish officers in 1940 in the Katyn forest, and extermination elsewhere in the Soviet Union of a further 10,000 officers and intellectuals deported by the invading armies of Hitler's Russian ally...". British officials took these documents as an indication of what could be expected of the monument's inscription.

[50] In 1980, Margaret Thatcher was prime minister, and she had few qualms about offending the Soviet Union. Thatcher approved a memorial to Soviet and Yugoslav citizens forcibly repatriated after the war; its location was the Cromwell Road Triangle, renamed Yalta Memorial Garden. She did so despite Foreign Office objections that such a memorial constituted a criticism of previous government actions; she also dismissed Soviet diplomatic protests.

proposed memorial caused indignation in the Soviet Union, claiming that the planned inscription was a distortion of facts, and asking the British government to influence the council to refuse permission. Douglas-Home stated that the government had no ability to intervene, noted that the government did not approve the inscription, and pointed out that the memorial would be in an out-of-the-way site and would not attract much attention; he then advised Smirnovsky to remain quiet about it and it would go unnoticed.[51]

Late in 1975, the Borough offered a site in Gunnersbury Cemetery well back from the entrance and not visible from nearby roads. But Warsaw and Moscow were unequivocal in insisting that the very existence of a memorial would be a problem.[52] Polish Ambassador Artur Starewicz had taken his objections to the council only to be rebuffed; he then petitioned the Mayoress of Kensington and Chelsea to intervene. Starewicz claimed that the inscription and emblem were slanderous, offensive, and insulting. This petition also failed. Moscow decided to forego official declarations on the matter but informed Western governments that the memorial was provocative and was calculated to damage international relations. Meanwhile, contributions flowed in from the United Kingdom and abroad. Émigrés throughout the United Kingdom made donations, as did British sympathizers; the Polish American Congress's Katyń Memorial Fund Commission alone raised over $20,000.

On the morning of Saturday, September 18, 1976, more than eight thousand people converged on Gunnersbury Cemetery for the unveiling. Dozens of banners from military, scouting, and social organizations fluttered in the breeze. Ostrowski, Sabbat, the Council of Ministers, and *Rada Narodowa* members were joined by the leaders of the Katyn Memorial Fund, British guests, representatives from several embassies,[53] representatives from the Czechoslovak, Hungarian, Lithuanian, Latvian, and Ukrainian exile communities, and members of the clergy. Lord Barnby delivered a speech, followed by Ostrowski and Lord St. Oswald. When they had concluded their remarks, Maria Chełmecka, widow of a Katyń victim, unveiled the monument, revealing these inscriptions:

---

[51] S. W. Martin of the Eastern European and Soviet Department proposed this to Polish diplomat Janusz Zabłocki. After some thought, Zabłocki rejected the idea, particularly if the site were the Polish cemetery in Newark-on-Trent.

[52] At the time the Soviet Union was pressuring the British government to block construction of the memorial, the KGB was covertly supplying arms to the Official Irish Republican Army, making Soviet complaints regarding construction of the memorial rather precious.

[53] A representative from the American embassy attended, as did representatives from Bolivia, Brazil, Colombia, Liberia, South Africa, and Uruguay.

"Sumienie świata wola o świadectwo prawdzie"[54]

"In remembrance of 14,500 Polish prisoners of war who disappeared in 1940 from camps at Kozielsk, Starobielsk, and Ostaszkow of whom 4,500 were later identified in mass graves at Katyn near Smolensk."

No official representative from Britain's government attended; it cited a lack of conclusive evidence that the killings were the work of the Soviet Union. A few members of Parliament, including Winston Churchill's grandson, attended in an unofficial capacity, and Conservative leader Margaret Thatcher chose to send a representative. The War Office forbade attendance by uniformed military personnel, but a number of retired British officers attended in full uniform.

Britain's media covered the event extensively. Television and radio news reported from Gunnersbury, and most newspapers ran articles and commentary, many of which were critical of the British government's refusal to send a representative; *The Daily Telegraph* asserted that the government had bowed to Soviet pressure. There was no official comment from Warsaw, nor was there any mention in Poland's press. But Britain's ambassador in Warsaw noted that the Polish people were very much aware of the monument's construction, were pleased that it had been built, and harbored some disappointment that Britain's government had not been more supportive.

In late February 1978, three hundred delegates from Polish communities across the United Kingdom assembled at POSK for *Ogólny Zjazd Polaków w W. Brytanii* (General Congress of Poles in Great Britain). Sabbat laid out their tasks: elect representatives to *Rada Narodowa* and adopt resolutions defining the position of Poles in Great Britain in the fight for independence. Delegates heeded Sabbat's earlier call for greater involvement of the younger generation; the average age of those elected to *Rada Narodowa* was forty-four, with only one over the age of sixty. They held lively and at times heated discussions on the situation in Poland, issues within the émigré community, and the state of international affairs. *Ogólny Zjazd Polaków* delegates paid their own expenses; they also contributed several hundred pounds of their own money to support free speech and human rights activities in Poland.

---

[54] English translation: *"The conscience of the world calls for the truth."*

V Rada Narodowa completed its five-year term in May 1978; later that month, *VI Rada Narodowa* was formed. With 105 members, it was considerably smaller, although like its predecessor it was composed of elected representatives, members designated by political parties and social groups, and presidential appointees.[55] Zygmunt Szadkowski was elected chairman in its opening session. *VI Rada Narodowa* had a five-year term.

In his remarks, Ostrowski noted that several elected members were from the younger generation; he viewed this as a positive sign that those born abroad were taking interest in the cause. He urged establishment of *Rada* branches in countries with significant émigré populations and cautioned against the concept of reducing the government-in-exile to encompass only the presidency. He outlined a clear vision of *Rada Narodowa's* responsibilities: "The nation in the country, through various forms of action and various trends, demands to ensure at least basic human and civil rights. Poles in the country do not have these rights, although they are guaranteed both by domestic regulations and by international agreements. The National Council, as a democratic organ of Free Poland, must, in this fight, express the will and aspirations of the Nation."[56]

Ostrowski saw the government-in-exile's role as the leader of émigré organizations striving for a free and independent homeland: "In the action of coordinating the activities of Polish organizations in the world, we want to see, above all, support and help for the fight for freedom and independence of Poland, for which the main responsibility lies with the factors of Polish independence emigration with the constitutional authorities in the first place."[57]

Prior to the opening session, Sabbat and the Council of Ministers resigned to allow a new government to be formed in consultation with *Rada Narodowa*. Sabbat was appointed again. Most of his previous ministers had positions in the new government, and they were joined by several new members.

---

[55] In *VI Rada Narodowa*, 30 members were elected, 44 were appointed by political parties, and 19 were appointed by veterans' organizations. Ostrowski named nine members, one of whom was a representative of religious denominations. A new category was AK veterans, three of whom sat on the *Rada*.

[56] PAT, "Przemówienie Prezydenta Rzeczypospolitej dr. Stanisława Ostrowskiego na inauguracyjnym Rady Narodowej Rzeczypospolitej Polskiej" ("Speech by the President of the Republic of Poland, Dr. Stanisław Ostrowski, at the inaugural meeting of the National Council of the Republic of Poland"), Nr. 5/78, Londyn, 19 czerwca 1978r, AJPIA 701/9/13, No. 96.

[57] PAT, "Przemówienie Prezydenta Rzeczypospolitej dr. Stanisława Ostrowskiego na inauguracyjnym Rady Narodowej Rzeczypospolitej Polskiej," Nr. 5/78, Londyn, 19 czerwca 1978r, AJPIA 701/9/13, No. 96.

In September 1978, Cardinal Wyszyński and Cardinal Wojtyła received the unexpected news that they would be returning to Rome. They had been there only one month earlier for the conclave that had elected Venice's Cardinal Luciani to the papacy, but on the thirty-third day of his pontificate, Pope John Paul was found dead in his apartment. Both knew that finding a replacement would be a challenge; it had been difficult enough to reach agreement on Luciani. Since Pope Adrian VI's death in 1523,[58] every pope had been an Italian; following that precedent, the assembled cardinals began by considering Italian candidates but had no success. Cardinal Franz König of Austria suggested looking to another country. He had a specific person in mind.

Since the start of the conclave, crowds had gathered in St. Peter's Square and strained to catch a glimpse of smoke from the narrow chimney protruding from the roof of the Sistine Chapel. For two days they had been disappointed by the sight of black smoke. Shortly after 6 p.m. on October 16, wisps of white smoke wafted from the chimney, signaling that a new pope had been chosen, and the crowd buzzed with speculation. The suspense was broken an hour later. Karol Wojtyła stepped onto the loggia of St. Peter's Basilica and was introduced as Pope John Paul II. His election galvanized Polish society, and spontaneous celebrations erupted throughout his homeland. Crowds poured into the streets, sang hymns and patriotic songs, waved Polish flags, and packed into churches. For PZPR, it was a debilitating shock. At a stroke, most of its efforts to undermine the Roman Catholic Church had been negated, and its project to supplant it with *Kościół Polskokatolicki*, which to date had shown sparse results, was dealt a ruinous blow. For Moscow, the news was alarming. A pope from a Soviet Bloc nation represented a direct contradiction to its atheistic program, and John Paul II had the potential to reawaken religious sentiments far beyond Poland.

Émigré Poles shared the enthusiasm of their countrymen. An emotional Kazimierz Sabbat opened the October 21 *Rada Narodowa* meeting with the words "*Habemus Papam Carolem Cardinalem*" and declared the pope's election a momentous event for Poles everywhere. Ostrowski, the Council of Ministers, and *Rada Narodowa* sent greetings to the new pope, and Sabbat met him in the Vatican on January 24, 1979. Sabbat would refer to Pope John Paul II frequently in his speeches, stressing his role in encouraging the opposition in Poland.

In John Paul II, Poles saw a highly visible person who would bring attention to the Polish cause, and they were correct. A slew of articles,

---

[58] Pope Adrian VI was Dutch; he was the first (and to date only) pope from the Netherlands.

books, and films about Wojtyła were hurriedly prepared that reminded the West of Poland's fate. Poland was claiming a larger place in Western consciousness.

Ostrowski never wavered from his pledge to leave office after seven years. Early in 1979, after confirming that Raczyński remained acceptable, he issued a statement upholding the 1972 decree appointing him and declaring that he would leave office on April 8. In his final speech to *Rada Narodowa* on April 7, Ostrowski reiterated his opposition to proposals that would alter the Republic's structure and end legalism. On the final day of his presidency, he urged exile groups to set aside their differences and expressed his desire for unity.

He remained involved in Polish affairs. He supported the opposition in Poland, met with Pope John Paul II on several occasions, and continued his activities in émigré organizations, particularly those related to his home city. On November 21, 1982, Ostrowski attended a commemoration of the 64th anniversary of the defense of Lwów. As he was being driven home afterwards, he collapsed in his seat. His driver rushed him to Charing Cross Hospital; he died there the next day. His funeral was in St. Andrzej Bobola Church. In his eulogy, Minister of Internal Affairs Edward Szczepanik gave him the title *Stanisław Zgodliwy* (Stanisław the Peacemaker) in recognition of his work to unite the émigré community. He was buried in the Polish Military Cemetery in Newark-upon-Trent on December 4.[59]

---

[59] In 1987, a plaque dedicated to Stanisław Ostrowski was unveiled in the Żoliborz district of Warsaw, an unusual honor for an exile politician in what was still People's Poland.

The Pretender

BACK IN 1972, on the afternoon of Ostrowski's inauguration, Minister of Justice Sylwester Karalus and Head of the Civil Chancellery Paweł Jankowski were examining two photocopied documents. Before them was former government minister and *Rada RP* member Juliusz Sokolnicki claiming that he, not Ostrowski, was Zaleski's successor and offering the photocopies as proof. One appeared to be a decree appointing him president dated September 22, 1971; the other, *Dziennik Ustaw Nr. 1*, dated April 7, 1972, included the decree. Karalus and Jankowski had no doubt that both were fabrications. As head of the civil chancellery, Jankowski maintained the president's official documents, and he knew that Zaleski had never submitted such a decree.[1] As minister of justice, Karalus was responsible for the content of *Dziennik Ustaw*. Not only had he not authorized publication of such a decree, he had published *Dziennik Ustaw Nr. 1* for 1972 on March 25. It was clear that Sokolnicki was attempting to perpetrate a fraud. They rejected his claim, dismissed him, and issued a statement declaring his documents to be false:

> In connection with the photostats of alleged official documents circulating in London, sent out by Mr. Juliusz Sokolnicki, we state that "the order of September 22, 1971, on the appointment of the successor of the President of the Republic of Poland" and "Dziennik Ustaw R.P. of April 7, 1972, with this order" are forgeries. There has never been such an order of the President of the Republic of Poland, which should be in the files of the Civil Chancellery of the President of the Republic of Poland, and such a Journal of Laws of the Republic of Poland has never been issued by order of the Minister of Justice.[2]

Sokolnicki retreated. He declared that he would resign from the presidency and sent Ostrowski a letter on April 11 stating that he recognized him as the legitimate president. But the matter was far from closed.

---

[1] No original of the decree in the photocopy was found in 43 Eaton Place, at Zaleski's residence, or among Zaleski's papers donated to the Hoover Institute. It should be remembered that August Zaleski had headed Raczkiewicz's civil chancellery and thus was intimately familiar with protocols and procedures for presidential decrees.

[2] Polska Agencja Telegraficzna, "Oświadczenie w sprawie krążących falsyfikatów" ("Statement on the circulating forgeries"), Nr. 3/72, Londyn, 7 kwietnia 1972 r., located in the archives of Instytut Piłsudskiego w Nowym Jorku (Józef Piłsudski Institute of America, New York), 701/9/13, No. 35.

Juliusz Sokolnicki's official biography indicated that he was born in Pińsk on December 16, 1920, studied history in Warsaw at *Uniwersytet Józefa Piłsudskiego* in 1937 and 1938, and was drafted into the Polish Army in 1939. Taken prisoner by the Red Army in 1939, he escaped, joined an underground group, and was arrested by the Gestapo. After a spell in Pawiak prison,[3] he was deported to a forced labor camp in occupied France[4] but was released due to poor health. He made his way to Warsaw, resumed anti-German and anti-Soviet activities in an organization called *Grupa Wolnych* (Free Group), and then joined AK. He rapidly rose through the ranks, beginning as a lieutenant in 1942, advancing to captain in 1943, and attaining the rank of lieutenant colonel by the end of the war. On April 2, 1942, he married Anna Nowak[5] in the town of Kraśnik, a few kilometers from Lublin; she died from mushroom poisoning fifteen months later, leaving him with an infant daughter.

That Juliusz Sokolnicki was born in Pińsk on December 16 is not in doubt; what is debatable is the year. His assertion that he was born in 1920 is contradicted by parish records indicating that the actual date was 1925,[6] and this five-year difference has great bearing on the veracity of his subsequent claims. Had Sokolnicki been born in 1920, in the autumn of 1937 he would have been sixteen years old, not an unreasonable age to start university studies, but his 1925 birthdate made him eleven years old at the time he claimed to have enrolled. His accounts of wartime military service are likewise problematic. Using his actual birth date, he would have been a lieutenant at the age of seventeen, a captain at eighteen, and a lieutenant colonel at nineteen. This would have been an extraordinary achievement, yet there is no evidence that he attended cadet school; without such education it was not possible to be an officer. No records have been found that corroborate his claim to have served in AK. A different version of events holds that he worked for a German company in Warsaw but, under pressure to sign the Volksliste,[7] fled to Kraśnik. This places him in Kraśnik at the time he claimed to have married Anna Nowak, but there is no record of their marriage. That Nowak gave birth to their daughter is not disputed,

---

[3] Warsaw's Pawiak prison was used as a Gestapo prison during the war.
[4] Sokolnicki claimed to have been held in a labor camp in Metz.
[5] Anna Nowak was born on July 24, 1914.
[6] Sokolnicki also claimed his parents had married in 1919; according to historian and genealogist Tomasz Lenczewski, a search of the parish archives showed that they were actually married in 1922.
[7] Signing the Volksliste meant declaring oneself to be German.

although Nowak died a few weeks later—not in 1943 as Sokolnicki contended—and Sokolnicki left his daughter in the care of a woman named Jadwiga Tańska.[8]

Little is known of Sokolnicki's activities and whereabouts in 1943 and 1944. He resurfaced in Żyrardów early in 1945, where on February 7, at the age of nineteen,[9] he married Tatiana Kotlińska, age thirty-four. From there, accounts again vary; he may have been a policeman in Żyrardów or an official of the registry and passport office in Lublin and later relocated to Szczecin. It is clear, however, that in early 1946 Sokolnicki abandoned his wife and left Poland accompanied by his mother. Through Czechoslovakia, he made his way to Germany and then Italy. He attempted to enlist in the Second Polish Corps but was rejected. He found work with the Polish Red Cross and accompanied the Corps when it departed Italy for the United Kingdom.

Sokolnicki settled in a modest flat in London and held a series of mundane jobs including laborer in a costume jewelry factory, gas meter reader, railroad maintenance worker, and shop assistant at Tesco. In 1947, he presented himself at the Polish consulate and volunteered to testify in a political trial.[10] In 1948, he married Florence Amelia Rosling without troubling himself to obtain a divorce from his wife in Poland.[11] He also involved himself in émigré politics. He joined LNP, but when that group's president Michał Grażyński signed the unification act, he quit and, with several like-minded opponents of Sosnkowski's reconciliation efforts, founded *Konwent Walk o Niepodległość* (KWN, Convention for the Fight for Independence). He was a KWN representative in the first *Rada Rzeczypospolitej Polskiej*, but after a 1955 dispute with chair Jerzy Ścibor-Kamiński, Sokolnicki established *Ruch Odrodzenia Narodowego* (RON, National Rebirth Movement); he would be a member of the second, third, and fourth *Rada RP* as an RON representative.

It was while Sokolnicki was involved with KWN that he came to SB's attention. Perceiving him to be a leading activist of KWN, LNP, and other *Sanacja*-oriented organizations, with extensive contacts among influential figures, SB opened an investigation into him in 1954, assigning him the code name *Mikron*. Agents in Poland located Tatiana Kotlińska and learned that

---

[8] Jadwiga Tańska was the wife of the administrator of the Zamoyski estate in Kwiatkowice.
[9] On his marriage certificate, Sokolnicki stated his age as 24 and claimed to be a bachelor, not a widower.
[10] The defendant was Stefan Rybicki. Sokolnicki did not testify, but he left a written statement with the consulate declaring his willingness to appear in court.
[11] Sokolnicki and his new wife Florence had four children together.

she and Sokolnicki had never divorced. They also found Jadwiga Tańska. She divulged that in the late 1940s she had received several letters from Sokolnicki; in them he depicted himself as an important political figure. She bluntly described him as a narrow-minded, foolish man who liked to drink, and she gave specific examples of his behavior. SB constructed a profile that depicted Sokolnicki as a weak man of poor character who typically sought the easiest path through life, reveled in even the most insignificant achievements, and held no strong political beliefs; his employment as a factory laborer provided barely enough income to support his wife and their four children in impoverished conditions. Armed with this information, SB formulated a plan to entice him to cooperate by promising a fixed payment of £40 to £50 a month; if he were to refuse, his wife in Poland would accuse him of bigamy and he would be threatened with deportation. Sokolnicki agreed to cooperate and received a salary. In 1956, ahead of Khrushchev's visit to London, Sokolnicki provided his contact with written reports on émigré activities, addresses of several hundred émigrés, and a list of non-Polish activists planning to participate in the protest march.

What Sokolnicki did next stunned the émigrés and SB. In August 1956, he walked into the offices of *Dziennik Polski i Dziennik Żołnierz* and announced that he had been in contact with SB over the previous six months. He provided details about their meetings and claimed that, in exchange for his cooperation, he would be paid £150 per month and would be appointed to a ministerial post when he returned to Poland. He stated that he was to provide names and addresses of people in Poland with whom exile politicians corresponded and was to persuade Zaleski to appoint a successor who would return to Poland immediately after taking office. His explanation for maintaining contact with PRL intelligence was that he wanted to learn about Warsaw's intentions and methods abroad.

Repercussions were few. SB broke contact with him. *Rada RP* declared that "he acted in a manner inconsistent with the honor and dignity of a member of the Council of the Republic of Poland," but his only punishment was to be barred from participating in *Rada* session for the remainder of his term of office; this was a minor penalty, as *Rada's* term ended a few months later. His transgressions were soon forgotten; he was appointed to *II Rada RP* as a RON representative. In January 1967, Zawisza appointed him minister of information and documentation; he retained that position in Muchniewski's Council of Ministers and took on the additional responsibility of minister of national affairs. It was in the latter capacity that Sokolnicki overreached his authority in a manner that resulted in his dismissal.

In 1971, Sokolnicki established contacts with groups of Germans displaced from the Recovered Territories and agreed that post-communist Poland should return to its prewar borders. This gave great hope to the Germans, but neither Zaleski, Muchniewski, nor Minister of Foreign Affairs Jerzy Gawenda were privy to his talks.[12] Word of his agreement reached Juliusz Szygowski, the government's representative in the United States, and on November 20 he sent a report containing specific information and incriminating details to London. Sokolnicki was dismissed from his government posts on November 25.[13]

His personal life was equally tumultuous. In 1955 he and Florence separated; their divorce was final in 1957. He married Joyce Teresa George Norton a few weeks later, and they had one son. This marriage lasted only slightly longer. They divorced in 1970, and he married Elizabeth Mary Mayall in November 1971.

At the time he approached Jankowski and Karalus, Sokolnicki had already written to politicians, newspapers, and press agencies around the world announcing his presidency, and copies of the nomination document he presented had been plastered on advertising posts around Polish London. About six months after he wrote to Ostrowski to resign his claim to the presidency, he decided to take legal action. Jankowski and Karalus received letters from a law firm notifying them that Sokolnicki was demanding that they retract their April 9 statement, apologize, and pay compensation for moral damage. In October, Jankowski and Karalus replied. They provided their basis for declaring Sokolnicki's documents to be fraudulent; Karalus included copies of the first two issues of *Dziennik Ustaw* for 1972. After reviewing their responses, the law firm withdrew from the case, and Sokolnicki ceased to seek legal remedies.[14]

Sokolnicki contacted Ostrowski, declared that he was the legitimate president, demanded that Ostrowski recognize him, and offered him the position of prime minister. Sokolnicki later claimed that he offered Ostrowski the presidency, but he refused to negotiate. On November 17, he declared himself

---

[12] Sokolnicki later contradicted this in correspondence with *Gazeta Wyborcza* editor Adam Michnik. He claimed that he believed that reconciliation with the Germans was a necessary precondition to German acceptance of the Oder–Neisse border.

[13] In the announcement of his dismissal, there is no indication that he resigned. When a government minister resigned, *Dziennik Ustaw* announcements typically noted that the departure was a resignation.

[14] These letters from Jankowski and Karalus were published in "*Komunikat Rządu R.P. z dnia 18 kwietnia 1977*" ("Communiqué of the Government of the Republic of Poland of 18 April 1977").

"President of Free Poland in Exile" and issued a decree in his self-published newspaper *Głos Wolnej Polski* (*Voice of Free Poland*) dismissing Urbański and Kopański from their respective posts of prime minister and inspector general of the armed forces and appointing his own government and inspector general. And he proffered a discharge certificate from the Polish Armed Forces that referred to him as Lieutenant Colonel Juliusz Sokolnicki.[15]

Apart from recognition of his claim, what Sokolnicki needed was money. With no access to *Skarb Narodowy* or 43 Eaton Place,[16] he had to obtain funds elsewhere, and he started with sources he had been cultivating since at least 1971, Germany's *Bund der Vertriebenen* (BdV, Federation of Expellees) and West German politician Herbert Czaja.[17] In December, Sokolnicki addressed a group of expellees in Hanover and proposed that Poland's borders should be restored to those in place in 1939 and that Germany and Poland should unite against the Soviet Union. His speech was received enthusiastically. That same day, he met privately with Czaja to obtain financial support.

Jadwiga Tańska had described Sokolnicki as a fool, but her impression was based on the callow young man she knew during the war. Tańska was incorrect; Sokolnicki was not a fool but an opportunist. His experiences in Italy had convinced him of the importance of name, position, and status. After his attempt to enlist in the Second Polish Corps failed, he obtained employment in the Polish Red Cross by implying that he and Michał

---

[15] This document is reproduced in Michael Subritzky-Kusza's *History of the Polish Government (In Exile) 1939–1990* (Three Feathers Publishing Co., Papakura, New Zealand, 1996), p. 48. It is the only documentary evidence offered to support Sokolnicki's claim of military service.

[16] Any designs Sokolnicki had on 43 Eaton Place were dashed by the lack of a decree from Zaleski. Since Jankowski had not received a decree appointing Sokolnicki as Zaleski's successor, he had no reason to provide Sokolnicki's name to Cytadela (Eaton Place) Limited's legal representation to place him in line to acquire Zaleski's shares in the trust. As the government stated:

> The building at 43 Eaton Place in London, where the President's seat is located, belongs to 'Cytadela Ltd.' company registered by English law. From the legal point of view, the ownership is set in such a way that each President of the R.P. owns 99.5% of shares. The name of the successor of the President is reported from time to time by the law firm so that only the designated successor acquires the shares. The shares currently belong to the President R.P. dr. Stanisław Ostrowski. Pan Sokolnicki, having no legal basis, could not apply for the right to take over the building.

See "Komunikat Rządu R.P. z dnia 18 kwietnia 1977," AJPIA 701/9/13, No. 105.

[17] Herbert Czaja was originally from Cieszyn; his ethnic background was a mix of German, Czech, and Polish. He attended German schools, belonged to German organizations in the Second Republic, and was a member of a German political party. He served in the German Army during the war; afterwards, he was forcibly relocated to West Germany. He served as president of the Federation of Expellees, was a member of the Bundestag, and consistently opposed recognition of the postwar Polish–German border. After German reunification, he took the position that the job was incomplete, as the Recovered Territories remained within Poland's borders, and proposed creating from them an autonomous area under international control.

Sokolnicki, Poland's ambassador to Turkey, were related.[18] He took this further in London, claiming that he was related to former Foreign Minister and former Ambassador to the United Kingdom Konstanty Skirmunt and to Bohdan Podoski, one of the primary authors of the April Constitution and a judge at *Sądy Obywatelskie na Obczyźnie*. Sokolnicki's decision to back Zaleski over Sosnkowski and to align himself with *Zamek* was a matter of opportunism and not rooted in political convictions, as was his part in creating KWN and RON. In each case, Sokolnicki gained visibility, position, and status; eventually, his efforts resulted in his appointment to two ministerial positions. His account of his supposed nomination was impossible to verify. He claimed that Zaleski was unhappy with the direction that unification talks had taken, summoned him in September 1971, and confided in him that he was reconsidering his decision to appoint the seventy-nine-year-old Ostrowski based on concerns that Ostrowski was too old, would be too willing to concede to *Zjednoczenie Narodowe,* and would be easily manipulated by them, particularly those responsible for *Sprawa Bergu*.[19] Sokolnicki then claimed that Zaleski offered him the presidency, although he insisted on keeping the appointment confidential for fear of disrupting unification talks; Sokolnicki said that he accepted and that Zaleski gave him a photocopy of the decree.[20] Sokolnicki claimed that he then voluntarily resigned from his government posts.

---

[18] Although they shared a family name, Michał Sokolnicki was descended from a different line than Juliusz Sokolnicki.

[19] Sokolnicki's claim that Zaleski was concerned that Ostrowski would be manipulated by the people behind *Sprawa Bergu* echoed the events of 1954, although the political landscape of 1972 was quite different, as SN, the party central to the Berg controversy, was now rejecting legalism. It is not clear if this would have been known to Zaleski at the time of his alleged meeting with Sokolnicki; he claimed their meeting took place on September 22, five days after the first meeting between the *Zamek* and *Zjednoczenie Narodowe* unification committees.

[20] Sokolnicki's supporters have expended considerable effort to bolster his claim that the photocopy he presented was of an authentic decree. In his book, Michael Subritzky-Kusza declared that examination of the photocopy proved that it had been written on official government stationery using a typewriter that belonged to the government, that the signature matched other instances of Zaleski's signature, and that the presidential seal was authentic. He reproduced a letter from one Lee D. MacMahon certifying that the signature was Zaleski's; on pages 50 and 51, he reproduced the photocopied document in question embellished with endorsements of its authenticity given by a John Holman and a Jon L. Dunkerley, both of whom Subritzky-Kusza presents as having "the authority in Britain to verify documents" (see note on page 49; no specific credentials are provided). In his letter, MacMahon used the postnominal "KtB (y)", indicating his claim to the hereditary title of "Knight Bachelor (Yugoslavia)," a chivalric order of dubious authenticity. (Subritzky-Kusza himself claimed membership in orders of questionable legitimacy.) Notable by its absence from his book is a discussion regarding the whereabouts of (or fate of) the original decree. As no original was ever found in 43 Eaton Place or in Zaleski's residence, and as Sokolnicki used at least two documents to justify his claim, on both of which Zaleski's signature was identical, it is reasonable to conclude that Sokolnicki fabricated the decree. Sokolnicki was minister of information and documentation for several years and had access to official stationery, a typewriter, documents with Zaleski's signature and seal, and a photocopier. It would have been quite simple for him to fashion a photocopy that appeared to be an image of a genuine presidential decree; it would have been equally simple to prepare a discharge certificate.

Sokolnicki's account contained a modicum of plausibility. Although Zaleski had taken many steps towards unification in 1971,[21] he had made comparable moves before he rejected *Akt Zjednoczenia Narodowego* in 1953. Choosing Sokolnicki as his successor, however, was less plausible. Sokolnicki may have served in two governments and *Rada RP*, but he was not widely known among the émigré community and, outside of PRL intelligence, Anna Nowak's family, Tatiana Sokolnicki and her family, and Jadwiga Tańska, he was unknown in Poland.

What mattered to Sokolnicki, though, was that his explanation resonated with a small émigré faction distrustful of people associated with *Zjednoczenie Narodowe*. This group, staunch *Zamek* adherents upset with what they perceived to be a defeat at the hands of the opposition, was to form the core of Sokolnicki's constituency. It was among them that he found people with whom he would populate his government.[22] Of more tangible value were people enamored with symbols of rank and status. Sokolnicki himself was one of them, as demonstrated by his postwar efforts to infer a shared lineage with several prominent Poles. In the 1960s, he became involved in a subculture of international traders of decorations and titles; by the early 1970s, he was calling himself a count, using the Nowina heraldry, and styling his surname Nowina-Sokolnicki.[23] For Sokolnicki, the presidency was a source of prestige and money. Prestige came from the title of president and from decorations and ranks, a fitting example being his promotion of himself to the rank of brigadier general.[24] Money flowed in from people who coveted a decoration, a high military rank, or a government position[25] and were willing to pay for it,[26] particularly since Zaleski had issued awards sparingly. He promoted three of his supporters, none of whom had commanded a unit

---

[21] Specifically, Zaleski had authorized talks with *Zjednoczenie Narodowe*, appointed Muchniewski to lead a commission to explore unification, dissolved *IV Rada R.P.* and replaced it with *Rada Stanu*, and rescinded his nomination of *Zamek* loyalist Aleksander Zawisza, replacing him with Ostrowski.

[22] According to Lenczewski, not all members of Sokolnicki's governments were aware of their positions. Some learned of this from third parties.

[23] Claiming the Nowina heritage is the least problematic of these, as there was a Sokolnicki line descended from the original families. Prepending Nowina to his name is more questionable, as none of the Sokolnickis known to have descended from the Nowina line had used the form "Nowina-Sokolnicki." Most problematic was his use of the title "Count." No member of his branch of the family received that title, and he was of a different line from the last Count with the Sokolnicki name.

[24] Sokolnicki promoted himself to the rank of brigadier general in August 1978.

[25] Polish-Canadian columnist Witold Lilenthal reported that a person who claimed the title of deputy prime minister and minister of foreign affairs in Sokolnicki's government offered him a government ministry and the Commander's Cross of the Order of Polonia Restituta for $800.

[26] Lenczewski contends that Sokolnicki was obtaining income from the sale of ranks and decorations.

larger than a platoon,[27] to the rank of general. Sokolnicki paid to have his biography included in directories such as *Who's Who*, *Dictionary of International Biography*, and *Debrett's Distinguished People of Today* and bestowed awards and honors on people whose favor he wanted.

In July 1976, a body calling itself "*Organizacja Bojowa Wolna Polska*—'Free Poland' Combat Organization" registered with the Department of Justice in Washington, D.C., "as a foreign representative of the Government of the Republic of Poland in Exile with its seat in London, in accordance with the Foreign Agents Registration Act."[28] It had been formed in New York and was not connected to the government-in-exile. Szygowski informed the Attorney General's office that this new organization was not authorized to act on the government's behalf or to register as its agent, and the government issued an official statement declaring that "*Organizacja Bojowa Wolna Polska* cannot be and is not a foreign representative of the Government, that the Government will not and cannot be held responsible for its acts." The government also noted that the organization advocated what it called "direct combat" and engaged in actions of questionable legality.[29]

In its publication, the bilingual *Wolna Polska – Free Poland*, *Organizacja Bojowa Wolna Polska* advocated tactics quite different from those employed by the government-in-exile. It called for direct action against communist regimes and called for volunteers, specifically people of military age and particularly those who had been arrested in People's Poland for political reasons. Behind *Organizacja Bojowa Wolna Polska* and *Wolna Polska – Free Poland* stood Konstanty Zygfryd Hanff. Born in Częstochowa in 1926 to a German father and an Armenian mother, he served in the German military during the war (although he later claimed to have been working for Polish intelligence) and applied for German citizenship in 1943. By his account, his service in the German military was less than exemplary; he claimed arrest by the Gestapo on unfounded charges; after his release, he deserted, was captured by the Germans, and was sent to the front in a penal battalion. He was then captured by the Red Army and spent several years in prison and in a gulag until deportation to Poland in 1948. He was permitted to emigrate in 1969.

---

[27] A typical platoon consists of thirty to forty soldiers.
[28] PAT, "Organizacja Bojowa Wolna Polska" ("Free Poland Combat Organization"), Nr. 15/76, Londyn, 12 października 1976r., AJPIA 701/9/13, No. 79.
[29] PAT, "Organizacja Bojowa Wolna Polska," Nr. 15/76, Londyn, 12 października 1976r., AJPIA 701/9/13, No. 79.

Despite Hanff's aggressive rhetoric, no insurrections were launched in Poland, nor is there evidence that he had fostered creation of any underground groups.[30] Instead, he engaged in provocations. Under the pseudonym Anatol Karewicz,[31] he mailed dozens of letters to Polish diplomatic and consular employees in the United States questioning the recipients' loyalty to the communist regime and offering the opportunity to collaborate with his organization; he also sent a threatening letter to a highly placed consular official.[32] Additionally, Hanff sent letters to the Swedish and Norwegian ambassadors to the United States offering to provide lists of Polish intelligence agents operating in their countries.

Hanff caused a diplomatic rift between Poland and the United States. Polish officials lodged complaints about his actions with their American counterparts, and the FBI began investigating him and his organization. Allegations appeared that Hanff had denounced AK members and Jews to the Germans during the war, that he had participated in killing Jews, and that he was actually an agent of communist Poland.[33] American officials attempting to investigate charges of war crimes received no cooperation from Warsaw,

---

[30] In December 1975 and January 1976, Hanff met with prominent Polonia figures in Chicago and "had alluded to the fact that 'Wolna Polska' had an organization in Poland which was reported to be preparing some kind of action aimed at the overthrow of the regime. In one of his talks, Hanff claimed to be in contact with a well-organized and militant underground in Poland." All of those he spoke with refused his overtures "because it would mean that a few unarmed and ill-advised individuals in Poland would be thrown against the Polish Army, which would be suicidal and no real aid to the cause of Polish freedom." See Federal Bureau of Investigation, Chicago, Illinois, "Polish Intelligence Activities in the United States," April 21, 1976 (File No. CG 100-17864). https://www.cia.gov/readingroom/docs/HANFF%2C%20KONSTANTY%20%20%20VOL.%201_0021.pdf

[31] Department of State memo from Verne F. St. Mars, Acting Deputy Assistant Secretary for Security, to Deputy Director for Operations, Central intelligence Agency, subject, Free Poland - Special Report Nr 3, October 22, 1976. In the background information section of this memo, the alias Anatol Karewicz is attributed to Hanff. In a June 1976 telegram from the American embassy in Warsaw to the Department of State, the embassy official made this comment about the name Karewicz: "If it is a pseudonym, the name 'Karewicz' is presumably based on 'kara,' which means 'execution' or 'sentence.'" See June 1976 telegram from American Embassy Warsaw to Secretary of State, subject: "Protection of Polish officials in the US: activities of 'Free Poland.'" https://www.cia.gov/readingroom/docs/HANFF%2C%20KONSTANTY%20%20%20VOL.%201_0031.pdf

[32] The most common letter opened with, "We absolutely do not believe in your complete devotion to the Soviet regime. On the contrary: we believe that you are ready to serve in the matter of freeing Poland from the yoke of occupation." In his letter to Consul Janusz Kuczawski, he wrote "...we are preparing a memorandum on the subject of tactical mistakes systematically committed by your disinformation section and about the insufficient professional education of the employees of that section in New York posts and at the consulate in Chicago as well. This memorandum shall be send [sic] to the highest-responsible official of the MSW in Warsaw, immediately after its final completion. In case you would like to learn some fragments of that memorandum, especially in the part referring to you personally, we ask you to not hesitate to write us." See Report of Andrew D. Skroch, Federal Bureau of Investigation, Field Office File #: 185-499. https://www.cia.gov/readingroom/docs/HANFF%2C%20KONSTANTY%20%20%20VOL.%201_0017.pdf

[33] Hanff did not let the charges in Tydzień go unchallenged. He threatened editor Jerzy Myssura with a defamation lawsuit and contended that information in his article proved he was connected to SB. The matter was dropped, although it is noteworthy that Hanff was not alone in his suspicions about Myssura. Copies of Tydzień could be found in the waiting room of the New York consulate, constituting endorsement of that paper. See Federal Bureau of Investigation, New York, New York, "Konstanty Zygfryd Hanff - Internal Security – Poland," Chicago, Illinois. Polish Intelligence Activities in the United States, August 20, 1976. https://www.cia.gov/readingroom/docs/HANFF%2C%20KONSTANTY%20%20%20VOL.%201_0043.pdf

raising speculation that he was in fact a PRL agent. Hanff was interviewed by the FBI and claimed that he disavowed violence and that his letters to Polish officials were no more than an offer of an alternative to service to Warsaw.

None of these investigations or allegations deterred Hanff; he launched a new campaign in 1977. He mailed letters to American politicians and FBI officials on what appeared to be official stationery from several Soviet Bloc embassies, signed with the names of actual diplomats stationed in those embassies. One contained disparaging accusations about some Polish diplomats. Another letter appeared to be from the Polish ambassador and was addressed to the Soviet ambassador, rescinding an invitation to a social function. Other letters on Polish embassy stationery were sent to American businessmen who had visited Poland; the letters stated that their conduct in Poland was disgusting and that they would be barred from visiting Poland again. Hanff also had plans for a more public provocation. He planned to call the Polish consulate in New York or the Polish ambassador to the United Nations from JFK International Airport, claiming to be a professor who had just arrived from Poland and asking for the whereabouts of the delegation that was to meet him. Presumably, someone would be dispatched to the airport for him, and he would start an altercation and accuse them of trying to kidnap him. He continued to publish provocative items in *Wolna Polska – Free Poland*, such as a 1977 feature, "Polish Communist Intelligence Officer Serves as Under Secretary General of United Nations in New York," which was rife with sordid and sensationalist allegations leveled at Polish diplomats.

Hanff and *Wolna Polska - Free Poland* recognized Sokolnicki's claim to the presidency and unflinchingly promoted him; frequently, his photo adorned the front page. *Wolna Polska* was essentially the official organ of Sokolnicki and his coterie.

Sokolnicki adamantly maintained that Ostrowski was a usurper and that his government was illegitimate, as did his followers.[34] In 1976, he added accusations of corruption.

A letter titled "*Do Społczeństwa Polskiego w Świecie*" ("To the Polish Society in the World") appeared in mailboxes of émigré organizations and individual Poles throughout the West. It alleged irregularities in payments from *Skarb Narodowy* to the government in 1973 and 1974. Its author was

[34] For example, Michael Subritzky-Kusza titled a section of his book "Usurper Government-in-Exile" to discuss Ostrowski.

Sokolnicki. Three *Rada Narodowa* members raised the issue at a session in October. *Rada* chair Franciszek Wilk rejected their motion, citing NIK audits that showed no delays or shortfalls. Treasury Minister Szadkowski and *Skarb Narodowy's* oversight board (*Główna Komisja Skarbu Narodowego*) were compelled to issue statements refuting Sokolnicki's allegations.

In September 1977, Gierek was on a state visit to France. His official itinerary included a stop at the Arc de Triomphe to lay a wreath at the Tomb of the Unknown Soldier. After placing his wreath, Gierek walked towards a group of banners representing military units and veterans' organizations; among them were Polish standards. He greeted the Poles; among them was Antoni Zdrojewski, whom Sokolnicki had appointed to the rank of *generał broni*[35] two years earlier. Polish newspapers reported that Gierek and Zdrojewski had a brief and cordial talk. A few months later, General Mieczysław Grudzień traveled from Warsaw to Paris to participate in the unveiling of a monument. Again, Zdrojewski was in attendance, as was Sokolnicki; he had also been present at the Arc de Triomphe. This time, Sokolnicki and Gierek exchanged greetings.

Sokolnicki made further efforts to extend his influence. In February 1978, he sent letters to President Carter and his security advisor proposing a new plan for Europe that included returning East Prussia to Germany and Wilno and Lwów to Poland. Most of the American government was unaware of Sokolnicki and his claim to the presidency,[36] and officials in Washington had to contact representatives of the government-in-exile for clarification.

The presence of Sokolnicki and Zdrojewski at the Paris events and their friendly talks with Gierek fueled the indignation of Polish veterans already incensed by Sokolnicki's trade in promotions and military decorations, which he sold for prices ranging from less than one hundred dollars to several thousand dollars. He awarded *Virtuti Militari* to over three hundred people, including Germans who had taken part in the September 1939 invasion. Those with whom he hoped to gain influence and friendship received decorations for free.[37] In April 1977, Generals Bohusz-Szyszko, Maczek, and Duch warned veterans about Sokolnicki's activities, equating them to PRL intrigues against émigrés. His actions were condemned at

---

[35] "*Generał Broni*" translates to "General of Arms." The corresponding rank in western armies is Lieutenant General.

[36] The FBI, however, was certainly aware of Sokolnicki and his claims; it learned about them while investigating Konstanty Hanff and his organization.

[37] Some of the German recipients had served on the battleship *Schleswig-Holstein*, which had fired some of the first shots on September 1, 1939.

the 1978 *Ogólny Zjazd Polaków w W. Brytanii*. This was followed by a meeting of PSZ leaders and *Virtuti Militari* recipients at the Sikorski Museum. Attendees passed a resolution calling on veterans to oppose Sokolnicki's "harmful and destructive activity," disseminate previously issued proclamations among the émigré community, educate those unaware of the state of affairs, and disassociate themselves from Sokolnicki, his associates, and his supporters. Eight generals and nineteen leaders of veterans' organizations signed the resolution.

By this time, Zenon Janasiak had more questions than answers. He did not know how Sokolnicki funded his activities, nor did he understand why Zdrojewski was so friendly with Gierek and Grudzień in Paris or why Sokolnicki attended both events. Many émigrés may have shared these questions, but Janasiak, Sokolnicki's minister of foreign affairs since 1975 and prime minister since 1976, should have had some insight. From these unanswered questions and his other observations, he concluded that he was supporting the wrong president. Janasiak contacted Sabbat in March 1978 and declared that he was severing ties with Sokolnicki. In a letter to Ostrowski, he concluded that Sokolnicki's government lacked legitimacy, was destructive, and was engaged in activities detrimental to the cause of Polish independence. Janasiak took it on himself to warn the émigré community about Sokolnicki's activities.

Sokolnicki was undaunted by the condemnations and by Janasiak's defection. In April, he appointed a new prime minister, and he continued to mete out promotions and decorations. He was not going to fade into obscurity; rather, he would continue to disrupt exile politics and the émigré community.

The Elder Statesman

Edward Raczyński,
President of the Republic of Poland 1979-1986

WINDING THROUGH WIELKOPOLSKA, the Warta River is one of Poland's defining waterways, so much so that it is mentioned in the second verse of the national anthem. From its source in the Silesian uplands, it courses through Częstochowa and Poznań until it flows into the Odra. Just over twenty kilometers upstream of Poznań, the Warta passes a few dozen meters from a cultural treasure. Amid carefully tended gardens and lawns stands a yellow-and-cream neo-Baroque palace topped with a terra cotta roof; two gracefully curved wings partially enclose a courtyard. This is Rogalin Palace, seat of the Raczyński family.

In the mid-nineteenth century, Rogalin was managed by Roger Maurycy Raczyński.[1] In his twenties he had an affair with Zenaida Lubomirska that resulted in a son, Edward Aleksander. Lubomirska, a member of the powerful Lubomirski family, was already married, so Roger married Maria Ernestyna Gotschall, who had agreed to raise Edward as her child. During the January Uprising, Roger supplied weapons and funds to the Poles; after its defeat he moved to Paris to avoid arrest and either exile or execution.

Edward remained in Poland, and in his youth he became acquainted with Róża Potocka, herself a member of a formidable family. They wanted

---

[1] In 1824, Prussian King Frederick Wilhelm III bestowed the hereditary title of count on Roger Maurycy Raczyński.

to marry, but his family was strongly opposed. In time, he yielded to their pressure and ended the relationship. In 1868, Róża married Władysław Krasiński,[2] member of another prominent family, but their marriage did not last long. Władysław had been diagnosed with tuberculosis shortly before they married and died in 1873. Their children Adam, Elżbieta Maria, and Zofia had also contracted tuberculosis, and after Władysław's death, Róża moved her family to the healthier climate of Zakopane.

Edward married Krasiński's sister Maria Beatrix Krasińska in 1877; they had one son, Karol. Their marriage was also ill-fated. Maria also contracted tuberculosis and died in 1884, and Róża took responsibility for Karol. Both Edward and Róża were now widowed and free to pursue their relationship; after a respectable mourning period, they married in 1886. In 1889, their first son, Roger Adam, was born in Warsaw. Their second son, Edward Bernard, was born in Zakopane on December 19, 1891. Roger and Edward spent their early years in Rogalin and in family residences in Kraków. They both graduated from *liceum* in Kraków and studied at Leipzig University;[3] from there, their paths diverged.[4] Edward continued his education at the London School of Economics and *Uniwersytet Jagielloński* (Jagiellonian University) in Kraków, receiving his doctorate in law in 1915.

From an early age, Edward wanted to serve the Polish cause. He credited his parents with instilling this ethic in him and his brother. He was drawn to military service but feared he would not be accepted due to a vision issue. His residence in Kraków made him a subject of the Austro-Hungarian Empire, and he was conscripted into its army but failed his medical exam. Undeterred, in early 1918 he volunteered for *Polski Korpus Posiłkowy* (PKP, Polish Auxiliary Corps), a Polish formation in the Austro-Hungarian Army. This time, he managed to avoid the vision examination and was admitted to cadet school.[5] When the war ended, Corporal Raczyński and his fellow cadets had the pleasure of disarming German soldiers, escorting them to the train station, and evicting them from newly independent Poland.

In the spring of 1919, Raczyński and his fellow cadets were given new orders. Most were posted in cities and towns to train new recruits, but he

---

[2] Władysław Krasiński's father, Zygmunt Krasiński, was one of Poland's great romantic poets.

[3] In post-war Europe, Leipzig was in East Germany; from 1953 until the unification of East and West Germany, Leipzig University was known as Karl Marx University.

[4] Roger Raczyński served in the Ministry of Foreign Affairs, in the Ministry of Agriculture, and as Poland's ambassador to Romania until November 1940, when Romania was pressured to join the Tripartite Pact and close the Polish embassy. Roger then joined the Greek government-in-exile and served as a minister; he died in Athens in 1945.

[5] He attended cadet school in Ostrów Mazowiecka.

was sent to a military mission in Bern, Switzerland. There he was nominated to be one of the secretaries of the legation in Copenhagen.[6] Quite by chance, he had become a diplomat. His next assignment was to the Polish embassy in London, where he met Lady Joyous Markham, daughter of a British coal mining magnate. They were married in 1925, and he was reassigned to Warsaw and appointed to head a department within the Ministry of Foreign Affairs.

His wife died in 1931. In 1932, he married again. He and his new wife, Cecylia Maria Jaroszyńska, had three daughters: Wanda (born in 1933),[7] Wirydianna (born in 1935), and Katarzyna (born in 1939). Also in 1932, he was appointed representative to the League of Nations. Raczyński's assignment in Geneva ended when he was named ambassador to the United Kingdom in 1934, where he had the challenge of representing Polish interests in a country where Piłsudski and his government were not well regarded.

Raczyński held a critical role as ambassador to a major power during a time of political turbulence. Germany and the Soviet Union were aggressively expanding their militaries and adopting increasingly assertive foreign policies. In 1939 Raczyński had the formidable task of creating a military alliance with the United Kingdom, historically not an ally of Poland. In his meetings with Foreign Secretary Lord Halifax, Raczyński outlined the threat that Germany presented to the United Kingdom and the whole of Europe. His persistent arguments were bolstered on August 23 when Germany and the Soviet Union announced their non-aggression pact.[8] Two days later, Raczyński and Halifax signed the Polish–British Alliance. This agreement was as surprising and unexpected to Germany and the Soviet Union as the Molotov–Ribbentrop Agreement had been to the West. Hitler postponed his planned invasion of Poland for a week to analyze the alliance and the United Kingdom's expected response.

During the war, Raczyński continued as ambassador to the United Kingdom. After the Sikorski–Maisky agreement was signed in 1941, Raczyński replaced August Zaleski as minister of foreign affairs. Raczyński later opined that the United Kingdom had been in a position to obtain concessions from Stalin regarding the future landscape of Europe but failed to capitalize on this opportunity since it was simply happy to gain a powerful ally.

---

[6] Doubtless, his fluency in French, English, and German had some bearing on this posting.
[7] Wanda Raczyńska married Captain Ryszard Dembiński; he was chairman of the Polish Institute and Sikorski Museum in London from 1979 until 2003.
[8] This was the Molotov–Ribbentrop Agreement.

After Sikorski's death, Mikołajczyk retained Raczyński as ambassador to the United Kingdom, and he held that position through the end of the war. He had to vacate the embassy, and he knew he could not return to Rogalin. His manor had survived the war but suffered depredations. German occupiers had confiscated it and used it as a school for the Hitler Youth. The library's contents had been moved to Poznań for safekeeping but were destroyed during a bombing raid. Rogalin itself was spared from destruction, although it stood abandoned until Warsaw decided that estates such as Rogalin presented an opportunity to advance its propaganda. It was seized and made a branch of the National Museum in Poznań in 1949; its purpose was to illustrate the exploitation of the masses by the wealthy few.

Raczyński continued to serve the Polish cause as an émigré. He had chaired the Polish Research Centre in London since 1940 and continued to serve in this role until 1965, when it merged with the General Sikorski Historical Institute to form the Polish Institute and Sikorski Museum. He served as the merged organization's chair from 1965 until 1976. He represented Poland on the Interim Treasury Committee for Polish Questions from 1945 until 1947 and was Honorary Chief Polish Advisor to the Ministry of Labour from 1952 to 1956. He was one of the founders of *Rada Trzech* and was a member until it was dissolved. He capitalized on his firsthand knowledge of European events in the 1930s and 1940s by writing several books. In 1948, he published *The British–Polish Alliance, Its Origin and Meaning*, followed by *Our Independence and the Constitution* in 1950. In 1960, he published his wartime experiences and issued an English-language edition in 1962 under the title *In Allied London*. His last book on this era was *Od Narcyza Kulikowskiego do Winstona Churchilla*, a collection of documents from his time as ambassador to the United Kingdom. He also wrote about his family. In 1969, he published a history of Rogalin palace titled *Rogalin i jego mieszkańcy*; he also published *Pani Róża*, a biography of his mother. Lastly, he had an abiding interest in poetry. He published his translation of Omar Khayyám's *Rubayat* in 1960.

Cecylia died in London in October 1962. A few years later, he began a relationship with Aniela Lilpop Mieczysławska but they did not marry; she was separated but not divorced from her husband, Witold Mieczysławski. In 1967, Raczyński moved to a house at 8 Lennox Gardens. Its location was ideal: the Polish Institute and Sikorski Museum was less than a mile to the north, 43 Eaton Place was about a half mile east, the Brompton Oratory was little more than a quarter mile away, and Daquise, one of his favorite restaurants, was a half mile to the west.

In 1979, Edward Bernard Raczyński became president of the Polish government-in-exile at the age of eighty-eight. About one hundred people assembled at 43 Eaton Place to witness the transfer of authority. In his brief remarks, Raczyński noted that although the émigrés had no power to influence events, their collective voice, heard throughout the world, "proclaims Poland's right to independence, demands free elections and respect for individual rights." He affirmed the government's strong support "...for the postulates put forward by fearless patriots in the country by the communist authorities' lofty declarations made in the constitution of the People's Republic of Poland and signed by the Warsaw regime in the final act of the Helsinki Conference." He closed by affirming his intent to leave office after completing a seven-year term, although he allowed that he was "...not optimistic enough to believe that, due to my age, I will be able to fulfill my term."[9] Raczyński was very much the elder statesman of the government-in-exile and was well known in Poland.

His term began as the Vatican and Warsaw were negotiating Pope John Paul II's visit. PZPR feared that a papal visit would arouse religious and nationalistic sentiments. Moscow's counsel was to deny permission, but Gierek knew that would lead to widespread discontent in an already volatile environment. Warsaw agreed to host John Paul II in June. From the moment his plane landed in Warsaw until his departure nine days later, the Polish-born Pope was greeted by massive crowds. His route from the airport into the city was lined with hundreds of thousands waving flags and banners and covering the streets of his motorcade with flowers. His Mass in Warsaw's *Plac Zwycięstwa* (Victory Square)[10] drew so many people that the crowds spilled over into the adjacent streets. After Warsaw, he visited Gniezno, Częstochowa, Auschwitz, Kalwaria Zebrzydowska, Wadowice, Nowy Targ, and Kraków. Moscow and Warsaw were right to fear his presence. In nine days, he inspired and united the Polish people, a task the communists had been unable to accomplish in thirty-five years.

One day prior to the pope's arrival in Warsaw, Raczyński and his government issued a declaration welcoming him to Poland and stating their

---

[9] "Przemówienie Prezydenta Rzeczypospolitej Edwarda Raczyńskiego" ("Speech by the President of the Republic of Poland, Edward Raczyński"), *DzU RP* Nr. 4 (Londyn), 26 czerwca 1979r., s. 20–21.
[10] After the Papal Mass, the communist authorities were determined to prevent *Plac Zwycięstwa* from becoming a place of veneration and turned it into a parking lot. As much as parking spaces were needed in central Warsaw, people refused to park there. After the fall of communism, *Plac Zwycięstwa* was resurfaced with stone and renamed *Plac Marszałka Józefa Piłsudskiego* (Piłsudski Square).

aspirations for his visit: "Together with the entire Polish Nation, we would like to welcome the first ever visit of the Vicar of Christ in our country. This overwhelms us with joy and gratitude to John Paul II. We believe that this will be a breakthrough on the road to real religious freedom in Poland and respect for human rights and will bring Poland closer to the day of freedom."[11]

Raczyński chose to keep Sabbat as prime minister. Sabbat retained several people from his previous council of ministers and added a few new names. On the day Sabbat and his ministers took their oaths, Raczyński gave a brief speech. He declared that their very presence was a powerful symbol and a protest against Moscow. He exhorted them not to boast about their titles but rather to take pride in their actions. Sabbat declared that John Paul II provided the West with the moral leadership it had lacked since the war. *Rada Narodowa* chairman Zygmunt Szadkowski recounted a conversation with a person who felt that the election of John Paul II relieved émigrés of further political responsibilities; Szadkowski contended that, on the contrary, it was time for them to redouble their efforts. His argument was strengthened by the changing political climate. Britain had a new, staunchly anti-communist prime minister, Margaret Thatcher. British accommodation and appeasement of Moscow had ended; Thatcher hammered that point home by sending an official representative to the Katyń Memorial for a ceremony marking the fortieth anniversary of the Soviet invasion. In December 1979, the Soviet Army rolled into Afghanistan to prop up its communist government, sparking a wave of protests and sanctions from Thatcher and other Western leaders.[12]

Raczyński emphasized the need to support the Polish opposition. He repeatedly reminded his fellow émigrés of their duty to their country, and he provided them with the means to show their support. Under his guidance, *Obywatelski Komitet Zbiórki na Pomoc Ofiarom Wydarzeń Czerwcowych* was transformed into the more general *Fundusz Pomocy Robotnikom* (Workers' Relief Fund) to provide aid to persecuted workers and their families, and he founded *Fundusz Wolności Słowa* (Freedom of Speech Fund) to assist underground publishers. Both collected funds in the West and discreetly channeled them to appropriate recipients. At the beginning of 1980,

---

[11] PAT, "Oświadczenie w Sprawie Wizyty Papieża w Polsce" ("Statement on the Pope's Visit to Poland"), Nr. 3/79, Londyn, 5 lipca 1979, AJPIA 701/9/13, No. 100.

[12] These included trade embargoes against the Soviet Union and a boycott of the 1980 Summer Olympic Games in Moscow by seventy-four nations, most notably the United States, Canada, China, Japan, and West Germany. Moscow returned the favor, leading a boycott of the 1984 Summer Olympic Games in Los Angeles under the guise of security concerns and purported anti-Soviet hysteria; fourteen nations did not participate.

Raczyński, Sabbat, and Minister of Homeland Affairs Edward Szczepanik merged both funds into *Fundusz Pomocy Krajowi* (FPK, National Assistance Fund). In September, London hosted *Światowy Zjazd Jedności z Walczącym Krajem* (World Congress of Unity with the Fighting Homeland).[13] Three hundred and fifty-two delegates from eighteen countries assembled to determine how émigrés could assist Poles at home. Raczyński addressed the attendees, declaring that unity with the country remained a primary obligation, commending activists in Poland, and calling Pope John Paul II a new source of hope. He continued in this vein at the commemoration of the thirtieth anniversary of *Skarb Narodowy*, noting that it had enabled the London government to assist the opposition. Raczyński and Sabbat also continued Ostrowski's work with other exile governments. In November, they signed a declaration with the Ukrainian exile government stating their goal of independence for both nations, pledging mutual respect, and supporting one another in the struggle to regain independence. Both governments agreed to maintain contact to strengthen cooperation.

Sabbat's rise had earned him some enmity. Juliusz Szygowski, the government-in-exile's representative in the United States since 1955, was one of his most fervent opponents. They did not enjoy a good relationship,[14] and Szygowski contended that Sabbat's appointment as prime minister led to a decline in trust among émigrés and a corresponding increase in Sokolnicki's influence in America.

Sabbat visited the United States in August 1979 in advance of *Światowy Zjazd Jedności z Walczącym Krajem* and met with Szygowski during his trip. It did not go well. Sabbat requested Szygowski's resignation for failing to raise sufficient American support for the conference, for not planning to attend it himself, and for not generating adequate opposition to Sokolnicki. In response, Szygowski wrote to Raczyński charging that Sabbat had erred by appointing two widely discredited people to lead the conference; he also made several insinuations against Sabbat's character. He expressed his view that Sabbat should step down and stated that he would offer his resignation after Sabbat left office. However, Raczyński was more inclined

---

[13] Kazimierz Sabbat was one of its organizers.
[14] The poor state of relations between Sabbat and Szygowski was well known. An FBI memo regarding Konstanty Hanff contained the following passage: "*Dr. Juliusz Szygowski of Evanston, Illinois, who is a diplomatic representative in the United States of the Polish Government-in-Exile, has been instructed to inform the office of the Attorney General in Washington, D.C., that Hanff does not have any authorization to act on behalf of the Government-in-Exile or to register as their agent under the Foreign Agents Registration Act. It is possible that Dr. Szygowski has not yet followed these instructions as his attitude towards Mr. Sabbat has not been too friendly lately.*" See "Polish Intelligence Activities in the United States Internal Security – Poland," United States Department of Justice, Federal Bureau of Investigation, Chicago, Illinois, January 4, 1977, file no. CG 100-17864.

to believe Sabbat, particularly as Szygowski was known to have been in contact with Konstanty Hanff for some time. Further, Raczyński was not one to have conditions dictated to him by his subordinates. He issued a decree referring to Szygowski's resignation[15] and dismissing him from his position. Szygowski responded with insinuations about Raczyński; the civil chancellery was compelled to issue a statement in response.

At the very time Pope John Paul II was in Poland, Sokolnicki was reviving the Order of St. Stanislas.[16] King Stanisław August Poniatowski had created it in 1765 as a charitable order for members of the nobility. During the Partitions, the Russian Empire awarded it to Russians and their Polish collaborators; it was abolished in the aftermath of the Bolshevik Revolution. Independence-minded Poles considered it irredeemably corrupted in Russian hands, and in newly independent Poland it was not revived; in its place, the government created *Order Odrodzenia Polski* (Order of Polonia Restituta, also known as the Order of the Rebirth of Poland). The Order of St. Stanislas was a forgotten artifact until Sokolnicki hit upon the idea of resuscitating it.

Sokolnicki had long known that a market for chivalric titles existed among affluent people who fancied themselves knights or counts, and he knew what they were willing to pay. He set prices ranging from $150 to over $1,000, depending on the class of the order desired, and business was brisk. He continued to award titles without charge to people whose influence he sought, such as Lech Wałęsa and Father Henryk Jankowski,[17] both of whom received the Order of St. Stanislas in 1980.

Lowering food prices in 1976 quelled societal unrest at the cost of worsening the economic crisis. Warsaw kept consumer prices artificially low through increasingly large subsidies funded by loans from Western nations, but exports failed to bring in sufficient hard currency to adequately

---

[15] In October, Szygowski issued a statement about his dismissal, noting that his resignation was contingent on Sabbat's resignation.

[16] Sokolnicki re-founded the Order of St. Stanislas on June 9, 1979.

[17] Father Henryk Jankowski had a mixed reputation. He was the primary force behind the restoration of *kościół św. Brygidy* (St. Brigid's Church) in Gdańsk, destroyed by the Red Army in 1945 and left in ruins until 1970. During August 1980, went to the shipyard daily to offer Mass; later, he was appointed as chaplain to *Solidarność*. He also received and distributed aid from the West. He was, however, somewhat prone to ostentation. He spoke German well and earned extra money by taking Germans on guided tours of Gdańsk, leading to a more lavish life than one would normally expect from a priest and bringing the disapproval of his superior at the parish where he served prior to his assignment at *kościół św. Brygidy*. He owned a Mercedes, but during the strikes he left it at home and took a borrowed Fiat 125p to the shipyard.

service this debt, so further loans were obtained to keep afloat. In short, Poland was living on credit.

Quite a lot of credit, as it happened. By 1980, Poland owed a staggering $24.1 billion to Western lenders, and it had to be repaid in their currencies. Poland was now inextricably dependent on exports to the West; every dollar, pound, franc, mark, or lira earned from exports was used to service debt. Exacerbating the problem, Polish industry had grown increasingly reliant on Western technology, and imports had to be paid for with Western currency. Several issues prevented Poland from achieving its needed level of exports. Global economic activity was stagnant; in 1979, Poland's economy contracted for the first time since the war.[18] Manufactured goods such as automobiles and appliances were typically of lesser quality and technologically inferior to those produced by Western companies and had to be sold as "value for money" products, bringing lower profits. Food, coal, and raw materials were in demand, but exporting too much meant shortages at home. Lastly, Poland, like all Soviet Bloc nations, was compelled to export a significant proportion of its products to the Soviet Union at exploitative exchange rates. Products that could have been sold at a profit in the West were sold at a loss to the Soviet Union; essentially, Warsaw was subsidizing Moscow.

Insolvency and default were very real possibilities. Western creditors, fearing the loss of some or all of their capital, negotiated revisions that lowered payments in the short term to allow Poland flexibility to get its fiscal affairs in order, but it was not enough. Even with lower debt payments, inflows of Western currency were insufficient to pay interest and import items needed for manufacturing, so imports had to be reduced. This caused industrial output to fall, and fewer manufactured goods were available for export. Reduced exports meant lower Western currency receipts, which further impeded Poland's ability to pay its debts and stabilize its economy. Poland was caught in a downward economic spiral. Gierek and his advisors had few options. He chose to reduce domestic spending.

Without warning, the government sharply increased food prices and raised work norms on July 1. Strikes immediately followed. Factory managers were instructed to bring strikes under control and were permitted to grant wage increases of ten to fifteen percent if needed. KSS "KOR" issued calls for workers to avoid public protests and demonstrations, fearing that such events would lead to violent repressions. Workers took that advice and confined their protests to their workplaces. By mid-July,

---

[18] In 1979, Poland's economy shrank by 2 percent.

Gierek believed he had matters under control and departed for a vacation in the Crimea and a visit to Moscow for meetings with Brezhnev and an appearance at the Olympic Games,[19] but he had misread the situation. Strikes continued to erupt; the most famous occurred at the same Gdańsk shipyard that had gone on strike in 1970. Crane operator Anna Walentynowicz was fired on August 9 for participating in an illegal union. She lost her pension rights five months before her planned retirement. Five days later, three workers arrived early at the shipyard and hung posters demanding her reinstatement and increased wages for all workers. Their demands were refused, and the workers formed a strike committee; they were joined by Lech Wałęsa, an electrician who had also been fired from the shipyard for illegal union activity. The workers occupied the shipyard and formed *Międzyzakładowy Komitet Strajkowy* (MKS, Interfactory Strike Committee). Backed by advisors from KSS "KOR," MKS drafted a list of twenty-one demands that went well past questions of pay rates. These included the right to form independent trade unions, a guarantee of the right to strike, freedom of speech, reinstatement of workers and students dismissed for striking or protesting, release of political prisoners, and significant economic reforms. On August 31, the government conceded, and MKS transformed itself into an independent trade union: *Niezależny Samorządny Związek Zawodowy "Solidarność"* (NSZZ "Solidarność," Independent Self-Governing Trade Union "Solidarity").

Most émigrés responded enthusiastically.[20] FPK sent food, clothing, medical supplies, and money.[21] Assisted by émigrés, *Solidarność* activists established *Grupa Działania NSZZ "Solidarność" w Wielkiej Brytanii* (Action Group of NSZZ "Solidarność" in Great Britain) and Biuro Informacyjne Solidarności w Londynie (Solidarity Information Office in London). Poland's opposition had friends among British society as well. In August 1980, a group of activists cooperating with the Labour Party formed Polish Solidarity Campaign.[22] This was followed by "British Solidarity with Poland," which cooperated with the government-in-exile, and "Solidarity with Solidarity," an apolitical organization.

---

[19] In the Moscow Olympic Games, Władysław Kozakiewicz set a world record in the pole vault, winning a gold medal in the process. He did so despite constant jeering and whistling that the mostly Soviet spectators rained down on him and other non-Soviet athletes. After his record-setting jump, he made a rude gesture to the crowd. For that, he almost lost his medal, but he became a hero at home.

[20] Some "*Solidarność*" members and some of its advisors from KSS "KOR" were former PZPR members, and many were socialists. This caused some émigrés to be wary of the movement.

[21] From late 1980 until the end of 1981, FPK sent more than £100,000 in cash and goods to Poland.

[22] Fortuitously, Polish Solidarity Campaign took its name before the Polish organization began to use the name "*Solidarność.*"

Lech Wałęsa had become the face of *Solidarność*. His image could be found in newspapers, magazines, and on television news programs throughout the West. He had been named 1980's Man of the Year by *The Financial Times, The Observer*, and *Die Welt*. People were intrigued by the emergence of this young shipyard worker with the distinctive mustache as a powerful adversary of the Soviet system, and he was in demand. Labor organizations lined up to pay for him to give speeches in their countries, and he readily obliged, looking to win further support for the union. His first foreign trip was to Rome; he was received by Pope John Paul II in a private audience. His travels also took him to France, Switzerland, and as far as Japan. During a stopover in London, he met with Raczyński, illustrating the regard Wałęsa had for him.

In light of Raczyński's advanced age and fading health, succession was an urgent concern. On the day he took office, he nominated Sabbat to succeed him, although this was a contingency in case he died before he could consult with the political parties and agree on a permanent successor.[23] He asked each party to propose two candidates; from them he would choose the next president. The most notable were Stefan Korboński and Stefan Soboniewski,[24] both of whom had support from several political parties and veterans' organizations. By February 1980, Korboński, a resident of the United States, emerged as the leading contender, but he did not want to travel to London unless his nomination was certain. As with Szygowski, Raczyński was not about to accept conditions. He interpreted this as a refusal.

Raczyński also looked to Poland. In early 1980, he proposed that Jan Józef Lipski, one of the signers of *List 59* and a founding member of KOR, succeed him, but Lipski turned him down. He later offered the position to Professor Aleksander Gieysztor,[25] Janusz Onyszkiewicz,[26] Władysław

---

[23] Article 21 of the April Constitution provided a process for electing a new president if the incumbent were to die in office: "*If the President of the Republic dies before his seven-year term of office expires, or if he resigns his office, the Speaker of the Senat shall immediately summon the Assembly of Electors, so that they may select a candidate for the Presidency; in the event that he proposes another candidate himself, he shall call a referendum.*" As there was no *Senat* in exile and *Rada Narodowa* was only a consultative body, there was no constitutional provision for electing a president if the office fell vacant without a successor named. Raczyński's age and health made naming a successor an immediate concern.

[24] Stefan Soboniewski was a veteran of the September campaign and evacuated to the West. He was one of the founders of SPK and was an EZN member.

[25] Aleksander Gieysztor was an AK and WiN veteran and headed the history department at *Uniwersytet Warszawski*.

[26] Janusz Onyszkiewicz had been involved with KOR and the underground publisher *Aneks*.

Bartoszewski,[27] and Leszek Moczulski;[28] they all declined as well. Raczyński decided that Sabbat would remain his successor. This provoked sharp reaction from some émigré politicians. American activists were particularly incensed, seeing the appointment of the little-known Sabbat over the more prominent Korboński as a perpetuation of London's dominance over émigré politics. PSL threatened to suspend participation in government bodies unless the nomination was reconsidered, but Raczyński held firm.

PZPR was in the unusual position of having to prove its relevance. Most Poles considered Pope John Paul II to be the nation's highest moral authority and viewed *Solidarność*, with over ten million members, as their true representative. Thousands resigned their Party membership, and many who remained also joined *Solidarność*. Needing to repair its image, PZPR again turned to Sikorski. 1981 was the centenary of his birth, and PZPR planned a flurry of events, honors, and activities that would culminate with his interment in Kraków. On March 17, Moczar announced plans during an interview with a reporter from the newspaper *Życie Warszawy*; later that month, Poland's ambassador in London asked the British government for assistance in facilitating the transfer of Sikorski's remains.

Standing in the way was Stanisław Leśniowski, Sikorski's son-in-law. He was executor of Helena Sikorska's will, and the general's body could not be moved without his permission. Raczyński remained opposed to the move, and he telegrammed Leśniowski with the message, "The Warsaw regime is seeking to transfer the body of General Sikorski to Poland. All our emigration is against it. Can I ask you for help from the office? We count on your refusal to transfer."[29] Leśniowski had no intention of acceding to Warsaw's request; the day after he received Raczyński's telegram, he replied, "I confirm the refusal to transport General Sikorski's remains to Poland."[30] Raczyński followed up with a letter of thanks that cut to the core of the issue: "This matter has taken on political significance in Poland and is being exploited by Moczar and his people appearing to be patriots. The Polish society here does not want to let the general's name be

---

[27] Władysław Bartoszewski had been a prisoner at Auschwitz, an AK solder, a member of Żegota, a veteran of the Warsaw Uprising, a postwar member of PSL, a prisoner of MBP, a journalist, and a correspondent for Radio Free Europe. He was under regular surveillance by the security apparatus.
[28] Leszek Moczulski was one of the founders of ROPCiO, founder of KPN, and for six years had been imprisoned by the Warsaw authorities.
[29] Tarka, "Rozgrywka nad trumną" ("Game over the Coffin"), *Dzieje Najnowsze*, Rocznik XLII 2010, 3, s. 71.
[30] Tarka, "Rozgrywka nad trumną," *Dzieje Najnowsze*, Rocznik XLII 2010, 3, s. 71.

abused by this 'mafia' and wants the general's corpse to return to a truly free Poland."[31] Raczyński had a further concern: if Warsaw were to obtain Sikorski's remains, it would likely demand the collections held by the Polish Institute and Sikorski Museum.

Raczyński contacted the Home Office and several Members of Parliament including Bernard Braine, Winston Churchill Jr., and Lord Barnby to make the Republic's position clear. *Rada Organizacji Kombatanckich*, a council of veterans' organizations, feared that Sikorski would be used as propaganda and issued a statement declaring that his remains could be returned to Poland only when the nation was governed by leaders chosen in free elections. As in the early 1970s, émigré and British newspapers followed developments intently.

Warsaw made plans as if the matter was settled. It released a program of events that included a public viewing of Sikorski's coffin[32] followed by a procession to Wawel and internment in the cathedral crypt. The Polish foreign minister brought the matter to Britain's foreign minister and was referred to the Home Office. After Braine intervened, permission to move Sikorski's remains was denied.

Émigré Poles conducted a series of events for Sikorski's centenary, including unveiling a plaque on Rubens Hotel, Sikorski's wartime headquarters. Warsaw abandoned the entire program. The only reminder of its plans was an empty marble sarcophagus in the cathedral crypt.

In less than three years, Pope John Paul II had become immensely popular. Catholics and non-Catholics were drawn to his charisma, humor, and down-to-earth manner, and crowds flocked to him. In fine Roman weather late in the afternoon of May 13, 1981, thousands packed into St. Peter's Square hoping to catch a glimpse of him. Shortly after five, his open-top Fiat "Popemobile" entered with him riding in the back. As his vehicle passed through the crowds on the north side of the square, four shots rang out, and he collapsed into the arms of his secretary and friend from Kraków, Bishop Stanisław Dziwisz. Clinging to life, he was rushed to Gemelli Polyclinic and underwent six hours of surgery.[33] The news quickly spread around the world. Nowhere was the shock greater than in Poland

---

[31] Tarka, "Rozgrywka nad trumną," *Dzieje Najnowsze*, Rocznik XLII 2010, 3, s. 71.

[32] *Barbakan Krakowski* is a stone defensive structure that is one of the few remnants of Kraków's medieval defensive walls.

[33] Although the surgery was successful, Pope John Paul II would suffer lingering aftereffects from the attack for the remainder of his life.

and Polonia. People across the country and in Polish communities around the world poured into churches to offer their prayers for his recovery.

After the initial shock came suspicion. Considering the course of events that followed the papal visit and the traditional (though rarely used of late) Soviet practice of eliminating troublesome people, talk of a Soviet plot spread.[34] With it came further distrust of PZPR and the security apparatus. The gap between *Solidarność* and the Warsaw government grew.

Little more than two weeks later, Poland was rocked again, this time by news of Cardinal Stefan Wyszyński's death after a brief struggle with cancer. Three days after the Pope had been shot, Wyszyński received the sacrament of Extreme Unction; after it had been administered, he said to those by his bed that he believed he should share in the sufferings of the Holy Father.

Edward Gierek was forced to resign on September 6, 1980, a few days after the Gdańsk agreement was signed. His replacement, Stanisław Kania, lasted barely a year. Next was General Wojciech Jaruzelski, a former gulag prisoner and First Polish Army veteran.[35] Jaruzelski's past gave no indication that he was a reformer, and *Solidarność* leaders were wary of him.

Their suspicions were correct. After the Gdańsk agreement had been signed, Jaruzelski ordered his general staff to plan for martial law in October. Although it wasn't implemented, in November the Ministry of Internal Affairs began to ready internment facilities for opposition leaders. The following February, military and security forces conducted training exercises to determine how martial law would be implemented. *Solidarność* considered a general strike in March after *Milicja* officers had detained and beaten union delegates, but the strike was called off after Wałęsa negotiated a settlement. Soviet concerns also grew, and more than six hundred Soviet Army tanks were quietly sent to Poland. Thousands of posters announcing martial law were printed in the Soviet Union and secretly transported to Warsaw.

Late in the evening of December 12, the government approved martial law and outlawed *Solidarność*.[36] At midnight, ZOMO arrested thousands of *Solidarność* leaders and other opposition activists and hauled them off

---

[34] Pope John Paul II's would-be assassin, Turkish national Mehmet Ali Ağca, continually changed his story about who backed the plot. He had claimed collaboration with or had been linked to agents from the Bulgarian Committee for State Security, the East German Stasi, the KGB, and Iran.

[35] Jaruzelski was said to hold a grudge against General Anders since Anders had not waited longer before evacuating the Second Polish Corps from the Soviet Union; had Anders waited longer, Jaruzelski reasoned, he would have left with the Corps. Instead, Jaruzelski later joined Berling's army.

[36] Jaruzelski later insisted that the Polish Army was deployed and martial law was declared to prevent a Soviet invasion. Soviet leaders have denied this.

to prisons and internment camps. Tanks and troops took control of the streets. At 6 a.m., *Polskie Radio* and *Telewizja Polska* broadcast a speech by Jaruzelski declaring martial law and announcing military administration.[37]

Raczyński was quick to issue a statement condemning Jaruzelski's actions. Western journalists called on 43 Eaton Place for information; on December 13 alone Sabbat gave more than a dozen interviews. By the end of December, Raczyński and Sabbat had been interviewed by British, American, French, and German television networks, radio stations, and newspapers. Raczyński helped organize demonstrations across the UK, including a picket at the embassy. On December 18, he and Sabbat outlined the government-in-exile's response in a document titled "Appeal to the Free World." They called for international condemnation of martial law, demanded release of political prisoners, urged resumption of dialogue between Jaruzelski's government and *Solidarność* and the Church, requested economic and diplomatic sanctions, and appealed for humanitarian aid for the Polish people. Anti-*Solidarność* and anti-government-in-exile propaganda emanating from Moscow and Warsaw was another concern, and Raczyński used public events and interviews with the press to counter such messages and to encourage émigrés and other sympathizers to support underground *Solidarność* and people suffering under martial law. A new organization, *Fundacja Pomocy Medycznej* (Medical Assistance Foundation), sent five truckloads of medical supplies to Poland in the first two months of 1982 alone.

More organizations sprang up to provide material relief and to fund education, underground publishing, and *Solidarność*; others assisted those who had escaped to the West to avoid persecution. They established channels to bring materials and money into the country; frequently, Catholic relief organizations were employed in this task. Printing equipment and electronics were surreptitiously imported through Sweden.[38] Sabbat and Szczepanik planned to create an economic aid program to be implemented if repression weakened. Their proposal would rely on the World Bank and the International Monetary Fund and was modeled on the postwar Marshall Plan.[39]

---

[37] Unfortunately for them, Jaruzelski and his associates had chosen a name with undesirable associations. Appending the letter "a" to the abbreviation WRON resulted in the word *wrona* (crow), which was bad enough; worse, *wrona* was a common derogatory appellation for the Gestapo during the war.

[38] *Fundusz Pomocy Krajowi* had created financial structures that enabled them to channel contributions from organizations such as the Polish American Congress into the country.

[39] In 1948, Warsaw wanted to accept Marshall Plan aid from the United States but was prevented from doing so by Stalin.

On the morning of Friday, May 28, 1982, Cardinal Basil Hume and 3,500 others massed on the tarmac of London Gatwick Airport and strained to catch a glimpse of an Alitalia aircraft. Their excitement built as it came into view and landed; it reached its crescendo at 8 a.m., when the plane rolled to a stop and Pope John Paul II emerged from the door, descended the steps, and kissed the ground. For the first time, a sitting pope was on British soil. After a brief welcome ceremony, he traveled to Westminster Cathedral and celebrated Mass. Among those greeting the Pope were Raczyński, Sabbat, and his wife, Anna. On Saturday, Cardinal Hume hosted a reception at his residence; Raczyński and the Sabbats were present. As they mingled with the other guests, John Paul II approached them and initiated a conversation; this was seen as a rare distinction.

Crystal Palace Stadium in south London often hosted large crowds, but usually not as early in the day as on Sunday, May 30. That morning, 24,000 elderly war veterans, other émigrés, refugees, and their children and grandchildren filled the stadium. Many wore military uniforms or traditional ethnic clothing; some carried flags and banners. They had come for a Mass offered by the Pope for the émigré community. In his sermon, the Pope declared them to be an integral and vital part of Poland that speaks of Poland as it was and should be. Raczyński, Sabbat, and other émigré leaders sat near the altar. After completing his sermon,[40] the Pope walked over to greet them. After London, Pope John Paul II visited Coventry, Liverpool, Manchester, York, Edinburgh, Glasgow, and Cardiff. Émigré Poles could be seen at every public event.

Pope John Paul II made it understood that the Vatican was very interested in the exile government's activities, and Raczyński took the opportunity to make use of this newfound attention. He wrote to the Pope later that year to make him aware of the plight of the Polish diaspora in West Germany, at that time the second-largest concentration of expatriate Poles in the West. Raczyński was concerned that they were in danger of losing their national identity and was seeking help to strengthen their cultural ties with Poland and Polonia. Shortly after, he received a letter from the Vatican Secretariat of State informing him that the Pope had made Cardinal Józef Glemp responsible for their care.[41]

---

[40] As the Crystal Palace Stadium Mass was primarily intended for émigré Poles, Pope John Paul II delivered his sermon in the Polish language. He spoke for 36 minutes; *Rzeczpospolita Polska* printed the transcript in its June 1982 issue.
[41] Pope John Paul II elevated Archbishop Glemp to the cardinalate in 1983.

Although months of careful preparation preceded martial law, SB had not arrested everyone on its list; several prominent *Solidarność* leaders eluded capture and were operating underground. In April 1982, they formed *Tymczasowa Komisja Koordynacyjna NSZZ "Solidarność"* (TKK, Temporary Coordinating Commission of NSZZ "Solidarność") to coordinate activities of regional *Solidarność* groups. TKK released a statement announcing that it would enter into negotiations with the government after all internees were released and amnesty was granted to those who had been sentenced. Its offer went unanswered. TKK also threatened a general strike if the legal standing of *Solidarność* was revoked. With the anniversary of the Gdańsk agreement approaching, TKK called for protests. PZPR and the government urged the public to disregard TKK's appeal, asked for calm, and issued dire warnings. In a televised statement, Minister of Internal Affairs General Czesław Kiszczak made thinly veiled threats of tragic consequences and promised further "lessons." Posters appeared warning against protests, and party activists cautioned workers to avoid demonstrations. These warnings had little effect. On August 31, nationwide protests broke out; more than four thousand were arrested and at least seven were killed. Afterwards, tensions continued to simmer. Curfews remained in effect, military units patrolled the streets and factories, and propaganda was incessant. But TKK persisted, aided by Raczyński and his government.

Despite difficulties in assisting illegal organizations, émigré Poles and sympathizers continued to send aid, in no small part due to exhortations from Raczyński, Sabbat, and *Rada Narodowa*. *Fundusz Pomocy Krajowi* used its channels to fund the union, educational organizations, and underground publishers; over one hundred opposition activists, students, and scientists received stipends. *Fundusz Wolności Słowa* stepped up purchases of printing equipment and supplies and used a broad network to bring these goods into Poland. A *Solidarność* activist drove cars laden with collected equipment to various points in Europe; from there, couriers took the equipment into the country using various means, including hiding it in shipments of foreign aid. Jerzy Giedroyc of *Kultura* funded the purchase of a refrigerated truck that had a false wall; half a ton of materials could be secreted behind it. Giedroyc estimated that about one hundred copy machines were brought into Poland in this truck before its driver, a French trade union activist, was arrested. Jaruzelski made several attempts to co-opt Wałęsa, but he refused to collaborate. Eventually bowing to international pressure, Jaruzelski released him in November but kept him under constant surveillance.

While Raczyński and his government were organizing financial, material, and political support, Sokolnicki was occupied with other matters. In 1982, he established *Polska Niezależna Brygada Rezerwy* (Polish Independent Reserve Brigade), an honorary military unit of émigrés, providing him with the basis to award military ranks. He also asserted that he was a leader of *Solidarność*, earning a rebuke from 43 Eaton Place. In January 1983, he issued a decree refashioning *Order Odrodzenia Polski* into *zakon rycerski Rzeczypospolitej Polskiej* (Order of Chivalry of the Republic of Poland). This new order gave its holders the right to use the title of "Sir."[42] As with the Order of St. Stanislas, this honor and title was available for a price.

Having already claimed noble heritage, the title of count, the presidency, and the position of Grand Master of the Order of St. Stanislas, Sokolnicki added another honorific to his collection. On May 27, 1983, he was ordained and consecrated a bishop in the Apostolic Episcopal Church.[43] He was assigned as deputy to that church's bishop in the United Kingdom, as bishop for the Polish-speaking community in the United Kingdom,[44] and as missionary bishop for the Bahamas. Two months later, he married Margaret O'Docherty, his fifth wife.[45]

Sokolnicki was doing quite well for himself. He had long since ceased menial labor, and in the years after he declared himself president, he moved from his small flat in an unfashionable part of London to a house in the far more pleasant surroundings of Colchester.

Friedrich Zimmermann, West Germany's minister of internal affairs, was in Munich on January 29, 1983, addressing a constituency that German politicians could not easily ignore. This was an organization of Germans who had lived east of the Oder–Neisse Line prior to 1945 and never accepted their expulsion. To them, the treaties of 1950 and 1970 were irrelevant; bolstering their position, Washington still had not formally recognized the border.

---

[42] Article 96 of the March Constitution specifically prohibited such titles: "*The Republic of Poland does not recognize privileges of birth or of estate, or any coats of arms, family or other titles, with the exception of those of learning, office, or profession.*" This provision was not included in the April Constitution.

[43] The Apostolic Episcopal Church is affiliated with the Old Catholic Church. In 1979, Sokolnicki gave state awards to Archbishop Bertil Persson and to Most Reverend Kermit Poling. There is no documentation that Sokolnicki attended a seminary.

[44] Although Sokolnicki was appointed as bishop to the Polish-speaking adherents of the Apostolic Episcopal Church, there is scant evidence of such a community in that church.

[45] Elizabeth Mary Mayall, Sokolnicki's fourth wife, had died in March 1982.

Expellees had been a potent force in West German politics since the 1950s, when most major political parties issued statements refusing to accept the new border. The 1970 Treaty of Warsaw may have been the official position of their government, but expellees continued to proclaim their right to return to their pre-1945 homes; some published anti-Polish propaganda and what were purported to be current maps of Germany showing the borders of 1914.

In Munich, Zimmermann declared that he considered the border to be temporary and assured the group that the government would oppose domestic political programs that did not take into account areas east of the Oder and Neisse. His comments were widely reported in the West German press. The government-in-exile viewed Zimmerman's statements as revisionist and contrary to the Treaty of Warsaw. The government issued a statement declaring the border to be inviolable, and its delegate submitted a protest to the West German government and to leaders of the political parties represented in the Bundestag.

VI Rada Narodowa was nearing the end of its term, and preparations were underway to form the next *Rada*. In June, the government announced plans for a 122-member *Rada*, consisting of fifty-two delegates from political parties, twenty-six from social, cultural, and veterans' organizations, thirty elected members, and fourteen presidential appointees, of whom four were representatives of religious organizations. *VII Rada Narodowa* convened for the first time on December 17. Raczyński, Sabbat, and Minister of Émigré Affairs Walery Choroszewski also announced creation of a sixty-six-member *Rada* branch in the United States; twenty-six members were elected, twelve represented political parties, ten represented other organizations, and eighteen were presidential appointees. They coordinated the terms of office for this new branch and the Canadian branch to end simultaneously with *VII Rada Narodowa*.

After 1979's *Światowy Zjazd Jedności z Walczącym Krajem*, its coordinating body, *Rada Koordynacyjna Polonii Wolnego Świata* (Coordination Council of the Polish Diaspora of the Free World), continued its ambitious program of advocacy for the rights of Poles and education on Polish culture and history. In 1984, it sponsored *II Światowy Zjazd Polonii Wolnego Świata* (Second World Congress of Polonia in the Free World). The event was held in London from May 8 through 12; again, Raczyński was its patron.

Pope John Paul II remained distressed by martial law and the outlawing of *Solidarność* and wanted to visit his homeland again. For its part, PZPR wanted to bring stability and calm back to the country and agreed to allow him to return. Officially, his visit was to commemorate the six hundredth anniversary of the arrival of the icon of Our Lady of Jasna Góra and to beatify three Poles.[46] They agreed on a visit from June 16 to June 23, although the Pope's insistence on a meeting with Wałęsa threatened to derail the trip. Eventually, permission for a private meeting was approved, and the Pope met with Wałęsa and his family near Zakopane. On July 22, Jaruzelski ended martial law.

Jaruzelski had successfully forestalled a public appearance of Wałęsa with the Pope; no transcripts of their meeting or photographs of them together were released. But Wałęsa was undeterred. He met with TKK leadership and maintained contacts with union structures. Hopes that he would disappear from Western consciousness were dashed on October 5, 1983, with news from Oslo that he would be awarded the Nobel Peace Prize. Fearing he would not be permitted to return to Poland, Wałęsa did not travel to Norway; instead, his wife, Danuta, and son, Bogdan, accepted the award on his behalf. His speech was read by Bohdan Cywiński, a *Solidarność* activist living in the West during martial law. Afterwards, Wałęsa applied for employment at the shipyard as an electrician.

Repression continued after martial law ended. Harassment and arrest of *Solidarność* figures and opposition activists occurred regularly; the most notorious case was that of Father Jerzy Popiełuszko. He was unofficial chaplain to *Solidarność* members in a Warsaw steel mill and distributed aid from *Fundusz Pomocy Krajowi*. His sermons frequently referenced political prisoners, repressions, and injustice. SB regularly harassed him, but he refused to back down. One October evening, he was returning to Warsaw from Bydgoszcz when he and his driver were abducted. The driver escaped, but Father Popiełuszko was beaten, gagged, and thrown from a dam into the Wisła. His body was recovered several days later. Over 250,000 attended his funeral. A wave of outrage swept the country and the West; it intensified when it became known that his abductors and murderers were SB officers from a secretive unit that targeted the Roman Catholic Church.[47]

---

[46] In Kraków he beatified Rafał Kalinowski and Albert Chmielowski; in Poznań he beatified Urszula Ledóchowska.

[47] The officers belonged to *Samodzielna Grupa "D" Departamentu IV MSW* (Independent Group "D" of the Fourth Department of the Ministry of the Interior), *Grupa Operacyjna do Zadań Dezintegracyjnych* (Operational Group for Disintegrative Tasks). Its mission was to penetrate and disrupt religious groups.

Four officers were arrested, put on trial, and convicted.

Exile authorities and journalists condemned Warsaw for Popiełuszko's death. *Kultura* obtained and published official court documents giving his driver's account of events and a detailed chronicle of the trial.

For forty years, the Yalta agreements had been the subject of perennial grievance among exiles. A handful of American and British politicians would periodically call on their governments to reject Yalta, but nothing came of these efforts. A desire for peaceful relations with Moscow, rooted in fear of Soviet military power, overrode concerns over the fates of Soviet Bloc nations. A new generation of Western politicians and activists saw the Soviet Union differently. Behind Moscow's imposing facade, they saw a rotten edifice nearing collapse, led by a calcified Communist Party that had brought the Soviet Union to the verge of bankruptcy. Human rights groups that formed in the wake of the Helsinki Final Agreement aimed to hold Soviet leadership to account for human rights abuses. Moscow was suspected of compelling Jaruzelski to impose martial law and of complicity in the assassination attempt on Pope John Paul II.

Raczyński, Sabbat, and their counterparts in other exile governments and committees agreed to coordinate their actions for the fortieth anniversary of the Yalta agreements. Exile governments from Czechoslovakia, Hungary, Poland, and Romania jointly issued an appeal to the British and American governments demanding repudiation of the Soviet Union's interpretation of the Yalta agreement and support for self-determination and sovereignty of central and eastern European nations. The Czechoslovak and Polish exile governments directly lobbied Margaret Thatcher and Ronald Reagan. Their cooperation encouraged Raczyński, and he pressed on with efforts to create alliances with other exile governments.

Having concluded an agreement with the Ukrainian government-in-exile in 1979, Raczyński set his sights on a similar understanding with Czechoslovakia. In June 1985, he invited representatives of the Council of Free Czechoslovakia to meet with members of the government-in-exile. Raczyński recalled past relations between the two nations and the wartime effort to abandon old animosities and create a confederation. He declared that Poland's goal was to live in peace with its neighbors and that the path forward was close, friendly cooperation; he went on to state that although exile leaders were unable to put these ideas into practice, they could count on a positive reception from Czechoslovak and Polish citizens. He concluded with a call to begin discussions: "When we start friendly conversations again, when we define together what we are striving to improve our own situation and our nations, history may record that in London, this year, something happened, that new thoughts appeared in our joint effort and cooperation."[48]

Father Jan Lang, president of the émigré Czechoslovak human rights organization Naarden Movement, followed Raczyński with comments emphasizing the historical, cultural, and religious links between their nations and outlined a vision where their federation would grow to include other neighboring states.

On January 19, 1986, precisely forty-four years after the 1942 declaration, two representatives of the Council of Free Czechoslovakia, Mojmir Povolny, Chairman of the Executive Committee, and Rudolf V. Frastacki, Chairman of the General Assembly,[49] signed a new declaration with Raczyński and Sabbat declaring their intention to facilitate creation of a friendly and peaceful union of central and eastern European states.[50] This statement acknowledged the need to cooperate to ensure the freedom of their nations in a post-communist era. Former adversaries who now shared a common fate in the Soviet Bloc were banding together to establish a foundation for a post-Soviet world.

In late February 1985, Cardinal Glemp embarked on a pastoral visit to Poles in the United Kingdom. On the 21st, he arrived at Heathrow and was greeted by Cardinal Basil Hume; from there he flew to Edinburgh. For ten days he traveled around the country, meeting members of the English and Scottish hierarchy and émigré Poles. Towards the end of his visit, he returned to London and met privately with Raczyński to discuss events in Poland; like John Paul II, Glemp considered émigré political activities to be valuable and necessary. Glemp also attended a public meeting in the hall of Christ the King Roman Catholic Church, a Polish parish in Balham. Raczyński was unable to attend, so Sabbat read his speech, which assured Glemp of émigrés' continued assistance and support for him and his priests. Sabbat went on to add his own comments; he recalled periods in history when the primate served

---

[48] "Komunikat Kancelarii Cywilnej Prezydenta R.P. o obiedzie polsko-czechosłowackim" ("Announcement of the Civil Chancellery of the President of the Republic of Poland on the Polish-Czechoslovak dinner"), *DzU RP* No. 3 (Londyn), 27 lipca 1985 roku, s. 37–38.
[49] Mojmir Povolny was chairman of the Executive Committee, and Rudolf V. Frastacki was chairman of the General Assembly of the Council of Free Czechoslovakia.
[50] Hubert Ripka, who signed the 1942 document for Czechoslovakia, died in 1958.

as Poland's leader during interregnums and linked those times to communist Poland, asserting that émigrés looked to Wyszyński and now to Glemp to lead the nation in the fight for truth and human rights.

In its thirty-five-year existence, *Polskie Towarzystwo Naukowe na Obczyźnie* had held countless meetings, lectures, and discussions, published yearbooks, and organized one general congress, 1970's *Kongres Kultury Polskiej na Obczyźnie*. In the early 1980s, PTNO's president Edward Szczepanik decided it was time for another congress.

Szczepanik, a native of Suwałki, graduated from *Szkoła Główna Handlowa w Warszawie* (Main School of Economics in Warsaw) in 1936, went on to study at the London School of Economics, and then returned to Warsaw to join the faculty at his alma mater. As a reserve officer, he was called to active duty in 1939; he crossed into Lithuania to avoid capture and was interned there. He was then captured by the Red Army in 1940 and sent to a gulag on the Kola peninsula. Freed in the amnesty, he joined the Second Polish Corps and served as an artillery officer. After the war, he resumed studies at the London School of Economics, eventually earning a PhD, and taught at Polish University College. While in London, he was the first president of *Instytut Badania Zagadnień Krajowych* (Research Institute for the Contemporary Affairs of Poland). From there, he moved to Hong Kong, where he taught at the university and worked for the United Nations. He then worked for the Harvard University Advisory Team in Karachi, Pakistan, and later moved to Rome to work as a senior economist for the United Nations. He returned to the United Kingdom in 1978 for a position at the University of Sussex and then taught at PUNO. In 1981, Szczepanik became president of PTNO and accepted a position as minister of home affairs under Prime Minister Sabbat; in 1982, he again took charge of *Instytut Badania Zagadnień Krajowych*.

As the new president of PTNO, Szczepanik organized II *Kongres Kultury Polskiej na Obczyźnie* under Raczyński's patronage. Held in London, the six-day conference opened on September 14, 1985, with a brief speech by Raczyński. He emphasized the importance of culture, stating, "For Poland, plundered and tormented for forty-six years, it is a precious treasure."[51] More than 500 participants from twenty countries, including

---

[51] "Komunikat Kancelarii Cywilnej Prezydenta R.P. o Kongresie Kultury Polskiej w Londynie" ("Announcement of the Civil Chancellery of the President of the Republic of Poland on the Polish Culture Congress in London"), *DzU RP* No. 4 (Londyn), dnia 11 listopada 1985 roku, s. 47.

Poland, attended; 150 papers were submitted on topics ranging from history and philosophy to Polish contributions to science and technology. Over the subsequent five years, *Polska Fundacja Kulturalna* published ten volumes containing the works of *II Kongres*.

At ninety-four years of age, Raczyński was blind and almost completely deaf; his daughters and grandchildren would read him mail, documents, and newspapers. Despite these maladies, Szczepanik noted that he had an extremely quick mind. He remained popular with émigrés and friends of Poland, having met with Jan Nowak-Jeziorański, poet and Nobel honoree Czesław Miłosz, composer Andrzej Panufnik, poet Józef Łobodowski, and British historian Norman Davies. Western television and radio journalists regularly sought him for interviews and comments. Raczyński's seven-year term concluded on April 8, 1986. He confirmed Sabbat as his successor and stepped down. His parents had imparted in him a deep devotion to serving his nation. It resulted in a career that spanned sixty-eight years, culminating in the presidency.

The Scoutmaster

Kazimierz Sabbat,
President of the Republic of Poland 1986-1989

AT 43 EATON Place on April 8, 1986, Poland's exile government exuded a sense of stability. For the second time, a sitting president had voluntarily stepped down after completing his seven-year term and was succeeded by his appointed successor without opening new rifts. A level of political maturity and normalcy had been achieved.

This is not to say that the new president was the choice of all émigré factions. Sabbat had faced sharp criticism while prime minister, with detractors specifically questioning his qualifications and emphasizing his relative anonymity in Poland. But those clamoring for the next president to come from the opposition at home did not know that everyone in Poland to whom Raczyński had offered the position had rejected it, and those preferring an émigré who was also well-known in Poland had few viable options. They also did not see the qualities that Raczyński recognized in Sabbat.

Kazimierz Sabbat was born on February 27, 1913, in Bieliny Kapitulne,[1] a small town near Kielce.[2] He was the fifth of nine children; his father was

---
[1] In post-communist Poland, Bieliny Kapitulne is known simply as Bieliny.
[2] At the time of Sabbat's birth, Bieliny Kapitulne was in the Russian partition.

a church organist, and his mother ran a farm. He attended primary school in Tursko Wielkie, and in 1925, he was sent to Mielec to attend *gymnasium*. Sabbat earned very good grades and was active in school organizations. At the age of fourteen, he joined ZHP and participated in scouting camps and rallies. He received his diploma in 1932, attended Reserve Officer Cadet School in Kielce, and enrolled at *Uniwersytet Warszawski* to study law, but he had to delay his studies until he had earned enough to pay for his education. He worked in administrative jobs for the next three years and was able to resume his studies in 1935.

In 1936, he joined the university's Academic Circle of Senior Scouts and later became director. With his assistance, eight more senior scouting circles were formed in other Warsaw universities. He studied at *Szkoła Nauk Politycznych w Warszawie* (School of Political Science in Warsaw) in 1938; also that year, he was appointed to the position of junior scoutmaster and founded *Kuźnica Harcerska*, a body to coordinate their activities. Sabbat organized scouting events and courses, including camps in Romania and Hungary.[3] He was awarded a law degree in June 1939.

Scouting's ideals and discipline appealed to Sabbat, and he believed that applying them on a broader scale would benefit Poland. He outlined his vision in an article published in the magazine *Brzask*.[4] ZHP president Michał Grażyński was impressed by his proposals and offered him a position as his personal secretary beginning in the autumn of 1939; Sabbat accepted. Before starting, he attended a scouting camp in Hungary and another in Poland. On August 31, he traveled to Kielce. The next morning, Sabbat awoke to news of the German attack. He was mobilized and ordered to report to Czortków[5] in the Podole region. It took him nearly two weeks to make the three-hundred-mile journey, and he arrived shortly before the Red Army attacked. Czortków was only a few kilometers from the Soviet border and its capture was imminent, so Sabbat and his unit were ordered to head to Hungary. They crossed the border at Jabłonica and were disarmed and interned.

ZHP's commander, also an internee, persuaded the Hungarians to place Sabbat in a camp designated for scouts and appointed him deputy commander. Internment camps were generally comfortable, and the

---

[3] Aleksander Kamiński later created *Szare Szeregi*.
[4] *Brzask* was a publication of *Związek Polskiej Młodzieży Demokratycznej* (Association of Polish Democratic Youth) and supported Piłsudski and his followers.
[5] According to Sabbat's daughter, Anna Sabbat-Świdlicka, and his biography on the website of Bieliny, Sabbat was called up to a unit in Czortków; Krzysztof Tarka's article states that Sabbat was mobilized to a reserve center in Kopyczyńce. Czortków and Kopyczyńce are only about 12 km apart, so this is a minor discrepancy.

authorities were friendly, but boredom and inactivity were the norm; the close proximity of vineyards and wineries added drunkenness to the mix. Sabbat's assignment was to combat this by applying his scouting experience. In short order, he organized two youth teams, a family circle, and a civilian group based on scouting regulations. His work was very effective—so much so that in December 1939 he was appointed scoutmaster and assigned to Budapest.

Although Sabbat's programs were achieving positive results, he wanted to rejoin the fight, and his prewar scouting contacts helped him escape. He left Hungary in late December and reported for duty in France in January 1940. He was assigned to the navy as a training instructor but was transferred to the 10th Armored Cavalry Brigade under General Stanisław Maczek. France provided little support until Germany attacked; then, Maczek received the equipment he had been pleading for. His brigade had several successes but was not large enough to be a decisive factor. Sabbat was wounded in action and taken to a hospital. Realizing that France would not stop the German advance and that he would likely be captured, he planned another escape. With his head wrapped in bandages, he slipped out of the hospital, made his way to the port of St.-Jean-de-Luz,[6] and managed to board a ship bound for Liverpool. He was again placed under Maczek's command in the newly formed First Polish Armored Division, posted to the division's base in Scotland, and assigned to educational and cultural duties. He began to organize scout teams, and in December 1940, Sabbat and other scout instructors held a conference in Perth and formed *Tymczasowy Naleczny Komitet Harcerski* (TNKH, Temporary Supreme Scouting Committee) as a body to coordinate scouting activities outside Poland.

At first, relations between TNKH and the military were difficult due to issues that predated the war. Michał Grażyński, ZHP's commander, had been a *Sanacja* supporter. He was appointed to the government on September 5, 1939, and evacuated to Romania with the rest of the government. Upon arrival in the United Kingdom, he was sent to Bute. Since ZHP had been led by a person imprisoned on *Wyspa Wężów*, its successor was viewed with distrust.[7]

---

[6] The rest of Maczek's unit continued to fight; however, the French units it accompanied had either been defeated or were retreating, and Maczek was surrounded and without fuel. Determined to escape, he broke his unit into small groups and had them slip through enemy lines to rejoin Allied forces. Maczek and many of his men escaped through Vichy France, North Africa, and Portugal on their way to the United Kingdom. Most of those who didn't make it out of France joined Polish and French resistance groups in France and Belgium.

[7] After Sikorski's death, a British government inquiry, and closure of the prison camp on Bute, Grażyński was released and reinstated into the army.

TNKH regained the military's trust and began to receive government funding. In April 1943, Sabbat was transferred to London and assigned to youth affairs. Thousands of children had been evacuated from the Soviet Union during formation of the Second Polish Corps, and the government needed to protect them and provide for their education. Sabbat formed scout teams and implemented scouting structures among the refugee children. He also became acquainted with members of the exile government and involved himself in politics. He disagreed with Mikołajczyk's return to Poland and sided with his opponents in London.[8]

After the war, Sabbat remained in London, joined SPK and the Polish Resettlement Corps, and continued to work in scouting. He traveled to refugee camps in Italy and Germany, and in early 1946, he organized a meeting in Enghien, France, of scouting centers outside Poland. There, they formed ZHP pgK and resolved to continue work in exile. Sabbat was chosen to lead the senior scouting organization, and later that year he organized a convention of "old scouts" at Lake Como in Italy.[9] ZHP pgK expanded its activities across the diaspora, and in 1947, Sabbat became its foreign commissioner. However, a conflict with Warsaw emerged. Warsaw opposed exile organizations that claimed to represent Polish interests and used its influence to have ZHP pgK expelled from international scouting organizations. Sabbat continued to represent ZHP pgK at international meetings and rallies as an unofficial delegate or as a guest of a recognized delegation. He also successfully lobbied SPK to accept scouts as members.

In 1948, Sabbat was discharged from PRC and founded Limba Trading Company Ltd. with his demobilization pay. Initially, Limba sold blankets and quilts from his residence in Fulham; the firm later began to manufacture quilts, duvet covers, sheets, pillows, pillowcases, and bed linens. Limba operated out of his new house in Putney; the business later moved to 230 Brompton Road, across from the Brompton Oratory. Limba was very successful and employed a number of émigrés. Sabbat also made its premises available for scout meetings.

On June 4, 1949, Kazimierz Sabbat married Anna Sulikowa, the eldest daughter of General Nikodem Sulik. They were married at Brompton

---

[8] For his part, Mikołajczyk did little to endear himself to the exile community. At a PSL congress in November 1945, he condemned the uncompromising attitude of the government-in-exile towards TRJN and its Soviet sponsors; he also denounced the NSZ's post-war actions against TRJN authorities and the Red Army occupiers.
[9] At the Lake Como meeting, Sabbat met Ryszard Kaczorowski, who would later hold a position in Sabbat's Council of Ministers.

Oratory and had four children: three daughters (Anna, born in 1950,[10] Jolanta, born in 1952, and Alina, born in 1955) and one son (Jan, born in 1957). With their earnings from Limba, the Sabbats purchased a large house at 38 Parkside in Wimbledon, but it was more than a family residence. Many émigrés needing a place to stay while they looked for work and housing found room with them. Their generosity extended to family members in Poland to whom they regularly sent parcels. Sabbat joined *Niezależna Grupa Społeczna* (NGS, Independent Social Group) in 1949 and supported Sosnkowski's efforts to conclude a unification agreement with Zaleski. When that failed, Sabbat was appointed to TRJN as an NGS representative. In 1954, he was appointed to manage financial matters for EZN and served in this role until 1967.

Sabbat's growing prominence attracted SB interest. He had first come to the attention of the security apparatus shortly after the war, when he and Zygmunt Szadkowski were organizing scouting in exile. Agents collected information on their activities and political positions, but no attempt was made to recruit them. By March 1963, SB understood Sabbat to be a leading figure in NGS and opened a file on him, assigning him the codename *Kanon*. As SB delved into his activities, an officer learned that he had been in regular contact with two government functionaries, Henryk and Janina Jaślan. Henryk, a provincial court employee, met Sabbat when they studied law at *Uniwersytet Warszawski*. Janina, a foreign language instructor at the Main School of Foreign Service, was a frequent guest at the Sabbat house during her stays in London. Henryk accompanied her on one trip and reunited with his former classmate; afterwards they corresponded. In 1964, an SB officer contacted Janina and questioned her about their relationship. He learned that Henryk and Kazimierz discussed politics and events in Poland and that Henryk regularly sent him newspapers and magazines, but he was unable to uncover any information that could be used against Sabbat. SB located his relatives in Poland, but they were no more useful to their effort than Janina Jaślan had been, and the investigation went dormant.

At 1962's *Zjazd Polaków w Wielkiej Brytanii*, Sabbat presented a paper titled *"Rola emigracji w walce narodu o niepodległość"* ("Role of Emigration in the Nation's Struggle for Independence"). He defined the role of émigrés as helping their fellow Poles at home, reminding the West of the Yalta

---

[10] Anna later worked in the Polish Section of Radio Free Europe along with her husband, Andrzej Świdlicki.

betrayal, and pushing for economic assistance for Poland. His paper had considerable influence; many of his proposals made their way into the final resolutions, and his reputation among émigrés grew.

His organizational talents were highly regarded within Zjednoczenie Narodowe. Along with EZN chairman Adam Ciołkosz, he organized 1966's Światowy Zjazd Polski Walczącej. Sabbat opened the meeting by emphasizing émigrés' primary objective—serving the cause of Polish independence—and reminding attendees of the democratic nature of the émigré community and their commitment to unity. This was the last major event under Ciołkosz's leadership. He had chaired EZN since early 1956, and after ten years in charge, he stepped down in December 1966. Rada Trzech chose Sabbat as EZN's new leader, appointing him in January 1967, but it took two months of negotiations to form a new cabinet. At the root of these difficulties was SN. Its leadership was aiming to carve out a larger role for itself and had become more assertive. Less than a month after Sabbat's appointment, SN threatened to withdraw from Zjednoczenie Narodowe and scuttled his plans for new elections to RJN. Its efforts to marginalize Sabbat failed, and he presented his list of EZN members to Rada Trzech in March.

Prior to being named chairman of EZN, Sabbat found it difficult enough to allocate his time among his family, political activities, Limba Trading Company, and ZHP pgK; now, it was impossible. His only choice was to end his work with ZHP pgK. He expressed his debt to scouting in his letter of resignation. He continued with Limba, but he gave less attention to the firm than was needed and it began to suffer.

As EZN's chairman, Sabbat shaped and directed its policies using the political program he defined in his 1962 paper as his basis. In 1969, he presented his views to a wider audience in the pages of Kultura. Its April issue featured a nine-page article by Sabbat, "Rola polityczna emigracji" ("The Political Role of Emigration"), which outlined his view of the duties of the diaspora and its relationship with Poland. He saw the initial job of Poles at home as survival, rebuilding the country, and maintaining Polish identity in the face of Sovietization; in time, this developed into influencing events in Poland and applying pressure on the regime. The diaspora was free Poland's voice, its advocate for independence in the West, and a counterweight to the PRL. He noted that although exiled political parties represented diverse viewpoints, they were united on essential matters. Sabbat's article provided opposition activists in Poland with insight into resources available to émigrés and illustrated that SB had been unsuccessful in its efforts to disrupt and weaken the émigré community.

Sabbat had been instrumental in the early stages of unification talks, but in mid-1971, LNP and SPK maneuvered him to the sidelines. Despite his prominence in EZN, for the first four years after unification, Sabbat had no consequential government role. Urbański did not appoint him to either of his Councils of Ministers; his only position was a seat in V Rada Narodowa. He had reservations about the unification agreement, particularly the lack of a defined term of office for the president and the continued use of what he considered anachronistic titles, such as Minister of National Defense and Minister of Justice. He preferred EZN's method of adopting resolutions over the *Zamek* system of presidential decrees, and he disagreed with Urbański's hierarchical governing style, considering it less democratic than EZN's governance.

In his first speeches as prime minister, Sabbat asserted that the government-in-exile continued to serve a vital purpose and noted that Poles had not accepted the government installed by the Soviet Union. He declared that the diaspora should set challenging goals for itself, most notably gaining the support of Western governments for the opposition. He cultivated good relationships with Radio Free Europe and *Kultura* and with the European Community. Sabbat made his first trip to the United States and Canada in 1977 and met with the chair of the House Foreign Affairs Committee, Congressman Clement Zablocki.

Sabbat's first Council of Ministers was dissolved in June 1978, and Ostrowski asked him to form a new government. It lasted less than a year and concluded its work with the end of Ostrowski's presidency. Raczyński chose to retain Sabbat as prime minister, and Sabbat conducted a minor reform of ministries, doing away with the Ministry of Information and Documentation completely and reshaping the Ministry of Religious Denominations, Education and Culture into the Ministry of Education and Culture. He also revived the Ministry of Emigration Affairs, last seen in Urbański's first Council of Ministers, and he renamed the Ministry of National Defense as the Ministry of Military Affairs. He continued to face sharp criticism, particularly from SN and from émigrés in the United States. Some former *Zamek* adherents refused to back him, seeing him as one of the "rebels" and as yet more proof that *Zjednoczenie Narodowe* supporters had taken possession of the government-in-exile at their expense.

In 1977, the SB reopened its file on Sabbat. It was particularly interested in him since the government-in-exile was supporting opposition groups; recruiting a deep contact in London would be a potential opening to penetrating opposition groups and therefore was of great interest. Again, they were unsuccessful.

As the end of Raczyński's term drew near, a group of Sabbat's opponents unleashed a fresh round of attacks on him and on the government-in-exile itself. New York's *Nowy Dziennik* newspaper was the locus, printing a series of articles questioning the principle of legalism and criticizing Sabbat. Juliusz Szygowski and Jerzy Jur-Lerski criticized Sabbat and questioned why a candidate from Poland was not chosen.[11]

On April 8, 1986, seven years to the day since he took office, Raczyński arrived at 43 Eaton Place, submitted his resignation, thanked those present for their support, and asked them to give their support and trust to his successor. Holding the original copy of the April Constitution in his hand, Sabbat then took the oath of office; afterwards, he gave a brief speech. He reaffirmed the government-in-exile's role with respect to Poland: "My first thought at this particular moment, like all of us, goes to the country. Everything we do in the name of maintaining the legal continuity of the sovereign Republic of Poland and its authorities in exile, we do with the country in mind and in the conviction that in this way we serve well the cause of freedom, independence and democracy in Poland."[12] Sabbat then thanked Raczyński for his lifetime of service to Poland and for the thirty years of guidance Raczyński had given him; he also thanked those from whom he had "…learned the difficult art of politics," a politically diverse group that included Sosnkowski, Grażyński, Adam Ciołkosz, Tadeusz Bielecki, Anders, and Bór-Komorowski. Lastly, he credited scouting: "I must also mention here the scouting movement, which taught me to serve God, Poland, and my neighbors."[13] He confirmed that he would limit his term to seven years and follow the guidelines of *Umowa Paryska*, closing with an affirmation that the government-in-exile existed to serve Poland.

A large and diverse group attended Sabbat's inauguration, including members of his Council of Ministers and *Rada Narodowa*, the president of *Skarb Narodowy*, leaders of veterans' organizations, government delegates to Canada, Australia, Argentina, Switzerland, Belgium, New Zealand, Italy, and the United States, and members of the Polish clergy in the United Kingdom. British friends of the exile government were there, as were

---

[11] Jur-Lerski was probably unaware that Raczyński had offered the presidency to several candidates from Poland, all of whom declined.

[12] "Przemówienie Prezydenta Rzeczypospolitej Kazimierza Sabbata podczas obejmowania urzędu po złożeniu przysięgi" ("Speech by the President of the Republic of Poland, Kazimierz Sabbat, upon taking office after taking the oath"), *DzU RP* No. 2 (Londyn), dnia 19 kwietnia 1986 roku, s. 39.

[13] "Przemówienie Prezydenta Rzeczypospolitej Kazimierza Sabbata podczas obejmowania urzędu po złożeniu przysięgi," *DzU RP* No. 2 (Londyn), dnia 19 kwietnia 1986 roku, s. 40.

representatives from the Council of Free Czechoslovakia, the Ukrainian government-in-exile, and émigré groups from Lithuania, Latvia, Estonia, Romania, Hungary, and Yugoslavia. Bishop Szczepan Wesoły[14] celebrated a Mass for the homeland at St. Andrew Bobola Church; later, the Sabbats hosted a reception.

Sabbat had taken charge of a reinvigorated government. Ostrowski and Raczyński had consolidated government structures, revived émigré interest in exile politics and *Skarb Narodowy*, began providing material support for the opposition at home, renewed international visibility of the government, and reestablished relations with other exile governments. Sabbat built on their accomplishments by strengthening London's position as the political center for the diaspora and recruiting younger people into government.

During his time as prime minister, Sabbat regularly traveled to Polish communities in Western Europe, and he visited the United States in 1980.[15] He solicited funds for *Skarb Narodowy* and implored his audiences to support the opposition in Poland. His visits strengthened the connection between émigré communities and 43 Eaton Place, and the increased contributions enabled London to continue financial and material support for opposition organizations. The government-in-exile nurtured an extensive network of contacts in Poland, ensuring it was well informed about developments at home. This flow of information enabled 43 Eaton Place to lobby Western governments and organizations on Poland's behalf. Sabbat and his family hosted opposition activists visiting London and invited émigré Poles and British supporters to meet them. He believed that the émigré community had no right to tell the opposition in Poland what to do; rather, its role was to support them, provide information to the Western press, and maintain contact with members of Parliament. He stipulated that the government would only support organizations seeking to effect change through peaceful means.

Children and grandchildren of postwar émigrés comprised a growing proportion of government volunteers. In a 1977 article in *Dziennik Polski i Dziennik Żołnierza*, Sabbat attributed their involvement to a desire to assist their homeland, inspired by the actions of their counterparts in Poland,

---

[14] Bishop Szczepan Wesoły was assigned by Cardinal Wyszyński in 1980 as his delegate for pastoral care of émigré Poles.
[15] In 1980, Sabbat visited New York, New Jersey, Illinois, and Connecticut.

and he entrusted them with positions of responsibility. Thus, younger exiles organized protests, issued press releases, and briefed Western journalists. Sabbat's lengthy involvement in scouting had given him useful experience in communicating with and motivating young people. Those who worked with him described him as an enthusiastic person who would inspire people but refrained from directing them in a controlling manner.[16]

London's support of *Solidarność* and other opposition groups incurred Warsaw's wrath. It fought back by attacking the government-in-exile's reputation with claims that the exiles were funded by American and British intelligence agencies. Government-in-exile press releases had long included declarations that its activities were funded by donations, and now Sabbat and others made a point to note in their speeches that émigrés themselves were the source of government funds.

Edward Szczepanik, minister of national affairs in Sabbat's third and fourth Council of Ministers, took on the responsibility of heading the government.[17] At the installation of Szczepanik's Council of Ministers, Sabbat remarked that the government-in-exile was indispensable to the cause of independence, noting its renewed importance to the opposition and its relevance in Poland. He quoted an underground *Solidarność* newspaper that underscored London's significance and noted that even PRL spokesman Jerzy Urban, usually quick to mock the government-in-exile, did not ridicule the most recent presidential transition. He closed by directing Szczepanik and his government to help the opposition, maintain contacts in the country, keep the Polish cause alive in the West, work with the diaspora and other émigré groups, and bring the next generation and recent refugees into their activities. In his comments, Szczepanik echoed Sabbat's instructions and also noted the necessity of nurturing Polish culture abroad and advocating for Poles who remained in the Soviet Union.

Szczepanik, Minister of Foreign Affairs Zygmunt Szkopiak, and Minister of Emigration Matters Zbigniew Scholtz strengthened the network of international representatives. In addition to delegates throughout the United Kingdom, the Republic of Ireland, the United States, Canada, Australia, France, and West Germany, by the late 1980s, the government could boast of representations in nations as distant and disparate as Sweden, Uruguay, Venezuela, Argentina, and Japan.

---

[16] It should be noted that these views were not universally held. Sabbat's biographer Jacek Danel described him as "despotic at times."

[17] Unsurprisingly, there were no SN members in Szczepanik's Council of Ministers.

Sokolnicki persisted in his efforts to legitimize his claim to the presidency by engaging with the Polish opposition and with other exile bodies. He and Hanff cultivated connections with two underground organizations, *Konfederacja Polski Niepodległej* (KPN) and *Solidarność Walcząca* (Fighting Solidarity). Their association with KPN did not last long, but Hanff's *Wolna Polska – Free Poland* championed *Solidarność Walcząca* leader Kornel Morawiecki in its pages.

In 1986, Hanff convened a meeting in New York with representatives from Albanian, Bulgarian, Croatian, Czechoslovak, Estonian, and Romanian exile bodies. Along with Sokolnicki's Free Poland in Exile, they formed the Central European Community (CEC). Hanff served as its coordinator and secretary. In September, this organization released the Multilateral Agreement of the Central European Community, which outlined their intentions to expose disinformation and propaganda, oppose staged elections, lobby Western governments, and provide mutual support.[18] Signing on behalf of Sokolnicki's organization was William K. Viekman, who gave his title as Acting Minister of Foreign Affairs of the Government of the Republic of Poland in Exile. He later took Hanff's position as secretary and coordinator.[19]

The CEC appeared to fill the void when ACEN was dissolved, but appearances were deceiving. None of the CEC's member organizations had been in ACEN, and most were of questionable legitimacy. Bulgaria was represented by the Bulgarian National Front and Croatia by the Independent State of Croatia; both organizations were founded by Nazi collaborators.[20] CEC member Interim Government of Republic of Czechoslovakia in Exile was not affiliated with the Council of Free Czechoslovakia, a former ACEN member that had been founded in 1948. A Ukrainian group had been accorded associate membership pending organization of a provisional exile government, but the Ukrainian government-in-exile already existed. Estonia's government-in-exile was a CEC member, but its authority was not recognized by the Estonian diplomatic service, still officially

---

[18] In the document, Hanff was listed as "Coordinator and Secretary of the Council H. E. Konstantin Siegfried Baron von Hanff, PhD., Undersecretary of State of the Government of Republic of Poland in Exile."

[19] Little information can be found on William K. Viekman. A person with that name had written a book on an American railroad, and a person giving his name as William K. Viekman, GCDE GCBS, had written an article titled "The Succession of Hassan I Durrani 1977" for *The Augustan* (issue no. 85, published 1979), the journal of The Augustan Society, a group engaged in the fields of chivalry and heraldry. Viekman's postnominals and his article in *The Augustan* indicate a person interested in orders and titles, much like Sokolnicki.

[20] The Bulgarian National Committee issued warnings about the Bulgarian National Front and cautioned that it was not a legitimate representative of the diaspora.

recognized as the nation's legitimate representative by the United States, the United Kingdom, and several other nations.[21]

In January 1987, the government-in-exile found it necessary to issue a new statement concerning Sokolnicki, reiterating previous warnings, noting the ongoing damage and confusion he was causing, and addressing his latest venture. Sokolnicki had issued a decree the previous March establishing what he called an "extraordinary criminal tribunal" with its seat in Warsaw and jurisdiction across all of Poland. He asserted that this body would be used to bring communists to justice for "crimes of murder on political grounds, physical and mental abuse of defenseless citizens and betrayal of national interests." The government condemned his statement, calling his action "a diversion and a provocation."[22]

As Moscow continued to insert itself into fresh political conflicts around the world, its European empire showed signs of advanced decay. Yet Western supporters of the Soviet Union denied that *Solidarność* and other opposition groups indicated widespread dissatisfaction with the Soviet system; they contended that the nations of Central Europe were not sufficiently mature for democracy and were fortunate to enjoy Moscow's benevolent oversight.

Sabbat took exception to this narrative and directly challenged it on May 6, 1987, at the government's commemoration of the May 3 Constitution:

> You can sometimes hear the argument that our countries are not mature enough for democracy to the same extent as the countries of Western Europe. Sometimes it is an excuse for abandoning Central and Eastern Europe. It must therefore be remembered that democracy in our countries is as old, sometimes older, and the democratic practices in our countries between the two world wars were not worse than in the countries of Western Europe.[23]

---

[21] As the United States never recognized the Soviet Union's 1940 incorporation of Estonia, Latvia, or Lithuania, the diplomatic legations of these nations were permitted to function.

[22] "Oświadczenie Rządu R.P. na Uchodźstwie w sprawie działalności Juliusza Sokolnickiego" ("Statement of the Polish Government in Exile regarding the activities of Juliusz Sokolnicki"), *DzU RP* No. 1 (Londyn), dnia 4 lutego 1987 roku, s. 7–9.

[23] "Komunikat Kancelarii Cywilnej Prezydenta Rzeczypospolitej z dnia 6 maja 1987 roku o obchodzie Święta 3 Maja" ("Announcement of the Civil Chancellery of the President of the Republic of Poland of 6 May 1987 on the celebration of the May 3 Holiday"), *DzU RP* No. 2 (Londyn), dnia 15 lipca 1987 r., s. 26–27.

Bernard Braine, Poland's long-time friend in Parliament, noted that Poland's aristocracy renounced their privileges in the May 3 Constitution, rebutting long-running PZPR claims. Braine ended his remarks with a call for reforms inspired by the May 3 Constitution.

In early July, *Rada Narodowa* released a series of resolutions. Mikhail Gorbachev, the new leader of the Soviet Union, had called for a discussion of "blank pages" in Polish–Soviet history, and *Rada* provided a list of events that required explanation, ranging from Moscow's unilateral violation of Polish–Soviet treaties to wartime deportations, massacres, and betrayals, its coverup of the Chernobyl nuclear disaster, and its failure to protect the language and cultural rights of Poles in the Soviet Union.[24] *Rada Narodowa* also expressed its pleasure over Pope John Paul II's visit to Poland the previous month, stating, "…this and the previous pilgrimage strengthened the moral and spiritual forces necessary to maintain the personality and culture of the Polish nation."[25]

Poland's government-in-exile had attained its highest visibility since wartime. Western politicians, government officials, and journalists rediscovered 43 Eaton Place and found it to be a useful source of information and perspectives that could not be obtained from official Warsaw sources. Sabbat used this atmosphere to strengthen London's preeminence in exile politics.

Vatican interest in the government-in-exile was revived, as evidenced by the Pope's 1982 London meetings with Raczyński and Sabbat and private audiences granted to Sabbat in the Vatican. Archbishop Luigi Barbarito, apostolic pro-nuncio to Great Britain, met with Sabbat, members of the government, leaders of Polish organizations, and Polish clergy in July 1987. Sabbat conveyed the government's gratitude for the Holy See's lengthy postwar recognition. In response, Barbarito thanked Sabbat and his family for hosting him at their home, discussed the plight and strong faith of émigré Poles, and thanked Polish veterans for their part in the liberation of his native Italy. The Holy See's renewed interest further enhanced the profile of 43 Eaton Place.

In Warsaw, Jaruzelski was under pressures unlike any his predecessors had experienced. Martial law, suppression of *Solidarność*, jailing of political opponents, and a deteriorating economy had further eroded society's already

---

[24] *Rada Narodowa's* resolution did recognize that language and cultural rights were afforded the Polish minority in the Vilnius region of Lithuania.

[25] "Rezolucja Rady Narodowej z dnia 4 lipca 1987 roku" ("Resolution of the National Council of July 4, 1987"), *DzU RP* No. 2 (Londyn), dnia 15 lipca 1987 r., s. 29–31.

low trust of PZPR, and dissidents used the Helsinki agreements as a weapon against it. Western sanctions worsened an already poor economy.[26] The exile government was funding the opposition, hosting dissidents and introducing them to Western politicians, and publicizing events that Jaruzelski would have preferred to go unnoticed. His options were limited, as Gorbachev had his hands full trying to maintain Moscow's influence while reviving his flagging economy. Jaruzelski was going to have to solve his own problems.

In 1986, he proposed a social consultative council that would include Wałęsa, Catholic clerics, and intellectuals, but Wałęsa refused to participate, as did most other invitees. He attempted to recruit Pope John Paul II to help, requesting that he use his upcoming 1987 visit to calm society, highlight PRL's positive accomplishments, reinforce the Polish character of the Recovered Territories, and show at least general support for the regime's initiatives. Papal influence, Jaruzelski reasoned, could lead society to endorse the PZPR program and get Western sanctions lifted. The Pope did not adhere to Jaruzelski's desired program. Instead, he spoke of human rights, decried the effect of poor economic conditions on families, exhorted young people to reject materialism, critiqued Marxism, and spoke of freedom and its concomitant responsibilities.

Jaruzelski realized that he had to look to Wałęsa and *Solidarność*. Internal PZPR studies concluded that the tenuous social peace would soon collapse under mounting economic pressures and concluded that Wałęsa must be offered a position on his consultative council. Such a move would solve many problems. First, Wałęsa was considered to be a national leader by Western governments and met with visiting dignitaries; giving him a quasi-official role would normalize his status somewhat. Second, Wałęsa's presence would give an image of legitimacy to the council while also making him and *Solidarność* share culpability with the government for unrest and economic hardships. Third, were Wałęsa to refuse, the government would appear to have made a good faith attempt to engage him and could portray him and *Solidarność* as uninterested in resolving Poland's problems. *Solidarność*, understanding that the regime was seeking social support, revised its strategy; it would now cooperate with anyone who wanted to carry out reforms, regardless of their political beliefs. Underground *Solidarność* structures were then dissolved and replaced with *Tymczasowa Rada NSZZ Solidarność* (Provisional Council of *NSZZ Solidarność*), a still-illegal organization that aimed to foster reforms.

---

[26] It is notable that, in 1986, Wałęsa, Bronisław Geremek, and Tadeusz Mazowiecki had publicly appealed to the American government to drop sanctions on Poland.

Jaruzelski remained convinced that a Marxist-Leninist government allied with the Soviet Union was the correct path, and he decided to use October Revolution commemorations to reinvigorate PZPR. Celebrations were ordered throughout the country, and it fell to the government-in-exile to bring this to Western attention. In an October statement, it informed the émigré press, Western media, and Western governments that Poles were compelled to celebrate this event and reminded them of the deleterious effects of the Bolshevik Revolution, particularly the transformation of nations blessed with rich farmlands and an abundance of mineral resources into economic wastelands. It also highlighted Moscow's undiminished commitment to world revolution and its previous alliance with Hitler.

In November, a group of activists announced the revival of PPS, a political party not seen in Poland since its predecessor's forced merger into PZPR in 1948. SB agents attempted to disrupt the party's founding congress but were unable to thwart the release of its political declaration that included its intention to reshape Polish politics by introducing political pluralism and freedom of association. KOR founder and longtime political activist Jan Józef Lipski chaired the party's Supreme Council. *Rada Narodowa* noted this as "an important step towards political pluralism in the country."[27]

Its optimism was tempered by the regime's imprisonment of two *Solidarność Walcząca* leaders, Kornel Morawiecki and Hanna Łukowska-Karniej. In its resolution, *Rada Narodowa* appealed to Western governments and organizations to intervene with Warsaw for their release, calling it a violation of human and civil rights and proof of the regime's fight against democratization; *Rada Narodowa* went on to condemn the ongoing harassment of opposition activists and asked émigré Poles to continue contributions to *Skarb Narodowy* and *Fundusz Pomocy Krajowi*.

Jaruzelski also decided to take his program directly to the people. He called a referendum for November 29 asking voters to support a radical economic recovery program and greater political involvement for ordinary citizens. A "yes" vote by a simple majority of registered voters was needed to approve each question. The questions were phrased to have broad appeal. But PZPR had uncharacteristically exposed itself to the risk that the vote would not go as planned. Certainly, society wanted political and economic reform, but to many, the idea of a referendum seemed redundant. In the pages of the underground newspaper *Tygodnik Mazowsze*,

---

[27] "Rezolucja Rady Narodowej Rzeczypospolitej Polskiej z dnia 12 grudnia 1987 roku" ("Resolution of the National Council of the Republic of Poland of December 12, 1987"), *DzU RP* No. 4 (Londyn), dnia 21 grudnia 1987 roku, str. 49–50.

Wałęsa opined that there was no need to ask Poles whether they wanted reforms, as they had made their desires evident in August 1980. *Solidarność* and other opposition groups called for a boycott, and for PZPR, voter turnout became a concern. Only 67 percent of those eligible voted. Both questions received a majority of votes cast, but the total count of "yes" votes for each question fell short of the number of votes needed for approval.[28] For the first time since the postwar imposition of communism, a Soviet-sponsored regime had lost a vote.

As Raczyński had, Sabbat first looked to Poland for a successor. In 1987, he offered the presidency to Władysław Bartoszewski, Leszek Moczulski, and Janusz Onyszkiewicz.[29] All declined. He would need to select someone from the diaspora and consulted with the political parties and *Rada Narodowa* to identify an acceptable candidate. They agreed on Minister of Internal Affairs Ryszard Kaczorowski.

Kaczorowski, a retired accountant, was a veteran of the Second Polish Corps and a scouting activist; Sabbat had first met him at a scouting event some forty years earlier. Kaczorowski's appointment was announced in January 1988. Few if any objections to his appointment were heard.

As Sabbat was planning presidential succession, Sokolnicki was seeking to extend his influence, and he set his sights on Wałęsa and those close to him. Mieczysław Wachowski, Wałęsa's driver, his personal assistant prior to martial law and later his personal secretary, received the rank of *generał brygady* (brigadier general).[30] Father Henryk Jankowski, who had already received the Order of St. Stanislas from Sokolnicki in 1980,[31] was given the rank of *kontradmirał*.[32] To Wałęsa himself, Sokolnicki awarded the Polonia Restituta.[33]

---

[28] At the time of the referendum, there were 26,201,169 registered voters in Poland. Both questions needed to receive 13,100,585 "yes" votes to be approved; this was just over 50% of the number of registered voters. Question 1 received 11,601,975 "yes" votes (44% of eligible voters), and question 2 received 12,127,621 (46% of eligible voters).

[29] 43 Eaton Place did not keep records of Sabbat's offers. His offers to Bartoszewski, Moczulski, and Onyszkiewicz were confirmed by Jacek Danel in correspondence and conversations with Bartoszewski, Moczulski, and Jolanta Sabbatówna. It is possible that Sabbat offered the presidency to others in Poland as well.

[30] Wałęsa would later appoint Wachowski to a series of positions in his government.

[31] Jankowski had been awarded Krzyż Komandorski Orderu Odrodzenia Polski (Commander's Cross of the Order of Polonia Restituta) in 1984 by Raczyński.

[32] Poland's naval rank of "*kontradmirał*" is the equivalent of rear admiral in Western navies.

[33] Sokolnicki bestowed the rank of general on Menachem Begin, once a corporal in the Second Polish Corps who had been permitted to leave the Polish Army during their time in Palestine. He gave the same rank to Julian Polan-Haraschin, a Stalinist-era judge who imposed death sentences on more than sixty AK veterans.

Well over one million Poles remained scattered throughout the vast reaches of the Soviet Union. Some were former gulag prisoners not permitted to return after their release, others were deportees who had not been able to leave with either Anders or Berling, others were more recent deportees, and some had simply stayed put when the borders shifted. After the repatriation program of the 1950s ended, Warsaw made no effort to intervene on their behalf. Moscow considered them to be Soviet citizens, and Warsaw dared not interfere in the Soviet Union's internal affairs. Although Warsaw would not speak for them, others did. Cardinal Wyszyński and the Roman Catholic clergy in Poland regularly raised the question of their status, as did *Kultura* and other émigré publications. On occasion, Western journalists would query Polish officials on the matter. Invariably they were told that Poles in the Soviet Union did not need special care, that Polish schools and cultural centers existed and Polish-language publications received government subsidies.

Rada Narodowa advocated for Poles in the Soviet Union and used its resolutions to make émigrés and the West aware of their fate, as exemplified by their February 1988 resolution:

> [*Rada Narodowa*] calls on all Polish centers in the world to continue to demand, from the governments and societies of the countries of our settlement, interventions to defend human rights for Poles in the USSR. The Russification of the Polish element within the present borders of the USSR did not cease, despite Gorbachev's proclamation of "glasnost" in international affairs. Poles are still treated there as citizens of a lower category and deprived of any opportunities for national cultural life and religious practices.[34]

Discontent with Soviet domination was spreading throughout the Bloc, despite efforts to contain the so-called "Polish contagion."[35] In 1988, Bulgaria

---

[34] "Rezolucja Rady Narodowej R.P." ("Resolution of the National Council of the Republic of Poland"), *DzU RP* No. 2 (Londyn), dnia 22 lutego 1988 r., s. 18–19.

[35] Czechoslovakia heavily guarded its border with Poland to prevent dissidents from illicitly crossing or from bringing illegal publications into the country. In the Podhale area near Zakopane, bemused hikers and tourists on the Polish side of the border were treated to the sight of Czechoslovak soldiers groaning under heavy packs as they patrolled mountain trails a few yards away.

permitted multiple candidates to run in local elections. In response to pressure from the American government over human rights abuses, Romania's Nicolae Ceaușescu renounced "most favored nation" trading status with the United States; in response, silent protests were held outside many Romanian embassies in Bloc nations on February 1. These events were noted in the government-in-exile's May 3 commemorations. Sabbat mentioned the Romanian protests in the context of increased cooperation between independence movements in Bloc nations; he went on to note the growth of underground publications, organized protests, and support for religious freedom in most of the captive nations. He concluded his remarks with a refutation of traditional communist charges of bourgeois Polish imperialism: "Thank you to all of you for wanting to share this anniversary with us, especially bearing in mind that the *Sejm* which passed the May 3rd Constitution consisted of representatives of the Commonwealth of Nations, that apart from Poles, also Lithuanians, Ukrainians and Belarusians participated in it."[36]

Rada Narodowa issued a series of resolutions, some familiar, others new. It continued to call for Western intervention for prisoners such as Kornel Morawiecki, Hanna Łukowska-Karniej, and Jan Andrzej Górny, decried the indifference of Western governments to the plight of Bloc nations, advocated for the rights of Poles in the Soviet Union, and implored people to contribute to *Skarb Narodowy* and *Fundusz Pomocy Krajowi*. To these, it added criticisms of PZPR's economic policy and a warning to émigrés about "the increasing penetration of Polish refugees by the regime which, under false pretenses of patriotism and communication with the Motherland, wants to weaken the political activity of the independence emigration."[37]

PZPR's economic policy was no more popular among émigrés than it was at home. Those structural issues that led to the upheavals of 1970, 1976, and 1980 remained unresolved; as a consequence, the economy continued to deteriorate, debt mounted, and the regime was again faced with a crisis. Choosing to follow the path of Gomułka and Gierek, Jaruzelski raised prices. As in 1970 and 1976, food price increases precipitated a fresh round of strikes, and loss of production only worsened the crisis. Jaruzelski could not afford to have strikes continue, but his plan to introduce

---

[36] "Oświadczenie Prezydenta Rzeczypospolitej i Rządu na Uchodźstwie z dnia 3 maja 1988 roku w sprawie strajków w Kraju" ("Statement of the President of the Republic of Poland and the Government in Exile of 3 May 1988 regarding strikes in the country"), *DzU RP* No. 3 (Londyn), dnia 27 czerwca 1988 roku, s. 37–38.

[37] "Rezolucja Rady Narodowej R.P. z dnia 27 lutego 1988 roku w sprawie Kraju" ("Resolution of the National Council of the Republic of Poland of 27 February 1988 regarding matters in the Country"), *DzU RP* No. 3 (Londyn), dnia 27 czerwca 1988 roku, s. 35–36.

government-affiliated unions to replace *Solidarność* had failed dismally. He had long blamed *Solidarność* for economic and societal disruptions, but now he was compelled to do something he found distasteful: he had to work with it. Jaruzelski and Wałęsa struck a bargain: if *Solidarność* were to call off the strikes, the government would bring it into negotiations on its legal status, on the economy, and on elections. Jaruzelski was in the awkward position of needing to negotiate with the very people he had ordered jailed in 1981. For Wałęsa and his associates, this was an opening not seen since Mikołajczyk had returned to Poland in 1945. Poland could have legitimate (albeit limited) political plurality, and *Solidarność* had an opportunity to regain recognition, paving the way for resumption of legal activities. Jaruzelski's motives were less pure. By bringing *Solidarność* into negotiations, he could apportion blame to it for subsequent economic hardships. Some opposition activists recognized this and expressed concerns in the underground press that *Solidarność* was being used.

While the regime was preparing for talks with the opposition, Sabbat and Szczepanik were engaged in a series of meetings designed to reinforce the authority of the government-in-exile, expand its activities, and increase émigré support for the opposition in Poland. Szczepanik's meetings were close to London; however, Sabbat embarked on a lengthy journey.

In late August 1988, Sabbat and his wife departed London. Their first stop was Pennsylvania for a rally of Polish scouts. From there they traveled to California for a meeting organized by *Skarb Narodowy* and then flew to Australia. Throughout September they made stops in Sydney, Canberra, Melbourne, Geelong, Hobart, Adelaide, and Brisbane. Sabbat met with émigré groups, government-in-exile representatives, veterans' groups, and scouting circles, visited Polish parishes and schools, laid wreaths at Polish and Australian war memorials, and was hosted at several receptions and dinners. He also made several appearances on émigré radio programs, and his visit was covered by émigré newspapers.

Interest in Sabbat extended beyond the Polish community. Soon after his arrival, he discussed the activities of Poland's government-in-exile in an interview on Australian television. At the end of September, the municipality of Ashfield honored him at the "Civic Reception for the President of Poland." Among the attendees were the deputy speaker of the Federal Parliament, a number of MPs, mayors of nearby municipalities, and other prominent Australians. On October 6, the Sabbats returned to London.

They had been away for forty-three days and traveled over 25,000 miles, and he had more travels planned.

On September 5, Szczepanik convened a meeting of government-in-exile delegates from Europe, North America, and Oceania at Fawley Court.[38] Joining them were members of the government, the chairmen of *Rada Narodowa* and *Skarb Narodowy*, the presidents of SPK and ZPWB, and émigré political party leaders. Szczepanik prepared an ambitious agenda. His overriding theme was the situation in Poland and the diaspora's role in supporting the opposition in its struggle for independence and democracy. The group reviewed the state of *Skarb Narodowy* and its role in making assistance to the Polish opposition possible; it discussed lobbying efforts with Western governments and the role of the newly-created "Central Bureau for International Relations of Free Poles,"[39] relations with other exile governments, the need to postpone questions regarding borders until the involved nations attained sovereignty, and the welfare of the estimated four million Poles in the Soviet Union. It sponsored a British–Polish symposium attended by Norman Raddaway, formerly Britain's ambassador in Warsaw, Norman Davies, professor of Polish history at the University of London, Leszek Kołakowski, professor of philosophy at Oxford, Leopold Łabędź, editor of the Sovietological magazine *Survey*, representatives of the British Foreign Office, and numerous English and Polish guests from London. Members of the British press covered the symposium. Afterwards, delegates planned the upcoming *Rada Narodowa* elections, discussed how to help new refugees from Poland and integrate them into émigré communities, and considered their options to re-engage émigré groups that placed little emphasis on supporting the Polish opposition.

Relations with other exile governments had been a topic at Fawley Court, and a few weeks later Sabbat and Szczepanik concluded another agreement with an exile government. The Polish and Estonian governments-in-exile prepared a joint declaration recognizing that both nations had a common goal of liberation from Soviet domination and that this created bonds of solidarity between them.[40] They agreed that freedom and sovereignty of their nations and all nations in the region was in their common interest and pledged to work together to achieve this goal. Both

---

[38] Delegates came from Australia, Austria, Belgium, France, the Netherlands, Canada, West Germany, New Zealand, the United States, Switzerland, Sweden, and Italy.

[39] The Central Bureau for International Relations of Free Poles was created in 1987 to facilitate "regular contacts with the authorities of countries with large Polish communities." Government-in-exile representatives in these countries also served as secretaries of the Bureau.

[40] This same Estonian government had joined Sokolnicki's Central European Community a few years earlier.

governments jointly announced the agreement on November 6. Szczepanik and his minister plenipotentiary for Polish-Baltic affairs joined the president of the Republic of Estonia, the Estonian prime minister, and the chairman of the Estonian National Council in signing a declaration.

Brooklyn's Greenpoint was undoubtedly the most Polish neighborhood in New York City. Polish shops, businesses, restaurants, and clubs lined Greenpoint Avenue and its adjacent streets, and several Polish parishes were situated in the area. As if to underscore its predominant ethnic character, entry from the north required crossing the Pulaski Bridge.

In the early 1980s, the idea of a Katyń memorial in New York City began to gather momentum, and it seemed fitting to build it in Greenpoint. A recent immigrant, Marian Gołębiewski, took a leading role in forming *Komitet Budowy Pomnika Katyńskiego* (Committee for the Construction of the Katyń Memorial). Gołębiewski had served in AK and later in WiN; he was arrested in 1946 and endured interrogations and imprisonment. After his release in the post-Stalin thaw, he supported underground groups (most notably ROPCiO), worked for *Solidarność*, and was arrested and briefly detained when martial law was imposed. He emigrated in 1982, wrote for émigré publications, and joined Sokolnicki's government.[41] His fellow committee members were Bronisław Baranowski, Leon Wiśniewski, and Konstanty Hanff, who served as chairman and organized fundraising.[42]

By late 1988, thousands of dollars had been collected, but there was nothing to show for it, and concerned donors and community leaders demanded an explanation. In response, Hanff resigned and appointed Baranowski as his replacement. Wiśniewski retained his position of treasurer, and Hanff named Gołębiewski to be secretary and deputy chairman. The funds remained unaccounted for.

Magdalenka, a leafy village about twenty kilometers from central Warsaw, seemed out of place in a socialist country. Its large houses and their spacious yards, often obscured from view by high fences and thick stands of trees, stood in stark contrast to Poland's modest farming villages, let alone the drab, crowded apartment blocks found in nearly every city and town. Its residents, high-ranking party, government, and military officials,

---

[41] Gołębiewski claimed the title of Minister of State under Sokolnicki's prime minister Jan Libront.
[42] Hanff's title under Libront was Minister of Foreign Affairs.

enjoyed an atmosphere comparable to the luxurious surroundings of prewar capitalists and landowners that PZPR propaganda so frequently condemned. Fittingly, a government conference center was located in Magdalenka; here, Wałęsa and several other opposition leaders began meetings with PZPR and government officials late in 1987 to plan what came to be known as *Okrągły Stół* (Round Table talks). Opposition representatives were compelled to accept the precondition that any proposals had to fit within the existing government framework as established in the 1952 Constitution. By January, they had agreed on a framework and discussion areas. Twenty-five delegates would participate: thirteen from PZPR and the government, ten from the opposition, and two observers.[43] They would commence their meetings on February 6.

Skepticism abounded. Several prominent *Solidarność* activists suspected that the talks were orchestrated by Moscow, that opposition delegates were carefully selected for their perceived malleability, and that the talks were designed to safeguard communist power.[44] Sabbat also took a cautious position. He saw the regime's offer of shared responsibility as a ploy to maintain control while apportioning blame to the opposition:

> It is being considered to admit the opposition to be jointly responsible for the state of the country, even in the *Sejm*, but so that the Party always has a guaranteed majority and decision. It is said that the party must have at least 60 percent of the seats. There are convinced supporters of such a partnership who believe that it is better than nothing, that at least one can speak and criticize in public. There are also opponents.[45]

Sabbat did not expect PZPR to willingly relinquish control: "The communist party will not give up power [...]. It will not keep any agreements.

---

[43] One of the observers was from the Roman Catholic Church; the other was from *Kościół Ewangelicko-Augsburski*, a Lutheran denomination.

[44] Andrzej Gwiazda, a participant in the 1968 and 1970 protests, one of the founders of *Solidarność*, believed that Moscow had arranged the talks. Anna Walentynowicz, whose firing in 1980 was one of the causes of the 1980 strike in Gdańsk, called the talks a successful communist operation that ensured no communists would be held to account for their conduct. Janusz Korwin-Mikke, a former *Solidarność* advisor, later claimed that PZPR and the opposition agreed that rightist parties would not be permitted to have power. Jan Olszewski, a lawyer who had advised the opposition during the Round Table talks, later claimed that fundamental issues had been decided before the talks began. Others claimed that all opposition representatives leaned to the political left, including some former PZPR members.

[45] "Przemowienie Prezydenta Rzeczypospolitej podczas spotkania noworocznego w dniu 1 stycznia 1989 roku" ("Speech by the President of the Republic of Poland during the New Year's meeting on January 1, 1989"), *DzU RP* No. 1 (Londyn), dnia 17 stycznia 1989 r., s. 15–21.

All agreements are only a maneuver in a period of weakness, a maneuver that is not taken seriously, as shown by the unilateral cancellation of the Gdańsk Agreement of 1981."[46] He did, however, detect a glimmer of hope: "On the other hand, even such an attempt to infringe on the Party's monopoly may be significant. It will testify to the weakening of the Party's power."[47]

The talks were contentious.[48] As Sabbat expected, PZPR wanted to share responsibility while maintaining control. In effect, it wanted to create another satellite party. Over six weeks, opposition delegates struggled to win concessions, eventually gaining much more than PZPR wanted to concede. *Solidarność* was legalized, censorship was ended, and the presidency would be restored, as would a 100-seat *Senat*. Of the 460 *Sejm* seats, 161 would be open for free elections; the remainder would be reserved for PZPR, ZSL, and SD. Elections for the *Sejm* seats and for the *Senat* would be held in June. The opposition formed *Komitet Obywatelski "Solidarność"* (Citizens' Committee *"Solidarność,"* or KO "S") as its political coalition.[49]

While the Round Table talks were in progress, Warsaw took another step to ingratiate itself with society, both at home and with the émigré community. On March 15, 1989, Prime Minister Mieczysław Rakowski repealed the 1946 resolution depriving General Władysław Anders of his citizenship.

Sokolnicki had his own thoughts. He proposed *Rada Regencyjna* (Regency Council), a transitional body that would serve as the interim government. Its members would be Jaruzelski, Cardinal Glemp, and himself. His proposition received no response.

In London, two elections were on the horizon: the *Sejm* and *Senat* election and elections to *VIII Rada Narodowa*. Planning for the latter had been underway since the second half of 1988; seats had been allocated, election ordinances had been published, and ballots were printed. That such a thing was even possible confounded Warsaw. Ever since Stalin authorized Polish communists to create ZPP in 1943, it had incessantly endeavored to infiltrate

---

[46] "Przemowienie Prezydenta Rzeczypospolitej podczas spotkania noworocznego w dniu 1 stycznia 1989 roku," *DzU RP* No. 1 (Londyn), dnia 17 stycznia 1989 r., s. 15–21.
[47] "Przemowienie Prezydenta Rzeczypospolitej podczas spotkania noworocznego w dniu 1 stycznia 1989 roku," *DzU RP* No. 1 (Londyn), dnia 17 stycznia 1989 r., s. 15–21.
[48] Talks were held in the neoclassical palace at Krakowskie Przedmieście 46/48. At the time, this was the seat of the Council of Ministers. In 1994, it became the official seat of the president.
[49] *Komitet Obywatelski "Solidarność"* (Solidarity Citizens' Committee, or *KO "S"*) was also known as *Obywatelski Komitet Wyborczy* (Citizens' Electoral Committee).

the exile government, co-opt its members, and sow discord. It looted its assets and unrelentingly attacked, undermined, belittled and ridiculed the exile government. And its efforts had failed. Not only did the exile government still exist, it had become more relevant both in the West and among the opposition in Poland. Worse, it was providing funds and supplies to *Solidarność*. Sabbat noted this in his 1989 New Year's greeting, stating:

> The communist regime in Poland was expecting that the Polish government-in-exile would eventually dissolve. The regime has relegated us to the dustbin of history many times. Our hosts in dispersed countries also expected it, seeing us as either blind or as irresponsible advocates for the Cold War. And here, after 50 years, we not only endure, but our activity has been strengthened and renewed. There has been a revival in exile. Political leadership enjoys a broader support than it did for many years before. Our presence in the country was revived, where the re-emerging political currents proclaim the program of Poland's independence and see its expression in the government-in-exile as the Image of the Nation.[50]

He returned to this theme in his April 1 speech at the opening of a meeting of ZPWB's 1989 congress: "…We are the subject of an offensive by the regime. It seemed and so it was said that we were thrown into the dustbin of history, that emigration did not matter, while it turns out how important emigration is, since so much attention is paid to emigration and so many efforts are made to win it. Apparently our role was not that small."[51]

He asserted that émigrés had the right and indeed the obligation to speak for Poland and defended the uncompromising attitude adopted by much of the diaspora. Sabbat cited General Maczek's response to Rakowski, who had issued an official apology to him: "At this point, it is difficult to refrain from citing the beautiful example of the old commander of the 1st Armored Division, my commander, General Maczek, who replied to the regime overtures: '40 years too late.'"[52]

---

[50] "Przemówienie Prezydenta Rzeczypospolitej podczas spotkania noworocznego w dniu 1 stycznia 1989 roku," *DzU RP* No. 1 (Londyn), dnia 17 stycznia 1989 r., s. 15–21.

[51] "Przemowienie Prezydenta Rzeczypospolitej na otwarciu Zjazdu Zjednoczenia Polskiego w Wielkiej Brytanii w dniu 1 kwietnia 1989 roku" ("Speech by the President of the Republic of Poland at the opening of the Congress of the ZPWB on April 1, 1989"), *DzU RP* No. 2 (Londyn), dnia 1 kwietnia 1989 roku, s. 34–36.

[52] "Przemowienie Prezydenta Rzeczypospolitej na otwarciu Zjazdu Zjednoczenia Polskiego w Wielkiej Brytanii w dniu 1 kwietnia 1989 roku," *DzU RP* No. 2 (Londyn), dnia 1 kwietnia 1989 roku, s. 34–36.

On April 30, émigrés elected thirty representatives from the United Kingdom, Norway, Sweden, Denmark, the Netherlands, Belgium, Luxembourg, Switzerland, Austria, and Italy to *Rada Narodowa*. Political parties and groups appointed fifty-two representatives, social, scientific, cultural, educational, and youth organizations designated twenty-six, and Sabbat selected ten additional representatives from the United Kingdom and four from religious organizations. *VIII Rada Narodowa* would convene for the first time on June 10, the same date that Sabbat, Szczepanik, and Scholtz announced appointments to *Rada Narodowa* branches in the United States, Canada, and West Germany.

Sabbat, Szczepanik, and the Council of Ministers remained skeptical about the elections in Poland. They did not believe that PZPR was above manipulating the election; the regime's conduct from its earliest days up to the present illustrated the lengths to which it was willing to go to maintain its grip on power. These were still not the "free and unfettered" elections promised forty-five years earlier. Émigrés would be permitted to vote at consulates, and although this election presented a chance to deal a blow to PZPR's monopoly on power, the government-in-exile was concerned that the regime would seize the opportunity to penetrate and disrupt the émigré community. It issued a statement recognizing that voting was an individual decision, advising those who voted to exercise caution with consulate officials, and asking them to support KO "S" and other independent candidates.

KO "S" conducted an energetic campaign, making use of whatever means it had at its disposal. Much of its funding came from the West, particularly from the Polish American Congress. A new newspaper, *Gazeta Wyborcza*,[53] began publication after the Round Table agreements and served as the voice of KO "S" in the weeks leading to the election. Television and radio broadcast time was allotted, campaign rallies were held, and posters appeared on walls, fences, and even tram cars. Invariably, posters for individual KO "S" candidates featured a photo with Wałęsa, although he did not stand for election.[54] The most famous poster bore an image of the American actor Gary Cooper from the 1952 film *High Noon*.

---

[53] *Gazeta Wyborcza's* very name testified to its initial mission; it translates to "Election Gazette." Its first issue was published on May 8, 1989, with the motto "*Nie ma wolności bez Solidarności*" ("There is no freedom without Solidarity").

[54] When asked why he was not running, Wałęsa reportedly replied that he wanted to leave the *Sejm* to others who were more qualified.

Dressed as a sheriff, Cooper had the *Solidarność* logo on his vest above his badge, and in his right hand was a folded paper bearing the word "*wybory*" ("elections"). At the bottom were the words "*W SAMO POŁUDNIE 4 CZERWCA 1989*" ("High Noon, June 4, 1989").[55] The message was clear: it was PZPR's time of reckoning.

Behind the display of confidence, KO "S" had no idea what to expect. True, a large segment of society had been members of *Solidarność*, but that was eight years ago, before martial law and before the organization was declared illegal. *Solidarność* had continued to operate underground, but there was no way to gauge support with any semblance of accuracy. Further, the most extreme opposition groups[56] disagreed with the Round Table agreements and called for a boycott of the election; no one knew what response they would get. To complete the picture, PZPR's conduct during the 1989 election campaign was reminiscent of PPR's actions in 1947. KO "S" posters were torn down, often by *Milicja* officers or local government officials. Slanderous articles about KO "S" candidates appeared in government-run newspapers,[57] and TVP (*Telewizja Polska*, the state-run television service and the only television broadcaster permitted to operate in the PRL) broadcast pro-PZPR propaganda and attacks on the opposition. *Gazeta Wyborcza* was plagued with insufficient allocations of paper, and opposition television and radio programs were aired at irregular times. A number of opposition candidates and activists were physically assaulted; others were arrested. These actions confirmed the fears expressed by the London government in May. KO "S" figured that it would win perhaps twenty seats.

Meanwhile, PZPR radiated confidence. It was running well-known candidates, including non-political figures such as celebrities and sports stars, against what it saw as a splintered opposition. Indeed, PZPR leaders were so convinced of their imminent success that they privately worried that they might win most, if not all, of the contested seats, thus dashing their carefully crafted plans to introduce a small opposition group into government to give the appearance of legitimacy and to apportion blame.

On Sunday, June 4, 1989, Poland turned out to vote. The results were stunning. KO "S" candidates won all 161 open *Sejm* seats and 99 of the

---

[55] Tomasz Sarnecki, a 22-year-old graphic designer, used the poster originally issued for the film's 1959 release in Poland as the basis for the campaign poster.
[56] Groups calling for a boycott of *Sejm* and *Senat* elections were *Solidarność Walcząca* (Fighting Solidarity), *Federacja Młodzieży Walczącej* (Federation of Fighting Youth), *Liberalno-Demokratyczna Partia "Niepodległość"* (Liberal Democratic Party "Independence"), and *PPS-Rewolucja Demokratyczna* (PPS-Democratic Revolution).
[57] Such articles appeared in *Trybuna Ludu*, *Życie Warszawy*, *Żołkieta Wolności*, and other official newspapers.

100 *Senat* seats; the other *Senat* seat was won by a *Solidarność* supporter. Society's rejection of PZPR could not have been clearer. And the Party was in shock. On Monday, the PZPR Central Committee Secretariat met to determine what went wrong and plan damage control. Minister of Internal Affairs Kiszczak bluntly assessed the situation as a total disaster for PZPR and a shock to the opposition.

Their discussion revealed PZPR's lack of understanding of the mood of the country. Zygmunt Czarzasty, secretary of the Central Committee of the PZPR, stated that an analysis of election results showed that they had the character of a plebiscite or referendum, something that PZPR had not anticipated. For that matter, PZPR did not even understand the frame of mind of its own members. Election results showed that a significant proportion of PZPR members and government functionaries did not vote for PZPR candidates. Some Central Committee members chose to blame the Roman Catholic Church; they had assumed that the Church would adopt a neutral stance, but after receiving reports of clergy support for KO "S", their discussion agenda included an item about considering talks with Primate Glemp. Central Committee members also worried that there would be public demonstrations by KO "S" supporters that would get out of hand. They needn't have been concerned; the opposition's astounded leaders took pains to avoid triumphant rhetoric for fear of provoking a harsh response.

While the campaign was underway, scores of Poles once again made the trek to the cemetery on the slopes of Monte Cassino. It had been forty-five years since the Second Polish Corps had forced the German Army from the hill, and Sabbat joined the group of veterans who came to pay their respects to fallen comrades. The following day, he was granted a private audience with Pope John Paul II; they discussed the current state of affairs in Poland. Sabbat and his family attended Mass in the Pope's private chapel, and later that day the Pope held a general audience for Poles to commemorate the anniversary of Poland's victory.

Jaruzelski had previously scheduled a mid-June trip to London and Brussels, and in the lead-up to the election, there seemed to be no reason to question his plans. Only two days before the vote, Prime Minister Thatcher's office confirmed his official visit on June 10 and 11, 1989. After PZPR's electoral defeat, the advisability of his trip was called into question. It was discussed at the June 4 Central Committee Secretariat meeting, but in the end, he went ahead with his travels and arrived in London on June 10.

Coinciding with Jaruzelski's arrival in London, *Rada Narodowa* issued a resolution. It declared that the end of communism in Poland was imminent, as evidenced by the Round Table agreements and the election results. It went on to make a specific statement on Jaruzelski's visit: "In connection with the current visit of Wojciech Jaruzelski to Great Britain, *Rada Narodowa R.P.* declares that he has no right to represent the Polish Nation."[58]

Rada Narodowa's objections notwithstanding, Jaruzelski secured promises of British support for International Monetary Fund aid, rescheduled debt payments from Poland's creditors, and British funds to support training and guidance in the transition towards democracy and a market economy. Jaruzelski also brought up the perennial question of returning General Sikorski's remains to Poland and was informed that the time was not yet right and that the matter would continue to be reviewed as the situation in Poland evolved.

Sabbat was continuing his work to expand awareness of the government-in-exile. In June, he traveled to Boulder, Colorado, and delivered a series of lectures on Polish history at the University of Colorado, an institution noted for its Central East European Studies Program. The program's director was Professor Edward Rożek, a veteran of the First Polish Armored Division and a member of the US branch of *Rada Narodowa*.

With the exception of a brief period in 1956, for over forty years the *Sejm* had been little more than a veneer providing PRL with the appearance of a legitimate democracy. Apologists would point out that seats were held by representatives from three parties—PZPR, ZSL, and SD—plus a bloc of independents; this was their proof that Poland was not under one-party rule. They refrained, however, from mentioning that ZSL, SD, and the independents were all controlled by PZPR.[59] In practice, this meant that PZPR made decisions and the *Sejm* obediently gave its approval.

After the 1989 elections, the *Sejm* became interesting. Fears that Jaruzelski would nullify election results were not realized, and KO "S" was now the second-largest party, holding only twelve fewer seats than PZPR itself; the remainder were held by five PZPR-affiliated parties.[60] PZPR considered

---

[58] "Rezolucja Rady Narodowej R.P. z dnia 10 czerwca 1989 roku w sprawie sytuacji w Kraju" ("Resolution of the National Council of the Republic of Poland of June 10, 1989, on the situation in the country"), *DzU RP* No. 4 (Londyn), dnia 29 czerwca 1989 roku, s. 61.
[59] PZPR referred to ZSL, SD, and the independents as their allies.
[60] A total of 126 seats were not held by PZPR or KO "S". ZSL had 76, SD had 27, and three nominally Catholic parties held the remainder: *Stowarzyszenie "Pax"* had 10, *Unia Chrześcijańsko-Społeczna* had 8, and *Polski Związek Katolicko-Społeczny* held the remaining 5.

this group as its guarantee that it would continue to control the *Sejm*.[61]

Poland's new president was to be elected by the *Sejm*, and PZPR proposed Jaruzelski. He wavered; at first, he refused to run, but later he gave in. KO "S" representatives subjected him to several hours of arduous questioning; an unrepentant Jaruzelski refused to apologize for declaring martial law or imprisoning *Solidarność* activists and defended Poland's participation in the 1968 invasion of Czechoslovakia.

On July 19, the *Sejm* convened to elect Poland's new president. PZPR would only permit Jaruzelski to be considered but quickly discovered that it could not control every aspect of the proceedings. PZPR had not anticipated that Wałęsa and KO "S" deputies would be able to persuade a large number of deputies from PZPR's allied parties to break with it. After a six-and-one-half-hour session that included nine separate ballots interspersed with procedural squabbles, Jaruzelski was elected president by a single vote.

PZPR got its president, but in the process, it learned that it could not impose its will any longer in the *Sejm*, and its erstwhile allies in ZSL and SD showed that they could and would act independently.

Sabbat, the government, and *Rada Narodowa* did not consider Jaruzelski to be a democratically elected president, nor did they believe that independence had been achieved. Still, it was plain to them that the end of communism was near. Five days before Jaruzelski's election, Sabbat asked his daughter Jolanta when she would be going to Poland. He thought that the time had come.

Sabbat spent July 19 at 43 Eaton Place monitoring the lengthy *Sejm* proceedings, meeting with members of his government, and talking with a representative of the opposition. Around seven in the evening, he left for home and began his half-mile walk to the Sloane Square underground station. At about twenty minutes past seven, he collapsed and fell to the sidewalk. Bystanders immediately came to his aid and summoned an ambulance. He was rushed to Westminster Hospital, but it was too late. He had died of heart failure.

Condolences poured in to his family and to 43 Eaton Place from Poland and from émigré communities around the world.[62] One day before his funeral, Sabbat's casket arrived at Westminster Cathedral and was

---

[61] Jaruzelski attempted to persuade *Solidarność* to join a coalition with the PZPR bloc, but his proposal was rejected.
[62] *Solidarność* and other opposition groups sent their condolences.

placed in the Lady Chapel. It was covered with the presidential banner and remained overnight beneath an image of Our Lady of Ostra Brama, an offering made by Polish pilots in 1944. That evening, St. Andrew Bobola Church was filled for a memorial Mass.

At half past ten in the morning of Friday, July 28, 1989, Sabbat's casket was transferred from the Lady Chapel to the main altar for his funeral. Thousands were in attendance, with dozens of regimental and scouting banners lining the nave. Bishop Szczepan Wesoły celebrated Mass and delivered a sermon; at the conclusion, a team of scouts bore his casket to the waiting hearse. Sabbat's casket was lowered into its grave at Gunnersbury Cemetery near the Katyń Monument, and a handful of soil from Katyń was scattered on his grave. His funeral ended with the mournful sound of the traditional scouting hymn "*Idzie Noc.*"[63]

Sabbat had earned the respect of British politicians and intellectuals as a legitimate representative of Polish émigrés, a champion of European integration, and a supporter of NATO. Major British newspapers printed his obituary, and in a sign that Poland was indeed changing, the official media noted his passing.

---

[63] The melody and words of "*Idzie Noc*" ("Night is Coming") will be familiar to Americans, as it shares the tune of "Taps" and has similar lyrics. Likewise, many British and Canadian scouting organizations have songs that use the same melody and similar words.

Exile's Last President

Ryszard Kaczorowski,
President of the Republic of Poland 1989-1990

ON JULY 19, 1989, a rapt audience at the Westminster Theatre watched intently as the second act of Oscar Wilde's *An Ideal Husband* concluded.[1] The house lights came up, and much of the crowd went outside to enjoy the warm summer evening. Among them were Ryszard Kaczorowski and his wife Karolina Kaczorowska, at the theater to celebrate their thirty-seventh wedding anniversary. As they milled about on the pavement, they noticed a car rapidly approaching. It screeched to a stop in front of them, and Zygmunt Szkopiak and Włodzimierz Olejnik hurriedly exited and rushed to them.[2] Szkopiak advised Kaczorowski that he was needed urgently at 43 Eaton Place. Their night at the theater ended prematurely.

Head of the Civil Chancellery Bohdan Wendorff had remained at 43 Eaton Place after Sabbat left and continued to work into the evening. At about eight, he was interrupted by sharp knocking on the front door. He rose from his desk, walked to the door, and saw a policeman on the stoop. The officer advised him that Sabbat had collapsed and had been taken to Westminster Hospital. Wendorff hurriedly locked the door,

---

[1] Westminster Theatre was located at 12 Palace Street. It was heavily damaged in a 2002 fire. Its remnants were demolished after a campaign to rebuild it failed. The St. James Theatre (later renamed The Other Palace) was built on its site.
[2] Szkopiak was minister of foreign affairs and Olejnik was undersecretary in the Ministry for Homeland Affairs.

climbed into the police car, and was driven to the hospital. On his arrival, the duty nurse informed Wendorff that, despite all efforts to revive him, Sabbat had died. Wendorff was driven back to Eaton Place by the police. He first called Sabbat's wife; he then summoned government officials. After ascertaining Kaczorowski's whereabouts, he sent Szkopiak and Olejnik to collect him.

When Kaczorowski and his wife arrived, Wendorff advised them that Sabbat had died. Kaczorowski decided to take the oath of office that evening. Wendorff gathered the necessary documents, took them into the hall, and placed them on a table covered with a red cloth, a copy of the constitution, lit candles, and a crucifix. By ten, most of those whom Wendorff contacted had arrived. At around 10:15, with about thirty people present, the act of swearing in the next president began. Wendorff advised the assembled group of Sabbat's death, reviewed the constitutional act providing for the appointment of a presidential successor, and showed the group the original of Sabbat's decree appointing his successor. Kaczorowski then took the oath of office, signed the documents, and made a few brief comments. Shortly after 11 p.m., the ceremony concluded. Ryszard Kaczorowski was president of the Republic of Poland.

Poland had been independent for little more than a year when Ryszard Kaczorowski was born in Białystok on November 26, 1919, making him the only president of the government-in-exile to be born in independent Poland.[3] In his youth he was involved in ZHP and rose to the rank of scoutmaster. At the age of fifteen, he enrolled in a private school; after graduation, he worked in a shop and continued his scouting work. In late August 1939, Kaczorowski was appointed deputy commander of ZHP's emergency medical service in Białystok.

On September 1, German aircraft appeared in the skies above Białystok. Scouts were deployed to assist the military and police. Kaczorowski's duties included clearing rubble from the rail station. As the German Army approached, the city's defense commander ordered older scouts to report to the Polish Army commander in Wołkowysk; they were put to work patrolling the area. After a few days, the scouts traveled by train to Baranowicze, arriving on the evening of September 16. In the morning, after learning that the Red Army had invaded, they bicycled to Nowogródek

---

[3] Wojciech Jaruzelski, elected president of the Polish People's Republic earlier that day, was also born in the Second Republic.

and saw Soviet tanks in the main square.[4] The group then made its way back to Białystok, now under Soviet occupation.

As elsewhere in Poland, resistance organizations quickly formed. In mid-October, Kaczorowski was one of the organizers of an underground scouting group. He made a risky trip to Warsaw to make contact with national scouting leaders but was unsuccessful. However, *Szare Szeregi* found the Białystok group. Kaczorowski served as regional liaison between *Szare Szeregi* and ZWZ, enrolled in school as a cover, and took over as regional commander when his superior's arrest was imminent. Kaczorowski was at school on July 17, 1940, when he was summoned to the administrator's office and arrested by the NKVD on the charge of being a British spy. Following the NKVD's logic, Robert Baden-Powell, founder of the scouting movement, had been a British spy in South Africa, and Kaczorowski was a scoutmaster; therefore, Kaczorowski was clearly a British spy.

Initially jailed and interrogated in Białystok, Kaczorowski was transported to the NKVD prison in Mińsk and endured six months of interrogation. After a two-day trial, he was found guilty of joining *Szare Szeregi* and conspiring to overthrow Soviet rule in western Byelorussia. He was sentenced to death on February 1, 1941. He and three fellow condemned prisoners were held in an underground cell and were repeatedly pressured to sign a petition asking for mercy. All refused. After one hundred days, Kaczorowski learned that his sentence was commuted to ten years of imprisonment, accompanied by loss of public rights and seizure of his property. His sentence was to be served in Kolyma, a brutally cold region in the far east of the Soviet Union.

Transit began with the sound of keys rattling at the cell door. All prisoners stood, the door was flung open, and a guard barked an order to prepare for transport. Prisoners were summoned by name and patronymic in the usual Russian manner: "*Kaczorowski, Ryszard, son of Wacław.*" He gathered his meager belongings, navigated his way through the other prisoners, and was marched to the back of a steel-gray, windowless police van,[5] already overflowing with other deportees. He squeezed his way into the van and stood silently while the guards checked and rechecked their paperwork. Finally, the doors were swung closed and locked, the van's engine rumbled to life, and it lurched away from the dock. After a brief but rough

---

[4] Wołkowysk, Baranowicze, and Nowogródek were located in the territories incorporated into the Soviet Union, and all three cities are now in independent Belarus. Wołkowysk is now called Vawkavysk, Baranowicze is now Baranavichy, and Nowogródek is Novogrudok.

[5] NKVD vans used to transport prisoners were often referred to as "Black Marias." They were windowless and typically had "Bread" or some other similarly innocuous inscription on the sides.

and uncomfortable drive, the van entered the grounds of a rail station and was backed up to a railcar located well out of sight of the station building. Prisoners stepped directly from the van into the railcar. Straw was strewn about the floor, and a hole in the corner served as a latrine. Light and ventilation came from a small window covered with an iron grate near the top of the car. When the car was filled, a guard slammed the door shut and locked it. Loading complete, the guards organized the paperwork to transfer custody of the prisoners and the train lumbered out of the station.

Thus began Kaczorowski's monotonous journey on the Trans-Siberian Railway. The train trundled across the vast expanse of the Soviet Union; once or twice a day, the train would stop and prisoners would be provided with rations, usually a piece of dried fish or salted herring, possibly a small piece of bread, and some water. Some days, there were no rations to be had and the prisoners went hungry. Many prisoners were unable to endure the tight, unsanitary conditions and meager food and died en route. Their bodies were left alongside the tracks.

After about five weeks, Kaczorowski's train pulled into Vladivostok. Guards unlocked the railcar door, slid it open, and ordered the prisoners to disembark. They poured out of their squalid temporary prison into the moist air of the Sea of Japan, but there was no time to rest. They were marched into a cordon of guards and dogs and ordered to squat. A guard blared that anyone standing up would be shot. They remained hunched down for hours while guards from their train handed over documents to transit camp guards and accounted for any deaths along the way. With all prisoners accounted for and bureaucratic tasks complete, prisoners were ordered to their feet and marched to a transit camp. In an environment reminiscent of a slave market, they were evaluated by labor camp officials and assigned to specific camps. They then waited for the next leg of their travels.

For Kaczorowski and others destined for camps in Siberia's far northeast, this required an ocean journey. On embarkation day, prisoners were rousted from their barracks and marched in columns to ships docked at the port at Nakhodka. They filed on board and descended into the dark, dank hold. When the ship was fully loaded with prisoners and cargo, the hatches were locked. Their route took them northward, keeping close to Soviet territory and carefully avoiding Japanese waters. For the prisoners, there was no distinction between day and night. The rumble of the ship's engines was constant, the air was foul and stifling, and political prisoners such as Kaczorowski did their best to avoid falling into the clutches of criminal prisoners, who thought nothing of robbing them, wagering their possessions in card games, or even killing them.

Eight days later, the ship's engines fell silent. They had docked in Nagaev Bay. The prisoners, squinting as they emerged into daylight, were marched to a transit camp in the city of Magadan. As they marched, guards barked out what became a familiar order: "One step to the left or to the right will be considered an attempt to escape, and we will shoot instantly." In transit camps, Poles were segregated from other prisoners. All underwent delousing, had their heads shaved, and had their clothes disinfected; they then waited to be dispatched to their labor camps.

Kaczorowski and his fellow prisoners were awakened early one morning, commanded to gather their belongings, and ordered outside. As they waited in the cold air, guards again exchanged paperwork; when all was ready, the prisoners were ordered into the back of an open truck, and they headed north on the Kolyma Highway. They took the highway across the Magdanka River until they reached the town of Palatka. There they turned off and began to slowly follow narrow mountain trails, easing their way along steep drops. They passed Ust-Omchug, turned west, and continued to the Tenika River. They crossed the river, followed it until it neared its confluence with the Kolyma River, and stopped where the Duskan River flowed into the Tenika. Prisoners were ordered out of the truck and marched five kilometers up steep hillsides until they reached their destination: the Duskanya gold mine.[6] This last trip to traverse the four hundred kilometers from Magadan took about two days. Kaczorowski was eleven thousand kilometers from home.

His job was to dig for gold. He began at four in the morning and worked until nine in the evening, digging four cubic meters of earth using only hand tools.[7] Camp officials had no concern for worker safety, prisoners worked in the same rags they slept in, barracks were frigid and overcrowded, and rations were insufficient to support heavy labor. Kaczorowski and his fellow prisoners were quite literally being worked to death.[8] Their only glimmer of hope was whispered news that Polish military units remained in action. He later recalled that "…by some miracle we heard the news that the Polish Army was fighting the Germans in Africa, that

---

[6] The Duskanya gold mine was located along the Duskan River in the Tenkinsky District of the Magadan Oblast.
[7] Kolyma soil was particularly rich in gold, yielding between 10 and 15 grams of gold per cubic meter of earth. Kaczorowski would have dug about 380 cubic meters of earth during his time in Duskanya; this calculates to about 4.75 kilograms of gold, worth about $5,170 on the world market in 1941.
[8] Robert Conquest estimated that every ton of Kolyma gold cost about 1,000 human lives.

Poland had not yet died. I don't need to add what it meant to us, how much such news comforted us and sustained in us the strength we needed to survive."[9]

Brutal conditions and excessive labor norms were taking their toll on Kaczorowski. His youth, strength, and good health kept him alive, but he did not believe he could withstand an extended stretch in Duskanya. His salvation arrived just over a month after he began work at the mine with the German invasion of the Soviet Union. When word of the Sikorski–Maisky agreement reached Duskanya in early September, Kaczorowski was transferred to lighter work.[10] On October 12, he was released and departed for Magadan with a group of 260 Poles. That they made it to Magadan at all was miraculous; of the 10,000 to 12,000 Polish prisoners exiled to Kolyma, only 583 survived to take advantage of the amnesty.

Their search for the Polish Army was hampered by indifferent and unhelpful Soviet officials, and accurate information was difficult to come by. They spent more than five months moving westward, searching for any sign of the Polish Army. They passed through Omsk and then moved south to the Kyrgyz SSR. There they learned that part of the army was in the Uzbek SSR. On March 27, they arrived in Margilan and were greeted by members of the Polish Army. Kaczorowski was assigned to 9 *Dywizja Piechoty* (9th Infantry Division). Evacuation of Polish Army units from Margilan was already underway, and Kaczorowski departed with his unit only a few days after joining. He and his fellow prisoners had narrowly made it to freedom.

Kaczorowski's arms and hands had been so badly damaged by mining that he had difficulty with basic drills. For the rest of his life, he would be unable to fully close his hands. He was assigned to a communications company and began to organize scouting units in his free time. He was part of the Second Polish Corps as it made its way through Italy. At Monte Cassino, he organized the Polish Army's communications center and was the first to broadcast that the Corps had taken the hill. After the war, he settled in the United Kingdom, joined PRC, and learned English. He found work as an accountant in a British firm and resumed his involvement with scouting. While working in ZHP pgK, he met Karolina Mariampolska,

---

[9] "Przemówienie Prezydenta Rzeczypospolitej Polskiej Ryszarda Kaczorowskiego na obchodzie 50-lecia powstania Samodzielnej Brygady Strzelców Karpackich w dniu 1 kwietnia 1990 roku" ("Speech by the President of the Republic of Poland, Ryszard Kaczorowski, at the celebration of the 50th anniversary of the establishment of the Independent Carpathian Rifle Brigade on April 1, 1990"), *DzU RP* No. 2 (Londyn), dnia 1 listopada, 1990 roku, s. 28–30.

[10] Kaczorowski arrived at Duskanya in late May and was transferred to lighter labor after news of the amnesty was announced in that camp. He would have worked at digging for about 95 days.

a native of Stanisławów.[11] Her father had been sent to a gulag, and she and her mother were deported to Siberia.[12] When amnesty was granted, she and her mother managed to reach the Polish Army and were evacuated with them. She was sent along with other children to Camp Koja, a refugee camp created by the government-in-exile in Uganda; there, she attended Polish school. She later moved to London with other refugees and enrolled at the University of London. After graduation, she worked as a schoolteacher and became involved with ZHP pgK. Kaczorowski and Mariampolska married in 1952, and they had two daughters, both of whom became involved in scouting.

In addition to scouting, Kaczorowski was active in SPK, ZPWB, POSK, PMS, *Instytut Polskiej Akcji Katolickiej* (Polish Institute of Catholic Action), and *Rada Koordynacyjna Polonii Wolnego Świata* (Coordinating Council of Poles in the Free World). After thirty-five years, he retired from his accountancy career. He now had more time to devote to scouting, and he traveled to Australia to inspect Polish scouting units. On his return to London, Prime Minister Sabbat offered him the position of minister without portfolio in his Council of Ministers. Szczepanik chose to retain him in his first Council of Ministers, appointing him minister of homeland affairs, where his primary duty was to maintain contacts with Poland; he was also appointed secretary of *Fundusz Pomocy Krajowi*. In 1988 Sabbat appointed Kaczorowski to be his successor, and in 1989 he joined *Rada Narodowa* as an NGS representative.

No guests were present at Kaczorowski's inauguration, nor was there a Mass or reception. Continuing the government's functions took precedence over pomp and ceremony. As was customary, Prime Minister Edward Szczepanik tendered his resignation. Kaczorowski had no intention of making a change and reappointed him after perfunctory consultations with the political parties.

A sense of optimism had emerged at 43 Eaton Place, although it was tempered with the knowledge that Jaruzelski and PZPR still held power and could respond sharply if their monopoly on power was threatened. London expected Jaruzelski to ignore his agreements with *Solidarność* and advised the opposition to proceed with caution.

---

[11] After the Soviet invasion in 1939, Stanisławów was forcibly incorporated into the Soviet Union and renamed Stanislav. In 1962, the city was again renamed, this time to Ivano-Frankivsk.
[12] Her parents were Franciszek Mariampolski and Rozalia Mariampolska.

In Warsaw, Minister of Internal Affairs Kiszczak was not optimistic. He contemplated forty-five years of UB and SB records and concluded that if they fell into the hands of the opposition, they would be used to hold him and his officers to account. In July, SB Commander General Henryk Dankowski held a telephone conference with his subordinates and recommended that they destroy all "useless" materials. They understood what he meant and began to purge files. Many were hauled to paper mills and pulped; others were burned or shredded.[13] In Kielce, a fire broke out in SB's offices and raged all day. Few documents related to the 1946 Kielce Pogrom survived. These actions could not be kept concealed, and by January Kiszczak was under mounting pressure. In late January, he issued an order prohibiting the destruction of working, operational, and archival documents. Yet destruction continued, albeit on a smaller scale. In total, an estimated fifty to sixty percent of SB's files were destroyed, although some files containing information on prominent people were kept for political blackmail.

In August, Jaruzelski came to understand how far his power had declined when he appointed Kiszczak as his prime minister. Kiszczak had been minister of internal affairs since July 1981. He oversaw *Milicja*, SB, and ZOMO and worked with Jaruzelski to plan martial law. Much of society held him responsible for the resulting deaths and internments. KO "S", ZSL, and SD refused to cooperate with him, and Kiszczak resigned. Jaruzelski had no choice but to appoint a prime minister acceptable to KO "S" and asked Wałęsa for nominations. Wałęsa submitted the names of three *Solidarność* advisors. Jaruzelski chose Tadeusz Mazowiecki,[14] whom he had ordered to be arrested back in 1980.[15] Mazowiecki was overwhelmingly approved in an August 24 *Sejm* vote,[16] making him the first prime minister in

---

[13] On October 30 alone, the Warsaw SB offices hauled 10 tonnes of files to a paper mill. Others were shredded or burned. Over the winter of 1989–1990, the SB building in Siedlce burned so many documents in its furnace that it had no need for other fuel.

[14] From the late 1940s until 1955, Mazowiecki had been a member of PAX. He founded the newspaper *Wrocławski Tygodnik Katolików* (*Wrocław Catholic Weekly*), and as its editor he wrote and published a condemnation of Bishop Kaczmarek, charging him with conducting "activities hostile to the national interest and social progress in the pre-war period, during the occupation and in People's Poland," with "breaking trust in the durability of the people's power and new social relations in Poland," and with being "involved in cooperation with American intelligence centers." He was later expelled from PAX and began to distance himself from the government. He served three terms in the *Sejm* as a representative of the Catholic organization *Znak*. In 1968 he handed a student petition to the marshal of the *Sejm* protesting the cancellation of Mickiewicz's *Dziady*. He was not permitted to run for re-election after he called for investigations into the government's conduct in the 1970 events. He aligned himself with the opposition, advised *Solidarność*, edited the *Tygodnik Solidarność* weekly, was interned during martial law, and was an opposition representative at the Round Table talks.

[15] The other two were Bronisław Geremek and Jacek Kuroń.

[16] A total of 378 deputies voted in favor of Mazowiecki, 4 voted against, and 41 abstained. As PZPR held 255 seats, this indicates that a large number of its deputies voted for him.

Warsaw in forty-three years who was neither a PPR/PZPR member nor a member of an allied party; further, he was the first non-communist prime minister in a Soviet Bloc country in over forty years. But PZPR was not completely devoid of power. To form his government, Mazowiecki had to concede three crucial positions to PZPR: deputy prime minister, minister of internal affairs, and minister of defense.[17]

In his first *Sejm* speech as prime minister, Mazowiecki declared a categorical break with the past through his doctrine for post-communist Poland in what became known as the *gruba linia* (thick line) policy: "We draw a thick line on what has happened in the past. We will be responsible only for what we have done to help extract Poland from her current predicament, from now on."[18] Mazowiecki had taken a conciliatory approach that gave top priority to extracting Poland from its economic crisis and rejected holding people responsible for their actions under communism.[19] Thus, he relegated the actions of Jaruzelski, Kiszczak, and many others to the past and considered them irrelevant.[20] His stance was widely unpopular in Poland and among émigrés; a prevalent view was that *gruba linia* amounted to an amnesty that would forestall efforts to hold communist-era authorities accountable for their actions.

Kaczorowski portrayed the events of 1989 as mostly positive: "…the June elections gave the society the opportunity to express its true opinion. The elections, treated by voters as a national referendum, showed the voters' maturity and political discernment. Before the elections, the regime's propaganda proclaimed that Poles were incapable of and afraid of democracy. This accusation is made against a nation which will soon

---

[17] Kiszczak held the position of deputy prime minister and retained his post of minister of internal affairs, leaving Milicja, SB, and ZOMO under communist control. General Florian Siwicki, a Politburo member, was minister of defense.

[18] Speech of Tadeusz Mazowiecki in the *Sejm*, August 24, 1989. See "*Sprawozdanie Stenograficzne z 6 posiedzenia Sejmu Polskiej Rzeczypospolitej Ludowej w dniach 23 i 24 sierpnia 1989 r.*" ("*Stenographic Report of the 6th Session of the Sejm of the Polish People's Republic on August 23 and 24, 1989*"), (Zakł. Graph. Tamka, Warszawa, 1989), łam 86.

[19] The term "lustration" was frequently heard in former Bloc nations as they emerged from communism. Lustration was an examination of government records to bring light on citizens' actions under communism and could potentially be used to disqualify people from government service or to deny them government pensions or other benefits. In declaring *gruba linia*, Mazowiecki was rejecting lustration. A fundamental problem with lustration was fabricated police reports and files, known as *fałszywki*. To discredit opposition activists, SB officers would create a *fałszywka* that included false information about the subject's work an informer or undercover agent. *Fałszywki* were numerous, and in a lustration process they could be used to unjustly bar a person from government office. Lech Wałęsa and Władysław Bartoszewski are two prominent examples of people for whom a *fałszywka* existed.

[20] Considering Mazowiecki's earlier writings, his membership in PAX, and his service in the PZPR-controlled *Sejm*, *gruba linia* may have been intended to protect himself as well.

celebrate its 500th anniversary of parliamentarism [...]."[21] He expressed his hopes at the 1989 SPK congress: "June 4, 1989, became a turning point in the history of the country. [...] With the formation of the government of Tadeusz Mazowiecki and the taking over of some of the ministries by *Solidarność* activists, a new situation has emerged, to which we attach new hopes together with the society in the country."[22]

However, Kaczorowski viewed the situation as fragile. His optimism was tempered with concerns that Poland effectively remained under PZPR control and his disagreement with Mazowiecki's *gruba linia*. He would not permit the government-in-exile to cooperate with Warsaw until communist control had completely ended and outlined his conditions at the SPK congress: "We cannot allow the institutions and agencies of emigration, built with such difficulty, to be taken over and used to break the unity of independence emigration. The main goal of this emigration is a free and independent Poland, and only to such a government, which will be elected in universal and free elections and which will be the only center of power in sovereign Poland, will we deposit the symbols of the Republic of Poland entrusted to our care."[23] *Rada Narodowa* shared his apprehensions but allowed that it was "...in the national interest to strengthen the contacts of this emigration with independent social and cultural organizations in the country, whose independence character does not raise any doubts."[24]

As the power of *Solidarność* leaders grew, the importance of 43 Eaton Place to them declined. In late November, Wałęsa arrived in London. He visited POSK, met with émigré organizations, called on Raczyński, and attended Mass at the Polish parish in Ealing.[25] He did not meet with Kaczorowski or Szczepanik.[26] This snub did not change Kaczorowski's commitment to help those at home. With winter fast approaching and the economy still in shambles, ZPWB launched a fresh appeal for funds in

---

[21] "Przemówienie Prezydenta Rzeczypospolitej na otwarcie w dniu 5 września 1989 roku III Zjazdu Światowego Wolnych Polaków pod hasłem 'Nadal w służbie Rzeczypospolitej Polskiej,'" *DzU RP* No. 6 (Londyn), dnia 15 grudnia 1989 roku, s. 114–116.

[22] "Przemówienie Prezydenta Rzeczypospolitej na Zjeździe Stowarzyszenia Polskich Kombatantów w W. Brytanii, w Londynie 27 października 1989" ("Speech by the President of the Republic of Poland at the Congress of the Polish Ex-Combatants Association in Great Britain, London, 27 October 1989"), *DzU RP* No. 6 (Londyn), dnia 15 grudnia 1989 roku, s. 119–121.

[23] "Przemówienie Prezydenta Rzeczypospolitej na Zjeździe Stowarzyszenia Polskich Kombatantów w W. Brytanii, w Londynie 27 października 1989," *DzU RP* No. 6 (Londyn), dnia 15 grudnia 1989 roku, s. 119–121.

[24] "Rezolucja" ("Resolution"), *DzU RP* No. 6 (Londyn), dnia 15 grudnia 1989 roku, s. 122–123.

[25] Wałęsa attended Mass at *parafia pw. NMP Matki Kościoła na Ealingu w Londynie* (Parish of Our Lady, Mother of the Church at Ealing in London). The church is located on Windsor Road.

[26] In 1981, Wałęsa met with Raczyński during a stop in London, but at the time Wałęsa was a private citizen.

November. Called *Komitet Doraźnej Pomocy Krajowi – Help Poland Fund*,[27] it was chaired by Kaczorowski; Raczyński, Maczek, and Rudnicki all voiced their support. By end of January, Poles in the United Kingdom had contributed more than £300,000.

Despite this help, Mazowiecki followed Wałęsa's lead during his official visit to London in February. Kaczorowski invited him to 43 Eaton Place; he declined. Mazowiecki's itinerary included a visit to POSK. Kaczorowski offered an informal meeting at that venue, but he canceled at the last minute. Their only contact was a brief telephone conversation.[28] Kaczorowski was diplomatic. *Tygodnik Solidarność* interviewed him, and when the topic of Mazowiecki's visit to London was broached, he noted that the existence of two presidents placed him in an awkward position. Mazowiecki's opinion of the London government was confirmed by Zdzisław Najder, a literary historian who had been in the United Kingdom when martial law was declared. Najder remained in exile, worked for Radio Free Europe, and returned to Poland in 1989. He had extensive interactions with Wałęsa and Mazowiecki and later stated that Mazowiecki's government had little regard for 43 Eaton Place and viewed the exile government as nothing more than a symbolic body.

As one Bloc nation after another rejected communism, they embarked on a flurry of activity to remove communist names and symbols and to revise communist-era constitutions.[29] On December 29, 1989, the *Sejm* adopted a resolution changing the official name of the state from the Polish People's Republic to the Republic of Poland, restoring the crown to the eagle on the national emblem, and removing wording from the constitution that enshrined PZPR's leading role and declared that Poland must have a socialist economy. London continued to take a cautious stance. The government-in-exile viewed these actions as symbolic, warned that they meant nothing without fundamental changes, and reiterated its readiness to assist in ridding Poland of its communist government.

---

[27] *Komitet Doraźnej Pomocy Krajowi* translates to "Committee for Urgent Help for Poland."

[28] Mazowiecki attended a state dinner with Margaret Thatcher on February 13. Thatcher made a passing reference in her speech to the Polish government's presence in London during the war and to the presence of the Polish émigré community. She did not mention the government-in-exile's continued presence and work in London. Mazowiecki made no reference to the exile government or the émigré community.

[29] Late in 1989, Czechoslovakia changed its official name from "Czechoslovak Socialist Republic" (ČSSR) to "Czech and Slovak Federative Republic" and removed the clause from its constitution declaring the communist party's leading role. Romania revised its name from "Socialist Republic of Romania" to "Romania" and removed the communist emblem from its flag. In 1990, the Hungarian People's Republic renamed itself "Republic of Hungary," and the People's Republic of Bulgaria became "Republic of Bulgaria." Like Romania, Bulgaria removed the communist emblem from its flag.

Jaruzelski's gambit had failed spectacularly, and PZPR had become incapable of defending itself. Ordinary citizens began to occupy the thousands of PZPR buildings across the country to prevent party functionaries from plundering valuables and from removing or destroying files.[30] In these chaotic circumstances, PZPR met in late January for its eleventh congress. Party leaders had intended to focus on restructuring and revitalizing PZPR, but at the end of the tumultuous proceedings, PZPR voted to dissolve itself. Many of its centrist leaders went on to form *Socjaldemokracja Rzeczypospolitej Polskiej* (SdRP, Social Democracy of the Republic of Poland); it was the legal successor of PZPR and inherited control of PZPR assets. This reconstituted party financed its activities in no small part through a substantial loan from the Communist Party of the Soviet Union. SdRP's most prominent leaders were former Politburo members Leszek Miller, Mieczysław Rakowski, and Aleksander Kwaśniewski, a minister under Jaruzelski. Most of those who did not join SdRP, particularly those advocating more leftward political positions, created *Polska Unia Socjaldemokratyczna* (Polish Social Democratic Union).[31]

PZPR's former allies charted new courses. ZSL renamed itself *Polskie Stronnictwo Ludowe "Odrodzenie"* (PSL "Odrodzenie," Polish People's Party "Rebirth"). SD retained its name but replaced most of its leaders.

London issued another statement regarding contact with Warsaw. It declared that changes in the official name of the state and the constitution did not alter London's policy regarding contacts with the Warsaw government; members of the exile government and *Rada Narodowa* were prohibited from visiting Poland or maintaining contacts with representatives from the Warsaw government unless authorized by 43 Eaton Place. Further cautions were advised regarding SdRP and *Polska Unia Socjaldemokratyczna*. The government warned, "The dissolution of the communist party known as PZPR on February 2 this year and the creation of two supposedly 'social democratic' parties in its place should not delude anyone that its former members will suddenly cease to serve purposes contrary to the good of the Polish nation. Therefore, Poles living abroad should still avoid contacts with them and

---

[30] Apparently, a large group of citizens did not subscribe to Mazowiecki's *gruba linia* policy.

[31] Later in 1990, a group of hardline communists formed a new and unapologetically communist party, *Związek Komunistów Polskich "Proletariat"* (Union of Polish Communists "Proletariat"). It opposed adoption of capitalist economics, advocated re-nationalization of industries and health care and elimination of the *Senat*, and was against Poland's accession into the European Union and its membership in NATO. This party never won a *Sejm* seat and was disbanded in 2002. A segment of its members then founded *Komunistyczna Partia Polski* (Communist Party of Poland, or KPP), which, like its predecessor, was unpopular.

with their 'nomenklatura.'"[32] However, the government-in-exile recognized the need to grow contacts with academic, scientific, and social organizations and encouraged private travel.

Soviet power was rapidly collapsing. In October, anti-communist protests erupted in East Germany. Berlin pleaded to Moscow for military intervention, but Gorbachev refused. Protests spread throughout East Germany, thousands stormed border checkpoints in Berlin, and the East German police and military stood down and did not hinder them. The Berlin Wall had been breached. German reunification was inevitable, but unfinished business remained. There had never been a peace conference at the end of the Second World War, and a final settlement had to be negotiated by the victorious allies.[33] As the senior member of the anti-German wartime alliance[34] and with an imposed border with Germany, Poland could reasonably expect to be part of the negotiations, but one final slight awaited Warsaw. Governments invited to the talks were from East Germany, West Germany, the United Kingdom, France, the Soviet Union, and the United States. Poland had been excluded. Both Polish governments were profoundly concerned; once again, large and powerful nations were negotiating the fate of Poland and other nations without their participation or consent. Mazowiecki and Minister of Foreign Affairs Krzysztof Skubiszewski petitioned the participating governments to permit Germany's neighbors to participate in the conference. In London, Szczepanik's government reminded the West of Poland's fate in the hands of others: "Remembering painfully the Yalta pact and its procedure of dictating Poland's fate by strangers, Poles both at home and abroad firmly demand that the principle 'nothing about us without us' be respected."[35]

The government-in-exile demanded inclusion of all nations bordering Germany, acceptance of the Polish–German border, and Poland's admission into the European Community. It also called for an alliance of Central

---

[32] "Oświadczenie Rządu w sprawie łączności z Krajem" ("Statement of the Government on Communication with the Country"), *DzU RP* No. 2 (Londyn), dnia 1 listopada, 1990 roku, s. 31–32.
[33] The Yalta agreements assigned spheres of influence in Europe, and provisional borders were drawn at Potsdam, but no final settlement had been concluded. The provisional borders remained the *status quo* for 45 years.
[34] Poland was unquestionably the senior member of the anti-German alliance, having been at war since the German invasion on September 1, 1939. France and the United Kingdom joined the fight on September 3, the Soviet Union joined the alliance on June 22, 1941, when it was invaded by its erstwhile German ally, and the United States entered the war on December 7, 1941.
[35] "Stanowisko Rządu w sprawie zjednoczenia Niemiec" ("The Government's position on the reunification of Germany"), *DzU RP* No. 2 (Londyn), dnia 1 listopada, 1990 roku, s. 33–34.

European nations as envisaged in the Polish–Czechoslovak declaration of 1986. Émigré publications exhorted their readers to write to the participating governments demanding Poland's inclusion, resulting in a deluge of letters. Embarrassed Western governments were compelled to respond. At the first session, all six governments agreed to include Poland, but only in discussions regarding the Polish–German border. Polish representatives were excluded from all other negotiations, including those setting limits on German military strength.

For nearly fifty years, the Soviet Union doggedly maintained that Katyń was a German crime committed in 1941, and its Polish clients permitted only Moscow's version of events to be presented. Mazowiecki broached the subject during a state visit to Moscow in November, calling it a wound that had not healed; he then visited Katyń and called for moral compensation for the victims. On April 12, 1990, Gorbachev admitted Soviet culpability. Two days later, TASS followed with a statement confirming that the massacre took place in 1940 and affixing blame on Beria, Merkulov, and the NKVD.

The government-in-exile responded swiftly. First, on April 13, Szczepanik issued a declaration directed at Moscow. He spelled out the government's expectations:

> We are now demanding the identification of previously unknown places of execution of a further ten thousand prisoners of war from Ostaszków and Starobielsk. We want to provide them all with a military funeral and celebrate them with a tribute to the Polish nation. We demand an official and solemn apology from the Soviet authorities. We demand material compensation from the Soviet Union for the closest members of the murdered families. We also demand that the names of all Soviet citizens who participated in the decision collection, planning and execution of this monstrous crime be revealed and punished.[36]

He closed with a demand for information on Poles deported into the Soviet Union during and after the war:

---

[36] "Oświadczenie Prezesa Rady Ministrów w sprawie przyznania się ZSSR do mordu w Katyniu z dnia 13 kwietnia 1990 r." ("Statement of the Prime Minister on the USSR's admission of responsibility for the Katyn massacre of April 13, 1990"), *DzU RP* No. 2 (Londyn), dnia 1 listopada, 1990 roku, s. 34–35.

Unfortunately, the above postulates do not exhaust the entire account of the population losses inflicted on Poland by the Soviets. In particular, we must not forget the fate of the approximately two million compatriots deported deep into the Soviet Union in 1940–1941 under terrible conditions, from where only a small part escaped. We cannot ignore the terrible fate of the thousands of soldiers of the Home Army illegally deported to the USSR in later years. We want to know the names of all Polish citizens killed, martyred and died on inhuman Soviet soil. We demand compensation for their families and for the Polish Nation for their labor and toil—bloodily forced by the Soviets during many years of persecution.[37]

Two weeks later, the Council of Ministers followed up with a statement intended for those who concealed the crime: "The Government of the Republic of Poland in Exile expects that the current state authorities in Warsaw strongly condemn all Polish citizens who, within 50 years of the crime, contributed to hiding it or shifting the blame for it onto the Germans, and expects that the surviving among them will be removed from any participation in Polish public life, while those persecuted for preaching the truth will receive compensation."[38]

Western governments that participated in the cover-up were not forgotten: "The Government of the Republic of Poland in Exile states that some Western governments concealed the truth known to them or even blamed the Germans for this crime and calls on them to make amends to the Polish people by helping them to recover from the Soviets." The Government closed with an expression of "… deep gratitude to all compatriots and foreigners for the political, journalistic and publishing work, thanks to which this monstrous Soviet crime lived for half a century in the conscience of the world, and finally led to the admission of the culprits."[39]

In July, *Rada Narodowa* passed a resolution calling for compensation from Moscow and urging Mazowiecki's government to pursue justice for the victims:

From the Kremlin rulers, who finally admitted after 50 years that the Katyń massacre was committed by the NKVD organs, we demand that

---

[37] "Oświadczenie Prezesa Rady Ministrów w sprawie przyznania się ZSSR do mordu w Katyniu z dnia 13 kwietnia 1990 r.," *DzU RP* No. 2 (Londyn), dnia 1 listopada, 1990 roku, s. 34–35.

[38] "Oświadczenie Rządu R.P. na Uchodźstwie z dnia 23 kwietnia 1990 roku" ("Statement of the Polish Government in Exile of April 23, 1990"), *DzU RP* No. 2 (Londyn), dnia 1 listopada, 1990 roku, s. 35–36.

[39] "Oświadczenie Rządu R.P. na Uchodźstwie z dnia 23 kwietnia 1990 roku," *DzU RP* No. 2 (Londyn), dnia 1 listopada, 1990 roku, s. 35–36.

our nation and members of the families of the murdered be properly compensated. We expect that the government of Tadeusz Mazowiecki will not cease making further efforts to reveal by the Kremlin further places of execution as soon as possible, based on reliable documents and testimonies of witnesses to the murders, and not to abandon the action aimed at punishing the perpetrators of these monstrous crimes.[40]

Moscow had finally admitted responsibility, but that was all. No compensation was paid. Some perpetrators were still alive, but none were brought to justice.[41] Mazowiecki's government stayed true to *gruba linia* and did not prosecute Poles who had participated in the coverup.

Back in New York, amidst allegations of missing funds, Konstanty Hanff had resigned from Greenpoint's Katyń memorial committee, but the matter was not closed. Thousands of dollars had not been accounted for, and Hanff's associates Marian Gołębiewski and Bronisław Baranowski remained in charge of the committee along with treasurer Leon Wiśniewski. With no answers forthcoming, irate contributors and community leaders called a meeting for Saturday, May 5, 1990, at *Dom Narodowy*.[42]

Gołębiewski and Baranowski attended the meeting and were confronted by allegations that they had failed to communicate the status and plans for the monument to its contractors and that they had illicitly transferred funds from the Committee's account at Chemical Bank into an account at the credit union in *Centrum Polsko-Słowiańskie* (Polish and Slavic Center)[43] without the consent or involvement of Wiśniewski. Gołębiewski and Baranowski left the meeting without defending or even discussing their actions and were replaced with a new chairman and secretary; Wiśniewski was also relieved of his duties.[44]

On Monday, the new chairman, secretary, and treasurer, accompanied by Wiśniewski and an attorney, met with credit union officials to revoke Gołębiewski's and Baranowski's access to the committee's account.

---

[40] "Rezolucja Rady Narodowej RP z dnia 28 lipca, 1990 r." ("Resolution of the National Council of the Republic of Poland of July 28, 1990,"), *DzU RP* No. 2 (Londyn), dnia 1 listopada, 1990 roku, s. 42–44.
[41] Remnants of the Communist Party of the Soviet Union and other factions repudiated Gorbachev's admission, denied the authenticity of the Beria memo, and continued to adhere to the Stalinist line that Katyń was a German crime.
[42] Greenpoint's *Dom Narodowy* (National Home) is located at 261 Driggs Avenue.
[43] The account was with the Polish & Slavic Federal Credit Union.
[44] The committee's new leaders were Bolesław Skaradziński (chairman), Zygmunt Czerwiński (secretary), and Lucjan Rutkowski (treasurer).

The next day, Gołębiewski and Baranowski visited the credit union and learned that they were no longer authorized to withdraw committee funds. They then proceeded to meet with a lawyer. Their lawyer drafted a letter claiming they had been illegally removed from the board. Another public meeting was planned for May 26 at *Dom Narodowy*, and donors were asked to bring proof of their payments.

While this meeting was being planned, Gołębiewski was making plans of a different sort. Having emigrated from Poland in 1982 to escape martial law, he now reversed course and returned to Poland, placing himself beyond the reach of the committee.[45]

Poland's citizens enthusiastically welcomed their newly regained political pluralism. In short order, KO "S", SD, reemergent prewar parties such as PPS and SN, and successors of PZPR and ZSL were joined by an array of new parties. Elections for local government offices were held in May 1990; KO "S" and other opposition parties scored impressive victories across the nation.

This rapid emergence of new parties coincided with mounting calls for Jaruzelski to step down, and this worried Wałęsa and his advisors. While they would welcome the end of Jaruzelski's presidency, continuing fragmentation of the opposition had resulted in over a dozen new parties to date, and if each were to propose its own presidential candidate, it was quite possible that SdRP could leverage PZPR's remnants to propel their candidate to victory. Wałęsa had the ability to block SdRP from claiming the presidency. In April, he was asked by a reporter from *Polska Agencja Prasowa* if he intended to run for the presidency, and he stated that he did. Shortly thereafter, Poland's public opinion polling agency *Centrum Badania Opinii Społecznej* (Public Opinion Research Center, or CBOS)[46] conducted a poll asking who should be president; Jaruzelski came in third and Wałęsa was fourth.[47]

Constituent republics of the Soviet Union began to follow the lead of Bloc nations. In 1988, Estonia held the Soviet Union's first free elections, and

---

[45] No public Katyń memorial was built in Greenpoint.
[46] CBOS was a relatively new organization. It was created in 1982 by one of Jaruzelski's advisors.
[47] Prime Minister Tadeusz Mazowiecki was supported by 24% of those polled. Bronisław Geremek came in second at 19%, followed by Jaruzelski 16.6%. Interestingly, at 16.1%, Wałęsa received less support than Jaruzelski.

its new parliament declared sovereignty in November 1988. Lithuania followed with free elections in February 1990; on March 11, Lithuania declared independence. Their declaration renewed the question of Poland's eastern borders. Lithuania's large Polish minority made Polish–Lithuanian relations and the border a question of paramount interest to émigré Poles.[48] *Rada Narodowa* issued a resolution welcoming the declaration and noting the need for Lithuania to respect the rights of ethnic Poles living within its borders.

The border question resurfaced in May. Mazowiecki's Minister of Foreign Affairs Krzysztof Skubiszewski made an unofficial visit to London, and a reporter asked him about his government's stance on Poland's eastern borders. He replied that Poland made no claims to territories that had been absorbed by the Soviet Union. Kaczorowski, Szczepanik, and the government were alarmed by his comment and were concerned that it would be taken as an official declaration of his acceptance of the Yalta border and therefore a territorial concession to the Soviet Union. They issued a corrective statement:

> During a private stay in London, the Minister of Foreign Affairs in the government of Tadeusz Mazowiecki, prof. Krzysztof Skubiszewski, at a press conference on May 10 this year, said that Poland has no claims to its former eastern lands. […] Statements about the territorial integrity of a state do not fall within the competence of ministers, if they are not based on relevant resolutions of sovereign parliaments. […] The eastern border of Poland with its neighbors can only be changed by free and sovereign parliaments of these countries.[49]

A deeper concern was that Skubiszewski was demonstrating a lack of political maturity, a growing concern about Mazowiecki's ministers among members of the exile government.

At the same time Skubiszewski made his troublesome comments, another minister in Mazowiecki's government was in London. Aleksander

---

[48] Despite numbering somewhere between one million and four million (Soviet census data is unreliable and unofficial estimates vary greatly), Poles were not considered to be an official minority in the Soviet Union and were not granted language or cultural rights. The only exception was in the Lithuanian SSR, where a large Polish presence remained in Vilnius (formerly Wilno) and the surrounding area. Poles who remained in territories that had been annexed to the Byelorussian SSR and Ukrainian SSR and those who had been deported to other Soviet republics were afforded no such rights.

[49] "Stanowisko Rządu w sprawie polskich ziem wschodnich" ("The Government's position on the Polish eastern territories"), *DzU RP* No. 2 (Londyn), dnia 1 listopada, 1990 roku, s. 36–37.

Hall, head of *Ministerstwo ds. Współpracy z Organizacjami Politycznymi i Stowarzyszeniami* (Ministry of Cooperation with Political Organizations and Associations), became the first official from Mazowiecki's government to pay a visit to 43 Eaton Place. On May 11, he met with Kaczorowski and Szczepanik to review the political situation in Poland and discuss contacts between Poland and the émigré community. Although his visit was unofficial, Hall's meeting marked the first contact between a member of Mazowiecki's government with the exile authorities.

Jaruzelski's opponents had been waiting for an opportunity to replace him, and the April CBOS poll provided an impetus. In July, deputies from several parties began to gather signatures on a petition calling on him to resign. Two days after they started, Jaruzelski signaled his willingness to leave office. Wałęsa called for early elections, and by mid-September his proposal received widespread support in the *Sejm*. Jaruzelski submitted a draft constitutional act shortening his term of office and introducing general elections to choose the next president.

Wałęsa was convinced that Poland needed a unifying figure in the elections, and believed he was he the only person who could fill that role. He declared his candidacy using the motto "*Nie chcę, ale muszę*" ("I don't want to, but I must"). His concerns that the opposition was fragmented were valid; sixteen candidates expressed their desire to run for the presidency.[50] Of the sixteen, only six managed to collect enough signatures necessary to be placed on the ballot: Włodzimierz Cimoszewicz from SdRP, Roman Bartoszcze of PSL, Leszek Moczulski from KPN, Canadian businessman Stanisław Tymiński, Mazowiecki, and Wałęsa.

Presidential campaigns were a new phenomenon in Poland. Most candidates chose to unleash personal attacks on their opponents in lieu of campaigning on policy; Mazowiecki was the exception. Émigré PPS leader Lidia Ciołkosz decried the level of discourse and attributed it to a lack of political experience.

---

[50] The sixteen candidates were Roman Bartoszcze (PSL); Jan Bratoszewski, a retired attorney from Radom; Janusz Bryczkowski (*Polska Partia Zielonych*, Polish Green Party); Włodzimierz Cimoszewicz (SdRP); Gabriel Janowski (*NSZZ RI "Solidarność,"* "Rural Solidarity"); Janusz Korwin-Mikke (*Unia Polityki Realnej*, Real Politics Union); Tadeusz Mazowiecki (independent); Edward Mizikowski (a *Solidarność* activist from Huta Warszawa); Leszek Moczulski (KPN); Kornel Morawiecki (*Partia Wolności*, Freedom Party); Józef Onoszko (*Stowarzyszenia Rozwoju Wyższej Świadomości "Refugium,"* Association for the Development of Higher Awareness "Refugium"); Władysław Siła-Nowicki (SP); Bolesław Tejkowski (*Polska Wspólnota Narodowa*, Polish National Community); Waldemar Trajdos, Łódź resident and former employee of insurance company PZU; Stanisław Tymiński (independent); and Lech Wałęsa.

Few of the reforms or concessions that *Solidarność* won during its legal existence survived martial law. *Trybunał Konstytucyjny* (Constitutional Tribunal) was one of the exceptions. Instituted to assess the constitutionality of actions taken by government agencies, within a few years its responsibilities were expanded to review the constitutionality of laws. In 1990, Mieczysław Tyczka, the tribunal's president, was forwarded an unusual letter from the United Kingdom. Its author, Juliusz Sokolnicki, presented himself as the president of Free Poland in Exile and offered to hand over his powers to a president chosen in free elections. As the letter's addressee was unfamiliar with Sokolnicki, he did not know how to respond. The letter was passed to various government officials until it landed on Tyczka's desk.

For eighteen years, a small minority of émigrés regarded Sokolnicki as the legitimate exile president and fervently defended his claim; many had received awards, titles, and military ranks from him. With Poland's presidential election approaching, Sokolnicki saw the opportunity to validate his claim to the presidency and the honors he had awarded.

None of those who had reviewed his letter were swayed by his assertions. They passed the letter onward to whomever they thought could adjudicate the matter, and it eventually came to Tyczka; he determined that he had no authority to accept Sokolnicki's offer or his claim to the exile presidency. In his reply to Sokolnicki, Tyczka declared that he and *Trybunał Konstytucyjny* had no competence to consider the matter. In effect, this meant that Warsaw considered Kaczorowski to be the émigré president.

Throughout the 1980s, Sokolnicki had endeavored to curry favor with influential people in Poland; unfortunately for him, none advocated for him, and his efforts to create a support base in Poland had come to nothing. Awards, honors, and military ranks dispensed by him would not be recognized in post-communist Poland. Sokolnicki was undeterred. He awarded military ranks to several more people in 1990.

The upcoming presidential election brought to the forefront questions of how and when the government-in-exile's mission would be complete. Kaczorowski felt that émigrés had knowledge and experience that would be vital for post-communist Poland and expanded on their continuing role in a November speech:[51]

---

[51] This speech was delivered at an SPK congress in New Jersey.

Many of us ask whether the pace of changes taking place in Poland is sufficient and how to respond to political disputes and fights taking place in the country. Political emigration has always recognized the separation of roles between a struggling country and emigration. Emigration carried out its activities for the freedom of Poland, and the country expanded the scope of freedom with the means available there. It is still our responsibility to watch over and cautiously assess the situation in the country. If we had failed, we would never have been forgiven for not having warned of the dangers when we had complete freedom and the ability to observe. The return to full democracy is fraught with difficulties largely due to the forty-five years of communist totalitarian rule. It destroyed the citizen's sense of responsibility for the state and people's ability to coexist. Success will not be complete if you do not apply democracy in life and teach that democracy is much more than holding elections or ruling by a majority of votes, that it is also about being, tact, a sense of civic responsibility and respect for the opponent.[52]

As the campaign progressed, Wałęsa understood that he had a strong chance to be elected president and began to think past the election to the inauguration and the formal transfer of power. He had no desire to accept the office from Jaruzelski, but he had an alternative at hand. Accepting power from Kaczorowski would simultaneously reject PRL's legitimacy and establish continuity with the Second Republic. Wałęsa decided that this was the best course of action and dispatched Zdzisław Najder to 43 Eaton Place. On October 12, he met with Kaczorowski and informed him that, if elected, Wałęsa would prefer to take power from him rather than Jaruzelski.

London's policy, set by Raczkiewicz in 1945, was that the government-in-exile would end its work when the exile president was able to hand over power to a president elected by the people of Poland in a free and democratic election. The April Constitution did not provide for presidential election by popular vote;[53] therefore, fulfilling Raczkiewicz's objective would require amending or replacing the April Constitution, actions that could only be undertaken by the *Sejm*. Thus, the government-in-exile and

---

[52] "Przemówienie Prezydenta Rzeczypospolitej na Zjeździe Stowarzyszenia Polskich Kombatantów 15 września 1990 roku w Perth Amboy" ("Speech by the President of the Republic of Poland at the Congress of the Polish Combatants Association on September 15, 1990, in Perth Amboy"), *DzU RP* No. 4 (Londyn), dnia 20 grudnia 1990 roku, s. 88–91.

[53] Under the April Constitution, the president was chosen by an assembly of electors appointed by the *Sejm* and *Senat*.

Rada Narodowa assumed that decommunization would proceed in five steps: first, withdrawal of Soviet troops from Poland; second, fully free *Sejm* and *Senat* elections; third, adoption of a new constitution; fourth, the presidential election; and finally, formal handover of power from the exile president to the newly elected president. *Rada Narodowa* reiterated this position in a resolution issued in late July:

> Polish independence emigration is the only one in the world that, based on the constitution of its own country [...], retained the foundations of legalism, i.e., continuity of the authorities and organs of the sovereign Polish State, headed by the President of the Republic. The 1935 Constitution, together with *Umowa Paryska,* is still in force. Due to the change in the current political conditions after the war, Poland requires a new constitution, which can only be adopted by the representation of the Polish nation, elected in democratic five-adjective elections.[54] Therefore, adoption of a new, democratic electoral law is of fundamental and most important significance for our nation. The present "35 percent" *Sejm* cannot pass a Constitution.[55]

Poland's new politicians gave little if any thought to the April Constitution or to London's plan. The government was functioning under what was known as the April Novelization, a revision of the much-amended 1952 Constitution; indeed, an amendment to the April Novelization that truncated Jaruzelski's term and introduced presidential elections by popular vote was the reason Najder and Kaczorowski were meeting. Poland was following a different path; first came free elections to local offices, then the presidential election; after that, legislative elections would be held, and a new constitution could be written and implemented. Ridding the nation of Jaruzelski was the priority.

Najder had placed Kaczorowski in a difficult position, but he concluded that he had to accept Najder's plan. The presidential election would occur and a new president would take office with or without his participation; choosing not to attend the inauguration would be ruinous to the government-in-exile's image. He declared his readiness to travel to Warsaw at the invitation of the newly elected president, whomever that would be, and to hand over the insignia of presidential power. After their initial discussion,

---

[54] Five-adjective elections, also known as five-point electoral law, is a Polish term referring to elections that are universal, direct, equal, proportional, and anonymous (i.e., secret ballot).
[55] "Rezolucja Rady Narodowej z dnia 28 lipca, 1990 r." ("Resolution of the National Council of July 28, 1990"), *DzU RP* No. 2 (Londyn), dnia 1 listopada, 1990 roku, s. 42–44.

Rada Narodowa chairman Zygmunt Szadkowski and Minister of Homeland Affairs Ryszard Zakrzewski joined the meeting and demanded free and democratic legislative elections as soon as possible.

Kaczorowski's statement was broadcast on Polish radio later that day. *Rada Narodowa* debated the matter at its October 19–20 meeting, and Szczepanik pointed out that Kaczorowski's statement applied to all presidential candidates, not only Wałęsa. At the conclusion of its meeting, *Rada Narodowa* issued a resolution reiterating that legislative elections must be held as soon as possible to "…create the necessary conditions for the transfer of the office of President Ryszard Kaczorowski to the newly elected President."[56] Lidia Ciołkosz voiced her objections in the pages of *Orzeł Biały*, declaring that Kaczorowski's decision disrupted the logical order of events. Kaczorowski addressed this conflict at a meeting with the American branch of *Rada Narodowa*:

[…] Before political emigration, a dilemma was faced: where to recognize that the goal set by us had been fulfilled? We expected that, in accordance with the wishes of the people, the Soviet troops would leave our country, that elections to both Legislative Chambers would be called, that a Constituent Assembly would be convened, which in turn would amend the Constitution or adopt a new one. This, in turn, will give rise to the election of the President of the Republic of Poland. Forty-five years have passed since President Władysław Raczkiewicz's statement and we found ourselves in a completely different political configuration, which he was unable to predict. […] We are looking forward to this breakthrough moment when completely free, democratic elections will result in the fully representative legislative bodies of the nation, its *Sejm* and *Senat*. But before that, free and universal elections for the office of President were announced. The order of things has been changed, and this will put us in a new situation, not planned by us.[57]

Other pieces critical of Kaczorowski's position appeared in *Dziennik Polski i Dziennik Żołnierza* and other émigré publications, but Kaczorowski

---

[56] "Uchwała Rady Narodowej R.P. z dnia 20 października 1990 r." ("Resolution of the National Council of the Republic of Poland of October 20, 1990"), *DzU RP* No. 4 (Londyn), dnia 20 grudnia 1990 roku, s. 97.

[57] "Przemówienie Prezydenta Rzeczypospolitej Ryszarda Kaczorowskiego na spotkaniu z Oddziałem Rady Narodowej R.P. w U.S.A. w Boulder, Colorado" ("Speech by the President of the Republic of Poland, Ryszard Kaczorowski, at a meeting with the Branch of the National Council of the Republic of Poland in the U.S.A. in Boulder, Colorado"), *DzU RP* No. 4 (Londyn), dnia 20 grudnia 1990 roku, s. 92–95.

held to his decision. He expanded on his decision in an interview with the Polish Section of the BBC, stating that the exile government had no other option but to accept this order of events.

Two other candidates followed Wałęsa's lead. On November 4, Kaczorowski met with Mazowiecki's representative, Aleksander Hall, and on November 14 he met with Grzegorz Hajdarowicz from Moczulski's campaign. Kaczorowski made the same pledge to them as he had to Najder. Both envoys also met with Szadkowski and other exile authorities and received the same demand for free legislative elections.

The objective of Najder's meeting with Kaczorowski was to enable Wałęsa, if elected, to avoid accepting power from Jaruzelski. Najder achieved his goal, but in so doing, he elevated the image of the government-in-exile in Poland. Media coverage of the meeting sparked extraordinary interest in the exile government. Journalist Jerzy Bukowski detected opportunism in Wałęsa's interest in Kaczorowski, recalling that neither Wałęsa nor Mazowiecki had met with him during their recent visits to London, but he did not condemn Wałęsa's actions; in his view, accepting power from Jaruzelski would confer undeserved dignity on the PRL era. Jerzy Giedroyc of *Kultura* considered Wałęsa's outreach to Kaczorowski to be more a move to distance himself from Jaruzelski than a recognition of the legitimacy of the government-in-exile. Regardless of Bukowski's and Giedroyc's concerns, regard for the London government by the people of Poland was at its highest point since the 1940s.

Popular sentiments in Poland towards the government-in-exile may have been on the rise, but many of the nation's new politicians viewed London as little more than a source of funds. Requests ranged from subsidies for schools to scholarships, funds for publications, and political campaign contributions. Exile politicians had experience in diplomacy, keen insights into how Western democracies function, and valuable contacts, but with very few exceptions, their advice was not sought. Szczepanik expressed his frustration in an interview with *Tygodnik Powszechny*, suggesting that Poland viewed émigrés as milk cows dispensing dollars and pounds and ignored their knowledge and experiences.

43 Eaton Place's popularity with guests from Poland stood in contrast to the dearth of visitors to Colchester. No government functionaries, representatives of presidential candidates, or activists called on Sokolnicki. His *Rada Regencyjna* proposal had fallen flat, and his lack of relevance and recognition in Poland did not bode well for his legitimacy or for that of the ranks, honors, and awards he had dispensed. On November 11, he

attempted to reassert his relevance by issuing "*Akt przekazania suwerennej władzy*" (Act of Transferring Sovereign Power):

> We, Juliusz Nowina-Sokolnicki,[58] President of the Republic of Poland in Exile from April 6, 1972, on the basis of a nomination issued on September 22, 1971, by the late August Zaleski, President of the Republic of Poland in Exile, in accordance with Article 24 of the Constitution of 1935, the Ministers of State and other State Dignitaries whose signatures are placed under this Act, we transfer all sovereign power that the Republic of Poland in Exile had so far, as continuator of the Second Republic of Poland established in 1918, to the hands of the Republic of Poland with its seat in Warsaw, and also, in accordance with Article 24 of the Constitution of 1935, on behalf of ourselves and on behalf of all claimants to the nomination received from the late President A. Zaleski, we irrevocably appoint as legal successor to the office of the President of the Republic a person who will be legally elected as a result of general elections scheduled for November 25, 1990, and we hand over the office of the President upon his swearing-in, thus entrusting the new President and the Government appointed by him the same sovereign power we have so far exercised under the Constitution of 1935.

"*Akt przekazania suwerennej władzy*" was received by the presidential civil chancellery in Warsaw on December 9 and was disregarded.

---

43 Eaton Place is little more than two miles from Poland's embassy at 47 Portland Place, but the ideological difference between them was vast until Tadeusz de Virion was appointed ambassador in 1990.[59] On November 5, de Virion took Marshal of the *Senat* Andrzej Stelmachowski on the short trip to Eaton Place to meet with Kaczorowski. This was the first meeting between an exile president and Poland's ambassador to the United Kingdom. Stelmachowski was responsible for planning the presidential inauguration, and they discussed the transfer of authority, conclusion of the government-in-exile's mission, and repatriation of the insignia of presidential power, including presidential seals, the original of the April

---

[58] In an unusual idiosyncrasy, Sokolnicki referred to himself in the first-person plural in "*Akt przekazania suwerennej władzy.*" This convention is typically affected only by monarchs.

[59] Tadeusz de Virion was an AK veteran and had fought in the Warsaw Uprising. After the war, he became an attorney. During martial law, he represented several opposition activists who were brought to trial.

Constitution, and the flag that had flown over Warsaw's Royal Castle at the time Poland was invaded. All had been evacuated from Poland along with Mościcki and his government.[60]

Stelmachowski had gone to the trouble to gain an understanding of exile politics, and de Virion had briefed him well about émigré objections to Kaczorowski's statement. He held a press conference after their meeting; when asked about the transfer of insignia, he displayed a high level of sensitivity. He stated that the insignia could be transferred after the presidential election or after *Sejm* and *Senat* elections and that he did not want this issue to be the cause of a split in the émigré community.

It was up to Kaczorowski to resolve the matter. On November 26, he chaired a meeting with Szczepanik, the Council of Ministers, *Rada Narodowa* chairman Szadkowski, *Skarb Narodowy* president Ludwik Łubieński, and political party leaders. Their meeting was "devoted to the exchange of views in connection with political changes taking place in the country."[61] Despite some opposition, Kaczorowski received the support he needed, and one week later he appointed a delegation that would travel to Warsaw to finalize conditions for transferring the insignia of office. Chaired by Szadkowski, the delegation also included Jerzy Morawicz, Zygmunt Szkopiak, and Jerzy Zaleski.

On the last Sunday in November, Western journalists fanned out across Poland to report on the latest milestone in the collapse of communism, Poland's presidential election. The following day, *Państwowa Komisja Wyborcza* (State Electoral Commission) released its official results. Wałęsa received the most support, taking just under 40 percent of the votes cast. Next came Stanisław Tymiński at 23 percent. Mazowiecki came in a distant third, receiving 18 percent; following him was Cimoszewicz at about 9 percent and Bartoszcze at about 7 percent. Moczulski, with 2.5 percent, came in last.

These results contained several surprises. Mazowiecki received far less support than expected, and Cimoszewicz was unable to capture all of the former PZPR vote. The biggest shock was Tymiński. He portrayed himself

---

[60] The items included in what was referred to as the presidential insignia were the flag that few over the Royal Castle at the outbreak of the war, the original parchment copy of the April Constitution, three metal seals with the inscription Prezydent Rzeczypospolitej (one for ink, one for lacquer, and one for embossing paper), and three metal seals of varying sizes bearing the inscription "Kancelaria Senatu." Also included were the insignia of the orders *Orzeł Biały* and *Polonia Restituta*.

[61] "Komunikat Kancelarii Cywilnej Prezydenta Rzeczypospolitej" ("Announcement from the Civil Chancellery of the President of the Republic of Poland"), *DzU RP* No. 4 (Londyn), dnia 20 grudnia 1990 roku, s. 100.

as an outsider bringing new solutions that would launch Poland into a new era of prosperity, and he created an air of mystery and intrigue by always carrying a black briefcase that he claimed contained secret papers that would ruin his opponents. As no candidate received a simple majority of the votes cast, *Państwowa Komisja Wyborcza* announced a runoff election. On Sunday December 9, Poland would vote again; this time their only choices were Wałęsa or Tymiński.

Tymiński's success brought scrutiny. Newspapers published results of their investigations into his dealings, and TVP broadcast a program examining his private life. The candidates met once for a televised debate. Tymiński threatened Wałęsa with the contents of his now-famous briefcase, but he was not prepared for his opponent's response. Wałęsa leaned forward and snapped, "I demand immediate publication of these documents, absolutely, right now." Startled, Tymiński answered, "Perhaps we can talk privately," but Wałęsa refused to back down, declaring: "No. If you accuse me, show the documents." For the remainder of the debate, Tymiński was peppered with questions about his employment of former SB officers on his campaign staff, a fact Wałęsa used to draw a link between Tymiński and Poland's former communist structures. After the debate ended, Tymiński canceled his scheduled appearance at a second televised debate. Revelations about Tymiński, coupled with his behavior during the runoff campaign, caused alarm across most political parties and drove Mazowiecki, Bartoszcze, and Moczulski to endorse Wałęsa. London was sufficiently concerned to drop its neutrality and openly endorse Wałęsa:

> The Government of the Republic of Poland in Exile did not take a position towards candidates seeking election by the nation for the office of the President of the Republic of Poland. However, in the current situation, the Government of the Republic of Poland in Exile considers it its duty to warn our compatriots in the country against the incalculable consequences of putting into unknown hands the highest Office of the Republic of Poland in the second vote on December 9 this year. We hope this time voters will support the only acceptable candidate: Lech Wałęsa, leader of *Solidarność*. We call on all our compatriots in the country to participate in these elections as much as possible, which are an important step on the way to Poland's restoration of full sovereignty.[62]

---

[62] "Stanowisko Rządu Rzeczypospolitej na Uchodźstwie wobec wyborów prezydenckich w Kraju" ("The position of the Government of the Republic of Poland in Exile on the presidential elections in the country"), *DzU RP* No. 4 (Londyn), dnia 20 grudnia 1990 roku, s. 99.

General Rudnicki joined the effort, issuing an "Open Letter to the Polish Nation" in the pages of *Dziennik Polski i Dziennik Żołnierza*. Wałęsa handily defeated Tymiński, receiving nearly three quarters of the vote.

Szczepanik and Szadkowski informed Kaczorowski that the government and *Rada Narodowa* supported his decision to transfer power to Wałęsa. Kaczorowski sent Wałęsa a congratulatory telegram. He then convened a meeting with Szczepanik, the Council of Ministers, Szadkowski, Łubieński, and political party leaders to further plan for the inauguration. Later that week, Stelmachowski invited the London delegation to Warsaw. They met with Stelmachowski and Jacek Merkel, head of Wałęsa's chancellery, on December 17 and 18 in the *Senat* building to discuss "the principles and forms of transferring the legal continuity of the Second Republic to the newly elected President and the presidential insignia connected with it."[63] During their stay, Stelmachowski appeared on Polish television and discussed émigré affairs.

As the Warsaw meeting began, Szczepanik and his Council of Ministers assembled. Transferring power remained controversial among some émigrés, and the government sought a means to make it more palatable. They told Kaczorowski that he should go to Warsaw to transfer his authority and the presidential insignia provided that Wałęsa met four conditions: that he would personally request Kaczorowski to do so, that he would justify the urgency of the transition, that he would set a date for fully free *Sejm* and *Senat* elections, and that he would permit members of the exile government to accompany Kaczorowski.

Stelmachowski's two-day meeting concluded with an announcement of the plan of events. He would host the ceremony at the Royal Castle on December 22. Wałęsa and Kaczorowski would sign a protocol proclaiming the transfer of presidential authority and the insignia; the protocol would also declare that *Rada Narodowa* would continue to function until legislative elections the following year. Both Wałęsa and Kaczorowski agreed to the plan, and that same day Stelmachowski invited Kaczorowski to Warsaw.

On June 29, 1945, Władysław Raczkiewicz had established the conditions to complete the government-in-exile's mission. On December 20, 1990, Ryszard Kaczorowski issued a decree declaring that it had completed

---

[63] "Komunikat Kancelarii Cywilnej Prezydenta Rzeczypospolitej w sprawie terminu, zasad i formy przekazania nowo wybranemu Prezydentowi ciągłości prawnej II Rzeczypospolitej oraz związanych z tym insygniów prezydenckich" ("Announcement of the Civil Chancellery of the President of the Republic of Poland regarding the date, principles and form of transferring the legal continuity of the Second Polish Republic and the related presidential insignia to the newly elected President"), *DzU RP* No. 4 (Londyn), dnia 20 grudnia 1990 roku, s. 101–102.

its mission. He dismissed Szczepanik and dissolved his government. Kaczorowski issued a series of decrees and letters that day. He dissolved *Skarb Narodowy* and established a liquidation commission. He appointed members to *Komisja Likwidacyjna Rządu Rzeczypospolitej* (Liquidation Commission of the Government of the Republic) and to *Komisja Likwidacyjna Skarbu Narodowego* (Liquidation Commission of the National Treasury). He sent dismissal letters to Szczepanik and all government ministers; he thanked Szczepanik for his many years of service and for his efforts to create an atmosphere of camaraderie and harmony. One day later, he dismissed Bohdan Wendorff from his position as head of the civil chancellery, an office he had held since 1975,[64] and thanked him for his service and dedication. Wendorff's dismissal was effective on December 22; he still had work to do in the transfer of insignia. Kaczorowski then issued his final message to the diaspora:

COUNTRYMEN!

On June 29, 1945, the then-President of the Republic of Poland, Władysław Raczkiewicz, issued a message in London to the Polish nation. In this address, the President announced that he would transfer his office to a successor elected by the people in free and unfettered elections as soon as they could be held.

Poland has waited over forty-five years for this day. My predecessors in the office of the President of the Republic of Poland—August Zaleski, Stanisław Ostrowski, Edward Raczyński and Kazimierz Sabbat—repeated Władysław Raczkiewicz's statement. When I assumed this high office on July 19, 1989, I did not know when I would be able to hand it over to a successor chosen by the nation.

Unexpected rapid political changes in Poland significantly shortened our waiting time. Here on December 9 this year, the Polish nation, by an overwhelming majority of votes, chose Lech Wałęsa, the leader of the legendary "Solidarność," as President of the Republic of Poland.

I wish our worthy successor strength, health, and happiness in carrying out his difficult duties in this crucial period in the history of our nation.

---

[64] Wendorff headed the civil chancellery for four presidents. His extended tenure earned him the sobriquet "*klucznik Zamku*" ("gatekeeper of the Castle").

By handing over the office of the President of the Republic of Poland and the insignia connected with it tomorrow to Lech Wałęsa at the Royal Castle in Warsaw, I will place in his complete care the independent, free, democratic, and just Poland for which the soldiers of September 1939, the Polish Armed Forces in the West and the heroic Home Army fought. Above all else to them I offer deep reverence today.

I will give President Lech Wałęsa the sovereignty over independent emigration, which fulfilled its mission by carefully preserving the idea of an independent Poland. It did not manage to achieve all of its political goals. They will be taken over by political parties rising in a free country.

Finishing my activities and thinking about my predecessors as President of the Republic of Poland, I can say with deep gratitude that in the difficult half-century work in exile, none of them compromised their oath of allegiance to our Republic. May their loyalty to the Nation, their faithfulness to its laws and traditions become a signpost that will save us all from fragmentation and will firmly unite us in the service of Poland.

The grateful memory of the nation will also forever remain the enormous and highly devoted effort of its two generations of political emigration and freedom movements in the country.

By handing over the office of the President of the Republic of Poland from London to Warsaw, we confidently cry out:

Long live the sovereign Republic of Poland![65]

Early on Saturday, December 22, 1990, Ryszard and Karolina Kaczorowski and their family left their house in Willesden for the Ealing Broadway underground station and boarded a train headed to Heathrow. At the airport, they were escorted to an area designated for private flights. Waiting

---

[65] "Orędzie Prezydenta Rzeczypospolitej Ryszarda Kaczorowskiego wydane w Londynie, dnia 21 grudnia 1990 roku" ("Address by the President of the Republic of Poland, Ryszard Kaczorowski, issued in London on December 21, 1990"), *DzU RP* Nr. 5 (Londyn), dnia 22 grudnia 1990 r., s. 126–127.

for them were Ambassador de Virion, Stelmachowski's representative Senator Andrzej Celiński, and Wałęsa's representative Senator Jarosław Kaczyński. Kaczorowski was accompanied by about fifty people, including members of the government and *Rada Narodowa*, leaders of exile political parties, veterans' organizations, social organizations, and eminent émigrés. Bohdan Wendorff oversaw transportation of the presidential insignia. Minister of Information Walery Choroszewski chose to remain in London, citing his personal opposition to the transfer as well as objections from the émigré community and from within Poland.

Stelmachowski had arranged for LOT Polish Airlines to provide an aircraft. The plan was to time the flight so it crossed into Polish airspace at the very moment Jaruzelski surrendered power, but their flight was delayed and they arrived at Warsaw's military airport a few minutes late. A group of government officials, including Stelmachowski, awaited them, along with a number of high-ranking military officers, an honor guard, and a military orchestra. The pilot brought their aircraft to a stop, its door was opened, and stairs were put in place. As Kaczorowski emerged, the orchestra's drummers began a cadence. When his feet touched the ground, the orchestra commenced the national anthem, and he was addressed as *"pan Prezydent"* ("Mr. President"). After brief greetings, the entourage was transported to Warsaw. A villa near *Pałac Belwederski* (Belweder Palace, the presidential residence) was placed at Kaczorowski's disposal. Most of the others were taken to a hotel; Wendorff and the insignia were driven directly to the Royal Castle to prepare for the ceremony.

At 3:40 p.m., Kaczorowski and his wife were welcomed at the Royal Castle. Twenty minutes later, Lech and Danuta Wałęsa arrived. After a short conversation, Wałęsa, Kaczorowski, and Stelmachowski entered the Assembly Hall and took their places. Stelmachowski opened the proceedings with a brief speech:

> We are gathered to participate in the ceremony of handing over the presidential insignia of the Second Republic of Poland to Lech Wałęsa, the President of the Republic of Poland, who was sworn in today and chosen by the will of the nation. But I think there is something more to this act. It is an act of recognition for the struggle of thousands of combatants remaining outside the country. It is an act of recognition for those who carried the banner and proclaimed the slogans of independence, even when we, here in the country, had to remain silent. Finally, it is an act of recognition for all those who were able to believe

in Poland and bring hope for her resurrection, even against all circumstances. *Contra spem sperare*⁶⁶ —it is a very difficult thing, and yet those who came here from far away were able to testify to this with their attitude. Thanks to them for that. I also believe that today's act is a milestone in building the foundations of the Third Republic, drawing refreshing lifeblood from the tradition and the earlier, older, and the latter, newer Republic; it is a recognition that we have returned to a free Poland, struggling with many adversities, but nevertheless sovereign. From now on, we will join our efforts and—I believe it deeply—we will have a homeland that is not only free but also prosperous, not only democratic but also just.⁶⁷

Kaczorowski followed with his comments:

I come from London to the Royal Castle in Warsaw, destroyed by foreign violence, but rebuilt from rubble by the efforts of an unbending nation. I arrive surrounded by comrades in arms fighting for a homeland that is truly free and sovereign, sincerely democratic, just for all. I am coming to the reborn Poland to hand over the state insignia of the Second Republic to the freely elected President Lech Wałęsa. For many years, from the tragic year 1939, these insignia were both the proof of our legality and a symbol of our faith in the reconstruction of our martyred country. The legitimate Polish authorities outside the country ceased to be recognized by the diplomatic chancelleries of foreign governments, but they were accredited in Polish hearts both in the homeland and abroad. This jewel of patriotic fidelity to that which did not perish shone with a special glow in the depths of the national night. In handing over these insignia, together with the banner of the Republic which once flew over this castle, I see in them the golden key to a better future for this, our beloved native land.⁶⁸

---

⁶⁶ The Latin phrase "*Contra spem sperare*" translates as "To hope against hope."
⁶⁷ "Przemówienie Marszałka Senatu Rzeczypospolitej, prof. Andrzeja Stelmachowskiego na uroczystości przekazania insygniów prezydenckich na Zamku Królewskim w Warszawie w dniu 22 grudnia 1990 roku" ("Speech by the Marshal of the Senate of the Republic of Poland, Professor Andrzej Stelmachowski, at the ceremony of handing over the presidential insignia at the Royal Castle in Warsaw on December 22, 1990"), *DzU RP* Nr. 5 (Londyn), dnia 22 grudnia 1990 r., s. 112–113.
⁶⁸ "Przemówienie Prezydenta Rzeczypospolitej na Uchodźstwie Ryszarda Kaczorowskiego na uroczystości przekazania insygniów prezydenckich nowoobranemu Prezydentowi Lechowi Wałęsie na Zamku Królewskim w Warszawie w dniu 22 grudnia 1990 roku" ("Speech by the President of the Republic of Poland in Exile, Ryszard Kaczorowski, at the ceremony of handing over the presidential insignia to the newly elected President Lech Wałęsa at the Royal Castle in Warsaw on December 22, 1990"), *DzU RP* Nr. 5 (Londyn), dnia 22 grudnia 1990 r., s. 113.

Wałęsa then spoke:

We are experiencing a special moment. On September 2, 1939, the President of the Republic of Poland left the Castle on a long journey. Today, after many years, this journey has come to an end. The President of the Republic in Exile, a symbol of our sovereignty, is back at the Castle, in his seat. He returned here with the insignia of state power after "years abroad. [...] You carried the banner of freedom with pride. You have fulfilled the greatest patriotic duty towards the Motherland. Poland emerged victorious from this historical trial, not diminished in her rights. We are still far from normal. We are at its beginning. We must build a democratic, independent and prosperous Poland. A Poland with a clear political and economic system. So right now, as the march towards Europe is accelerating, we will need help and multiple examples in the political and commercial, industrial and cultural spheres. There must be an exchange on all levels. And we will not get there without the help of our Polish institutions scattered all over the world, without Poles willing to participate in the life of the country. [...] The Polish authorities in exile have fulfilled their historic mission with dignity and victory. Once again, I thank the President for everything.[69]

Lech Wałęsa and Ryszard Kaczorowski at the Royal Castle in Warsaw, December 22, 1990. *Photo by PAP / Alamy stock photo.*

---

[69] "Przemówienie nowobranego Prezydenta Rzeczypospolitej Lecha Wałęsy na uroczystości przekazania insygniów prezydenckich na Zamku Królewskim w Warszawie w dniu 22 grudnia 1990 roku" ("Speech by the newly elected President of the Republic of Poland, Lech Wałęsa, at the ceremony of handing over the presidential insignia at the Royal Castle in Warsaw on December 22, 1990"), *DzU RP* Nr. 5 (Londyn), dnia 22 grudnia 1990 r., s. 114.

Wałęsa and Kaczorowski then proceeded to the table where the presidential insignia were displayed. The event concluded with the playing of the national anthem. After a brief break, Wałęsa, Kaczorowski, and the guests proceeded to the Cathedral of St. John the Baptist for Mass. Archbishop Bronisław Dąbrowski addressed his sermon to the government-in-exile, likening their time in exile to the Advent season:

> It was your longing for your homeland, for this kingdom of Mary, that led you on the path of penance. The longing for a free homeland was the dominant feature of your aspirations, sacrifices and desires. So you went on a path of penance, fraught with suffering and pain, and finally, after fifty years, you have reached the goal of meeting your brothers in the heart of Mary's kingdom. [...] Today, Poland says thanks, heartfelt thanks, "God bless you," expresses gratitude—for the heroism of the Polish soldier, for remaining as witnesses at all ends of the earth, convinced that Poland is alive, that Poland endures, fights, that Poland prays. [...] Thank you, thank you, that you fought for the independence of Poland, that you told the truth about Poland, that you fought for the freedom of the Church, for the release of the imprisoned Primate [...] testifying that Poland was betrayed by the Allies, convinced that "Poland has not yet perished." [...] Mr. President, your visit, the presence of you and your faithful companions, begins a new chapter in the history of Poland. You close the book of Poland of the Second Republic, and you are a link on the road to the Third Republic...[70]

Later that evening, Stelmachowski accompanied his guests to *Dom Polonii*, seat of *Stowarzyszenie "Wspólnota Polska"* (Association "Polish Community"), a new organization created to strengthen ties between Poland and Polonia. There, several hundred guests greeted the London contingent, shared *opłatek*,[71] and exchanged Christmas greetings. On Sunday, Kaczorowski hosted a lunch at *Kasyno Garnizonowe*[72] for Stelmachowski,

---

[70] "Uzupełniające Informacje do Czesci II, Dział Nieurzedowy Dziennika Ustaw Rzeczypospolitej No. 5 z dnia 22 grudnia 1990 roku" ("Supplementary Information to Part II, Unofficial Section of the Journal of Laws of the Republic of Poland No. 5 of 22 December 1990"), *Dziennik Ustaw Rzeczypospolitej Polskiej*, Londyn, s. 3–6.

[71] *Opłatek* is an unleavened wafer traditionally shared before the Christmas Eve dinner. Outside of a Christmas Eve dinner such as Kaczorowski and his group participated in, an *opłatek* ceremony is an exchange of Christmas greetings.

[72] *Kasyno Garnizonowe* was located at Aleja Jana Chrystiana Szucha 29. In Poland, a *kasyno* was a rest and recreation center where military personnel could avail themselves of food, entertainment, and relaxation. A *kasyno* typically had a kitchen and dining room, meeting rooms, a library, and a game room.

Senat Vice Marshal Dr. Zofia Kuratowska, and other guests from Poland. Attending were members of the last exile government, *Rada Narodowa* members, *Skarb Narodowy* chairman Łubieński, Anna Sabbatowa, Irena Andersowa, General Klemens Rudnicki, and Bernard Braine. Afterwards, the Kaczorowski family and most of the London contingent departed for the airport.

Exiles and the Third Republic

43 EATON PLACE had endured as the symbol of free Poland and had been at the center of émigré politics since 1945. It had been the site of five presidential inaugurations, hundreds of Council-of-Ministers meetings, and dozens of commemorations of national holidays and solemn events. It had been visited by opposition activists from Poland, representatives from other exile governments and committees, and members of Parliament. For years, the president had hosted members of the government, *Rada Narodowa*, *Skarb Narodowy*, political parties, and émigré organizations at the beginning of each year to deliver his customary greetings.

On January 1, 1991, more than two hundred people arrived at 43 Eaton Place for the final celebration. Kaczorowski opened by remembering those who preceded him and thanking those who had served or supported the exile government:

> [...] Thinking about my predecessors as President of the Republic, I can say with deep gratitude that in the difficult half-century work in exile, none of them compromised their oath of allegiance to our Republic. May their loyalty to the Nation, their faithfulness to its laws and traditions become a signpost that will save us all from shattering and will firmly unite us in the service of Poland. The grateful memory of the nation will also forever remain the enormous and highly devoted effort of her two generations of political emigration and freedom movements in the country. I would like to thank all those who have never lost faith in Poland.[1]

Szczepanik followed with thanks for Kaczorowski for his service. He then honored the long line of exile prime ministers and called for documentation of the government-in-exile's activities:

> As we stand today at the end of a long phase of independence in exile, we can perhaps say that the time has come to commemorate our

---

[1] "Przemówienie Prezydenta Ryszarda Kaczorowskiego" ("Speech by President Ryszard Kaczorowski"), *Uzupełniające Informacje do Czesci II, Dział Nieurzedowy Dziennika Ustaw Rzeczypospolitej No. 5 z dnia 22 grudnia 1990 roku*, Londyn, s. 7–8.

achievements for future generations through historical publications, films, archives and museum collections. Our efforts to mobilize Polish refugees to work for independence should be documented. It is necessary to describe our presentation and defense of Polish interests in the international arena. Above all, we should consolidate our political, moral, material and cultural assistance to our countrymen in the country in their struggle for independence, freedom, wholeness, justice, and democracy.[2]

He concluded by recalling the opening words of the April Constitution that obliged each generation with increasing the strength and dignity of Poland and declaring that emigration had fulfilled its duty well.

General Rudnicki then made a brief comment: "Perhaps the biggest thing that could happen to us soldiers of the Second Polish Republic was the celebration of December 22 in Warsaw at the Royal Castle, the magnificent *Te Deum Laudamus* in our wonderful diocesan basilica of St. John the Baptist. We have been waiting forty-five years for this to finish this military service with arms in hand and to make what happened on December 22 possible."[3]

Szadkowski recounted the experiences of his delegation in its preparatory trip to Warsaw, starting with its unexpected greeting at the airport by government officials, military units, and a military orchestra. He finished by thanking Kaczorowski for his service and reminding him that his work was not complete by quoting Wałęsa: "Mr. President, your role in the life of the nation is not over yet, I will be in touch with you both on a private and business basis."[4]

Kaczorowski returned to the podium for his final comments. He again expressed his gratitude to members of the government, *Rada Narodowa*, *Skarb Narodowy*, political parties, and émigré organizations; he also thanked Bohdan Wendorff, Edward Raczyński, General Rudnicki, Bishop Wesoły, and Ambassador de Virion. He then concluded the final New

---

[2] "Przemówienie ostatniego Prezesa Rady Ministrów na Uchodźstwie. prof. dr. Edwarda Szczepanika" ("Speech by the last Prime Minister in Exile, Prof. Dr. Edward Szczepanik"), *Uzupełniające Informacje do Czesci II, Dział Nieurzedowy Dziennika Ustaw Rzeczypospolitej No. 5 z dnia 22 grudnia 1990 roku*, Londyn, s. 9–11.

[3] "Przemówienie gen. dyw. Klemensa Rudnickiego" ("Speech by Major General Klemens Rudnicki"), *Uzupełniające Informacje do Czesci II, Dział Nieurzedowy Dziennika Ustaw Rzeczypospolitej No. 5 z dnia 22 grudnia 1990 roku*, Londyn, s. 11.

[4] "Przemówienie Przewodniczącego Rady Narodowej Rzeczypospolitej Polskiej, Zygmunta Szadkowskiego" ("Speech by the Chairman of the National Council of the Republic of Poland, Zygmunt Szadkowski"), *Uzupełniające Informacje do Czesci II, Dział Nieurzedowy Dziennika Ustaw Rzeczypospolitej No. 5 z dnia 22 grudnia 1990 roku*, Londyn, s. 11–14.

Year event at 43 Eaton Place: "It is our last meeting, and it is Christmas time. So I would like to break *opłatek* with you, wishing all gathered here a happy New Year, all personal well-being and the best results in the service of Poland."[5]

After *opłatek*, the crowd slowly dispersed. Many lingered, taking a last look around. When the last guest had departed, the lights were extinguished and the door to *Zamek* was locked.

The following day, work to conclude the government-in-exile's affairs began in earnest. Szczepanik chaired *Komisja Likwidacyjna Rządu Rzeczypospolitej Polskiej*, and most of its members had been ministers in his government. They had much to do. They had to dispose of 43 Eaton Place and its contents, including government archives, and end publication of official government journals. They had to close nine ministries, twenty delegate offices,[6] the civil chancellery, NIK, *Rada Narodowa*, and its branches in the United States, Canada, and West Germany. *Komisja Likwidacyjna* deposited government archives at the Polish Institute and Sikorski Museum.[7] Books with no archival value were donated to *Biblioteka Polska* at POSK. The director of Warsaw's Royal Castle visited 43 Eaton Place and identified items of historical significance, including portraits of the exile presidents, paintings, artifacts, memorabilia, furnishings, and carpets; these were donated to the Castle. Other significant items were given to the Polish embassy on Portland Place. Publication of *Dziennik Ustaw RP*, *Polish Affairs*, and *Rzeczpospolita Polska* was ended. *Komisja Likwidacyjna* created the Polonia Aid Foundation Trust (PAFT), a nonpolitical organization chartered to provide financial assistance for educational, cultural and historical activities in the Polish émigré community.

Skarb Narodowy chairman Ludwik Łubieński headed *Komisja Likwidacyjna Skarbu Narodowego* (Liquidation Commission of the National Treasury).[8] Its members had to liquidate Danina Polska Ltd., close its more than one hundred local committees, and disburse assets exceeding

---

[5] "Na zakończenie uroczystości Prezydent Ryszard Kaczorowski wygłosił jeszcze następujące przemówienie" ("At the end of the ceremony, President Ryszard Kaczorowski delivered the following speech"), *Uzupełniające Informacje do Czesci II, Dział Nieurzedowy Dziennika Ustaw Rzeczypospolitej No. 5 z dnia 22 grudnia 1990 roku*, Londyn, s. 14–15.

[6] At the time of liquidation, the government-in-exile had delegates in Argentina, Australia, Austria, Belgium, Brazil, Canada, Chile, Denmark, France, West Germany, Holland, Italy, Mexico, New Zealand, South Africa, Zimbabwe, Sweden, Switzerland, the United States, and Venezuela.

[7] Szadkowski disagreed with this decision. He wanted the archives to be transferred to Warsaw.

[8] Łubieński had left Poland with Minister of Foreign Affairs Józef Beck in September 1939. From Romania, he got to France and was detained at Cerizay. In the United Kingdom, he returned to active duty and headed Poland's maritime mission in Gibraltar; he was an eyewitness to the crash of Sikorski's aircraft. After the war, he held various government positions, served in *Rada Narodowa*, and was the last chair of *Komisja Główna Skarbu Państwa*.

£500,000.⁹ Jerzy Ostoja-Koźniewski, the last minister of the treasury and a member of *Komisja Likwidacyjna Rządu Rzeczypospolitej Polskiej*, asked Wałęsa for his instructions on dispersing *Skarb Narodowy's* assets. Wałęsa advised him to leave them in London. After deducting liquidation expenses, Ostoja-Koźniewski transferred the remainder to PAFT.

Rada Narodowa members from PPS and PSL complained that *Komisja Likwidacyjna* was undemocratic as it had no representatives from some parties. Szczepanik countered that it was not a political body and only oversaw matters regarding property, personnel, documentation, archives, and publishing; he went on to state that it would consult *Rada Narodowa* until its dissolution. His assurances did not convince the more strident *Rada* members, particularly Lidia Ciołkosz and Władysław Szkoda, who continued to insist on expansion of *Komisja Likwidacyjna*. Their objections culminated in a demand that *Komisja* submit itself to the control of NIK and *Rada Narodowa*. *Rada* chairman Szadkowski went so far as to travel to Warsaw in an unsuccessful attempt to enlist the support of Stelmachowski; he then created a consultative committee intended to coordinate with *Komisja*. This failed to achieve its intended purpose, and at the end of April, a *Rada* member proposed that the two bodies no longer meet. *Komisja Likwidacyjna* readily agreed, but it continued to be criticized by *Rada Narodowa*.

PAFT also came under *Rada Narodowa* criticism. Szadkowski claimed that its legal structure and staff did not meet émigrés' needs. Szczepanik rejected this contention, noting that PAFT had been established by Kaczorowski in agreement with *Rada Narodowa*; at PAFT's inception, *Rada Narodowa* was allocated four trustees to its board, agreed to how it would function, and agreed that it would be apolitical.

This left the matter of 43 Eaton Place. Poland's embassy on Portland Place had sufficient space to meet the government's needs; likewise, POSK comfortably accommodated émigré organizations. *Zamek* was no longer needed. *Komisja Likwidacyjna* dissolved Cytadela (Eaton Place) Ltd., and, with Wałęsa's consent, donated the lease to PAFT.[10]

---

[9] *Skarb Narodowy* had a 12-member main commission and committees worldwide. In the United Kingdom alone, there were 50 local committees and 28 *Skarb* representatives; there were another 16 committees in the nations of Western Europe, 24 in the United States, 17 in Canada, and 12 in Australia. Argentina and Brazil each had two committees, and New Zealand, South Africa, Venezuela and Zimbabwe each had one *Skarb* committee.

[10] Like most other émigré organizations, PAFT maintained its offices in POSK and had no use for 43 Eaton Place. However, the lease on 43 Eaton Place was quite valuable due to its highly desirable location. PAFT sold the lease to further fund its operations.

Transitioning to a market economy was an agonizing process and quite painful for the people of Poland. Price controls and subsidies were ended, exchange rate controls for the *złoty* were eliminated, and a new taxation plan was implemented. Food and other consumer goods were now in plentiful supply, but at far higher prices. Warsaw labored under the enormous debt accumulated by Gierek, and exports to the West were hampered by EU regulations. Wałęsa needed economic and political help and sought it in London.

In April 1991, Wałęsa became the first head of a post-communist nation to make a state visit to the United Kingdom. He was treated with the utmost respect; he stayed at Windsor Palace for three nights as the guest of Queen Elizabeth II and was feted by her at a state dinner at Claridge's Hotel. Outside of such activities, he successfully obtained some debt relief, convinced the British to pay for an investment bank to consult with his government on privatization, and received Prime Minister John Major's backing for associate membership in the European Union.[11]

Wałęsa had not forgotten the former exile government. He insisted on a visit with Raczyński, and he asked Kaczorowski to accompany him to No. 10 Downing Street. Kaczorowski introduced himself; Major smiled and said, "You do not have to introduce yourself, we know you perfectly well."

Free and unfettered legislative elections, promised since Yalta, were finally scheduled for October 27, 1991, but the electoral law disappointed the émigré community: only those citizens living abroad for less than five years were eligible to vote. *Rada Narodowa* unsuccessfully attempted to influence Warsaw to change the law. Postwar political émigrés, even those who never accepted citizenship in their new homelands, were ineligible.

An astounding 111 parties fielded candidates; of them, twenty-nine were represented in the new *Sejm* and twenty-two in the *Senat*. No party took an absolute majority in either house. Tadeusz Mazowiecki's *Unia Demokratyczna* (Democratic Union) received the most support, winning the most seats in both houses. *Sojusz Lewicy Demokratycznej* (SLD, Democratic Left Alliance), a merger of SdRP and several minor left-wing parties, was the second largest party in the *Sejm* but only seventh largest in *Senat*. A remnant of KO "S" running under the *Solidarność* banner took the second-most *Senat* seats, but it was only the ninth largest *Sejm* party. Stanisław Tymiński had remained in Poland and created his own organization,

---

[11] In 2012, the Republic of Poland completed repayment of all debt accumulated under Edward Gierek.

Partia X (Party X); it won three *Sejm* seats. The rest were held by familiar parties such as PSL, KPN, and SP, Catholic parties, and myriad other political, regional, and ethnic entities.[12] Fragmented though the *Sejm* and *Senat* were, they had been freely elected. NIK and *Rada Narodowa*, the final remaining bodies of the Second Republic, could now conclude their work.

NIK chairman Stanisław Borczyk had been in charge of that body for only about two years, having taken over on November 1, 1989. He ended NIK's operations on December 8, 1991. That same day, *Rada Narodowa* met for the final time in the theater at POSK. In attendance were Kaczorowski, Szczepanik, de Virion, and Consul General Janusz Kochanowski. Guests from Poland included Stelmachowski, *Senat* Deputy Marshal Alicja Grześkowiak, Minister of State Dr. Andrzej Zakrzewski, head of the *Senat* Chancellery Wojciech Sawicki, and *Sejm* deputy Leszek Moczulski. Letters from Wałęsa and the *Sejm* and *Senat* marshals were read, and Stelmachowski paid tribute to émigré activists who had not lived to see a free Poland, noting their inspiring stubbornness and perseverance. Szczepanik thanked *Rada Narodowa* for its years of service. *Rada Narodowa* passed its final resolution, declaring itself dissolved, paying tribute to all who had devoted their lives to the Polish cause, and offering ongoing help to Poland and to Poles abroad.

Liquidation was complete on December 31, 1991. The following March, Ambassador de Virion invited members of *Komisja Likwidacyjna Rządu Rzeczypospolitej Polskiej* to the embassy and presented them with letters from Wałęsa:

> Sir,
>
> It is my pleasant duty to thank you for the effort you put into the work of the Liquidation Committee.
>
> This is an extraordinary moment: the final closure of a chapter so important in the history of the Republic of Poland and Emigration. Usually, at such moments, a feeling of relief comes along with nostalgia. I think the more appropriate word is fulfillment. The long-term struggle ended victoriously. A joint fight, although we struggled in different places.

---

[12] One new party that gained international attention was *Polska Partia Przyjaciół Piwa* (PPPP, Polish Beer-Lovers' Party). Founded by satirist Janusz Rewiński, its goal was to promote beer drinking over vodka consumption, thus fighting alcoholism. Although its origins were based in humor, PPPP proposed higher taxes on hard liquor and championed environmental reforms to ensure clean water.

Concern for the dignity, continuity of the state, civic honor and national pride was passed on to the next generations of Poles. Most importantly—in the homeland.

I have said many times, and I would like to say it again: it is a personal honor for me that it happened during my presidency.

Thank you for the effort and work done.

To greetings from Warsaw, I add wishes for your best health.

Lech Wałęsa[13]

Thorough nationalization of industry and property in the late 1940s had given the new Polish government more challenges. It now had control of overstaffed, inefficient businesses offering products and services targeted at Soviet Bloc customers. They were outdated and uncompetitive in the West. Warsaw wanted to rid itself of these firms, as well as the thousands of houses, manors, and palaces seized by the communists, and the preference was return them to the original owners or their heirs. In many cases, this was impossible as the owners had died during the war or under communism,[14] yet the government painstakingly worked to identify the rightful proprietors. Finding the legitimate owner of Rogalin, however, was quite simple. Wałęsa had visited him in London and knew his address.

Edward Raczyński regained title to Rogalin, but his poor health made it impossible for him to personally assess its condition. He learned that although Rogalin was intact, it bore the scars of fifty years of occupation, abuse, and neglect. The communist authorities had chosen to preserve it as a museum, but under their stewardship it was subjected to indifferent maintenance and badly executed restoration work unfaithful to its design. After conferring with his daughters, he established the Raczyński

---

[13] "Komisja Likwidacyjna..." ("Liquidation Commission..."), *Uzupełniające Informacje do Częsci II, Dział Nieurzedowy Dziennika Ustaw Rzeczypospolitej No. 5 z dnia 22 grudnia 1990 roku*, Londyn, s. 16–17.

[14] In the early 1990s, it became somewhat common for Germans to arrive unannounced at houses in Poland and declare that they were going to petition the government for the return of their property; this was a particular problem in Gdańsk and the Recovered Territories. The status of formerly Jewish-owned properties was more problematic, as most of the owners had perished in the Holocaust or in combat. It would take decades to resolve many of these cases.

Foundation at the National Museum in Poznań and transferred ownership of Rogalin to it.[15] The foundation took responsibility for restoring and maintaining the palace and grounds and for care of its library and art collection.[16]

Few people live to their ninety-ninth birthday; marriages involving people who have attained this age are quite rare indeed. In 1991, at age ninety-nine, Edward Raczyński married for the third time. His new wife was Aniela Lilpop Mieczysławska. She and her husband Witold Mieczysławski had been separated for several decades; she and Raczyński had been companions for nearly thirty years, and they finally married when Witold died. On December 19, Raczyński reached his one-hundredth birthday. He received greetings from Wałęsa, John Major, and other world leaders; Queen Elizabeth II awarded him an honorary knighthood. The following day, the Raczyński Foundation was officially registered in Poland.

Now that a freely elected *Sejm* had been seated, work could begin on a new constitution. Writing it was a significant undertaking; a draft would have to be reviewed by branches of the government and independent legal scholars, revised as needed, and reviewed again, a process expected to take several years.[17] A short-term solution was needed to further distance the nation from the 1952 PRL Constitution. This was the so-called *Mała Konstytucja z 1992* (Small Constitution of 1992), a revision of the 1952 document codifying the preeminent role of government institutions, the precepts of liberal multiparty democracy, and an economic system based on free market principles. *Mała Konstytucja* was not what émigrés expected, but they were not allowed input. The team appointed to write it did not include anyone from the émigré community, and throughout the process none of the authors sought the opinions or perspectives of any émigrés. In his November 1990 interview with *Tygodnik Powszechny*, Szczepanik expressed the disappointment felt by many émigrés who stood ready to share their experiences and knowledge only to be ignored.

Szczepanik and other former government and *Rada Narodowa* members were further disappointed about Warsaw's disregard of the April Constitution. As the document at the center of the government-in-exile's

---

[15] The Raczyński Foundation was officially registered on December 20, 1991, the day after Raczyński's one-hundredth birthday.
[16] The collection numbered about 450 paintings and other works of art that had survived the war and the communist period.
[17] The new constitution did not come into effect until October 1997.

existence, there was an expectation that Warsaw would recognize it in some way, such as by symbolically adopting it, even if for only a few hours. In 1990, Wałęsa and most of his fellow presidential candidates wanted to receive power and the symbols of state from Kaczorowski; one could conclude that this indicated respect for the April Constitution. But no such act was forthcoming, and Szczepanik was unable to influence Warsaw in this regard. Nor did the April Constitution merit reference in the new constitution. It was mentioned only in a 1996 draft, and that reference was deleted in the final document.

Thousands of Poles died in foreign lands during and after the war, and many expressed their wishes to be laid to rest in Poland when it became possible. In 1989, it was. Juliusz Ulrych, minister of communications under Składkowski at the outbreak of the war, had died in London in 1959. In 1989, his remains were reburied in Warsaw. Składkowski himself had died in London in 1962, and he was reburied in Warsaw's Powązki Military Cemetery in 1990. On September 27, 1990, the remains of General Bolesław Wieniawa-Długoszowski were reburied in Kraków's Rakowicki Cemetery alongside other members of the Polish Legions. In 1991, Minister of Foreign Affairs Józef Beck was reinterred in Powązki. In June 1992, the remains of Ignacy Jan Paderewski were transported to Warsaw; on June 29, the fifty-first anniversary of his death, he was reburied in the crypt of the Cathedral Basilica of St. John the Baptist.[18] In September 1992, the remains of General Michał Tokarzewski-Karaszewicz were reburied in Powązki. Later that year, the remains of General Kazimierz Sosnkowski were returned to Poland. His family, friends, and supporters had petitioned the government to allow his repatriation, and they obtained the necessary permission for his burial in the crypt of the Warsaw cathedral, where he was reinterred on November 12, 1992. Ignacy Mościcki's family had received permission from Warsaw in 1984 to repatriate his remains, but the Swiss government refused to allow it. In 1993, Wałęsa revisited the matter. This time, there were no obstacles from Switzerland, and his remains were reinterred in the crypt of the Warsaw cathedral.

The matter of Władysław Sikorski's reburial arose again. This time, it was proposed by the British government during a 1991 visit by Minister

---

[18] Paderewski's body was buried in Warsaw, but his heart remained in the United States. It was encased in a bronze sculpture in the National Shrine of Our Lady of Częstochowa, near Doylestown, Pennsylvania.

of Foreign Affairs Krzysztof Skubiszewski. Later that year, de Virion petitioned the British government to permit the move. Discussions proceeded slowly through 1992 and came to a halt when ZPWB and SPK, not opposed to the move in 1991, reversed their positions, although they allowed that if Warsaw decided to proceed, they would not object. Another complication arose in February 1993. *Rada Ochrony Pamięci Walk i Męczeństwa* (Council for the Protection of Struggle and Martyrdom Sites) adopted a resolution to stop repatriation of the remains of the prominent and meritorious. Wałęsa rendered these developments and statements moot in July with his announcement that Sikorski's remains would be returned. On September 17, 1993, Sikorski was reburied in the marble sarcophagus that had sat empty in the crypt at Wawel since 1981.[19] The following year, the remains of General Tadeusz Bór-Komorowski were moved from Gunnersbury Cemetery to Warsaw's Powązki Military Cemetery. In 2000, the remains of Stanisław Mikołajczyk were moved from the United States to *Cmentarz Zasłużonych Wielkopolan* (Cemetery of Meritorious Wielkopolans) in Poznań.

Some prominent exiles who lived to see the end of the PRL died overseas but were buried in Poland. General Klemens Rudnicki lived long enough to have the satisfaction of returning to his newly free homeland, and he lived another eighteen months after the ceremony at the Royal Castle. He died in London in June 1992 at the age of ninety-five and was permitted to be buried in Rakowicki. Edward Raczyński died in London on July 30, 1993, at age 101. His funeral was held in London, and his remains were buried in the chapel crypt at Rogalin alongside his parents. His family donated the contents of his office to the Raczyński Foundation, and it was reconstructed in the north wing of Rogalin. It contains his furniture, family photographs, portraits of ancestors, and personal belongings, including his London address book containing Winston Churchill's telephone number. General Stanisław Maczek chose a different resting place. He died in Edinburgh on December 11, 1994, at age 102, and like Anders, he chose to be buried with his soldiers. His grave is in the Polish military cemetery in Breda.

Despite the collapse of their Moscow-backed governments, the Soviet military was an ongoing problem for Poland, Czechoslovakia, Hungary, and eastern Germany. Soviet Army units remained at their posts in these

---

[19] Among the attendees at Sikorski's reburial were Ryszard Kaczorowski, Queen Elizabeth II, and Prince Philip.

countries, causing uncertainty and constituting a barrier to full independence from Moscow. Mazowiecki began to push for withdrawal in 1990. The Soviet military agreed and began a gradual drawdown. In 1991, Soviet military units were completely removed from Hungary and Czechoslovakia, but thousands of soldiers remained in Poland. On December 8, 1991, the presidents of Russia, Ukraine, and Belarus signed an agreement declaring the Soviet Union to be dissolved. On December 25, Gorbachev resigned; that night the Soviet flag was lowered at the Kremlin in Moscow, and the Russian flag was raised in its place. The Soviet Army was now the Russian Army.

Throughout 1992, Poland and Russia planned the final withdrawal. Warsaw wanted the departure date of the last Russian troops to be September 17, 1993, the anniversary of the Red Army invasion in 1939, but the last train did not depart until the following morning. At the official ceremony on the seventeenth, Wałęsa called September 17 a painful date in Polish history and declared that the withdrawal marked the end of an era in Polish–Russian relations. Russian Ambassador Yuri Kashlev stayed true to the Soviet version of events, declaring that Russian soldiers were leaving Poland with a clear conscience. At 5:41 the following morning at a train station in east Warsaw, General Vladimir Ivanovich Bryzgun stepped aboard a train car, gave a final salute, and closed the door as the train left the station. The ceremony was poorly received in Russia.

The Russians left behind hundreds of military cemeteries containing the graves of more than one million Soviet soldiers. Warsaw and Moscow agreed to respect and maintain military cemeteries within their borders, but Soviet war memorials became a point of contention. Memorials emblazoned with Soviet symbols could be found in every city and town, and Poles typically viewed these as reminders of their time of subjugation. The *Sejm* enacted a law ordering such monuments to be removed. Moscow was quick to object, restating its line that the Soviet Union had saved Poland from fascism and expressed its concern that war graves would be desecrated. Poland had to assure Russia that its military cemeteries would be well cared for and went on to promise that Soviet memorials integral to acemetery would be preserved. Poland also reached an agreement with independent Ukraine to permit restoration of the Lwów Eaglets cemetery. Ukraine permitted its restoration, while Poland paid for refurbishment and maintenance.

Juliusz Sokolnicki did not fade quietly into obscurity. His copious distribution of awards, titles, government ministries, and military ranks had created an unwanted headache. Demands for recognition of rank, service, or title flowed into Warsaw, and the government was faced with the task of informing the claimants that their honors were worthless. The problem reached such proportions that in 1994, Wałęsa's press spokesman had to issue a statement:

> Article 11 of Bill 1 of 25 October 1991, while giving the President and Minister of Defence of the Polish Republic the power and obligation to promote to military [knightly] rank, also recognises this power as being bestowed by Authority of the Polish Republic up to 22 December 1990. The phrase "the Authority of the Polish Republic" should be understood to mean the organs of the state institutions abroad [i.e., in London] based on the Polish Constitution of 23 April 1935. It therefore recognises as Presidents of the Polish Republic General Bolesław Wieniawa-Długoszowski, Władysław Raczkiewicz, August Zaleski, Stanisław Ostrowski, Edward Raczyński, Kazimierz Sabbat, and Ryszard Kaczorowski, as well as the state organs appointed by them. According to the Constitution of 23 April 1935 and historical fact they are the successors of President Ignacy Mościcki.
>
> The last mentioned, President Ryszard Kaczorowski, acknowledges that, following free elections in Poland and the election of the President [Wałęsa] in 1990, the activities of the President-in-Exile terminated when he handed the insignia of the Second Polish Republic to President Lech Wałęsa.
>
> With this in mind, it should be stated that Mr. Juliusz Nowina-Sokolnicki did not possess the authority of the Polish Republic and therefore his activities purporting to be actions of the state (as a result of calling himself President-in-Exile) cannot be honoured, and according to Article 11 of Bill 1, the ranks granted by him are not recognised.
>
> Andrzej Drzycimski
> State Secretary Press Spokesman for the President of the Polish Republic

Sokolnicki dismissed the criticism and defended himself by contrasting his actions with those of the PRL, claiming that his award of a few thousand medals was nothing compared to the eight million decorations dispensed by the communists.

Having declared that he had transferred his presidential powers, Sokolnicki was no longer able to award military ranks or government offices. His remaining source of income was the Order of St. Stanislas, now fragmented into several competing factions. He added the stipulation that the Grand Master had to be a member of his family, thereby transforming what he originally portrayed as a state honor into his personal property. As Grand Master, he continued to sell titles. The order did involve itself in charitable works and contributed to the construction of *Golgota*, a 33-meter-high building near the villages of Kałków and Godów commemorating the martyrdom of the Polish nation. A tablet listing donors included the Order and Sokolnicki: "Knights and Ladies of the Order of Saint Stanislaus, who work for charity among the most needy, under the leadership of the Grand Master of the Order, President of the Republic of Poland in Exile, Count Juliusz Nowina-Sokolnicki."

Konstanty Hanff remained in Sokolnicki's service. In the late 1990s he wrote a series of books titled *Rewizja historii* (Revision of History) documenting the history of Sokolnicki's government and the CEC. These were published in Poland and were intended to present Sokolnicki's version of history to the Polish people.

Sokolnicki could declare himself to be Poland's exile president in the United Kingdom without fear of legal consequences, but that was not the case in Poland. Dorota Arciszewska-Mielewczyk, a senator from Gdynia, visited *Golgota* in 2006 and was astounded to see Sokolnicki referred to as president on the donor tablet. She brought the matter to the attention of the *Senat* and Minister of Justice Zbigniew Ziobro. On the *Senat* floor, she read the inscription from the *Golgota* tablet and asked by what right Sokolnicki uses the title of president, claims the title of Grand Master of the Order of St. Stanislas, and distributes decorations. The Ministry of Justice evaluated her charges, ruled that his actions were illegal, and referred the case to the police in nearby Starachowice for further action. But nothing further happened. The prosecutor in Starachowice refused to pursue the case. Senator Arciszewska-Mielewczyk complained to the minister of justice, but to no avail.

Gazeta Wyborcza ran an article in 2008 titled *"Wielki Mistrz"* ("The Great Master") detailing Sokolnicki's claim to the presidency and his actions since 1972, including his talk in Hanover, his meeting with German politician Herbert Czaja, his sale of honors, awards, and offices, and his activities as Grand Master. Sokolnicki responded with a letter to *Gazeta Wyborcza* editor

Adam Michnik laying out his claim to the presidency, declaring that he was in possession of the original of his nomination and had offered to take it to Warsaw, hurling invectives at Ostrowski, Raczyński, Sabbat, and Kaczorowski, denying having met Czaja, disputing the details of the Hanover meeting,[20] denying having decorated former German soldiers with Polish medals, and threatening legal action against the newspaper.

In 2009, Sokolnicki was eighty-three years of age and in failing health. He transferred the office of Grand Master of the Order of St. Stanislas to a distant cousin, Jan Zbigniew Potocki, and on August 15 he declared Potocki to be the successor of the President of the Republic of Poland should an emergency arise, contradicting his 1990 "Act of Transferring Sovereign Power." Sokolnicki died in Colchester on August 17, 2009, at the age of eighty-four.[21] He was cremated, and his ashes were brought to Poland. On September 26, his ashes were placed in the crypt of *Sanktuarium Matki Bożej Bolesnej Królowej Polski,* the church where the *Golgota* monument was located. In attendance were about 150 members of his order, several priests and military veterans, and a firefighter's orchestra. No state authorities attended his burial. Despite his claim in the letter to Michnik, no original of his purported nomination has surfaced.

Decommunization brought economic pain and uncertainty and incessant political squabbles as the nation learned how to function as a free-market democracy. Economic impacts were the immediate concern of most Poles. In a period of rampant price inflation, workers worried about earning enough money to support themselves and their families; their concerns were compounded by restructuring and privatization of large concerns that often resulted in thousands of lost jobs. It took most of the 1990s for the economy to completely stabilize. On the positive side, Poles now enjoyed a free press that had no qualms about criticizing the government or public figures and often ran exposés on the nation's once-powerful communist leaders. New newspapers, magazines, radio stations, and television networks proliferated, covering seeming every conceivable point of view, and books appeared on the market delving into aspects of national history that had been banned from discussion in the PRL. Government oversight of religious matters ended. And communist place names disappeared.

---

[20] In his letter to Michnik, Sokolnicki claimed he chaired a Polish delegation at a conference in Hanover in January 1972. In her article, Bożena Aksamit placed him there in December 1972.

[21] *Polityka* incorrectly reported his age as 89; Sokolnicki's official biography was probably consulted for this information.

Since the time of Bierut, streets, parks, public squares, schools, and factories had been adorned with the names of communist luminaries, heroes, and events. The name of Bierut himself had been affixed to the University of Wrocław in 1952, but it reclaimed its initial postwar name, *Uniwersytet Wrocławski,* in 1989. After that, changes came quickly. Common names such as *Ulica 22 Lipca* (July 22 Street, named after the founding date of PKWN) and *Ulica 1 Maja* (May 1 Street) disappeared from the map, either reverting to their prewar names or adopting names unthinkable in the PRL. Warsaw's *Plac Zwycięstwa* (Victory Square), where Pope John Paul II had offered Mass during his first pilgrimage, was renamed *Plac Marszałka Józefa Piłsudskiego* (Piłsudski Square), and *Plac Dzierżyńskiego*, named after the founder of the Cheka, reverted to its prewar name of *Plac Bankowy* (Bank Square). Kraków's *Ulica Rewolucji Kubańskiej* (Cuban Revolution Street) in Nowa Huta was renamed *Aleja Jana Pawła II* (John Paul II Avenue), as was Częstochowa's *Aleja Lenina* (Lenin Avenue). Vladimir Lenin's name, once ubiquitous, disappeared from sites around the country and was replaced with a variety of names, including that of General Anders and others suppressed or scorned in the PRL, such as Bór-Komorowski, Raczkiewicz, Ostrowski, Sosnkowski, and Arciszewski. Names of opposition figures and organizations also appeared, such as *Aleja Solidarności* (*Solidarność* Avenue, in several cities), *Ulica Zbyszka Godlewskiego* in Elbląg, and *Ulica Janka Wiśniewskiego* in Gdynia.

Statues of communist heroes also came down. Beginning in 1989, statues and memorials of communist luminaries were removed and either placed in storage or destroyed. In many cases, they were replaced with memorials to people who could not be commemorated in the PRL or to victims of communism, including many memorials for the Katyń victims.[22] Official holidays were likewise revised. The *Sejm* dismissed Jaruzelski's objections and voted to remove the July 22 holiday *Narodowe Święto Odrodzenia Polski* (National Day of the Rebirth of Poland) from the calendar in 1990. Later, holidays commemorating the defeat of Germany (May 9) and the October Revolution (November 7) were ended, while celebrations of the May 3 Constitution and the November 11 Independence Day were restored.

Reminders of the government-in-exile's extended stay in London are readily found. In addition to the Hotel Rubens plaque commemorating Sikorski, one was installed on 43 Eaton Place informing passersby of its role

---

[22] Some statues of communist notables such as Lenin, Marx, Engels, Dzierżyński, and Bierut were preserved at *Galeria Sztuki Socrealizmu* (Gallery of Socialist Realist Art) on the grounds of the Zamoyski palace and museum in Kozłówka, near Lublin. The Gallery occupies one of the palace buildings and part of its garden.

as "Seat of the President and the Polish Government-in-Exile 1945–1990," and another on 8 Lennox Gardens reading, "Count Edward Raczynski (1891–1993), Polish Statesman, lived here 1967–1993." A less overt memorial was at the Imperial War Museum in Duxford; a Hawker Hurricane fighter plane at the entrance was painted with the markings of the 302 Squadron.[23]

There were still slights. In 1993, an imposing Battle of Britain Memorial was built near Dover featuring the insignia of the RAF squadrons that fought. At its unveiling, a reporter noticed that two squadrons had been excluded: 302 and 303, the two all-Polish squadrons. Those responsible claimed it was an oversight and quickly added the missing insignia.

The enduring memorial of the government-in-exile's time in London was the continued presence of Poles themselves. The United Kingdom was their home, and their presence could be seen in many ways: at the newsagents, where copies of *Dziennik Polski* were sold, at Daquise and other restaurants, at Polish grocery shops and bookstores, at clubs such as *Ognisko Polskie*, and at POSK. They would remain a presence, and their numbers would be bolstered after Poland joined the European Union in 2004 and some of their countrymen came to the United Kingdom for work.

Ryszard Kaczorowski remained a resident of London, but he never accepted British citizenship. He kept small busts of Józef Piłsudski and General Maczek and an urn of soil from Katyń on his desk. He closely monitored events in Poland and visited frequently; in the process, he became well known but did not involve himself in politics. In 1994, Prime Minister Waldemar Pawlak proposed Kaczorowski as minister of defense, but his idea was ridiculed in the Polish press. Kaczorowski extracted Pawlak from further controversy by declining the offer, stating that he could not accept the proposal due to his age.

Kaczorowski received several honorary degrees and was awarded honorary citizenship of many provinces, districts, cities, and towns. He viewed these not as personal honors but as honors for all political émigrés. He served as chairman of PAFT and held seats on the boards of several organizations in Poland. He also founded *Instytut Strategii Polskiej* (Polish Institute of Strategy) in Warsaw.

On April 10, 2010, Kaczorowski boarded the presidential aircraft in Warsaw for a flight to Smolensk. He had been invited to join President

---

[23] In February 2018, the airplane was repainted with the markings of 242 Squadron, a non-Polish unit.

Lech Kaczyński and his contingent for a memorial service marking the seventieth year since the Katyń massacres. Thick fog shrouded Smolensk–Severnyy Airport that morning, and as the plane descended, it struck several treetops and crashed a short distance from the runway. All ninety-six passengers and crew died.

Ryszard Kaczorowski's funeral was held in Warsaw's Cathedral of St. John the Baptist. He was buried in the crypt of *Świątynia Opatrzności Bożej* (Temple of Divine Providence) in Warsaw's Wilanów district.

As the centennial of Poland regaining independence approached, the government prepared a lengthy program of commemorations and celebrations. Among them was *Misja: Wolna Polska* (Mission: Free Poland), a project to expand knowledge of the exile government. On November 3, 2022, its final phase began with the exhumation of the remains of Raczkiewicz, Zaleski, and Ostrowski. They were flown to Warsaw and buried in a new section of the crypt, *Mauzoleum Prezydentów Rzeczypospolitej na Uchodźstwie* (Mausoleum of the Presidents of the Republic of Poland in Exile) alongside Kaczorowski and the symbolic tombs of Raczyński and Sabbat.[24] Artifacts from the exile presidents are displayed in a nearby chamber. At their reburial, Prime Minister Mateusz Morawiecki remarked, "After a long journey [the presidents] are returning to their homeland. They are coming where they belong. Now, they will forever witness the truth, continuation and dream of a great Poland." He called them "…the depositaries of memory and the continuity of the Polish state, and guardians of hope."

---

[24] The families of Raczyński and Sabbat declined to have their remains moved to the crypt.

Changing the Course of an Avalanche

AT POTSDAM IN 1945, the Soviet Union, the United States, and the United Kingdom solemnly declared that Poland's Second Republic no longer existed. Władysław Raczkiewicz, his government, and thousands of exiles chose to differ. For the next forty-five years, the government continued to function, enjoying little international recognition, receiving no material support from any Western government or international body, and having no standing with the United Nations or the European Union.[1] Frequently, it was characterized as irrelevant, an anachronism, or a mere symbol. It withstood PRL intrigues, Western indifference, internal discord, and schisms. It supported émigré Poles throughout the West, provided aid to people in Poland, supported the opposition, spoke for those exiled into the Soviet Union, and advocated for a free Poland with Western governments. It not only survived; it outlasted its presumed replacement.[2] Recalling the words of poet Czesław Miłosz, it is fair to state that the exile government indeed changed the course of an avalanche.[3]

Poland's exile government bore no resemblance to the caricatures offered by Warsaw or the superficial analyses that occasionally surfaced in Western newspapers. 43 Eaton Place was center of a surprisingly large and sophisticated organization with extensive contacts in Poland and a global network of representatives. It served as a valuable, albeit informal, source of information to the British and American governments, connected opposition activists with Western government and media contacts, and provided aid to victims of communist repression. It fostered an environment where culture could develop without censorship, a free press could function, a broad range of political viewpoints could be expressed, and where prewar political parties could continue to operate.

Among the many Cold War–era exile governments and national committees, only the Polish government-in-exile was a direct continuation of

---

[1] Although TRJN, PNKD, and *Rada Polityczna* received British and American funds from NCFE, ACEN, or for intelligence operations such as *Sprawa Bergu*, the Polish government-in-exile received none.
[2] Poland's government was in exile for fifty-one years, three months, and six days. Counting from PKWN's proclamation on July 22, 1944, until the *Sejm* changed the state's name back to the Republic of Poland, PRL existed for forty-five years, five months, and seven days.
[3] From his poem *Treatise on Morality*: "And even if you're like a pebble on the ground, / Together with many other pebbles / You can change the course of an avalanche."

the pre-Soviet government. Its lineage was a perennial annoyance to the communist regime, as evidenced by Warsaw's many attempts to create division and discord in emigration and in its mostly unsuccessful efforts to entice exile government figures to return to Poland and recognize PRL. Not only did the very existence of the London-based government undermine Warsaw's legitimacy, its incessant calls for free elections were an embarrassment that exposed regime claims of near-universal support as blatant lies, and its support of dissidents and opposition groups threatened communist hegemony.

None of this would have been possible were it not for the persistence and determination of the exiles. Seven served as president,[4] fifteen as prime minister, dozens as ministers, scores as undersecretaries, desk officers, in NIK, in the chancellery, in the judiciary,[5] or in other functions, hundreds as *Rada* representatives, and hundreds more as *Skarb Narodowy* representatives. Thousands voted in *Rada* elections, contributed to *Skarb Narodowy*, answered appeals to provide relief to opposition groups and people persecuted by the regime, attended official events, appeared at demonstrations, and wrote letters to Western journalists and government figures. As Pope John Paul II noted, they had created Poland outside of Poland.

They did not have to do any of this. Most were already hard-pressed to learn new languages, develop marketable skills, find work, and support their families. They could have used the few pounds, dollars, francs, marks, or lira they set aside for *Skarb Narodowy* for more immediate needs, they could have spent their spare time with family and friends rather than volunteer, and they could have dismissed *Rada* elections as irrelevant. Yet they contributed their money, turned out to vote, and offered their time and paid their own expenses. The government-in-exile would not have survived without them.

That so many supported the exile government is remarkable, but it begs the question: Why did they? What drove them to sacrifice their time and money for an unrecognized government that had no real authority? While every person had their own reasons, a general understanding can be attained by viewing the question through the perspective of history.

Prior to 1918, when Poland regained independence, a Polish state was simultaneously a memory and an objective. Poles fought in uprisings, resisted Russification and Germanization, preserved their language and

---

[4] This count of seven exile presidents includes General Bolesław Wieniawa-Długoszowski.
[5] Although the judicial system had been dormant for many years, its institution should be counted as one of the exile government's achievements.

culture, and safeguarded their national ethos. They taught their children their nation's history and taught them to revere heroes such as Tadeusz Kościuszko and Prince Józef Poniatowski and their own ancestors, immersing them in stories of courage, determination, and self-sacrifice. They drew inspiration from writers such as Adam Mickiewicz, Stanisław Wyspiański, and Henryk Sienkiewicz.[6] In this mix of national, familial, and fictional heroes, there was an abundance of inspiration for budding patriots, and countless Poles drew on it during the Great War and in the ensuing struggles against Germany and the Soviet Union. They treasured independence, and when Poland was again invaded, occupied, and partitioned, their love of their nation and their willingness to sacrifice for it drove them to fight in the underground, evacuate to France and Britain, or find their way across the Soviet Union to join the Second Polish Corps. Those who had firsthand experience of Soviet captivity knew what their countrymen were experiencing. Those who had escaped to the West were frustrated that they had fought to liberate Italy, France, Belgium, and the Netherlands but were unable to free their own nation and considered their job to be incomplete. They also drew inspiration from home. Most had families, friends, and neighbors in Poland who refused to acquiesce, and they could do no less.

A flag epitomizes their dedication and resolve. Late in 1939, a group of Air Force officers in France decided to create a standard that would be sewn in Poland and brought to the West to symbolize the unity between home and the exile military.[7] Their design made its way to Wilno by way of Switzerland, and sympathetic diplomats from neutral countries obtained damask fabric and gold and silver thread in Berlin and used their diplomatic bags to bring these items to Wilno. It was sewn under conditions of absolute secrecy in convents and by a small number of families; they completed their work in June 1940. The standard consisted of a red cross superimposed on a square of white cloth. On one side, an image of Our Lady of Ostra Brama was in the center; above was a white eagle, below were the words "*Bóg, Honor, Ojczyzna*" ("God, Honor, Homeland"). On the other side, an image of St Thérèse of Lisieux was in the center to symbolize the Air Force's presence in France. Above, "*Wilno 1940*" was embroidered,

---

[6] In the 1880s, Sienkiewicz wrote a series of three novels "to uplift the hearts" of his countrymen. *Ogniem i mieczem* (*With Fire and Sword*) was set during the Cossack Rebellion, *Potop* (*Deluge*) took place during the Swedish invasion, and *Pan Wołodyjowski* (*Sir Wołodyjowski*) was set in the ensuing Turkish invasion. Together, the books are known as *Trylogia Sienkiewicza* (*Sienkiewicz's Trilogy*), or simply *Trilogy*). His protagonists placed the good of their nation above their personal aspirations.
[7] A military standard is a flag or pennant that identifies a unit.

and below were the words "Miłość Żąda Ofiary" ("Love Demands Sacrifice"). By the time it was completed, France had fallen, and the standard was brought to London through Berlin and Stockholm by a courier from the Japanese consulate in Wilno. It was mounted on a flagstaff topped with an eagle made from gold and silver rings and coins contributed by Polish airmen.[8] In June, Sikorski officially received the standard at the RAF airfield at Swinderby; he presented it to the commander of the Polish Air Force, who in turn presented it to the 300 Bomber Squadron, the first Polish squadron formed in the RAF. Every three months thereafter, it was transferred to another squadron to allow all squadrons the honor of displaying it.[9]

"Miłość Żąda Ofiary." In these three words lay the answer to what drove the exiles to support their government for the forty-five years, five months, and twenty-two days since it lost most Western recognition. It is the reason they served in the government, *Rada*, and *Skarb Narodowy*. It is the reason they contributed their time and money, voted, and taught their children their language, history, and culture. It is the reason they sent food, clothing, medicine, and money to family and friends and provided aid to victims of repression and their families. They did it because love demands sacrifice.

---

[8] This eagle was made in the United Kingdom by the jeweler Spinks & Co.
[9] After the war, the standard was preserved in London's Polish Institute and Sikorski Museum. On September 4, 1992, it was brought to Warsaw; Lech Wałęsa received it in a ceremony in Piłsudski Square. It is on display at the Polish Air Force Museum in Dęblin.

Abbreviations and Terms

ACEN	Assembly of Captive European Nations
AJPIA	Archives of the Józef Piłsudski Institute of America
AK	*Armia Krajowa* (Home Army)
AL	*Armia Ludowa* (People's Army)
BBWR	*Bezpartyjny Blok Współpracy z Rządem* (Nonpartisan Bloc for Cooperation with the Government)
BCh	*Bataliony Chłopskie* (Peasants' Battalions)
CBKP	*Centralne Biuro Komunistów Polski* (Central Bureau of Polish Communists)
Cheka	All-Russian Extraordinary Commission, predecessor to the NKVD and KGB
CIA	Central Intelligence Agency
CKON	*Centralny Komitet Organizacji Niepodległościowych* (Central Committee of Independence Organizations)
Delegatura	The exile government's structure in occupied Poland
DzU RP	*Dziennik Ustaw Rzeczypospolitej Polskiej* (Journal of Laws of the Republic of Poland), the official journal of laws, government acts, and ordinances
DzU PRL	*Dziennik Ustaw Polskiej Rzeczypospolitej Ludowe* (Journal of Laws of the Polish People's Republic), the official journal of laws, government acts, and ordinances in communist Poland
EZN	*Egzekutywa Zjednoczenia Narodowego* (Executive of National Unity)

FOM	*Fundusz Obrony Morskiej* (Maritime Defense Fund)
FON	*Fundusz Obrony Narodowej* (National Defense Fund)
IPN	*Instytut Pamięci Narodowej* (Institute of National Remembrance)
ITC	Interim Treasury Committee for Polish Affairs
KGB	Committee for State Security (*Komitet gosudarstvennoy bezopasnosti*, the Soviet secret police from 1954–1991)
KL	*Koło Lwowian* (Circle of Lwów)
KNAPP	*Komitet Narodowy Amerykanów Polskiego Pochodzenia* (National Committee of Americans of Polish Extraction)
KO "S"	*Komitet Obywatelski "Solidarność"* (Citizens' Committee "Solidarność")
KOR	*Komitet Obrony Robotników* (Workers' Defense Committee)
KPN	*Konfederacja Polski Niepodległej* (Confederation of Independent Poland)
KPP	*Komunistyczna Partia Polski* (Communist Party of Poland)
kresy	"Borderlands," referring to Poland's eastern provinces annexed by the Soviet Union in 1939
KRN	*Krajowa Rada Narodowa* (State National Council)
KRP	*Krajowa Reprezentacja Polityczna* (National Political Representation)
KSS "KOR"	*Komitet Samoobrony Społecznej "KOR"* (Committee for Social Self-Defense "KOR")

KWN	*Konwent Walk o Niepodległość* (Convention for the Fight for Independence)
LNP	*Liga Niepodległości Polski* (Polish Independence League)
MBP	*Ministerstwo Bezpieczeństwa Publicznego* (Ministry of Public Security)
MKS	*Międzyzakładowy Komitet Strajkowy* (Interfactory Strike Committee)
Milicja	*Milicja Obywatelska* (Citizens' Militia)
MO	Abbreviation for *Milicja Obywatelska*
Monitor Polski	Official Gazette of the Republic of Poland, the prime minister's official journal
NCFE	National Committee for a Free Europe
ND	*Narodowa Demokracja* (National Democracy)
NGS	*Niezależna Grupa Społeczna* (Independent Social Group)
NiD	*Polski Ruch Wolnościowy Niepodległość I Demokracja* (*Polish Freedom Movement Independence and Democracy,* abbreviated as *PRW NiD* or as *NiD*)
NIE	*Niepodległość* (Independence, an anti-communist structure in AK)
NIK	*Najwyższa Izba Kontroli* (Supreme Audit Office)
NKVD	*People's Commissariat for Internal Affairs* (*Narodnyy komissariat vnutrennikh del*, the Soviet secret police from 1934–1946)
NSZ	*Narodowe Siły Zbrojne* (National Armed Forces)

NZW	*Narodowe Zjednoczenie Wojskowe* (National Military Union)
OPW	*Obóz Polski Walczącej* (Camp of Fighting Poland)
ORMO	*Ochotnicza Rezerwa Milicji Obywatelskiej* (Volunteer Reserve of the Citizens' Militia)
OZN	*Obóz Zjednoczenia Narodowego* (Camp of National Unity)
PAC	Polish-American Congress
PAL	*Polska Armia Ludowa* (Polish People's Army)
PAP	*Polska Agencja Prasowa* (Polish Press Agency)
PAT	*Polska Agencja Telegraficzna* (Polish Telegraphic Agency)
PKB	*Państwowy Korpus Bezpieczeństwa* (National Security Corps)
PKP	*Polityczny Komitet Porozumiewawczy* (Political Coordinating Committee)
PKWN	*Polski Komitet Wyzwolenia Narodowego* (Polish Committee of National Liberation)
POSK	*Polski Ośrodek Społeczno-Kulturalny* (Polish Social and Cultural Association)
POW	*Polska Organizacja Wojskowa* (Polish Military Organization)
PPP	*Polskie Państwo Podziemne* (Polish Secret State)
PPR	*Polska Partia Robotnicza* (Polish Workers' Party)
PPS	*Polska Partia Socjalistyczna* (Polish Socialist Party)

PPS-WRN	*Polska Partia Socjalistyczna – Wolność, Równość, Niepodległość* (Polish Socialist Party - Freedom, Equality, Independence)
PRC	Polish Resettlement Corps (*Polski Korpus Przysposobienia i Rozmieszczenia*)
PRCUA	Polish Roman Catholic Union of America
PSL	*Polskie Stronnictwo Ludowe* (Polish People's Party)
PSL "NW"	*PSL "Nowe Wyzwolenie"* (Polish People's Party "New Liberation")
PSzP	*Polski Sztab Partyzancki* (Polish Partisan Staff)
PTNO	*Polskie Towarzystwo Naukowe na Obczyźnie* (Polish Scientific Society Abroad)
PUCAL	Polish University College Association Limited
PUNO	*Polski Uniwersytet na Obczyźnie* (Polish University in Exile)
PZN	*Polskie Zjednoczenie Narodowe* (Polish National Union)
PZPR	*Polska Zjednoczona Partia Robotnicza* (Polish United Workers' Party)
RAF	Royal Air Force
RJN	*Rząd Jedności Narodowej* (Council of National Unity), representative body in wartime Poland subordinated to the government-in-exile *Rada Jedności Narodowej* (Provisional Council of National Unity), exile representative body in opposition to August Zaleski
ROPCiO	*Ruch Obrony Praw Człowieka i Obywatela* (Movement for Defense of Human and Civic Rights)

RTRP	*Rząd Tymczasowy Rzeczypospolitej Polskiej* (Provisional Government of the Republic of Poland)
SB	*Służba Bezpieczeństwa* (Security Service)
SD	*Stronnictwo Demokratyczne* (Alliance of Democrats)
SDKPiL	*Socjaldemokracja Królestwa Polskiego i Litwy* (Social Democracy of the Kingdom of Poland and Lithuania)
Sejm	Lower house of Poland's parliament (from 1946–1990, the only house)
Senat	Upper house of Poland's parliament (did not exist from 1946–1989)
SL	*Stronnictwo Ludowe* (People's Party)
SL "*Wolność*"	*Stronnictwo Ludowe "Wolność"* (People's Party "Freedom")
SN	*Stronnictwo Narodowe* (National Party)
SP	*Stronnictwo Pracy* (Labor Party)
SPK	*Stowarzyszenie Polskich Kombatantów* (Association of Polish Combatants)
Szare Szeregi	Grey Ranks (underground scouting organization)
SZP	*Służba Zwycięstwu Polski* (Service for Poland's Victory)
Światpol	*Światowy Związek Polaków z Zagranicy* (World Association of Poles Abroad)
TASS	Telegraph Agency of the Soviet Union (*Telegrafnoye agentstvo Sovetskogo Soyuza*)
TON	*Tajna Organizacja Nauczycielska* (Secret Teaching Organization)

TRJN	*Tymczasowy Rząd Jedności Narodowej* (Provisional Government of National Unity), the Soviet-backed government in postwar Poland *Tymczasowa Rada Jedności Narodowej* (Provisional Council of National Unity), an exile representative body in opposition to August Zaleski
TVP	*Telewizja Polska* (Polish Television)
UB	*Urząd Bezpieczeństwa* (Department of Security)
UdSW	*Urząd do Spraw Wyznań* (Office for Religious Affairs)
WiN	*Zrzeszenie Wolność i Niezawisłość* (Freedom and Independence Association)
WRON	*Wojskowa Rada Ocalenia Narodowego* (Military Council of National Salvation)
ZHP	*Związek Harcerstwa Polskiego* (Polish Scouting Association)
ZHP pgK	*Związek Harcerstwa Polskiego działający poza granicami Kraju* (Polish Scouting Organization Operating Outside the Country)
ZOMO	*Zmotoryzowane Odwody Milicji Obywatelskiej* (Motorized Reserves of the Citizens' Militia)
ZPE	*Zjednoczenia Polek na Emigracji* (Union of Polish Women in Exile)
ZPP	*Związek Patriotów Polskich* (Union of Polish Patriots)
ZPWB	*Zjednoczenie Polskie w Wielkiej Brytanii* (Federation of Poles in Great Britain)
ZSL	*Zjednoczone Stronnictwo Ludowe* (United People's Party)
ZWZ	*Związek Walki Zbrojnej* (Union of Armed Struggle)

ŻOB	*Żydowska Organizacja Bojowa* (Jewish Combat Organization)

ŻZW	*Żydowski Związek Wojskowy* (Jewish Military Union)

Bibliography

BOOKS

Anders, Władysław. *An Army in Exile*. MacMillan & Co., 1949.

Andres, Christopher, and Vasily Mitrokhin. *The Sword and the Shield: The Mitrokhin Archive and the Secret History of the KGB*. Basic Books, 2001.

Anstruther, F. C. *Old Polish Legends*. Hippocrene Books Inc., New York, 1991.

Bór-Komorowski, Tadeusz. *The Secret Army*. The Battery Press, Inc., 1984.

Checinski, Michael. *Poland: Communism, Nationalism, Anti-Semitism*. Karz-Cohl Publishing Inc., 1982.

Ciechanowski, Jan. *Defeat in Victory*. Doubleday & Company, Inc., 1947.

Cienciala, Anna M. (ed.). *Katyn: A Crime Without Punishment*. Yale University Press, 2007.

Conquest, Robert. *Kolyma: The Arctic Death Camps*. Oxford University Press, 1980.

———. *The Great Terror: A Reassessment, 40th Anniversary Edition*. Oxford University Press, 1990, 2008.

Courtois, Stéphane, Jean-Louis Panné, Andrzej Paczkowski, Karel Bartosek, Jean-Louis Margolin, and Nicolas Werth, *The Black Book of Communism: Crimes, Terror, Repression*. Harvard University Press, 1999.

The Crime of Katyń: Facts & Documents. London: Polish Cultural Foundation, 1965.

Curry, Jane Leftwich (ed. and trans.). *The Black Book of Polish Censorship*. Random House, 1984.

Davies, Norman. *Europe: A History*. Oxford University Press, 1996.

———. *God's Playground: A History of Poland, Volume I*. Columbia University Press, 1982.

———. *God's Playground: A History of Poland, Volume II*. Columbia University Press, 1982.

———. *Trail of Hope*. Osprey Publishing, 2015.

———. *White Eagle Red Star: The Polish–Soviet War 1919–20*. Orbis Books (London) Ltd., 1983.

Doucette, Siobhan. *Books Are Weapons: The Polish Opposition Press and the Overthrow of Communism*. University of Pittsburgh Press, 2017.

Fiedler, Arkady, and Jarek Garliński (translator). *303 Squadron: The Legendary Battle of Britain Fighter Squadron*. Aquila Polonica, 2010.

Friszke, Andrzej. *Życie Polityczne Emigracji (Druga Wielka Emigracja 1945–1990 cz. I)*. Warszawa: Biblioteka Więzi, 1999.

Garliński, Józef. *Poland in the Second World War*. Hippocrene Books Inc., New York, 1985).

Glass, Ruth (ed.). *London: Aspects of Change*. MacGibbon and Kee, 1964.

Habielski, Rafał. *Życie Społeczne i Kulturalne Emigracji (Druga Wielka Emigracja 1945–1990 cz. III)*. Warszawa: Biblioteka Więzi, 1999.

Habielski, Rafał (ed.). *Poczet Prezydentów Rzeczypospolitej Polskiej na Uchodźstwie w latach 1939–1990*. Białystok: Instytut Pamięci Narodowej, 2015.

Iranek-Osmecki, Kazimierz. *The Unseen and Silent*. Sheed and Ward, 1954.

Iwanow, Nikołaj, and Ewa Siwoń (trans.). *Zginli, bo byli Polakami - Koszmar "operacji polskiej" NKWD 1937–1938 / Killed for Being Poles - Horrors of the "Polish Operation" Conducted by the NKVD in 1927–1938*. Poznań: REBIS Publishing House Ltd., 2017.

Jaroszyńska-Kirchmann, Anna D. *The Exile Mission: The Polish Political Diaspora and Polish Americans, 1939–1956*. Ohio University Press, 2004.

Jędrzejewicz, Wacław. *Piłsudski: A Life for Poland*. Hippocrene Books Inc., New York, 1982.

Kádár Lynn, Katalin (ed.). *The Inauguration of Organized Political Warfare Cold War Organizations sponsored by the National Committee for a Free Europe / Free Europe Committee*. Helena History Press, LLC, 2013.

Kaliński, Janusz, and Joanna Rohozinska-Michalska (trans.). *Economy in Communist Poland – The Road Astray*. Warsaw: Institute of National Remembrance, 2014.

Karpiński, Jakub. *Countdown: The Polish Upheavals of 1956, 1968, 1970, 1976, 1980*. Karz-Cohl Publishers Inc., 1982.

The Katyn Forest Massacre, Hearings before the Select Committee to conduct an investigation of the facts, evidence, and circumstances of the Katyn Forest Massacre. United States Government Printing Office, 1952.

Kemp-Welch, A. *Poland Under Communism: A Cold War History.* Cambridge University Press, 2008.

Kersten, Krystyna. *The Establishment of Communist Rule in Poland, 1943–1948.* University of California Press, 1991.

Kochanski, Halik. *The Eagle Unbowed.* Harvard University Press, 2012.

Korboński, Stefan. *The Polish Underground State.* Hippocrene Books, Inc., 1978, 1981.

Laba, Roman. *The Roots of Solidarity.* Princeton University Press, 1991.

Lane, Arthur Bliss. *I Saw Poland Betrayed.* The Bobbs-Merrill Company, 1948.

Lepak, Keith John. *Prelude to Solidarity: Poland and the Politics of the Gierek Regime.* Columbia University Press, 1988.

Lukas, Richard C. *Bitter Legacy: Polish-American Relations in the Wake of World War II.* The University Press of Kentucky, 1982.

Łukasiewicz, Juliusz, and Wacław Jędrzejewicz (ed.). *Diplomat in Paris.* Columbia University Press, 1970.

Michta, Andrew A. *Red Eagle: The Army in Polish Politics, 1944–1988.* Hoover Institution Press, 1990.

Mikołajczyk, Stanisław. *The Pattern of Soviet Domination.* Sampson Low, Marston & Co., Ltd., 1948.

Miłosz, Czesław. "Traktat moralny" ("Moral Treatise"), *Światło dzienne*, Instytut Literacki, 1953.

Moody, John, and Roger Boyes. *The Priest and the Policeman: The Courageous Life and Cruel Murder of Father Jerzy Popieluszko.* Summit Books, 1987.

The Moscow Trial of the 16 Polish Leaders. London: Liberty Publications, 1945.

My tu żyjemy jak w obozie warownym. Listy PPS-WRN Warszawa-Londyn 1940–1945. Puls Publications Ltd., 1992.

Nazi–Soviet Relations, 1939–1941: Documents from the Archives of The German Foreign Office. Department of State, 1948.

Olson, Lynne, and Stanley Cloud. *A Question of Honor*. Alfred A. Knopf, 2003.

Ostrowski, Stanisław, Danuta B Łomaczewska, and Zbigniew M. Chmielowski (ed.). *Dnie Pohańbienia, Wspomnienia z lat 1939-1941*. Warszawa: Towarzystwo Miłośników Lwowa i Kresów Południowo-Wschodnich, Oddział Stołeczny, Warszawa, 2002–2003.

Patterson, Archibald L. *Between Hitler and Stalin: The Quick Life and Secret Death of Edward Śmigły-Rydz Marshal of Poland*. Dog Ear Publishing, 2010.

Persak, Krzysztof, and Łukasz Kamiński (eds.). *A Handbook of the Communist Security Apparatus in East Central Europe 1944–1989*. Warsaw: Institute of National Remembrance, 2005.

Peszke, Michael Alfred. *The Polish Underground Army, the Western Allies, and the Failure of Strategic Unity in World War II*. McFarland & Company Inc., 2005.

Pienkos, Donald E. *For Your Freedom Through Ours: Polish American Efforts on Poland's Behalf, 1863–1991*. East European Monographs, 1991.

———. *PNA: Centennial History*. East European Monographs, 1984.

Piesakowski, Tomasz. *The Fate of Poles in the USSR 1939–1989*. Gryf Publications Ltd., 1990.

Pleszak, Frank. *Two Years in a Gulag*. Amberley Publishing, 2013.

Polish Educational Foundation in North America. *Kielce – July 4, 1946 – Background, Context and Events*. Toronto and Chicago: The Polish Educational Foundation in North America, 1996.

Polish Government-in-Exile. London: Caldra House Limited, 1989.

Polish–Soviet Relations, 1918–1943. Polish Embassy, 1943.

Raczyński, Edward. *In Allied London: The Wartime Diaries of the Polish Ambassador*. Weidenfeld and Nicolson, 1962.

Republic of Poland Ministry of Foreign Affairs. *The Mass Extermination of Jews in German Occupied Poland*. Hutchinson & Co. (Publishers) Ltd., 1942.

Rogalski, Wiesław. *The Polish Resettlement Corps 1946–1949: Britain's Polish Forces*. Helion & Company Limited, 2019.

Ruane, Kevin. *To Kill a Priest, The Murder of Father Popiełuszko and the Fall of Communism*. Gibson Square Books Ltd., 2004.

Rudnicki, Klemens. *The Last of the War Horses*. Bachman & Turner, 1974.

Siemaszko, Karol. *Sąd Obywatelski w Londynie. Organizacja i orzecznictwo*. Poznań: Wydawnictwo Rys, 2013.

Sikorski, Radek. *Full Circle*. Simon & Schuster, 1997.

Slany, William, and Rogers P. Churchill (eds.). *Foreign Relations of the United States, 1947, Eastern Europe; The Soviet Union, Volume IV*. United States Government Printing Office, 1972.

Stachura, Peter D. *The Poles in Britain 1940–2000: From Betrayal to Assimilation*. Frank Cass Publishers, 2004.

Steven, Stewart. *The Poles*. Macmillan Publishing Company, 1982.

Stypulkowski, Zbigniew. *Invitation to Moscow*. Walker and Company, 1951.

Subritzky-Kusza, Michael. *History of the Polish Government (In Exile) 1939–1990*. New Zealand: Three Feathers Publishing Co., 1996.

Sukiennicki, Wiktor. *Facts and Documents Concerning Polish Prisoners of War Captured by the U.S.S.R. during the 1939 Campaign*. London, 1946.

Swianiewicz, Stanisław. *In the Shadow of Katyn*. Witold Publishing, Canada, 2002.

Swoger, Gordon. *The Strange Odyssey of Poland's National Treasures, 1939–1961*. Dundurn, 2004.

Sword, Keith. *The Formation of the Polish Community in Great Britain 1939–50*. London: Caldra House Ltd., 1989.

Szkopiak, Zygmunt C. (ed.). *The Yalta Agreements - Documents Prior to, During and After the Crimea Conference 1945*. London: Polish Government-in-Exile, 1986.

Torańska, Teresa. *"Them": Stalin's Polish Puppets*. Harper & Row, 1987.

Turkowski, Romuald. *Parlamentaryzm polski na uchodźstwie 1945–1972*. Warszawa: Wydawnictwo Sejmowe, 2001.

———. *Parlamentaryzm polski na uchodźstwie 1973–1991*. Warszawa: Wydawnictwo Sejmowe, 2002.

Wałęsa, Lech. *A Way of Hope*. Henry Holt and Company Inc., 1987.

Wat, Aleksander. *My Century*. Norton & Company, Inc., 1990.

Watt, Richard M. *Bitter Glory: Poland and its Fate, 1918 to 1939*. Simon and Schuster, 1979, 1982.

Weiser, Benjamin. *A Secret Life.* PublicAffairs, 2004.

Williamson, David G. *The Polish Underground, 1939–1947.* Pen & Sword Books Limited, 2012.

Wojdon, Joanna. *White and Red Umbrella.* Helena History Press, 2015.

Wood, E. Thomas, and Stanislaw M. Jankowski. *Karski: How One Man Tried to Stop the Holocaust.* John Wiley & Sons, Inc., 1994.

Zamoyski, Adam. *Paderewski.* Atheneum, 1982.

———. *The Forgotten Few.* John Murray, 1995.

Zawodny, J. K. *Death in the Forest.* University of Notre Dame Press, 1962.

Journals and Periodicals

The American Political Science Review

Archiwum Emigracji

The Augustan

Biuletyn Instytutu Pamięci Narodowej (Biuletyn IPN)

Biuletyn Koło Lwowian

Biuletyn Stowarzyszenie-Klub Kawalerów Orderu Wojennego Virtuti Militari

The Chicago Tribune

Dzieje Najnowsze

Dziennik Polski (London)

Dziennik Polski i Dziennik Żołnierza

The Economist

Express Wieczorny

Free Poland – Wolna Polska

Gazeta Wyborcza

Glaukopis

Głos Ludu

The Guardian

Humanities and Social Sciences

The Independent

Klio. Czasopismo poświęcone dziejom Polski i powszechnym

Kultura (Paris)

Kurier Historyczny

Kurier Poranny

The London Gazette

The Los Angeles Times

Maclean's

Narodowiec (France)

The New Criterion

Niedziela

Nowy Czas

Nowy Dziennik (New York)

Orka

Orzeł Biały (London)

Pamięć i Sprawiedliwość

The Pittsburgh Press

Polish Affairs

Polish American Studies

The Polish Review

POLITEJA. Pismo Wydziału Studiów Międzynarodowych i Politycznych Uniwersytetu Jagiellońskiego

Polityka

Polska Zbrojna Historia

Polska Walcząca

Przegląd Historyczny

Przegląd Historyczno-Wojskowy

Przegląd Naukowo-Metodyczny

Przegląd Polonijny

Przegląd Polsko-Polonijny – The Poland-Polonia Review

Robotnik Wybrzeża
Rocznik Historii Prasy Polskiej
Rzeczpospolita
Rzeczpospolita Polska
Słowo
Samostanowienie – Kwartalnik Polityczny
Studia Historyczne
The Telegraph
Time
The Times (London)
Tribune
Trybuna (London)
Trybuna Ludu
Trybuna Robotnicza
Tygodnik Polski
Tygodnik Powszechny
Tygodnik Przegląd
Tygodnik Solidarność
The Washington Post
Wiadomości (London)
WIĘŹ
Wprost
Zeszyty Historyczne
Zeszyty Naukowe WSOWL
Żołkieta Wolności
Życie Warszawy

Government Publications and Press Releases

Source names are listed in their language of publication. If a source is published in multiple languages, its name is given in all languages referenced in this work. When multiple sources share a name, the city of publication is provided to distinguish between them.

Bankoteka

Biuletyn Informacyjny

Dziennik Ustaw Rzeczypospolitej Polskiej (Londyn)

Dziennik Ustaw Rzeczypospolitej Polskiej (Lublin)

Dziennik Ustaw Rzeczypospolitej Polskiej (Warszawa)

Information Bulletin of the Polish Government-in-Exile

Monitor Polski

Polska Agencja Prasowa

Polska Agencja Telegraficzna / Polish Telegraph Agency

TASS

Archives

Archives of the Józef Piłsudski Institute of America

Archiwum Akt Nowych

Archiwum Instytutu Literackiego (Maisons-Lafitte)

Archives of the Polish Institute and Sikorski Museum (PISM)

Archiwum Instytutu Pamięci Narodowej (AIPN)

Archiwum Senatu RP

Central Intelligence Agency FOIA (Freedom of Information Act)

Department of State (United States)

Federal Bureau of Investigation

Hansard (UK Parliament)

Ministerstwo Spraw Zagranicznych

Margaret Thatcher Foundation

National Archives (United Kingdom)

National Historical Archives of Belarus (Национальный Исторический Архив Беларуси)

Polish Roman Catholic Union of America (Chicago)

Senat Rzeczypospolitej Polskiej

Truman Library

Documents

Bierut, Bolesław. "*Dekret o własności i użytkowaniu gruntów na obszarze m. st. Warszawy,*" 1945.

Central European Council. "Multilateral Agreement of the Central European Community," 1986.

Churchill, Winston and Roosevelt, Franklin. *Atlantic Charter*, 1941.

Gomułka, Władysław. "*O co walczymy?*" *(Deklaracja Programowa Polskiej Partii Robotniczej)*, 1943.

Hanff, Konstanty Z. Letter to Bronisław Baranowski, Mjr. Leon Wiśniewski, and Płk. Marian Gołębiewski dated January 20, 1989.

Inter-Allied Council Statement on the Principles of the Atlantic Charter: September 24, 1941.

Paulus VI, "*Episcoporum Poloniae coetus,*" 1972.

Potsdam Agreement, 1945.

Rada Jedności Narodowej. "O co walczy Naród Polski?", 1944.

Reddaway, Norman. "Memorandum of 28 September 1976 to The Right Honorable Anthony Crosland MP, Foreign and Commonwealth Office, from Norman Reddaway, British Ambassador to Poland," 1976.

Constitutions of Poland

1919: Small Constitution of 1919 *(Mała Konstytucja z 1919 roku)*

1921: Constitution of the Republic of Poland *(Konstytucja Rzeczypospolitej Polskiej)*, also known as the March Constitution *(Konstytucja marcowa)*

1926: Act of August 2, 1926, amending and supplementing the Constitution of the Republic of Poland of March 17, 1921 *(Ustawa z dnia 2 sierpnia 1926 r. zmieniająca i uzupełniająca Konstytucję Rzeczypospolitej z dnia 17 marca 1921 r.)*, also known as the August Novelization *(Nowela sierpniowa)*

1935: Constitutional Act of April 23, 1935 *(Ustawa Konstytucyjna z dnia 23 kwietnia 1935 r.)*, also known as the April Constitution *(Konstytucja kwietniowa)*

1947: Constitutional Act of February 19, 1947, on the structure and scope of activities of the highest bodies of the Republic of Poland *(Mała Konstytucja z 1947 roku (Ustawa Konstytucyjna z dnia 19 lutego 1947 r. o ustroju i zakresie działania najwyższych organów Rzeczypospolitej Polskiej)*, also known as the Small Constitution of 1947 *(Mała Konstytucja z 1947)*

1952: Constitution of the Polish People's Republic *(Konstytucja Polskiej Rzeczypospolitej Ludowej)*, also known as the July Constitution *(Konstytucja lipcowa)*

1989: Act of April 7, 1989, amending the Constitution of the Polish People's Republic *(Ustawa z dnia 7 kwietnia 1989 roku o zmianie Konstytucji Polskiej Rzeczypospolitej Ludowej)*, also known as the April Novelization *(Nowela kwietniowa)*

1992: Constitutional Act of October 17, 1992, on mutual relations between the legislative and executive authorities of the Republic of Poland and on local government *(Ustawa Konstytucyjna z dnia 17 października 1992 r. o wzajemnych stosunkach między władzą ustawodawczą i wykonawczą Rzeczypospolitej Polskiej oraz o samorządzie terytorialnym)*, also known as the Small Constitution of 1992 *(Mała Konstytucja z 1992 r.)*

1997: Constitution of the Republic of Poland *(Konstytucja Rzeczypospolitej Polskiej z dnia 2 kwietnia 1997 r.)*

Online Resources

Abbey-Principality of San Luigi, "The Most Revd. Juliusz Nowina-Sokolnicki." https://san-luigi.org/2013/06/06/the-most-revd-juliusz-nowina-sokolnicki/

"Archiwum Feliksa Rembiałkowskiego," Muzeum Dyplomacji i Uchodźstwa Polskiego Uniwersytetu Kazimierza Wielkiego w Bydgoszczy. http://muzeum.niezurawski.pl/feliksrembialowski.php

"Afera" Bergu (1). July 16, 2012. www.salon24.pl/u/chris1991/434219,afera-bergu-1

Biegus, Zosia and Jurek. "Penley, Llanerch Panna and Iscoyd Park Polish Hospitals." www.polishresettlementcampsintheuk.co.uk/penley.htm

Bretan, Juliette. "Moved Away, Then Faded Away: Polish Interwar Artists After WWII." culture.pl/en/article/moved-away-then-faded-away-polish-interwar-artists-after-wwii

Chodakiewicz, Marek Jan. "The Legacy of Hopelessness: Katyń and Smolensk," speech delivered at the Second Polonia Forum, Doylestown, PA, April 18, 2015. www.iwp.edu/kosciuszko-chair-center-for-intermarium-studies/2015/05/04/dr-chodakiewicz-speaks-about-katyn-and-smolensk-at-the-second-polonia-forum/

Dowell, Stuart. "On this day, 79 years ago, Poland was invaded by the Soviet Union following a secret deal between Stalin and Hitler," The First News, September 17, 2018. https://www.thefirstnews.com/article/on-this-day-79-years-ago-poland-was-invaded-by-the-soviet-union-following-a-secret-deal-between-stalin-and-hitler-2277#:~:text=Soviet%20invasion%20of%20Poland%2C%201939.%20Advance%20of%20the,of%20this%20bastard%20of%20the%20Treaty%20of%20Versailles".

Drogosz, Andrzej i Cedro, Aneta. "Kazimierz Sabbat 1913–1989." www.bieliny.pl/asp/kazimierz-sabbat,154,1

Fischer, Benjamin B. "The Katyn Controversy: Stalin's Killing Field," April 14, 2007. www.cia.gov/static/5a3e46e77b3c417a15bcf927e7b049cc/Stalins-Killing-Field.pdf

Gasior, Mariusz. "The Polish Pilots Who Flew in the Battle of Britain," Imperial War Museums, London. www.iwm.org.uk/history/the-polish-pilots-who-flew-in-the-battle-of-britain

Gniadek, Waldemar. "Bolesław Wieniawa Długoszowski – lekarz, generał, wolnomularz." http://doi.org/10.25121/MR.2020.23.3.109

Kister, Anna Grażyna. "Stalinowska partia w partii: Centralne Biuro Komunistów Polskich w ZSRR," July 8, 2014. historia.interia.pl/polska-walczaca/news-stalinowska-partia-w-partii-centralne-biuro-komunistow-polsk/podglad-wydruku,nId,1464768

Kopeć, Krzysztof. "Fundusz Obrony Narodowej – FON." 11/2010. krzysztofkopec.pl/dokumenty/Fundusz_Obrony_Narodowej.pdf

Koper, Sławomir. "Bolesław Wieniawa-Długoszowski." zbiam.pl/artykuly/boleslaw-wieniawa-dlugoszowski/

Komunikat. www.videofact.com/pomnik_kat_skandal.html

Kowalski, Waldemar. "Kryzys prezydencki 1939 roku." https://muzhp.pl/wiedza-on-line/kryzys-prezydencki-1939-roku (accessed 9/5/2025)

Kozłowski, Tomasz. "The Security Service's Last Task." polishhistory.pl/the-security-services-last-task/

"The Literary Institute." kulturaparyska.com/en/article/history

Lenczewski, Tomasz. "Juliusz Nowina-Sokolnicki - Uwagi do biografii." tomaszlenczewski.pl/teksty/historia/juliusz-nowina-sokolnicki/

Lenczewski, Tomasz. "Oszust genealogiczny." tomaszlenczewski.pl/teksty/genealogia-2/oszust-genealogiczny/

Lipińska, Grażyna. www.17september1939.com

Magola, Miroslaw. "Interview with Daphne Urbanska, widow of Marek Urbanski, son of Alfred Urbański, Prime Minister of Poland 1972–1976," February 5, 2014. cupdf.com/document/interview-with-daphne-urbanska-widow-of-marek-urbanski-son-of-alfred-urbanski-conducted-by-miroslaw-magola.html?page=3

Mazowiecki, Tadeusz, speech in *Sejm*, August 24, 1989. "*Sprawozdanie Stenograficzne z 6 posiedzenia Sejmu Polskiej Rzeczypospolitej Ludowej w dniach 23 i 24 sierpnia 1989 r.*" (Zakł. Graph. Tamka, Warszawa, 1989), łam 86. https://orka2.sejm.gov.pl/StenogramyX.nsf/0/259278CD28DE3BBDC1257D20002CC6FD/$file/006_000006771.pdf

Mirowicz, Ryszard, and Gregory P. Dziekonski (editor and translator). *Edward Rydz-Śmigły: A Political and Military Biography*. digital.lib.washington.edu/researchworks/bitstream/handle/1773/22699/Rydz-Smigly.pdf?sequence=1

Mokrzycka-Pokora, Monika. "Kazimierz Dejmek 17.05.1924—31.12.2002." *culture.pl/en/artist/kazimierz-dejmek*

"Nazwy do Zmiany, ul. Berlinga Zygmunta," *ipn.gov.pl/pl/upamietnianie/dekomunizacja/zmiany-nazw-ulic/nazwy-ulic/nazwy-do-zmiany/37003,ul-Berlinga-Zygmunta.html*

Nowak, Joanna. "London Office of Edward Raczyński." *rogalin.mnp.art.pl/en/page/london-office*

Pietraszka, Irka S. i Żmudzki, Michał K. "Wieniawa-Długoszowski – Ułan i Poeta." *jpilsudski.org/artykuly-personalia-biogramy/wspolpracownicy-rodzina-otoczenie-jozefa-pilsudskiego/item/2044-wieniawa-dlugoszowski-ulan-i-poeta*

Paczkowski, Andrzej. "Referendum z 30 czerwca 1946 r. Próba wstępnego bilansu." *www.kedyw.info/wiki/Andrzej_Paczkowski,_Referendum_z_30_czerwca_1946_r._Próba_wstępnego_bilansu*

The Polish Institute and Sikorski Museum. *www.pism.org.uk/history*

"Report to Congress on the Crimea Conference, March 1, 1945." *www.presidency.ucsb.edu/documents/address-congress-the-yalta-conference*

Sabbat-Świdlicka, Anna. "Hm. Kazimierz Sabbat." *www.zhpharcerki.org/organizacja_harcerek/egazetka_6/instruktorzy/sabbat.htm*

Słomińska, Sylwia. "Wieluń, 1 września 1939 r." *www.szynkielow.amr.pl/artykuly.php?artykul=194*

Sprawozdanie Stenograficzne z 23. posiedzenia Senatu Rzeczypospolitej Polskiej w dniach 13 i 14 grudnia 2006 r., Senat Rzeczypospolitej Polskiej VI kadencja (Warszawa 2007 r., ISSN 0867-261X), s. 121–122. *http://ww2.senat.pl/k6/dok/sten/023/spr23.pdf*

Starowieyski, Łukasz. "He Did Not Return on a White Horse. General Władysław Anders." *polishhistory.pl/he-did-not-return-on-a-white-horse-general-wladyslaw-anders/*

Szcześniak, Andrzej Leszek. "Historia Fundusz Obrony Narodowej," *www.fon.com.pl/historia-fon/*

Szukała, Michał. "Prof. M. Wołos: Wieniawa-Długoszowski był uosobieniem tego, co polskie" (31.08.2017), *niepodlegla.dzieje.pl/artykul/prof-m-wolos-wieniawa-dlugoszowski-byl-uosobieniem-tego-co-polskie*

"The Tehran Conference, 1943." *history.state.gov/milestones/1937-1945/tehran-conf*

Tomczyk, Paweł. "140 lat temu urodził się Bolesław Wieniawa-Długoszowski." *dzieje.pl/wiadomosci/140-lat-temu-urodzil-sie-boleslaw-wieniawa-dlugoszowski*

"Upamiętnienie Władysława Raczkiewicza w Gruzji," Ministerstwo Kultury i Dziedzictwa Narodowego." *www.gov.pl/web/kultura/upamietnienie-wladyslawa-raczkiewicza-w-gruzji*

"The Wartime Experiences of an RNR Officer." *W2 People's War. www.bbc.co.uk/history/ww2peopleswar/stories/33/a8999833.shtml*

Wójtowicz, Norbert. "Juliusz Nowina-Sokolnicki (1920–2009)." *www.legitymizm.org/nowina-sokolnicki*

"Zarys instytucji referendum jako formy demokracji bezpośredniej. Referendum ogólnokrajowe w Polsce." Kancelaria Senatu Biuro Analiz i Dokumentacji, OT-620, Maj 2013. *https://www.senat.gov.pl/gfx/senat/pl/senatopracowania/50/plik/ot-620_internet.pdf*

"ZOMO – 'bijące' serce partii." April 13, 2009. *wiadomosci.dziennik.pl/wydarzenia/artykuly/145811,zomo-bijace-serce-partii.html*

Films and Multimedia Resources

Jagodziński, Konrad and Chmura, Agnieszka. "Republic in Exile, Episode 4: Solidarity," 2015. *https://www.youtube.com/watch?v=UE6KGBcPKrI&list=PLpGkvbzPcKIlYZLK3tapD7OGyx5I4Fl_S&index=4*

Jagodziński, Konrad and Chmura, Agnieszka. "Republic in Exile, Episode 5: Free Poland," 2015. *https://www.youtube.com/watch?v=mAcNj5fSMVM&list=PLpGkvbzPcKIlYZLK3tapD7OGyx5I4Fl_S&index=5*

Acknowledgements

This book would not have been possible without the support and encouragement of my wife Brenda or the interest in Polish history instilled in me by my parents Stanley and Elizabeth. My thanks to the team at Hippocrene Books for all of their hard work that brought this book to publication. I also wish to thank Dr. Kornelia Tancheva and Renée Pekor at the University of Pittsburgh for their support and Peter Kracht at the University of Pittsburgh for his guidance.

Index

Page numbers followed by n indicate footnotes.

A

Academic Circle of Senior Scouts (University of Warsaw), 318
Academy of Fine Arts (Berlin), 36
Accord of Democratic Parties, see *Porozumienie Stronnictw Demokratycznych (PSD)*
ACEN. See *Assembly of Captive European Nations*
ACEN Inc., 247
Action Group of NSZZ "Solidarność" in Great Britain, see *Grupa Działania NSZZ "Solidarność" w Wielkiej Brytanii)*
Adamczyk, Arkadiusz, 55n24
Adesko, Thaddeus, 118n7
Adria restaurant (Warsaw), 39n23
Adrian VI, 277
afera Bergu (Berg affair) or *Sprawa Bergu* (Berg matter), 174–176, 185, 193–194, 199, 201, 214n31
Afghanistan, 298
Ağca, Mehmet Ali, 306n34
Agreement Concerning the Demarcation of the Established and the Existing Polish–German State Frontier, see Treaty of Zgorzelec
Agreement of Mutual Assistance, 20–21
AK. See *Armia Krajowa*
Akcja Antyk, 100
Akcja Burza (Operation Tempest), 107
Akcja N, 94n8
Aksamit, Bożena, 396n20
Akt Zjednoczenia Narodowego (National Unity Act), 192–196, 199, 229, 231, 234, 243, 286
AL. See *Armia Ludowa*
Albania, 203, 260n19
Alexander III, 8
Alexander Nevsky Cathedral, 7n3
Alexandrowicz, Janusz Witold, 230
Allied forces, 121
  Battle of Britain, 94, 116
  invasion of Germany, 138–140
  invasion of Italy, 138–139
  Operation Market Garden, 140
  Potsdam conference, 142–144
  and Warsaw Uprising, 116
Alt-Eiche, 21
American Polish Labor Council, 117n5
American Polonia, 259
American Slav Congress, 117n5
Anders, Irena, 239
Anders, Władysław, 238–239
  and *Akt Zjednoczenia Narodowego* (National Unity Act), 195–196
  Battle of Monte Cassino, 108–109
  burial, 239, 392
  citizenship, 158, 339
  as commander in chief, 65–72, 81–83, 96n14, 97, 117, 139, 149, 158, 166–167, 203, 254–255, 306n35
  and Council of Ministers, 226
  and Danina Polska Ltd., 187
  death, 239
  division between Zaleski and, 182, 230–231, 237–238
  and Jaruzelski, 306n35
  and Klimkowski, 223
  and *Komitet Pomocy Rodakom w Kraju* (Committee to Aid Compatriots in the Country), 214
  libel cases, 222–224
  London office, 202
  and Poles in Soviet Union, 87
  political affiliation, 158
  and POSK, 235
  and presidential succession, 166–167
  principles of unification, 229
  protests, 205
  on *Rada Trzech* (Council of Three), 196–197
  and Sabbat, 324
  and *Skarb Narodowy*, 188
  support for Israel, 236
  support for POSK, 235
  support for Sosnkowski, 116
  and Tomaszewski, 182
Andersowa, Irena, 381
Andorra, 260n19
Andrews, George D., 169
Andrzejewski, Jerzy, 271n45
Anglo–Polish Society, 210
anti-Catholic prejudice, 158
anti-Polish sentiments, 157–158
antisemitism, 155–156, 236
Apostolic Episcopal Church, 310
"Appeal to the Free World," 307
April Constitution. See Constitution
April Novelization, 368
Arbuz (Watermelon) (codename), 216–217, 228
Arc de Triomphe, 290
Arciszewska-Mielewczyk, Dorota, 395
Arciszewski, Melania, 112, 127, 130
Arciszewski, Mirosław, 52n17
Arciszewski, Tomasz, 111–112, 122, 138, 144, 163, 166–168, 172–173, 196–197, 202
Argasiński, Tadeusz, 52n17
Argentina, 193n3
Armenia, 269n36
Armia Krajowa (AK, Home Army), 78–79, 85–86, 99–100, 106, 110–112, 376
  command, 123
  deportations, 361
  dissolution, 124
  Operation Tempest *(Akcja Burza)*, 107
  operations to release comrade prisoners, 138
  publications and monuments related to, 215
  strength of, 124n20
  veterans of, 136–138, 176–178, 184, 205–206, 215, 276n55
  Warsaw Uprising, 113–118
Armia Ludowa (AL, People's Army), 103–104, 107, 114, 124n20
Armia Małopolska, 26–27
Armia Narodowa (National Army), 56
Arran, Lord, 272n48
Artystów Polskich (Association of Polish Artists), 36n14

Assembly of Captive European Nations (ACEN), 203–204, 226, 247, 327, 401n1
Association of Friends of the Polish Village in America, see *Związek Przyjaciół Wsi Polskiej w Ameryce*
Association of Polish Airmen in London, see *Stowarzyszenie Lotników Polskich w Londynie*
Association of Polish Artists, see *Artystów Polskich*
Association of Polish Democratic Youth, see *Związek Polskiej Młodzieży Demokratycznej*
Association of Polish Engineers in Great Britain, see *Stowarzyszenie Techników Polskich w Wielkiej Brytanii*
Association of Polish Socialists Abroad, see *Związek Socjalistów Polskich na Obczyźnie*
Association of Polish Stage Artists, see *Związek Artystów Scen Polskich*
Association of Polish Youth, see *Związek Młodzieży Polskiej*
Association "Polish Community", see *Stowarzyszenie "Wspólnota Polska"*
Athworth, John, 222
Atlantic Charter, 72, 83, 105, 118, 125
Attlee, Clement, viii, 143, 151–152, 156–158
Auschwitz concentration camp, 56, 62, 94n8, 114
Australia, 91, 193n3, 335–336, 353
Austria, 14n26, 19, 148
Austria-Hungary, 3n1, 8–9
Austro-Hungarian Army, 294

B
Babiński, Wacław, 221
Baden-Powell, Robert, 349
Bagiński, Kazimierz, 54, 130, 133–134, 171, 174
Balastis, Maria, 36n12
Balkan States, 264
Baltavia, 169–170
Baltic Sea, 21n35
Bańczyk, Stanisław, 232n28, 264
Bank Handlowy w Warszawie, 34n5, 166
Bank of Montreal, 221–222
Bank Polski, 25–26

Bank Powszechna Kasa Oszczędności (Bank PKO), 224–225
Banque de France, 25–26
las Baran (Ram's Forest), 119
Baranowski, Bronisław, 337, 362–363
Barbakan Krakowski, 305n32
Barbarito, Luigi, 329
Barnby, Lord, 272n48, 274, 305
Bartel, Kazimierz, 15
Bartoszcze, Roman, 365, 372–373
Bartoszewski, Władysław, 303–304, 332, 355n19
Bataliony Chłopskie (BCh, Peasants' Battalions), 55, 78, 85, 106–107, 118, 124, 136–138
Battle of Britain, 94, 116
Battle of Britain Memorial, 398
Battle of Grunwald, 233
Battle of Lenino, 96–97
Battle of Monte Cassino, 108–109, 352
The Battle of Russia, 77n61
Battle of Warsaw, 222
BBC, 62, 272, 370
BBC1, 267
BBC2, 272
BBWR. See *Bezpartyjny Blok Współpracy z Rządem*
BBWR (*Bezpartyjny Blok Współpracy z Rządem*, Nonpartisan Bloc for Cooperation with the Government), 15–18
BCh, see *Bataliony Chłopskie*
BdV, see *Bund der Vertriebenen*
Beck, Józef, 18, 20–21, 28–29, 39n24, 52n17, 53, 385n8, 391
Begin, Menachem (Mieczysław Biegun), 101n23, 332n33
Belgium
  German invasion of, 58
  government-in-exile, 2, 28n15, 60
  and independent Poland, 20
  Inter-Allied Council, 72
  liberation of, 403
Belweder Palace, see *Pałac Belwederski*
Belzec death camp, 85
Benelux countries, 193n3
Beneš, Edvard, 141n1
Berenson, Bronisława, 36–38
Berenson, Leon, 36–37
Bereza Kartuska prison, 17, 198

Berg affair or Berg matter, see *afera Bergu*
Beria, Lavrentiy, 66, 73, 91, 100n20, 189, 360
Berlin, Germany, 140
Berlin Wall, 359
Berling, Zygmunt, 67, 70–71, 75, 82–83, 95–97, 107, 115
Berman, Jakub, 74n52, 75, 102–103, 131
Bessarabia, 58
Bezpartyjny Blok Współpracy z Rządem (BBWR, Nonpartisan Bloc for Cooperation with the Government), 15–18
Biblioteka Polska (Polish Library), 234–235, 255, 385
Bielicki, Tadeusz, 51, 175, 196–197, 210, 324
Bieliny Kapitulne, 317
Bień, Adam, 129–130, 133
Biernacka, Barbara (Maria), 74n50
Biernacki, Bolesław, 74n50
Bierut, Bolesław
  as activist, 73
  assassination attempt, 162
  brutal regime, 124, 129, 151, 162–163, 189, 206, 216
  death, 205–206
  internment, 240
  as NKVD agent, 74, 162n39
  Potsdam conference, 143–144
  as PPR leader, 86–87, 104, 120, 124, 129, 134–135, 151, 159–160, 178–179
  presidential election of, 159–160
  statues of, 397n22
  and Warsaw Uprising, 115
Bierut, Wojciech, 74n50
Bierut Decree, see *Dekret Bieruta*
Bissell, Clayton, 93n6
Biuletyn Informacyjny (Information Bulletin), 31
Biuro Informacyjne Solidarności w Londynie (Solidarity Information Office in London), 302
Biuro Polityczne (Political Bureau), 26n1
The Black Book of Poland, 62
Black Madonna, 214–215
Black Marias, 349–350
Błaszczyk, Henryk, 155, 156n31
Błaszczyk, Walenty, 156n31
Blok Demokratyczny (Democratic Bloc), 152–153, 160–161
blood libel, 155n30
Bobkowski, Aleksander, 52n17

Bohemia and Moravia, 19
Bohusz-Szyszko, Zygmunt, 67, 70, 208n24, 210, 290
Bojczuk, Michał, 259
Bolesław Bierut University of Wrocław, see *Uniwersytet Wrocławski im. Bolesława Bieruta*
Bolshevik Revolution, 300, 331
Bolshevism, 12, 149n19
Bonnet, Georges, 24–25
Bór-Komorowski. *See* Komorowski, Tadeusz
Borczyk, Stanisław, 258n16, 388
borders
  Atlantic Charter, 72
  Curzon Line, 105–106, 109, 120–122, 125, 127
  after Great War, 11–12
  Locarno Treaties, 14
  Oder–Neisse Line, 83, 105, 123, 147, 159, 225, 283n12, 310–311
  Polish–German border, 259, 359–360
  Potsdam Agreement, 143–144, 241
  after Second World War, 147
  Sikorski–Maisky Pact, 64–65
  Treaty of Warsaw, 241
  Treaty of Zgorzelec, 186
  US recognition of, 158–159
  Yalta agreements, 125, 128–129, 364
Bortnowski, Władysław, 208n24
Boruta-Spiechowicz, Mieczysław, 70, 245
The Boys from Stalingrad, 77n61
Braine, Bernard, 305, 329, 381
Brandt, Willy, 241
Bratoszewski, Jan, 365n50
Braun, Jerzy, 141–142
Brazil, 193n3
Breslau University, 147
Brett, Robert E., 26
Brezhnev, Leonid, 233n31, 302
Brezhnev Doctrine, 262
British Solidarity with Poland campaign, 302
British War Graves Commission, 239
Brompton Cemetery, 202
Brompton Oratory, 205, 211, 296, 320–321
Brońska, Wanda, 189n49
Brooke, Alan, 139
Brown, George, 272n48
Bryczkowski, Janusz, 365n50
Bryja, Wincenty, 168–169, 169n8

Brystiger, Julia, 74n52
Bryzgun, Vladimir Ivanovich, 393
Brzask, 318
Brześć (now Brest), 30n19
Brzeski, Tadeusz, 199
Brzesko, 36n13
Brzeszczyński, Stefan, 258n16
Bucharest, 25–26
Bucher, Roy, 272n48
Bugnanin, Nikolai, 110
Bukojemski, Leon, 71n43
Bukowski, Jerzy, 370
Bulganin, Nikolai, 204
Bulgaria, 174, 203, 357n29
Bulgarian National Committee, 327n20
Bulgarian National Front, 327
Bulgarians, 205
Bund der Vertriebenen (BdV, Federation of Expellees), 284
Burdenko, Nikolai, 100
Burdenko Commission (Extraordinary State Commission for Ascertaining and Investigating Crimes Perpetrated by the German-Fascist Invaders and their Accomplices), 100, 150
Burhardt-Bukacki, Stanisław, 42
Butyrka Prison, 133n41, 252–253
Byelorussia, 12, 349
Byelorussian SSR, 364n48
Byelorussians, 18, 69, 80–81
Byrnes, James, 143–144, 159

C

Cadogan, Alexander, 89
Călinescu, Armand, 34n5
Calvas, Stefania, 36–37, 38n18
Cambridge University, 210n27
Camp Koja, 353
Camp of Fighting Poland, see *Obóz Polski Walczącej*
Camp of National Unity, see *Obóz Zjednoczenia Narodowego*
Camus, Albert, 181
Canada
  émigré seats in *Rada Rzeczypospolitej Polskiej*, 193n3
  Rada branch in, 311, 341, 385
  relations with Poland, 150, 220–222, 323
  relations with Soviets, 298n12
Capra, Frank, 77n61
The Captive Mind (Miłosz), 177n20

Caritas, 176–177
Carol II, 28–29, 33–36, 42
Carter, Jimmy, 290
Carter, John F., 90
Cathedral of St. John the Baptist (Warsaw), 380, 391, 399
Catherine II of Russia, 7
Caxton Hall, 188
CBKP, see *Centralne Biuro Komunistów Polski*
CBOS, see *Centrum Badania Opinii Społecznej*
Ceaușescu, Nicolae, 334
CEC. See Central European Community
Cecilienhof Palace, 142–143
H. Cegielski Metal Industry Complex in Poznań, National Enterprise, see *Zakłady Przemysłu Metalowego H. Cegielski w Poznaniu, Przedsiębiorstwo Państwowe*
Celiński, Andrzej, 377
Cemetery of Meritorious Wielkopolans, see *Cmentarz Zasłużonych Wielkopolan*
Cemetery of the Defenders of Lwów, see *Cmentarz Obrońców Lwowa*
censorship, 160, 168, 236–237, 271, 339
Central Bureau for International Relations of Free Poles, 336
Central European Community (CEC), 327–328, 336n40, 395
Central Intelligence Agency (CIA), 173–175, 247
Centralne Biuro Komunistów Polski (CBKP, Central Bureau of Polish Communists), 103–104
Centralny Komitet Organizacji Niepodległościowych (CKON, Central Committee of Independence Organizations), 26, 55
Centrolew coalition, 16
Centrum Badania Opinii Społecznej (CBOS, Public Opinion Research Center), 363
Centrum Polsko-Słowiańskie (Polish and Slavic Center), 362
Cerizay, France, 53–54, 123
Chaciński, Józef, 130, 133–134
Chamberlain, Neville, 19, 30–31
Champetier de Ribes, Auguste, 35–36, 40–43
Charing Cross Hospital (London), 278

INDEX

Charta 77 (Charter 77), 269n36
Cheka, 37, 180n32. *See also* KGB; NKVD
Chełm, liberation of, 110
Chełmecka, Maria, 274–275
Chemical Bank, 362
Chernobyl, 329
Chez Sophie, 211
China, Republic of, 72, 131, 150, 203, 298n12
Chita region, 253–254
Chmielowski, Albert, 312n46
Choroszewski, Walery, 311, 377
Christ the King Roman Catholic Church (Balham), 314
Christian Democracy Party, see *Stronnictwo Chrześcijańskiej Demokracji*
Christian Democratic Union of Central and Eastern Europe, 203
Chrześcijańska Demokracja, 227
Church of Saints Peter and Paul (Lwów), 148n18
Churchill, Winston, 145n12, 392
　and Anders, 139
　Atlantic Charter, 72, 83, 105, 118, 125
　and Curzon Line, 105–106, 120–122
　Declaration on Liberated Europe, 125
　and invasion of France, 58
　and Katyń massacre, 89–90, 94–95
　and Mikołajczyk, 120–122, 140, 170
　and Poland's provisional government, 134–135
　Potsdam conference, 143
　and Second Polish Corps, 80
　and Sikorski, 83, 97
　and Sikorski–Maisky Pact, 64–65
　and Sosnkowski, 111, 116
　Soviet policy, 62–63
　timeline of major events, viii
　victory celebration, 151–152
　Yalta agreements, 124–129
Churchill, Winston (grandson), 272n48
Churchill, Winston, Jr., 239n37, 305
CIA, see Central Intelligence Agency
Cichociemni (Silent and Unseen), 112n34
Ciechanowski, Jan, 83
Ciepliński, Łukasz, 206
Cieszyn Silesia, 11–12, 14
Cimoszewicz, Włodzimierz, 365, 365n50, 372–373
Ciołkosz, Adam, 197, 205, 210, 260n20, 265–270, 322–324
Ciołkosz, Lidia, 210, 265, 365, 369, 386
Citizens' Committee "Solidarność", see *Komitet Obywatelski "Solidarność" KO "S"*
Citizens' Court in London, see *Sąd Obywatelski w Londynie*
Citizen's Courts Abroad, see *Sądy Obywatelskie na Obczyźnie*
Citizens' Militia, see *Milicja Obywatelska*
citizenship rights, 158, 226, 239, 246, 257
Civic Committee of the Collection to Aid the Victims of June Events, see *Obywatelski Komitet Zbiórki na Pomoc Ofiarom Wydarzeń Czerwcowych*
Civil Division court, see *Wydział Cywilny*
CKON. *See Centralny Komitet Organizacji Niepodległościowych*
Claridge's Hotel, 387
Clark, Mark, 239n37
Cmentarz Obrońców Lwowa (Cemetery of the Defenders of Lwów), 249, 256
Cmentarz Zasłużonych Wielkopolan (Cemetery of Meritorious Wielkopolans), 392
Cold War, 77n61, 173–174
Comintern. *See* Communist International (Comintern)
Committee for Social Self-Defense "KOR", see *Komitet Samoobrony Społecznej "KOR"*
Committee for the Construction of the Katyń Memorial, see *Komitet Budowy Pomnika Katyńskiego*
Committee for the Defense of the Eastern Borderlands, 48
Committee of Solidarity with the Democratic Movement, 271
Committee of the Three, see *Komitet Trzech*
Committee of Underground Independence Organizations, see *Komitet Porozumiewawczy Organizacji Niepodległościowych*
Committee to Aid Compatriots in the Country, see *Komitet Pomocy Rodakom w Kraju*
communism
　anti-Polish propaganda, 137
　collapse of, 357, 372–376
　governments, 202–203
　Nazi opposition to, 20
　in Poland, 72–79, 103–104, 152–155, 216n38, 344
Communist International (Comintern), 73–75, 78–79
Communist Party of Poland, see *Komunistyczna Partia Polski*
Communist Party of the Soviet Union, 73, 103, 204, 313, 358, 362n41
Confederation of the Nation. *See Konfederacja Narodu*
Conference on Security and Co-operation in Europe (CSCE), 260–262, 264, 266–267
Congress of Poles in Great Britain, see *Zjazd Polaków w Wielkiej Brytanii*
Congress of Polish Culture and Science Abroad, see *Kongres Kultury i Nauki Polskiej na Obczyźnie*
Constitution (1952), 265
April 1935 Constitution, 367–368
　Article 1, 262
　Article 12, 64
　Article 13, 17, 167
　Article 21, 303n23
　Article 23, 196
　Article 28, 50n7
　Article 31, 50n9
　original document, 324, 371–372
　Polish commitment to, 123, 202, 229, 243, 262, 271
　Polish communist obsession with, 216–217
　recognition of, 50, 202, 229, 243
　socialist disregard of, 173
　Soviet disregard of, 95, 103, 110, 123–124, 234
　timeline of major events, vii
　Warsaw's disregard of, 390–391
March 1921 Constitution, 13, 17, 110, 310n42
May 3 1791 Constitution, 7, 328–329, 334, 397
Constitution Day, 150
Constitutional Tribunal, see *Trybunał Konstytucyjny*

consular passports, 178
Continental Food Supply, 208n24
Convention for the Fight for Independence, see *Konwent Walk o Niepodległość*
Cooper, Gary, 341–342
Coordinating Council of Poles in the Free World, see *Rada Koordynacyjna Polonii Wolnego Świata*
Council for the Protection of Struggle and Martyrdom Sites, see *Rada Ochrony Pamięci Walk i Męczeństwa*
Council of Academic Technical Schools, see *Rada Akademickich Szkół Technicznych*
Council of Free Czechoslovakia, 313–314, 327
Council of Ministers
  and borders, 120–122
  and division between *Zamek* and *Zjednoczenie Narodowe*, 230
  and elections in Poland, 341
  and Katyń massacre, 361
  and Katyń Memorial, 274–275
  and loss of recognition, 144
  members of, 258
  official seat, 339n48
  and POSK, 262–263
  support for, 263–264, 267
  support for John Paul II, 277
  and VI Rada Narodowa, 276
  and Wałęsa, 374
  and Yalta agreements, 125–126
Council of National Unity, see *Rada Jedności Narodowej*
Council of Polish Political Parties, see *Rada Polskich Partii Politycznych*
Council of State, see *Rada Państwa*
Council of State of the Republic of Poland, see *Rada Stanu Rzeczypospolitej Polskiej*
Council of Three, see *Rada Trzech*
Council of Veterans' Organizations, see *Rada Organizacji Kombatanckich*
Crimean Conference (Yalta conference), 124–129
Cripps, Stafford, 59, 65
Croatia, Independent State of, 327
Cromwell Road, London (Polish Corridor), 208

Crystal Palace Stadium (London), 308
CSCE, see Conference on Security and Co-operation in Europe
Cuba, 150, 216
Curzon Line, 12, 109, 120–122, 125, 127
Cymbarewicz, Franciszek, 216n35
Cyrankiewicz, Józef, 225, 241
Cytadela (Eaton Place) Limited, 235, 284n16, 386
Cytadela Warszawska (Warsaw Citadel), 7–8
Cywiński, Bohdan, 312
Czaja, Herbert, 284
Czarnecki, Kamil, 238–239, 246
Czarnecki, Marian, 238–239
Czarnowski, Eugeniusz, 130, 133
Czarzasty, Zygmunt, 343
Czechoslovakia
  borders, 11–14, 333n35
  communist control of, 169, 202–203, 237
  constitution, 265n28
  German annexation of, 19
  government-in-exile, 2, 60, 83, 313–314, 327
  governments, 14n26
  Inter-Allied Council, 72
  and NCFE, 174
  official name, 357n29
  opposition movement, 269n36
  relations with Poland, 14, 131, 141, 237, 241n38, 313–314
  Soviet invasion of, 237, 241n38, 260–261, 345
  Soviet occupation of, 237, 392–393
  Soviet withdrawal from, 393
Czechs, 205
Czeremosz River (now Cheremosh River), 25
Czerwiński, Paweł, 216n37
Czerwiński, Witold, 244, 260n20, 269n39
Czerwiński, Zygmunt, 362n44
Czerwone maki na Monte Cassino (Red Poppies on Monte Cassino), 211n28
Czerwony Sztandar (Red Banner), 73
Częstochowa, Poland, 214–215, 397
Czortków, 318

D

D-Day, 109
Dąb-Biernacki, Stefan, 54, 84
Dąbrowski, Bronisław, 380
Dąbrowski, Mieczysław, 169n8
The Daily Telegraph, 240, 275
Daily Worker, 115, 222n8
Daladier, Édouard, 19, 25, 42
Danel, Jacek, 326n16
Danilewiczowa, Maria, 234
Danina Polska Ltd., 187–188, 385–386
Dankowski, Henryk, 354
Danzig, 11, 13–14, 21, 30
Daquise (restaurant), 210, 296, 398
Dargas, Antoni, 244
Davies, Norman, 23n1, 47n1, 316, 336
Davis, Walpole, 169–170
Dayan, Moshe, 236
Days of Glory, 77n61
de Monzie, Anatole, 42–43
de Virion, Tadeusz, 371–372, 377, 384, 388, 392
debt relief, 146, 300–301, 334–335, 387
Declaration on Liberated Europe, 125
Defense Committee of the Eaglets Cemetery, 256
Dekret Bieruta (Bierut Decree), 151
Delegatura Rządu Rzeczypospolitej Polskiej na Kraj (Government Delegation for Poland, *Delegatura*), 57, 79, 86, 99–100, 105–110, 124, 142
Delegatura veterans, 136–138
Delmar-Czarnecka, Irena, 238–239
Dembiński, Ryszard, 295n7
Dembiński, Stefan, 210, 229–231
Democratic Bloc, see *Blok Demokratyczny*
Democratic Concentration, see *Koncentracja Demokratyczna*
Democratic Left Alliance, see *Sojusz Lewicy Demokratycznej*
Democratic Union, see *Unia Demokratyczna*
Denmark, 58
Department of Security. See *Urząd Bezpieczeństwa*
deportations, 7–8, 20, 29, 47, 56–57, 62, 65, 91, 127, 136–138, 142, 333, 360–361, 364n48
Desa, 178

d'Estaing, Valéry Giscard, 263
Detroit, Michigan, 258
Dewey, Thomas, 117
Die Welt, 303
Dimitrov, G. M., 231
Dimitrov, Georgi, 103–104, 206n20
Dingell, John, 117, 118n7
displaced persons, 142, 148, 283
Divine Mercy College (Fawley Court, Buckinghamshire), 209
Długosz, Jan, 36n10
Wieniawa-Długoszowski, Bolesław, vii, 33, 35–46, 391, 394, 402n4
Dmowski, Roman, 9–11, 18
"Do Społczeństwa Polskiego w Świecie" ("To the Polish Society in the World") (Sokolnicki), 289–291
Dolanowski, Mikołaj (Jerzy Hryniewski), 194, 245, 269n39
Dołęga-Modrzewski, Stanisław, 182
Dom Narodowy (National Home), 362–363
Dom Polonii, 380
Dom Polski (Polish Home), 211
Dorpat (now Tartu), Estonia, 48n2
Douglas-Home, Alec, 273–274
Dowding, Hugh, 60–61
Dowgiałło, Krzysztof, 242n41
Drozdowski, Wacław, 39n22
Drzycimski, Andrzej, 394
Dublin, Ireland, 216
Duch, Bronisław, 229–231, 290
Dudziński, Kazimierz, 67, 71, 74–75
Duff House Sanatorium (Ruthin Castle), 163
Dunglass, Lord, 127
Dunkerley, Jon L., 285n20
Duplessis, Maurice, 221
Duskanya gold mine, 351
9 *Dywizja Piechoty* (9th Infantry Division), 352
Dzerzhinsky, Felix, 37, 75n56
Dziady (Forefathers' Eve), 236, 354n14
Dziennik Polski (Detroit), 44, 199
Dziennik Polski (Polish Daily), 62
Dziennik Polski i Dziennik Żołnierza, 62n36, 184, 191–192, 195, 197n9, 198, 204–205, 209, 223, 245, 268, 282, 325–326, 369–370, 374
Dziennik Ustaw, 283
Dziennik Ustaw Nr. 1, 279
Dziennik Ustaw Rzeczypospolitej Polskiej (Journal of Laws of the Republic of Poland), 9n9, 163, 167, 256, 258, 385
Dziennik Żołnierza (Soldier's Daily), 62n36
Dzierżyńska, Zofia, 75
Dzierżyński, Feliks, 75n56, 212, 397n22
Dziob, Frank, 118n7
Dziwisz, Stanisław, 305

E

Earle, George, 100–101
East Germany (German Democratic Republic), 186–187, 202–203, 359
École Supérieure de Guerre (French war college), 18
economic policy, 213, 236, 241, 267–268, 300–302, 334–335, 387, 396–398
economic strike (1970), 242–243
The Economist, 2
Eden, Anthony, 63, 89–90, 97, 120–121, 130–131, 143–144
Egypt, 236, 267
Egzekutywa Zjednoczenia Narodowego (EZN, Executive of National Unity), 176n17, 196–197, 200–202, 243–244, 321–322
Eisenhower, Dwight, 191
elections
 five-adjective (five-point electoral law), 368
 free, 152, 199–200, 387
 presidential, 372–374
 Rada, 199–200, 225
 Sejm, 152–155, 159–162, 206, 216, 339–343, 387–388
 Senat, 339–343, 387–388
Eliot, T. S., 181
Elizabeth II, 387, 390, 392n19
Embassy of the People's Republic of Poland (London), 1, 144, 183–184
émigré community
 citizens' courts, 184–185
 clubs, 210
 and CSCE, 260–261
 daily life, 209
 division, 219–247
 and free elections in Poland, 387
 fundraising, 187–188, 258, 269–270, 298–299, 302, 309, 325–326, 331
 and Glemp, 314–315
 and John Paul II, 277–278, 308
 legalists, 172–174
 in London, 208–212
 and Mikołajczyk, 170–171
 official representatives, 224–225
 protests, 205
 and provisional government, 134
 and PZPR, 302n20
 role of, 203, 321–322, 325, 340
 seats in *Rada Rzeczypospolitej Polskiej*, 193n3
 Sikorski's centenary events, 305
 support for Polish opposition, 335–337
 support for unification, 192
 and transfer of power to Wałęsa, 374
 unskilled laborers, 208–209
émigré culture, 210–211
émigré press, 181, 199, 225, 333, 360
Endecja. See *Narodowa Demokracja*
England. See United Kingdom
Episcoporum Poloniae coetus, 259–260
Estonia, 58, 203, 205, 264, 327–328, 336–337, 363–364
Estonian National Council, 337
ethnic minorities, 11–12, 18, 148
European Community, 323, 359–360
European Economic Community, 257
European Union, 387, 398, 401
Executive of National Unity, see *Egzekutywa Zjednoczenia Narodowego*
exiles. See also émigré community; Polish Government-in-Exile
 burials in Poland, 392
exports, 267, 301, 387
Express Wieczorny, 232
Extraordinary State Commission for Ascertaining and Investigating Crimes Perpetrated by the German-Fascist Invaders and their Accomplices, see Burdenko Commission
EZN, see *Egzekutywa Zjednoczenia Narodowego*

F

fabricated reports and files, see *fałszywki*
facilities, 234–235, 246
Fact-Finding Commission to Enquire into Recent Events in Poland, 52–53
Falaise, battle at, 109
fałszywki (fabricated reports and files), 355n19
fascism and fascists, 20, 118, 130, 137, 393
FBI (Federal Bureau of Investigation), 288–289, 299n14
February Revolution, 48
Fedak, Stepan, 14n25
Federacja Młodzieży Walczącej (Federation of Fighting Youth), 342n56
Federacja Ruchów Demokratycznych (Federation of Democratic Movements), 226, 259. See also *Polskie Zjednoczenie Narodowe*
Federal Bureau of Investigation (FBI), 288–289, 299n14
Federal Republic of Germany (West Germany), 186–187, 189
Federation of Democratic Movements, see *Federacja Ruchów Demokratycznych*
Federation of Expellees, see *Bund der Vertriebenen*
Federation of Fighting Youth, see *Federacja Młodzieży Walczącej*
Federation of Poles in Great Britain, see *Zjednoczenie Polskie w Wielkiej Brytanii*
Fejgin, Anatol, 189–190, 215
Fiat automobiles, 300n17, 305
Fiderkiewicz, Alfred, 221
Fieldorf, Emil, 99, 206
Fighting Solidarity, see *Solidarność Walcząca*
financial and material assets, 144–146. See also treasury
The Financial Times, 303
Finder, Paweł, 73, 102–103
Finland, 58
First General Congress of Military Poles, 48
First Polish Army, 115
First Polish Corps in Russia, see *I Korpus Polski w Rosji*
First Republic. See Polish-Lithuanian Commonwealth
FitzGibbon, Louis, 271–272, 272n48
five-adjective elections (five-point electoral law), 368
flags, 357n29, 403–404
Flato, Stanisław, 177
Flondor, 34–35
Floyar-Rajchman, Henryk, 45
FOM, see *Fundusz Obrony Morskiej*
FON, see *Fundusz Obrony Narodowej*
food prices, 213, 236, 241, 267–268, 300–302, 334–335, 387, 396
Ford, Gerald, 264
Fornalska, Małgorzata, 102
"Four Freedoms" (Roosevelt), 118
Fourteen Points, 10–11
FPK, see *Fundusz Pomocy Krajowi*
France
 battle at Falaise, 109
 and CSCE, 260n19
 émigré community, 185n42, 193n3
 German invasion of, 58
 government-in-exile, 2, 60
 government of Germany by, 186
 governments, 14n26
 and independent Poland, 9, 14, 18, 20–21
 and Inter-Allied Council, 72
 and invasion of Poland, 24–28, 30–32
 Kasprzycki–Gamelin Convention, 21n35
 liberation of, 403
 Locarno Treaties, 14
 Nuremburg trials, 149–150
 Poles in, 403
 Polish Army in, 33, 44, 53–54
 Polish government in, 53, 58–60
 relations with Germany, 359
 relations with Poland, 40–43, 141, 163
 timeline of major events, vii, viii
Franczak, Józef, 176n18
Frankowski, Feliks, 24, 33
Frastacki, Rudolf V., 314
fraud, 279–291
Frederick Wilhelm III, 293n1
Free City of Danzig, 14
Free Europe Committee, 203–204, 247
Free French Army, 72
Free Group, see *Grupa Wolnych*
Free Poland, see *Wolna Polska*
Free Poland in Exile, 327
free press, 396
Freedom and Independence, see *Zrzeszenie Wolność i Niezawisłość*
Freedom of Speech Fund, see *Fundusz Wolności Słowa*
Fregata, 225
French Army, 25, 108–109
French Navy, 26
French North Africa, 54
French war college, see École Supérieure de Guerre
Front Morges, 18, 40, 71
Fundacja Pomocy Medycznej (Medical Assistance Foundation), 307
fundraising, 187–188, 197, 258, 266, 331, 402
 Katyń Memorial Fund, 272, 273n49, 274
 Komitet Doraźnej Pomocy Krajowi – Help Poland Fund, 357
 for Polish opposition, 298–299, 307–308, 325, 331, 356–357
 for Polish workers, 269–271, 298–299
Fundusz Obrony Morskiej (FOM, Maritime Defense Fund), 16–17
Fundusz Obrony Narodowej (FON, National Defense Fund), 19, 26, 176–178, 263
Fundusz Pomocy Krajowi (FPK, National Assistance Fund), 299, 302n21, 308, 312, 331, 353
Fundusz Pomocy Robotnikom (Workers' Relief Fund), 298
Fundusz Wolności Słowa (Freedom of Speech Fund), 298, 308

G

Gabszewicz, Aleksander, 229–231
Gafencu, Grigore, 33–34
Galantiere, Lewis, 231
Galeria Sztuki Socrealizmu (Gallery of Socialist Realist Art), 397n22
Galinat, Edmund, 31
Gallery of Socialist Realist Art, see *Galeria Sztuki Socrealizmu*
Gamelin, Maurice, 21, 24–25
Garbusiński, Tadeusz, 52n17
Garda de Fier (Iron Guard), 34n5
Gaś, Adam, 222–223

Gawenda, Jerzy, 240, 244, 258n16, 262, 283
Gawlina, Józef, 205, 214
Gazeta Ludowa, 160, 168
Gazeta Niedzielna, 209, 268
Gazeta Polska, 202
Gazeta Powszechna, 202
Gazeta Warszawska, 39n22
Gazeta Wyborcza, 283n12, 342, 395–396
Gdańsk, Poland, 147, 300n17. *See also* Danzig
Gdańsk Agreement, 339
Gdańsk Shipyard, see *Stocznia Gdańska*
Gdynia, Poland, 13–14, 21n35, 242
General Congress of Poles in Great Britain, see *Ogólny Zjazd Polaków w W. Brytanii*
General Division (court), see *Wydział Ogólny*
General Sikorski Historical Institute, 144–145, 223n9, 296
Generalne Gubernatorstwo (General Government), 32
George VI, 60, 90, 151–152
Georgia, 269n36
Geremek, Bronisław, 330n26, 354n15, 363n47
German Army, 7n4, 24, 30–32
German Democratic Republic (East Germany), 186–187
German Invasion of Poland, 61–62
German Occupation of Poland – Extract of Note Addressed to The Allied and Neutral Powers, 62
Germanization, 56
Germany
  aggression, 19, 58
  anti-Polish propaganda, 139
  borders, 14, 147
  displaced Poles in, 148
  foreign occupation of, 147, 221n5, 392–393
  foreign policy, 19
  and independent Poland, 9, 11–12, 14, 16, 20–21
  invasion of Poland, vii, 1, 23–29, 295
  invasion of Soviet Union, vii, 63, 253
  and Katyń massacre, 89–90, 93–95, 100–101
  Lebensraum ("living space"), 56n27
  Locarno Treaties, 14
  non-aggression pact with Poland (1934), 16
  occupation of Poland, 3, 7–9, 30–32, 56, 84–85
  postwar administration of, 128
  reunification of, 359
  surrender of, 150
  timeline of major events, vii
  Treaty of Non-Aggression (Molotov–Ribbentrop Pact), 20–21, 27–28, 105, 295
  war on US, 77
Germany, Federal Republic of (West Germany), 186–187
Gestapo, 62, 86, 102, 107
Ghent, France, 140
Giedroyc, Jerzy, 181, 235, 308, 370
Gierek, Edward, 243, 263–268, 272n47, 290–291, 301–302, 306, 387
Gieysztor, Aleksander, 303–304
GL, see *Gwardia Ludowa*
Gleiwitz, 21
Glemp, Józef, 308, 314–315, 339
Glinka, Xawery, 212
Głos Ludu, 137–138
Głos Powszechny, 202, 211–212
Głos Wolnej Polski (Voice of Free Poland), 284
Głowacki, Janusz, 224n10
Główna Komisja Skarbu Narodowego, 266
Główna Rada Polityczna (GRP, Main Political Council), 31, 54–55, 58
Głuchowski, Janusz, 52n17, 116
Głuchowski, Krzysztof, 188n46
Gniezno, 5
Godlewski, Zbigniew, 242n41
Goetel, Ferdynand, 93n7
gold mining, 351
gold reserves, 25–26, 59, 146
Gołębiewski, Marian, 337, 362–363
Golgota, 395–396
Gombrowicz, Witold, 181
Gomułka, Władysław
  as activist, 73
  arrest of, 189
  as first secretary, 215–216, 233–237, 240–243
  as PPR leader, 86, 102–104, 132, 134–135, 152–153, 178
  support for, 104, 152–153, 215, 235–237
Gorbachev, Mikhail, 329–330, 360–362, 362n41, 393
Górczyński, Eustachy, 71n43
Gorky, 124n18
Gorski, Martin, 129
Gotschall, Maria Ernestyna, 293
Gottwald, Klement, 206n20
Government Delegation for Poland. *See Delegatura Rządu Rzeczypospolitej Polskiej na Kraj*
Government of the Republic of Poland in Exile. *See* Polish Government-in-Exile
Grabowski, Mateusz, 210
Grabowski, Witold, 52n17
M. B. Grabowski Foundation, 210n27
Grabski, Stanisław, 143–144
Grabski, Władysław, 14n24, 49, 120n13, 134
Graham, Alan, 102n24, 127, 136
Gray Ranks, see *Szare Szeregi*
Grażyński, Michał, 123, 191–192, 281, 318–319, 324
Great Britain. *See* United Kingdom
Great October Socialist Revolution Day, 150
Great Purge, 189n49
Great Terror, 19–20
Great War, 3, 7n4, 11–12, 28n15, 48, 403
Greece, 2, 11n16, 20, 72, 128
Greenpoint (Brooklyn, NY), 337, 362, 363n45
Greenwood, Arthur, 126–127
Griffs, Stanton, 169
Grodyński, Tadeusz, 52n17
Grosvenor Hotel (Edinburgh), 208n24
Grot-Rowecki, Stefan. *See* Rowecki, Stefan
GRP. *See Główna Rada Polityczna*
gruba linia (thick line) policy, 355–356, 358n30, 361–362
Grubiński, Wacław, 212
Grudzień, Mieczysław, 290–291
Grupa Działania NSZZ "Solidarność" w Wielkiej Brytanii (Action Group of NSZZ "Solidarność" in Great Britain), 302
Grupa Inicjatywna PPR (PPR Initiative Group), 76, 78–79
Grupa Operacyjna do Zadań Dezintegracyjnych (Operational Group for Disintegrative Tasks), 312n47
Grupa Wolnych (Free Group), 280
Gryf Publications Ltd., 209

Grześkowiak, Alicja, 388
Grzywacz, Andrzej, 52n15
Grzybowski, Wacław, 27
gulags, 29, 91, 136–137, 253, 351–352
Gunnersbury Cemetery, 274, 346
Gwardia Ludowa (GL, People's Guard), 78–79, 85–87, 103, 106-107
Gwardia Ludowa WRN (People's Guard of the WRN), 56, 78

H

Habsburg Empire, 6–7
Hague Conference on Reparations, 166
Hajdarowicz, Grzegorz, 370
Hájek, František, 93n7
Halifax, Lord, 24, 36, 40–41, 60, 295
Hall, Aleksander, 364–365, 370
Haller, Józef, 12, 37, 43, 51n11, 52–53, 65
Haller, Stanisław, 65, 67, 93
Hammersmith, 235
"Hands Off Russia" campaign, 149n19
Haneman, Jan, 103
Hanff, Konstanty Zygfryd, 287–289, 290n36, 299–300, 327, 337, 362, 395
Hanke (Woliński), Hugon (codename *Ważny*), 194, 200–202, 207, 219
Hara, Mieczysław, 246
Haren (Maczków), 186n43
Harriman, Averell, 120–121, 125–126
Harvard University Advisory Team, 315
Harvard University *The August Zaleski Lectures in Modern Polish History*, 247
Haskoba, 208, 224–225
Hawker Hurricane, 398
Hejnał mariacki, 108–109
Hel Peninsula, 30
Hełczyński, Bronisław, 260n20
Helsinki Final Act, 264–265, 313
Hemar, Marian, 210–211
Hemar Theater, 211
Herling-Grudziński, Gustaw, 181
High Noon (1952), 341–342
Hitler, Adolf, 16, 19–21, 24, 56n27, 62, 106, 140, 295
Hitler Youth, 296

Hitlerite collaborators, 118
Hlond, August, 34–35, 41–42
HMS *Arethusa*, 58
Hochlinden, 21
holidays, 150–151, 210, 397
Hollywood, 77–78
Holman, John, 285n20
Holocaust, 84–85, 138, 155–156, 389n14
Holodomor, 19–20
Holy Family Church, see *Kościół Najświętszej Rodziny*
Holy Family of Nazareth Convent School (Pitsford, Northamptonshire), 209
Holy See, 216, 220, 329
Home Army. *See Armia Krajowa*
Hoover Institution Library (Stanford University), 247
Hopkins, Harry, 132, 134
Hospital of St. John and St. Elizabeth (London), 247
Hotel Francuski, 162
House Committee on Foreign Affairs (US), 232, 323
Hryniewski, Jerzy (Mikołaj Dolanowski), 194–195, 197, 245, 269n39
Hulewiczowa, Maria, 169n8
Hume, Basil, 308, 314
Hungarians, 205
Hungary
  Communist government, 203
  constitution, 265n28
  government-in-exile, 313
  governments, 14n26
  and invasion of Poland, 27–28
  and NCFE, 174
  official name, 357n29
  Soviet occupation of, 159–160, 215n33, 392–393
  Soviet withdrawal from, 393
Hyde Park (London), 243

I

I Korpus Polski w Rosji (First Polish Corps in Russia), 48
Imach, Roman, 71n43
Imperial Russian Army, 48
Imperial War Museum (Duxford), 398
imports, 301
independence, vii, 3, 5–21, 48, 348
Independence Day (November 11), 10, 150, 397
Independent Group "D" of the Fourth Department of the Ministry of the Interior, see *Samodzielna Grupa "D" Departamentu IV MSW*

1st Independent Parachute Brigade, see *1 Samodzielna Brygada Spadochronowa*
Independent Publishing House NOWA, see *Niezależna Oficyna Wydawnicza NOWA*
Independent Self-Governing Trade Union "Solidarity", see *Niezależny Samorządny Związek Zawodowy* "Solidarność," NSZZ "Solidarność"
Independent Social Group, see *Niezależna Grupa Społeczna*
Independent Social Movement, see *Niezależny Ruch Społeczny*
industry, 13, 16, 102, 168, 172, 179, 186–187, 212–213, 267, 301, 389
Information Bulletin, see *Biuletyn Informacyjny*
Instytut Badania Zagadnień Krajowych (Research Institute for the Contemporary Affairs of Poland), 315
Instytut Literacki, 181, 224, 235
Instytut Polskiej Akcji Katolickiej (Polish Institute of Catholic Action), 353
Instytut Strategii Polskiej (Polish Institute of Strategy), 398
intelligence operations, 175–176
Inter-Allied Council, 72
Interfactory Strike Committee, see *Międzyzakładowy Komitet Strajkowy*, MKS
Interim Government of Republic of Czechoslovakia in Exile, 327
Interim Treasury Committee for Polish Affairs (ITC), 144–146, 296
International Lenin School, 75n55
International Monetary Fund, 307, 344
International Peasant Union (IPU), 203, 231–232
International Red Cross, 68, 89–90, 94–95, 110
International World Court of Justice, 203
IPU (International Peasant Union), 203, 231–232
Iran, 80–82, 101
Iraq, 182
Ireland, Republic of, 150, 216
Iron Guard, see *Garda de Fier*

Islamic community, 18
Isle of Snakes (*Wyspa Wężów*), 61, 319
Israel, 236, 267
The Issue to be Avoided (BBC2), 272
Italy
  Battle of Monte Cassino, 108–109
  liberation of, 403
  Locarno Treaties, 14
  Polish advance through, 101–102, 108–109, 139, 148, 255
  relations with Poland, 44
ITC (Interim Treasury Committee for Polish Affairs), 144–146, 296
Ivano-Frankivsk, 353n11
Ivanov, Colonel-General. *See* Serov, Ivan
Iwaniuk, Jan, 74. *See also* Bierut, Bolesław
Izvesta, 76

J

Jablunka Pass, 21
Jadwiga, Queen, 6
Jagiellonian dynasty, 6
Jagiellonian University (*Uniwersytet Jagielloński*), 294
Jan III Sobieski, 6
Jan Kazimierz University (*Uniwersytet Jana Kazimierza*), 147, 250, 256
Janasiak, Zenon, 291
Janek Wiśniewski padł ("Janek Wiśniewski Fell"), 242n41
Janikowski, Stanisław, 42
Jankowski, Henryk, 300, 332
Jankowski, Jan Stanisław, 99, 113, 129–130, 133, 141–142
Jankowski, Paweł, 235, 279, 283
Janowski, Gabriel, 365n50
January Uprising (1863–1864), 7, 36, 47–48, 293
Januszajtis, Marian, 70
Japan, 77, 298n12
Jaroszewicz, Piotr, 74n52, 87, 162, 268
Jaroszyńska, Cecylia Maria, 295–296
Jaruzelski, Wojciech, 96n13, 306–308, 312–313, 329–335, 339, 343–345, 348n3, 353–355, 358, 363–365
Jasiński, Tadeusz, 29n18
Jasiukowicz, Stanisław, 129–130, 133
Jaślan, Henryk and Janina, 321

Jasna Góra, 214–215, 233, 312
Jędrychowski, Stefan, 73, 74n52
Jędrzejewicz, Janusz, 123
Jędrzejewicz, Wacław, 45
Jessel, Toby, 272n48
Jewish Combat Organization (*Żydowska Organizacja Bojowa*, ŻOB), 78, 85
Jewish Military Union (*Żydowski Związek Wojskowy*, ŻZW), 56
Jewish-owned properties, 389n14
Jews
  emigration from Poland, 237
  Holocaust, 84–85, 138, 155–156, 389n14
  "The Mass Extermination of Jews in German Occupied Poland" (Raczyński), 84–85
  in Second Polish Corps, 69, 81–82, 101
  in Second Republic, 18
  segregation of, 32
Jogaila, Grand Duke of Lithuania, 6
John Paul, 277
John Paul II, 1, 2, 57n29, 297–299, 303–307, 312–313, 329
  and Jaruzelski, 330
  and Sabbat, 277, 298, 308, 343
  support for, 277–278, 308
  support for Polish Government-in-Exile, 402
John XXIII, 220
Jordan, 236
Josef Stalin Metal Works in Poznań (*Zakłady Metalowe im. Józefa Stalina w Poznaniu*, ZISPO), 213, 216n34
Josef Stalin Palace of Culture and Science (*Pałac Kultury i Nauki im. Józefa Stalina*), 188
Journal of Laws of the Republic of Poland, see *Dziennik Ustaw Rzeczypospolitej Polskiej*
Jubiler, 178
judicial system, 184–185
Jur-Lerski, Jerzy, 324
Jutro Polski (Poland Tomorrow), 122–123, 209

K

Kaczmarek, Czesław, 180n30
Kaczorowska, Karolina, 347, 376–377
Kaczorowski, Ryszard, 3, 320n9, 348–353, 388, 392n19
  border concerns, 364
  death and funeral, 398–399

  final celebration remarks, 383–385
  final message to the diaspora, 375–376
  fundraising, 357
  and Mazowiecki, 357
  and presidency, 332
  as president, 347–348, 353–381, 394
  as scoutmaster, 348–349, 352–353
  timeline of major events, ix
  transfer of power to Wałęsa, 367–371, 374–381
  and Wałęsa, 387
Kaczyński, Jarosław, 377
Kaczyński, Lech, 29n18, 399
Kaganovich, Lazar, 215n32
Kąkolewnica, 119
Kalinowski, Rafał, 312n46
Kaliński, Emil, 52n17
Kamiński, Aleksander, 318n3
Kania, Stanisław, 306
Kapitaniak, Zygmunt, 142n4, 142n6
Karalus, Sylwester, 258n16, 279, 283
Karewicz, Anatol (pseudonym), 288
Karski, Jan, 85
Kasprzycki, Tadeusz, 52–53
Kasprzycki–Gamelin Convention, 21n35
Kasyno Garnizonowe, 380
Katowice, 212, 215
Katyń massacre, 89–97, 100–101, 110, 138, 204, 213, 215n32, 250n4, 251n5
  Death in the Forest: The Story of the Katyn Forest Massacre (Zawodny), 237
  The Issue to be Avoided (BBC2), 272
  Katyn: A Crime Without Parallel (Zawodny), 271–272
  Little Katyń (Mały Katyń), 119
  Mazowiecki and, 360–362
  Nuremburg trials, 150, 156n31
  Select Committee to Conduct an Investigation and Study of the Facts, Evidence, and Circumstances of the Katyn Forest Massacre (Madden Committee), 203
Katyń Memorial, 272–275, 298, 337, 362
Katyn Memorial Fund, 272, 273n49, 274
Katyń Memorial Fund Commission, 274
Katyń Monument, 346

Kazimierz Wielki (Casimir the Great), 6
Kellogg–Briand Pact, 166
Kelly, Edward, 117
Kent, Duke of, 210
Kerr, Archibald Clark, 125–126, 131
KGB, 37n15, 274n52. *See also* Cheka; NKVD
Kharkov, 93
Khayyam, Omar, 296
Khrushchev, Nikita, 204–205, 206n19, 215, 235, 282
Kielce Pogrom, 155–156, 180n30, 354
Kiernik, Władysław, 134, 135n45
Kingdom of Poland, 9
King's College, 165
Kissinger, Henry, 264
Kiszczak, Czesław, 309, 343, 354–355
Klaipėda region, 19
Klimkowski, Jerzy, 223–224
Klub Lotników Polskich (Polish Airmen's Club), 210
Kmicic-Skrzyński, Ludwik, 208n24
KNAPP, see *Komitet Narodowy Amerykanów Polskiego Pochodzenia*
KNP, see *Komitet Narodowy Polski*
KO "S" (*Komitet Obywatelski "Solidarność,"* Citizens' Committee *"Solidarność"*), 339, 341–345, 354–355, 363
Kobylański, Kazimierz, 130, 133
Koc, Adam, 5, 18, 41–43, 51, 77n59
Kochanowski, Janusz, 388
Kociołek, Stanisław, 242–243
Koestler, Arthur, 181, 271n45
Kołakowski, Leszek, 336
Koło Lwowian (Lwów Circle), 255
Kołodziej, Antoni, 134
Kołodziejski, Henryk, 134
Kolyma, 349–352
Kolyma Highway, 351
Komisja Likwidacyjna Rządu Rzeczypospolitej Polskiej (Liquidation Commission of the Government of the Republic of Poland), 375, 385, 388–389
Komisja Likwidacyjna Skarbu Narodowego (Liquidation Commission of the National Treasury), 375, 385–386

Komisja Scaleniowa (Unification Commission), 240, 243–244
Komisja Skarbu Narodowego, 258
Komisja Tymczasowa Okresu Przejściowego (Temporary Committee for the Transitional Period), 257–259
Komitet Budowy Pomnika Katyńskiego (Committee for the Construction of the Katyń Memorial), 337, 362–363
Komitet Doraźnej Pomocy Krajowi – Help Poland Fund, 356–357
Komitet Główny Milenium Polski Chrześcijańskiej w Kanadzie (Main Committee of the Millennium of Christian Poland in Canada), 229n18
Komitet Narodowy Amerykanów Polskiego Pochodzenia (KNAPP, National Committee of Americans of Polish Extraction), 45, 171
Komitet Narodowy Polski (KNP, Polish National Committee), 9–10, 165
Komitet Obrony Robotników (KOR, Workers' Defense Committee), 133n41, 269–271
Komitet Obywatelski "Solidarność" (KO "S," Citizens' Committee *"Solidarność"*), 339, 341–345, 354–355, 363
Komitet Pomocy Rodakom w Kraju (Committee to Aid Compatriots in the Country), 214
Komitet Porozumiewawczy Organizacji Niepodległościowych (KPON, Committee of Underground Independence Organizations), 55
Komitet Samoobrony Społecznej "KOR" (KSS "KOR," Committee for Social Self-Defense "KOR"), 269n36, 270–271, 301–302
Komitet Trzech (Committee of the Three), 177
Komorowski, Tadeusz (Bór-Komorowski)
  as military commander, 99, 113–117, 186n43, 205
  and POSK, 235

  as prime minister, 168, 182, 184
  protest march, 205
  Rada Trzech tenure, 202
  reburial, 392
  and Sabbat, 324
  social club, 210
  and Sosnkowski, 116
  support for POSK, 235
  as underground leader, 55
  as upholsterer, 168n7, 208n24
Komunistyczna Partia Polski (KPP, Communist Party of Poland), 38, 73–74, 358n31
Konarski, Feliks (Ref-Ren), 211
Koncentracja Demokratyczna (Democratic Concentration), 168, 170–172
Konecki family, 34–35
Konfederacja Narodu (KN, Confederation of the Nation), 55
Konfederacja Polski Niepodległej (KPN), 327, 388
Kongres Kultury i Nauki Polskiej na Obczyźnie (Congress of Polish Culture and Science Abroad), 234
Kongres Kultury Polskiej na Obczyźnie, 315
II Kongres Kultury Polskiej na Obczyźnie, 315–316
König, Franz, 277
Konstytucja Polskiej Rzeczypospolitej Ludowej, 188
Konwent Walk o Niepodległość (KWN, Convention for the Fight for Independence), 219, 227, 281
Kopański, Stanisław, 116, 152, 157, 210, 235, 257–258
KOR, see *Komitet Obrony Robotników*
Korboński, Stefan
  and ACEN, 247
  as *Delegat*, 141
  escape from Poland, 168–169, 171n13
  and Mikołajczyk, 204, 232
  and presidency, 303
  and PSL, 174, 187, 257n14
  on *Sejm*, 161–162
  travel to Washington, 171
  US office, 187
Korean War, 203
Korsak, Władysław, 52n17
Korwin-Mikke, Janusz, 365n50
Kościół Najświętszej Rodziny (Holy Family Church), 245
Kościół Polskokatolicki (Polish Catholic Church), 180–181

INDEX

Kościół św. Andrzeja Boboli (St. Andrew Bobola Church), 211, 239, 247, 256, 278
kościół św. Brygidy (St. Brigid's Church), 300n17
Kościuszko, Tadeusz, 7, 96n12, 403
Kościuszko Uprising (1791), 7
Kot, Stanisław, 51n12, 53, 59, 67–70, 111, 254
Kotlińska, Tatiana, 281–282
Kotowicz, Zygmunt, 211–212
Kowalski, Władysław, 134
Kowel (Kovel), 74n51
Kozakiewicz, Władysław, 302n19
Kozelsk prison camp, 91–93
KPN (*Konfederacja Polski Niepodległej*), 327, 388
KPON (*Komitet Porozumiewawczy Organizacji Niepodległościowych*, Committee of Underground Independence Organizations), 55
KPP, see *Komunistyczna Partia Polski*
Krajowa Rada Narodowa (KRN, State National Council), 102–104, 110, 135, 216n38
Krajowa Reprezentacja Polityczna (KRP, National Political Representation), 99–100, 107
Kraków, Poland, 13, 32, 222, 305n32, 397
Kraków *województwo*, 49
Krasicki, Jan, 74n52
Krasińska, Elżbieta Maria, 294
Krasińska, Maria Beatrix, 294
Krasińska, Zofia, 294
Krasiński, Adam, 294
Krasiński, Władysław, 294
Krasiński, Zygmunt, 294n2
Krasnoyarsk, 253
Krasowski, Józef, 142n4, 142n6
kresy wschodnie (eastern borderlands), 12
KRN, see *Krajowa Rada Narodowa*
Kronika, 212, 227–228
KRP, see *Krajowa Reprezentacja Polityczna*
Krynica, 222
Krzyż Komandorski Orderu Odrodzenia Polski (Commander's Cross of the Order of Polonia Restituta), 332n31
Krzyżanowski, Adam, 134

KSS "KOR" (*Komitet Samoobrony Społecznej "KOR,"* Committee for Social Self-Defense "KOR"), 269n36, 270–271, 301–302
Kuczawski, Janusz, 288n32
Kukiel, Marian, 9, 54, 89, 98–101, 111n32, 176–178, 210
Kukliński, Bogdan, 261n24
Kukliński, Ryszard, 261
Kukliński, Waldemar, 261n24
Kukuliński, Franciszek, 71n43
Kultura, 181, 192, 199, 208n22, 224, 235, 271n44, 313, 322–323, 333, 370
    fundraising for Poland, 270, 308
Kultura warszawska, 224
Kuniczak, Stanisław, 258n16
Kuratowska, Zofia, 381
Kurier Poranny, 15n27
Kuroń, Jacek, 354n15
Kuropieska, Józef, 177
Kutaisi, Georgia, 47
Kutrzeba, Stanisław, 134–135
Kuty, 25
Kuźnica Harcerska, 318
Kwapiński, Jan, 146n16, 172
Kwaśniewski, Aleksander, 358
Kwiatkowski, Eugeniusz, 52n17
Kwiatkowski, Michał, 222–223
Kwiecień, Marcin, 52n15
KWN, see *Konwent Walk o Niepodległość*
Kycia, Marceli, 223–224
Kyrgyz SSR, 352

L

Łabędź, Leopold, 336
labor camps, 253, 351–352
Labor Party. See *Stronnictwo Pracy*
labor strikes, 216, 242–243, 268, 301–302
labor unions, 213, 302
Labour Party, 302
Ładoś, Aleksander, 43, 51n11, 52–53
Lalande, Jeanne-Liliane, 38nn17–18
Lampe, Alfred, 74n52, 95, 102
land reform, 172, 186–187, 389
Lane, Arthur Bliss, 156n31, 161, 171, 180n30
Lang, Jan, 314
Lange, Oskar, 104, 111n32
Langner, Władysław, 250
Latinik, Franciszek, 12
Latvia, 12, 27–28, 58, 203, 264, 328n21

Latvians, 205
League of Air and Anti-Gas Defense. See *Liga Obrony Powietrznej i Przeciwgazowe*
League of Nations, 11, 229n21, 295
League of Nations Council, 166
Lebanon, 25–26, 150, 216
Lebedev, Viktor, 109–110
Lebensraum ("living space"), 56n27
Ledóchowska, Urszula, 312n46
legalists and legalism, 172–174, 191–192, 202, 258, 271, 278, 324
Legiony Polskie (Polish Legions), 9
Legnica, 148
Leipzig University, 294
Lenczewski, Tomasz, 286n22
Lenin, Vladimir, 12, 212, 213n29, 397
Lenin Shipyard in Gdańsk (*Stocznia Gdańska im. Lenina*), see *Stocznia Gdańska*
Leninism, 331
Łepkowski, Stanisław, 34–35, 42–43
Les champeaux cemetery (Montmorency), 238n36
Lesinski, John, 129
Leśniakowa, Maria, 269n39
Leśniowski, Stanisław, 304–305
Leśniowski family, 26
Levytsky, Dmytro, 251–252
libel cases, 115, 155n30, 183–185, 207, 222–224
Liberal Democratic Party "Independence", see *Liberalno-Demokratyczna Partia "Niepodległość"*
Liberalno-Demokratyczna Partia "Niepodległość" (Liberal Democratic Party "Independence"), 342n56
Lieberman, Herman, 51
Life magazine, 77–78, 94
Liga Niepodległości Polski (LNP, Polish Independence League), 123, 191–192, 194, 219, 257, 281, 323
Liga Obrony Powietrznej i Przeciwgazowe (LOPP, League of Air and Anti-Gas Defense), 17n32
Lilenthal, Witold, 286n25
Limba Trading Company Ltd., 208, 320–322

Link, William, 129
Lipiński, Edward, 265, 269–270
Lipski, Jan Józef, 303, 331
Liquidation Commission of the Government of the Republic of Poland, see *Komisja Likwidacyjna Rządu Rzeczypospolitej Polskiej*
Liquidation Commission of the National Treasury, see *Komisja Likwidacyjna Skarbu Narodowego*
Lis, Józef, 71, 75
List 59 (Letter of 59), 265–266
Litauer, Stefan, 59, 111
Lithuania, 19, 203, 220
  opposition movement, 269n36
  Polish-Lithuanian Commonwealth, 6
  relations with Poland, 11–12, 14, 27–28, 30, 364
  relations with Poland in exile, 266
  Soviet invasion and annexation of, 58, 264, 328n21
Lithuanian SSR, 119, 364n48
Lithuanians, 205, 334
Little Katyń, see *Mały Katyń*
Little Moscow, see *Mała Moskwa*
Litvinov, Maxim, 101–102
Litwinowicz, Aleksander, 52n17
Livytskyi, Mykola, 266
Lloyd, Selwyn, 205
LNP, see *Liga Niepodległości Polski*
Łobodowski, Józef, 316
Locarno Treaties, 14
London, England
  9 Princes Gardens, 234–235
  43 Eaton Place, 1–3, 197, 200, 235, 385–386, 397–398
  capital of Poland, 1–3, 60–61
  Citizens' Court in London (*Sąd Obywatelski w Londynie*), 184–185
  Embassy of the People's Republic of Poland, 1–3, 144, 183–184
  émigré community, 148, 208–212
  Polish Corridor, 208, 235n33
  protest marches, 205
  victory parade, 151–152
London School of Economics, 294, 315
Łopianowski, Narcyz, 71, 75
LOPP. See *Liga Obrony Powietrznej i Przeciwgazowe*

LOT Polish Airlines *(Polskie Linie Lotnicze LOT)*, 224–225, 377
Łubieński, Ludwik, 29n16, 372, 374, 381, 385–386
Lublin, Poland, 32
Lublin Committee, 110–111, 120, 125
Lublin prison (NKVD), 137
Lubodziecki, Stanisław, 230
Lubomirska, Zenaida, 293
Lubomirski, Eugeniusz, 272n48
Lubyanka prison, 37, 38n19, 65, 74, 129, 132, 199, 251–252
Łuck (now Lutsk), 25
Ludowe Wojsko Polskie (LWP, Polish People's Army), 107, 140, 162, 178
Łukasiewicz, Juliusz, 20–21, 24–25, 33–36, 40–42, 123
Łukowska-Karniej, Hanna, 331
Luksemburg, 212
lustration (term), 355n19
Luxembourg, 2, 58, 72
Lwów (now Lviv), 11–12, 27, 121, 147–148, 249–251, 256
Lwów Circle *(Koło Lwowian)*, 255
Lwów Eaglets, 249, 256, 393
Lwów i Wilno, 198–199
LWP, see *Ludowe Wojsko Polskie*

M

Mabledon Hospital, 211
Machalski, Tadeusz, 227–228
Mackiewicz, Stanisław, 176, 198–199, 202, 206–208, 210
MacMahon, Lee D., 285n20
Maczek, Stanisław, 109, 140, 186n43, 208n24, 290, 319, 340, 392, 398
Maczków (Haren), 186n43
Madden, Ray, 203
Madden Committee (Select Committee to Conduct an Investigation and Study of the Facts, Evidence, and Circumstances of the Katyn Forest Massacre), 203
Magdalenka, Poland, 337–338
Main Committee of the Millennium of Christian Poland in Canada, see *Komitet Główny Milenium Polski Chrześcijańskiej w Kanadzie*
Main Political Council. See *Główna Rada Polityczna*
Maisky, Ivan, 72, 98, 101–102

Sikorski–Maisky Pact, vii, 64–65, 76, 166, 199, 202, 251n6, 253, 352
Majdanek concentration camp, 137
Major, John, 387, 390
Mała Konstytucja z 1947 (Small Constitution of 1947), 162
Mała Konstytucja z 1992 (Small Constitution of 1992), 390
Mała Moskwa (Little Moscow), 148
Mała Ziemiańska cafe (Warsaw), 38
Małcużyński, Witold, 221–222
Mały Katyń (Little Katyń), 119
Manifesto of the Council of National Unity to the Polish and Allied Nations, see *Rada Jedności Narodowej do Narodu Polskiego i do Narodów Zjednoczonych*
March Constitution. See Constitution
Mariampolska, Karolina, 352–353
Mariampolska, Rozalia, 353n12
Mariampolski, Franciszek, 353n12
Maritime Defense Fund, see *Fundusz Obrony Morskiej*
Markham, Joyous, 295
Markov, Marko, 93n7
Marshall Plan, 307
martial law, 306–307, 312–313, 329–330, 354–355, 366
Marxism, 8, 331
"The Mass Extermination of Jews in German Occupied Poland" (Raczyński), 84–85
mass graves, 119
Matłachowski, Jan, 142n4, 142n6
matryoshkas, 162
Matuszewski, Ignacy, 45
Mauzoleum Prezydentów Rzeczypospolitej na Uchodźstwie (Mausoleum of the Presidents of the Republic of Poland in Exile), 399
May 3 Constitution. See Constitution
Mayall, Elizabeth Mary, 283, 310n45
Mazowiecki, Tadeusz, 330n26, 354–365, 370–373, 387
MBP, see *Ministerstwo Bezpieczeństwa Publicznego*
McCreery, Richard, 139
McEwen, John, 127

McGovern, John, 106, 128
Mead, James, 117
media coverage, 2
Medical Assistance
  Foundation, see *Fundacja Pomocy Medycznej*
Mednoye, 93
memorials, 393, 397
Mercedes automobiles, 300n17
Merkel, Jacek, 374
Merkulov, Vsevolod, 66, 70, 100, 360
Mexico, 150
Michałowski, Stanisław, 130, 133
Michnik, Adam, 283n12, 396
Mickiewicz, Adam, 236, 403
Mieczysławska, Aniela Lilpop, 296, 390
Mieczysławski, Witold, 296, 390
Miedziński, Bogusław, 196
Międzyzakładowy Komitet Strajkowy (MKS, Interfactory Strike Committee), 302
Mierzwa, Stanisław, 130, 133n41
Miesięcznik Literacki, 38
Mieszko I, 6, 233
Mikołajczyk, Stanisław
  and Anders, 223
  as deputy prime minister, 60
  escape from occupied Poland, 168–171
  and IPU, 231–232
  and Korboński, 204, 232
  opposition to, 320
  as PNKD leader, 197
  Potsdam conference, 143–144
  PPR campaign against, 160–161
  as prime minister, 98–99, 105, 109–117, 120–123, 134–135, 139–140, 153, 158–162, 171–172
  as *Rada Narodowa* vice chair, 51
  reburial, 392
  and referendum, 153
  and *Sejm* elections, 159–162
  and Sosnkowski, 98–99, 111
  support for national committee, 172–174
  US support, 170–171, 174, 187
  and Warsaw Uprising, 115–117
Mikoyan, Anastas, 91, 215n32
Milicja Obywatelska (MO, Citizens' Militia), 119, 155, 160, 216, 242, 267–268, 306, 354–355
militarization, 16
military administration, 307

military chaplains, 69
military decorations, 286–287, 290–291, 394–395
Military Organization. See *Organizacja Wojskowa*
military ranks, 310, 332, 366
military standard, 403–404
military veterans
  and Mieszko's baptism, 233
  opposition to Sokolnicki, 290–291
  Rada Organizacji Kombatanckich (Council of Veterans' Organizations), 305
  and Six-Day War, 236
  Soviet persecution of, 136–138, 206
  Stowarzyszenie Polskich Kombatantów (SPK, Polish Combatants' Association), 149, 183–184, 210, 263, 320, 323, 353
Miller, Leszek, 358
Miloslavić, Eduard, 93n7
Miłosz, Czesław, 177n20, 271n45, 316, 401
Minc, Hilary, 74n52, 95, 103
Ministerstwo Bezpieczeństwa Publicznego (MBP, Ministry of Public Security), 123–124
Ministry of Education and Culture, 323
Ministry of Emigration Affairs, 323
Ministry of Information and Documentation, 61–62, 323
Ministry of Military Affairs, 323
Ministry of National Defense, 323
Ministry of Public Security, see *Ministerstwo Bezpieczeństwa Publicznego*
Ministry of Religious Denominations, Education and Culture, 323
Mińsk prison, 349
Miracle of Częstochowa, 214–215
Misja: Wolna Polska (Mission: Free Poland), 399
Mission to Moscow, 77n61
Mizikowski, Edward, 365n50
MKS, see *Międzyzakładowy Komitet Strajkowy*
MO, see *Milicja Obywatelska*
Moczar, Mieczysław, 73, 235–237, 304
Moczulski, Leszek, 304, 332, 365, 370–373, 388
Modelski, Izydor, 52–53
modernization, 267

Modzelewski, Zygmunt, 143–144
Mołojec, Bolesław, 73–74, 79
Molotov, Vyacheslav
  and borders, 143–144
  and invasion of Poland, 27, 30
  and Katyń massacre, 90–91, 215n32
  and Mikołajczyk, 120
  and Polish communists, 104
  and Polish officers in captivity, 70, 91
  and United Nations, 131
  and Warsaw Uprising, 115
  and Yalta agreements, 127
  and Yalta Agreements, 125–126
Molotov–Ribbentrop Pact (Treaty of Non-Aggression), 20–21, 27–28, 105, 295
Mongolia, 252
Monitor Polski (Polish Monitor), 9n9, 35–36, 50
Monte Cassino, 343
  Battle of Monte Cassino, 108–109, 352
  Polish Military Cemetery, 239
Montgomery, Lord, 140
Montmorency, France, 238
Moore–McCormack Steamship Lines, 169
Moraczewski, Jędrzej, 13
moral destruction, 137
morale, 84
Moravia, 19
Morawicz, Jerzy, 372
Morawiecki, Kornel, 327, 331, 365n50
Morawiecki, Mateusz, 399
Morawski, Kajetan, 52n17
Morawski, Marian, 71
Morrison, Herbert, 84
Mościcki, Ignacy
  attacks on, 198
  and independent Poland, 15, 18–19
  and invasion of Poland, 25–29, 32, 372
  as president, 15, 18–19, 25–29, 32–36, 41–44, 49, 372
  presidential successors, 394
  reinternment, 391
Moscow Helsinki Group, 269n36
Mossley Hill military hospital (Liverpool), 255
"most favored nation" trading status, 334
Motorized Reserves of the Citizens' Militia. See *Zmotoryzowane Odwody Milicji Obywatelskiej*
Motyl field, 111n33
Mount Olivet Cemetery (Washington, D.C.), 232

Movement for Defense of Human and Civic Rights, see *Ruch Obrony Praw Człowieka i Obywatela*
Muchniewski, Zygmunt, 230, 240, 243–244, 258n16, 282–283, 286n21
Muggeridge, Malcolm, 205
Multilateral Agreement of the Central European Community, 327
musicians, 215
Mussolini, Benito, 19, 44
Muzeum Narodowe (National Museum), 178, 296, 389-390
Myssura, Jerzy, 288n33

N

Naarden Movement, 314
Naczelnik Państwa, 13
Naczelny Polski Komitet Wojskowy (Supreme Polish Military Committee, *Naczpol*), 48
Nagy, Ferenc, 232
Najder, Zdzisław, 357, 367–370
Najwyższa Izba Kontroli (NIK, Supreme Audit Office), 182, 388
Nakoniecznikow-Klukowski, Bronisław, 52n17
Narodowa Demokracja (ND, National Democrats), 8–9, 13, 16
Narodowe Siły Zbrojne (NSZ, National Armed Forces), 78–79, 85, 106–107, 124
  operations to release comrade prisoners, 138
  veterans of, 136–138, 206
  Warsaw Uprising, 114, 118
Narodowe Święto Odrodzenia Polski (National Day of the Rebirth of Poland), 150, 397
Narodowe Zjednoczenie Wojskowe (NZW, National Military Union), 138
Narodowiec, 222–224
Narodowy Bank Polski (NBP, National Bank of Poland), 178
Narutowicz, Gabriel, 13–14
Nasz Znak, 212
national anthem, 131, 205, 293, 380
National Archives, 220–221
National Armed Forces. See *Narodowe Siły Zbrojne*
National Army, see *Armia Narodowa*
National Assistance Fund, see *Fundusz Pomocy Krajowi*

National Bank of Poland, see *Narodowy Bank Polski*
national committee concept, 172–174
National Committee for a Free Europe (NCFE), 173–174, 203–204, 231, 401n1
National Committee of Americans of Polish Extraction, see *Komitet Narodowy Amerykanów Polskiego Pochodzenia*, KNAPP
National Council of the Republic of Poland. See *Rada Narodowa Rzeczypospolitej Polskiej*
National Day of the Rebirth of Poland, see *Narodowe Święto Odrodzenia Polski*
National Defense Fund, see *Fundusz Obrony Narodowej*
national delegations, 203–204
National Democrats, see *Narodowa Demokracja*
national flag, 371–372
National Gallery of Art, 13–14
national holidays, 150–151, 210, 397
National Home, see *Dom Narodowy*
National Library (Warsaw), 32
National Military Union, see *Narodowe Zjednoczenie Wojskowe*
National Museum, see *Muzeum Narodowe*
National Party. See *Stronnictwo Narodowe*
National Political Representation, see *Krajowa Reprezentacja Polityczna*
National Rebirth Movement, see *Ruch Odrodzenia Narodowego*
National Security Corps, see *Państwowy Korpus Bezpieczeństwa*
National Shrine of Our Lady of Częstochowa (Doylestown, PA), 391n18
National Socialist Party (Nazi party), 16, 56n27
National Theater, see *Teatr Narodowy*
National Treasury. See *Skarb Narodowy*
National Unity, see *Zjednoczenie Narodowe*
National Unity Act, see *Akt Zjednoczenia Narodowego*
National Victory Day, 150

nationalization, 102, 150–151, 168, 172, 179, 212–213, 389
NATO (North Atlantic Treaty Organization), 261
Navy Mutual Aid Association, see *Samopomoc Marynarki Wojennej*
Nazi collaborators, 327
Nazi Germany, 20
Nazi party (National Socialist Party), 16, 56n27
NBP, see *Narodowy Bank Polski*
NCFE (National Committee for a Free Europe), 173–174, 203–204, 231, 401n1
ND, see *Narodowa Demokracja*
Neave, Airey, 272n48
Netherlands, 2, 58, 72, 140, 403
Neubersteich, 21
New Horizons, see *Nowe Widnokręgi*
New Year's speeches, 266, 340
New York City, New York
  NCFE headquarters, 203–204
  Pulaski Day Parade, 117
New Zealander forces, 108–109
Newsweek, 94
NGS, see *Niezależna Grupa Społeczna*
NiD. See *Polski Ruch Wolnościowy Niepodległość i Demokracja*
NIE, 99
Niesłuchowska, Jadwiga, 48
Niewiadomski, Eligiusz, 13–14
Niezależna Grupa Społeczna (NGS, Independent Social Group), 257, 321, 353
Niezależna Oficyna Wydawnicza NOWA (Independent Publishing House NOWA), 271n45
Niezależny Ruch Społeczny (Independent Social Movement), 219, 227
Niezależny Samorządny Związek Zawodowy "Solidarność" (NSZZ "Solidarność," Independent Self-Governing Trade Union "Solidarity"), 133n41, 302, 309, 312, 330
NIK, see *Najwyższa Izba Kontroli*
Nixon, Richard, 264n27
NKVD (*Narodnyy komissariat vnutrennikh del*, People's Commissariat for Internal Affairs). See also Cheka; KGB
  actions against Polish resistance, 62, 68–70, 106–107, 127–129, 142
  arrests, 55, 129, 141

Black Marias (vans), 349–350
invasion of Poland, 29, 123–124, 251
Katyń massacre, 100, 203, 250n4, 251n5, 360–362
Kielce pogrom, 155–156, 180n30, 354
leadership, 66
Mały Katyń (Little Katyń), 119
Order No. 00485, "On the liquidation of Polish sabotage and espionage groups and units of the POW," 19–20
and Poles in Soviet Union, 87
Polish communists in, 74
prisons, 37n16, 91, 137, 349
propaganda, 77–78
pursuit of underground soldiers, 162–163
Sachsenhausen concentration camp, 150n21
Villa of Bliss (Malakhovka), 71, 74–75
and Wasilewska, 96
Nobel Peace Prize, 312
noble conspiracy, 230
Noël, Léon, 34–35, 39–40
Nonpartisan Bloc for Cooperation with the Government, see Bezpartyjny Blok Współpracy z Rządem
nonviolence, commitments to, 241
North Atlantic Treaty Organization (NATO), 203, 261
North Korea, 203
The North Star, 77n61
Northern Bukovina, 58
Northern Group of Forces, 148
Norton, Joyce Teresa George, 283
Norway, 2, 58, 72
Notebooks of History, see Zeszyty Historyczne
November Uprising (1830–1831), 7
NOWA, 271n45
Nowa Kultura, 224
Nowak, Anna, 280–281
Nowak, Stanisław, 258n16
Nowak-Jeziorański, Jan, 136, 245, 271n45, 316
Nowe Widnokręgi (New Horizons), 73, 75–76
Nowicki, Stanisław, 177–178
Nowogródek Cavalry Brigade, 223
Nowogródek województwo, 49
Nowotko, Marceli, 73–74, 79, 212
Nowy Dziennik (New York), 324

NSZ. See Narodowe Siły Zbrojne
NSZZ Solidarność (Niezależny Samorządny Związek Zawodowy "Solidarność," Independent Self-Governing Trade Union "Solidarity"), 133n41, 302, 309, 312, 330
nuclear era, 151n24
Nuremburg trials, 149–150, 155
NZW, see Narodowe Zjednoczenie Wojskowe

O

"O co walczy Naród Polski?" ("What is the Polish Nation Fighting For?") (RJN), 108
"O co walczymy?" (PPR), 108
Oblicze Tygodnia, 212
Obóz Polski Walczącej (OPW, Camp of Fighting Poland), 76, 77n59
Obóz Zjednoczenia Narodowego (OZN, Camp of National Unity), 18, 77n59
The Observer, 303
Obywatelski Komitet Zbiórki na Pomoc Ofiarom Wydarzeń Czerwcowych (Civic Committee of the Collection to Aid the Victims of June Events), 269–271, 298
Ochab, Edward, 73, 74n52
Ochotnicza Rezerwa Milicji Obywatelskiej (ORMO, Volunteer Reserve of the Citizens' Militia), 155, 160–161, 216, 237, 267–268
October Revolution commemorations, 331, 397
Oder River, 143–144
Oder–Neisse Line, 83, 105, 123, 147, 159, 225, 283n12, 310–311
Odgłosy, 212
O'Docherty, Margaret, 310
Odzierzyński, Władysław, 182, 193–197, 200–201, 210
Office for Religious Affairs, see Urząd do Spraw Wyznań
Officer Concentration Station Rothesay, see Stacja Zborna Oficerów Rothesay
Official Documents Concerning Polish–German and Polish–Soviet Relations 1933–1939 – Polish White Book, 61–62
Official Irish Republican Army, 274n52
Ognisko Polskie (Polish Hearth), 210–211, 269, 398

Ogólny Zjazd Polaków w W. Brytanii (General Congress of Poles in Great Britain), 275, 291
Okhrana, 48
Okrągły Stół (Round Table talks), 338–339, 344, 354n14
Okulicki, Leopold, 69, 99, 123–124, 129–130, 133
Olejniczak, Jan, 118n7
Olejnik, Włodzimierz, 347
Olszowski, Stefan, 273–274
Olympic Games, 298n12, 302
O'Malley, Owen, 90
Onoszko, Józef, 365n50
Onyszkiewicz, Janusz, 303–304, 332
OPEC, 267
Operation Canned Goods, 24n2
Operation Himmler, 24n2
Operation Keelhaul, 156n32
Operation Konserve, 24n2
Operation Market Garden, 140
Operation Tempest, see Akcja Burza
Operational Group for Disintegrative Tasks, see Grupa Operacyjna do Zadań Dezintegracyjnych
opłatek, 380, 385
Opole, 147
OPW, see Obóz Polski Walczącej
Orbis, 209, 225
Order Odrodzenia Polski (Order of Polonia Restituta, also known as the Order of the Rebirth of Poland), 300, 332
Order of Chivalry of the Republic of Poland, see zakon rycerski Rzeczypospolitej Polskiej
Order of St. Stanislas, 300, 310, 332, 395
Organizacja Bojowa Wolna Polska—'Free Poland' Combat Organization, 287
Organizacja Wojskowa (OW, Military Organization), 26n1
Organization of Ukrainian Nationalists (OUN), 17
Orka, 232
Orlov, Alexander, 74
ORMO, see Ochotnicza Rezerwa Milicji Obywatelskiej
ORP Orzeł, 17
ORP Ślązak, 101
Orthodoxy, 7, 18, 69
Orwell, George, 181
Orzeł Biały, 209–211, 369

Osóbka-Morawski, Edward, 103, 110, 115, 134–136, 143–144
Ossolineum, 147–148
Ossoliński, Józef, 147
Ostashkov camp, 91
Ostashkov prisoners, 93
Ostoja-Koźniewski, Jerzy, 386
Ostrowska, Kamila, 250, 255
Ostrowska, Maria, 249
Ostrowski, Michał, 249
Ostrowski, Stanisław, 244
   accusations of corruption against, 289–291
   and CSCE, 266
   fundraising for KOR, 269–270
   and John Paul II, 277
   and Katyń Memorial, 274–275
   legalism, 278
   military, medical, and government service, 249–256
   opposition to, 263–264
   "Polski Nowy Rok w Londynie" ("Polish New Year in London") speech (1975), 266
   as president, 249, 256–278, 286n21, 323, 325, 375, 394
   presidential succession, 257, 278, 283–284
   reburial, 399
   Stanisław Zgodliwy (Stanisław the Peacemaker), 278
   support for, 263–264
   timeline of major events, ix, viii
   and VI Rada Narodowa, 276
Ostrowski, Stanisław Kazimierz, 36n14
Oświęcim Concentration Camp, 56, 62
OUN (Organization of Ukrainian Nationalists), 17
Our Lady of Jasna Góra, 214–215, 312
Our Lady of Ostra Brama, 346
OW. See *Organizacja Wojskowa*
Oxford University, 210n27
OZN, see *Obóz Zjednoczenia Narodowego*

P

PAC (Polish American Congress), 117–118, 129, 159, 171, 274, 307n38, 341
Paderewski, Ignacy Jan
   activism, 9–10
   death, 71–72
   government service, 13, 18, 34, 41–43, 49, 51, 219
   reburial, 391

PAFT (Polonia Aid Foundation Trust), 385–386, 398
Pahlavi, Mohammad Reza, 80n65
Pająk, Antoni, 202, 204, 211, 219, 227–229
Pająk, Jadwiga, 227n16
Pająk, Maria, 227n16
Pajdak, Antoni, 129–130, 133, 269n35
PAL, see *Polska Armia Ludowa*
Pałac Belwederski (Belweder Palace), 377
Pałac Kultury i Nauki (Palace of Culture and Science), 188, 215
Palace of the Council of Ministers (Warsaw), 241
Palestine, 101, 237n35
Palkin, Aron, 161n37
Pan-Slav Committee, 75
Pan-Slavic Committee, 75
Państwowa Komisja Wyborcza (State Electoral Commission), 372
Państwowy Korpus Bezpieczeństwa (PKB, National Security Corps), 57
Panufnik, Andrzej, 316
Papée, Kazimierz, 220, 237, 259–260
parafia pw. NMP Matki Kościoła na Ealingu w Londynie (Parish of Our Lady, Mother of the Church), 356n25
Paris Agreement, see *Umowa Paryska*
Paris Commune Shipyard, see *Stocznia im. Komuny Paryskiej*
Paris Peace Conference, 10, 165, 219
Parish of Our Lady, Mother of the Church, see *parafia pw. NMP Matki Kościoła na Ealingu w Londynie*
Partia X (Party X), 387–388
Partition, 6–8, 30, 221n6, 300, 403
partyzanci (partisans), 235–236
PAT, see *Polska Agencja Telegraficzna*
patriotic priests, 179–180
Patton, George, 46
Paul VI, 233, 260
Pawiak prison (Warsaw), 280
Pawlak, Waldemar, 398
PAX Association, see *Stowarzyszenie PAX*
PAX priests, 220n4

Peasants' Battalions, see *Bataliony Chłopskie*
Pękala, Julian, 181n34
People's Army, see *Armia Ludowa (AL)*
People's Guard, see *Gwardia Ludowa*
People's Guard of the WRN, see *Gwardia Ludowa WRN*
Persson, Bertil, 310n43
Petherick, Maurice, 127–128
Philip (Prince of Wales), 392n19
Piasecki, Julian, 52n17
Piast dynasty, 6
Piątkowski, Mateusz Jan, 23n1
Piekałkiewicz, Jan, 86
Piekiełko cafe, 210–211
Pieracki, Bronisław, 17
Pieśń o Janku z Gdyni ("Song about Janek from Gdynia"), 242n41
PIH, see *Polski Instytut Historyczny*
Pilecki, Witold, 206
Piłsudski, Bronisław, 8n6
Piłsudski, Józef
   and Długoszowski, 39
   as marshal, 5, 8–21, 36–39, 66
   and Raczkiewicz, 49
   support for, 45, 73, 123, 199, 318n4, 398
Piłsudski, Romuald, 136
Piłsudski, Rowmund, 210
Józef Piłsudski Institute (New York and London), 255–256
Piłsudski Square, see *Plac Marszałka Józefa Piłsudskiego*
Piłsudski's Legions, 18, 67, 255
Pitschen, 21
Pius XII, 201, 220
PKB, see *Państwowy Korpus Bezpieczeństwa*
PKN, see *Polski Komitet Narodowy*
PKP (*Polityczny Komitet Porozumiewawczy*), see *Polityczny Komitet Porozumiewawczy*
PKP (*Polski Korpus Posiłkowy*), see *Polski Korpus Posiłkowy*
PKWN, see *Polski Komitet Wyzwolenia Narodowego*
Plac Marszałka Józefa Piłsudskiego (Piłsudski Square), 397
Plac Zwycięstwa (Victory Square), 297, 397
place names, 212–213, 215–216, 357, 396–397
Płońska, Janina, 240
PMS, 353

PNCC (Polish National Catholic Church), 180n31
PNKD, see *Polski Narodowy Komitet Demokratyczny*
PNKK (*Polski Narodowy Kościół Katolicki*, Polish National Catholic Church), 180
Podoski, Bohdan, 123, 285
Polan-Haraschin, Julian, 332n33
Poland
  Agreement of Mutual Assistance, 20–21
  archives, 144–146, 177, 385n7
  borders. *See* borders
  Communist government, 202–203
  cultural artifacts, 220–222
  émigré community. *See* émigré community
  ethnic composition, 148
  financial and material assets, 144–146
  food prices, 213, 236, 241
  foreign occupation of, 3, 7–9, 30–32, 56, 84–85, 99–100, 142, 147–148, 150–155, 164, 188, 215, 306, 403
  German invasion of, vii, 1, 23–29, 250–251, 295
  German relations, 359–360, 403
  gold reserves, 25–26, 59, 146
  independent, vii, 3, 5–21, 48, 348
  Inter-Allied Council, 72
  Kingdom of, 9
  London capital, 1–3, 60–61
  martial law, 306–307, 312–313
  name changes, 357
  reburials in, 391–392
  Second Republic. *See* Second Republic
  Sikorski–Maisky Pact, vii, 64–65, 76, 166, 199, 202, 251n6, 253, 352
  silver reserves, 263
  Soviet invasion of, vii, 2–3, 29–32, 250
  Soviet system imposed on, 206, 212–215
  Soviet withdrawal from, 393
  standard of living, 267
  Third Republic, 383–399
  timeline of major events, vii–ix
  treaty of alliance and friendship with Soviet Union, 136
Poland Tomorrow, see *Jutro Polski*
Poling, Kermit, 310n43
Polish Affairs, 197, 385

Polish Affairs and Problems of Central & Eastern Europe, 197
Polish Airmen's Club, see *Klub Lotników Polskich*
Polish-American community, 170–171, 187
Polish American Congress (PAC), 117–118, 129, 159, 171, 274, 307n38, 341
Polish and Slavic Center, see *Centrum Polsko-Słowiańskie*
Polish Armed Forces, 10–11, 44
  Air Force, 60–61, 109, 152, 398, 404
  10th Armored Cavalry Brigade, 319
  1st Armored Division, 109, 140, 148, 186n43, 200, 319, 340
  campaign encouraging soldiers to return to Poland, 156–158
  in captivity, 91
  General Staff, 177
  1st Tadeusz Kościuszko Infantry Division (*1 Polska Dywizja Piechoty im. Tadeusza Kościuszki*), 96–97
  9th Infantry Division (*9 Dywizja Piechoty*), 352
  Katyń massacre, 89–95, 97, 100–101
  Navy, 60, 109
  in Poland, 213
  1 Samodzielna Brygada Spadochronowa (1st Independent Parachute Brigade), 140
  Second Polish Corps. *See* Second Polish Corps
  Sovietization of, 178–181
  Supreme Council, 48
  in UK, 59–61
  veterans of. *See* military veterans
Polish Armed Forces in the West, 2, 33, 60, 203–205, 376
Polish Autocephalous Orthodox Church, 179n29
Polish Auxiliary Corps, see *Polski Korpus Posiłkowy*, PKP
Polish Aviators' Cemetery (Newark-upon-Trent), 229–230
Polish Beer-Lovers' Party, see *Polska Partia Przyjaciół Piwa*
Polish Catholic Church, see *Kościół Polskokatolicki*
Polish Catholic Mission, see *Polska Misja Katolicka*
Polish Combatants' Association, see

Stowarzyszenie Polskich Kombatantów
Polish Committee for Cooperation and Security in Europe, 260–261
Polish Committee of National Liberation, see *Polski Komitet Wyzwolenia Narodowego*
Polish communists, 72–76, 78–79, 103–104
Polish contagion, 333–335
Polish Corridor (London), 208, 235n33
Polish Daily, see *Dziennik Polski*
Polish Educational Society, see *Polska Macierz Szkolna*
Polish Fortnightly Review, 61–62
Polish Freedom Movement Independence and Democracy. *See Polski Ruch Wolnościowy Niepodległość i Demokracja*
Polish Government-in-Exile
  abandonment of, 113–140
  "Appeal to the Free World," 307
  changing the course of an avalanche, 401–404
  conclusion of affairs, 385
  discord, 165–190
  discord to division, 190–217
  dissolution of, 375
  division, 219–247
  into exile, 47–87
  funding, 401
  fundraising, 187–188, 197, 258, 266, 325, 331, 402
  international recognition of, 141–146, 150, 216n37, 260, 329, 401
  last president of, 347–381
  length of service, 401n2
  London seat, 1–3, 145, 183–184, 401
  mission, 374–375
  presidency of, 33–46
  publicity, 267
  refusal to disband, 141–164
  relations with British government, 205
  role of, 276
  support for Wałęsa, 373
  and Third Republic, 383–399
  timeline of major events, vii–ix
  troublesome alliances, 89–112
"Polish Government-in-Exile" (BBC1), 267
Polish Hearth, see *Ognisko Polskie*
Polish Home, see *Dom Polski*
Polish Hospital No. 3 (North Wales), 255

Polish Independence League, see *Liga Niepodległości Polski*
Polish Independent Reserve Brigade, see *Polska Niezależna Brygada Rezerwy*
Polish Institute and Sikorski Museum, 202, 223n9, 291, 296, 305, 404n9
Polish Institute of Catholic Action, see *Instytut Polskiej Akcji Katolickiej*
Polish language, 7–8, 30, 165, 209
Polish-language publications, 181–184, 209–212, 222, 333
Polish Library, see *Biblioteka Polska*
Polish-Lithuanian Commonwealth, 6–7, 10n10
Polish Medical Association in London, see *Związek Lekarzy Polskich w Londynie*
Polish Military Cemetery (Monte Cassino), 239
Polish Military Cemetery (Newark-upon-Trent), 247, 278
Polish Monitor, see *Monitor Polski*
Polish National Alliance, 117, 187
Polish National Catholic Church (PNCC), 180n31
Polish National Catholic Church, see *Polski Narodowy Kościół Katolicki*
Polish National Committee, see *Komitet Narodowy Polski*, KNP
Polish National Committee, see *Polski Komitet Narodowy*
Polish National Democratic Committee, see *Polski Narodowy Komitet Demokratyczny*
Polish National Fund, 261n22
Polish National Union. See *Polskie Zjednoczenie Narodowe*
"Polish New Year in London", see *"Polski Nowy Rok w Londynie"* speeches
Polish People's Army, see *Ludowe Wojsko Polskie*
Polish People's Army, see *Polska Armia Ludowa*
Polish People's Party, see *Polskie Stronnictwo Ludowe*
Polish People's Party "Rebirth", see *Polskie Stronnictwo Ludowe "Odrodzenie,"*

Polish People's Republic, see *Rzeczpospolita Polska Ludowa*
Polish Polytechnic, 234
Polish Red Cross, 68, 94, 130, 210, 229n21, 281, 284–285
Polish Relief Fund, 10n12
Polish Research Centre (London), 210, 296
Polish Resettlement Corps (PRC, *Polski Korpus Przysposobienia i Rozmieszczenia*), 157–158, 163, 320, 352
Polish Roman Catholic Union of America, 171
Polish Scouting Association, see *Związek Harcerstwa Polskiego*
Polish Scouting Organization Operating Outside the Country, see *Związek Harcerstwa Polskiego poza granicami Kraju*, ZHP pgK
Polish Seamen's Union, 134
Polish & Slavic Federal Credit Union, 362n43
Polish Social and Cultural Association. See *Polski Ośrodek Społeczno-Kulturalny*
Polish Social Democratic Union, see *Polska Unia Socjaldemokratyczna*
Polish Socialist Party – Freedom, Equality, Independence, see *Polska Partia Socjalistyczna – Wolność, Równość, Niepodległość*, PPS-WRN
Polish Society of Arts and Sciences Abroad, see *Polskie Towarzystwo Naukowe na Obczyźnie*
Polish Solidarity Campaign, 302
Polish Telegraphic Agency, see(*Polska Agencja Telegraficzna*
Polish United Workers' Party. See *Polska Zjednoczona Partia Robotnicza*
Polish University Abroad *(Uniwersytet Polski za Granicą)*, 209n25
Polish University College, 210, 315
Polish University College Association Ltd. (PUCAL), 234
Polish University in Exile *(Polski Uniwersytet na Obczyźnie*, PUNO), 209, 234, 263, 315

Polish Workers' Party. See *Polska Partia Robotnicza*
Polish–British Alliance, 295
Polish–Soviet War (1919–1920), 12–13, 30–31, 38, 48, 65, 73, 149n19, 157n33, 249, 252
Politburo, 131, 268
Political Bureau, see *Biuro Polityczne*
Political Council, see *Rada Polityczna*
political parties, 363, 387
Polityczny Komitet Porozumiewawczy (PKP, Political Coordinating Committee), 58, 99
Polityka, 396n21
Polkowski, Józef, 220–222
Polonia Aid Foundation Trust (PAFT), 385–386, 398
Polonia Theater, 211
Polska (newspaper), 70
Polska Agencja Prasowa, 363
Polska Agencja Telegraficzna (PAT, Polish Telegraphic Agency), 59, 130, 132, 138, 211, 222, 257
Polska Armia Ludowa (PAL, Polish People's Army), 87
1 Polska Dywizja Piechoty im. Tadeusza Kościuszki (Polish 1st Tadeusz Kościuszko Infantry Division), 96–97
Polska Fundacja Kulturalna, 316
Polska Macierz Szkolna (Polish Educational Society), 209
Polska Misja Katolicka (Polish Catholic Mission), 211
Polska Niezależna Brygada Rezerwy (Polish Independent Reserve Brigade), 310
Polska Organizacja Wojskowa (POW, Polish Military Organization), 5
Polska Partia Przyjaciół Piwa (PPPP, Polish Beer-Lovers' Party), 388n12
Polska Partia Robotnicza (*PPR*, Polish Workers' Party), 75–79, 101–107. See also *Blok Demokratyczny*; *Polska Zjednoczona Partia Robotnicza*
  campaign against Mikołajczyk and PSL, 160–161
  Central Committee, 86–87
  Głos Ludu, 137–138
  graffiti campaigns against, 100n19
  "O co walczymy?", 108
  in occupied Poland, 152–155

and provisional government, 134–135
and *Sejm* elections, 160–161
"*Trzy Razy Tak*" ("Three Times Yes", 3xTAK) campaign, 153–154
and Warsaw Uprising, 113
Polska Partia Socjalistyczna (PPS, Polish Socialist Party), 8, 13–15, 74, 86, 110, 122, 171–172, 363. *See also* Blok Demokratyczny; Koncentracja Demokratyczna; Polska Zjednoczona Partia Robotnicza; Polskie Zjednoczenie Narodowe; Rada Polityczna
and *Akt Zjednoczenia Narodowego* (National Unity Act), 195–196
legalist position, 172
in occupied Poland, 31
and Poland's provisional government, 135
Porozumienie Stronnictw Demokratycznych (PSD, Accord of Democratic Parties), 172–173
and presidency, 192–193
and reconciliation, 257
revival, 331
Wolność, 202
and Zaleski's presidency, 167–168
Polska Partia Socjalistyczna – Wolność, Równość, Niepodległość (PPS-WRN, Polish Socialist Party – Freedom, Equality, Independence), 56, 78
Polska Unia Socjaldemokratyczna (Polish Social Democratic Union), 358
Polska Walcząca, 183–184
Polska Zjednoczona Partia Robotnicza (PZPR, Polish United Workers' Party), 206, 215, 235–237, 302n20, 353, 356
Central Committee, 343
dissolution, 358–359
economic policy, 241, 334–335
election campaign, 341–342
formation, 178–179
and John Paul II, 277, 297, 304, 306, 312
and *List 59*, 265
objective, 179
Okrągły Stół (Round Table talks), 338–339
protests against, 236–237, 242–243
reinvigoration, 331

and *Sejm*, 344
and Sikorski, 304–305
strategy against religion, 179–180, 214–215
and TKK, 309
Polski Instytut Historyczny (PIH, Polish Historical Institute), 149
Polski Komitet Narodowy (PKN, Polish National Committee), 102–103
Polski Komitet Wyzwolenia Narodowego (PKWN, Polish Committee of National Liberation), vii, 110–111, 115, 118–122, 216n38. *See also* Rząd Tymczasowy Rzeczypospolitej Polskiej
Polski Korpus Posiłkowy (PKP, Polish Auxiliary Corps), 294
Polski Korpus Przysposobienia i Rozmieszczenia (Polish Resettlement Corps, PRC), 157–158, 163, 320, 352
Polski Narodowy Komitet Demokratyczny (PNKD, Polish National Democratic Committee), 174, 187, 197, 203, 232, 401n1
Polski Narodowy Kościół Katolicki (PNKK, Polish National Catholic Church), 180
"*Polski Nowy Rok w Londynie*" ("Polish New Year in London") speeches, 266, 340
Polski Ośrodek Społeczno-Kulturalny (POSK, Polish Social and Cultural Association), 235, 246, 255, 353, 356–357, 386, 398
Ogólny Zjazd Polaków w W. Brytanii (General Congress of Poles in Great Britain), 275
opening, 262–263
Polski Ruch Wolnościowy Niepodległość i Demokracja (Polish Freedom Movement Independence and Democracy, PRW NiD or NiD), 136, 171–172. *See also* Koncentracja Demokratyczna; Rada Polityczna
Trybuna, 136, 209
Polski Sztab Partyzancki (PSzP, Polish Partisan Staff), 104
Polski Uniwersytet na Obczyźnie (PUNO, Polish University in Exile), 209, 234, 263, 315
Polski Związek Katolicko-Społeczny, 344n60

Polskie Linie Lotnicze LOT (LOT Polish Airlines), 224–225, 377
Polskie Państwo Podziemne (Polish Secret State), 57, 141–142
Polskie Radio, 307
Polskie Stronnictwo Ludowe (PSL, Polish People's Party), 134–135, 160–161, 168, 171–174, 187, 231–232, 388. *See also* Polski Narodowy Komitet Demokratyczny
Jutro Polski, 209
Nasz Znak, 212
Orka, 232
Porozumienie Stronnictw Demokratycznych (PSD, Accord of Democratic Parties), 172–173
and presidency, 304
and reconciliation, 257
Polskie Stronnictwo Ludowe Nowe Wyzwolenie (PSL NW, PSL New Liberation), 160
Polskie Stronnictwo Ludowe "Odłam Jedności Narodowej," 226, 264
Polskie Stronnictwo Ludowe "Odrodzenie" (PSL "Odrodzenie," Polish People's Party "Rebirth"), 358
Polskie Stronnictwo Ludowe "Piast" (PSL "Piast," Polish Peasant Party "Piast"), 13–14, 153
Polskie Towarzystwo Naukowe na Obczyźnie (PTNO, Polish Society of Arts and Sciences Abroad), 255, 315–316
Polskie Zjednoczenie Narodowe (PZN, Polish National Union), 259, 264, 269n40
Pomerania, 11, 21
Pomorskie *województwo*, 49
Poniatowski, Józef, 258n16, 403
Poniatowski, Juliusz, 52n17
Poniatowski, Stanisław August, 300
Poniatowski Bridge, 15
Popiel, Karol, 134–135, 160, 232
Popiełuszko, Jerzy, 312–313
Poplavsky, Stanislav, 213
Popular National Union, see Związek Ludowo-Narodowy
population transfers, 147–149
Porozumienie Stronnictw Demokratycznych (PSD, Accord of Democratic Parties), 172–173

Portugal, 216n37
POSK. See Polski Ośrodek Społeczno-Kulturalny
POSK News (Wiadomości POSK), 235
Potemkin, Vladimir Petrovich, 27
Potocka, Róża, 293–294
Potocki, Jan Zbigniew, 396
Potsdam Agreement, 142–144, 146, 159, 241
Povolny, Mojmir, 314
POW. See Polska Organizacja Wojskowa
Powązki Cemetery (Warsaw), 240, 272n47
Powązki Military Cemetery (Warsaw), 391–392
Poznań protests (1956), 213–215
Poznań region, 21
Poznański, Karol, 235
PPPP, see Polska Partia Przyjaciół Piwa
PPR. See Polska Partia Robotnicza
PPR Initiative Group, see Grupa Inicjatywna PPR
PPS. See Polska Partia Socjalistyczna
PPS-Rewolucja Demokratyczna (PPS-Democratic Revolution), 342n56
PPS-WRN, see Polska Partia Socjalistyczna – Wolność, Równość, Niepodległość
Pragier, Adam, 40, 195, 227, 260n20
Pravda, 89
Prawin, Jakub, 74n52
PRC, see Polish Resettlement Corps
presidency, 17–21, 33–46, 188, 339n48
presidential campaigns, 365
presidential decrees, 17, 323
presidential insignia, 371–380
Presidential Palace (Warsaw), 241n38
presidential seals, 371–372
presidential succession, 17, 303n23
prisoners of war, 93, 138, 360
privatization, 387, 396
PRL, see Rzeczpospolita Polska Ludowa
propaganda, 77–78, 94, 100–102, 106–107, 137–139, 307
Protectorate of Bohemia and Moravia, 19

Protestant Action Society, 158
protests
  anti-censorship (1968), 236–237
  economic strike (1970), 242–243, 268
  Jasna Góra pilgrimage (1956), 214–215
  London (1953), 205
  against martial law, 307–309
  Poznań (1956), 213–215
  student, 216, 236–237, 243
  workers' (1976), 268
Provisional Council of National Unity, see Tymczasowa Rada Jedności Narodowej (London)
Provisional Council of NSZZ Solidarność, see Tymczasowa Rada NSZZ Solidarność
Provisional Government of National Unity. See Tymczasowy Rząd Jedności Narodowej
Provisional Government of the Republic of Poland. See Rząd Tymczasowy Rzeczypospolitej Polskiej
Prussian Empire, 6–7
PRW NiD. See Polski Ruch Wolnościowy Niepodległość i Demokracja
Prytytski, Siarhei, 104
Przegląd Kulturalny, 224
Przegląd Polski (Polish Review), 175
Przewłocki, Marian, 208n24
Przeździecki, Wacław, 70, 75n53
PSD. See Porozumienie Stronnictw Demokratycznych
PSL. See Polskie Stronnictwo Ludowe
PSL New Liberation, see Polskie Stronnictwo Ludowe Nowe Wyzwolenie
PSL-NKW, 232
PSL NW, see Polskie Stronnictwo Ludowe Nowe Wyzwolenie
PSL "Odłam Jedności Narodowej" ("Group of National Unity"), 174
PSL "Odrodzenie", see Polskie Stronnictwo Ludowe "Odrodzenie"
PSL "Piast." See Polskie Stronnictwo Ludowe "Piast"
PSzP (Polski Sztab Partyzancki, Polish Partisan Staff), 104
PTNO, see Polskie Towarzystwo Naukowe na Obczyźnie

public opinion
  anti-Catholic, 158
  anti-Polish, 157–158
  attitude towards Soviets, 203
  Poland's image in the West, 105–106
  support for government-in-exile, 370–371
Public Opinion Research Center, see Centrum Badania Opinii Społecznej)
Public Security Offices, see Urzędy Bezpieczeństwa Publicznego
PUCAL (Polish University College Association Ltd.), 234
Pulaski, Kazimierz, 117n6
Pulaski Day, 117
PUNO (Polski Uniwersytet na Obczyźnie, Polish University in Exile), 209, 234, 263, 315
Putrament, Jerzy, 177–178
Pużak, Kazimierz, 130, 133
PZN. See Polskie Zjednoczenie Narodowe
PZPR. See Polska Zjednoczona Partia Robotnicza

Q
Quebec Provincial Museum, 221–222

R
Raczkiewicz, Benedykt, 47–48, 53
Raczkiewicz, Josef, 48
Raczkiewicz, Ludwika, 48
Raczkiewicz, Władysław
  birth and early years, 48–49
  burial site, 247
  death, 163
  and presidency, 41–43
  as president, 34, 47, 49–87, 94–99, 124, 138–141, 163–167, 193n2, 374–375, 394, 401
  presidential succession, 58, 111–112, 141, 163, 166–167
  private residence, 145
  Rada Narodowa Rzeczypospolitej Polskiej (National Council of the Republic of Poland), 51
  reburial, 399
  and Sosnkowski, 116–117
  timeline of major events, ix, vii, viii
  Umowa Paryska (Paris Agreement), 50
Raczyńska, Katarzyna, 295
Raczyńska, Wanda, 295

Raczyńska, Wirydianna, 295
Raczyński, Edward
  Aleksander, 293–294
Raczyński, Edward Bernard,
  210, 294–296, 316, 384
  and borders, 121
  burial site, 392
  condemnation of Jaruzelski's
    actions, 307
  death and funeral, 392
  as diplomat, 60, 70, 84–85,
    295–296
  fundraising, 357
  fundraising for KOR, 269–270
  and independent Poland, 20
  and invasion of Poland, 24
  and ITC, 145
  and John Paul II, 308
  and *Komitet Pomocy Rodakom
    w Kraju* (Committee to
    Aid Compatriots in the
    Country), 214
  and *List 59*, 265
  and loss of recognition, 144
  "The Mass Extermination of
    Jews in German Occupied
    Poland", 84–85
  memorial plaque, 398
  as Minister of Foreign
    Affairs, 83, 89, 141
  one-hundredth birthday, 390
  and POSK, 235
  and presidency, 35–36, 40–42,
    58, 257
  as president, 293, 297–316,
    324–325, 332n31, 375, 394
  presidential succession,
    303–304, 316–317, 324
  protests, 205
  on Rada Trzech (Council of
    Three), 196–197
  and Rogalin Palace, 389–390
  and Sabbat, 317, 323–324
  and Sikorski, 304–305
  support for POSK, 235
  symbolic tomb, 399
  timeline of major events,
    ix, viii
  and TKK, 309
  and unification, 240
  and Wałęsa, 356, 387
  and Lech Wałęsa, 303
  and Yalta agreements, 125–126
Raczyński, Karol, 294
Raczyński, Roger Adam,
  33–35, 40–42, 294
Raczyński, Roger Maurycy, 293
Raczyński family, 293
Raczyński Foundation,
  389–390, 392
*Rada Akademickich Szkół
  Technicznych* (Council
  of Academic Technical
  Schools), 234

Rada Jedności Narodowej (RJN,
  Council of National Unity),
  107–108, 111, 142, 168n5,
  191–192, 225–226
*Rada Jedności Narodowej do
  Narodu Polskiego i do Narodów
  Zjednoczonych* (Manifesto
  of the Council of National
  Unity to the Polish and
  Allied Nations), 142
*Rada Koordynacyjna Polonii
  Wolnego Świata* (Coordinating
  Council of Poles in the Free
  World), 311, 353
*I Rada Narodowa
  Rzeczypospolitej Polskiej*
  (National Council of the
  Republic of Poland), 51,
  59–61, 65, 83, 199
*II Rada Narodowa
  Rzeczypospolitej Polskiej*, 83,
  111, 123
*III Rada Narodowa
  Rzeczypospolitej Polskiej*, 173,
  182, 187, 193–194, 199, 219
*IV Rada Narodowa
  Rzeczypospolitej Polskiej*, 187,
  199–200, 225
*V Rada Narodowa
  Rzeczypospolitej Polskiej*, 259,
  265, 267–270, 274–277, 323
*VI Rada Narodowa
  Rzeczypospolitej Polskiej*, 276,
  308, 311
*VII Rada Narodowa
  Rzeczypospolitej Polskiej*, 311,
  329, 331, 333–336
*VIII Rada Narodowa
  Rzeczypospolitej Polskiej*,
  339–341, 344, 356, 361–364,
  368–369, 374, 377, 386–388
*Rada Ochrony Pamięci Walk i
  Męczeństwa* (Council for the
  Protection of Struggle and
  Martyrdom Sites), 392
*Rada Organizacji
  Kombatanckich* (Council of
  Veterans' Organizations), 305
Rada Państwa (Council of
  State), 188, 244–245
Rada Polityczna (Political
  Council), 174–176, 187,
  192–193, 196, 203, 401n1
Rada Polskich Partii Politycznych
  (Council of Polish Political
  Parties), 138
Rada Regencyjna (Regency
  Council), 9–10, 339, 370
Rada Rzeczypospolitej Polskiej
  (Rada RP), 193–194, 199–201,
  219, 234–235, 281–282

*II Rada Rzeczypospolitej Polskiej
  (II Rada RP)*, 219, 227, 282
*III Rada Rzeczypospolitej Polskiej
  (III Rada RP)*, 227, 230
*IV Rada Rzeczypospolitej Polskiej
  (IV Rada RP)*, 245
*Rada Stanu Rzeczypospolitej
  Polskiej* (Council of State
  of the Republic of Poland),
  240, 257
Rada Trzech (Council of
  Three), 196–197, 202, 222,
  229, 234, 243–244, 257, 296
Raddaway, Norman, 336
Radio Free Europe, 173–174,
  189–190, 203, 214, 232, 237,
  245, 257–258, 321n10, 323
Radio Kościuszko *(Tadeusza
  Kościuszki)*, 75–76, 89, 110,
  113
Radio Warsaw, 176
Radkiewicz, Stanisław, 74n52
Radom, Poland, 32
Radziwiłł, Stanisław, 229
Raikes, Victor, 127–128
railroads, 13, 79–80, 92, 350
Railwaymen's Union, 15
Rakowicki Cemetery
  (Kraków), 391
Rakowski, Mieczysław,
  339–340, 358
Ram's Forest, see *las Baran*
Rataj, Maciej, 14n23
RBP, see *Resort Bezpieczeństwa
  Publicznego*
reactionaries, 118
Reagan, Ronald, 313
Recovered Territories, 147,
  180, 186–187, 259
Red Army
  attack on Finland, 58
  and independent Poland,
    12, 20
  invasion of Germany,
    138–140, 221n5
  invasion of Poland, 2, 27–30,
    56–57, 66, 107, 251
  liberation of Chełm, 110
  Northern Group of Forces,
    148
  occupation of Germany, 147
  occupation of Poland, 142,
    147, 151, 213–215, 306,
    392–393
Polish 1st Tadeusz Kościuszko
  Infantry Division *(1 Polska
  Dywizja Piechoty im. Tadeusza
  Kościuszki)*, 96–97
Polish communist support
  for, 73
Polish division, 73–75. See
  also Second Polish Corps
Target Vistula, 12

Ukrainian Front, 251
  and Warsaw Uprising, 113–117
  withdrawal from Poland,
    159–160, 393
Red Army Day, 94
Red Banner, see Czerwony
  Sztandar
Red Corner, 70–71
Red Cross, 89–90
Red Poppies on Monte
  Cassino, see Czerwone maki
  na Monte Cassino
refugee camps, 149, 175, 353
refugees, 148, 157–158, 320
Regency Council (Rada
  Regencyjna), 9–10, 370
Rembertów prison (NKVD),
  138n48
reparation payments, 143
repatriation, 215, 333
  demands for, 135, 138, 391
  population transfers, 147–149
  requirements for, 157–158
representation, 203
repression, 312–313
Republic of Poland
  (Rzeczpospolita Polska). See
  Second Republic
Research Institute for the
  Contemporary Affairs of
  Poland, see Instytut Badania
  Zagadnień Krajowych
resistance, 85–87
resistance organizations, 349
Resort Bezpieczeństwa
  Publicznego (RBP, Resort of
  Public Security), 123–124
Retinger, Józef, 65
Rewiński, Janusz, 388n12
Reynaud, Paul, 58
Rhineland, 19
Ribbentrop, Joachim von,
  20, 127
  Treaty of Non-Aggression
    (Molotov–Ribbentrop Pact),
    20–21, 27–28, 105, 295
Riflemen's Association, see
  Związek Strzelecki
Rioni River, 47
Ripka, Hubert, 83, 314n50
RJN, see Rada Jedności
  Narodowej
Robotnik (The Worker), 8
Rode, Maksymilian, 181
Rogalin Palace, 293, 296,
  389–390, 392
Roja, Bolesław, 12
Rokossovsky, Konstantin,
  119, 148, 178–179, 213, 216
Rola-Żymierski, Michał, 103,
  143–144, 189
Roman, Antoni, 52n17

Roman Catholic Church, 8,
  15, 214, 220, 259–260, 277,
  312, 343
Roman Catholic priests, 69,
  179–180
Romania
  Communist government, 203
  constitution, 265n28
  government-in-exile, 313
  governments, 14n26
  and independent Poland,
    11n16, 12, 20
  and invasion of Poland,
    25–29, 32
  and NCFE, 174
  and occupied Poland, 34–35,
    43
  official name, 357n29
  protests, 334
  Soviet invasion and
    annexation of, 58
  US relations, 334
Romer, Tadeusz, 90–91,
  120n13, 121
Romkowski, Roman, 215
Rómmel, Juliusz, 31, 223
RON, see Ruch Odrodzenia
  Narodowego
Roosevelt, Eleanor, 71
Roosevelt, Franklin
  Atlantic Charter, 72, 83, 105,
    118, 125
  Declaration on Liberated
    Europe, 125
  "Four Freedoms," 118
  and Katyń massacre, 90,
    100–101
  support for Poles and Poland,
    43, 71–72, 85, 105, 109–110,
    117–118, 121, 128–129,
    158–159, 170n10
  timeline of major events, viii
  Yalta conference, 124–126,
    128–129
ROPCiO, see Ruch Obrony
  Praw Człowieka i Obywatela
Rose, Adam, 52n17
Rosen-Zawadzki, Kazimierz,
  71n43
Rosling, Florence Amelia,
  281, 283
Rothesay, Isle of Bute, 61, 84,
  123
Round Table talks, see
  Okrągły Stół
Rowecki, Stefan, 31, 55, 76
Royal Air Force (RAF), 24–25,
  239
  Polish squadrons, 60–61, 109,
    152, 398, 404
Royal Albert Hall, 204
Royal Army (British Army),
  84, 108–109

Royal Castle (Warsaw), 178n26,
  372, 374, 377–379, 384
Royal Courts of Justice
  (London Law Courts), 222
Royal Hungarian Army, 114n3
Royal Navy, 25, 60
Różański, Józef, 74n52, 215
Rożek, Edward, 344
Rozmarek, Charles, 117–118,
  129, 131, 159, 171, 187, 214
RTRP, see Rząd Tymczasowy
  Rzeczypospolitej Polskiej
Rubens Hotel (London), 145,
  305, 397
Rubin, Władysław, 246
Rubinstein, Artur, 131, 210
Ruch Obrony Praw Człowieka
  i Obywatela (ROPCiO,
  Movement for Defense of
  Human and Civic Rights),
  133n41, 270–271
Ruch Odrodzenia Narodowego
  (RON, National Rebirth
  Movement), 219, 227, 281
Rudenko, Roman, 150
Rudnicki, Klemens, 55, 210,
  357, 374, 381, 384, 392
Russia, 10, 48, 155n30
Russian Army, 7n4, 393
Russian Civil War, 149n19
Russian Empire, 3, 6–9, 47–48
Russian language, 148, 213, 252
Russian National Liberation
  Army (SS Sturmbrigade
  RONA), 114n3
Russian Orthodox Church, 8,
  180n32
Ruthin Castle, 163
Rutkowski, Bolesław, 74. See
  also Bielecki, Tadeusz
Rutkowski, Henryk
  (Wojciech), 74n50
Rutkowski, Lucjan, 362n44
Rybicki, Stefan, 281n10
Rydz-Śmigły, Edward, 12,
  18–21, 25, 33–34, 50–55,
  76–77
Rynkiewicz, Artur, 269n39
Rząd Tymczasowy
  Rzeczypospolitej Polskiej (RTRP,
  Provisional Government
  of the Republic of Poland),
  123–125, 131–136, 142
Rzeczpospolita Polska (Republic
  of Poland). See Second
  Republic
Rzeczpospolita Polska Ludowa
  (PRL, Polish People's
  Republic), 188, 208n22, 212,
  216n38, 259–260, 348n3,
  401n2

Rzeczpospolita Polska – Republic of Poland (biweekly), 212, 308n40, 385
Rzymowski, Wincenty, 143–144

S

Sabbat, Alina, 321
Sabbat, Anna, 308, 321
Sabbat, Jan, 321
Sabbat, Jolanta, 321, 345
Sabbat, Kazimierz, 270, 291, 317–321
  and CSCE, 260n20, 266
  death and funeral, 345–348
  and EZN, 197
  as EZN chairman, 236–237, 240, 243–244, 322–323
  and John Paul II, 277, 298, 308, 343
  Kanon (SB codename), 321, 323–324
  and Katyń Memorial, 274–275
  Limba Trading Company Ltd., 208, 320–322
  New Year's greeting (1989), 340
  and *Ogólny Zjazd Polaków w W. Brytanii* (General Congress of Poles in Great Britain), 275
  opposition to, 324
  organizational skills, 234–235, 322
  and presidency, 304
  as president, 317, 324–346, 375, 394
  presidential succession, 332, 348, 353
  as prime minister, 271, 274–277, 298–300, 307–309, 311, 314–315, 323–325
  and *Rada Narodowa*, 276
  as scoutmaster, 318–320, 322, 324, 326
  symbolic tomb, 399
  timeline of major events, ix
  Western travels, 335–336, 344
Sabbatowa, Anna, 381
Sachsenhausen concentration camp, 150n21
Sąd Obywatelski w Londynie (Citizens' Court in London), 184–185
Sądy Obywatelskie na Obczyźnie (Citizen's Courts Abroad), 184–185
Saint-Exupéry, Antoine, 181
Saint-Omer, France, 140
Salisbury, Lord, 272n48
Salomea, Marianna, 74n50

1 Samodzielna Brygada Spadochronowa (1st Independent Parachute Brigade), 140
Samodzielna Grupa "D" Departamentu IV MSW (Independent Group "D" of the Fourth Department of the Ministry of the Interior), 312n47
Samopomoc Marynarki Wojennej (Navy Mutual Aid Association), 210
San River, 187n44
Sanacja government, 15–20, 39–40, 45, 51–55, 73, 123, 198, 208n22
  sanctions, 298, 307, 330
Sanktuarium Matki Bożej Bolesnej Królowej Polski, 396
Sanok, 186–187
Sapieha, Adam, 57n29, 134, 199n14
Sapieha, Eustachy, 199, 219
Saratov, 76
Sarnecki, Tomasz, 342n55
Sas-Skowroński, Mieczysław, 235
Sawicki, Wojciech, 388
SB. See *Służba Bezpieczeństwa*
Schleswig-Holstein, 23–24, 290n37
Scholtz, Zbigniew, 258n16, 326, 341
Ścibor-Kamiński, Jerzy, 281
Scotland, 60, 99, 158
Scotland Yard, 212
scouting, 318, 324, 348–349, 352–353
SD, see *Stronnictwo Demokratyczne*
SDKPiL, see *Socjaldemokracja Królestwa Polskiego i Litwy*
SdRP, see *Socjaldemokracja Rzeczypospolitej Polskiej*
Second Czechoslovak Republic, 19
Second Polish Corps, 65–71, 79–84, 94–98, 237, 281, 315, 351–352, 403
  advance through Italy, 101–102, 108–109, 139, 148, 255
  Battle of Monte Cassino, 108–109, 352
  campaign encouraging soldiers to return home, 156–158
  discontent, 87
  ethnic composition, 69, 80–81
  Katyń massacre, 97
  medical supplies, 69, 80
  in Middle East, 101, 182, 237n35, 255
  military hospitals, 255
  Polish communists in, 75–76
  rations and equipment, 81–82, 96, 101
  in Soviet Union, 89, 223, 253–254
  uniforms, 69
Second Republic, 10–16, 142, 202, 230
  Government-in-Exile. See Polish Government-in-Exile
  international recognition of, 401
  timeline of major events, vii–ix
Second World Congress of Polonia in the Free World (*II Światowy Zjazd Polonii Wolnego Świata*), 311
Second World War, 3
Secret Teaching Organization. See *Tajna Organizacja Nauczycielska*
Security Service. See *Służba Bezpieczeństwa*
Sejm (parliament)
  dissolution, 50
  elections, 152–155, 159–162, 206, 216, 339–343, 387–388
  exile. See *Rada Narodowa Rzeczypospolitej Polskiej*
  in independent Poland, 7, 14–17
  and official name of Poland, 357
  political parties, 344–345, 387–388
  in PRL, 188
  timeline of major events, vii
Sejm Chancellery, 265
Select Committee to Conduct an Investigation and Study of the Facts, Evidence, and Circumstances of the Katyn Forest Massacre (Madden Committee), 203
Senat
  elections, 339–343, 387–388
  in independent Poland, 14–17
  Marszałek Senatu (Marshal of the Senate), 49
  political parties, 387–388
  PPR abolition campaign, 153–155
  restoration of, 339
Serov, Ivan, 30, 56–57, 129, 133, 151
Service for Poland's Victory. See *Służba Zwycięstwu Polski*
Seyda, Marian, 51n11, 64
Siberia, 253

Sidor, Kazimierz, 103
Sienkiewicz, Henryk, 403
Siewierski, Janusz, 71n43
Sikorska, Helena, 26, 144–145, 202, 223–224, 239–240, 245, 304–305
Sikorski, Franciszek, 250
Sikorski, Radoslaw, 256n11
Sikorski, Stanisław, 26
Sikorski, Władysław
  and Atlantic Charter, 72
  centenary events, 305
  death and funeral, 97–98, 223
  and independent Poland, 9, 12, 18, 20–21
  and invasion of Poland, 26–29
  and Katyń massacre, 90, 94–95
  and occupied Poland, 35
  as prime minister and commander in chief, 23, 35, 39–44, 49–55, 58–60, 63–72, 76, 79–87, 97, 145n12, 198, 208n22, 223
  reburial, 240, 245, 304–305, 344, 391–392
  and resistance, 86
  and Second Polish Corps, 79–84
  timeline of major events, vii
  Umowa Paryska (Paris Agreement), 50
  and Zaleski, 166
  and ZPP, 95
Sikorski–Maisky Pact, vii, 64–65, 76, 166, 199, 202, 251n6, 253, 352
Sikorski's tourists, 53
Siła-Nowicki, Władysław, 365n50
Silent and Unseen, see *Cichociemni*
silver reserves, 263
Simon, John, 24
Sinclair, John, 272n48
Singer, Bernard, 183–184, 207
Siwicki, Florian, 355n17
Six-Day War, 236
Skaradziński, Bolesław, 362n44
Skarb Narodowy (National Treasury), 335–336
  fundraising, 187–188, 197, 258, 266, 270, 325, 331, 402
  liquidation of, 375, 385–386
  Main Commission, 191–194
  revenues, 197, 266
  thirtieth anniversary commemoration, 299
Skarb Narodowy Rzeczypospolitej Polskiej, 258
Skarb Narodowy Zjednoczenia, 197, 258

Skirmunt, Konstanty, 285
Składkowski, 33, 391
Skokowski, Julian, 113
Skrzeszewski, Stanisław, 74n52
Skrzyński, Aleksander, 49
Skubiszewski, Krzysztof, 359, 364, 392
SL *(Stronnictwo Ludowe)*, 31, 86, 110, 122, 135. See also *Blok Demokratyczny*
SL *"Wolność"*, 173
Śląsk region, 21
Sławoj-Składkowski, Felicjan, 52n17, 53
SLD, see *Sojusz Lewicy Demokratycznej*
Słomińska, Sylwia, 23n1
Słotwina, 36n13
Slovak Republic, 19
Słowo, 198
Służba Bezpieczeństwa (SB, Security Service), 190, 215, 222–226, 309, 312, 331
  Arbuz (Watermelon) case, 216–217, 228
  document destruction, 354
  fabricated reports and files *(fałszywki)*, 355n19
  Kanon case, 321, 323–324
  Kielce Pogrom, 354
  Mikron case, 281–282
  Ważny (Important) case, 200–202
Służba Zwycięstwu Polski (SZP, Service for Poland's Victory), 31, 54–55
Small Constitution of 1947 *(Mała Konstytucja z 1947)*, 162
Small Constitution of 1992 *(Mała Konstytucja z 1992)*, 390
Smirnovsky, Mikhail, 273–274
SN. See *Stronnictwo Narodowe*
Sobczyk, Waldemar, 212
Soboniewski, Stefan, 260n20, 303
Social Democracy of the Kingdom of Poland and Lithuania, see *Socjaldemokracja Królestwa Polskiego i Litwy*
Social Democracy of the Republic of Poland, see *Socjaldemokracja Rzeczypospolitej Polskiej*
Socialist Realism, 179, 215, 397n22
Socialist Revolution Day, 150
Socjaldemokracja Królestwa Polskiego i Litwy (SDKPiL, Social Democracy of the Kingdom of Poland and Lithuania), 8

Socjaldemokracja Rzeczypospolitej Polskiej (SdRP, Social Democracy of the Republic of Poland), 358, 363
Sojusz Lewicy Demokratycznej (SLD, Democratic Left Alliance), 387
Sokolnicki, Juliusz, viii, 279–291, 300, 310, 327–328, 332, 339, 366, 370–371, 394–396
Sokolnicki, Michał, 284–285
Sokorski, Włodzimierz, 74n52
Soldier's Daily, see *Dziennik Żołnierza*
Solidarity Information Office in London, see *Biuro Informacyjne Solidarności w Londynie*)
Solidarity with Solidarity, 302
Solidarność (Solidarity), 2–3, 300n17, 302–313, 326, 329–335, 366
  Okrągły Stół (Round Table talks), 338–339
  political party, 387
  timeline of major events, viii
  underground operations, 342
Solidarność Walcząca (Fighting Solidarity), 327, 331, 342n56
Solina Dam, 187n44
Song of Russia, 77n61
Sosabowski, Stanisław, 140, 208n24, 210
Sosnkowski, Kazimierz, 34n4, 51, 59, 324
  as commander in chief, 83n69, 98–99, 111–112, 116–117
  death, 238
  and independent Poland, 5, 9, 12
  and invasion of Poland, 26–27
  and *Komitet Pomocy Rodakom w Kraju* (Committee to Aid Compatriots in the Country), 214
  Operation Tempest *(Akcja Burza)*, 107
  popularity, 191
  and presidency, 192–193, 197
  principles of unification, 191–192, 234
  and Raczkiewicz, 49–50, 60, 64, 83–84, 168n6
  reinterment, 391
  Sanacja affiliation, 51n11
  and Warsaw Uprising, 116–117
  and Zaleski, 191–196
South African forces, 108–109
South Ealing Cemetery, 227
sovereignty, 204

Soviet Army. *See* Red Army
Soviet Bloc, 188–189, 269n36, 277, 301, 334
Soviet secret police. *See* NKVD
Soviet Union. *See* Union of Soviet Socialist Republics
Sovietization, 178–181, 212–215
SP. *See Stronnictwo Pracy*
Spa Conference (1920), 11–12
Spain, 150, 216, 237, 260n19
Speakers' Corner (Hyde Park), 243
The Spectator, 94
SPK, see *Stowarzyszenie Polskich Kombatantów*
Społeczny Komitet Antykomunistyczny (Public Anticommunist Committee), 99–100
Sprawa Bergu (Berg matter) or *afera Bergu* (Berg affair), 174–176, 185, 193–194, 199, 201, 214n31, 401n1
Spychalski, Marian, 103, 189
Šrámek, Jan, 97
Srokowski, Włodzimierz, 230–231
SS *Eocene*, 25–26
SS Sturmbrigade RONA (Russian National Liberation Army), 114n3
St. Andrew Bobola Church (*Kościół św. Andrzeja Boboli*), 211, 239, 247, 256, 278, 325, 346
St. Brigid's Church (*kościół św. Brygidy*), 300n17
St. James Theatre (later The Other Palace), 347n1
St. Mary Abbot's Hospital, 182
St. Mary's Catholic Cemetery, Kensal Green, 182
St. Oswald, Lord, 272n48, 274–275
St. Pancras Town Hall, 192
St. Petersburg Imperial University, 48
Stachiewicz, Wacław, 54
Stacja Zborna Oficerów Rothesay (Officer Concentration Station Rothesay), 61
Stalin, Josef, 16, 19–20, 30n20, 62–65, 70, 212
  border demands, 102n24, 105–106, 109, 120–121
  command post, 254n8
  criticism of, 204
  Declaration on Liberated Europe, 125
  erasure from Poland, 215
  and Katyń massacre, 89–90, 100n20
  and Mikołajczyk, 120–121
  oversight of Poland, 188–189
  and Polish communists, 73, 75n54
  and Polish officers in captivity, 91
  and Polish provisional government, 134
  Potsdam conference, 143
  and Rokossovsky, 178–179
  and Second Polish Corps, 79–83
  and *Sejm* elections, 159–160, 161n37
  and Sosnkowski, 111
  and Soviet propaganda, 106–107
  timeline of major events, viii
  and Trial of the Sixteen, 132–133
  Uncle Joe, 77–78
  and United Nations, 131
  and US aid, 307n39
  and Warsaw Uprising, 114–115
  Yalta conference, 124–126
  and ZPP, 95–97
Stalinist wedding cake style, 188n47
Stalinogród, 212, 215
Stańczyk, Jan, 51n11, 53, 134
Stanford University Hoover Institution Library, 247
Stanislav, 353n11
Stanisławów, 353n11
Starewicz, Artur, 274
Starobelsk camp, 91, 93
Stars and Stripes, 94
Starszewski, Jan, 197
Starzewski, Jan, 236, 258n16
Starzewski, Jerzy, 240
Starzyński, Teofil, 118n7
Stasi, 189
Staszewski, Stefan, 206n19
State National Council, see *Krajowa Rada Narodowa*
Stelmachowski, Andrzej, 371–374, 377–381, 386–388
Stemler, Józef, 130, 133
Stettin, 144
Stettinius, Edward, 131
Stevenson, Adlai, 191
Stewart, Donald B., 93–94
Stocznia Gdańska (Gdańsk Shipyard), 242–243, 242n40, 302
Stocznia im. Komuny Paryskiej (Paris Commune Shipyard), 242
Stolypin, Pyotr, 92n3
Stolypin cars, 92
Stowarzyszenia Lotników Polskich, 245
Stowarzyszenie Lotników Polskich w Londynie (Association of Polish Airmen in London), 229–230
Stowarzyszenie PAX (PAX Association), 179–180, 344n60, 354n14
Stowarzyszenie Polskich Kombatantów (SPK, Polish Combatants' Association), 149, 183–184, 210, 263, 320, 323, 353, 392
Stowarzyszenie Techników Polskich w Wielkiej Brytanii (Association of Polish Engineers in Great Britain), 234
Stowarzyszenie "Wspólnota Polska" (Association "Polish Community"), 380
Strasburger, Henryk, 51n12, 59, 145–146
Straszewicz, Czesław, 181
Stratton House (London), 145
Strauss, Henry, 128
Stronnictwo Chrześcijańskiej Demokracji (Christian Democracy Party), 219, 227
Stronnictwo Demokratyczne (SD), 31, 110, 171–172, 178, 339, 344–345, 354–355, 358, 363. *See also Koncentracja Demokratyczna; Polski Narodowy Komitet Demokratyczny*
Stronnictwo Ludowe (SL), 31, 86, 110, 122, 135. *See also Blok Demokratyczny*
Stronnictwo Ludowe "Wolność" (SL "Wolność"), 173
Stronnictwo Narodowe (SN, National Party), 16–18, 31, 56, 78, 122, 193, 264, 363. *See also Polskie Zjednoczenie Narodowe; Rada Polityczna* and *Akt Zjednoczenia Narodowego* (National Unity Act), 195–196
  intelligence operations, 175–176
  opposition to unification, 244, 258–259
  and reconciliation, 257
  and Sabbat, 322–323, 326n17
Stronnictwo Narodowo-Demokratyczne, 13n21
Stronnictwo Pracy (SP, Labor Party), 18, 122, 135, 153, 160, 171–172, 200, 388. *See also Koncentracja Demokratyczna; Polski Narodowy Komitet*

Demokratyczny; Polskie Zjednoczenie Narodowe
 Foreign Committee, 173
 opposition to unification, 258–259
 Popiel's branch, 232
 Porozumienie Stronnictw Demokratycznych (PSD, Accord of Democratic Parties), 172–173
 and reconciliation, 257
 spinoffs, 219
Stroński, Stanisław, 35, 40–43, 51n10, 52–53, 83–84
Strzałkowski, Wiesław, 258n16, 267
student protests, 216, 236–237, 243
Stypułkowski, Zbigniew, 130, 133, 197, 205
Subritzky-Kusza, Michael, 285n20, 289n34
Sudetenland, 19
Sulik, Nikodem, 320
Sulikowa, Anna, 320–321
Sullivan, Gael, 170n10
Summer Olympic Games, 298n12, 302
Supreme Audit Office, see *Najwyższa Izba Kontroli*
Supreme Council of the Polish Armed Forces, 48
Supreme Polish Military Committee. See *Naczelny Polski Komitet Wojskowy*
Survey, 336
Sweden, 212
Swianiewicz, Stanisław, 91–92
Światło, Józef, 162n39, 189–190
Światowy Zjazd Jedności z Walczącym Krajem (World Congress of Unity with the Fighting Homeland), 299
II Światowy Zjazd Polonii Wolnego Świata (Second World Congress of Polonia in the Free World), 311
Światowy Zjazd Polski Walczącej (World Congress of Fighting Poland), 233–234, 322
Światowy Związek Polaków z Zagranicy (World Association of Poles Abroad, Światpol), 49
Świątynia Opatrzności Bożej (Temple of Divine Providence), 399
Świderski, Bolesław, 227–228
Świdlicki, Andrzej, 321n10
Świerz-Zaleski, Stanisław, 220–221

Świętosławski, Wojciech, 52n17
Syria, 236, 267
Szadkowski, Zygmunt, 276, 290, 298, 321, 369–374, 384–386
Szare Szeregi (Gray Ranks), 31, 318n3, 349
Szczecin, Poland, 144n11, 242
Szczepanik, Edward, 299, 307, 315–316
 conclusion of government-in-exile's affairs, 385–388
 and constitution, 390
 final celebration remarks, 383–384
 as prime minister, 326, 335–336, 341, 353, 359–361, 364, 369, 372–375
Szczerbiec (coronation sword), 220–221
Szczypiorski, Stanisław, 71n43
Szembek, Jan, 52n17
Szkoda, Władysław, 386
Szkopiak, Zygmunt, 326, 347, 372
Szostak, Józef, 38n20
SZP. See *Służba Zwycięstwu Polski*
Szumigalski, Włodzimierz, 71n43
Szygowski, Juliusz, 283, 299–300, 324
Szymański, Jerzy, 55

T

Tadeusza Kościuszki (Tadeusz Kościuszko Radio Station, Radio Kościuszko), 75–76, 89, 110, 113
Taganka prison, 37n16
Tajna Organizacja Nauczycielska (TON, Secret Teaching Organization), 57
Tańska, Jadwiga, 281–282, 284
Target Vistula (Red Army), 12
Tarka, Krzysztof, 228n17
TASS, 59, 115, 188–189, 360–362
Tatar, Stanisław, 123, 177–178
Tatars, 69
Taylor, Ernest, 130
Tazab, 208, 224–225
Teatr Narodowy (National Theater), 236
Teatr Ref-Ren, 211
Tejkowski, Bolesław, 365n50
Telewizja Polska (TVP), 307, 342, 373
Temple of Divine Providence (*Świątynia Opatrzności Bożej*), 399

Temporary Board of Frontier Areas, 48
Temporary Committee for the Transitional Period, see *Komisja Tymczasowa Okresu Przejściowego*
Temporary Coordinating Commission of NSZZ "Solidarność", see *Tymczasowa Komisja Koordynacyjna NSZZ "Solidarność"*
Temporary National Treasury Commission, see *Tymczasowa Komisja Skarbu Narodowego*
Temporary Supreme Scouting Committee, see *Tymczasowy Naleczny Komitet Harcerski*, TNKH
Terné, Zofia, 211
Testament Polski Walczącej (Testament of Fighting Poland), 142
Thatcher, Margaret, 273n50, 298, 313, 343–344, 357n28
thick line policy, see *gruba linia*
Thierry, Adrien, 40–41
Third Republic, 383–399
Thomas, William Bain, 157
Three Russian Girls, 77n61
Thugutt, Mieczysław, 135n45
Time magazine, 62, 77–78
The Times of London, 132, 271–272
Timoshenko, Semyon, 251
Tito, 141n2
TKK, see *Tymczasowa Komisja Koordynacyjna NSZZ "Solidarność"*
TNKH, see *Tymczasowy Naleczny Komitet Harcerski*
Tokarzewski-Karaszewicz, Michał, 31, 55, 101n23, 116, 256, 391
Tomala, Michał, 71n43
Tomaszewski, Tadeusz, 166–167, 182–184
Tomb of the Unknown Soldier (Arc de Triomphe), 290
TON. See *Tajna Organizacja Nauczycielska*
Topolski, Feliks, 210
trade unions, 213, 242, 302
Trades Union Congress, 158
Trajdos, Waldemar, 365n50
Trąmpczyński, Wojciech, 134
Trans-Iranian Railway, 80
Trans-Siberian Railway, 350

treasury
  gold reserves, 25–26, 59, 146
  Interim Treasury Committee for Polish Affairs (ITC), 144–146
  National Treasury (*Skarb Narodowy*), 187–188, 191–192, 194, 197, 266
  silver reserves, 263
  Temporary National Treasury Commission (*Tymczasowa Komisja Skarbu Narodowego*), 201
  unified, 257–258
Treaty of Non-Aggression (Molotov–Ribbentrop Pact), 20–21, 27–28, 105, 295
Treaty of Riga, 12, 64, 95, 222
Treaty of Versailles, 19, 30
Treaty of Warsaw, 240–241, 311
Treaty of Zgorzelec (Agreement Concerning the Demarcation of the Established and the Existing Polish–German State Frontier), 186
Trial of the Sixteen, 132–134, 138, 150, 204
TRJN. *See Tymczasowy Rząd Jedności Narodowej*
Truman, Harry, viii, 134, 143, 158–159
Trybuna, 136, 209
Trybuna Ludu, 176, 342n57
Trybunał Konstytucyjny (Constitutional Tribunal), 366
"*Trzy Razy Tak*" ("Three Times Yes", 3xTAK) campaign, 153–154
tsarist Russia, 155n30
Turkey, 6, 20, 150
TVP (*Telewizja Polska*), 307, 342, 373
Tyczka, Mieczysław, 366
Tydzień, 288n33
Tygodnik, 202
Tygodnik Mazowsze, 331–332
Tygodnik Polski, 183–184, 207
Tygodnik Solidarność, 354n14, 357
Tymczasowa Komisja Koordynacyjna NSZZ "Solidarność" (TKK, Temporary Coordinating Commission of NSZZ "Solidarność"), 309, 312
Tymczasowa Komisja Skarbu Narodowego (Temporary National Treasury Commission), 201

Tymczasowa Rada Jedności Narodowej (TRJN, Provisional Council of National Unity) (London), viii, 196–197, 200, 225
Tymczasowa Rada NSZZ Solidarność (Provisional Council of NSZZ Solidarność), 330
Tymczasowy Naczelnik Państwa (Provisional Chief of State), 10
Tymczasowy Naleczny Komitet Harcerski (TNKH, Temporary Supreme Scouting Committee), 319–320
Tymczasowy Rząd Jedności Narodowej (TRJN, Provisional Government of National Unity) (Warsaw), 125, 135, 137–138, 321, 401n1
  diplomats, 145–146
  foreign relations, 149–151
  international recognition of, 141
  and Kielce pogrom, 155
  meeting space, 202
  nationalization of Poland, 150–151
  and repatriation, 158
  Sejm elections, 159–162
  transfer of Poland's embassy to, 144
  US support, 158–159
Tymiński, Stanisław, 365, 372–374, 387–388
Tyszyński, Leon, 71n43

U

UB. *See Urząd Bezpieczeństwa*
UBP, see *Urzędy Bezpieczeństwa Publicznego*
UdSW, see *Urząd do Spraw Wyznań*
Uganda, 353
Ukraine
  government-in-exile, 299, 313, 327
  Holodomor, 19–20
  and independent Poland, 11–12, 18
  opposition movement, 269n36
  Orange Revolution, 256n12
  Organization of Ukrainian Nationalists (OUN), 17
  relations with Poland, 393
  relations with Poland in exile, 266, 299
Ukrainian Front, 251
Ukrainian Military Organization (UVO), 14, 17

Ukrainian SSR, 119, 364n48
Ukrainians, 18, 69, 80–81, 334
Ulica Łącki, 251
Ulrych, Juliusz, 52n17, 391
Umowa Paryska (Paris Agreement), 50, 98, 192, 229, 243, 256, 324, 368
underground operations, 54–58, 70, 142, 162–163, 309. *See also* Warsaw Uprising
underground publishers, 298, 308
underground *Sejm*, 107–108
Unia, 141
Unia Chrześcijańsko-Społeczna, 344n60
Unia Demokratyczna (Democratic Union), 387
Uniate priests, 69
unification
  Akt Zjednoczenia Narodowego (National Unity Act), 192–196, 229, 231, 234, 243, 286
  noble conspiracy for, 230
  opposition to, 244, 258–259
  principles of, 191–192, 229, 243
  unified treasury, 258
  Zamek plan, 229–230, 240, 244–245
Unification Commission (*Komisja Scaleniowa*), 240, 243–244
Union of Armed Struggle, see *Związek Walki Zbrojnej*
Union of Legionnaires, see *Związek Legionistów Polskich*
Union of Participants of the Polish Resistance Movement in France, see *Związek Uczestników Polskiego Ruchu Oporu we Francji*
Union of Polish Communists "Proletariat", see *Związek Komunistów Polskich "Proletariat"*
Union of Polish Patriots, see *Związek Patriotów Polskich*
Union of Soviet Socialist Republics (USSR, Soviet Union)
  administration of Germany, 186
  administration of Recovered Territories, 186–187
  aggression, 58, 70–71
  annexation of Poland, 56–57
  and Atlantic Charter, 83
  dissolution of, 393
  German invasion of, vii, 79n64, 253
  and independent Poland, 12, 16, 19–21

INDEX

Inter-Allied Council, 72
invasion of Afghanistan, 298
invasion of Czechoslovakia,
  260–261, 345
invasion of Poland, vii, 2–3,
  27–32
Katyń massacre, 89–97,
  100–101, 360–362
Kozelsk prison camp, 91–92
nationalization of Poland,
  150–151
non-aggression pact with
  Poland (1932), 16
Nuremburg trials, 149–150
occupation of Hungary, 215n33
occupation of Poland,
  150–155, 164, 306
opposition to, 265–266
Order No. 00485, "On
  the liquidation of Polish
  sabotage and espionage
  groups and units of the
  POW" (NKVD), 19–20
Poles in, 56–57, 68, 86–87,
  91, 142, 148, 204, 215, 329,
  333–336, 360–361, 364n48
Polish Army in (Second
  Polish Corps), 65–71, 75–76,
  79–83
Polish–Soviet War, 12–13,
  30–31, 38, 48, 65, 73
power, 203
propaganda, 77–78, 101–102,
  136–138, 307
relations with Germany,
  240–241, 359
relations with Poland, vii,
  14–16, 19–21, 77, 89–112,
  329, 401
relations with UK, 152,
  272–273
relations with West, 72, 203–
  204, 247, 260–262, 264, 298
reparation payments, 143
Sikorski–Maisky Pact, vii,
  64–65, 76, 166, 199, 202,
  251n6, 253, 352
and Six-Day War, 236
support for PPR, 86–87
timeline of major events, vii
and Trans-Iranian Railway,
  80
treaty of alliance and
  friendship with Poland, 136
Treaty of Non-Aggression
  (Molotov–Ribbentrop Pact),
  20–21, 27–28, 105, 295
Treaty of Riga, 12
and United Nations, 131
war crimes, 203
and Warsaw Uprising, 115
Union of the Eastern
  Territories (Związek Ziem
  Wschodnich), 219, 227

United Kingdom
  Agreement of Mutual
    Assistance, 20–21
  alliance with Komitet
    Narodowy Polski, 9
  campaign encouraging Polish
    soldiers to return to Poland,
    156–158
  and Długoszowski, 41
  émigré community, 208–212
  government of Germany
    by, 186
  and independent Poland, 20
  Inter-Allied Council, 72
  Interim Treasury Committee
    for Polish Affairs (ITC),
    144–146
  and invasion of Poland,
    24–26, 30–31
  and Katyń massacre, 89–90,
    94, 101
  Locarno Treaties, 14
  May 22 Mass, 233
  Operation Keelhaul, 156n32
  Polish population, 59, 170,
    357, 403
  relations with Germany, 359
  relations with Poland, 141,
    144, 149, 152, 156–160,
    163–164, 273–274, 295, 325,
    366, 387, 401
  relations with Soviets, 149,
    152, 203–204, 272–273, 298
  relations with TRJN, 146
  and Second Polish Corps, 80
  support for Poland, 60–61, 69,
    105–106, 120–121, 125, 133
  support for Stalin, 63
  timeline of major events, viii
  and Trans-Iranian Railway,
    80
  and United Nations, 131
  US support, 72
  war on Japan, 77
  and Warsaw Uprising, 114
United Nations, 131, 150,
  203–204, 315, 401
United Nations Charter, 150
United Nations Declaration,
  131
United People's Party, see
  Zjednoczone Stronnictwo
  Ludowe
United States
  anti-German alliance
    support, 72
  Battle of Monte Cassino,
    108–109
  Department of Defense,
    173–174, 203
  Department of State, 173–174
  Federal Bureau of
    Investigation (FBI), 288–289,
    299n14

government of Germany
  by, 186
House Committee on Foreign
  Affairs Subcommittee on
  Europe, 232
and Katyń massacre, 94,
  100–101
Operation Keelhaul, 156n32
Polish community, 170–171
Rada branch in, 311, 341, 344,
  369, 385
relations with Germany, 359
relations with Poland, 141,
  159–160, 164, 264, 288–289,
  323, 325, 330n26, 335–337,
  401
relations with Soviets, 203,
  247, 298n12
Select Committee to Conduct
  an Investigation and Study
  of the Facts, Evidence, and
  Circumstances of the Katyn
  Forest Massacre (Madden
  Committee), 203
and Six-Day War, 236
support for Poland, 120–121,
  125, 133, 170, 229n19, 259
timeline of major events, viii
and United Nations, 131
war on Japan, 77
and Warsaw Uprising, 114
United States Holocaust
  Museum, 156n31
University College London,
  210n27
University of Colorado, 344
University of Dorpat, 48
University of Fribourg, 44
University of London, 353
University of Stirling, 210n27
University of Sussex, 315
University of Tartu, 48n2
Uniwersytet Jagielloński
  (Jagiellonian University), 294
Uniwersytet Jana Kazimierza
  (Jan Kazimierz University),
  147, 250, 256
Uniwersytet Polski za Granicą
  (Polish University Abroad),
  209n25
Uniwersytet Stefana Batorego,
  147
Uniwersytet Warszawski
  (University of Warsaw), 207,
  236–237, 250, 318, 321
Uniwersytet Wrocławski
  (University of Wrocław), 147,
  179n28, 397
Uniwersytet Wrocławski im.
  Bolesława Bieruta (Bolesław
  Bierut University of
  Wrocław), 179n28
Upper Silesia, 11–12, 14

Urban, Jerzy, 326
Urbański, Alfred, 257–258, 266–267, 271, 323
Urbański, Franciszek, 130, 133–134
Uroczysko Baran, 119
Ursus, 268–269
Urząd Bezpieczeństwa (UB, Department of Security), 124, 137, 142, 162–163, 175–176, 179–180, 206
  dissolution, 189–190
  and Kielce pogrom, 155
Urząd do Spraw Wyznań (UdSW, Office for Religious Affairs), 181
Urzędy Bezpieczeństwa Publicznego (UBP, Public Security Offices), 124
USS *Maine* Memorial (Arlington National Cemetery), 72
Utnik, Marian, 177–178
UVO (Ukrainian Military Organization), 14, 17
Uzbek SSR, 352

V

van Vliet, John H., 93–94
Vatican, 150, 179–180, 220, 237, 259, 297
  relations with Poland, 308, 329
  relations with PRL, 259–260
Versailles, France, 10–11
Vichy France, 71
Victoria, Australia, 258
Viekman, William K., 327
Vienna, Austria, 6
Villa of Bliss (Malakhovka), 71, 74–75
Vilnius (formerly Wilno), Lithuania, 30, 364n48
Virtuti Militari, 290–291
Voice of Free Poland, see *Głos Wolnej Polski*
Volunteer Reserve of the Citizens' Militia, see *Ochotnicza Rezerwa Milicji Obywatelskiej*, ORMO
Vonnegut, Kurt, 271n45
Voroshilov, Kliment, 91
Vyshinsky, Andrey, 68, 70

W

Wachowski, Mieczysław, 332
Wajda, Roman, 234–235, 246, 263
Walentynowicz, Anna, 302
Wałęsa, Bogdan, 312
Wałęsa, Danuta, 312, 377

Wałęsa, Lech
  fałszywki (fabricated reports and files), 355n19
  and Jaruzelski, 309, 330, 335
  and John Paul II, 303, 312
  and Kaczorowski, 367–371, 384
  and labor strikes, 242–243, 302, 306, 335
  in London, 356
  nominations for prime minister, 354–355
  Okrągły Stół (Round Table talks), 338–339
  as president, 151n25, 332n30, 387–394, 404n9
  presidential campaign, 363, 365–367
  presidential election, 372–374
  presidential inauguration, 374–376
  and Raczyński, 303, 390
  and Sokolnicki, 300, 332
  and *Solidarność*, 303, 306, 331–332, 335
  support for, 341, 345, 372–373
  timeline of major events, ix, viii
  transfer of power to, 374–381
Wańkowicz, Melchior, 51n13
Warsaw, Poland, 13
  Battle of Warsaw, 222
  customs duties, 224–225
  evacuation of, 114
  German occupation of, 32, 114n3
  place names, 297, 397
  reconstruction of, 188
  Treaty of Warsaw, 240–241, 311
Warsaw Citadel, see *Cytadela Warszawska*
Warsaw Ghetto, 78, 85
Warsaw Ghetto Uprising, 85, 137–138
Warsaw Pact, 261
Warsaw Uprising, 113–119, 139, 215
Warta River, 293
Washington, George, 117n6
Wasilewska, Wanda, 73, 75, 95–96, 103, 110, 115
Wat, Aleksander, 38
Wawel Castle, 220–222
Wawel Cathedral, 240
Ważny (Important) (codename), 200–202
Wendorff, Bohdan, 235, 347–348, 375, 377, 384
Wesoły, Szczepan, 325, 346, 384
West Germany (Federal Republic of Germany), 186–189, 193n3, 226, 240–241, 359
  borders, 310–311
  Rada branch in, 341, 385

  relations with Poland, 259
  relations with Soviets, 298n12
West Ukrainian People's Republic, 11–12, 249
Western Byelorussia, 30
Western press, 2–3, 213–214
Western public opinion, 62–63, 105–106
Westminster Cathedral, 233–234, 239, 308
Westminster Hospital, 347
Westminster Theatre, 347
"What is the Polish Nation Fighting For?", see "*O co walczy Naród Polski?*"
White armies, 149n19
White City Stadium, 233
White Cross Society, 10n12
Whitehall News, 136
Wiadomości, 45n27, 198–199, 209
Wiadomości POSK (POSK News), 235
Wicherkiewicz, Tadeusz, 71n43
Wielkopolska, 11–14
Wieluń, Poland, 23
Wierusz-Kowalski, Tadeusz, 52n17
Wierzbiański, Bolesław, 197
Wilde, Oscar, 347
Wilhelmshaven, Germany, 140
Wilk, Franciszek, 231–232, 259, 260n20, 264, 269n39, 290
Wilno (Vilnius) region, 11–12, 14, 27, 30, 48–49, 121
Wilson, Woodrow, 10–11
WiN, see *Zrzeszenie Wolność i Niezawisłość*
Windsor Palace, 387
Wiśniewski, Janek, 242n41
Wiśniewski, Leon, 337, 362
Wiszniewski, Stanisław, 258n16
Witos, Andrzej, 110
Witos, Wincenty, 15, 18, 134
Władysław II Jagiełło, 6
Wojciechowski, Stanisław, 14–15
Wójcik, Stanisław, 232n28
Wojtyła, Karol, 57n29, 199n14, 233, 245, 277–278
Woliński (Hugon Hanke, codename *Ważny*), 200–202
Wolna Polska (Free Poland), 95–96
Wolna Polska – Free Poland, 287, 289, 327
Wolność, 202
Wołowska, Honorata, 118n7

Workers' Defense Committee, see *Komitet Obrony Robotników*
workers' protests, 268–270, 298–299
Workers' Relief Fund *(Fundusz Pomocy Robotnikom)*, 298
workers' strikes, 216, 242–243, 268, 301–302
World Association of Poles Abroad. See *Światowy Związek Polaków z Zagranicy*
World Bank, 307
World Congress of Fighting Poland, see *Światowy Zjazd Polski Walczącej*
World Congress of Unity with the Fighting Homeland, see *Światowy Zjazd Jedności z Walczącym Krajem*
World Disarmament Conference, 166
Wprost, 45n27
Wrocław, Poland, 147
Wrocławski Tygodnik Katolików (Wrocław Catholic Weekly), 354n14
WRON, 307n37
Wycech, Czesław, 135n45
Wydawnictwo Biblioteka Historyczna i Literacka, 271n45
Wydział Cywilny (Civil Division) court, 185
Wydział Ogólny (General Division) court, 185
Wyspa Wężów (Isle of Snakes), 61, 319
Wyspiański, Stanisław, 403
Wyszyński, Stefan, 220, 245, 277
 arrest of, 189, 206
 attacks on, 181
 call for resolution of differences, 229
 death, 306
 and deportees, 333
 and Mieszko's baptism, 233
 release of, 215
 support for, 213–214, 315

Y

Yalta agreements, 125–129, 139, 159, 170n10, 313, 359n33, 364
Yalta conference (Crimean Conference), 124–129
Yalta Memorial Garden, 273n50
Yangi-Yul (Yangiyo'l), 80
Yezhov, Nikolai, 252

youth affairs, 320, 326
Ypres, France, 140
Yugoslavia, 126n24, 128, 131
 Communist government, 203
 government-in-exile, 2
 governments, 14n26
 and independent Poland, 11n16
 Inter-Allied Council, 72
 and NCFE, 174
 relations with Poland, 141
 relations with UK, 152

Z

Ząbkowski, Ludwik, 210, 240, 244
Zablocki, Clement, 323
Zabłocki, Janusz, 274n51
Zachariasiewicz, Władysław, 259
Zakłady Metalowe im. Józefa Stalina w Poznaniu (ZISPO, Josef Stalin Metal Works in Poznań), 213, 216n34
Zakłady Przemysłu Metalowego H. Cegielski w Poznaniu, Przedsiębiorstwo Państwowe (H. Cegielski Metal Industry Complex in Poznań, National Enterprise), 216n34
zakon rycerski Rzeczypospolitej Polskiej (Order of Chivalry of the Republic of Poland), 310
Żakowski, Józef, 134
Zakrzewski, Andrzej, 269n39, 388
Zakrzewski, Ryszard, 369
Zaleszczyki (now Zalishchyky), 25
Zaleska, Ewelina, 247
Zaleska, Zofia, 216–217
Zaleski, August
 and *Akt Zjednoczenia Narodowego* (National Unity Act), 192–196, 199, 230–231, 286
 Arbuz (SB codename), 216–217, 228
 and British–Soviet talks, 204
 and citizens' courts, 184–185
 and Cytadela, 235
 as diplomat, 165–166
 division between Anders and, 182, 230–231, 237–238
 on émigré communities, 222
 final days and death, 247
 and invasion of Poland, 9
 as Minister of Foreign Affairs, 43, 52, 59, 63–65, 166
 New Year's speeches, 266n31
 opposition to, 173, 230–231
 and Poznań protests, 214
 and presidency, 34–35, 41–42

 as president, 40, 163–204, 211, 214–219, 225–231, 235–240, 243–245, 266n31, 283, 375, 394
 presidential succession, 182, 192–196, 199, 219, 240, 244, 256, 279, 286
 reburial, 399
 Sanacja affiliation, 51, 166
 and *Skarb Narodowy*, 188
 and Sosnkowski, 191–196
 and Srokowski, 230n26
 support for, 200, 229n19
 timeline of major events, ix, viii
Zaleski, Jerzy, 260n20, 372
Zaleski, Paweł, 171
The August Zaleski Lectures in Modern Polish History (Harvard University), 247
Zambrowski, Roman, 74n52
Zamek (Castle), 197, 201–202, 205, 212, 386
 constitutional authority, 226
 and cultural treasures, 222
 division between *Zjednoczenie Narodowe* and, 230–234, 237–240
 financial position, 216–217
 presidential decrees, 323
 pro-*Zamek* political entities, 219
 reconciliation with *Zjednoczenie Narodowe*, 256–258
 relations with West Germany, 226
 structure of, 243
 unification plan, 229–230, 240, 244–245
Zamorski, Józef, 208n24
Zamość, 186–187
Zamość area, 85
Zamoyski, Adam, 272n48
Zamoyski, Maurycy, 13
Zamoyski, Stefan, 272n48
Zaremba, Władysław, 232n28
Zaremba, Zygmunt, 142n4, 142n6
ZASP, see *Związek Artystów Scen Polskich*
Zawadowski, Zygmunt, 216n36
Zawadzki, Aleksander, 73, 74n52, 103–104
Zawisza, Adam. See Rydz-Śmigły, Edward
Zawisza, Aleksander, 39, 45–46, 219, 227, 230, 237, 240, 244, 282, 286n21
Zawodny, Janusz, 237–238, 271–272
Zdrojewski, Antoni, 228, 290–291

Żegota, 57
Żeligowski, Lucjan, 177–178
Żenczykowski, Tadeusz, 207, 269n39
Zeszyty Historyczne (Notebooks of History), 224
Zet, see *Związek Młodzieży Polskiej*
Zgoda prison, 137
ZHP, see *Związek Harcerstwa Polskiego*
ZHP pgK, see *Związek Harcerstwa Polskiego poza granicami Kraju*
Zhukov, G. S., 69–70, 81–82, 130, 132
Zieliński, Karol, 269n39
Zimmermann, Friedrich, 310–311
Ziobro, Zbigniew, 395
ZISPO (*Zakłady Metalowe im. Józefa Stalina w Poznaniu*, Josef Stalin Metal Works in Poznań), 213, 216n34
Zjazd Polaków w Wielkiej Brytanii (Congress of Poles in Great Britain), 225, 321–322
Zjednoczenie Narodowe (National Unity), 197, 225–226, 230–240, 244–245, 256–258, 271, 322–323
Zjednoczenie Polskie w Wielkiej Brytanii (ZPWB, Federation of Poles in Great Britain), 184, 205, 340, 353, 392
Zjednoczone Stronnictwo Ludowe (ZSL, United People's Party), 178, 339, 344–345, 354–355, 358
Żmigrodzki, Józef, 260n20
Zmotoryzowane Odwody Milicji Obywatelskiej (ZOMO, Motorized Reserves of the Citizens' Militia), 176n18, 216, 237, 267–268, 306–307, 354–355
Znak, 354n14
ŻOB (*Żydowska Organizacja Bojowa*, Jewish Combat Organization), 78, 85

Żółkieta Wolności, 342n57
Żołnierz Wolności, 239
ZOMO. See *Zmotoryzowane Odwody Milicji Obywatelskiej*
ZPP, see *Związek Patriotów Polskich*
ZPWB, see *Zjednoczenie Polskie w Wielkiej Brytanii*
ZPWP, see *Związek Przyjaciół Wsi Polskiej w Ameryce*
Zrzeszenie Wolność i Niezawisłość (WiN, Freedom and Independence), 138, 155, 162, 174–176, 206
ZSL, see *Zjednoczone Stronnictwo Ludowe*
Żuławski, Zygmunt, 134–135
ZUPRO, see *Związek Uczestników Polskiego Ruchu Oporu we Francji*
Związek Artystów Scen Polskich (ZASP, Association of Polish Stage Artists), 210
Związek Harcerstwa Polskiego (ZHP, Polish Scouting Association), 31, 318–319, 348
Związek Harcerstwa Polskiego poza granicami Kraju (ZHP pgK, Polish Scouting Organization Operating Outside the Country), 209, 320, 322, 353
Związek Komunistów Polskich "Proletariat" (Union of Polish Communists "Proletariat"), 358n31
Związek Legionistów Polskich (Union of Legionnaires), 255
Związek Lekarzy Polskich w Londynie (Polish Medical Association in London), 255
Związek Ludowo-Narodowy (Popular National Union), 13, 16
Związek Młodzieży Polskiej (Zet, Association of Polish Youth), 48
Związek Patriotów Polskich (ZPP, Union of Polish Patriots), 95–97, 102–104, 339–340

Związek Polskiej Młodzieży Demokratycznej (Association of Polish Democratic Youth), 318n4
Związek Przyjaciół Wsi Polskiej w Ameryce (ZPWP, Association of Friends of the Polish Village in America), 232n29
Związek Socjalistów Polskich na Obczyźnie (Association of Polish Socialists Abroad), 219, 227
Związek Strzelecki (Riflemen's Association), 37
Związek Uczestników Polskiego Ruchu Oporu we Francji (ZUPRO, Union of Participants of the Polish Resistance Movement in France), 228
Związek Walki Czynnej (ZWC, Association for Active Struggle), 9, 37
Związek Walki Zbrojnej (ZWZ, Union of Armed Struggle), 55–56, 78, 349
Związek Ziem Wschodnich (Union of the Eastern Territories), 219, 227
Zwierzyński, Aleksander, 130, 133
Życie, 209
Życie Warszawy, 239, 304, 342n57
Żydowska Organizacja Bojowa (ŻOB, Jewish Combat Organization), 78, 85
Żydowski Związek Wojskowy (ŻZW, Jewish Military Union), 56, 85
Zygmunt II August, 6
Zyklon-B gas, 62
Zyndram-Kościałkowski, Marian, 49, 52n17
ŻZW (*Żydowski Związek Wojskowy*, Jewish Military Union), 56

www.ingramcontent.com/pod-product-compliance
Lightning Source LLC
Jackson TN
JSHW072121231125
94517JS00002B/2